TREATING THE LIFETIME HEALTH EFFECTS OF CHILDHOOD VICTIMIZATION

Second Edition

Kathleen Kendall-Tackett, Ph.D., IBLC, FAPA

CRI
Civic Research Institute
4478 U.S. Route 27 • P.O. Box 585 • Kingston, NJ 08528

By Civic Research Institute, Inc.
Kingston, New Jersey 08528

Printed in the United States of America

Library of Congress Cataloging in Publication Data
Treating the lifetime health effects of childhood victimization/Kathleen Kendall-Tackett, Ph.D.

ISBN 978-1-887554-90-9

Library of Congress Catalog Card Number 2012954874

This book is dedicated to Cindy Castro, my awesome prayer warrior.
I could not have done it without you. You rock!

To God be the glory!

"Adult disease prevention begins with reducing early toxic stress. . . . An increasing amount of research in neuroscience, social epidemiology, and the behavioral sciences suggests that a reduction in the number and severity of early adverse experiences will lead to a decrease in the prevalence of a wide range of health problems."

— J. P. Shonkoff, W. T. Boyce, and B. S. McEwen. (2009). Neuroscience, Molecular Biology, and the Childhood Roots of Health Disparities: Building a New Framework for Health Promotion and Disease Prevention. *Journal of the American Medical Association, 301*(21), 2252–2259

Acknowledgements

This book was first conceived in a rainstorm. I was doing a brief presentation at a Brandeis University alumni author reception. Deborah Launer, of Civic Research Institute, was on her way to another meeting but was trapped because of torrential rain. We've always considered our meeting providential. The rest, as they say, is history. She has been a highly supportive guide as I worked my way through this project. A simple "thank you" seems inadequate for all her help and support.

I also want to thank Lori Jacobs for her careful copyediting of this new version of my book. Having been a copyeditor myself I know how hard that job can be. I appreciate her hard work on my behalf.

This book would not have been possible without the incredible wealth of research in both child maltreatment and health psychology. It is because of these researchers' hard work that I had such a rich source to mine. I'm especially appreciative for the work of the following people: Vincent Felliti, Robert Anda, Jan Kiecolt-Glaser, Ken Wallston, Tim Smith, Bruce McEwen, Vicki Helgeson, Bruce Perry, Cathy Widom, David Finkelhor, Doug Drossman, and Jane Leserman.

In addition, I wish to thank my colleagues from the American Psychological Association's Division of Trauma Psychology: Terry Keane, Chris Courtois, Steve Gold, Sandra Mattar, Beth Rom-Rymer, Joan Cook, Laura Brown, and Sherry Hamby. I am inspired by the passion you bring to the work of psychological trauma. It has truly been an exciting journey. I can't wait to see what the future holds for this field.

Finally, I wish to thank my husband, Doug, and my sons, Ken and Chris. As always, I am grateful to have you in my life. I appreciate that you gave me the time and space to complete the second edition of a book I have always jokingly called (but is not too far from the truth) my *magnum opus*.

— K. K.-T.

Acknowledgements

About the Author

Kathleen Kendall-Tackett, Ph.D., IBCLC, FAPA, a health psychologist and an International Board Certified Lactation Consultant, is the owner and Editor-in-Chief of Praeclarus Press, a new small press specializing in women's health. Dr. Kendall-Tackett is a research associate at the Crimes Against Children Research Center at the University of New Hampshire, clinical associate professor of pediatrics at Texas Tech University School of Medicine in Amarillo, Texas, and a Fellow of the American Psychological Association in both the Divisions of Health and Trauma Psychology. She is a founding associate editor of the journal *Psychological Trauma* and currently Editor-in-Chief of *Clinical Lactation*. Dr. Kendall-Tackett is author of more than 310 journal articles, book chapters, and other publications and author or editor of 22 books in the fields of trauma, women's health, depression, and breastfeeding, including *Depression in New Mothers* (2nd ed.) (2010), and *The Psychoneuroimmunology of Chronic Disease* (2010). She is a founding officer of the American Psychological Association's Division of Trauma Psychology and is currently President-elect.

Dr. Kendall-Tackett received bachelor's and master's degrees in psychology from California State University, Chico, and a doctorate from Brandeis University in social and developmental psychology. She has won several awards, including the Outstanding Research Study Award from the American Professional Society on the Abuse of Children. She was named Distinguished Alumna, College of Behavioral and Social Sciences, California State University, Chico. In 2011, she received the John Kennell & Marshall Klaus Award for Excellence in Research from DONA International, and the Community Faculty Award from the Department of Pediatrics, Texas Tech University School of Medicine. Her web sites are *UppityScienceChick.com*, *BreastfeedingMadeSimple.com*, *KathleenKendall-Tackett.com*, and *PraeclarusPress.com*.

Foreword

Richard D. Krugman, M.D.

The year 2012 marked the 100th anniversary of the founding of the Children's Bureau and the 50th anniversary of C. Henry Kempe's article: "The Battered Child Syndrome" (Kempe, Silverman, Steele, Droegmeuller, & Silver, 1962). And a decade has passed since the first edition of this volume was published. There is a lot more going on with regard to research on the biological basis of abusive and neglectful behavior, but not much has happened in the real world to change either how we approach the problem of child abuse and neglect or how we effectively treat those who are victims of maltreatment. There is a more research on the neurobiology and neuroimmunology of abusive and neglectful behavior, but the child protection system in the United States deals with the hundreds of thousands of abused and neglected children and their families with not much more success than in previous decades.

Dr. Kendall-Tackett does a wonderful job updating the increasing research information on the significant health effects of childhood victimization. Many of us have pled for more attention from the National Institutes of Health (NIH) for logarithmic increases in funding of work similar to that described and documented in these pages. Sadly, a decade later, the amount of funding from this research engine has been stuck at 0.1% ($30 million of a $31 billion NIH budget) (see "Estimates of funding . . .," 2012). Given the magnitude of the morbidity and mortality attributable to the consequences of child maltreatment, more clearly needs to be done, although the fiscal predicament faced by the U.S. Congress as of 2013 suggests that the likelihood of changing this failure-to-thrive situation is not very likely.

If progress is to be made to address this gap, something will need to unstick the status quo in how our country addresses the problem of child maltreatment. Given the addictive nature of how the current revenue flows in well-worn ways—the vast majority of resources going to the child protective services systems that are housed in public child welfare and human services agencies are supporting efforts to identify victims but rarely support treatment, and only in those cases in which the abuse or neglect is intrafamilial. When abuse occurs outside the family (as it does more often than not for boys who are sexually abused), there is practically no treatment available. And, in spite of all the data on the long-term consequences of maltreatment, the child protection system is episodic, and unavailable for the long haul of support needed by these children and families.

One can only hope that this situation will change before the next edition of this compendium. In the meanwhile, health and mental health professionals need to understand what is in these pages, and national child advocacy organizations need to come together to ensure that there is an expansion of the resources available for research similar to that within these pages.

— Richard D. Krugman, M.D.
Distinguished Professor of Pediatrics
Vice Chancellor for Health Affairs
Dean, University of Colorado School of Medicine
January 28, 2013

References

"Estimates of funding for various research, condition, and disease categories (RCDC)" [Table]. *National Institutes of Health Reporter*, Feb. 13, 2012. Available online at: *http://report.nih.gov/categorical_spending.aspx.*

Kempe, C. H., Silverman, F. N., Steele, B. F., Droegmueller, W., & Silver, H. K. (1962). The battered child syndrome. *Journal of the American Medical Association, 18*(1), 17–24.

Preface

I vividly remember when I first learned about the connection between childhood abuse and health. I was attending grand rounds at our local hospital, back in the mid-1990s. The speaker was talking about various aspects of the mind-body connection. She mentioned a study that linked irritable bowel syndrome to child sexual abuse. I was stunned. I had been around the child sexual abuse literature *for years*, and I had never heard this before. Little did I know that that brief sentence, said almost in passing, was to lead to some of the most fascinating work of my career. It started that day, and it is ongoing. Since writing the first edition of this book (published in 2003), I have since edited five books covering various aspects of victimization, trauma, and physical health (Banyard, Edwards, & Kendall-Tackett, 2009; Kendall-Tackett, 2004, 2005, 2010; Kendall-Tackett & Klest, 2010). I also have had the privilege of being a founding officer in the American Psychological Association's Division of Trauma Psychology and serving as an associate editor on their new journal, *Psychological Trauma*. I have watched the topic of trauma and health really come of age. There have been many exciting developments in this field.

My initial interest in this topic coincided with my own medical odyssey. At that time I heard that lecture, I was going through a lengthy medical process that eventually culminated in a diagnosis of systemic lupus erythematosus. I've often joked that it was my crash course in American medical practice, as I bounced between various specialists trying to figure out what was wrong. I learned firsthand what it was like to have a chronic pain condition. I also learned what it was like to have vague, but debilitating, symptoms without an obvious cause. During that process, I had some great—and not-so-great—health care providers, and a few who doubted whether I was really sick (a frequent problem for people with autoimmunity).

My experience also provided many opportunities to talk with my fellow patients. Because I was "one of them," these men and women would tell me things they would never say to their health care providers. Seventeen years later, I still find this to be true. I also found that patients, upon learning that I was a family-violence researcher, would tell me about their past experiences of abuse and neglect, and they were quite interested in learning about the connection between these experiences and their current health problems. To this day, my experiences as a patient do inform my views. When talking about patients, it is never "them" for me; it is always "us."

All these experiences were molding my thinking on the impact of abuse on health. It was clear from reading the research that people who experienced childhood abuse had higher rates of illness. Even the first small study I conducted with Ken Ness and Roberta Marshall demonstrated this. One of our initial findings was on the occurrence of diabetes in people who had been physically or sexually abused (Kendall-Tackett & Marshall, 1999). To understand our findings, we put them in the context of abuse as a chronic stressor, and suddenly the pieces seemed to fit. The much larger Adverse Childhood Experiences (ACE) study had similar findings, not only for diabetes but for illnesses ranging from cancer to skeletal fractures. All these were more likely in abuse survivors (Felitti et al., 1998). The emerging field of psychoneuroimmunology has also been important in understanding these effects.

Chronic pain in abuse survivors seems to be a particularly robust finding, and it has shown up repeatedly as an effect of past abuse. Neuroscience research has demonstrated that traumatic events can actually alter the brain and body, and the body becomes more sensitive to sensations. There is even evidence that suggests that abuse survivors have lower pain thresholds. Although we still don't know the exact mechanism for this effect, some highly intriguing possibilities have been raised.

Inflammation is proving to be an absolutely essential part of understanding the mechanisms that influence the health of abuse survivors. That literature has grown substantially since the first edition of this book, and you will see it woven throughout the chapters. The psychoneuroimmunology research has demonstrated not only that inflammation has a causal role in chronic diseases, such as cardiovascular disease and diabetes, but that psychological processes can actually cause inflammation. Understanding this process is also key to thinking about prevention of health problems in abuse survivors (Kendall-Tackett, 2009, 2010).

WHY DOES CHILD ABUSE MAKE PEOPLE SICK?

Recent studies have established that child abuse makes people sick. The next logical question to ask is "why." A health psychology and psychoneuroimmunology framework can help us answer that question and reveals many possible mechanisms by which abuse could influence health. Some are obvious, but most are fairly subtle. Any given survivor could have several of these operating at once. In fact, in all likelihood, not only would there be several at work, but they would be synergistic and would influence each other for an even more harmful effect.

The framework I use came about by combining research from child maltreatment and health psychology/behavioral medicine fields. Combining those two large literatures proved to be a mammoth task. But it led to some interesting findings. For example, an interest in religiosity led me to variables such as hope, forgiveness, and finding meaning in suffering. The relational difficulties of adult survivors led me to rejection sensitivity, unmitigated agency and communion, the internal working model, and the health effects of mistrust and hostility. A look at homelessness led me to socioeconomic status, learning disabilities, and problems in school. I often characterized this project as working on a giant jigsaw puzzle. But instead of cardboard puzzle pieces, I was assembling components of the human psyche. The final picture was as complex and fascinating as human beings themselves. In the end, I grouped these possible influences into five pathways. Each of these can have a negative impact on health alone and can interact with the others. The five pathways are as follows:

- *Physiological Pathways.* Trauma changes the body. The sympathetic nervous system becomes more reactive. Levels of stress hormones and inflammatory cytokines become dysregulated. Pain thresholds are lower. Children are especially vulnerable to these changes, and the changes are more likely to occur when trauma is severe.
- *Behavioral Pathways.* Abuse survivors are more likely to engage in harmful behaviors, especially substance abuse and high-risk sexual activity. This pathway has the most empirical support of all the ones I considered.

A relatively new line of research considers the flip side of harmful behaviors: health-enhancing ones. Although only a few studies have been conducted, these results suggest that adult survivors are less likely to participate in health-promoting behaviors as well.

- *Cognitive Pathways.* Abuse survivors are more likely to have negative beliefs about themselves and others. These studies are some of the most interesting in this book, and they can explain some of the difficulties that otherwise high-functioning survivors face. Negative beliefs can undermine health and may also lead to harmful behaviors and harmful relationships. Yet, we often don't take these beliefs as seriously as we should because they are not as dramatic as harmful behaviors. Nevertheless, the detrimental effects are very real.
- *Social Pathways.* Adult survivors often have difficulties in their adult relationships. One of the more extreme manifestations of this is revictimization. But there were many more subtle manifestations including divorce, marital disruptions and social isolation. Adult survivors are more likely to be poor, to have a hard time in school, and to be homeless than are their non-abused counterparts. Even behavior that we might label as "codependent" can be the result of childhood abuse. Moreover, all these social difficulties can have a negative impact on health.
- *Emotional Pathways.* Depression and posttraumatic stress disorder (PTSD) are common sequelae of past abuse. We have known for many years that depression suppresses the immune system and causes myriad health problems. It can even increase the risk of heart attacks. Recent research has revealed similar negative health consequences for PTSD. We are used to thinking about PTSD and depression as outcomes, but we also need to think of them as mechanisms that can lead to poor health.

FORMAT OF THE BOOK

Throughout this book, I have followed a simple formula. For each variable, I first show how it pertains to abuse survivors and then how it is related to health. On some topics, such as substance abuse or high-risk sexual behavior, there are dozens of studies. I have listed them all for completeness, but even skimming these longer sections is enough to get the picture. On other topics, the literature is somewhat limited but suggestive of future studies.

In the final section, I have provided clinical guidelines for working with this population in health care settings. I focused on health care rather than traditional mental health settings since health problems are more likely to surface there. However, I have written these clinical chapters in such a way that I hope mental health professionals will find them useful as well. There is a schism in our country between mental and physical health. It has improved somewhat. But there is still more to do. My goal is to promote a more collaborative and holistic approach to treating the concerns of abuse survivors. The first chapter in this section focuses on general issues that arise in treating adult survivors. The next three chapters are on the clinical management of the three most common conditions that adult survivors manifest—depression, PTSD, and chronic pain.

WHY THIS WORK IS IMPORTANT

When reviewing these research studies, I encourage you to remember the real people behind the numbers—the people whose lives have been shattered by childhood abuse. The health problems of this population can sometimes seem overwhelming. You might be tempted to give up hope. But there is much you can do to help.

Early in my training, I attended a weeklong seminar on the treatment of child sexual abuse at the Institute for the Community as an Extended Family (now the Giarretto Institute). At that time, it was the only facility in the country that offered training on treating incest. Many of the clients seen there were highly symptomatic. Yet, one of the trainers said something I have never forgotten. She told us that we must communicate our belief in our clients' capacity for wellness—that it is indeed possible to recover from past abuse, and to have a life that becomes strong in the broken places. We must communicate this hope to the patients who seek our care. Although many have complex medical conditions, they can be well. Even with chronic and disabling conditions, it is possible to manage symptoms and function better. This is the message that we must bring. My desire is to support you in that task.

— Kathleen Kendall-Tackett, Ph.D., IBCLC, FAPA
Amarillo, Texas
June 17, 2012

References

Banyard, V. L., Edwards, V. J., & Kendall-Tackett, K. A. (Eds.). (2009). *Trauma and physical health: Understanding the effects of extreme stress and of psychological harm*. London, UK: Routledge.

Felitti, V. J., Anda, R. F., Nordenberg, D., Williamson, D. F., Spitz, A. M., Edwards, V., et al. (1998). Relationship of childhood abuse and household dysfunction to many of the leading causes of death in adults. The Adverse Childhood Experiences (ACE) Study. *American Journal of Preventive Medicine, 14*(4), 245–258.

Kendall-Tackett, K. A. (Ed.). (2004). *Health consequences of abuse in the family: A clinical guide for evidence-based practice*. Washington, DC: American Psychological Association.

Kendall-Tackett, K. A. (Ed.). (2005). *Handbook of women, stress and trauma*. New York: Brunner-Routledge.

Kendall-Tackett, K. A. (2009). Psychological trauma and physical health: A psychoneuro-immunology approach to etiology of negative health effects and possible interventions. *Psychological Trauma, 1*(1), 35–48.

Kendall-Tackett, K. A. (Ed.). (2010). *The psychoneuroimmunology of chronic disease*. Washington, DC: American Psychological Association.

Kendall-Tackett, K. A., & Klest, B. (Eds.). (2010). *Trauma, dissociation and health*. London, UK: Routledge.

Kendall-Tackett, K. A., & Marshall, R. (1999). Victimization and diabetes: An exploratory study. *Child Abuse and Neglect, 23*, 593–596.

Table of Contents

Chapter 8: Social Pathways I—Social Networks, Support, and Relationships

Chapter 9: Social Pathways II—Poverty and Homelessness

Chapter 10: Social Pathways III—Revictimization

Chapter 11: Emotional Pathways I—Depression

Chapter 12: Emotional Pathways II—Posttraumatic Stress Disorder

Chapter 13: Individual Differences in the Expression of Symptoms

Chapter 14: Pain I—Overview of Chronic Pain in Abuse Survivors

Chapter 15: Pain II—Chronic Pain Syndromes in Adult Survivors of Childhood Abuse

Chapter 16: Perinatal Effects of Childhood Abuse

Chapter 17: Clinical Approaches to Abuse Survivors in Health Care Settings

Chapter 18: Clinical Management of Depression in Health Care Settings

Chapter 19: Clinical Management of Posttraumatic Stress Disorder

Chapter 1

Abuse Survivors in the Health Care System

> Abuse is not destiny. It is an appalling event that no child should have imposed on them. It places that child at greater risk of developmental disruption and of experiencing a range of problems in adult life. But fortunately, for many victims, these risks may not be realized. (Mullen, Martin, Anderson, Romans, & Herbison, 1994, p. 45)

Physician Vincent Felitti was asked to consult on a case involving a 70-year-old woman. She has hypertension, diabetes, and morbid obesity. She is chronically depressed and has never married. Felitti asks if she has ever been sexually assaulted or abused. She tells him that an older brother raped her at age 10. No health care provider had ever asked her before or tried to connect her current health problems with her past assault (Felitti, 2001)—and she is not alone.

Each year, thousands of children are beaten, raped, neglected, or killed by members of their own family. The National Violence Against Women Survey (Tjaden & Thoennes, 2000) found that in one year:

- 4 million women and 900,000 men are battered by intimate partners;

- 1.8 million elders and 1.7 million children are abused or neglected; and
- 1,500 women and 1,100 children die at the hands of a family member.

Data from a U.S. nationally representative sample of 1,467 children ages 2–17 also indicated that victimization of children is common (Finkelhor, Ormrod, & Turner, 2009). A staggering 88 percent of children and youth reported that they had been victimized at least once. The mean number of victimizations the children reported was 3.7. Not surprisingly, the higher the number of victimizations a child experienced, the more trauma symptoms he or she had. These findings highlight that children continue to be victimized at high rates in the United States, and that there are serious consequences associated with those experiences.

THE HEALTH OF ADULT SURVIVORS

The majority of reports on child victimization and health have focused on immediate consequences, such as injury. And these needs are substantial. According to the National Violence Against Women Survey, 39 percent of female victims of violence reported injuries. Approximately 500,000 women sought medical care for their injuries, and 62 percent of these women were seen in emergency departments (Tjaden & Thoennes, 2000). Family-violence-related injury leads to massive demands on the health care system.

Increasingly, however, researchers are beginning to understand that injuries represent the tip of the iceberg in terms of health effects. Indeed, the health care needs of people who have experienced previous abuse may vastly overwhelm the numbers of people who are seeking assistance for current injuries. Family violence has been related to a wide range of chronic diseases and conditions.

In the Adverse Childhood Experience (ACE) study, Felitti et al. (1998) found that subjects who experienced four or more types of adverse childhood events, including child abuse and exposure to domestic violence, were at significantly increased risk for such diverse conditions as ischemic heart disease, cancer, stroke, chronic bronchitis, emphysema, diabetes, skeletal fractures, and hepatitis. The childhood events they studied included psychological abuse, physical abuse, contact sexual abuse, exposure to substance abuse, parental mental illness, exposure to violent treatment of the mother or stepmother, and exposure to criminal behavior.

The ACE study results underscored the need to study abuse in the overall context of other types of abuse, maltreatment, and adversity. Dong et al. (2004) analyzed data from 8,629 adult members of a health maintenance organization (HMO). The researchers found that two-thirds of their participants reported at least one ACE. Among those who experienced at least one ACE, 81 percent to 98 percent had experienced more than one. Most had experienced from two to four other types.

Knowing about multiple types of ACEs allows researchers to study graded relationships between childhood exposures and health and social outcomes. Recent studies have revealed a relationship between ACEs and diseases, such as cardiovascular disease, diabetes, pulmonary conditions, chronic pain syndromes, and autoimmune disease. Many of these diseases are common, and can lead to premature mortality.

Cardiovascular Disease

Using data from the National Comorbidity Survey, researchers found that a history of childhood abuse increased the risk of cardiovascular disease. Interestingly, the link between child maltreatment and cardiovascular disease was especially strong for women, with maltreated women having a ninefold increase in cardiovascular disease compared to nonmaltreated women. Depression did not explain this relationship (Batten, Aslan, Maciejewski, & Mazure, 2004).

A recent meta-analysis of twenty-four studies (N = 48,801) found that physical and sexual child abuse increased the risk of adult-onset neurological and musculoskeletal conditions, respiratory problems, cardiovascular disease, gastrointestinal conditions, and metabolic disorders (Wegman & Stetler, 2009). The neurological and musculoskeletal conditions included migraines, broken bones, and arthritis. Metabolic disorders included diabetes and obesity. Cardiovascular problems included heart attack and stroke. Respiratory problems included asthma and bronchitis. There were no studies of neglect or emotional abuse in their review. Their findings suggested that the health effects of child abuse were greater for females than males, although males were underrepresented in the literature.

Diabetes

Data from the Nurses' Health Study II shows that physical and sexual abuse in childhood or adolescence increased the risk of Type 2 diabetes in adult women (Rich-Edwards et al., 2010). In this study, models were adjusted for age, race, body type at age 5, parental education, and parental history of diabetes. They found that the hazards ratio was 1.03 for mild physical abuse, 1.26 for moderate physical abuse, and 1.54 for severe physical abuse, including a 50 percent increase in risk for those who experienced severe abuse. There was a similar pattern for sexual abuse, with the highest hazards ratio for repeated forced sex. For example, girls who had experienced repeated forced sex had 69 percent higher risks of diabetes than girls who were not sexually abused. Moderate-to-severe physical or sexual abuse increased risk of Type 2 diabetes, and it did so in a dose-response way: The more severe the abuse, the more severe the symptoms. There was also an additive effect, with those who experienced both types of abuse at higher risk those who experienced only one type. Adult body mass index (BMI) explained some of the relationship between abuse and diabetes, but even BMI may be influenced by abuse experience. In this study, the physically and sexually abused girls had higher BMIs than did the non-abused girls. Further, the trajectories between abused and non-abused girls had grown wider by adulthood, particularly for the girls exposed to repeated forced sex in childhood or adolescence.

Pulmonary Conditions

Childhood adversity was also related to adult-onset asthma (Scott et al., 2008). This study included ten cross-sectional population surveys of adults (N = 18,303). The authors found that early-onset affective disorders also predicted asthma.

Exposure to chronic violence can also influence childhood lung dysfunction, as

Suglia, Ryan, Laden, Dockery, and Wright (2008) found in their study of 313 urban children. They found that girls who were exposed to high levels of parental verbal aggression had decreased lung function. The relationship between parental verbal aggression and lung function was in the same direction for boys, but it was not significant. These findings still appear even after adjusting for maternal education, child's age and race, tobacco exposure, and health factors including asthma, allergies, and respiratory infections. Exposure to community violence was not associated with increased lung function for girls, but it was for boys. Boys with the highest levels of exposure to community violence had significantly poorer lung function than boys in the lowest tertile, even after adjusting for other risk factors.

Chronic Pain Syndromes and Somatic Complaints

A study of 6,593 high school students in mainland China found that physical and sexual abuse was associated with higher levels of a number of physical symptoms including stomach pain, nightmares, poor appetite, shortness of breath, chest pain, dizziness, irregular menstruation, and suicidal ideation (Wong et al., 2009). This association was stronger when severity of the abuse was taken into account. Severe abuse led to stronger symptoms. Surprisingly, boys were more likely to experience severe physical maltreatment and sexual abuse than were girls.

In a study of 163 male and female psychiatric patients over the age of 50, Talbot and colleagues (Talbot et al., 2009) found that severe childhood sexual abuse (CSA) was associated with higher cumulative medical illness burden, worse physical functioning, and greater bodily pain. The effect of CSA on illness burden was comparable to adding eight years of chronological age. In terms of activities of daily living and bodily pain, sexual abuse was comparable to adding twenty years of chronological age. The authors concluded that early detection of patients' abuse histories could lead to that prevent or decelerate the progression of morbidity in this group.

Golding (1994) also found that women who had been sexually assaulted, as either children or adults, had significantly more health problems than did their non-assaulted counterparts. The women were at increased risk for diabetes, arthritis, and physical disability. Twenty-nine percent of assaulted women reported at least six medically explained symptoms, compared to only 16 percent of the non-assaulted women. When controlling for demographic characteristics, the odds of having at least six symptoms were three times greater for the assaulted women. Pain symptoms were more likely, as were neurological symptoms such as loss of voice, fainting, trouble walking, or paralysis.

A study of 3,568 randomly sampled, insured women, ages 18 to 64, found that childhood physical and sexual abuse increased the risk of somatic complaints (Bonomi, Cannon, Anderson, & Rivara, 2008). Women who were both physically and sexually abused before the age of 18 were at high risk for depression; joint pain; insomnia; fatigue; stomachache or abdominal pain; severe headaches; numb hands or feet; diarrhea; constipation; shortness of breath; facial pain; dizziness; nausea or vomiting; and chest pain. Women who had been both physically and sexually abused had three times the risk of severe depression. The researchers noted that their findings were consistent with the results of the ACE study, in that there was a graded relationship between abuse exposures and poor health in adulthood.

Autoimmune Disease

Data from the ACE Study found that cumulative childhood stress and a higher ACE score increased the risk of being hospitalized with a diagnosed autoimmune disease (Dube et al., 2009). Compared to people with no ACEs, a person with two or more ACEs was at 70 percent increased risk for Th1 diseases (such as insulin-dependent diabetes mellitus, irritable bowel syndrome, and idiopathic myocarditis), 80 percent increased risk for Th2 diseases (such as multiple sclerosis, Graves' disease, and celiac disease), and 100 percent increased risk for rheumatic diseases (such as lupus, rheumatoid arthritis, and scleroderma). The authors concluded that childhood adversities and traumatic stress increased the likelihood of hospitalization with a diagnosed autoimmune disease decades into adulthood and are consistent with previous studies showing a link between childhood adversities and inflammatory diseases.

PATTERNS OF HEALTH CARE USE

With high rates of chronic pain and illness, it should not surprise us to learn that survivors of child victimization have high rates of health care use. They make more visits to primary care physicians, specialists, and emergency departments. They report more symptoms, have more procedures and diagnostic tests, and have surgery more often—in our study, twice as much (Kendall-Tackett, Marshall, & Ness, 2000). Yet they are often very unhappy with the care they receive, and indeed they may be retraumatized by their health care providers.

Doctors' Visits

Abuse survivors go to the doctor more often than do their non-abused counterparts. In a sample of HMO patients, Felitti (1991) found that 22 percent of his abused sample had visited a doctor ten or more times a year compared with 6 percent of the control group. Ten visits a year was considered to be a pattern of high use of health care services.

During pregnancy, women with a history of child sexual abuse reported more health complaints, and used more health care services than did their non-abused counterparts (Grimstad & Schei, 1999). Similarly, Benedict, Paine, Paine, Brandt, and Stallings (1999) found that women with a sexual abuse history reported higher levels of depressive symptoms during pregnancy, negative life events, and physical and verbal abuse before and during pregnancy than their non-abused counterparts. Neither study, however, found higher rates of obstetric complications, low birthweight babies, or difficulties with newborn outcomes in abuse survivors.

In a study of patients with chronic headaches, 76 percent of the physically or sexually abused women had been hospitalized compared with 25 percent of the non-abused group (Domino & Haber, 1987). And women in a support group for sexual abuse survivors reported more pain and went to their family practitioners more often than did the women in comparison groups (Finestone et al., 2000).

The Impact of Severity

Severity of victimization is a powerful predictor of number of physician visits and total outpatient costs. In a sample of women recruited from a gastroenterology clinic (Leserman, Li, Drossman, & Hu, 1998), women who had experienced severe sexual or physical abuse had eight more health care visits than did non-abused subjects in the previous year. Those with moderate abuse had three more visits than did non-abused women. Severity of abuse history, number of medical symptoms, and functional disability explained 30 percent of the variance in health care visits. Women with severe abuse had more somatic symptoms and related disability, which led to greater use of health care services.

In another study (Leserman et al., 1997), severity was directly related to current health status. For women who reported sexual abuse, 24 percent of the variance in current health was explained by rape, serious injury during the abuse, and victimization by more than one perpetrator. For women who reported physical abuse, rape and multiple life-threatening incidents explained 39 percent of the variance.

Similar findings appeared in a study of criminal victimization (Koss, Koss, & Woodruff, 1991). Women in the victimized group had been raped, had been physically assaulted, or had suffered from a noncontact crime. When women were severely victimized, they made twice as many physicians' visits in the year after their victimization as did nonvictimized women. Number of visits to physicians increased 15–24 percent during the year of the crime, compared with only 2 percent for the nonvictims, and their outpatient costs were 2.5 times greater. Women who had been multiply victimized visited the doctor 6.9 times per year, compared with 3.5 times for the nonvictimized group. In analyzing body systems, there were greater numbers of symptoms reported across all systems except for eyes and skin. The largest effects were on gynecological symptoms, including sexual dysfunction.

Symptoms, Surgery, and Disability

Adult survivors report a high number of symptoms and surgeries and high levels of disability. In two studies of patients with chronic pain, those with a history of physical or sexual abuse had significantly more surgeries than did their non-abused counterparts (Domino & Haber, 1987; Drossman et al., 1990). Women in a support group for sexual abuse survivors reported more hospitalizations and surgeries than did comparison subjects (psychiatric outpatients and nurses) (Finestone et al., 2000).

Abuse survivors in our primary care study reported twice as many symptoms on a review of systems, and twice as many surgeries as age-matched non-abused controls (Kendall-Tackett, Marshall, & Ness, 2003). Similarly, in a large primary care practice, women who had been sexually abused reported significantly more symptoms and a greater intensity of symptoms than did their non-abused counterparts. They also reported significantly higher rates of lifetime surgery (Hulme, 2000). However, Cunningham, Pearce, and Pearce (1988) found no significant difference in the number of surgeries among sexual abuse survivors in their family-practice sample.

In a case study of seven women who had been sexually abused as children, Arnold, Rogers, and Cook (1990) found a mean of eight surgeries per patient. These patients had seen doctors in nineteen different specialties and had had a mean of eighteen contacts with physicians who were not psychiatrists. Despite all these medical interventions, the findings were normal 66 to 70 percent of the time. Felitti (1991) found no significant differences in number of surgical procedures done, with one exception: Women with a history of sexual abuse had had significantly more breast augmentation surgeries.

A series of studies from a gastroenterology practice indicated that both physical and sexual abuse were related to increased pain, somatic symptoms, number of surgeries, days in bed due to disability, and functional disability (Leserman et al., 1996). When abuse included serious injury, the results were even more pronounced (Leserman et al., 1997). Another study compared patients with irritable bowel syndrome to those with organic gastrointestinal conditions (Drossman, Li, Leserman, Toomey, & Hu, 1996). Drossman et al. found a nonsignificant trend toward increased number of physician visits and lifetime surgeries in those with a history of abuse. When considering the amount of variance accounted for by abuse history in health functioning, the numbers were initially fairly small, ranging from 1 percent to 10 percent. However, when only patients with severe abuse were considered, abuse history accounted for 63 percent of the variance for days in bed, 74 percent for number of physician visits, and 231 percent for lifetime surgeries.

INCREASED HEALTH CARE COSTS

When men and women go to the doctor more often, and have more surgeries, their health care costs increase. Not surprisingly, childhood abuse is associated with increased health care costs. In a primary care sample, women who had been sexually abused visited the primary clinic 1.3 times more often than did their non-abused counterparts, with a difference of $150 more in charges over a two-year period (Hulme, 2000).

Walker et al. (1999) also examined the cost of health care services for abuse survivors. They gathered a sample of 1,225 women members of an HMO and asked them to complete a Childhood Trauma Questionnaire. Women who reported any type of abuse and neglect had $97 more in health care costs. Women who reported sexual abuse had an additional $245 in costs, and had significantly higher primary care and outpatient costs. Women with a history of sexual abuse were twice as likely to visit the emergency department (ED) as women with no abuse history, and they were significantly more likely to visit the ED than women who were physically abused or neglected but not sexually abused. Women with any type of maltreatment experience were also twice as likely to seek mental health services as women with no history. And women who had experienced four or five types of abuse had nearly twice the outpatient and total costs over a five-year period (Walker et al., 1999).

More than ten years have passed since these studies were published. So the dollar amount the authors reported need to be adjusted for inflation. Even so, the per-patient costs appear fairly modest. However, when all abused patients are combined, the costs become substantial. Health care costs can also be calculated by looking at the costs of individual symptoms. Depression, posttraumatic stress disorder, and chronic pain are common and costly symptoms among abuse survivors. Although not all patients who have these symptoms were abused as children, a substantial proportion were, and these symptoms are responsible for a large percentage of health care costs. Understanding the cost of these symptoms may give a truer indication of health care costs associated with childhood victimization.

Depression

In a study of 6,000 primary care patients, depressed patients had significantly higher health care costs of all types, including specialty, inpatient, pharmacy, and laboratory, than did patients who were not depressed. The elevated costs remained even after the patients were no longer depressed (Simon, Ormel, VonKorff, & Barlow, 1995). In a ten-year longitudinal study, depressive symptoms were associated with increased outpatient visits, even when patients were no longer depressed, and even after controlling for age, sex, marital status, medical comorbidity, and patient status (Kimerling, Ouimette, Cronkite, & Moos, 1999). When depression accompanies other conditions, it significantly increases both mortality and morbidity associated with those conditions (Murberg, Bru, Svebak, Tveteras, & Aarsland, 1999).

In a study of veterans over age 60, medical costs were directly associated with depression. Medical costs for subjects in the highest quartile of depressive symptoms were $3,200 higher than those in the lowest quartile. In other words, those veterans reporting the most depression had costs that were 50 percent higher than those reporting the least amount (Druss, Rohbaugh, & Rosenheck, 1999).

Posttraumatic Stress Disorder

Posttraumatic stress disorder (PTSD) is also associated with increased health care costs. One study estimated that PTSD and other anxiety disorders cost the U.S. economy $42 billion per year. These patients were three to five times more likely to go to a doctor, and six times more likely to be hospitalized than those without anxiety disorders (Greenberg et al., 1999). In another study of female veterans with PTSD and a history of child maltreatment found that it was PTSD that increased the health care costs. History of maltreatment without PTSD did not increase the costs (Lang et al., 2006).

Chronic Pain

Pain is another symptom strongly associated with childhood abuse, and it too is a costly symptom. According to the U.S. Institute of Medicine, 116 million Americans suffer from chronic pain, and chronic pain accounts for $560 to $635 billion a year in medical costs (Committee on Advancing Pain Research, Care and Education & Institute of Medicine, 2011). Chronic-pain patients are five times more likely to use health care services than are patients without chronic pain (Becker et al., 1997). Further, one in four sick days are for pain, and this equals 50 million workdays lost per year (Brownlee & Schrof, 1997).

Just a brief look at the dollar amounts associated with these three conditions lets us know that childhood victimization is expensive, even if we conservatively estimate that only 25 percent of these patients are abuse survivors. And other costly conditions, including substance abuse or HIV (human immunodeficiency virus), have not even been considered.

HEALTH CARE PROVIDERS' RESPONSE

Abuse and trauma survivors come into a health care system that is not prepared to receive them. Providers often do not know what to do with or for them. In addition, there is rarely infrastructure in place for providers to make referrals. Finally, abuse survivors often have vague symptoms that come and go, and they may be labeled "difficult" by their providers.

A recent study of primary care providers found that many felt unprepared to deal with psychological trauma (Green et al., 2011). This study included a focus group of thirty-one primary providers who worked with a low-income, underserved population. They reported frequent contact with patients who had trauma histories. However, many indicated that they felt unprepared to deal with these patients. When asked to describe some "difficult" patients, they mentioned patients with mental illness or substance abuse. The physicians also had issues with patients with multiple, complex, or vague physical complaints, chronic pain, or obesity—in other words, the profile of many abuse survivors in the health care system. There were two main concerns: the physicians' lack of formal training in how to care for trauma survivors and their strong emotional reactions to some of these patients. By being less effective, the health care providers felt that working with trauma patients was contributing to their job stress. The authors suggested that additional training and appropriate treatment models could increase both the providers' effectiveness and their job satisfaction.

Some of the difficulties health care providers have with trauma patients may be due to their own experiences. The percentage of health care providers who are also abuse survivors appears to be higher than it is in the general population. For example, in data from the Nurses' Health Study II ($N = 67{,}853$), 54 percent indicated that they had experienced physical abuse in child or adulthood. In addition, 34 percent reported sexual abuse as a child or adolescent (Rich-Edwards et al., 2010).

A study of 176 hospital-based health care workers in Canada found that 68 percent had a history of one or more types of violence, abuse, or neglect: 33 percent before the age of 13 (Maunder, Peladeau, Savage, & Lancee, 2010). Health care workers with abuse histories reported more recent stressful life events (eleven vs. five over the previous six months) and greater psychological distress than providers who were not abused. Childhood adversity was also associated with more missed workdays and lower perceived social support. The authors concluded that childhood adversity is common among health care workers and associated with a higher number of life events, more psychological distress, and greater impairment.

Health care providers are not the only professional group with high rates of past abuse. In a study of urban development workers, 75 percent reported direct community violence victimization, 71 percent reported at least one ACE, and 14 percent met the diagnostic criteria for PTSD (Walling, Eriksson, Putman, & Foy, 2011). Urban development workers choose to live and work in impoverished neighborhoods with the goal of improving quality of life for underserved communities. Most of the organizations whose workers were included in this sample were faith-based. The most common ACEs they reported were parental separation or divorce, substance abuse in the household, mental illness in the household, and sexual abuse.

WHY CHILD VICTIMIZATION MAKES PEOPLE SICK

As we have seen, health problems occur more frequently among abuse survivors. Childhood abuse and victimization does indeed make people sick, which raises the intriguing question about why it occurs. Chapters 2 through 20 describe five possible pathways (physiological, behavioral, social, cognitive, and emotional) by which victimization can influence health. These chapters bring together research on the long-term effects of child abuse with research in health psychology. By looking at the long-term effects of childhood abuse in a new way, clinicians and researchers can begin to understand the mechanisms by which health problems occur. Adult survivors can be influenced by any or all of these, and the five types influence each other. Indeed, they form a complex matrix of interrelationships, all of which influence health.

As we recognize the complexity of the forces that lead to health, we must strive for an approach that addresses all five of these pathways. Health outcomes are unlikely to improve if we continue in the mind-set of treating mental health and physical health sequelae separately. Only by recognizing, and addressing, all these underlying factors can we hope to improve the health of adult survivors of childhood abuse.

References

Arnold, R. P., Rogers, D., & Cook, D. A. G. (1990). Medical problems of adults who were sexually abused in childhood. *British Medical Journal, 300*, 705–708.

Batten, S. V., Aslan, M., Maciejewski, P. K., & Mazure, C. M. (2004). Childhood maltreatment as a risk factor for adult cardiovascular disease and depression. *Journal of Clinical Psychiatry, 65*, 249–254.

Becker, N., Bondegaard, T. A., Olsen, A. K., Sjogren, P., Bech, P., & Eriksen, J. (1997). Pain epidemiology and health-related quality of life in chronic non-malignant pain patients referred to a Danish multi-disciplinary pain center. *Pain, 73*, 393–400.

Benedict, M. I., Paine, L. L., Paine, L. A., Brandt, D., & Stallings, R. (1999). The associations of childhood sexual abuse with depressive symptoms during pregnancy, and selected pregnancy outcomes. *Child Abuse and Neglect, 23*, 659–670.

Bonomi, A. E., Cannon, E. A., Anderson, M. L., & Rivara, F. P. (2008). Association between self-reported health and physical and/or sexual abuse experienced before age 18. *Child Abuse and Neglect, 32*, 693–701.

Brownlee, S., & Schrof, J. M. (1997). The quality of mercy. *U.S. News & World Report, March 17*, 54–67.

Committee on Advancing Pain Research, Care and Education & Institute of Medicine. (2011). *Relieving pain in America*. Washington, DC: National Academies Press.

Cunningham, J., Pearce, T., & Pearce, P. (1988). Childhood sexual abuse and medical complaints in adult women. *Journal of Interpersonal Violence, 3*, 131–144.

Domino, J. V., & Haber, J. D. (1987). Prior physical and sexual abuse in women with chronic headache: Clinical correlates. *Headache, 27*, 310–314.

Dong, M., Anda, R. F., Felitti, V. J., Dube, S. R., Williamson, D. F., Thompson, T. J., et al. (2004). The interrelatedness of multiple forms of childhood abuse, neglect, and household dysfunction. *Child Abuse and Neglect, 28*(7), 771–784.

Drossman, D. A., Leserman, J., Nachman, G., Li, Z., Gluck, H., Toomey, T. C., et al. (1990). Sexual and physical abuse in women with functional or organic gastrointestinal disorders. *Annals of Internal Medicine, 113*, 828–833.

Drossman, D. A., Li, Z., Leserman, J., Toomey, T. C., & Hu, Y. J. B. (1996). Health status by gastrointestinal diagnosis and abuse history. *Gastroenterology, 110*, 999–1007.

Druss, B. G., Rohbaugh, R. M., & Rosenheck, R. A. (1999). Depressive symptoms and health care costs in older medical patients. *American Journal of Psychiatry, 156*, 477–479.

Dube, S. R., Fairweather, D., Pearson, W. S., Felitti, V. J., Anda, R. F., & Croft, J. B. (2009). Cumulative childhood stress and autoimmune diseases in adults. *Psychosomatic Medicine, 71*(2), 243–250.

Felitti, V. J. (1991). Long-term medical consequences of incest, rape, and molestation. *Southern Medical Journal, 84*, 328–331.

Felitti, V. J. (2001). Reverse alchemy in childhood: Turning gold into lead. *Health Alert, 8*, 1–4.

Felitti, V. J., Anda, R. F., Nordenberg, D., Williamson, D. F., Spitz, A. M., Edwards, V., et al. (1998). Relationship of childhood abuse and household dysfunction to many of the leading causes of death in adults. The Adverse Childhood Experiences (ACE) Study. *American Journal of Preventive Medicine, 14*(4), 245–258.

Finestone, H. M., Stenn, P., Davies, F., Stalker, C., Fry, R., & Koumanis, J. (2000). Chronic pain and health care utilization in women with a history of childhood sexual abuse. *Child Abuse and Neglect, 24*, 547–556.

Finkelhor, D., Ormrod, R. K., & Turner, H. A. (2009). Lifetime assessment of poly-victimization in a national sample of children and youth. *Child Abuse and Neglect, 33*, 403–411.

Golding, J. M. (1994). Sexual assault history and physical health in randomly selected Los Angeles women. *Health Psychology, 13*, 130–138.

Green, B. L., Kaltman, S., Frank, L., Glennie, M., Subramanian, A., Fritts-Wilson, M., et al. (2011). Primary care providers' experiences with trauma patients: A qualitative study. *Psychological Trauma, 3*(1), 37–41.

Greenberg, P. E., Sisitsky, T., Kessler, R. C., Finkelstein, S. N., Berndt, E. R., Davidson, J. R. T., et al. (1999). The economic burden of anxiety disorders in the 1990s. *Journal of Clinical Psychology, 60*, 427–435.

Grimstad, H., & Schei, B. (1999). Pregnancy and delivery for women with a history of child sexual abuse. *Child Abuse and Neglect, 23*, 81–90.

Hulme, P. A. (2000). Symptomatology and health care utilization of women primary care patients who experienced childhood sexual abuse. *Child Abuse and Neglect, 24*, 1471–1484.

Kendall-Tackett, K. A., Marshall, R., & Ness, K. E. (2000). Victimization, healthcare use and health maintenance. *Family Violence and Sexual Assault Bulletin, 16*, 18–21.

Kendall-Tackett, K. A., Marshall, R., & Ness, K. E. (2003). Chronic pain syndromes and violence against women. *Women and Therapy, 26*, 45–56.

Kimerling, R., Ouimette, P. C., Cronkite, R. C., & Moos, R. H. (1999). Depression and outpatient medical utilization: A naturalistic 10-year follow-up. *Annals of Behavioral Medicine, 21*(4), 317–321.

Koss, M. P., Koss, P. G., & Woodruff, M. S. (1991). Deleterious effects of criminal victimization on women's health and medical utilization. *Archives of Internal Medicine, 151*, 342–347.

Lang, A. J., Laffaye, C., Satz, L. E., McQuaid, J. R., Malcarne, V. L., Dreselhaus, T. R., et al. (2006). Relationships among childhood maltreatment, PTSD, and health in female veterans with a history of child maltreatment. *Child Abuse and Neglect, 30*, 1281–1292.

Leserman, J., Drossman, D. A., Li, Z., Toomey, T. C., Nachman, G., & Glogau, L. (1996). Sexual and physical abuse history in gastroenterology practice: How types of abuse impact health status. *Psychosomatic Medicine, 58*, 4–15.

Leserman, J., Li, Z., Drossman, D. A., & Hu, Y. J. B. (1998). Selected symptoms associated with sexual and physical abuse history among female patients with gastrointestinal disorders: The impact on subsequent health care visits. *Psychological Medicine, 28*, 417–425.

Leserman, J., Li, Z., Drossman, D. A., Toomey, T. C., Nachman, G., & Glogau, L. (1997). Impact of sexual and physical abuse dimensions on health status: Development of an abuse severity measure. *Psychosomatic Medicine, 59*, 152–160.

Maunder, R. G., Peladeau, N., Savage, D., & Lancee, W. J. (2010). The prevalence of childhood adversity among healthcare workers and its relationship to adult life events, distress and impairment. *Child Abuse and Neglect, 34*, 114–123.

Mullen, P. E., Martin, J. L., Anderson, J. C., Romans, S. E., & Herbison, G. P. (1994). The effect of child sexual abuse on social, interpersonal, and sexual function in adult life. *British Journal of Psychiatry, 165*, 35–47.

Murberg, T. A., Bru, E., Svebak, S., Tveteras, R., & Aarsland, T. (1999). Depressed mood and subjective health symptoms as predictors of mortality in patients with congestive heart failure: A two-year follow-up study. *International Journal of Psychiatry in Medicine, 29*, 311–326.

Rich-Edwards, J. W., Spiegelman, D., Lividoti Hibert, E. N., Jun, H.-J., Todd, T. J., Kawachi, I., et al. (2010). Abuse in childhood and adolescence as a predictor of type 2 diabetes in adult women. *American Journal of Preventive Medicine, 39*(6), 529–536.

Scott, K. M., VonKorff, M., Alonso, J., Angermeyer, M. C., Benjet, C., Bruffaerts, R., et al. (2008). Childhood adversity, early-onset depressive/anxiety disorders, and adult-onset asthma. *Psychosomatic Medicine, 70*, 1035–1043.

Simon, G., Ormel, J., VonKorff, M., & Barlow, W. (1995). Health care costs associated with depressive and anxiety disorders in primary care. *American Journal of Psychiatry, 152*, 352–357.

Suglia, S. F., Ryan, L., Laden, F., Dockery, D. W., & Wright, R. J. (2008). Violence exposure, a chronic psychosocial stressor, and childhood lung function. *Psychosomatic Medicine, 70*, 160–169.

Talbot, N. L., Chapman, B., Conwell, Y., McCollumn, K., Franus, N., Cotescu, S., et al. (2009). Childhood sexual abuse is associated with physical illness burden and functioning in psychiatric patients 50 years of age or older. *Psychosomatic Medicine, 71*, 417–422.

Tjaden, P., & Thoennes, N. (2000). *Extent, nature, and consequences of intimate partner violence: Findings from the National Violence against Women Survey.* U.S. Department of Justice, Office of Justice Programs, National Institute of Justice.

Walker, E. A., Unutzer, J., Rutter, C. M., Gelfand, A., Saunders, K., VonKorff, M., et al. (1999). Costs of health care use by women HMO members with a history of childhood abuse and neglect. *Archives of General Psychiatry, 56*, 609–613.

Walling, S. M., Eriksson, C. B., Putman, K. M., & Foy, D. W. (2011). Community violence exposure, adverse childhood experiences, and posttraumatic distress among urban development workers. *Psychological Trauma, 3*(1), 42–49.

Wegman, H. L., & Stetler, C. (2009). A meta-analytic review of the effects of childhood abuse on medical outcomes in adulthood. *Psychosomatic Medicine, 71*, 805–812.

Wong, W. C. W., Leung, P. W. S., Tang, C. S. K., Chen, W.-Q., Lee, A., & Ling, D. C. (2009). To unfold a hidden epidemic: Prevalence of child maltreatment and its health implications among high school students in Guangzhou, China. *Child Abuse and Neglect, 33*, 441–450.

Chapter 2

Physiological Pathways I—The Neuropsychology of Childhood Abuse and Trauma

Children's brains and neurological systems mature at the most rapid rate during the first five years of life, but they continue to mature throughout childhood. Children are especially vulnerable to the impact of traumatic events due to their effect on young brain development (DeBellis, 2011; Heim & Nemeroff, 2009). "Traumatic events in adults can influence the mature brain, but in the developing brain they alter the neural systems in such a way that they create a lifetime of vulnerability" (Perry, 2001, p. 24). Similarly, Sherin and Nemeroff (2011) note that:

> There is a burgeoning literature documenting that early adverse experience, including prenatal stress and stress throughout childhood, has profound and

> long-lasting effects on the development of neurobiological systems, thereby "programming" subsequent stress reactivity and vulnerability to develop PTSD. (p. 273)

Teicher (2002) also noted that early trauma may result in permanent changes to the developing brain:

> Stress can set off a ripple of hormonal changes that permanently wire a child's brain to cope with a malevolent world. Through this chain of events, violence and abuse pass from generation to generation as well as from one society to the next. Our stark conclusion is that we see the need to do much more to ensure that child abuse does not happen in the first place, because once these key brain alterations occur, there may be no going back. (p. 75)

Over the past two decades, researchers have learned much about the effects of traumatic events on the brain and its development. Recent research has indicated that this relationship is more complex than it initially appeared, as Sherin and Nemeroff (2011) described:

> Efforts to identify neurobiological markers for PTSD originally presumed that abnormalities were acquired "downstream" from an exposure, as a consequence of traumatic experience. It could be, however, that certain abnormalities in the patient with PTSD simply represent pre-existing or "upstream" pathology that is functionally dormant and released by trauma exposure and detected thereafter upon investigation. (p. 264)

This argument may be more relevant to children who are victimized at older ages. But stress exposure that occurs in utero, or during early infancy, may have created vulnerabilities that were exacerbated by victimization experiences.

The goal of this chapter is to familiarize readers with the relevant structures of the brain, the normal stress response, and how trauma influences both of these. It is fairly brief because the role of physiological factors is woven throughout the remainder of this book; physiological pathways pertain to emotions, cognitions, behaviors, social relationships, chronic pain, and the perinatal period.

THE BRAIN AND NERVOUS SYSTEM

The nervous system includes the brain and the series of circuits that are involved in governing our responses to threatening or traumatic events. Here I provide a brief overview of these systems. Changes in the neural system underlie many of the sequelae of past abuse described in subsequent chapters.

Brain 101

The brain develops in a hierarchical and sequential fashion. The least complex regions develop first, with components becoming progressively more complex with development (Perry, 2001). This section briefly outlines some of the major areas of the brain and their functions. Table 2.1 also summarizes these components.

Table 2.1
Major Brain Components and Their Functions

Brain Region	Constituent Parts	Age of Greatest Developmental Activity	Age of Functional Maturity	Key Functions
Brainstem	Midbrain Cerebellum Pons Medulla oblongata	In utero	Infancy	Core physiological, state regulation, primary sensory processing
Diencephalon	Thalamus Hypothalamus	Infancy	Childhood	Motor control, secondary sensory processing
Limbic system	Amygdala Cingulate cortex Hippocampus Basal ganglia Caudate nucleus	Early childhood	Puberty	Memory, emotional regulation, primary sensory integration
Neocortex	**Cerebral cortex**			
	Frontal lobes Temporal lobes Parietal lobes Occipital lobes Corpus callosum	Childhood	Adult	Reasoning, problem solving, abstraction, secondary sensory integration

- *Brainstem.* The first area to develop is the brainstem. This area includes the midbrain, cerebellum, pons, and medulla oblongata. It regulates core body functions, such as breathing and sleep.
- *Diencephalon.* The next level to develop is the diencephalon, which includes the thalamus and hypothalamus. It is responsible for motor control, and secondary processing of sensory information.
- *Limbic system.* The limbic system includes several key players in the response to traumatic events, such as the cingulate cortex, which is related to pain perception, the amygdala and hippocampus, which are involved in learning and memory, and the basal ganglia. The limbic system is involved in emotional regulation, attachment, and primary sensory integration.
- *Neocortex.* The last area to develop is the neocortex. The neocortex is responsible for abstract reasoning, complex state regulation, attachment, mood regulation, and socialization.

Each of these areas of the brain has some role in the response to a threat (Perry & Pollard, 1998). The brainstem and diencephalon regulate autonomic and hypothalamic output, alter arousal, and help tune out other distracting information. The limbic system modulates recognition of facial expression and emotional reactivity, and the cortex interprets the threat and develops a plan.

Brainstem Nuclei

Other key structures include the aminergic nuclei of the brainstem, which synthesize the neurotransmitters serotonin, norepinephrine, and dopamine. The nuclei of interest are the locus coeruleus, which synthesizes norepinephrine, the raphe nuclei, which synthesizes serotonin, and the ventral tegmental nucleus, which synthesizes dopamine (Lovallo, 1997; Perry, Pollard, Blakley, Baker, & Vigilante, 1995; Sherin & Nemeroff, 2011).

The locus coeruleus is the key mediator of the fight-or-flight response, and it regulates the autonomic nervous system, the immune system, and HPA (hypothalamic-pituitary-adrenal) axis (Perry & Pollard, 1998; Sherin & Nemeroff, 2011). It contains 90 percent of the norepinephrine-containing fibers in the central nervous system and regulates attention, arousal, sleep-wake cycles, learning and memory, anxiety and pain, mood, and brain metabolism, and can influence almost every part of the brain. It projects to the prefrontal cortex, amygdala, hippocampus, hypothalamus, periaqueductal grey, and the thalamus. Norepinephrine also plays a role in encoding memories that aid in recognition of future danger (Bear, Connors, & Paradiso, 1996; DeBellis, 2011; Southwick, Bremner, Krystal, & Charney, 1994).

Serotonin (5HT) is a monoamine neurotransmitter synthesized from the amino acid tryptophan. Serotonin projects to several brain regions including the amygdala, stria terminalis, hippocampus, hypothalamus, and prefrontal cortex. It regulates sleep, appetite, sexual behavior, aggression and impulsivity, motor function, and analgesia. The serotonin system interacts with the corticotropin-releasing hormone (CRH) and norepinephrine (NE) systems to coordinate affective and stress responses, and altered serotonin transmission likely contributes to posttraumatic stress disorder (PTSD) symptoms, such as increased startle, impulsivity, and intrusive memories (Sherin & Nemeroff, 2011).

GABA (gamma-aminobutyric acid) is a principal inhibitory neurotransmitter of the central nervous system. It has anti-anxiety (anxiolytic) effects, and dampens the behavioral and physiological response to stress. It does so by inhibiting the CRH/NE circuits. Uncontrollable stress alters the GABA/benzodiazepine-receptor complex. Treatment with benzodiazepines does not prevent PTSD after exposure to psychological trauma (Heim & Nemeroff, 2009).

Neuropeptide Y also has stress-buffering and anxiolytic effects, and inhibits the CRH/NE circuits involved in stress and fear. It also reduces the release of NE from the sympathetic nervous system. Neuropeptide Y may also be involved in recovery from and resilience to traumatic events, and combat veterans with low levels of neuropeptide Y are more likely to develop PTSD than combat veterans without PTSD (Heim & Nemeroff, 2009).

Neurotransmitter changes in PTSD likely reflect sensitization of stress-mediating systems and/or decreased ability to restrain stress responses in order to regain homeostasis (Heim & Nemeroff, 2009).

Brain Circuitry Altered by Traumatic Events (Structural and Functional Anatomy)

Several areas comprise a neural circuit that mediates stress and fear conditions. These include the amygdala, hippocampus, anterior cingulate cortex, insula, and orbitofrontal region. Changes in these circuits have a possible link to the development of PTSD (Heim & Nemeroff, 2009; Sherin & Nemeroff, 2011; Teicher, 2002).

The hippocampus is one of the most malleable regions of the brain. It is involved in declarative memory and the contextual aspects of fear condition. Prolonged exposure to stress atrophies the hippocampus. Small hippocampal volumes were associated with severity of the trauma and memory impairments. Further, hippocampal deficits may activate and/or fail to shut down the stress response (Heim & Nemeroff, 2009). However, hippocampal atrophy, and the functional deficits that accompany it, can be reversed by treating with the selective serotonin reuptake inhibitor (SSRI) class of antidepressants (Bremner, 2005; Heim & Nemeroff, 2009; Sherin & Nemeroff, 2011; Teicher, 2002).

The amygdala is a structure in the limbic system. It is involved in emotional processing and the acquisition of the fear response (Heim & Nemeroff, 2009). It has a critical role in the fear response. Following threat exposure, it can become hyperresponsive to fear cues (Sherin & Nemeroff, 2011; Teicher, 2002). Patients with PTSD have a hyperresponsiveness of the amygdala in imaging studies in responding to traumatic cues. It also seems to be pick up on subliminally threatening cues in PTSD (Heim & Nemeroff, 2009).

The medial prefrontal cortex (PFC) is made up of the anterior cingulate cortex, subcallosal cortex, and the medial frontal gyrus. The medial PFC can inhibit the stress response and emotional reactivity to fear cues because of its connections to the amygdala. When patients have symptoms of PTSD, they often have reduced volumes of the PFC, including the anterior cingulate cortex (Heim & Nemeroff, 2009). A greater reduction in the PFC is related to greater symptom severity. However, treatment with SSRIs has been shown to restore medial prefrontal cortical activation patterns (Sherin & Nemeroff, 2011).

THE STRESS RESPONSE

The stress response is designed to preserve the life of the organism. Following is a description of these actions. It will be helpful in understanding how these processes change in the case of traumatic events (DeBellis, 2011; Kendall-Tackett, 2010; Lovallo, 1997).

Sensory Intake and Interpretation of the Environment

The process begins when a person perceives a potential threat. The thalamus directs information to the corresponding area of the cerebral cortex (e.g., visual information is directed to the part of the cerebral cortex responsible for processing visual information). The physiological response is the same for physical or psychological threat.

Generation of Emotions Based on the Appraisal Processes

Once the information has been referred to the appropriate area, the brain begins the process of evaluation. The portions of the brain that govern emotions and affective state include the PFC, amygdala, hippocampus, anterior cingulate cortex, and insular cortex (Bremner, 1999; Davidson, 2000). The frontal lobes, especially the PFC, attach meaning to events and consider possible consequences. The prefrontal areas, hippocampus, and amygdala generate emotions. The hippocampus is involved in learning and memory, whereas the amygdala gives emotional content to memories, especially those associated with fear and pain (Bear et al., 1996; DeBellis, 2011).

If the event is perceived as nonthreatening but requires action, the amygdala activates the adrenal-medulla system, resulting in increased secretion of norepinephrine. Cortisol levels are unaffected. If, however, the event is perceived as noxious, the hippocampus activates the HPA axis, and cortisol is released (Lovallo, 1997).

There is also evidence of a feed-forward circuit connecting the amygdala and hypothalamus to the locus coeruleus, such that CRH and NE interact. This interaction increases fear conditioning and encoding of emotional memories. It also enhances arousal and hypervigilance. This cascade is inhibited by glucocorticoids (DeBellis, 2011; Sherin & Nemeroff, 2011). With fear conditioning, neutral stimuli present at the initial traumatic event can provoke the same feeling of fear and terror (Davidson, 2000; Southwick et al., 1994). Finally, the anterior cingulate cortex responds and activates other brain circuits involved in emotions (Davidson, 2000).

Sympathetic Nervous System

The sympathetic nervous system responds to threat by releasing catecholamines (norepinephrine, epinephrine, and dopamine). This is the fight-or-flight response, and it occurs instantly after threat exposure (DeBellis, 2011). Both dopamine and norepinephrine derive from the amino acid tyrosine (Sherin & Nemeroff, 2011).

Norepinephrine is one of the principal mediators of the autonomic stress response and accounts for classic symptoms of PTSD including hyperarousal, heightened startle, and increased coding of fear memories (Sherin & Nemeroff, 2011). A cardinal feature of patients who have experienced traumatic events is sustained hyperactivity of the autonomic nervous system, including increased heart rate, blood pressure, and skin conductance level (Heim & Nemeroff, 2009). Because of this involvement, researchers have proposed using the adrenergic blocker propranolol to reduce PTSD severity after exposure to a traumatic event. Unfortunately, it did not prevent the development of PTSD in one study, but it did appear to block traumatic memory consolidation, which may have reduced the severity and chronicity of PTSD symptoms (Heim & Nemeroff, 2009). The International Society for Traumatic Stress Studies has identified propranolol as a promising treatment for possibly preventing PTSD after trauma exposure (Friedman, Cohen, Foa, & Keane, 2009).

HPA Axis

The HPA axis is central to the stress response. As such, it has been a major focus of trauma researchers (Sherin & Nemeroff, 2011). The HPA axis produces a cascade response, starting with the hypothalamus. The paraventricular nucleus of the hypothalamus releases CRH (also known as corticotropin-releasing factor, or CRF). CRH is the central regulatory neuropeptide that coordinates the neuroendocrine response to stress. It activates both the pituitary-adrenal axis and the sympathetic nervous system (Heim & Nemeroff, 2009; Miller, 1998). CRH causes the pituitary to release adrenocorticotropic hormone (ACTH) and beta-endorphin. ACTH signals the cortex of the adrenal glands to secrete cortisol (Lovallo, 1997).

The HPA axis has far-reaching effects on immunity, metabolism, and reproduction. This system returns to baseline a few hours after stress exposure. If stress continues, however, it becomes dysregulated, and patterns of either hyperactivity or hypoactivity appear (Corwin & Pajer, 2008). Hypocortisolemia is a hallmark symptom of PTSD, and it allows the sustained activation of the neural systems involved in fear processing, including CRH and NE (DeBellis, 2011; Heim & Nemeroff, 2009).

Inflammatory Response System

The final component of the stress response is the inflammatory response system, which responds to threat by increasing systemic inflammation (Corwin & Pajer, 2008; Kendall-Tackett, 2007). Researchers generally assess inflammation by measuring serum levels of proinflammatory cytokines, which are messenger molecules of the immune system (Miller, Cohen, & Ritchey, 2002). The proinflammatory cytokines that are most often measured in depression and trauma research are interleukin-1β (IL-1β), interleukin-6 (IL-6), and tumor necrosis factor-α (TNF-α). Researchers sometimes include other measures of inflammation in their studies. These include interferon-γ (IFN-γ), soluble-intercellular adhesion molecule (sICAM), fibrinogen, or C-reactive protein (CRP). Most of the research on the inflammatory response to stress comes from a field known as psychoneuroimmunology (Kendall-Tackett, 2010). The inflammatory response is a key mediator of the health effects of trauma.

Like other aspects of the stress response, the inflammatory response is meant to preserve the life of the organism. It has two main functions: fight infection and heal wounds. In anticipation of a possible threat, the body is prepared to mend itself. The difficulty occurs when the inflammatory response is chronically elevated. Most of this research has focused on depression. More recently, we have seen a similar effect with other negative emotional states, such as hostility or anger. As I describe in subsequent chapters, some negative mental states are more common in abuse survivors than in their non-abused counterparts. Although a fairly new area of study within the trauma field, I believe that inflammation will prove to be a key mediator between childhood abuse and adult health problems.

One of the original studies that established the link between chronic stress, inflammation, and severe health problems was not a study of trauma at all, but a sample of elderly men and women (average age = 70 years), half of whom were caring for a spouse with Alzheimer's (Kiecolt-Glaser et al., 2003). This study particularly focused on the proinflammatory cytokine IL-6, which has been linked to a number of chronic diseases, including cardiovascular disease, Type 2 diabetes, cancer, and overall functional decline. The impact of caregiving was such that IL-6 levels were four times higher in the caregivers versus age-matched non-caregivers. These levels remained elevated even after the spouse had died. At the end of the six-year follow-up, 78 of the 119 caregivers had died. These researchers concluded that chronic stress accelerated the risk of disease by prematurely aging the immune response.

Inflammation in Trauma Survivors. Inflammation levels have also been elevated in abuse survivors. Childhood maltreatment was shown to affect clinically relevant levels of C-reactive protein when measured twenty years after the abuse (Danese, Pariante, Caspi, Taylor, & Poulton, 2007). C-reactive protein is an acute-phase reactant that becomes elevated when there are high levels of proinflammatory cytokines. It is a general measure of inflammation. The participants ($N = 1{,}037$) were part of the Dunedin Multidisciplinary Health and Development Study, a study of health behavior in a complete birth cohort in Dunedin, New Zealand. Participants were assessed every two to three years throughout childhood, and every five to six years through age 32. The effect of child maltreatment on inflammation was independent of co-occurring life stresses in adulthood, early life risks, or adult health or health behavior. White blood cell count and fibrinogen were also elevated in those who experienced childhood physical or sexual abuse. Fibrinogen is concerning because it increases the "stickiness" of blood and increases clotting, which can increase the risk of both heart attack and stroke. Severity of abuse was related, in a dose-response way, to severity of inflammation.

At the thirty-two-year follow-up of the same cohort, the participants were assessed for the impact of childhood adversity on three age-related disease markers: major depression, high inflammation (C-reactive protein), and a cluster of metabolic risk factors that included overweight, high blood pressure, high cholesterol, low HDL cholesterol, high glycated hemoglobin, and low maximum oxygen consumption (Danese et al., 2009). "Childhood adversity" was defined as low socioeconomic status (SES), child maltreatment, and social isolation. They found that children exposed to childhood adversities were at high risk for all three disease markers. They had elevated risk of depression, high inflammation levels, and high rates of the metabolic risk factors. These risk factors were nonredundant, cumulative, and independent of other risk factors. They noted that childhood adversity has long-term effects on emotional, immune, and metabolic abnormalities.

In a related study, chronic family stress was related to an increased inflammatory response to an acute stress event in children with asthma (Marin, Chen, Munch, & Miller, 2009). This study included seventy-one children with asthma and seventy-six healthy control children. The children who had higher levels of chronic family stress had an increased production of IL-4, IL-5, and IFN-γ, the inflammatory cytokines related to asthma following an acute stress event. An example of an acute stress event included mother being fired from a job, father admitted to the hospital for depression, or a best friend moving away. The authors concluded that acute negative life events will have a particularly negative effect for the subgroup of children with asthma who are exposed to chronic family stress. The stress system is already overloaded, and when an acute event occurs, it leads to an exacerbation in symptoms. The same was not true for the healthy control children. These findings support the notion that children who are under stress are at greater risk for asthma exacerbations.

In a sample of fourteen otherwise healthy patients with PTSD, and a matched group on age and gender of fourteen patients without PTSD, von Kanel et al. (2006) investigated blood coagulation. They noted that PTSD increases risk of cardiovascular disease and that the mechanism for this relationship is not well understood. In this study, they investigated whether PTSD was associated with coagulation activity by measuring various clotting factors (FVII:C, FVIII:C, FXII:C), fibrinogen, and D-dimer in the plasma. They found that FVIII:C was predicted by hyperarousal severity and overall PTSD severity. In patients with PTSD, hyperarousal and overall PTSD severity predicted fibrinogen. The more severe the PTSD, the greater the concentration of these coalgulation factors. They concluded that PTSD may elicit hypercoagulability, even at subthreshold levels, and this may increase risk for cardiovascular disease in trauma survivors.

The aforementioned studies indicated that inflammation was related to increased rates of various diseases. Chronic inflammation was also found to have effects on cognitive ability in older adults. A sample of 2,312 men and women, ages 50–85, who were free of cardiovascular disease at the beginning of the study, were followed for five years (Marioni et al., 2009). The authors were studying whether C-reactive protein, fibrinogen, plasma viscosity, and hematocrit were related to cognitive decline five years later. The results indicated that C-reactive protein, plasma viscosity, and fibrinogen were related to cognitive decline by several measures, including general cognitive ability, nonverbal reasoning, executive function, processing speed, and mental flexibility.

Summary. Trauma, in general and child victimization in particular, have demonstrated negative impact on health. Psychoneuroimmunology (PNI) research suggests that inflammation is a possible mechanism by which trauma increases the risk of illness. Fortunately, inflammation can be specifically and easily addressed in health care settings. With information from these studies, practitioners can address health issues of trauma survivors—increasing their health and longevity in the process.

NEURONAL PLASTICITY

Neuronal plasticity is another construct that needs to be understood with regard to the health effects of child victimization. One of the hallmark features of neurons is that they change in response to external signals (Perry et al., 1995). This means that the brain is malleable. Changes that occur at the molecular level permit the neuron and neural systems to store information. The more frequently an experience occurs, the more indelible the impression and the internal representations. When stress is severe, uncontrollable, or chronic, the normal stress response becomes overactivated, fatigued, and no longer capable of restoring homeostasis (Perry & Pollard, 1998).

A fear response in children can organize neural systems. Indeed, experience becomes the filter through which all new information is processed. In reviewing the literature, Lovallo (1997) describes how traumatic stress has the largest impact on the central nervous system. The changes appear to be related to long-term alterations in frontal-limbic connections and alterations in feedback to the central nervous system from the brainstem aminergic nuclei. Experience may alter behavior in an adult, but it literally provides the organizing framework for a child. Because the brain is most malleable during these first five years, the child is most vulnerable to experience during that time.

Although it is adaptive for a child growing up in an abusive environment to become hypersensitive to external cues, this constant exposure to traumatic stress actually organizes the child's neural systems to adapt to a violent or chaotic environment. Adults exposed to traumatic events become sensitized and reactive to cues specifically related to their trauma. Children exposed to consistent trauma, in contrast, develop a generalized physiological hyperarousal, and all cues activate this system (Perry, 2001).

Sensitization

Sensitization is one type of change that is central to our understanding of neuronal plasticity. Sensitization is the process by which a previous experience of stress amplifies that organism's response to a new stressor. The brain adapts to adverse events by sensitizing neural circuits, and subsequent stressors cause an overreaction (Plotsky, Owens, & Nemeroff, 1998). Once sensitization has occurred, the same level of neural response can be triggered by less and less external stimulation (Perry et al., 1995) and generalized to broader categories of triggers.

Perry et al. (1995) noted that children who have experienced trauma exhibit a profound level of sensitization that can result in either hyperarousal or dissociation. These responses can be elicited by fairly minor stressors. Sensitization has been implicated in depression, PTSD, and chronic pain among adult survivors of childhood abuse (Miller, 2000). Trauma survivors may be hypersensitive to environmental and external events, and may hyperrespond, even in the face of nondangerous stimuli (Yehuda, 1999). Sensitization can also help explain why adults who were abused as children seem more vulnerable to stressors as adults.

For example, child abuse made combat veterans more vulnerable to PTSD. Bremner, Southwick, Johnson, Yehuda, and Charney (1993) compared rates of childhood abuse in Vietnam veterans with and without combat-related PTSD. They found higher rates of childhood physical abuse among veterans with PTSD compared with those without PTSD (26 percent vs. 7 percent). This association held even after controlling for the difference in level of combat exposure. It is important to note, however, that childhood abuse does not account for all PTSD among veterans. Seventy-four percent of those with PTSD did not report a history of abuse.

Another study showed similar findings (King, King, & Foy, 1996). In a group of Vietnam veterans, previous exposure to a traumatic event directly predicted PTSD and also exacerbated PTSD symptoms for high combat-exposed male soldiers. The traumatic events include accidents, assaults, and natural disasters. Family instability and childhood antisocial behavior had indirect effects. For women, in contrast, family instability was more predictive of PTSD, but only indirectly.

A similar finding was made among female rape survivors. In this study, women with a history of either physical or sexual assault had significantly lower cortisol response to a current rape than did women who did not have such a history (Resnick,

Yehuda, Pitman, & Foy, 1995). Low cortisol levels at intake predicted the development of PTSD three months later in response to the current rape (Yehuda, McFarlane, & Shalev, 1998a).

Sensitization may also explain why other adverse childhood events can create similar results to those found in cases of childhood abuse. For example, Roy (1996) reports that loss of a parent for at least one year before the age of 17 was significantly associated with chronic depression in women. In another study, parental loss also predicted health problems in middle-age adults. Parental divorce predicted a higher number of physical health problems for both men and women. But the relationship was mediated by income, education, drug use, and family support, and this was stronger for men than it was for women. In contrast, parental death predicted more autonomy for men and more depression in women (Maier & Lachman, 2000).

Changes in the HPA Axis

Chronic stress has been shown to alter components of the HPA axis (Yehuda et al., 1996). These alterations manifest themselves in many ways, including abnormal levels of stress hormones, such as norepinephrine and cortisol, specific changes in the number or sensitivity of receptors to these substances, and changes in certain brain structures such as the hippocampus (Lovallo, 1997; Southwick et al., 1994). Traumatic changes also cause chronic hypersecretion of CRH and ACTH, with accompanying adrenal and pituitary hypertrophy (Weiss, Longhurst, & Mazure, 1999).

CRH can mediate the association between early-life stress and the development of mood and anxiety disorders (Heim et al., 2000). CRH neurons are found in several key sections of the brain: the hypothalamus, neocortex, and the central nucleus of the amygdala. Enhanced release of CRH and sensitization of the CRH systems may account for symptoms of depression in response to current stress.

At the onset of trauma, high levels of cortisol may damage the hippocampus, and this damage can persist for many years and lead to a lower hippocampal volume on an MRI. The atrophy of the hippocampus may lead to hypothalamic inhibition, which results in elevated CRH and a blunted response to ACTH. This is the pattern seen in PTSD (Yehuda et al., 1996). The abnormally low levels of cortisol in PTSD may reflect a long-term change and adaptation to the high levels of cortisol initially. Thus acute stress may lead to hyperactivity of the CRH/HPA system, whereas chronic PTSD may lead to long-term dysregulation and indeed a different HPA/cortisol system. But the mechanism for this reaction is still unclear (Bremner, 1999).

Normally, glucocorticoids constrain the sympathetic nervous system and the catecholamine response to a stressful event. The catecholamines also curb the inflammatory response. But the catecholamines also regulate the HPA axis. Changes in either the catecholamine system or the HPA axis can profoundly affect how the catecholamines coordinate in response to stress. When describing the role of cortisol and catecholamines, Yehuda, Resnick, Schmeidler, Yang, and Pitman (1998b) noted that prior trauma appears to affect the cortisol response to stress. When this response is altered, the normal coordination between the cortisol and NE systems breaks down. An abnormally low cortisol level could also lead to changes in the processing of traumatic memories because it enhances the memory-potentiating effects of catecholamines in the formation of memories of the traumatic event. There is also the phenomenon of cortisol resistance, whereby someone under severe stress secretes high levels of cortisol, but the body does not respond because the individual has become cortisol resistant (Miller et al., 2002). This also means that cortisol will not contain or attenuate the inflammatory response system.

Evidence for HPA Alterations and Sensitization

Evidence for sensitization and alterations in the HPA axis comes from three types of studies: those with animals, infants, and children. This section contains a brief synopsis of a few of these studies. Additional evidence is included in subsequent chapters.

In a review of fifty animal studies of early loss, Hofer (1996) concluded that early loss (i.e., maternal separation) altered the normal function of the HPA axis. Early loss made the animals more vulnerable to both disease and subsequent stress and caused a widespread dysregulation of all functional systems.

In comparing a sample of thirteen depressed children who had been abused, thirteen depressed children who had not been abused, and thirteen normal control children, Kaufman et al. (1997) found that depressed abused children had significantly greater peak, total and net ACTH. It was only observed for those depressed abused children living in chronic adversity including marital violence, emotional abuse, poverty, or lack of family support. Most of these children experienced multiple types of abuse, with sexual and emotional abuse being the most common. The authors concluded that abuse experienced with ongoing stressors, and in the absence of positive supports, promoted a significant dysregulation of the HPA axis.

Novel Treatments Suggested by Biological Literature

Research into the psychobiology of traumatic events has suggested several promising avenues for treatment. For example, administration of hydrocortisone a short time after trauma exposure can prevent PTSD. It also helps simulate the normal circadian rhythm of cortisol and as such can be useful in the treatment of PTSD. The beta-adrenergic antagonist propranolol did not prevent the development of PTSD, but it did reduce symptom severity by blocking traumatic memory consolidation. Finally, the partial NMDA (N-Methyl-D-aspartate)-receptor antagonist DCS lessens the fear response in rodents, and has also helped patients with phobia undergoing treatment via exposure therapy. It is not yet known whether the drug enhances the outcomes of exposure therapy (Heim & Nemeroff, 2009). (See Chapters 17 to 20 for more on treatments.)

Summary

Traumatic events can change the neural systems of children and how they respond to subsequent stressors. Trauma affects several key areas of the brain, including the parts responsible for emotional regulation, attachment, learning, and memory. Each of these is important to understanding the effects of abuse on other areas of functioning. Chapter 3 describes another physiological symptom that is relevant to both trauma and health: sleep.

References

Bear, M. F., Connors, B. W., & Paradiso, M. A. (1996). *Neuroscience: Exploring the brain.* Baltimore, MD: Williams & Wilkins.

Bremner, J. D. (1999). Does stress damage the brain? *Biological Psychiatry, 45*, 797–805.

Bremner, J. D. (2005). The neurobiology of childhood sexual abuse in women with posttraumatic stress disorder. In K. A. Kendall-Tackett (Ed.), *Handbook of women, stress, and trauma* (pp. 181–206). New York: Brunner-Routledge.

Bremner, J. D., Southwick, S. M., Johnson, D. R., Yehuda, R., & Charney, D. S. (1993). Childhood physical abuse and combat-related posttraumatic stress disorder in Vietnam veterans. *American Journal of Psychiatry, 150*, 235–239.

Corwin, E. J., & Pajer, K. (2008). The psychoneuroimmunology of postpartum depression. *Journal of Women's Health, 17*(9), 1529–1534.

Danese, A., Moffitt, T. E., Harrington, H., Milne, B. J., Polanczyk, G., Pariante, C. M., et al. (2009). Adverse childhood experiences and adult risk factors for age-related disease: Depression, inflammation, and clustering of metabolic risk markers. *Archives of Pediatric and Adolescent Medicine, 163*(12), 1135–1143.

Danese, A., Pariante, C. M., Caspi, A., Taylor, A., & Poulton, R. (2007). Childhood maltreatment predicts adult inflammation in a life-course study. *Proceedings of the National Academy of Sciences USA, 104*(4), 1319–1324.

Davidson, R. J. (2000). Affective style, psychopathology, and resilience: Brain mechanisms and plasticity. *American Psychologist, 55*, 1193–1214.

DeBellis, M. D. (2011). Neurodevelopmental biology associated with childhood sexual abuse. *Journal of Child Sexual Abuse, 20*, 548–587.

Friedman, M. J., Cohen, J. A., Foa, E. B., & Keane, T. M. (2009). Integration and summary. In E. B. Foa, T. M. Keane, M. J. Friedman, & J. A. Cohen (Eds.), *Effective treatments for PTSD: Practice guidelines from the International Society for Traumatic Stress Studies* (pp. 617–642). New York: Guilford Press.

Heim, C., & Nemeroff, C. B. (2009). Neurobiology of posttraumatic stress disorder. *CNS Spectrums, 14*(1 Suppl. 1), 13–24.

Heim, C., Newport, D. J., Heit, S., Graham, Y. P., Wilcox, M., Bonsall, R., et al. (2000). Pituitary-adrenal and autonomic responses to stress in women after sexual and physical abuse in childhood. *Journal of the American Medical Association 284*, 592–597.

Hofer, M. A. (1996). On the nature and consequences of early loss. *Psychosomatic Medicine, 58*, 570–586.

Kaufman, J., Birmaher, B., Perel, J., Dahl, R. E., Moreci, P., Nelson, B., et al. (1997). The corticotropin-releasing hormone challenge in depressed abuse, depressed nonabused, and normal control children. *Biological Psychiatry, 42*, 669–679.

Kendall-Tackett, K. A. (2007). A new paradigm for depression in new mothers: The central role of inflammation and how breastfeeding and anti-inflammatory treatments protect maternal mental health. *International Breastfeeding Journal, 2*(6). Available online at: *http://www.internationalbreastfeedingjournal.com/content/2/1/6).*

Kendall-Tackett, K. A. (Ed.). (2010). *The psychoneuroimmunology of chronic disease*. Washington, DC: American Psychological Association.

Kiecolt-Glaser, J. K., Preacher, K. J., MacCallum, R. C., Atkinson, C., Malarkey, W. B., & Glaser, R. (2003). Chronic stress and age-related increases in the proinflammatory cytokine IL-6. *Proceedings of the National Academy of Sciences USA, 100*(15), 9090–9095.

King, D. W., King, L. A., & Foy, D. W. (1996). Prewar factors in combat-related posttraumatic stress disorder: Structual equation modeling with a national sample of female and male Vietnam veterans. *Journal of Consulting & Clinical Psychology, 64*, 520–531.

Lovallo, W. R. (1997). *Stress and health: Biological and psychological interactions*. Newbury Park, CA: Sage.

Maier, E. H., & Lachman, M. E. (2000). Consequences of early parental loss and separation for health and well-being in midlife. *International Journal of Behavioral Development, 24*(2), 183–189.

Marin, T. J., Chen, E., Munch, J. A., & Miller, G. E. (2009). Double-exposure to acute stress and chronic family stress is associated with immune changes in children with asthma. *Psychosomatic Medicine, 71*, 378–384.

Marioni, R. E., Stewart, M. C., Murray, G. D., Deary, I. J., Fowkes, F. G. R., Lowe, G. D. O., et al. (2009). Peripheral levels of fibrinogen, C-reactive protein, and plasmas viscosity predict future cognitive decline in individuals without dementia. *Psychosomatic Medicine, 71*, 901–906.

Miller, A. H. (1998). Neuroendocrine and immune system interactions in stress and depression. *Psychiatric Clinics of North America, 21*, 443–463.

Miller, G. E., Cohen, S., & Ritchey, A. K. (2002). Chronic psychological stress and the regulation of pro-inflammatory cytokines: A gulcocorticoid-resistance model. *Health Psychology, 21*, 531–541.

Miller, L. (2000). Neurosensitization: A model for persistent disability in chronic pain, depression, and posttraumatic stress disorder following injury. *NeuroRehabilitation, 14*, 25–32.

Perry, B. D. (2001). The neuroarcheology of childhood maltreatment: The neurodevelopmental costs of adverse chlidhood events. In K. Franey, R. Geffner & R. Falconer (Eds.), *The cost of child maltreatment: Who pays? We all do* (pp. 15–37). San Diego: Family Violence & Sexual Assault Institute.

Perry, B. D., & Pollard, R. (1998). Homeostasis, stress, trauma, and adaptation: A neuro-developmental view of childhood trauma. *Child and Adolescent Psychiatric Clinics of North America, 7*, 33–51.

Perry, B. D., Pollard, R., Blakley, T. L., Baker, W. L., & Vigilante, D. (1995). Childhood trauma, the neurobiology of adaptation, and "use-dependent" development of the brain: How "states" become "traits." *Infant Mental Health Journal, 16*, 271–291.

Plotsky, P. M., Owens, M. J., & Nemeroff, C. B. (1998). Psychoneuroendocrinology of depression: Hypothalamic-pituitary-adrenal axis. *Psychiatric Clinics of North America, 21*, 293–307.

Resnick, H. S., Yehuda, R., Pitman, R. K., & Foy, D. W. (1995). Effect of previous trauma on acute plasma cortisol level following rape. *American Journal of Psychiatry, 152*, 1675–1677.

Roy, A. (1996). Psychosocial factors and chronic depression. *Journal of Nervous and Mental Disease, 184*, 507–509.

Sherin, J. E., & Nemeroff, C. B. (2011). Post-traumatic stress disorder: The neurobiological implications of psychological trauma. *Dialogues in Clinical Neuroscience, 13*(3), 263–278.

Southwick, S. M., Bremner, J. D., Krystal, J. H., & Charney, D. S. (1994). Psychobiologic research in posttraumatic stress disorder. *Psychiatric Clinics of North America, 17*, 251–264.

Teicher, M. H. (2002). Scars that won't heal: The neurobiology of child abuse. *Scientific American, 286*(3), 68–75.

von Kanel, R., Hepp, U., Buddeberg, C., Keel, M., Mica, L., Aschbacher, K., et al. (2006). Altered blood coagulation in patients with posttraumatic stress disorder. *Psychosomatic Medicine, 68*(4), 598–604.

Weiss, E. L., Longhurst, J. G., & Mazure, C. M. (1999). Childhoood sexual abuse as a risk factor for depression in women: Psychosocial and neurobiological correlates. *American Journal of Psychiatry, 156*, 816–828.

Yehuda, R. (1999). Biological factors associated with susceptibility to posttraumatic stress disorder. *Canadian Journal of Psychiatry, 44*, 34–39.

Yehuda, R., Levengood, R. A., Schmeidler, J., Wilson, S., Guo, L. S., & Gerber, D. (1996). Increased pituitary activation following metyrapone administration in post-traumatic stress disorder. *Psychoneuroendicrinology, 21*, 1–16.

Yehuda, R., McFarlane, A. C., & Shalev, A. Y. (1998a). Predicting the development of posttraumatic stress disorder from the acute response to a traumatic event. *Biological Psychiatry, 44*, 1305–1313.

Yehuda, R., Resnick, H. S., Schmeidler, J., Yang, R.-K., & Pitman, R. K. (1998b). Predictors of cortisol and 3-methoxy-4-hydroxyphenylglycol responses in the acute aftermath of rape. *Biological Psychiatry, 43*, 855–859.

Chapter 3

Physiological Pathways II—Sleep Disturbances

Human beings need to sleep; in fact, it is essential to our survival. It is during sleep that the body repairs itself, recuperates from spent energies, and generates and stores energy reserves for future use (Hawkley, Preacher, & Cacioppo, 2010). Although sleep is a behavior, it is also a physiological process regulated by the brain stem, thalamus, hypothalamic hormones, and external stimuli, such as light. For these reasons, it can also be influenced by external events, such as childhood abuse (Hanson & Chen, 2010). Too little sleep, or sleep that is nonrefreshing, results in daytime fatigue, cognitive and behavioral impairments, and, ultimately, poor health (Hawkley, et al., 2010).

Sleep problems are common in abuse and trauma survivors, and it exerts an independent effect on health above and beyond that of depression or posttraumatic stress disorder (PTSD) (Krakow et al., 2000a; Roberts, Shema, Kaplan, & Strawbridge,

2000). Moreover, sleep difficulties actually exacerbate the effects of depression and PTSD (Krakow et al., 2000a). In addition, proinflammatory cytokines appear to have a role in regulating sleep, and the body responds to sleep deprivation by increasing proinflammatory cytokines (Groër et al., 2005; Wilson, Finch, & Cohen, 2002).

GOOD VS. DISTURBED SLEEP

Definition of Good Sleep

Sleep is a complex state that includes a number of dimensions: duration, continuity (the amount and distribution of sleep and wakefulness), architecture (the stages of sleep), and quality (perceptions of how soundly one sleeps or how rested one feels) (Mezick et al., 2008).

Additional parameters include:

- *Sleep latency.* This parameter refers to the number of minutes that it takes to get to sleep. In the general population, sleep latency of less than thirty minutes is characteristic of good sleep.
- *Total sleep time.* A total sleep time of approximately seven hours characterizes good sleep.
- *Sleep efficiency.* This parameter refers to the total time sleeping versus time in bed. Sleep efficiency of 85 percent is characteristic of good sleep (Fernandez-Mendoza et al., 2010).

What Is a Sleep Disorder?

It is equally important to have a definition of poor sleep, which is usually due to one or more sleep disorders. The term "sleep disorders" covers a wide range of problems. Some disorders are measured via patient questionnaire. Others need to be measured via polysomnographic studies, which record vital signs and other physiological measures during the night. A polysomnographic study includes an EEG (electroencephalogram) to measure brain wave activity, an EMG (electromyogram) to measure muscle activity, and an EOG (electro-oculogram) to measure eye movements. Other measures include respiratory airflow, blood oxygen saturation, pulse, heart rate, body position, and respiratory effort. Polysomnographic studies are necessary to detect problems, such as sleep-disordered breathing (e.g., sleep apneas), and sleep-movement disorders (e.g., restless-leg syndrome). Patients are often unaware of these problems, and so cannot report them via patient questionnaire. Sleep disorders can be grouped into three broad categories.

- *Insomnia.* Insomnia refers to an inability to either fall asleep (primary insomnia) or stay asleep (secondary insomnia). It is often precipitated by life stress, worrying, or depression. Insomnia can also be caused by lifestyle factors, such as daytime napping, excessive caffeine consumption, or exercise too close to bedtime.

- *Hypersomnia.* Hypersomnia refers to excessive daytime sleepiness and is a symptom associated with conditions such as sleep apnea.
- *Parasomnias.* Parasomnias are unusual behaviors that occur during sleep. These behaviors include sleep walking, bruxism (teeth grinding), and nightmares, which occur during REM (rapid eye movement) sleep.

EFFECTS OF VIOLENCE AND CHILDHOOD ADVERSITY ON SLEEP

Although disturbed sleep patterns are a relatively new area of study in the interpersonal-violence field, a number of studies have documented disturbed sleep patterns in men and women who have been abused. For example, in a European community sample, 68 percent of sexual abuse survivors reported having sleep difficulties, with 45 percent having repetitive nightmares (Teegan, 1999). In a French sample, 33 percent of teens who had been raped indicated that they "slept badly" compared with 16 percent of the nonassaulted comparison group. Of the assaulted teens, 28 percent had nightmares (compared with 11 percent), and 56 percent woke during the night, compared with 21 percent (Choquet, Darves-Bornoz, Ledoux, Manfredi, & Hassler, 1997).

Hulme (2000) found that sleep problems among female sexual abuse survivors were common in a primary-care sample. Fifty-two percent of sexual abuse survivors reported that they could not sleep at night (compared with 24 percent of the non-abused group), and 36 percent reported nightmares (compared with 13 percent). Intrusive symptoms were also common with 53 percent of sexual abuse survivors reporting sudden thoughts or images of past events (compared with 18 percent of the non-abused group).

Childhood adversities can also influence current sleep quality. Hanson and Chen (2010) investigated whether childhood family environment moderated the relationship between daily stress and sleep. The researchers included eighty-seven undergraduates in their study. They monitored the students' sleep for seven days, having each student keep a sleep diary and wear an Actiwatch that monitored their movements. As predicted, participants with more difficult family environments were more likely to experience poor sleep and increased cortisol on days where they experienced more stress. The students who described their parents as "warm" slept longer, and they had lower levels of cortisol.

Other types of family violence were also related to poor sleep quality. In a sample of battered women living in shelters ($N = 50$), 70 percent reported poor sleep quality, 28 percent went to bed very fatigued, and 40 percent woke up feeling very fatigued (Humphreys, Lee, Neylan, & Marmar, 1999). Moreover, 82 percent described one or more of the following characteristics of disturbed sleep: many wakings over the course of the night, restless sleep, and early-morning waking. Six described vivid nightmares that included recent incidents of abuse.

Similarly, Pidgeon et al. (2011) found that women exposed to intimate partner violence (IPV) were likely to have sleep disorders, including insomnia and nightmares. All of the women had filed protection orders against their partners. In this sample of 121 survivors of IPV, 46 percent had clinically significant insomnia and 32 percent had nightmares. In terms of insomnia subtype, 51 percent had moderate-to-severe sleep-initiation insomnia, 57 percent had middle-of-the-night insomnia, and 30 percent had moderate-to-severe complaints of early-morning waking. Depressed women had more severe PTSD, and were more likely to have both insomnia and nightmares than nondepressed women. When controlling for severity of PTSD symptoms, insomnia increased the risk of depression eightfold, and nightmares were associated with a twofold risk. Women in this sample may have viewed sleep as dangerous in that it limits their ability to monitor their surroundings. The implications of sleep disturbances are serious given their negative impact on decision making and self-care.

In a study of sleep disorders in sexual assault survivors, 80 percent had either sleep-breathing or sleep-movement disorders. Both of these disorders were linked to higher levels of depression and suicidality, and women who had both types of sleep disorders had the most severe symptoms. The authors speculated that fragmented sleep potentiated the symptoms for women after a sexual assault, stretching their fragile coping abilities to the breaking point (Krakow et al., 2000a).

This finding was replicated in a study of PTSD (Belleville, Guay, & Marchand, 2009). In a study of ninety-two volunteers with PTSD, two-thirds reported significant sleep difficulties. Results from a series of regression analyses revealed that sleep quality has an impact on PTSD symptom severity and perceived mental health. The relationship between sleep quality and PTSD symptoms remained even after controlling for sociodemographic factors (gender, age, marital status, income, and employment status), trauma-related characteristics, comorbid psychiatric conditions, alcohol, and use of psychotropic medications. Forty-nine percent had comorbid depression, and 41 percent had comorbid anxiety disorder. Sleep difficulties contributed uniquely to the variance in perceived mental health, but, surprisingly, sleep was not uniquely related to the variance for perceived physical health. These findings emphasize the important role sleep difficulties have in maintenance of PTSD symptoms.

POSSIBLE MECHANISMS FOR SLEEP DISTURBANCES

There are several possible mechanisms by which childhood abuse might be related to sleep problems. These mechanisms include beliefs, anxiety disorders, and depression.

Perfectionism and Parental Criticism

A study by Vincent and Walker (2000) compared thirty-two people with chronic insomnia to twenty-six healthy controls on a measure of perfectionism. The subjects with chronic insomnia were more likely to endorse items that indicated perfectionism. In addition, they were more likely to report doubts about actions, frequent parental criticism, and concern over mistakes. Higher levels of parental criticism were associated with delayed sleep onset. No other aspect of perfectionism was associated with sleep characteristics, including total sleep time or sleep quality. Parental criticism was also indirectly associated with sleep difficulties because it heightened presleep arousal.

Perfectionism was also higher in a sample of patients with chronic fatigue syndrome compared with healthy controls. In particular, concern over mistakes and doubts about actions were significantly higher. However, personal standards, parental expectations, and parental criticism were not significantly different between the two groups. Patients with chronic fatigue were also significantly more likely to report low self-esteem (White & Schweitzer, 2000).

Chronic Arousal

One debate among researchers studying insomnia is whether hyperarousal is cause or a consequence of chronic insomnia (Fernandez-Mendoza et al., 2010). People with chronic insomnia often have obsessive-ruminative personality traits, inadequate stress coping, and cognitive-emotional hyperarousal. In a sample of middle-age and young adults who were defined as good sleepers, the researchers demonstrated that cognitive-emotional hyperarousal was associated with vulnerability to insomnia. Those with vulnerability to insomnia tested high in presleep cognitive arousal, rumination, and emotion-oriented coping. The researchers also noted that middle-age adults may be more vulnerable because of increased sensitivity to stress hormones rather than simply an increase in life stress. Strategies for preventing insomnia include stress-inoculation programs, reduction of cognitive and somatic hyperarousal, and management of worry.

Rumination was related to longer sleep-onset latency after an acute stressor in a sample of seventy participants who were asked to give a five-minute speech in front of panel whose members would evaluate them (Zoccola, Dickerson, & Lam, 2009). Rumination is a tendency to replay and reexperience previous events. The researchers measured both trait rumination (a tendency to ruminate in general) and stressor-specific rumination. They found that both were related to a longer sleep latency, but neither measure was related to sleep duration or wakefulness.

Anger expression also influences sleep quality in patients with coronary heart disease (Caska et al., 2009). In this study, every standard deviation increase of anger suppression was associated with an 80 percent increase in poor sleep quality. This association remained strong after adjusting for demographics, comorbid conditions, lifestyle factors, medications, cardiac function, depressive symptoms, and anger. The authors concluded that anger suppression is associated with poor sleep quality in patients with coronary heart disease.

Research on differences in sleep quality by income or ethnicity also supports the notion that hyperarousal impacts sleep. In a study of 187 adults, Mezick et al. (2008) found that blacks had shorter sleep duration and lower sleep efficiency compared to whites. On average, they took twenty-five minutes to fall asleep compared to sixteen minutes for whites and Asians. In addition, they spent shorter amounts of time in Stage 3–4 sleep (3.6 percent vs. 6.8 percent for whites and Asians). These ethnic-group differences persisted even after controlling for socioeconomic status (SES). This study also found an impact of SES. Low SES was associated with longer sleep latency, more waking after sleep onset, and poorer sleep quality. The authors concluded that blacks may be at particular high risk for sleep problems, including shorter and less efficient sleep, and this increases their risk for serious health problems such as obesity, hypertension, and diabetes.

A study of perceived unfair treatment was also associated with poorer sleep quality, more daytime sleepiness, shorter sleep duration, lower sleep efficiency, and a smaller proportion of REM sleep in a study of 97 African-American and 113 white adults (Beatty et al., 2011). Sleep efficiency was measured by actigraph and polysomnograph. There were also differences by ethnicity, with blacks having shorter sleep time and lower sleep efficiency. Unfair treatment was associated with higher trait anger, trait anxiety, hostility, and nightly worry. But it was not associated with depressive symptoms. Perceptions of unfair treatment were related to sleep problems for both white and black participants.

Security of Relationships and Sleep Quality

Sleep is a highly social arrangement. Throughout human evolution, sleep—and the salubrious effect of sleep in particular—has relied on a safe sleep environment, a need that has typically been met by sleeping near loved ones. Given this evolutionary history, it is not surprising that social isolation, real or perceived, is related to poor sleep quality (Hawkley et al., 2010). In addition, feeling implicitly unsafe disrupts sleep by increasing the nightly microawakenings.

One way that problem relationships may impact health is by influencing sleep. Two recent studies have examined the relationship between the security of adult attachments and sleep quality. In addition to being a social arrangement, sleep is also a physiologically vulnerable state. In order to sleep soundly, people must feel safe so they can downregulate vigilance and alertness. And to do so, they must be secure in their social relationships with sleep partners (Troxel, Cyranowski, Hall, Frank, & Buysee, 2007). Two studies have examined the relationship between security of relationships with adult partners and sleep quality.

In the first study, seventy-eight married adults completed questionnaires about their sleep quality, quality of current partnership (secure vs. insecure attachment), and depression (Carmichael & Reis, 2005). The sleep questionnaire asked about seven aspects of sleep including perceived sleep quality, sleep latency (time to get to sleep), sleep duration, habitual sleep efficiency, sleep disturbances, and use of sleep medications. Using structural equation modeling, the researchers found that married participants who were anxious about their current relationships reported poorer sleep quality, even after controlling for depression. Women with insecure attachments rated their partners as emotionally unavailable and reported that they did not trust their partners. The researchers indicated that one limitation of their study was that they used a self-report measure of sleep, rather than assessing sleep directly via polysomnigraph, so they could not assess actual sleep architecture.

Troxel et al. (2007) addressed that limitation by using polysomnographic studies to assess sleep directly. In a study of 107 women with recurrent major depression, marital status and security of that relationship predicted quality and efficiency of sleep. If women had anxious attachments, particularly if they were separated or widowed, they had a significantly smaller percentage of Stage 3–4 sleep than women who were currently partnered and who had secure attachments. The authors noted the importance of Stage 3–4 sleep in protecting individuals from cardiovascular and metabolic diseases.

More recently, Troxel, Buysse, Hall, and Matthews (2009) found that happily married women reported fewer sleep problems than did women who were unhappily married, even after controlling for potential confounding variables, such as depressive and anxiety symptoms, and medication use. These sleep difficulties included difficulty falling asleep, nighttime wakenings, early-morning awakenings, and restless sleep. Based on earlier studies, the authors noted that women seem more prone to relational issues impacting their sleep. The data were collected from the Study of Women's Health Across the Nation (SWAN), and the study included a multiethnic, community-based sample of 2,148 middle-age women. These findings were strongest for Caucasian women, but this problem also existed, to a lesser extent, for African-American women.

Attachment style was related to quality of sleep in a community-based sample of seventy older adults (Verdecias, Jean-Louis, Zizi, Casimir, & Browne, 2009). In this study, participants with a preoccupied attachment style were more likely to report daytime napping, and use of sleep medications than were participants with secure, dismissive, and fearful attachments.

Loneliness has also been related to poor sleep quality (Hawkley et al., 2010). In a prospective study of 215 adults (mean age = 57.5 years), loneliness was related to daytime fatigue, low energy, and sleepiness. Daytime dysfunction also predicted subsequent loneliness. The authors concluded that the effect of loneliness on daytime dysfunction was independent of sleep duration, suggesting that the same amount of sleep is less effective when people feel more socially isolated.

Interestingly, sharing sleep with a spouse even increases the likelihood of adherence to CPAP (continuous positive airway pressure) treatment in obstructive sleep apnea (Cartwright, 2008). In this study of ten married men, investigated over a period of 4.6 months, Cartwright found that treatment adherence to CPAP in married men is strongly related to the frequency with which their partners sleep with them during their initial home treatment. This is an issue because many patients do not comply with their CPAP regimens. Adherence greatly improves the health of patients with sleep apnea. Along those same lines, Baron and colleagues found that marital conflict was related to CPAP adherence. Married men with high levels of conflict were less likely to adhere to CPAP use than married men with lower levels of conflict (Baron, Smith, Czajkowski, Gunn, & Jones, 2009)

Depression

Sleep difficulties intersect with depression in a number of ways. Data from a large sample of older adults ($N = 2,370$) indicated that sleep disorders were strongly associated with the risk of major depression. Early-morning waking was the sleep disturbance most consistently related to depression over time (Roberts et al., 2000). Sleep difficulties also predicted a longer course of depression. In a ten-year study of outcomes of depression treatment, those with severe fatigue and trouble sleeping were more likely to have a chronic course of depression (Moos & Cronkite, 1999).

Depression also impacts sleep architecture. Sleep architecture refers to the percentage of time that people spend in various sleep stages and the distribution of those stages throughout the night (Morin & Ware, 1996). The alteration most likely in depressed individuals is an alteration of REM-sleep parameters. Specifically, depressed people are more likely to have longer periods of REM earlier in the night than nondepressed people (referred to as a "short REM latency"). They are also likely to have increased percentages of REM sleep and less deep sleep as a result (Morin & Ware, 1996).

One study examined the relationship between sleep architecture and depression (Perlis et al., 1997). Using canonical correlation, the authors found that severe depression drastically reduced the amount of time spent in Stage 4 (delta) sleep. Further, depressed patients have more REM sleep, and REM sleep occurs earlier in the night (Perlis et al., 1997; Ware & Morin, 1997). Antidepressants, particularly tricyclics and MAO (monoamine oxydase) inhibitors, decrease percentage of REM sleep and prolong the latency to first REM sleep. Cognitive-behavioral therapy may also produce these changes (Ware & Morin, 1997).

Patients with depression and comorbid sleep disorders have poorer clinical outcomes than do patients who do not have sleep disorders. Some of these outcomes include poorer clinical attrition and remission rates and stability of response to treatment (Manber et al., 2008). Patients with sleep disturbances are more likely to have suicidal ideation. These previous findings indicate that insomnia inhibits depression treatment. Further, sleep issues do not always resolve with depression treatment, posing a serious threat of relapse. A stressor may precede insomnia. However, over time insomnia becomes a conditioned response, and it persists even after the stressor is removed. Anxiety about not being able to sleep may replace the earlier stressor. Insomnia is not simply a symptom of depression. It is a comorbid disorder that can hinder response to antidepressants.

Hall et al. (2000) studied fourteen healthy adults who met criteria for primary insomnia. They hypothesized that stress-related intrusive thoughts, subjective stress burden, and symptoms of depression would be positively correlated to indices of hyperarousal during sleep. These indices would include attenuation of deep (Stage 3–4) sleep, and lighter (heightened alpha and beta) sleep. They also hypothesized that subjective sleep complaints would be related to hyperarousal during sleep. Stress and depression increased hyperarousal, defined by less deep sleep and more light sleep. Subclinical depression also increased light sleep and was associated with poorer subjective sleep quality. The authors stipulated that degree of associated distress, as opposed to a simple dichotomous distinction (depression vs. no depression), may be what distinguishes primary insomnia versus insomnia related to another mental disorder. However, we must recognize that stress and insomnia form a bidirectional relationship.

Posttraumatic Stress Disorder

Sleep disorders are also common in PTSD, with disturbed sleep and nightmares as key symptoms (Morin & Ware, 1996). PTSD also appears to have a relationship to REM latency, but this relationship is unclear. Some survivors have a shortened REM latency, while others have a lengthened REM latency. The reactions of particular trauma survivors tend to vary by both the recency of the traumatic event and the severity of current PTSD (Morin & Ware, 1996).

Sleep problems may also keep symptoms of PTSD active. In a study of twenty-three patients who suffered from chronic nightmares and obstructive sleep apnea, patients who had completed a treatment program for their sleep problems ($N = 14$) were compared with patients who had dropped out of the program ($N = 9$). Twenty-one months later, those who completed the program had substantially improved sleep compared with those who had not. When the patients with PTSD were compared with the PTSD/no-treatment patients, those in the treatment group had 75 percent improvement in their PTSD symptoms. In contrast, the six patients in the PTSD/no-treatment group reported a 43 percent worsening of symptoms. The authors concluded that treating sleep difficulties appeared to also improve PTSD symptoms, and they recommended a full evaluation of sleep in patients with PTSD (Krakow et al., 2000b).

HOW SLEEP IMPACTS HEALTH

Poor sleep quality has a profound effect on health. It compromises immune, metabolic, and neuroendocrine function; chronically activates the HPA axis; and even increases mortality risk (Carmichael & Reis, 2005).

Sleep and the Stress Response

In a lab study, twenty healthy participants were in a within-subjects crossover-design study comparing a good night's sleep with a night of total sleep deprivation (Franzen et al., 2011). The day after each night, participants were exposed to a lab-induced stressor. The researchers found that there was a significant interaction between sleep deprivation and stress on systolic blood pressure. Sleep deprivation made people more vulnerable to stress and increased their systolic blood pressure. The authors speculated that sleep loss may increase cardiovascular risk by dysregulating stress physiology.

A twenty-year longitudinal study from Switzerland ($N = 591$) found that insomnia had a prevalence rate of 20 percent, and in about 40 percent of subjects with insomnia, it had become chronic (Buysse et al., 2008). Women had twice the risk of insomnia compared to men. Chronic insomnia predicted major depression, and major depression predicted insomnia at subsequent interviews. The prospective and longitudinal design of the study allowed the authors to determine the temporal relation between insomnia and depression, rather than to observe that they simply co-occurred.

In a meta-analysis of nineteen studies, Pilcher and Huffcutt (1996) found that sleep deprivation had a strong impact on functioning in three broad categories—motor functioning, cognitive functioning, and mood—with the most severe effect being on mood. Indeed, sleep-deprived subjects reported moods that were three standard deviations lower than their non-sleep-deprived counterparts. Sleep-deprived subjects performed at a level comparable to the lowest 10 percent of the non-sleep-deprived subjects. Interestingly, partial sleep deprivation was more damaging than total sleep deprivation. People with chronically poor sleep also have more car accidents. And among people with chronic conditions, lack of sleep predicted greater functional disability and decreased quality of life. Not surprisingly, people with poor sleep use more medical services than do their non-sleep-deprived counterparts (Stepanski, Rybarczyk, Lopez, & Stevens, 2003).

Metabolic Effects

McEwen (2003) reported that even short periods of sleep deprivation can elevate cortisol and glucose levels and can increase both insulin and insulin resistance. Sleep deprivation also provokes an inflammatory response since the body thinks it is under attack. Long-term sleep deprivation can seriously impair health. Suarez and Goforth (2010) also describe the importance of sleep in preventing cardiovascular and metabolic diseases.

This relationship is confirmed when examining data from a study on snoring (Dunai, Keszei, Kopp, Shapiro, & Mucsi, 2008). In a population survey from Hungary of 12,643 residents, loud snoring was related to significantly increased risk of hypertension, myocardial infarctions, and stroke after adjusting for age, sex, body mass index (BMI), diabetes, level of education, smoking, and alcohol consumption. Loud snorers also had higher rates of health care utilization. Sleep-disordered breathing was associated with increased catecholamines and inflammatory cytokines, including IL-6, C-reactive protein, and TNF-α.

A population study from Sweden ($N = 10{,}756$) found that snoring and witnessed sleep apneas increased the risk of diabetes mellitus in women but not in men (Valham et al., 2009). Women who reported that they snored had a 58 percent increase in diabetes. Witnessed sleep apnea resulted in a threefold increase in diabetes. These effects were adjusted for age, BMI, and waist circumference.

Short sleep duration has also been linked to metabolic syndrome in middle-age adults (Hall et al., 2008). Data were collected form the Adult Health Behavior Project registry and the participants were ages 30–54. Short sleep duration was related to abdominal obesity, elevated fasting glucose, and hypertriglyceridemia. The authors concluded that their data suggest that short sleep duration is a significant correlate of metabolic syndrome.

Sleep is also related to obesity. In a meta-analysis of forty-five studies of children and adults, including 634,511 participants worldwide, short sleep duration was related to obesity (Cappuccio et al., 2008). For children, the definition of "short sleep" was ten hours. For adults, the definition of "short sleep" was less than five hours. Although the authors acknowledged that their methodology did not allow them to elucidate a mechanism, there were several possibilities. First, short sleep may lead to obesity because of hormonal changes that lead to an increase in appetite and caloric intake. Short sleep is associated to reciprocal changes in leptin and ghrelin, which increases appetite and leads to obesity. In addition, inflammatory pathways are activated by short sleep.

Sleep and Pain

Sleep problems are common in pain patients. Smith, Perlis, Smith, Giles, and Carmody (2000) noted the overlap between sleep and pain, with the relationship most likely being bidirectional: Pain interferes with sleep and sleep disturbances increase the experience of pain. Sleep problems may also reduce a patient's ability to cope with chronic pain. In their study of fifty-one people with chronic pain, 88 percent reported some dissatisfaction with their sleep. Presleep cognitive hyperarousal was the best predictor of sleep quality, regardless of pain severity. This included racing thoughts, intrusive thoughts, depressive cognitions, and worry.

In a study of patients with fibromyalgia or rheumatoid arthritis, sleep was found to buffer the relationship between stress and negative affect, and the relationship between pain and both positive and negative affect (Hamilton, Catley, & Karlson, 2007). The researchers examined sleep and its role in allostatic load on pain patients. They were working under the assumption that sleep problems acted as a stressor, and were not simply the consequence of stressful life event. Allostatic load refers to wear and tear resulting from accumulated adaptational demands. It is the net effect of demands on the system and the overall health and resilience of that system. They noted that good-quality sleep minimizes allostatic load and becomes a biobehavioral resource. The patients who were getting poor sleep were more reactive to stress and pain, and restorative sleep had an important role in pain management. In contrast, the better sleepers were more resilient to both stress and pain. They concluded that restorative sleep moderates the stress response.

The results of Hamilton et al.'s (2008) study indicate that sleep is prospectively related to the next day's affect and fatigue. Negative affect follows even a single night of poor sleep. But the accumulated sleep debt appears more important to these negative events than does a single night of poor sleep. The results suggested that reactivity may be less important than the speed of recovery. For example, affective response to negative events may linger into the next day—unless the slate is wiped clean by longer-than-average sleep time. The consequences of inadequate sleep accrue over time. Successive nights of partial sleep deprivation lead to progressively worsened affect. Sleep duration and quality play central roles in day-to-day function for women with fibromyalgia, predicting mood, cognitions, and also pain. Sleep can also have an indirect relationship on social relationships and participation in health-promoting activities (Hamilton et al., 2008).

In a sample of 167 female rape survivors, participants were assessed for PTSD symptoms, depression, sleep disturbance, and frequency of self-reported health problems. They found that trauma-related sleep disorders had an independent impact on health, above and beyond that of depression and PTSD (Clum, Nishith, & Resick, 2001). The symptoms reported most often represented a wide range of body systems, but many reflected increased pain or other symptoms of hyperarousal. These included headaches (86 percent), upset stomach (75 percent), back pains (70 percent), pressure in head (70 percent), premenstrual problems (60 percent), stiff muscles (58 percent), racing heart (58 percent), and pain in stomach (57 percent).

Fatigue and exhaustion are also related to sudden cardiac arrest. In a case-control study, ninety-nine victims of sudden cardiac arrest were matched with healthy controls for age and gender. Family members of those who died were significantly more likely to report that the victims were exhausted in the weeks preceding their deaths and were less likely to express their emotions (Appels, Golombeck, Gorgels, de Vreede, & van Bruekelen, 2000). We need to interpret these results with caution, however, because the data were collected after the subjects had died. Family members who were still reeling from the shock of the sudden death of their loved ones may have remembered things differently, and this could have skewed the results. But the results are intriguing and raise the possibility of another severe consequence of sleep deprivation.

Inflammation and Sleep

Inflammation is an important mechanism by which sleep difficulties can cause health problems. Sleep problems increase rates of systemic inflammation. For example, in one study comparing depressed ($n = 22$) and nondepressed, age-matched controls ($n = 18$), depressed participants had significantly higher nighttime elevations of IL-6 and sICAM (Motivala, Sarfatti, Olmos, & Irwin, 2005). Depressed participants had lower total sleep time, prolonged sleep latency, and decreased Stage 2 sleep compared with controls. However, sleep characteristics, such as longer sleep latency, were associated with elevations in IL-6 and sICAM. Increases in REM sleep also increased IL-6 levels. The authors concluded that their findings support the relationship between sleep disturbance and inflammation, a relationship that was not accounted for by confounding factors such as age and BMI. Further, they noted that the relationship between sleep problems and inflammation is bidirectional (e.g., increased IL-6 may delay sleep onset), and sleep problems increase inflammation. These findings suggest that interventions that target sleep disorders may have a beneficial effect on inflammatory processes, which could lower risk of cardiovascular symptoms in patients with depression.

Obstructive sleep apnea is also associated with systemic inflammation including TNF-α, IL-6, adhesion molecules, and C-reactive protein (Ting et al., 2009). In a study of 263 patients from Taiwan with sleep-disordered breathing, Ting et al. (2009) found that sleep-breathing disorders may occur in the early morning and the increase is maintained for three to four hours. These patients are at particular risk for cardiovascular disease. There is evidence that sleep-breathing disorders are related to increased rates of inflammation, hypertension, metabolic syndrome, diabetes, and obesity. The results of Ting et al. indicated that patients whose post- and pre-overnight systolic blood pressures were elevated had more sleep respiratory disturbance, more inflammation, and higher metabolic syndrome indices than patients with sleep-breathing disorders without this pattern of morning increase in blood pressure. The patients with a morning surge showed many symptoms that patients with constant blood-pressure elevations showed, even though the patients with the morning surge did not have high blood pressure.

In a sample of 290 patients at high risk for obstructive sleep apnea, both major depression and anxiety disorders were related to increased inflammation (Einvik et al., 2011). C-reactive protein was highest in patients with comorbid depression and anxiety disorders. Neither disorder was related to low-level myocardial damage.

Poor sleep quality was found to be related to preterm birth in a prospective study of 166 pregnant women (Okun, Schetter, & Glynn, 2011). In this study, for every one-point increase on the Pittsburgh Sleep Quality Index, there was a 25 percent increase in the odds of preterm birth in early pregnancy and an 18 percent increase in later pregnancy. The authors speculated that sleep disturbances initiated inappropriate inflammatory responses, which may result in the premature activation of the normal processes associated with parturition. They suggested that improving maternal sleep may be a relatively simple way to reduce the risk for adverse pregnancy outcomes by ameliorating the negative effects of deleterious psychosocial (depressive) and biological (inflammatory) pathways.

Summary

Disturbed sleep in abuse survivors is frequently undiagnosed, may exacerbate depression and PTSD, and is related to increased health problems and decreased quality of life. These findings suggest that sleep should be evaluated in abuse survivors, and that sleep disorders not simply be attributed to either depression or PTSD. Improving sleep quality will likely result in lower levels of symptoms and improved health overall.

TREATMENT OF SLEEP DISORDERS

As described in the previous section, sleep is often compromised in abuse survivors, which increases the risk of health problems (Suarez & Goforth, 2010). Krakow et al. (2000b) noted that since sleep medicine is not well-integrated into trauma treatment, practitioners are often less effective than they could be if they also treated underlying sleep disorders.

To lessen the negative health effects of sleep problems, the first step is to assess abuse survivors for possible sleep disorders. Clinicians should ask about the onset of the sleep disorder. If clients have any psychiatric disorders, clinicians should ask about the temporal sequence of when the sleep disorder and psychiatric disorders manifested. Did the symptoms of the psychiatric disorder predate the onset of sleep problems or vice versa? Polysomnigraphic studies can also reveal whether there are any sleep-breathing or sleep-movement disorders that might be treated (Morin & Ware, 1996).

Treatment of insomnia may be challenging if abuse survivors consider their insomnia to be a survival advantage, in that it increases their ability to be vigilant in unsafe environments. Pidgeon et al. (2011) recommend that survivors' actual physical safety will need to be specifically addressed before addressing insomnia complaints. If the patients are safe but continue to feel unsafe at night, this issue can be addressed as part of insomnia therapy. Medications to treat insomnia may blunt vigilance, and this may concern clients who do not feel safe. Treatments need to include both pharmacological and behavioral treatments in a manner that provides relief from symptoms while assuring clients that they are safe. For men and women in currently abusive relationships, improved sleep may allow them to better cope with their current situation, make informed decisions about safety planning, ameliorate PTSD and depression symptoms, and increase their ability to seek other forms of treatment, including mental health care.

Interventions for sleep disorders include cognitive-behavioral approaches, assistive devices, and medications. Cognitive–behavioral approaches are the most common form of sleep treatments. In one recent review, it was effective for 70–80 percent of patients, and its effectiveness was comparable to sleep medications (Morin, 2004; Stepanski & Perlis, 2000). Cognitive-behavioral interventions help with sleep because they produce changes in REM sleep. Cognitive approaches can also address worrying and rumination that may be at the base of primary or secondary insomnia (Morin & Ware, 1996).

Cognitive-Behavioral Approaches

Cognitive therapy for insomnia includes three components—behavioral, cognitive, and educational—and can be most easily incorporated into standard trauma care. These include establishing regular bedtimes, not using the bed for anything but sleeping and sex, getting out of bed when unable to sleep, and eliminating naps during the day. There is also a relaxation component, which focuses on both autonomic relaxation techniques (e.g., progressive muscle relaxation) and cognitive techniques, that stops the worrying that keeps people from sleeping.

In one review, cognitive therapy was effective for 70–80 percent of patients, and was comparable to sleep medications (Morin, 2004; Stepanski & Perlis, 2000). Cognitive-behavioral interventions help with sleep because they produce changes in REM sleep. Cognitive approaches can also address worrying and rumination that may be at the base of primary or secondary insomnia (Morin & Ware, 1996). A combination of cognitive, behavioral, and stress-reduction approaches is effective for most patients with sleep disorders.

Manber et al. (2008) conducted a randomized trial with thirty patients who had both major depression and insomnia to test the efficacy of a cognitive-behavioral intervention on insomnia. This intervention was in conjunction with antidepressant treatment. The intervention included education about normal sleep, sleep in depression, circadian rhythms, and impact of substances, sleep restriction and stimulus control instructions, management of stress and cognitive and somatic arousals, cognitive restructuring, and instructions for avoiding relapse. The control group received education about sleep and sleep hygiene but no active components of cognitive therapy. The results indicated that patients who received both antidepressant treatment and the cognitive-behavioral intervention had a higher rate of remission of depression and insomnia than those who received medication and the control intervention. The sleep intervention had an impact on both sadness and anhedonia, the core symptoms of depression, and likely had impact on the other symptoms of depression, such as mood, concentration, energy, and coping.

In a study of veterans with PTSD, Ulmer, Edinger, and Calhoun (2011) found that combining cognitive therapy with an intervention designed to address PTSD-specific nightmares proved to be highly effective. Even with a small sample ($N = 22$), there were very large treatment effects for insomnia severity, sleep quality, and PTSD symptoms. Participants who received the trauma-specific intervention, in addition to cognitive-behavioral therapy, had a significant reduction in both insomnia and PTSD symptoms, although these symptoms did not completely remit.

Assistive Devices

For sleep apnea, and other types of sleep-breathing disorders, a CPAP device can be helpful. This small unit, which includes a facial mask or nasal cannulas, provides pressurized air to prevent the airway from collapsing while the patient sleeps. This ensures a better night's sleep. Some dental devices, such as a mandibular repositioning device, can also help keep the airway open during sleep. A sleep-medicine specialist can help determine whether a patient needs devices such as these. The physician and therapist should be aware that devices such as these might be especially difficult for some trauma survivors because they have elements reminiscent of the trauma (the assault/domestic violence survivor who was choked, the sexual abuse survivor who was forced to perform oral sex and who felt smothered during the experience). They may need to find alternative approaches that are easier to tolerate (C. Courtois, personal communication, January 3, 2009).

Medications

Although medications are not always part of trauma treatment, for patients with sleep disorders, the serotonin-2 antagonists/reuptake inhibitors (SARIs), such as trazadone (Desyrel) and nefazadone (Serzone), can be helpful adjuncts. When they are administered with SSRIs, SARIs boost the actions of the SSRIs and reverse medication-induced insomnia. Trazadone suppresses REM sleep, which can reduce the number of nightmares patients experience (Lange et al., 1999). In contrast, nefazadone increases REM sleep and may improve overall sleep quality in PTSD (Virani, Bezchlibnyk-Butler, & Jeffries, 2009). Both of these drugs may be too sedating for some patients, however (Friedman, 2001). For a more detailed discussion of medications for PTSD, see International Society for Traumatic Stress Studies (2009), and Chapter 19 (in this volume).

CONCLUSION

Sleep disorders are another common effect of abuse that can increase health problems in abuse survivors. By recognizing possible sleep disorders, practitioners can help patients minimize or even eliminate them. Addressing sleep disorders will likely result in lower levels of symptoms and improved health overall.

References

Appels, A., Golombeck, B., Gorgels, A., de Vreede, J., & van Bruekelen, G. (2000). Behavioral risk factors of sudden cardiac arrest. *Journal of Psychosomatic Research, 48*, 463–469.

Baron, K. G., Smith, T. W., Czajkowski, L. A., Gunn, H. E., & Jones, C. R. (2009). Relationship quality and CPAP adherence in patients with obstructive sleep apnea. *Behavioral Sleep Medicine, 7*(1), 22–36.

Beatty, D. L., Hall, M. H., Kamarck, T. W., Buysse, D. J., Owens, J. F., Reis, S. E., et al. (2011). Unfair treatment is associated with poor sleep in African American and Caucasian adults: Pittsburgh SleepSCORE Project. *Health Psychology, 30*(3), 351–359.

Belleville, G., Guay, S., & Marchand, A. (2009). Impact of sleep disturbances on PTSD symptoms and perceived health. *Journal of Nervous and Mental Disease, 197*(2), 126–132.

Buysse, D. J., Angst, J., Gamma, A., Ajdacic, V., Eich, D., & Rossler, W. (2008). Prevalence, course, and comorbidity of insomnia and depression in young adults. *Sleep, 31*(4), 473–480.

Cappuccio, F. P., Taggart, F. M., Kandala, N. B., Currie, A., Peile, E., Stranges, S., et al. (2008). Meta-analysis of short sleep duration and obesity in children and adults. *Sleep, 31*(5), 19–26.

Carmichael, C. L., & Reis, H. T. (2005). Attachment, sleep quality, and depressed affect. *Health Psychology, 24*, 526–531.

Cartwright, R. (2008). Sleeping together: A pilot study of the effects of shared sleeping on adherence to CPAP treatment in obstructive sleep apnea. *Journal of Clinical Sleep Medicine, 4*(2), 123–127.

Caska, C. M., Hendrickson, B. E., Wong, M. H., Ali, S., Neylan, T. C., & Whooley, M. A. (2009). Anger expression and sleep quality in patients with coronary heart disease: Findings from the Heart and Soul Study. *Psychosomatic Medicine, 71*, 280–285.

Choquet, M., Darves-Bornoz, J.-M., Ledoux, S., Manfredi, R., & Hassler, C. (1997). Self-reported health and behavioral problems among adolescent victims of rape in France: Results of a cross-sectional survey. *Child Abuse and Neglect, 21*, 823–832.

Clum, G. A., Nishith, P., & Resick, P. A. (2001). Trauma-related sleep disturbance and self-reported physical health symptoms in treatment-seeking female rape victims. *Journal of Nervous and Mental Disease, 189*, 618–622.

Dunai, A., Keszei, A. P., Kopp, M. S., Shapiro, C. M., & Mucsi, I. (2008). Cardiovascular disease and health-care utilization in snorers: A population survey. *Sleep, 31*(3), 411–416.

Einvik, G., Hrubos-Strom, H., Ranby, A., Hordhus, I. H., Somers, V. K., Omland, T., et al. (2011). Major depressive disorder, anxiety disorders, and cardiac biomarkers in subjects at high risk of obstructive sleep apnea. *Psychosomatic Medicine, 73*, 378–384.

Fernandez-Mendoza, J., Vela-Bueno, A., Vgontzas, A. N., Ramos-Platon, M. J., Olavarrieta-Bernardino, S., Bixler, E. O., et al. (2010). Cognitive-emotional hyperarousal as a premorbid characteristic of individuals vulnerable to insomnia. *Psychosomatic Medicine, 72*, 397–403.

Franzen, P. L., Gianaros, P. J., Marsland, A. L., Hall, M. H., Siegle, G. J., Dahl, R. E., et al. (2011). Cardiovascular reactivity to acute psychological stress following sleep deprivation. *Psychosomatic Medicine, 73*, 679–682.

Friedman, M. J. (2001). *Posttraumatic stress disorder: The latest assessment and treatment strategies*. Kansas City, MO: Compact Clinicals.

Groër, M. W., Davis, M. W., Smith, K. W., Casey, K., Kramer, V., & Bukovsky, E. (2005). Immunity, inflammation and infection in post-partum breast and formula feeders. *American Journal of Reproductive Immunology, 54*, 222–231.

Hall, M., Buysse, D. J., Nowell, P. D., Nofzinger, E. A., Houck, P., Reynolds, C. F., et al. (2000). Symptoms of stress and depression as correlates of sleep in primary insomnia. *Psychosomatic Medicine, 62*, 227–230.

Hall, M. H., Muldoon, M. F., Jennings, J. R., Buysse, D. J., Flory, J. D., & Manuck, S. B. (2008). Self-reported sleep duration is associated with the metabolic syndrome in midlife adults. *Sleep, 31*(5), 635–643.

Hamilton, N. A., Affleck, G., Tennen, H., Karlson, C., Luxton, D., Preacher, K. J., et al. (2008). Fibromyalgia: The role of sleep in affect and in negative event reactivity and recovery. *Health Psychology, 27*(4), 490–494.

Hamilton, N. A., Catley, D., & Karlson, C. (2007). Sleep and the affective response to stress and pain. *Health Psychology, 26*(3), 288–295.

Hanson, M. D., & Chen, E. (2010). Daily stress, cortisol, and sleep: The moderating role of childhood psychosocial environments. *Health Psychology, 29*(4), 394–402.

Hawkley, L. C., Preacher, K. J., & Cacioppo, J. T. (2010). Loneliness impairs daytime functioning but not sleep duration. *Health Psychology, 29*(2), 124–129.

Hulme, P. A. (2000). Symptomatology and health care utilization of women primary care patients who experienced childhood sexual abuse. *Child Abuse and Neglect, 24*, 1471–1484.

Humphreys, J. C., Lee, K. A., Neylan, T. C., & Marmar, C. R. (1999). Sleep patterns of sheltered battered women. *Journal of Nursing Scholarship, 31*, 139–143.

International Society for Traumatic Stress Studies. (Ed.). (2009). *Effective treatments for PTSD: Psychopharmacology for adults (Guideline 6)*. New York: Guilford Press.

Krakow, B., Artar, A., Warner, T. D., Melendez, D., Johnston, L., Hollifield, M., et al. (2000a). Sleep disorder, depression, and suicidality in female sexual assault survivors. *Crisis, 21*, 163–170.

Krakow, B., Lowry, C., Germain, A., Gaddy, L., Hollifield, M., Koss, M., et al. (2000b). A retrospective study on improvements in nightmares and post-traumatic stress disorder following treatment for co-morbid sleep-disordered breathing. *Journal of Psychosomatic Research, 49*(5), 291–298.

Lange, A., deBeurs, E., Dolan, C., Lachnit, T., Sjollema, S., & Hanewald, G. (1999). Long-term effects of childhood sexual abuse: Objective and subjective characteristics of the abuse and psychopathology in later life. *Journal of Nervous and Mental Disease, 187*, 150–158.

Manber, R., Edinger, J. D., Gress, J. L., San Pedro-Salcedo, M. G., Kuo, T. F., & Kalista, T. (2008). Cognitive behavioral therapy for insomnia enhances depression outcome in patients with comorbid major depressive disorder and insomnia. *Sleep, 31*(4), 489–495.

McEwen, B. S. (2003). Mood disorders and allostatic load. *Biological Psychiatry, 54*, 200–207.

Mezick, E. J., Matthews, K. A., Hall, M., Strollo, P. J., Buysse, D. J., Kamarck, T. W., et al. (2008). Influence of race and socioeconomic status on sleep: Pittsburgh SleepSCORE Project. *Psychosomatic Medicine, 70*, 410–416.

Moos, R. H., & Cronkite, R. C. (1999). Symptom-based predictors of a 10-year chronic course of treated depression. *Journal of Nervous and Mental Disease, 187*, 360–368.

Morin, C. M. (2004). Cognitve-behavioral approaches to the treatment of insomnia. *Journal of Clinical Psychiatry, 65*[Suppl. 16], 33–40.

Morin, C. M., & Ware, J. C. (1996). Sleep and psychopathology. *Applied and Preventive Psychology, 5*, 211–224.

Motivala, S. J., Sarfatti, A., Olmos, L., & Irwin, M. R. (2005). Inflammatory markers and sleep disturbance in major depression. *Psychosomatic Medicine, 67*(2), 187–194.

Okun, M. L., Schetter, C. D., & Glynn, L. M. (2011). Poor sleep quality is associated with preterm birth. *Sleep, 34*(11), 1493–1498.

Perlis, M. L., Giles, D. E., Buysse, D. J., Thase, M. E., Tu, X., & Kupfer, D. J. (1997). Which depressive symptoms are related to which sleep electroencephalographic variables? *Biological Psychiatry, 42*, 904–913.

Pigeon, W. R., Cerulli, C., Richards, H., He, H., Perlis, M., & Caine, E. (2011). Sleep disturbances and their association with mental health among women exposed to intimate partner violence. *Journal of Women's Health, 20*(12), 1923–1929. [E-publication]

Pilcher, J. J., & Huffcutt, A. I. (1996). Effects of sleep deprivation on performance: A meta-analysis. *Sleep, 19*, 318–326.

Roberts, R. E., Shema, S. J., Kaplan, G. A., & Strawbridge, W. J. (2000). Sleep complaints and depression in an aging cohort: A prospective perspective. *American Journal of Psychiatry, 157*, 81–88.

Smith, M. T., Perlis, M. L., Smith, M. S., Giles, D. E., & Carmody, T. P. (2000). Sleep quality and presleep arousal in chronic pain. *Journal of Behavioral Medicine, 23*, 1–13.

Stepanski, E. J., & Perlis, M. (2000). Behavioral sleep medicine: An emerging subspecialty in health psychology and sleep medicine. *Journal of Psychosomatic Research, 49*, 343–347.

Stepanski, E. J., Rybarczyk, B., Lopez, M., & Stevens, S. (2003). Assessment and treatment of sleep disorders in older adults: A review for rehabilitation psychologists. *Rehabilitation Psychology, 48*, 23–36.

Suarez, E. C., & Goforth, H. (2010). Sleep and inflammation: A potential link to chronic diseases. In K. A. Kendall-Tackett (Ed.), *The psychoneuroimmunology of chronic disease* (pp. 53–75). Washington, DC: American Psychological Association.

Teegan, F. (1999). Childhood sexual abuse and long-term sequelae. In A. Maercker, M. Schutzwohl, & Z. Solomon (Eds.), *Posttraumatic stress disorder: A lifespan developmental perspective* (pp. 97–112). Seattle, WA: Hogrefe & Huber.

Ting, H., Hsiao-Sui, L., Chang, S.-Y., Chung, A.-H., Kuan, P.-C., & Yuan, S.-C. (2009). Post- to pre-overnight sleep systolic blood pressures are associated with sleep respiratory disturbance, pro-inflammatory state and metabolic situation in patients with sleep-disordered breathing. *Sleep Medicine, 10*(7), 720–725.

Troxel, W. M., Buysse, D. J., Hall, M., & Matthews, K. A. (2009). Marital happiness and sleep disturbances in a multi-ethnic sample of middle-aged women. *Behavioral Sleep Medicine, 7*(1), 2–19.

Troxel, W. M., Cyranowski, J. M., Hall, M., Frank, E., & Buysee, D. J. (2007). Attachment anxiety, relationship context, and sleep in women with recurrent major depression. *Psychosomatic Medicine, 69*, 692–699.

Ulmer, C. S., Edinger, J. D., & Calhoun, P. S. (2011). A multi-component cognitive-behavioral intervention for sleep disturbance in veterans with PTSD: A pilot study. *Journal of Clinical Sleep Medicine, 7*(1), 57–68.

Valham, F., Stegmayr, B., Eriksson, M., Hagg, E., Lindberg, E., & Franklin, K. A. (2009). Snoring and witnessed sleep apnea is related to diabetes mellitus in women. *Sleep Medicine, 10*, 112–117.

Verdecias, R. N., Jean-Louis, G., Zizi, F., Casimir, G. J., & Browne, R. C. (2009). Attachment styles and sleep measures in a community-based sample of older adults. *Sleep Medicine, 10*, 664–667.

Vincent, N. K., & Walker, J. R. (2000). Perfectionism and chronic insomnia. *Journal of Psychosomatic Medicine, 49*, 349–354.

Virani, A. S., Bezchlibnyk-Butler, K. Z., & Jeffries, J. J. (2009). *Clinical handbook of psychotropic drugs*. Seattle, WA: Hogrefe.

Ware, J. C., & Morin, C. M. (1997). Sleep in depression and anxiety. In M. R. Pressman & W. C. Orr (Eds.), *Understanding sleep: The evaluation and treatment of sleep disorders* (pp. 483–503). Washington, DC: American Psychological Association.

White, C., & Schweitzer, R. (2000). The role of personality in the development and perpetuation of chronic fatigue syndrome. *Journal of Psychosomatic Research, 48*, 515–524.

Wilson, C. J., Finch, C. E., & Cohen, H. J. (2002). Cytokines and cognition—The case for a head-to-toe inflammatory paradigm. *Journal of the American Geriatrics Society, 50*, 2041–2056.

Zoccola, P. M., Dickerson, S. S., & Lam, S. (2009). Rumination predicts longer sleep onset latency after an acute psychosocial stressor. *Psychosomatic Medicine, 71*, 771–775.

Chapter 4

Behavioral Pathways I—Substance Abuse, Smoking, Obesity, and Eating Disorders

Adult survivors of childhood abuse are more likely than other adults to behave in harmful ways, and the health implications are staggering. More than 2 million Americans die each year from preventable causes. Behavior and lifestyle play a major role in heart disease, cancer, HIV (human immunodeficiency virus) infection, and injuries. The Centers for Disease Control and Prevention (2002) has identified risk behaviors that contribute dramatically to mortality. These risk behaviors include tobacco use, alcohol and drug use, high-risk sexual behaviors, and behaviors that result in violence or accidents. In 2005, approximately 467,000 preventable deaths in the United States were due to tobacco; 395,000 were due to high blood pressure, 190,000–216,000 were due to high glucose, overweight/obesity, and physical inactivity; and 90,000 were due to alcohol-related accidents or injuries (Danaei et al., 2009). The four most common causes of death were ischemic heart disease, lung cancer, stroke, and chronic obstructive pulmonary disease (COPD) (Danaei et al., 2009). Many of these behaviors and conditions are more common in abuse survivors than in the general population.

If harmful behaviors occurred by themselves, they would be bad enough. Unfortunately, they tend to co-occur (Dallam, 2001), thereby multiplying their harmful effects. In a review of the literature on psychosocial factors associated with cancer treatment and disease course, Anderson, Kiecolt-Glaser, and Glaser (1994) noted that harmful behaviors, such as sleep deficiencies, drug use, and alcohol intake can have a direct impact on the immune system and its ability to ward off pathogens. This chapter and Chapter 5 describe the risk behaviors that most commonly occur in abuse survivors.

The impact of child maltreatment on problem behavior can be seen in a study of 1,131 youth, ages 12–18 (Hazen, Connelly, Roesch, Hough, & Landsverk, 2009). In this study, youth were divided into three groups: low maltreatment; physical and emotional abuse; or sexual, physical, and emotional abuse. The youth in both maltreatment groups were more withdrawn and had more somatic symptoms, anxiety, and depression than did their nonmaltreated peers. In addition, they had more behavior problems of all types than did the nonmaltreated youth. Youth who had been sexually, physically, and emotionally abused had significantly higher levels of delinquent behaviors than did the low-maltreatment group. The authors recommended providing appropriate interventions for victimized youth as these early interventions could mitigate both short- and long-term effects of childhood abuse.

SUBSTANCE ABUSE

Adult survivors are at increased risk for abusing alcohol and drugs. A number of studies have found that a high percentage of substance abusers have a history of childhood abuse and maltreatment. I have divided these studies by type of sample. The findings are remarkably consistent across study type and population.

Population-Based and Community Samples of Adults

In a population-based sample of 1,411 female adult twins, Kendler et al. (2000) assessed the impact of child sexual abuse (CSA) on rates of substance abuse. Sexual abuse that included intercourse dramatically increased the occurrence of alcohol abuse (OR = 4.01, 95 percent CI, 2.33–7.96) and drug dependence (OR = 5.7, 95 percent CI, 3.04–10.69). But there were significant effects for major depression, generalized anxiety disorder, panic disorder, and bulimia nervosa. Controlling for dysfunctional family environment somewhat attenuated the effects of CSA on most psychiatric disorders and substance use. However, for disorders such as panic disorder and bulimia, the relationship with CSA was actually strengthened when accounting for the effect of dysfunctional parenting.

Swedish women were interviewed regarding early substance use. Sexual abuse before age 13, a history of psychiatric problems, early deviant behavior, and substance use before age 15 were all associated with alcohol dependence in adults. Sexual abuse was the strongest predictor of adult alcohol abuse (Spak, Spak, & Allebeck, 1997). In a national survey of 1,099 American women, women who had been sexually abused were significantly more likely to report recent intoxication, drinking-related problems, symptoms of alcohol dependence, and lifetime abuse of prescription and illicit drugs compared to women with no abuse history (Wilsnack, Vogeltanz, Klassen, & Harris, 1997).

Data from a community sample of 274 male adults revealed that severe child physical abuse increased the probability of alcohol abuse from 11 percent in the rest of the sample to 63 percent. If they were also sexually abused, the probability of alcohol abuse increased from 63 percent to 81 percent (Kinzl & Biebl, 1997). In a study of gay and bisexual men, those with a history of child sexual abuse were more likely to use psychoactive drugs than were non-abused men (Bartholow et al., 1994).

Samples From Primary Care Medical Practices

In a sample from a rural family practice (Springs & Friedrich, 1992), women with a history of sexual abuse were more likely to abuse drugs and to report that they needed to decrease the amount of alcohol they consumed. In two other primary care samples, men and women with a history of victimization were more likely to use recreational and intravenous (IV) drugs (Kendall-Tackett, Marshall, & Ness, 2000) and to report heavy drinking than were patients without an abuse history (Hulme, 2000). In the Adverse Childhood Experiences (ACE) study, men who experienced six or more adverse childhood experiences had a 4,600 percent increase in the likelihood of later becoming an IV drug user (Felitti, 2001).

Samples From Treatment Programs

A study from Sao Paulo, Brazil, compared histories of childhood traumas for four groups: patients with alcohol dependence, patients with drug dependence, patients with diagnosed depression or dysthymia, and a control group of healthy volunteers (Tucci, Kerr-Correa, & Souza-Formigoni, 2010). The researchers found that patients with either drug- or alcohol-abuse experienced more severe abuse (physical, sexual, and emotional) compared to patients with depression. The patients with depression reported higher levels of physical, sexual, and emotional abuse than the control volunteers. Women were more likely to have a history of abuse than men. In all cases, the frequency was higher among women than among men. Most of the patients had been under psychiatric care for at least two years, yet the majority of abuse survivors had never talked about abuse experiences with their psychiatrists. The researchers urged those working with these populations to do a thorough assessment of previous trauma as it seems to be common for patients in psychiatric care.

In a sample of teens in treatment for substance abuse, those with a history of sexual abuse demonstrated a more serious involvement with substances. Males in the sample also showed increased suicidal ideation and school failure (Blood & Cornwall, 1996). In a study of 146 men and women in residential drug abuse treatment,

Gutierres and Todd (1997) found that 79 percent of the women and 41 percent of the men reported a history of physical, sexual, or emotional abuse.

A study from Australia compared 967 opioid-dependent patients of an outpatient treatment program with a matched group of 346 non-opioid-dependent controls (Conroy, Degenhardt, Mattick, & Nelson, 2009). Both groups reported high rates of child maltreatment, but there was an even higher prevalence in the opioid-dependent group. For example, 56 percent of the opioid-dependent females reported penetrative CSA compared to 28 percent of the females in the control group. For physical abuse, approximately 58 percent of the opioid-dependent males and females reported physical abuse, compared to 36–42 percent of the control group (males and females, respectively). Men were more likely to report physical and emotional abuse, women were more likely to report sexual abuse, particularly among the opioid-dependent group. There was no difference in rates of neglect between the opiod-dependent and control groups. In another Australian study, Jarvis and Copeland (1997) found that the women in treatment for either drugs or past sexual abuse had elevated levels of anxiety, somatization, and dissociation, but not depression. Women who reported both sexual abuse and substance abuse were more likely to have attempted suicide.

A sample of thirty-five lesbians in treatment for alcohol problems (Hall, 1996) found that 46 percent of these women had been sexually abused. The abuse survivors had multiple issues including addictions, self-harm, isolation, self-loathing, sexual problems, depression, physical illness, and inability to work. The women who had not been abused had more positives in their lives, including stability in their work and social relationships. In recovery, they had better physical health. The non-abused women's alcohol problems seemed more circumscribed and more amenable to treatment. In contrast, recovery for the sexually abused women was more complicated, and these women required more comprehensive interventions (Hall, 1996).

Childhood abuse also predicted attrition from a drug and alcohol rehabilitation program. In a study of ninety-two patients in treatment for substance abuse, the potential for successful rehabilitation was weakened by a history of child abuse. The authors suggest that these clients' problems with authority and interpersonal relationships need to be addressed if they are to be successful in rehab (Palmer, Palmer, Williamson, & Michiels, 1995).

Samples With Children or Teens

In a study of Minnesota public school students ($N = 122{,}824$), in grades 6, 9, and 12, physical and sexual abuse were associated with increased likelihood of alcohol, marijuana, and other drug use. Use of multiple substances was highly elevated among abuse victims, with the highest rates for those who reported both types of abuse. Abuse victims started using substances earlier, gave more reasons for using, and indicated that they used substances to cope with painful emotions and to escape from problems (Harrison, Fulkerson, & Beebe, 1997).

Another study compared three groups: alcoholic teens, teens who abused alcohol but were not yet dependent, and a control group (Clark, Lesnick, & Hegedus, 1997). Alcohol abuse or dependence was six to twelve times more likely in teens who had been physically abused, and eighteen to twenty-one times more likely in teens who had been sexually abused. Sexual abuse was more common among the females, and physical abuse or violence was more likely among the males.

In France, boys who had been raped were more likely to report frequent drug and alcohol abuse than a comparison group of teens who had not been raped. This pattern did not appear for the girls (Choquet, Darves-Bornoz, Ledoux, Manfredi, & Hassler, 1997). And in a birth cohort sample of 1,265 18-year-olds in New Zealand, exposure to parental violence was related to alcohol use and dependence, marijuana abuse and dependence, and abuse of "other substances." This was dose-response effect: The higher the level of violence in the home, the higher the percentage of substance abusers in each category (Fergusson & Lynskey, 1997).

Other Clinical Populations

A sample of female sexual abuse survivors with posttraumatic stress disorder (Bremner et al., 1997) also had high rates of comorbid substance abuse. Seventy-one percent reported alcohol dependence, 36 percent reported marijuana dependence, 14 percent reported stimulant dependence, 29 percent reported opiate dependence, and 57 percent reported cocaine dependence.

In a study of psychiatric emergency department (ED) patients, sexual abuse survivors were ten times more likely to have a history of drug addiction and two times more likely to have been alcoholics than were non-abused psychiatric ED patients (Briere & Runtz, 1987). A study of low-income urban women with severe mental disorders found that early sexual abuse predicted alcohol and cocaine use, as well as prostitution. Childhood physical abuse predicted alcohol abuse (Goodman & Fallot, 1998).

Prospective Designs

A prospective study of 276 college women examined the impact of childhood victimization on revictimization risk (Messman-Moore, Ward, & Brown, 2009). The researchers were testing the theory that psychological dysfunction increased the risk for revictimization. They hypothesized that substance abuse and sexual behavior function as coping and tension-reduction strategies in response to posttraumatic stress disorder (PTSD) symptomatology. During the eight-month follow-up, 9 percent of the sample was raped. In 88 percent of the cases, substance abuse was involved. Factors that predicted rape were PTSD symptoms, substance abuse, and sexual behavior. The authors concluded that college women with PTSD symptoms are at greater risk of rape if they abuse substances in order to reduce their distress and self-medicate. They may also consume alcohol to reduce tension, and to improve social and sexual interactions. Although a high percentage of the sample reported childhood victimization, that by itself did not predict revictimization. Rather, PTSD symptoms did, likely due to prior victimization.

A prospective study of African-American sexual abuse survivors found that childhood physical abuse and multiple sexual victimizations were each associated with heavy and binge drinking. Multiple victimization and younger age at first assault were significant predictors of binge drinking. Older age at first assault predicted heavy drinking. Older age at first assault may have meant more physical force used, which is also related to increased symptomatology. These women were also more likely to have intrusive memories, and heavy drinking was an attempt to self-medicate. Binge drinking may have been related to an attempt to block a specific trigger or memory of the abusive experience, whereas heavy drinking may have been an attempt to cope with overall bad feelings (Jasinski, Williams, & Siegel, 2000).

In a prospective study of 672 abused and neglected children and 518 non-abused children, Widom and White (1997) found that abused or neglected girls were more likely to abuse substances and be arrested for violent crime than were the non-abused girls, even after controlling for parent alcohol or drug problems, parental arrest, childhood poverty, and ethnicity. Another study examined whether there was a causal relationship between child abuse and neglect and the subsequent development of alcoholism. Using causal modeling, Schuck and Widom (2001) were able to demonstrate a causal relationship between alcohol abuse and child maltreatment. They also found depression and using alcohol to cope as mediating the effects of alcohol abuse but not the other factors.

Possible Explanations for Substance Abuse in Adult Survivors

Why do survivors seem more prone to abuse substances than do their non-abused counterparts? A number of explanations have been offered.

Psychosocial Explanations. One possible explanation is that abuse survivors may drink or use drugs to self-medicate, subdue painful memories, or settle anxiety (Schuck & Widom, 2001). Adult survivors may also drink or use drugs to shore up flagging self-confidence and to relieve social anxiety. They may also abuse substances to enjoy a sense of power and control, however fleeting, or to relieve feelings of guilt. Abuse survivors may abuse substances to relieve anxiety about having sex or their sense of social isolation (Jasinski et al., 2000).

Biological Vulnerability. Psychosocial explanations most likely explain some substance use among abuse survivors. But these explanations do not tell the whole story. Neuroscience research has indicated that there may also be a biological vulnerability to substance abuse and addiction—especially in those who have experienced traumatic events. Addiction involves the dopamine-releasing neurons of the ventral tegmental area that extend to the nucleus accumbens and prefrontal cortex (Wickelgren, 1997). This "pleasure pathway" has projections to the limbic system and orbitofrontal cortex (Leshner, 1997). Researchers have questioned whether this pathway really involves pleasure because people persist in addictive behavior even after it is no longer pleasurable. A more likely possibility is that this pathway is involved in learning and memory rather than pleasure. It is the common element in all drug use and what keeps users taking drugs (Leshner, 1997).

Both sensitization of the brain (especially the ascending dopamine projections) and alterations in the HPA (hypothalamic-pituitary-adrenal) axis have been hypothesized as being factors in addiction. Sensitization of the brain can result in compulsive seeking of the drug that does not cause pleasure and is particularly of interest to us in that it frequently has a relationship to past traumatic events. Indeed, Nesse and Berridge (1997) noted the importance of both genetic factors and emotional experience in susceptibility to addiction, pointing to the high degree of comorbidity between substance use and PTSD. Susceptibility is correlated with dysregulation of the HPA axis, corticotropin-releasing hormone, and prolonged secretion of glucocorticoids in response to stress (Koob & LeMoal, 1997; Nestler & Aghajanian, 1997).

Up to this point, the research on the psychobiology of addiction has raised some intriguing possibilities but has not demonstrated a definite link. Future research may eventually demonstrate that traumatic events transform the brain to such an extent that it becomes highly vulnerable to addiction. Couple this with the psychosocial vulnerabilities and we see a population highly susceptible to addiction.

How Substance Abuse Affects Health

Substance abuse has long-range implications for health. Some of the more immediate effects are the danger of accident, injury, or violence (Trezza & Popp, 2000). Suicide risk among substance users is also high. Looking across studies, Trezza and Popp (2000) noted that lifetime suicide risk among alcoholics ranged from 3.4 percent to 43 percent, and completed suicides were twice as high as even a general psychiatric population. In addition, substance abusers were at increased risk for being the victims or recipients of violence, both of which increase their risk of injury and death.

Long-term substance abuse puts people in danger of heart and liver disease (Trezza & Popp, 2000) and a variety of social problems including employment difficulties, car accidents, and breakdown of social relationships. There is also an increased likelihood of homelessness among substance abusers and the participation in other harmful behaviors, including smoking and high-risk sexual activity, both of which are described in subsequent sections.

Substance use also increases the risk of sexual assault. Victims of alcohol-related sexual assault are more likely to believe that alcohol will confer certain positive advantages, such as feeling warmer and more romantic, sociable, powerful, sexual, and less inhibited. These beliefs are known as alcohol-outcome expectancies. In Marx et al.'s study of 176 female college undergraduates, victims of alcohol- and drug-related sexual assault reported more frequent and great alcohol consumption, and a greater endorsement of alcohol-outcome expectancies compared to nonvictims or women who were victims of non-alcohol or drug sexual assault (Marx, Nichols-Anderson, Messman-Moore, Miranda, & Porter, 2000). The authors speculated that this group may be at increased risk of sexual assault because they do not understand the extent to which increased levels of alcohol consumption lead to increased levels of impairment. They may not fully anticipate the negative effects of alcohol that increase risk for such experiences.

SMOKING

Smoking is also more likely among those with a history of abuse (DeWit, MacDonald, & Offord, 1999; Kendall-Tackett et al., 2000). In a sample from a rural family practice (Springs & Friedrich, 1992), sexual abuse predicted smoking. Women whose abuse started at an early age also began smoking at an early age. Indeed, the women who had been sexually abused started smoking 1.6 years earlier than did their non-abused counterparts. Sexual abuse, but not current age, predicted heavier smoking.

Physical abuse predicted smoking in a group of adolescents (ages 12–18) who were recruited from the New York State Department of Social Services. Smoking co-occurred with depression, conduct disorder, dysthymia, and drug abuse (Kaplan, Pelcovitz, Salzinger, & Weiner, 1998). Teens who reported a history of physical abuse were three times more likely to smoke than were non-abused teens in another study (Riggs, Alario, & McHorney, 1990). French teens who had been raped were significantly more likely to smoke than teens who had not been raped (Choquet et al., 1997). And, in a community sample of teenage girls, those who had been both physically and sexually abused were almost six times more likely to smoke than were their non-abused counterparts (Diaz, Simatov, & Rickert, 2000).

In a sample of women who had been sexually abused, 45 percent of abused women with PTSD smoked; in contrast, abused women without PTSD and non-abused women did not smoke at all (Lemieux & Coe, 1995). In a study of chronic pain, subjects who were abused as children or adults were significantly more likely to smoke (46 percent vs. 18 percent; Scarinci, McDonald-Haile, Bradley, & Richter, 1994). Norwegian women with a history of child sexual abuse were more likely to smoke during pregnancy (Grimstad & Schei, 1999).

Smoking was also asked about as part of the ACE study. The sample from this study included 9,215 mostly middle-age adults from a health maintenance organization (HMO). Even after adjusting for age, sex, race, and education, smoking was related to each type of childhood adversity. Those who had experienced five or more adverse childhood experiences were five times more likely to have started smoking before age 15, twice as likely to still be smoking, and almost three times more likely to be heavy smokers. Indeed, the effects of individual types of abuse on smoking were marginal. However, when all the types were considered together, there was a strong and graded relationship between the number of adverse childhood experiences and smoking (Anda et al., 1999; Felitti et al., 1998). Indeed, a person with a score of 4 or more adverse events was 390 percent more likely to have COPD than was a person with a score of 0. The only exception was one finding with regard to sexual abuse: Sexual abuse that happened before age 14 and antedated the age of smoking was associated with a fourfold increase in smoking initiation (Anda et al., 1999).

Exposure to domestic violence also dramatically increases the odds of smoking. In a birth cohort sample of 18-year-olds from New Zealand, Fergusson and Horwood (1998) found that smoking was more common in teens whose families had high levels of interparental violence. The teens with the highest levels of parental violence had the highest chance of smoking.

Why Abuse Survivors Smoke

Anda et al. (1999) raised the question of how people who have experienced adverse childhood events might "benefit" from the use of nicotine. They speculated that nicotine may be used as a psychoactive substance to help them regulate affect. People who suffered from adverse childhood experiences may be using nicotine to boost their mood. These authors did also find a strong, graded relationship in their data between depression in the past year and the number of adverse childhood experiences. Current smokers were always more likely to have had episodes of depression.

Ironically, although most smokers feel that cigarettes help them relieve stress, the reality is that stress levels of smokers are generally higher than those of nonsmokers. In reviewing a number of past studies, Parrott (1999) concluded that nicotine dependence causes stress. In general, smokers report being under more stress and having repeated negative moods throughout the day between cigarettes. Nicotine is a cholinergic agonist with sympathomimetic rather than sedative qualities. The apparent mood benefits of smoking only reflect the relief of withdrawal symptoms. Not surprisingly, quitting smoking actually decreased stress, although one's mood may be foul for a few weeks while in the process of quitting. Parrott (2000) points out that while people smoke, they feel normal, but in between cigarettes they feel depressed and anxious at a level that is worse than if they were not nicotine dependent. Though there is evidence of mood modulation as people smoke, there is little evidence of mood improvement.

Leventhal et al. (2010) considered the role of tobacco as a way to cope with negative moods and its relation to depression and obesity. Their thesis was that some people might use smoking, rather than food or sedentary behavior, to cope with depression. As such, it might moderate the link between depression and body mass index (BMI). In their population study of 41,654 U.S. adults, they found that major depression predicted obesity and high BMI in nonsmokers. But this was not true for smokers. Their findings confirmed their hypothesis that smoking moderated the link between depression and obesity.

How Smoking Affects Health

The health effects of smoking are well-known even among the general population. Smoking tobacco is the largest modifiable health risk among adults. It is responsible for over 467,000 deaths per year in the United States and for as much as $155 billion in direct and indirect medical costs (Centers for Disease Control and Prevention, 2002; Danaei et al., 2009).

Smoking accounts for a substantial portion of deaths from cardiovascular disease; stroke; pulmonary disease; and cancer of the lungs, larynx, esophagus, mouth, and bladder. It also increases vulnerability to cancer of the cervix, pancreas, and kidneys (Centers for Disease Control and Prevention, 2002; Dennis, Janssen, & Singer, 2004). It even affects the people around the smoker; secondhand smoke can cause chronic pulmonary disease and cancer (Connelly & Inni, 1998), and up to 300,000 American children suffer from infections of the respiratory tract due to secondhand smoke (Centers for Disease Control and Prevention, 2002).

In short, smoking alone can account for many of the health problems adult survivors face. But smoking tends to co-occur with other harmful behaviors.

OBESITY AND EATING DISORDERS

Adult survivors can also have patterns of disturbed eating. Two of the most common manifestations of these dysfunctional patterns are obesity and eating disorders, such as anorexia and bulimia. These are described next.

Obesity

A substantial percentage of the American population is either overweight or obese. Obviously, childhood abuse is not the sole cause. However, adult survivors do appear to be at increased risk. Three studies have found a link between child sexual abuse and obesity. In a family-practice study, Springs and Friedrich (1992) found that women who had been sexually abused were significantly more likely to be currently overweight (i.e., more than 40 percent over their ideal weight based on the Metropolitan Life Insurance tables).

In a study of 131 HMO patients with a history of incest, 60 percent of these patients were more than fifty pounds overweight, compared with 28 percent of the control group. Twenty-five percent were more than 100 pounds overweight compared with only 6 percent of the control group (Felitti, 1991). Felitti first became interested in the connection between abuse and obesity when he observed a correlation between a failure to lose weight in a weight-control program and a report of CSA. He compared this sample with age-matched women from the same medical population. Obesity co-occurred with depression and chronic pelvic pain, headache, and gastrointestinal distress.

In a sample of middle-age women ($N = 4{,}641$), obesity and depression were associated with a history of childhood physical and sexual abuse (Rohde et al., 2008). Adult women who reported a history of either physical or sexual abuse had twice the likelihood of current obesity and depression compared with the non-abused group. Controlling for age and ethnicity had only a minimal impact on the magnitude of the associations. Child physical abuse was not associated with depression for black, Hispanic, or American Indian participants. The association between obesity and depression was somewhat attenuated after controlling for sexual abuse and physical abuse history.

The difficulty abuse survivors have in losing weight also appeared in another study. King, Clark, and Pera (1996) compared twenty-two women with obesity who had a history of sexual abuse with a matched group of twenty-two women with obesity who had no history of abuse. All were enrolled in a hospital-based weight-loss program. The sexually abused women lost significantly less weight and had more episodes of nonadherence to their weight-loss plan. They also had lower self-efficacy than did the non-abused women (King et al., 1996).

Obesity may also be due to early maltreatment's impact on the stress responses, which affects how the brain regulates energy balance. If that is so, then the social and emotional aspects of the parent-child relationship may also affect obesity risk. In a study of 2,412 3-year-old children who were part of the Fragile Families and Child Wellbeing Study (Whitaker, Phillips, Orzol, & Burdette, 2007), researchers asked mothers questions about neglect, corporal punishment, and psychological aggression. They found that 18 percent of the children were obese. The prevalence of "any" episode of neglect, corporal punishment, and psychological aggression was 11 percent, 84 percent, and 93 percent respectively. Only neglect was related to obesity, and this association was still present even after controlling for income, number of children in the house, mother's race/ethnicity, education, marital status, maternal BMI, and prenatal smoking, as well as age and the child's sex and birthweight. Corporal punishment and psychological aggression were not associated with increased risk of obesity. The authors suggested that aspects of the parent-child relationship not related to diet and exercise may influence the risk of childhood obesity. Maintaining a healthy weight may be another positive outcome for children that could result from efforts to prevent child neglect.

Eating Disorders

Adult survivors also appear vulnerable to eating disorders. In the United States, eating disorders are most common among adolescents and young women. The National Institute of Mental Health (2000) estimated that 0.5 percent to 1 percent of women suffer anorexia nervosa, 1 percent to 3 percent have bulimia nervosa, and 0.7 percent to 4 percent have a binge-eating disorder. Prevalence in males is unknown. A number of past studies have found a relationship between child abuse and disordered eating, but the results have been mixed. Not all men and women with eating disorders are abuse survivors. But the experience of childhood abuse may increase risk of eating disorders for some.

In a primary care sample, women with a history of CSA were more likely to report eating too little, eating too much, and making themselves vomit than were women with no reported history. There was no significant difference in the number of women who reported that they were too thin from starving themselves, however (Hulme, 2000). In a large community sample, men and women who had been sexually assaulted were more likely to think they were "too fat," and to report one or more symptoms of anorexia and sudden weight change. The authors concluded that there was a relationship between a history of sexual assault and symptoms of eating disorders (Laws & Golding, 1996).

Miller, McClusky-Fawcett, and Irving (1993) found that significantly more young women diagnosed with bulimia reported sexual abuse after age 12 with an adult relative than did a group of matched controls. However, the relationship between sexual abuse prior to age 12 was non-significant. There were also high rates of dissociation and unusual mealtime experiences among the bulimic women. The authors conservatively suggest that sexual abuse may be related to the onset of bulimia for some women. Others have not found a relationship (Kinzl, Traweger, Guenther, & Biebl, 1994; Rorty, Yager, & Rossotto, 1994).

In a large sample of adolescents (grades 5–12), Ackard, Neumark-Sztainer, Hannan, French, and Story (2001) found that binge-and-purge behavior was twice as prevalent in girls as in boys and was significantly related to all types of child maltreatment. The associations were highest for boys and girls who had been both physically and sexually abused.

Van Gerko, Hughes, Hamill, and Waller (2005) collected data on 299 women who met the criteria for eating disorders according to the fourth edition of *Diagnostic and Statistical Manual of Mental Disorders* (American Psychiatric Association, 1994). Twenty-nine percent of the women in their sample reported a history of CSA. Sexual abuse was more common among women with atypical anorexia, but with relatively low rates among women with restrictive anorexia and binge eating. For women with nonpurging eating disorders (restrictive anorexia and binge eating), 17.4 percent reported sexual abuse. Of women with any purging behavior, 33.8 percent reported a history of sexual abuse. The abuse survivors had significantly higher levels of objective bingeing, vomiting, laxative abuse, and diuretic abuse. Age and BMI did not account for these group differences.

A summary of three different large samples of ninth- to twelfth-graders show similar results (Thompson, Wonderlich, Crosby, & Mitchell, 2001). In this study, the authors examined the relationship between sexual victimization and weight-regulation practices. Sexual victimization included victimization by both adults and peers, and increased the likelihood of purging and diet pill use. Sexually victimized girls were also more likely to choose multiple forms of weight regulation (i.e., exercise, dieting, diet pills, fasting, and purging) than their non-abused peers.

Eating Disorders and Comorbid Conditions. Eating disorders are often comorbid with other conditions in those who have a history of childhood abuse. Matsunaga et al. (1999) evaluated forty-four female patients who had been in recovery from bulimia nervosa for at least one year. Twenty of these patients had a history of physical or sexual abuse. Members of the abused group had higher levels of general psychopathology and were more likely to report interpersonal distrust. They also scored higher on measures of drive for thinness, body dissatisfaction, and ineffectiveness than the non-abused women. The abused women were also more likely to have comorbid PTSD and substance abuse. These results suggest that childhood abuse is not the cause of most cases of bulimia, but those who have experienced childhood abuse are a distinct subgroup that are prone to serious comorbid conditions.

A recent study of 753 women with anorexia nervosa explored the relationship between anorexia and comorbid PTSD (Reyes-Rodriguez et al., 2011). In this sample, 13.7 percent met the criteria for PTSD. They found that PTSD was more common in patients with purging anorexia compared with restricting anorexia. Sixty-four percent reported that a traumatic event preceded their anorexia. The most common types of trauma related to their PTSD were sexual traumas that occurred either during childhood or adulthood.

Another study had similar results (Holzer, Uppala, Wonderlich, Crosby, & Simonich, 2008). This study included seventy-one victims of sexual trauma and twenty-five control subjects. They found that there was a significant association between trauma history and eating disorders. The relationship between trauma and eating-disorder symptoms was lessened when PTSD was added to the regression model, suggesting that PTSD was mediating the link between sexual trauma and eating disorders. These findings were most pronounced for the physiological arousal and avoidance components of PTSD. The authors did note that since their data were cross-sectional, not longitudinal, they could not tell for certain whether PTSD actually mediated the relationship. But they suggested that it would be a possible avenue to explore in future studies.

Theories for Eating Disorders in Abuse Survivors. Thompson et al. (2001) speculated on several possible explanations for the relationship between sexual victimization and eating disorders. A history of sexual trauma may sensitize the body and increase the concerns about body issues in general. This may heighten awareness and dissatisfaction with body shape and size. Sexual trauma might also influence neurotransmitter systems, including those of serotonin, norepinephrine, dopamine, and endorphins. These may, in turn, create disturbances in eating behavior.

Eating disorders may also be related to serotonin levels. Serotonin pathways are related to satiety after eating, and medications that boost serotonin levels decrease food intake. Compared with healthy controls, women with bulimia are more likely to have diminished satiety after eating, and this could be due to lower levels of serotonin. To test this hypothesis, Jimerson et al. (1997) administered a serotonin-producing drug, which lowered the number of binge episodes in the bulimic group. The authors concluded that impaired central nervous system serotonin may contribute to or maintain disordered eating patterns in women with bulimia nervosa. Indeed, they noted that "altered central serotonin function may reflect a shared neurobiological diathesis across several psychiatric disorders" (p. 532).

How Obesity and Eating Disorders Impact Health

Overweight and obesity can influence health. People who are overweight are at higher risk for heart disease, stroke, diabetes, hyperlipidemia, gall bladder problems, and hypertension. Excess dietary fat has been linked with several cancers including breast, colon, prostate, and lung (Connelly & Inni, 1998; Stice, 2002). Obesity has not received as much attention as eating disorders, especially in regard to past victimization. But it is much more common than all eating disorders combined.

Eating disorders can also have a serious impact on health. Anorexia may lead to osteoporosis, cardiac arrhythmias, hypotension, depression, hypothermia, infertility, suicide, and even death (DeAngelis, 2002). Problems associated with bulimia include erosion of tooth enamel, cardiac arrhythmias, esophageal or gastric rupture, and aspiration of gastric contents. Other problems include cardiac and renal conditions due to blood chemistry imbalances (e.g., hypokalemia and a potassium imbalance) (Heffernan, 1998). The mortality and morbidity risks are substantial.

In summary, obesity and eating disorders do not affect all adult survivors. And not all people with these conditions have been abused. But a substantial proportion of adult survivors are more vulnerable to these conditions than those in the general population—and this can have a serious impact on health.

SUMMARY

Substance abuse, smoking, eating disorders, and obesity are all more common among abuse survivors than they are in the general population. Each of these behaviors can have a negative impact on health. In the next chapter, I describe two more types of high-risk behavior that can affect the health of abuse survivors: suicide and high-risk sexual activity.

References

Ackard, D. M., Neumark-Sztainer, D., Hannan, P. J., French, S., & Story, M. (2001). Binge and purge behavior among adolescents: Associations with sexual and physical abuse in a nationally representative sample: The Commonwealth Fund Survey. *Child Abuse and Neglect, 25*, 771–785.

American Psychiatric Association. (1994). *Diagnostic and statistical manual of mental disorders*

(4th ed.). Washington, DC: Author.

Anda, R. F., Croft, J. B., Felitti, V. J., Nordenberg, D., Giles, W. H., Williamson, D. F., et al. (1999). Adverse childhood experiences and smoking during during adolescence and adulthood. *Journal of the American Medical Association, 282*, 1652–1658.

Anderson, B. L., Kiecolt-Glaser, J. K., & Glaser, R. (1994). A biobehavioral model of cancer stress and disease course. *American Psychologist, 49*, 389–404.

Bartholow, B. N., Doll, L. S., Joy, D., Douglas, J. M., Bolan, G., Harrison, J. S., et al. (1994). Emotional, behavioral, and HIV risks associated with sexual abuse among adult homosexual and bisexual men. *Child Abuse and Neglect, 18*, 747–761.

Blood, L., & Cornwall, A. (1996). Childhood sexual victimization as a factor in the treatment of substance misusing adolescents. *Substance Use and Misuse, 31*, 1015–1039.

Bremner, J. D., Randall, P., Vermetten, E., Staib, L., Bronen, R. A., Mazure, C. M., et al. (1997). Magnetic resonance imaging-based measurements of hippocampal volume in posttraumatic stress disorder related to childhood physical and sexual abuse: A preliminary report. *Biological Psychiatry, 41*, 23–32.

Briere, J. N., & Runtz, M. (1987). Post sexual abuse trauma: Data and implications for clinical practice. *Journal of Interpersonal Violence, 2*, 367–379.

Centers for Disease Control and Prevention. (2002). *Targeting tobacco use: The nation's leading cause of death*. Atlanta: Author.

Choquet, M., Darves-Bornoz, J.-M., Ledoux, S., Manfredi, R., & Hassler, C. (1997). Self-reported health and behavioral problems among adolescent victims of rape in France: Results of a cross-sectional survey. *Child Abuse and Neglect, 21*, 823–832.

Clark, D. B., Lesnick, L., & Hegedus, A. M. (1997). Traumas and other adverse life events in adolescents with alcohol abuse and dependence. *Journal of the American Academy of Child and Adolescent Psychiatry, 36*, 1744–1751.

Connelly, M. T., & Inni, T. S. (1998). Principles of disease prevention. In A. S. Fauci, E. Braunwald, K. J. Isselbacher, J. D. Wilson, J. B. Martin, D. L. Kasper, et al. (Eds.), *Harrison's principles of internal medicine* (14th ed., pp. 46–48). New York: Mc-Graw-Hill.

Conroy, E., Degenhardt, L., Mattick, R. P., & Nelson, E. C. (2009). Child maltreatment as a risk factor for opioid dependence: Comparison of family characteristics and type and severity of child maltreatment with a matched control group. *Child Abuse and Neglect, 33*, 343–352.

Dallam, S. J. (2001). The hidden effects of childhood maltreatment on adult health. In K. Franey, R. Geffner & R. Falconer (Eds.), *The cost of child maltreatment: Who pays? We all do.* (pp. 1–14). San Diego: Family Violence & Sexual Assault Institute.

Danaei, G., Ding, E. L., Mozaffarian, D., Taylor, B., Rehm, J., Murray, C. J. L., et al. (2009). The preventable causes of death in the United States: Comparative risk assessment of dietary, lifestyle, and metabolic risk factors. *PLoS Medicine, 6*(4), e1000058.

DeAngelis, T. (2002). Promising treatments for anorexia and bulimia. *Monitor on Psychology, 33*, 38–41.

Dennis, C.-L., Janssen, P. A., & Singer, J. (2004). Identifying women at-risk for postpartum depression in the immediate postpartum period. *Acta Psychiatrica Scandanavica, 110*, 338–346.

DeWit, D. J., MacDonald, K., & Offord, D. R. (1999). Childhood stress and symptoms of drug dependence in adolescence and early adulthood. *American Journal of Orthopsychiatry, 69*, 61–72.

Diaz, A., Simatov, E., & Rickert, V. I. (2000). The independent and combined effects of physical and sexual abuse on health. Results from a national survey. *Journal of Pediatric and Adolescent Gynecology, 13*(2), 89.

Felitti, V. J. (1991). Long-term medical consequences of incest, rape, and molestation. *Southern Medical Journal, 84*, 328–331.

Felitti, V. J. (2001). Reverse alchemy in childhood: Turning gold into lead. *Health Alert, 8*, 1–4.

Felitti, V. J., Anda, R. F., Nordenberg, D., Williamson, D. F., Spitz, A. M., Edwards, V., et al. (1998). Relationship of childhood abuse and household dysfunction to many of the leading causes of death in adults. The Adverse Childhood Experiences (ACE) Study. *American Journal of Preventive Medicine, 14*(4), 245–258.

Fergusson, D. M., & Horwood, L. J. (1998). Exposure to interparental violence in childhood and psychosocial adjustment in young adulthood. *Child Abuse and Neglect, 22*, 339–357.

Fergusson, D. M., & Lynskey, M. T. (1997). Physical punishment/maltreatment during childhood and adjustment in young adulthood. *Child Abuse and Neglect, 21*, 617–630.

Goodman, L. A., & Fallot, R. D. (1998). HIV risk behavior in poor urban women with serious mental disorders: Association with childhood physical and sexual abuse. *American Journal of Orthopsychiatry, 68*, 73–83.

Grimstad, H., & Schei, B. (1999). Pregnancy and delivery for women with a history of child sexual abuse. *Child Abuse and Neglect, 23*, 81–90.

Gutierres, S. E., & Todd, M. (1997). The impact of childhood abuse on treatment outcomes of substance users. *Professional Psychology: Research and Practice, 28*, 348–354.

Hall, J. M. (1996). Pervasive effects of childhood sexual abuse in lesbians' recovery from alcohol problems. *Substance Use and Misuse, 31*, 225–239.

Harrison, P. A., Fulkerson, J. A., & Beebe, T. J. (1997). Multiple substance use among adolescent physical and sexual abuse victims. *Child Abuse and Neglect, 21*, 529–539.

Hazen, A. L., Connelly, C. D., Roesch, S. C., Hough, R. L., & Landsverk, J. A. (2009). Child maltreatment profiles and adjustment problems in high-risk adolescents. *Journal of Interpersonal Violence, 24*(2), 361–378.

Heffernan, K. (1998). Bulimia nervosa. In E. A. Blechman & K. D. Brownell (Eds.), *Behavioral medicine & women: A comprehensive handbook* (pp. 358–363). New York: Guilford Press.

Holzer, S. R., Uppala, S., Wonderlich, S. A., Crosby, R. D., & Simonich, H. (2008). Mediational significance of PTSD in the relationship of sexual trauma and eating disorders. *Child Abuse and Neglect, 32*, 561–566.

Hulme, P. A. (2000). Symptomatology and health care utilization of women primary care patients who experienced childhood sexual abuse. *Child Abuse and Neglect, 24*, 1471–1484.

Jarvis, T. J., & Copeland, J. (1997). Child sexual abuse as a predictor of psychiatric co-morbidity and its implications for drug and alcohol treatment. *Drug and Alcohol Dependence, 49*, 61–69.

Jasinski, J. S., Williams, L. M., & Siegel, J. A. (2000). Childhood physical and sexual abuse as risk factors for heavy drinking among African American women: A prospective study. *Child Abuse and Neglect, 24*, 1061–1071.

Jimerson, D. C., Wolfe, B. E., Metzger, E. D., Finkelstein, D. M., Cooper, T. B., & Levine, J. M. (1997). Decreased serotonin function in bulimia nervose. *Archives of General Psychiatry, 54*, 529–534.

Kaplan, S. J., Pelcovitz, D., Salzinger, S., & Weiner, M. (1998). Adolescent physical abuse: Risk for adolescent psychiatric disorders. *American Journal of Psychiatry, 155*, 954–959.

Kendall-Tackett, K. A., Marshall, R., & Ness, K. E. (2000). Victimization, healthcare use and health maintenance. *Family Violence and Sexual Assault Bulletin, 16*, 18–21.

Kendler, K. S., Bulik, C. M., Silberg, J., Hettema, J. M., Myers, J., & Prescott, C. A. (2000). Childhood sexual abuse and adult psychiatric and substance use disorders in women. *Archives of General Psychiatry, 57*, 953–959.

King, T. K., Clark, M. M., & Pera, V. (1996). History of sexual abuse and obesity treatment outcome. *Addictive Behaviors, 21*, 283–290.

Kinzl, J. F., & Biebl, W. (1997). Sexual abuse in people with alcohol problems. *British Journal of Psychiatry, 170*, 193.

Kinzl, J. F., Traweger, C., Guenther, V., & Biebl, W. (1994). Family background and sexual abuse associated with eating disorders. *American Journal of Psychiatry, 151*, 1127–1131.

Koob, G. F., & LeMoal, M. (1997). Drug abuse: Hedonic homeostatic dysregulation. *Science, 278*, 52–57.

Laws, A., & Golding, J. M. (1996). Sexual assault history and eating disorder symptoms among white, Hispanic, and African American women and men. *American Journal of Public Health, 86*, 579–582.

Lemieux, A. M., & Coe, C. L. (1995). Abuse-related posttraumatic stress disorder: Evidence for chronic neuroendocrine activation in women. *Psychosomatic Medicine, 57*, 105–115.

Leshner, A. I. (1997). Addiction is a brain disease. *Science, 278*, 45–47.

Leventhal, A. M., Mickens, L., Dunton, G. F., Sussman, S., Riggs, N. R., & Pentz, M. A. (2010). Tobacco use moderates the association between major depression and obesity. *Health Psychology, 29*(5), 521–528.

Marx, B. P., Nichols-Anderson, C., Messman-Moore, T. L., Miranda, R., & Porter, C. (2000). Alcohol consumption, outcome expectancies, and victimization status among female college students. *Journal of Applied Social Psychology, 30*(5), 1056–1070.

Matsunaga, H., Kaye, W. H., McConaha, C., Plotnicov, K., Pollice, C., Rao, R., et al. (1999). Psychopathological characteristics of recovered bulimics who have a history of physical or sexual abuse. *Journal of Nervous and Mental Disease, 187*, 472–477.

Messman-Moore, T. L., Ward, R. M., & Brown, A. L. (2009). Substance use and PTSD symptoms impact the likelihood of rape and revictimization in college women. *Journal of Interpersonal Violence, 24*(3), 499–521.

Miller, D. A., McClusky-Fawcett, K., & Irving, L. M. (1993). The relationship between childhood sexual abuse and subsequent onset of bulimia nervosa. *Child Abuse and Neglect, 17*, 305–314.

National Institute of Mental Health. (2000). *Brief notes on the mental health of children.* Washington, DC: Author.

Nesse, R. M., & Berridge, K. C. (1997). Psychoactive drug use in evolutionary perspective. *Science, 278*, 63–66.

Nestler, E. J., & Aghajanian, G. K. (1997). Molecular and cellular basis of addiction. *Science, 278*, 58–62.

Palmer, J. A., Palmer, L. K., Williamson, D., & Michiels, K. (1995). Childhood abuse as a factor in attrition from drug rehabilitation. *Psychological Reports, 76*, 879–882.

Parrott, A. C. (1999). Does cigarette smoking cause stress? *American Psychologist, 54*, 817–820.

Parrott, A. C. (2000). Cigarette smoking does cause stress. *American Psychologist, 55*, 1159–1160.

Reyes-Rodriguez, M. L., Von Holle, A., Ulman, T. F., Thornton, L. M., Klump, K. L., Brandt, H., et al. (2011). Posttraumatic stress disorder in anorexia nervosa. *Psychosomatic Medicine, 73*, 491–497.

Riggs, S., Alario, A. J., & McHorney, C. (1990). Health risk behaviors and attempted suicide in adolescents who report prior maltreatment. *Journal of Pediatrics, 116*, 815–821.

Rohde, P., Ichikawa, L., Simon, G. E., Ludman, E. J., Linde, J. A., Jeffery, R. W., et al. (2008). Associations of child sexual and physical abuse with obesity and depression in middle-aged women. *Child Abuse and Neglect, 32*(9), 878–887.

Rorty, M., Yager, J., & Rossotto, E. (1994). Childhood sexual, physical, and psychological abuse in bulimia nervosa. *American Journal of Psychiatry, 151*, 1122–1126.

Scarinci, I. C., McDonald-Haile, J., Bradley, L. A., & Richter, J. E. (1994). Altered pain perception and psychosocial features among women with gastrointestinal disorders and history of abuse: A preliminary model. *American Journal of Medicine, 97*, 108–118.

Schuck, A. M., & Widom, C. S. (2001). Childhood victimization and alcohol symptoms in females: Causal inferences and hypothesized mediators. *Child Abuse and Neglect, 25*, 1069–1092.

Spak, L., Spak, F., & Allebeck, P. (1997). Factors in childhood and youth predicting alcohol dependence and abuse in Swedish women: Findings from a general population study. *Alcohol and Alcoholism, 32*, 267–274.

Springs, F. E., & Friedrich, W. N. (1992). Health risk behaviors and medical sequelae of childhood sexual abuse. *Mayo Clinic Proceedings, 67*, 527–532.

Stice, E. (2002). The neglect of obesity. *Monitor on Psychology, 33*, 33.

Thompson, K. M., Wonderlich, S. A., Crosby, R. D., & Mitchell, J. E. (2001). Sexual victimization and adolescent weight regulation practices: A test across three community-based samples. *Child Abuse and Neglect, 25*, 291–305.

Trezza, G. R., & Popp, S. M. (2000). The substance user at risk of harm to self or others: Assessment and treatment issues. *Journal of Clinical Psychology, 56*, 1193–1205.

Tucci, A. M., Kerr-Correa, F., & Souza-Formigoni, M. L. O. (2010). Childhood trauma in substance use disorder and depression: An analysis by gender among a Brazilian clinical sample. *Child Abuse and Neglect, 34*, 95–104.

Van Gerko, K., Hughes, M. L., Hamill, M., & Waller, G. (2005). Reported childhood sexual abuse and eating-disordered cognitions and behaviors. *Child Abuse and Neglect, 29*, 375–382.

Whitaker, R. C., Phillips, S. M., Orzol, S. M., & Burdette, H. L. (2007). The association between maltreatment and obesity among preschool children. *Child Abuse and Neglect, 31*, 1187–1199.

Wickelgren, I. (1997). Getting the brain's attention. *Science, 278*, 35–37.

Widom, C. S., & White, H. R. (1997). Problem behaviors in abused and neglected children grown up: Prevalence and co-occurrence of substance abuse, crime and violence. *Criminal Behavior and Mental Health, 7*, 287–310.

Wilsnack, S. C., Vogeltanz, N. D., Klassen, A. D., & Harris, T. R. (1997). Childhood sexual abuse and women's substance abuse: National survey findings. *Journal of Studies of Alcohol, 58*, 264–271.

Chapter 5

Behavioral Pathways II—Suicide and High-Risk Sexual Activity

SUICIDE

Suicide and suicide attempts are also serious risks to health and more common in adult survivors. According to the National Institute of Mental Health (2000), the rate of suicide among adolescents and young adults in the United States has doubled since 1964. As of 1996, suicide was the third leading cause of death in this country for 15- to 24-year-olds, and the fourth leading cause of death for 10- to 14-year-olds. And the risk of suicide continues throughout life.

Relationship Between Abuse and Suicide

In data from the National Comorbidity Survey, men and women who reported child sexual abuse (CSA) had increased risk of suicide (Molnar, Berkman, & Buka, 2001). The National Comorbidity Survey is a representative study of prevalence, risk factors, and social consequences of psychiatric disorders in the United States with a large sample of 5,877 adults. The odds of suicide attempts for women were two to four times higher than for the non-abused group and four to eleven times higher for men. These effects held even after controlling for other lifetime adversities. The people at highest risk were those who experienced child rape. For women, 27 percent of those who experienced child rape reported suicide attempts, as did 31 percent of the men who reported child rape. This was compared to 3 percent of the total sample who had reported suicide attempts.

Childhood Adversities. A study from New Zealand of 1,000 young adults under age 25 explored the relationship between childhood physical and sexual abuse and mental health problems in early adulthood (Fergusson, Boden, & Horwood, 2008). They found that childhood abuse increased risks of suicidal ideation, suicide attempts between the ages of 16 and 25, depression, anxiety disorder, conduct disorder, and substance abuse. The relationship was no longer significant after controlling for family, social, and individual factors. However, CSA was still significantly associated with an increase in mental disorders. Severity of sexual abuse also made a difference. Those who had experienced attempted or completed penetration had 2.4 times the rates of mental disorders compared to those not exposed to CSA. CSA accounted for about 13 percent of the mental health problems. Physical abuse accounted for only about 5 percent.

Other childhood adversities were also related to suicide attempts (Molnar et al., 2001). For example, 45 percent of the people who attempted suicide reported that their mothers had major depression, and 25 percent reported paternal depression. Fifty-three percent of the adults in their sample reported five or more childhood adversities, compared with 24 percent among those who did not attempt suicide. Further, 79 percent of suicide attempts could be attributed to psychiatric disorders that preceded the attempt. The authors concluded that there was a strong association between child sexual abuse and suicidal behavior, partially but not wholly mediated by psychopathology, and that abuse survivors were a high-risk population for suicidal behavior (Molnar et al., 2001).

Sexual Victimization. A study of U.S. college women also found a link between sexual victimization and suicidality. Suicide risk was highest for women whose abuse experiences had included a combination of force and penetration: both indices of greater severity (Stepakoff, 1998). In a French study of teens (Choquet, Darves-Bornoz, Ledoux, Manfredi, & Hassler, 1997), subjects who had been raped were significantly more likely to report suicidal thoughts.

Another study examined suicide risk, physical and sexual abuse, and neglect in a randomly selected sample of 776 adolescents and adults. This sample was part of the large cohort of a seventeen-year longitudinal study that was initially recruited when cohort members were children. Subjects with a history of any type of maltreatment were three times more likely to become depressed or suicidal compared with subjects who had no maltreatment history. Family dysfunction increased risk for both depression and suicide in adolescence but not in adulthood. Of all abuse types, sexual abuse seemed to have a particularly noxious effect; subjects with a history of CSA had an eight times greater risk of repeated suicide attempts than did those with no history of sexual abuse (Brown, Cohen, Johnson, & Smailes, 1999).

In a study of college women, Thakkar and McCanne (2000) found that physical and sexual child abuse were related to suicidal ideation, and adult physical and sexual abuse were related to negative attitudes about life. In another study of undergraduates, participants who reported severe sexual or physical abuse reported more lifetime suicidality than did participants who reported mild abuse. Invasive sexual abuse and severe physical abuse were particularly related to suicidality. However, men and women who reported both types of abuse were not more suicidal than subjects who reported only one type (Bryant & Range, 1997).

College men and women in an introductory psychology class produced similar findings. In this study, researchers found that men and women who had been sexually abused as children, or who had been sexually victimized by a peer, were significantly more suicidal than were their nonvictimized peers (Peters & Range, 1995). Men and women had similar levels of suicidality, but women expressed more survival and coping beliefs and more fear of suicide. The sexually abused adults were more suicidal, were less able to cope, and felt less responsibility for their families than did the non-abused adults.

A study of homeless teens revealed high rates of suicide attempts (Ryan, Kilmer, Cauce, Watanabe, & Hoyt, 2000). Sixty-eight percent of the group that experienced both physical and sexual abuse had attempted suicide, compared with 41 percent of the physically abused group and 23 percent of the group with no abuse history. Sexual abuse alone was also highly related to suicide attempts, with 54 percent of sexually abused teens indicating that they had attempted suicide.

In a study of women patients in a primary care practice (Hulme, 2000), women with a history of CSA were significantly more likely to report hurting their body and thinking about killing themselves, but there was no significant difference in actual suicide attempts. In the Adverse Childhood Experience (ACE) study (Felitti et al., 1998), men and women with higher ACE scores attempted suicide twenty-three times more often. Participants who experienced four or more adverse childhood events were 460 percent more likely to be suffering from depression, and 1,220 percent more likely to have attempted suicide. In a European community sample, 43 percent of sexual abuse survivors had suicidal ideation and 14 percent had made suicide attempts (Teegan, 1999). Gay and bisexual men who had been sexually abused as children were also significantly more likely to have suicidal thoughts or actions (Bartholow et al., 1994).

Three studies of patients in the psychiatric emrgency room (ER) showed a relationship between childhood abuse and suicide attempts. Sixty-six percent of sexually abused psychiatric ER patients had attempted suicide compared with a 27 percent of those without a history (Briere & Zaidi, 1989). Physical and sexual abuse were related to homicidal and suicidal ideation and suicide attempts in another study of psychiatric ER patients, even after controlling for demographic variables (Briere, Woo, McRae, Foltz, & Sitzman, 1997). Another study of psychiatric inpatients had similar results (Read, 2001). Twenty-two percent of patients who did not disclose abuse indicated that they were suicidal compared with 64 percent of those who reported childhood physical abuse, 65 percent of those who reported sexual abuse, and 67 percent of those who reported both physical and sexual abuse. When data were analyzed for both gender and type of abuse, the strongest relationship was for men who had been sexually abused.

Other Comorbid Conditions. One recent study of CSA and depression did not find relationship between past abuse and suicide attempts. There was a relationship between suicide attempts, borderline personality disorder, and posttraumatic stress disorder (PTSD), however, and these conditions were more likely among sexual abuse survivors. The authors concluded that sexual abuse per se did not cause suicide attempts: CSA could be related because of these other comorbid conditions that increase risk (Zlotnick, Mattia, & Zimmerman, 2001).

The Health Effects of Suicide Attempts

The health effects of suicide are obvious. Perhaps less obvious are the health implications of suicide attempts. Suicide attempts involving drug overdoses or physical injury may have long-term health implications. Suicidal ideation and attempts also tend to co-occur with other problems that have a negative impact on health, including depression, substance abuse, eating disorders, and the topic of our next section: high-risk sexual behavior.

HIGH-RISK SEXUAL BEHAVIOR

Risky sexual behavior is the most highly documented form of harmful behavior in abuse survivors. This finding holds true for males and females, and it is consistent across the range of ethnic groups, income levels, and sexual orientations. The overwhelming majority of studies involve sexual abuse survivors. However, physical abuse and neglect also appear to be related, and can have an additive effect to sexual abuse.

Sexual abuse is related to a number of high-risk sexual behaviors. The most commonly occurring consequences include early initiation into consensual sexual activity, many sexual partners, and risky sexual practices (e.g., no condom and no contraception). Other consequences include abortion, sexually transmitted diseases (STDs), teen pregnancy, and early menarche. In a sample of thirty African-American women, higher posttraumatic stress symptoms were associated with more sexual partners, greater frequency of vaginal sex without a condom, and having sex while intoxicated (Munroe, Kibler, Ma, Dollar, & Coleman, 2010). PTSD symptoms were negatively correlated with perceived sexual control, but they were not correlated with sexual compulsivity or sensation seeking.

A sample from Sweden found an association between childhood or adolescent sexual abuse and sexual-risk behavior in a population study of 2,810 adults (Steel & Herlitz, 2005). In this sample, history of sexual abuse was associated with younger age at first intercourse, younger age at first diagnosis of STDs (chlamydia, HPV, gonorrhea, and herpes), higher rates of unintended pregnancies, greater likelihood of participation in group sex, greater likelihood of exchanging sex for money or other necessities, more frequent substance abuse in the past forty-eight hours, and higher likelihood of adult sexual and physical assault. Legal abortions were also higher in the sexually abused versus non-abused groups.

In a study of 248 sexual abuse survivors and a group of age-matched controls, the abuse survivors had more children, were younger at the time of their first pregnancy, and were more likely to have been pregnant at the age of 19 or younger (Mullen,

Martin, Anderson, Romans, & Herbison, 1994). Thirty-one percent of abuse survivors whose abuse included intercourse had a pregnancy early in marriage or were pregnant before they married.

Not every study has found a positive association between childhood abuse and sexual risk behaviors in adults. A survey of 1,428 low-income women (ages 18–40) seeking care at a family-planning clinic were asked about recent sexual history, and previous experiences of physical and sexual abuse (Littleton, Breitkopf, & Berenson, 2007). Contrary to previous studies, Littleton et al. did not find an association between childhood physical or sexual abuse and adult sexual-risk behaviors. They did find that intrafamilial sexual abuse was related to having had multiple sexual partners. In addition, a history of partner violence was associated with several sexual-risk behaviors, including multiple sexual partners in the past year and having sex after drinking or while using drugs. Depression or substance abuse did not account for this relationship.

CSA history was also related to increased rates of abortion in adolescence or early adulthood in a sample of 1,265 young adults in New Zealand (Boden, Fergusson, & Horwood, 2009). This study was part of a larger twenty-five-year birth-cohort study. They found that severity of the CSA experiences was significantly related to the number of abortions: Those exposed to severe CSA had twice as many abortions as did their non-abused counterparts, or those who experienced milder CSA. After adjusting for potential confounding variables, the magnitude of the association was only marginally significant. The authors concluded that their findings indicated a causal chain in which CSA leads to increased rates of pregnancy, which leads to increased rates of abortion. They noted that their findings are consistent with the wide number of studies that found that CSA increases the risk of high-risk sexual behavior, which increases the rates of pregnancy.

High-Risk Sexual Activity Among Special Populations

There have also been studies of sexual activity in distinct or high-risk populations. These include ethnic minorities, incarcerated youth, patients in treatment for STDs, and men and women who are at-risk for contracting HIV (human immunodeficiency virus).

In a sample of 250 at-risk women living in Atlanta, researchers examined the impact of child neglect on HIV-risk behaviors (Klein, Elifson, & Sterk, 2007). Criteria for "at risk" included living in a drug-infested area, being a drug user or having a relative who was, being in poverty, having less than a high school education, being unemployed, or having a criminal history. The researchers found that childhood neglect led to reduced self-esteem and the more religious the women reported themselves to be, the higher their self-esteem. Also, African-American women had higher self-esteem than women from any other ethnic group. Neglect was also associated with worsened attitudes about condom use and more involvement in HIV-risk behaviors. The neglect measure included both physical and emotional neglect. These data argue against a "traumatic sexualization" model, whereby only sexual abuse leads to later high-risk sexual behavior. Neglect involves being treated in a manner that communicates not mattering to others. Therefore, risky behavior does not matter, and these behaviors reflect abuse survivors' attempts to form human connections with others.

Puerto Rican and African-American adolescent males experience disproportionately higher rates of HIV infection than other groups. In a sample of 171 African-Americans and 187 Puerto Rican adolescent males, Voisin (2002) found that age, witnessing community violence, being a victim of community violence, and being sexually abused before the age of 13 were related to high-risk sexual behaviors. When examining high-risk sexual behaviors, current age, age at sexual onset, witnessing or being a victim of community violence, parents' educational level, and familial emotional support networks were related for African-American teens but not for Puerto Ricans. In contrast, for both African-American and Puerto Rican teens, large, supportive families were positively correlated with membership in non-kin networks with safer-sex norms. Further, among African Americans, those who were satisfied with the level of emotional support they received from their families, and who had families that had supported their achievements, were less likely to engage in HIV-sexual-risk behavior. In this study, HIV-sexual-risk behaviors were defined as sex without condoms, sex with girls who have concurrent sexual partners, sex after drug use, and a history of STDs in the past twelve months.

Consistent with the results of the above-cited study, Voisin et al. (2004) examined high-risk sexual activity in 270 detained male adolescents (ages 14–18). They found that adolescents who reported being in a gang were many times more likely to engage in high-risk sexual behavior, even compared to other detained youths. For example, they were 5.7 times more likely to have had sex, 3.2 times more likely to have gotten a girl pregnant, and nearly four times more likely to have been high on drugs or alcohol during sex.

Community violence is also related to high-risk sexual activity. In a sample of 120 male high school students in New York City, Voisin (2003) found that 59 percent had been robbed or mugged, 69 percent had received news of the mutilation or serious injury of someone close to them, 50 percent had experienced a violent incidence where they thought they would be killed, and 28 percent had been forced into sexual contact before the age of 13. The results of the study indicated that males who were victims of community violence were more likely than their non-exposed counterparts to engage in high-risk sexual activity. Self-efficacy did not appear to attenuate this relationship.

Voisin (2005) found that male and female adolescents in New York City ($N = 409$) who had been exposed to childhood sexual abuse, had witnessed family violence, or had been exposed to community violence were approximately three times more likely than nonexposed peers to engage in HIV-risky behavior than their nonexposed peers. The results from the logistic regression indicated that each of these types of violence was independently associated with high-risk sexual activity. A gender difference also appeared. Boys who experienced family violence were almost three times more likely than girls to report multiple sexual partners or using drugs during sex. There were no gender differences observed in the effects of witnessing family violence or having sex without a condom.

Theories Explaining High-Risk Sexual Behavior

In attempting to explain why high-risk sexual behaviors occur among abuse survivors, Fergusson, Horwood, and Lynskey (1997) identified two possible paths. The first is that a general level of family dysfunction—including family instability, impaired parent-child relationships, and social disadvantage—is associated with CSA and also with sexual risks in adolescence. The second is that exposure to CSA may encourage early-onset consensual activity that places adolescents at greater risk during their adolescence.

Cognitive Aspects of High-Risk Sex. Many of the mediators of sexual behavior are cognitive. The person must make an appraisal of potential risk and have the capacity to enact behaviors necessary to reduce that risk. The processes include such thoughts as the need for social acceptance, sexual-impulse control, and affective states. Shame and guilt are other possible mechanisms for high-risk sex (Parillo, Freeman, Collier, & Young, 2001). In a retrospective study, self-blame resulting from early childhood abuse predicted later vulnerability to exploitation as adults (Liem & Boudewyn, 1999). Early sexual abuse may set up and perpetuate a lifetime pattern of revictimization (Parillo et al., 2001).

Depression and Anger. Depression and anger are also possible links. People who are depressed or angry may engage in self-gratifying behaviors, including unsafe sexual practices or substance abuse, in order to distract themselves from these negative states. Distorted thinking may also reduce the sense of self-care and motivation to protect themselves. Interestingly, HIV-risky behavior was not related to depression, anxiety, and anger in a meta-analysis (Crepaz & Marks, 2001). The authors stated, however, that this lack of relationship may be due to methodological issues. For example, depression may need to be examined for a curvilinear relationship with unsafe sex; only the moderately depressed people engage in these practices because the very depressed may avoid any sexual contact and the people with mild depression still feel self-protective enough to avoid high-risk practices.

Low Self-Esteem and Self-Efficacy. Sexual-risk behaviors may also be due to impulsivity, low self-esteem, and powerlessness (Brown, Kessel, Lourie, & Ford, 1997). These behaviors may manifest as failure to set limits in sexual encounters, as when participants fail to discuss safe-sex activities or cannot resist pressures to engage in high-risk sexual behaviors. The authors suggested that techniques to improve communication skills and self-efficacy be added to standard treatment for teens who have been sexually abused.

Self-efficacy and security of relationships are both related to high-risk sexual activity. To reduce high-risk sexual behavior, a person must have a strong sense of self-efficacy (Murphy, Stein, Schlenger, Maibach, & National Institute of Mental Health Multisite HIV Prevention Trial Group, 2001). Self-efficacy that has safer sex as its outcome must address several issues. There must be perceived ability to negotiate condom use, and this negotiation can vary by reluctance of the partner, level of sexual arousal, whether either partner is intoxicated, whether the partner is new or former, and whether the partner is perceived as high or low risk.

A study of 165 African-American women found that sexually abused women were significantly more likely to worry about getting infected with HIV, believe that their partners did not care for them, and doubt the longevity of their relationships. They were also more likely to have been physically abused in the previous three months, have had a partner who became physically abusive when asked to wear a condom, and to have consumed three or more servings of alcohol at one time (Wingood & DiClemente, 1997).

Posttraumatic Stress Disorder. In a study of thirty African-American college women, PTSD symptoms were related to high-risk sexual activity (Munroe et al., 2010). There was a negative relationship between PTSD symptoms and sexual control. Compulsive sexual behavior and sexual-sensation seeking were not significantly related to PTSD symptoms. This suggests that those with PTSD may have propensities toward sex that are different from those of other people. Rather, higher PTSD symptoms may be associated with lower levels of control that make it difficult to negotiate safe sex in some, but possibly not all, sexual situations. In addition, lower perceived control was associated with more frequent vaginal sex without a condom, and greater likelihood of sex while under the influence of a substance. It was not related to the number of sexual partners. The authors noted that sexual situations presented difficult decisions and that, in situations involving risky sexual behaviors, perceptions of low control may relate to poor decision making and lack of efficacy.

Social-Learning Theory. Paul, Catania, Pollack, and Stall (2001) put forth a social-learning model of sexual risk taking. Sexual abuse overwhelms the victims, particularly if the experience was violent or forceful. Victims may have also been "punished" for any attempt made to get away or to evade the sexual contact. This sense of powerlessness, in turn, may become generalized to other situations, becoming "learned helplessness," low self-efficacy, and poor interpersonal regulation of adult sexual relationships.

Finkelhor and Browne (1985) put forth a similar explanation in their traumagenic dynamics model. According to this model, subjects sexually abused in childhood would, upon reaching adolescence or adulthood, replicate certain feelings and experiences learned from their abuse. Negative perceptions or stigmas are integrated into the self-concept. These perceptions facilitate the formation of repetitive or compulsive responses to abuse, being played out in situations that resemble it. The result is an overgeneralization of the abuse experience to other close relationships.

In a study of gay men, perceived sexual coercion was specifically related to later sexual risk. Men who had been "strongly coerced or forced" as children to participate in sexual activity were significantly more likely to report unprotected anal intercourse than men who reported no coercion or only mild coercion (Jinich et al., 1998). The men who were strongly coerced were also more likely to report HIV-positive status and had significantly higher levels of depressive symptoms.

Another outcome of sexual abuse, in particular, is its more direct influence on sexuality. Some of the positive aspects of the abuse experience (e.g., nurturance and attention) may reinforce the notion that sexuality is a means by which a person can get these positive factors in relationships. Compulsive sexual behavior may also become a means by which survivors deal with anxiety or other disturbing emotions, with orgasm providing the means for tension reduction. This type of sexuality is likely to lead to a higher number of sexual partners (Paul et al., 2001).

The Role of Substance Abuse. Mosack et al. (2010) investigated the mechanisms of HIV risk for women with and without a history of CSA. CSA survivors reported more unprotected intercourse and more STDs but not higher rates of intoxication during sex or higher prevalence of HIV. The frequency of unprotected sex was mediated by intoxication during sex and participating in sex work. Experiencing CSA makes women vulnerable to both drug addiction and "dissociated sexuality." They may not be aware of their right and capability to claim when, how, and with whom they are sexual. CSA was also related to a sexual external locus of control, which is the perception that the women's partner is in charge of sexual decision making on issues such as condom use.

Contrary to prediction, there was no significant difference in relationship power between those with a CSA history and those without. However, there were other risk factors in both groups, such as a high rate of homelessness, which could account for the lack of difference in findings. Locus of control and relationship power did play an important role in sexual risk taking for women with a CSA history. The authors noted that this underscores the difficulties for women in making healthy sexual decisions in relationships where they have no power. Among those with a history of CSA, an external locus of control in the relationship and in STD prevention was associated with engaging in sex work. In turn, sex work was related to being intoxicated during sex, and having more unprotected sex. Interventions should include an educational component describing maladaptive strategies, such as using drugs to dissociate during sex, and how these strategies can contribute to powerlessness and put these women at increased risk for HIV infection and revictimization (Mosack et al., 2010).

Health Effects of High-Risk Sexual Activity

Men and women who engage in high-risk sexual activity are at increased risk of developing sexually transmitted diseases. This was found in two studies with community samples in the United States (Felitti et al., 1998) and New Zealand (Fergusson, et al., 1997). Increased incidence of STDs among sexual abuse survivors was also found in a study of women currently in treatment for STDs (Thompson, Potter, Sanderson, & Maibach, 1997), and in two studies of gay and bisexual men (Bartholow et al., 1994; Jinich et al., 1998).

One of the principal concerns about engagement in high-risk sexual activity is the transmission of HIV. Not surprisingly, child maltreatment is also a risk factor for HIV infection (Dallam, 2001). In one U.S. study, more than 50 percent of HIV-positive adolescents had documented histories of sexual abuse, and 82 percent also had a history of substance abuse (Pao et al., 2000).

Women with a history of childhood abuse, particularly sexual abuse, have several characteristics that put them at high risk for HIV. As noted previously, they begin having sex at an earlier age, and have higher rates of teen pregnancy and substance abuse. They are four times more likely to be involved in prostitution, have greater difficulty in their sexual relationships, and have higher rates of violence and sexual victimization as adults than do non-abused women (Whitmire, Harlow, Quina, & Morokoff, 1998). High-risk sexual activity exposes men and women not only to HIV and other STDs but also to violence. All these can lead to poor health.

HIGH-RISK BEHAVIORS IN COMBINATION

Unfortunately, high-risk behaviors tend to co-occur. Depression and substance abuse were prominent in the life histories of 120 children and adolescents who committed suicide over a two-year period (Shaffer, Gould, Fisher, & Trautman, 1996). Sexual abuse was also associated with multiple risk behaviors in teenage runaways, including alcohol and drug use and high-risk sexual behavior (Rotheram-Borus, Mahler, Koopman, & Langabeer, 1996). The Commonwealth Fund Adolescent Health Survey found multiple high-risk behaviors in girls who had been abused. This study included a nationally representative sample of 3,015 girls, grades 5–12. Girls who had experienced both physical and sexual abuse were more likely to smoke, drink alcohol, use illicit drugs, and have a history of bingeing and purging (Diaz, Simatov, & Rickert, 2000).

A recent study of 257 adolescents indicated that four types of risky behavior—marijuana use, alcohol use, high-risk sexual behavior, and cigarette smoking—were related. All these behaviors were significantly related to each other, and cigarette use covaried with development of high-risk sexual behavior (Duncan, Strycker, & Duncan, 1999). A teen who was participating in one activity was also likely to be participating in the other three. Cigarette smoking, according to the study's authors, may be one of the most influential risk factors for adolescents, and therefore it deserves more attention than it is presently getting.

In summary, high-risk behaviors can affect health in a number of ways. All the high-risk behaviors described are more common in adult survivors and are more likely to occur in combination with each other, thereby multiplying their harmful effects.

References

Bartholow, B. N., Doll, L. S., Joy, D., Douglas, J. M., Bolan, G., Harrison, J. S., et al. (1994). Emotional, behavioral, and HIV risks associated with sexual abuse among adult homosexual and bisexual men. *Child Abuse and Neglect, 18*, 747–761.

Boden, J. M., Fergusson, D. M., & Horwood, L. J. (2009). Experience of sexual abuse in childhood and abortion in adolescence and early adulthood. *Child Abuse and Neglect, 33*, 870–876.

Briere, J. N., Woo, R., McRae, B., Foltz, J., & Sitzman, R. (1997). Lifetime victimization history, demographics, and clinical status in female psychiatric emergency room patients. *Journal of Nervous and Mental Disease, 185*, 95–101.

Briere, J. N., & Zaidi, L. Y. (1989). Sexual abuse history and sequelae in female psychiatric emergency room patients. *American Journal of Psychiatry, 146*, 1602–1606.

Brown, J., Cohen, P., Johnson, J. G., & Smailes, E. M. (1999). Childhood abuse and neglect: Specificity of effects on adolescent and young adult depression and suicidality. *Journal of the American Academy of Child and Adolescent Psychiatry, 38*, 1490–1496.

Brown, L. K., Kessel, S. M., Lourie, K. J., & Ford, H. H. (1997). Influence of sexual abuse on HIV-related attitudes and behaviors in adolescent psychiatric inpatients. *Journal of the American Academy of Child and Adolescent Psychiatry, 36*, 316–322.

Bryant, S. L., & Range, L. M. (1997). Type and severity of child abuse and college students' lifetime suicidality. *Child Abuse and Neglect, 21*, 1169–1176.

Choquet, M., Darves-Bornoz, J.-M., Ledoux, S., Manfredi, R., & Hassler, C. (1997). Self-reported health and behavioral problems among adolescent victims of rape in France: Results of a cross-sectional survey. *Child Abuse and Neglect, 21*, 823–832.

Crepaz, N., & Marks, G. (2001). Are negative affective states associated with HIV sexual risk behaviors? A meta-analytic review. *Health Psychology, 20*(4), 291–299.

Dallam, S. J. (2001). The hidden effects of childhood maltreatment on adult health. In K. Franey, R. Geffner, & R. Falconer (Eds.), *The cost of child maltreatment: Who pays? We all do* (pp. 1–14). San Diego: Family Violence & Sexual Assault Institute.

Diaz, A., Simatov, E., & Rickert, V. I. (2000). The independent and combined effects of physical and sexual abuse on health. Results from a national survey. *Journal of Pediatric and Adolescent Gynecology, 13*(2), 89.

Duncan, S. C., Strycker, L. A., & Duncan, T. E. (1999). Exploring associations in developmental trends of adolescent substance use and risky sexual behavior in a high-risk population. *Journal of Behavioral Medicine, 22*, 21–34.

Felitti, V. J., Anda, R. F., Nordenberg, D., Williamson, D. F., Spitz, A. M., Edwards, V., et al. (1998). Relationship of childhood abuse and household dysfunction to many of the leading causes of death in adults. The Adverse Childhood Experiences (ACE) study. *American Journal of Preventive Medicine, 14*(4), 245–258.

Fergusson, D. M., Boden, J. M., & Horwood, L. J. (2008). Exposure to childhood sexual and physical abuse and adjustment in early adulthood. *Child Abuse and Neglect, 32*, 607–619.

Fergusson, D. M., Horwood, L. J., & Lynskey, M. T. (1997). Childhood sexual abuse, adolescent sexual behaviors and sexual revictimization. *Child Abuse and Neglect, 21*, 789–803.

Finkelhor, D., & Browne, A. (1985). The traumatic impact of child sexual abuse: A conceptualization. *American Journal of Orthopsychiatry, 55*, 530–541.

Hulme, P. A. (2000). Symptomatology and health care utilization of women primary care patients who experienced childhood sexual abuse. *Child Abuse and Neglect, 24*, 1471–1484.

Jinich, S., Paul, J. P., Stall, R., Acree, M., Kegeles, S., Hoff, C., et al. (1998). Childhood sexual abuse and HIV risk-taking behavior among gay and bisexual men. *AIDS and Behavior, 2*, 41–51.

Klein, H., Elifson, K. W., & Sterk, C. E. (2007). Childhood neglect and adulthood involvement in HIV-related risk behaviors. *Child Abuse and Neglect, 31*(1), 39–53.

Liem, J. H., & Boudewyn, A. C. (1999). Contextualizing the effects of childhood sexual abuse on adult self- and social functioning: An attachment theory perspective. *Child Abuse and Neglect, 23*, 1141–1157.

Littleton, H., Breitkopf, C. R., & Berenson, A. (2007). Sexual and physical abuse history and adult sexual risk behaviors: Relationships among women and potential mediators. *Child Abuse and Neglect, 31*, 757–768.

Molnar, B. E., Berkman, L. F., & Buka, S. L. (2001). Psychopathology, childhood sexual abuse and other childhood adversities: Relative links to subsequent suicidal behaviour in the U.S. *Psychological Medicine, 31*, 965–977.

Mosack, K. E., Randolph, M. E., Dickson-Gomez, J., Abbott, M., Smith, E., & Weeks, M. R. (2010). Sexual risk-taking among high-risk urban women with and without histories of childhood sexual abuse: Mediating effects of contextual factors. *Journal of Child Sexual Abuse, 19*, 43–61.

Mullen, P. E., Martin, J. L., Anderson, J. C., Romans, S. E., & Herbison, G. P. (1994). The effect of child sexual abuse on social, interpersonal, and sexual function in adult life. *British Journal of Psychiatry, 165*, 35–47.

Munroe, C. D., Kibler, J. L., Ma, M., Dollar, K. M., & Coleman, M. (2010). The relationship between posttraumatic stress symptoms and sexual risk: Examining potential mechanisms. *Psychological Trauma, 2*(1), 49–53.

Murphy, D. A., Stein, J. A., Schlenger, W., Maibach, E., & National Institute of Mental Health Multisite HIV Prevention Trial Group. (2001). Conceptualizing the multidimensional nature of self-efficacy: Assessment of situational context and level of behavioral challenge to maintain safer sex. *Health Psychology, 20*(4), 281–290.

National Institute of Mental Health. (2000). *Brief notes on the mental health of children.* Washington, DC: Author.

Pao, M., Lyon, M., D'Angelo, L. J., Schuman, W. B., Tipnis, T., & Mrazek, D. A. (2000). Psychiatric diagnoses in adolescents seropositive for human immunodeficiency virus. *Archives of Pediatric and Adolescent Medicine, 154*, 240–244.

Parillo, K. M., Freeman, R. C., Collier, K., & Young, P. (2001). Association between early sexual abuse and adult HIV-risk sexual behaviors among community-recruited women. *Child Abuse and Neglect, 25*, 335–346.

Paul, J. P., Catania, J., Pollack, L., & Stall. (2001). Understanding childhood sexual abuse as a predictor of sexual risk-taking among men who have sex with men: The Urban Men's Health Study. *Child Abuse and Neglect, 25*, 557–584.

Peters, D. K., & Range, L. M. (1995). Childhood sexual abuse and current suicidality in college women and men. *Child Abuse and Neglect, 19*, 335–341.

Read, J. (2001). Child abuse and severity of disturbance among adult psychiatric inpatients. In K. Franey, R. Geffner, & R. Falconer (Eds.), *The cost of child maltreatment: Who pays? We all do* (pp. 103–112). San Diego: Family Violence & Sexual Assault Institute.

Rotheram-Borus, M. J., Mahler, K. A., Koopman, C., & Langabeer, K. (1996). Sexual abuse history and associated multiple risk behavior in adolescent runaways. *American Journal of Orthopsychiatry, 66*, 390–400.

Ryan, K. D., Kilmer, R. P., Cauce, A. M., Watanabe, H., & Hoyt, D. R. (2000). Psychological consequences of child maltreatment in homeless adolescents: Untangling the unique effects of maltreatment and family environment. *Child Abuse and Neglect, 24*, 333–352.

Shaffer, D. R., Gould, M. S., Fisher, P., & Trautman, P. (1996). Psychiatric diagnosis in child and adolescent suicide. *Archives of General Psychiatry, 53*, 339–348.

Steel, J. L., & Herlitz, C. A. (2005). The association between childhood and adolescent sexual abuse and proxies for sexual risk behavior: A random sample of the general population of Sweden. *Child Abuse and Neglect, 29*, 1141–1153.

Stepakoff, S. (1998). Effects of sexual victimization on suicidal ideation and behavior in U.S. college women. *Suicide and Life-Threatening Behavior, 28*, 107–126.

Teegan, F. (1999). Childhood sexual abuse and long-term sequelae. In A. Maercker, M. Schutzwohl, & Z. Solomon (Eds.), *Posttraumatic stress disorder: A lifespan developmental perspective* (pp. 97–112). Seattle, WA: Hogrefe & Huber.

Thakkar, R. R., & McCanne, T. R. (2000). The effects of daily stressors on physical health in women with and without a childhood history of sexual abuse. *Child Abuse and Neglect, 24*, 209–221.

Thompson, N. J., Potter, J. S., Sanderson, C. A., & Maibach, E. W. (1997). The relationship of sexual buse and HIV risk behaviors among heterosexual adult female STD patients. *Child Abuse and Neglect, 21*, 149–156.

Voisin, D. R. (2002). Family ecology and HIV sexual risk behaviors among African American and Puerto Rican adolescent males. *American Journal of Orthopsychiatry, 72*(2), 294–302.

Voisin, D. R. (2003). Victims of community violence and HIV sexual risk behaviors among African American adolescent males. *Journal of HIV/AIDS Prevention and Education for Adolescents and Children, 5*(3/4), 87–110.

Voisin, D. R. (2005). The relationship between violence exposure and HIV sexual risk behavior: Does gender matter? *American Journal of Orthopsychiatry, 75*(4), 497–506.

Voisin, D. R., Salazar, L. F., Crosby, R. D., DiClemente, R. J., Yarber, W. L., & Staples-Horne, M. (2004). The association between gang involvement and sexual behaviours among detained adolescent males. *Sexually Transmitted Infections, 80*(6), 440–442.

Whitmire, L., Harlow, L., Quina, K., & Morokoff, P. (1998). *Childhood trauma and HIV: Women at risk*. Philadelphia: Taylor & Francis.

Wingood, G. M., & DiClemente, R. J. (1997). Child sexual abuse, HIV sexual risk, and gender relations of African American women. *American Journal of Preventive Medicine, 13*, 380–384.

Zlotnick, C., Mattia, J., & Zimmerman, M. (2001). Clinical features of survivors of sexual abuse with major depression. *Child Abuse and Neglect, 25*, 357–367.

Chapter 6

Cognitive Pathways I—Beliefs About Self

What we believe about ourselves shapes our everyday lives. Self-conscious emotions, such as shame, embarrassment, and humiliation, can arise from the beliefs that others are negatively evaluating our selves or our social acceptability (Dickerson, 2011). These beliefs guide our actions and help us judge the dangerousness of situations. Beliefs are particularly influential when a situation is unclear or ambiguous (Snyder, Irving, & Anderson, 1991), and beliefs about self can be changed by childhood abuse: "Victimization activates negative self-images such that victims see themselves as weak, needy, frightened, and out of control. . . . Visions of the self as healthy, active, or strong may be necessary to regain a convincing sense of control" (Koss, 1990, p. 376).

This chapter and Chapter 7 describe beliefs about self that are influenced by childhood abuse. These beliefs include shame and self-blame, attributional style, self-esteem, and self-efficacy. Other self-beliefs include health perception and health locus of control. Each of these beliefs can influence health.

SHAME AND SELF-BLAME

Shame and self-blame are two overlapping constructs that have to do with the amount of responsibility a survivor takes for the abuse. Both are more common in adult survivors than in other adults.

Shame

Shame is the key emotional component of a coordinated psychobiological response to threats against the "social self," which responds to social evaluation or rejection. Evidence suggests that shame is related to submission and withdrawal and is accompanied by the urge to hide, escape, or "shrink into the floor" (Dickerson, Gruenewald, & Kemeny, 2004a). It involves feelings of self-contempt, and leaves people feeling exposed, vulnerable, and "defective." It is a painful emotion that usually results after conduct or circumstances that damage one's self-respect. It is internally derived and may be influenced, but not controlled, by attitudes perceived to be in the community (Persons, Kershaw, Sikkema, & Hansen, 2010).

Shame can develop as a result of early abusive experiences or other failures in parenting (Kessler & Bieschke, 1999), and it may be at the base of many of the symptoms observed in abuse survivors (Persons et al., 2010). It can be socially isolating, reinforce a sense of low self-worth (Feiring, Taska, & Lewis, 1998), and reduce health-related quality of life (Persons et al., 2010).

Shame may be adaptive in short-term situations where there is uncontrollable social threat. However, prolonged exposure to social threat could increase the risk of adverse health outcomes (Dickerson et al., 2004a). The experience of shame is the result of a person concluding that he or she has lost social value and is at risk for rejection by the community. For example, some of the items that can assess shame following sexual abuse include: "I struggle with feeling worthless because I've been sexually abused," "I hide my sexual abuse or rape experience(s) from others," and "Having been sexually abused/raped makes me want to hide, disappear, or even die."

In a critical review, Whiffen and MacIntosh (2005) examined the relationship between child sexual abuse (CSA) and emotional disturbance, such as depression, anxiety, and trauma, with the possible cognitive mediators that explain the relationship between the two. They reviewed nineteen studies and found that shame and self-blame; interpersonal difficulties, including insecure attachments; and use of avoidant coping strategies to cope with CSA had the strongest relationship to abuse sequelae, such as depression. There are more social and interpersonal difficulties following CSA, including less satisfaction with their current relationships, more divorce, more sexual problems, and insecurity in current relationships.

Other types of maltreatment are related to shame as well. In a sample of college undergraduates, parental emotional abuse was related to shame, overt hostility, and anger. Women reported higher levels of shame and guilt, and men reported higher levels of overt hostility and expressed anger. However, "shame proneness" was related to covert hostility and unexpressed anger for both men and women (Hoglund & Nicholas, 1995).

Consequences of Shame. Shame is common after disclosure of sexual abuse. In an outpatient group of sexually abused girls (ages 8–12), emotions such as fear, anger, shame, hostility, and guilt were more common than anxiety and depression (Carey, Kempton, & Gemmill, 1996). Feiring et al. (1998) found that shame and self-blame were strongly related to depression, self-esteem, and posttraumatic stress syndrome (PTSD) symptoms in the eight weeks following disclosure of sexual abuse. The sample included eighty-two children and sixty teens. Shame accounted for a significant amount of variance in symptoms even after age, gender, and abuse characteristics had been controlled for.

A study of 280 college students included measures of shame, guilt, and a history of psychological maltreatment (Webb, Heisler, Call, Chickering, & Colburn, 2007). Psychological maltreatment included emotional neglect, such as acting indifferent and failing to provide support; hostile rejection, such as screaming at or calling the child names; or isolating by discouraging social contact. They found that depression was related to both shame and guilt, but when shame was removed from the analysis, guilt was no longer correlated with depression. Psychological maltreatment was correlated with depression and shame, but not guilt.

Shah and Waller (2000) found three core beliefs that distinguished the depressed from nondepressed subjects: shame, self-sacrifice, and insufficient self-control. Depressed subjects were more likely to characterize their parents as uncaring and intrusive. These core beliefs mediated the relationship between poor parenting and depression.

Unfortunately, shame can also make relationships with others more difficult for abuse survivors. Fifty-six sexually abused girls (ages 12–15) were interviewed at the time of disclosure and one year later. Shame and self-blame influenced the girls' perceptions of how capable they were of forming satisfying relationships with peers, friends, and romantic partners (Feiring, Rosenthal, & Taska, 2000). Girls who blamed themselves for the abuse had less satisfaction with their same-sex friends but more satisfaction with their opposite-sex friends. Shame was related to lower perceptions of peer acceptance and close friendship.

Another study of 129 mothers whose children attended a special summer camp program for disadvantaged and at-risk families examined the impact of CSA history on shame-proneness and conflict with the current intimate partner (Kim, Talbot, & Cicchetti, 2009). The authors noted that shame can become chronic, coloring experiencees of self and others in painful ways that impede interpersonal responses, and as a result, it can produce hostile interpersonal responses, especially when others are seen as critical or rejecting. As predicted, they found that shame significantly mediated the association between childhood abuse and current interpersonal conflict. Women with a history of CSA reported more shame in their daily lives. Shame was related to higher rates of self-verbal aggression and physical aggression with intimate partners. The authors concluded that shame is a component in the conflicts of women with sexual abuse histories and should be specifically addressed in treatment.

Children who are subjected to "severe or humiliating abuse are at high risk of feeling bad about themselves at the very core of their being" (Whiffen & MacIntosh, 2005, p. 34), where shame becomes a part of their "permanent landscape." An individual who experiences shame expects others to be rejecting and scornful about their supposed defects. Thus, as adults, shame may be elicited as a response to both real and imagined mistreatment by others. The internalization of shame can lead survivors to withdraw from others in order to protect themselves from further humiliation or, alternatively, to attach to others to conceal their shame. Thus, shame may link the intrapersonal world to the interpersonal one, and it may isolate the survivor from the very relationships that could be used to manage distress and to create a more positive sense of self. Early experiences with abusive individuals seem to impair CSA survivors' ability to form close, trusting relationships. Whiffen and MacIntosh (2005) recommend that clinicians focus on softening shame, strengthening interpersonal relationships, and promoting active coping.

Shame and Attributional Style. In another study of forty-seven children and adolescents who were sexually abused, Feiring, Taska, and Lewis (2002) examined the role of shame and attributional style on adjustment following disclosure of sexual abuse one year later. The phenomenological experience of shame includes the desire to hide the damaged self from others, to disappear, or to die. Cognitive processes are linked to shame and how individuals evaluate their actions in relation to their standards and attributions about the self. People with a pessimistic attributional style experienced more shame and depression and had lower self-esteem than did people with a more optimistic world view.

Shame and attributional style account for additional variation in victims' adjustment one year following discovery. Children high in shame had more depressive symptoms, more PTSD symptoms, and lower self-esteem than children lower in shame. Attributional style showed small, but significant, moderating effects on the relationship between abuse severity, depressive symptoms, and self-esteem. Changes in shame and attribution each contributed to changes in adjustment. Children whose level of shame decreases show concomitant improvement in adjustment. Children who remain high in shame appeared to be at risk for the poorest adjustment over a year's time (Feiring et al., 2002).

Another study examined the additive effects of both CSA and current HIV (human immunodeficiency virus) infection (Persons et al., 2010) in a study of 247 HIV patients with a history of CSA. The results indicated that shame-related CSA plus current HIV was negatively related to health-related quality of life, physical well-being, global well-being, social and emotional well-being, and cognitive functioning. The authors concluded that shame was an important and modifiable predictor of health-related quality of life in HIV-positive populations, and that health care providers should be aware of the importance of shame and its impact on patient well-being.

Self-Blame

Self-blame is a construct that reflects self-criticism and low self-evaluation combined with a tendency to take responsibility for negative events. People who self-blame devalue their own thoughts and feelings (Ali et al., 2000). There are two main types of self-blame: characterological and behavioral. Characterological self-blame associates abuse with some enduring trait or characteristic, whereas behavioral self-blame focuses on behavior that may have led to the abuse. While behavioral blame is milder than characterological blame, both types increase distress. Self-blame has been studied in populations of teens, college students, and adults.

Studies of Teens and College Students. Zinzow, Seth, Jackson, Niehaus, and Fitzgerald (2010) studied 183 female undergraduates with a history of CSA and examined the impact of abuse and parental characteristics on attributions. Self-blame was positively correlated with abuse frequency, duration, and age of onset. Severe abuse predicted self-blame. Family blame occurred most often when the mother was unavailable or the abuse was perpetrated by a peer (e.g., "I blame my family for not doing more to protect me"). Perpetrator blame was positively correlated with abuse frequency and type and negatively correlated with age of onset. Family and perpetrator blame contributed above and beyond self-blame, abuse characteristics, and family environment to PTSD symptoms and general psychological adjustment, implying that these should be addressed in treatment as well.

In a college sample, 119 women indicated that they had been raped as adults. Forty-two percent of these women had also been sexually abused as children. The sexually abused women engaged in characterological self-blame (i.e., they thought that they had been abused because of some internal flaw within themselves). They also had more symptoms and used more negative coping strategies. They believed they deserved the rape and were bad people, not able to take care of themselves, and "victim types." These women also blamed society, feeling that the world was unsafe for women, that there were many emotionally disturbed people around, and that no one was ever available to help them when they needed it (Arata, 1999).

Another study found that self-blame mediated interpersonal sensitivity, hostility, and vulnerability to revictimization for sexual abuse survivors (Liem & Boudewyn, 1999). In this study, undergraduates who blamed themselves for CSA and abuse as adults had worse social functioning in adult relationships than those who did not. Self-blame was related to depression, low self-esteem, and self-destructiveness. Self-blame also predicted the need to control others in adult relationships, as well as interpersonal relationships characterized by interpersonal sensitivity, hostility, and paranoia.

Studies of Adults. In a qualitative study of forty sexual abuse survivors, women were more likely to self-blame if their abuse was chronic or they were younger when it started (Perrott, Morriss, Martin, & Romans, 1998). Women who coped alone had higher levels of psychiatric morbidity, as did women who had not worked through the abuse. Disturbingly, women in this study who reframed the abuse had better mental health but were significantly more likely to have a child who was also sexually abused. The authors speculated that this might be due to the possible development of ineffective parenting styles that made them less able to protect their children from a fate similar to their own. Dissociation and denial may have led these women to choose partners who were abusive to their children.

In a study of three types of chronic pain (Scarinci, McDonald-Haile, Bradley, & Richter, 1994), patients who had a history of abuse had significantly higher levels of self-blame, chronic tension, and pain stability than did pain patients who were not abused. The combination of self-blame, pain stability (i.e., that pain will not get better), and uncontrollability led to a sense of hopelessness. These beliefs intensified pain perceptions and contributed to functional disability.

Emotional abuse was highly correlated with self-blame and self-silencing in patients with gastrointestinal illness (Ali et al., 2000). Self-silencing refers to a tendency to "protect" intimate relationships by silencing certain thoughts, feelings, or actions. The intercorrelation between emotional abuse, self-blame, and self-silencing suggests that women who were emotionally abused were more prone to take responsibility for negative events and to inhibit self-expression. This pattern is stressful, which increases pain symptoms. A high percentage of these women were also physically or sexually abused.

Both shame and self-blame led to worse outcomes for female rape survivors who had also been sexually abused as children. These women were more likely to use disengagement as a coping method after being sexually assaulted as adults (Gibson & Leitenberg, 2001). Disengagement strategies included denial, wishful thinking, avoidance, and self-criticism.

All these strategies had an adverse impact on recovery. Women with a sexual abuse history were more likely to feel stigmatized, powerless, and betrayed than women without such a history. The authors hypothesized that preexisting feelings of badness and shame are confirmed by the most recent assault, giving them more evidence of being "damaged goods" (Gibson & Hartshome, 1996). The use of disengagement strategies may be their way of coping with these intensely negative feelings. Expressive coping (talking with others about their feelings) was associated with fewer symptoms, whereas self-destructive coping (thinking about killing themselves, drinking too much, blaming themselves) was associated with more.

Health Effects of Shame and Self-Blame

Shame and self-blame are often grouped together in studies of health effects of abuse. The health impact of shame and self-blame is indirect in that it makes people more vulnerable to four things that have a known impact on health:

1. Revictimization;
2. PTSD;
3. Depression; and
4. Eating disorders.

In a study of 548 college women, Kessler and Bieschke (1999) found a significant relationship between sexual abuse and later revictimization. Shame was significantly related to revictimization, whereas dissociation was not. The authors felt that shame needs to be specifically addressed in any treatment efforts designed to lower the risk of revictimization. Shame and guilt also appear to play an important role in the development of PTSD among battered women. Indeed, the psychological abuse that often accompanies physical abuse is focused on creating guilt and shame (Street & Arias, 2001).

Messman-Moore, Coates, Gaffey, and Johnson (2008) had a similar finding. An eight-month prospective study of 276 college women found that in one academic year, 9.5 percent reported rape and 11.7 percent reported verbal sexual coercion. Alcohol and marijuana use increased the risk for rape, whereas self-criticism and depression increased the risk for verbal coercion. Women's sexuality and sexual behavior, difficulties with self-confidence, identity, and boundaries were associated with both rape and verbal coercion. These results suggest that aspects of sexuality, such as shame regarding sexuality or using sex to meet other needs, may increase the risk for rape and verbal coercion.

Shame also is associated with whether victims of violent crime develop PTSD in response to the incident. At one month after the incident, subjects were asked about previous child physical or sexual abuse, their responses to the current crime, sense of shame, and their anger with others. Fear and helplessness were common reactions, and events that combined a high degree of fear with helplessness predisposed people to PTSD (Brewin, Andrews, & Rose, 2000). Shame and anger were the only independent predictors of PTSD at one month (Andrews, Brewin, Rose, & Kirk, 2000), and the effects were independent of intense fear, helplessness, and horror (Brewin et al., 2000). At six months, only shame predicted PTSD. The authors concluded that shame was an important component in the development of crime-related PTSD. These findings are consistent with previous research on shame as a mediator between childhood abuse and adult psychopathology (Brewin et al., 2000).

In a more recent study, 140 men and women participated in an online survey (Robinaugh & McNally, 2010). The sole inclusion criterion was whether they had experienced something that they remembered with guilt and shame. The most commonly reported incidents participants reported included betrayal of trust, harm inflicted on someone else (e.g., publicly ridiculing someone), or instigating a physical altercation. Shame and guilt were measured with the State Shame and Guilt Inventory. Shame concerned cognitions about the entire self. Guilt only concerned a specific action. Shame significantly predicted both depression and PTSD, whereas guilt was not related to either once the effects of shame were controlled for. The authors suggested that their findings indicated that shame was capable of eliciting intrusive and distressing memories that were characteristic of PTSD. They also suggested that shame-producing events are more likely to cause psychological distress when those events become central to one's identity and autobiographical narrative.

Shame may also have specific immunologic correlates. In a study of forty-nine individuals, thirty-one were assigned to write about a traumatic experience in which they blamed themselves and eighteen wrote about neutral experiences (Dickerson, Kemeny, Aziz, Kim, & Fahey, 2004b). Those in the shame/self-blame condition showed an increase in sTNFαRII, a measure of proinflammatory cytokine activity compared to those in the control condition. Those in the self-blame condition showed the highest levels of shame, which was related to inflammation. Cortisol levels were not associated with shame in this study but have been shown to be elevated in other studies (Dickerson et al., 2004a). Guilt and general negative emotions did not increase inflammation levels. The authors noted that sustained activation of the TNF-cytokine system can have long-term health effects in the context of inflammatory diseases. Shame may also promote goal disengagement, which can be adaptive in the face of uncontrollable situations or situations that require skills the person does not possess.

Shame and self-blame are both common among abuse survivors and may be the mechanism for symptoms these survivors manifest. Andrews (1997) investigated the role of shame in the relationship between childhood abuse and bulimia. In a community sample of young women (ages 15–25), she found a significant relationship between childhood abuse and shame that indicated that bodily shame could not be explained by bodily dissatisfaction. Child abuse showed a significant relation to bulimia, but once shame was controlled for, the relationship vanished. Andrews suggests that shame is a mediator between early abuse and bulimia.

Dysfunctional cognitions and negative thought-control strategies, such as worry and self-punishment, also play an important role in the maintenance of PTSD symptoms, highlighting the significance of dysfunctional cognitions associated with traumatic events (Bennett, Beck, & Clapp, 2009). They also cause problems with identifying current threats and include negative self-schemas, such as "I am incompetent and cannot handle stress," or beliefs about the world, "The world is a dangerous place." In a study of 295 men and women who had experienced a serious motor vehicle accident, there was a significant indirect relationship between PTSD and dysfunctional beliefs. More severe PTSD was associated with increases in worry and self-punishment. However, distraction proved to be an adaptive response resulting in lower levels of PTSD. The authors hypothesized that maladaptive thought control strategies interfere with the processing of traumatic material, which in turn maintains trauma symptoms.

The health effects of shame and self-blame are indirect. But given the association with depression, PTSD, and revictimization, these are beliefs the field should take seriously and address in treatment programs.

ATTRIBUTIONAL STYLE

People have a basic need to explain unusual, unexpected, or unwanted events. The way people interpret events is known as their attributional style. People whose style is predominantly negative (the pessimists) have learned to interpret events in a way that makes them more stressful, while those whose style is more positive (the optimists) are often buffered from stress.

People with a pessimistic attributional style make internal, global, and stable attributions about why negative events occurred (Abramson, Seligman, & Teasdale, 1978; Cutrona, 1983). Internal attributions mean that the cause of the negative event is within the person's control, or is due to some characteristic within the person. (This is similar to characterological self-blame described earlier.) Attributions are stable if they do not change over time or circumstances. Global characteristics are those that affect multiple areas of one's life. For example, loss of a job also affects personal relationships. Depression, anxiety, and intrusive symptomatology have been associated with internal, global, and stable causal attributions of blame for traumatic events (Barker-Collo, 2001).

Impact of Abuse on Attributional Style

Not surprisingly, childhood abuse can influence attributional style. Women who had been sexually abused were more likely to have internal, stable, and global attributional styles when confronted with stressful or adverse life events (Gold, 1986). In Gold's study, current functioning was related most strongly to women's attributions for negative events.

In a college sample of women who had been raped, women who had also been sexually abused made more global, stable, and internal attributions about the rape. Coping style was most predictive of current symptoms (Arata, 1999). In a study of female sexual abuse survivors, Barker-Collo (2001) found that the internal aspect of attributional style predicted adult symptomatology. Those women who blamed themselves had high levels of symptoms on the Trauma Symptom Checklist and were significantly more likely to have attempted suicide. These findings were particularly true for women who were abused by family members and those abused before age 10.

In a study of depressed women, Kuyken and Brewin (1999) found that abuse history was not directly related to attributional style or coping. However, women with intrusive memories of physical or sexual abuse had lower self-esteem, had a more negative attributional style, and were more likely to use avoidance as a coping style. When they controlled for severity of depression, abuse history and intrusive memories were both still associated with lower levels of positive self-esteem.

How Attributional Style Influences Health

There is a large body of literature that links attributional style to health. Attributional style is related to immune system function and recovery from illness. In a study of law students, optimism was associated with better mood, higher numbers of T cells, and higher natural killer cell cytotoxicity. Mood only partially accounted for this relationship (Segerstrom, Taylor, Kemeny, & Fahey, 1998).

The Health Effects of Optimism. A study of 340 men with a mean age of 70.9 years examined the relationship between optimism, inflammation, and endothelial function over time (Ikeda et al., 2011). These men were free of coronary disease. The researchers found that higher optimism scores were related to lower IL-6 and sICAM-1 across multiple time points. When they compared optimism and pessimism, pessimism had a stronger effect.

Optimism is both a state and a trait within the self-regulatory process, and when looking at behavioral change, different types of cognitions may be important at different stages of the health-behavior change process (Schwarzer, 1999). Some degree of risk perception can set the stage for subsequent contemplation and motivation to change, but it must be accompanied by other cognitions, outcome expectancies, and perceived self-efficacy. Someone with low self-efficacy will anticipate failure scenarios and worry about performance deficiencies and attempts prematurely. Optimistic self-efficacy visualizes success scenarios that guide action and let them persevere in the face of obstacles and recover quickly from unforeseen difficulties.

Researchers examined the role of attributional style on function of the immune system in HIV-positive gay men. The authors hypothesized that men's negative or pessimistic beliefs about themselves or the future would predict decline in their CD4 cells. Examining these cells is both diagnostic and prognostic; a rapid decrease in CD4 cells reflects HIV progression, and low numbers of the cells increase the risk of opportunistic infections. They indeed found that the more negative events were attributed to self, the faster the CD4 count declined. This was true even after controlling for CD4 count at baseline, depression, health behavior, high-risk sexual behavior, partner status, bereavement, and symptoms of HIV. Attributional style did not predict the development of AIDS, however (Segerstrom, Taylor, Kemeny, Reed, & Visscher, 1996).

In another study of HIV-positive gay men, even unrealistically optimistic beliefs about the future were associated with a less rapid course of the illness. Men who were "realistic" about their impending deaths tended to die a full nine months before their less-realistic peers. These results held true even after accounting for health habits, social support, depression, psychological distress, and adherence to treatment regimens (Taylor, Kemeny, Reed, Bower, & Gruenewald, 2000). Optimism has also been associated with a faster rate of recovery following a coronary bypass surgery, a faster return to normal life after discharge, and a better quality of life six months after surgery (Scheier et al., 1990).

Finally, a sixty-year longitudinal study of nuns has also demonstrated that optimism, reflected in positive-emotion words (happiness, hope, gratitude, love), is related to longevity. Researchers found that nuns who used more positive-emotion words in their handwritten, one-page autobiographies written at age 22 (a requirement for entry into the convent) had a 2.5-fold decrease in mortality sixty years later. Indeed, there was a 6.9 year difference in mortality between the highest and lowest quartiles of positive-emotion sentences (Danner, Snowdon, & Friesen, 2001).

The Impact of Subjective Well-Being. A construct related to optimism is subjective well-being. It too is related to health. Xu and Roberts (2010) studied the construct of subjective well-being. They discovered that it included three specific aspects: positive feelings, global life satisfaction, and domain life satisfaction. Subjective well-being and negative feelings were used to predict longevity using data from the Alameda County Study, a twenty-eight-year longitudinal study of 6,856 residents of Alameda County, California. The results indicated that all aspects of subjective well-being predicted all-cause and natural-cause mortality, even after controlling for demographic and baseline health covariates. These effects were tied to social networks.

Another study also examined whether personality traits impacted mortality. Grossardt, Bower, Geda, Colligan, and Rocca (2009) conducted a forty-year longitudinal study that examined the relationship between personality characteristics and all-cause mortality. The sample was a cohort of 7,216 residents of Minnesota. A total of 4,634 participants died during the follow-up. The researchers discovered that pessimistic, anxious, and depressive traits were associated with increased all-cause mortality for both men and women. The design of the study allowed researchers to determine whether negative personality traits in early life predicted mortality or whether these traits resulted from health problems later in life.

The researchers noted three possible causal mechanisms for their findings. The first is that there is a direct biological mechanism, such as through stress and depression, which leads to increased mortality risk. The second is that negative personality traits lead to poor self-care. And the third is that negative personality traits modify the progress of disease at its onset, portending a more negative prognosis than for someone with more positive personality traits. All three of these mechanisms are likely involved (Grossardt et al., 2009).

Cognitive Appraisals

Cognitive appraisal is involved in coping. When a problem is seen as amendable, the person is more likely to pursue problem-focused coping, which includes seeking support, cognitive engagement, acceptance, and meaning. In contrast, when a person perceives that nothing can be done to modify the stressful event, he or she is more likely to use avoidant coping. This includes suppression of thoughts and feelings, escapism, and dissociation.

Phanichrat and Townshend (2010) presented results of an interpretive phenomenological analysis of three males and four females who were CSA survivors. The focus was on coping strategies they used to recover from CSA. There were two key themes clusters: avoidant coping strategies and problem-focused coping

Avoidant coping is common following CSA, but it has been consistently related to psychological problems. Participants were asked open-ended questions: "What strategies do you use for your healing process?" "What was the turning point in your life when you realized you would recover?" "Can you provide insights into a fuller understanding of your coping strategy?" Participants initially used avoidant strategies in order to cope with the emotional impact, social stigma, and perceived negative self-image left in the wake of CSA. Healthier strategies were then employed that included cognitive reappraisal, reframing, externally attributing responsibility for the abuse, positive thinking, self-reflection, and acceptance strategies.

A positive attitude with hope, in particular, underpinned a turning point, which facilitated seeking support, positive cognitive engagement, and acceptance. The cognitive processes involved in recognizing that the abuse was not their fault was part of the positive cognitive engagement.

In the end, CSA survivors indicated that recovery is an arduous process and that traumatic experiences may surface and resurface. No single approach to coping works alone—a variety of techniques help. But successful coping may mean, as one survivor described it: "where it doesn't influence every moment of my waking life" (Phanichrat & Townshend, 2010, p. 75).

Moore, Varra, Michael, and Simpson (2010) studied stress-related growth, which refers to the extent to which a person's perspective and behaviors have positively changed because of a traumatic event. Positive reframing refers to altering one's thinking to find something positive in stressful situations. Their study included 203 male and female U.S. veterans receiving general or specialized PTSD care in Veterans Administration facilities in Washington State. Greater stress-related growth was associated with higher use of emotional processing and positive reframing in the two weeks prior to assessment. Emotional processing includes attempts to explore meanings and to come to an understanding of one's emotions. There was a curvilinear relationship. Those with the lowest and highest stress-related growth had the lowest PTSD and depression. Those reporting low stress-related growth and distress may not perceive the event as a crisis, making both growth and distress unlikely.

Centrality

Our autobiographical narratives act as a reference point for our experiences and attributions. Centrality refers to the extent to which a negative or traumatic event becomes central to one's identity or life story (Robinaugh & McNally, 2011). With regard to traumatic events, cognitive theorists have examined the importance of negative trauma-related self-appraisals. When traumatic events become the central reference point in a person's life, that person is at higher risk for developing PTSD.

To measure centrality, the Centrality of Events Scale (CES) was developed (Berntsen & Rubin, 2006). Some of the items on this scale include the following:

- I believe that people who haven't experienced this type of event think differently than I do.
- This event was a turning point in my life.
- My life story can be divided into two main chapters: One is before and one is after this event happened.
- This event has become a reference point for the way I understand new experiences.

In a study of 102 survivors of childhood sexual abuse, Robinaugh and McNally (2011) found that scores on the CES correlated with PTSD symptom severity, depression severity, and self-esteem, with higher scores related to increased symptomatology and lower self-esteem. The relation between CES scores and PTSD symptoms remained even after controlling for depression severity, self-esteem, age, intelligence, and dissociation.

Robinaugh and McNally (2011) also conducted a principal-components analysis and found three underlying factors. The first factor included items that tapped both centrality to identity and integration with other memories. Greater integration with other memories was related to more severe PTSD symptoms. The second factor included items regarding whether the traumatic event was a turning point in one's life (i.e., having been changed by the event). The higher the impact of the event, the more severe the PTSD symptoms. Finally, the third factor was the extent to which the survivors viewed their future through the lens of the traumatic event. The more survivors framed their futures by their past traumas, the higher the likelihood of PTSD symptoms. The authors suggested that believing that a traumatic event was central to one's future seems to be a particularly toxic belief to future mental health (Robinaugh & McNally, 2011).

Centrality of the traumatic event and posttraumatic cognitions also predicted PTSD symptoms in a sample of 514 undergraduates (Lancaster, Robriguez, & Weston, 2011). Lancaster et al. specifically tested the hypothesis that PTSD is maintained by an interaction between the person's posttraumatic appraisals of an event and his or her memory of the event. This interaction results in the ongoing belief that the world is a dangerous place. In addition, they tested whether centrality impacted the current sense of threat and subsequent PTSD symptoms. Examples of negative beliefs included the following: "I am bad." "I've lost my soul forever." "My whole nervous system is permanently ruined." "The world is completely dangerous."

Lancaster et al. (2011) found a positive relationship between posttraumatic cognitions, the centrality of the event, and symptoms of PTSD. Negative cognitions were the most significant predictor of PTSD. They also hypothesized about the effects of multiple or repeated events, noting that these could both increase the centrality of the event and change one's self-schema about both the self and world in some dramatic ways. They urged clinicians to understand that trauma was not simply a one-time distressing event. These lifetime experiences can become the reference point in the survivor's life narrative, and they can color survivor's view of all subsequent life experiences. Further, different types of trauma may have unique effects and each may require a separate assessment.

Rumination

Rumination refers to repetitive thoughts about the abuse and the negative emotions associated with it. Conway, Mendelson, Giannopoulos, Csank, and Holm (2004) studied the relationship between child and adult sexual abuse, intimidation, and rumination on sadness and dysphoria in a sample of 201 undergraduates. Consistent with previous research, abuse survivors were more likely to ruminate on sadness than were their non-abused counterparts. They also had higher scores on the Rumination on Sadness Scale and were more likely to ruminate when feeling sad regardless of the cause. The authors indicated that this is one possible way that abuse and victimization can lead to depression in adulthood. Rumination included thoughts such as, "I repeatedly analyze and keep thinking about the reasons for my sadness." From a stem question of "When I am sad, down, or feel blue . . . ." The authors note the cognitive-behavioral therapy (CBT) techniques for addressing ruminative styles in response to sadness may prove helpful in helping clients develop a more adaptive response. Problem-solving skills may also prove helpful.

HEALTH PERCEPTION

Health perception refers to whether people consider themselves to be healthy. Those beliefs can have a substantial impact on health and health behavior. Moreover, health perception is an important predictor of mortality (Wiest, Schuz, Webster, & Wurm, 2011).

Sexual abuse survivors, in one study, expressed less overall satisfaction with their health than did their non-abused counterparts (Moeller, Bachman, & Moeller, 1993). In our study of primary care patients, patients who had been abused were significantly less likely to describe themselves as healthy than were non-abused patients matched for age and sex (Kendall-Tackett, Marshall, & Ness, 2000).

In a meta-analysis of seven studies ($N = 10{,}000$), patients with a history of sexual assault were significantly more likely to describe their health as "poor." This result held true even after controlling for gender, ethnicity, or source of sample. Depression did not account for or mediate this association. Moreover, patients who had experienced multiple sexual assaults reported the worst health of all (Golding, Cooper, & George, 1997).

A prospective study found that trauma was related to self-rated health (Warshaw et al., 1993). Three groups of patients were compared: those with no trauma history; those with a trauma history but no PTSD; and those with a trauma history and PTSD. The types of trauma included child sexual and physical abuse, rape, witness to violence, war, assault, accident, and early separation from parents. Subjects who were in the trauma/PTSD group rated their health as significantly worse than those in the other two groups, and patients in the trauma/no-PTSD group had poorer self-rated health than did the group with no trauma history. Patients in all three groups had anxiety disorders.

PTSD also had a negative impact on health perceptions of veterans. In a study of aging veterans, PTSD was negatively correlated with health perceptions, vitality, social functioning, pain, and physical and mental health. Combat exposure did not account for these relationships (Schnurr & Spiro, 1999).

Health Effects of Health Perception

At first glance, what people think about their health might seem to make little difference. But health perception is related to day-to-day functioning, disability, even mortality. For example, health perception was significantly associated with four aspects of health: chronic disease, functional limitations, psychosomatic symptoms, and perceived discomfort or distress in one study (Simon, van de Mheen, Van der Meer, & Mackenbach, 2000). Perceiving themselves to be healthy was also protective against adverse outcomes for female teens who had been sexually abused (Chandy, Blum, & Resnick, 1996). Health perception predicted whether people would take protective measures against the sun. Those who perceived that their health was excellent were more likely to comply with sunscreen regimens or to avoid sun during peak sunlight hours (Weinstock, Rossi, Redding, Maddock, & Cottrill, 2000).

In a study of 3,124 German adults, ages 40 to 85, subjective well-being was examined as a predictor of mortality (Wiest et al., 2011). This study examined three aspects of subjective well-being: life satisfaction, positive affect, and negative affect. They found that life satisfaction and positive affect predicted mortality above and beyond the impact of physical health and demographic factors. This relationship diminished when self-rated health and physical activity were included in the model. They found that no aspect of subjective well-being accounted for mortality when covariates were controlled for. Self-rated health attenuated these factors. Regardless of age, gender, region, education, partner status, and physical health, people reporting high life satisfaction and positive affect lived longer.

Marital functioning was also related to self-rated health. Women who were positive about their marriages were more likely to describe their health as good than women who had low marital satisfaction. Women in positive marriages reported sleeping better and going to the doctor less frequently than women in less positive relationships. There was no impact of quality of marital relationship on sleep or going to the doctor for men, however (Kiecolt-Glaser & Newton, 2001).

People who suffered from panic attacks had worse health perception than a control group matched for age, gender, and ethnicity. Panic attack sufferers were more likely to worry about illness, be concerned about pain, and be afraid of diseases and death. For these patients, health perceptions affected quality of life, severity of panic attacks, and work disability (Katerndahl, 1999).

Health perception has also been shown to predict mortality. In a study of 3,500 Canadian senior citizens, those who rated their health as "poor" were almost three times more likely to die during the seven-year study as those who rated their health as "excellent." This proved to be a more accurate predictor of mortality than the objective rating of physicians (Mossey & Shapiro, 1982). Another study of 7,000 adults in California found similar results even after controlling for health behavior, depression, and social ties (Kaplan & Camacho, 1983).

How might health perception be related to actual mortality? One possible explanation is that patients actually knew something about their health that their doctors did not. Another possibility is how patients reacted to their perceived poor health. People who perceived their health to be poor might worry more, thereby creating actual health problems. In a study of older Americans, those who perceived their health status to be poor worried more than those who perceived that their health status was good. Interestingly, a similar pattern was found for those who perceived their financial status to be poor (Watari & Brodbeck, 2000).

Another study found a connection between subjective socioeconomic status (SES) and self-rated health. In a sample of pregnant multiethnic women, subjective SES was related to self-rated health for all groups. Subjective SES predicted self-rated health after taking into account actual income for white and Chinese-American women. For African-American women and Latinas, actual household income was the only predictor (Ostrove, Adler, Kuppermann, & Washington, 2000).

Health Locus of Control

A construct related to health perception is health locus of control. Health locus of control (HLC) describes people's sense of control over their health. Health beliefs fall into three general categories: health can be the result of people's own actions (internal control), under the control of powerful others, or due to fate or chance (Wallston, 2001). People high in internal control are more likely to engage in health-enhancing behaviors and to avoid harmful ones. HLC has been used as a construct in only one childhood abuse study, but it raises some intriguing possibilities for future research.

In a sample of low-income HIV-positive minority women, there was a high percentage of childhood abuse. In a multivariate analysis, powerful others and internal control were independent predictors of perceived health. The more external the focus, the worse the perceived health (Simoni & Ng, 2002). Given abuse survivors' experiences with powerful others, it stands to reason that they would consider their health to be outside their control.

Norman, Bennett, Smith, and Murphy (1998) examined the relationship between HLC and health behaviors, using a composite measure of alcohol consumption, smoking, exercise, and diet in a sample of 11,632 patients who participated in the Health in Wales Survey. According to the theory, individuals who believe that they have control over their health will be more likely to engage in health-enhancing behaviors and to avoid health-compromising ones. Their findings revealed that people who believed that their health was under their control performed a higher number of health behaviors than those who thought their health was in the hands of powerful others or was due to change. Those who believed their health was due to chance were the least likely to perform health behaviors.

HLC is also a factor in compliance with treatment. In a study of HIV-positive men, those who attributed their health status to fate or chance were significantly more likely to be depressed, feel hopeless, and be under stress. There was also a significant relationship between positive beliefs in doctors and others on their health care team and adherence to their treatment regimens (Evans, Ferrando, Rabkin, & Fishman, 2000).

SELF-ESTEEM AND SELF-EFFICACY

This final section describes the constructs of self-esteem and self-efficacy. These constructs overlap considerably. According to Tafarodi and Swann (1995), self-esteem includes both self-liking and self-efficacy. Self-efficacy refers to beliefs about how competent people feel they are. It is measured by questions such as "when expected problems occur, I can handle them well," and "when trying to learn something new, I soon give up if I am not successful." Low self-efficacy is measured with items such as "I do not handle myself well in social settings" and "It's difficult for me to make new friends" (Voisin, 2005). Efficacy beliefs influence the course of action people chose, how much effort is put into the action, how long they persevere, and how much they accomplish (Bandura, 1999). Self-efficacy is a good predictor of health behaviors (Wallston, 2001).

Self-esteem and self-efficacy are often grouped together in studies on childhood abuse, or they are used interchangeably. However, research indicates that childhood abuse affects both, and that both have an impact on health.

Self-Esteem Influenced by Childhood Abuse

In a study of patients in residential treatment for substance abuse, men and women who reported physical, emotional, or sexual abuse had significantly lower self-esteem than did the non-abused patients. Females who had been abused had the lowest self-esteem of all (Gutierres & Todd, 1997). In a primary care sample, 65 percent of women with a history of CSA indicated that they had low self-esteem and did not feel good about themselves compared with 31 percent of the non-abused group. Guilt was also common, with 60 percent of the abused group reporting guilt compared with 21 percent of the non-abused group (Hulme, 2000). Another study (Schuck & Widom, 2001) found that abuse survivors had significantly lower self-esteem than their non-abused counterparts and were significantly more likely to report that they felt worthless.

Brayden, Deitrich-MacLean, Dietrich, Sherrod, and Altemeier (1995) found that both mental well-being and physical self-esteem were influenced by childhood abuse. Women in this study were part of a longitudinal study on pregnancy and prenatal care in a group of low-income women. The sexually abused women had lower well-being and self-concept scores overall. When controlling for demographic factors and childhood nurturance, general well-being and physical self-concept were still related to previous sexual abuse. Physical self-concept refers to body image, health, physical appearance, skills, and sexuality.

In a sample of college students, Lopez and Heffer (1998) examined the impact of physical abuse on self-esteem and social competence. After controlling for ethnicity and SES, those who had been physically abused had the lowest self-concept. The experience of physical abuse led to a perception of lower parental support, which led to low self-esteem. Interestingly, physical abuse did not appear to affect social competence, which was measured by self-report of social skills.

Age at which the abuse occurred made a difference in terms of self-esteem. In a study of 190 runaways, males and females who were abused before age 13 had lower self-esteem than those abused after age 13 and those who were not abused (Rotheram-Borus, Mahler, Koopman, & Langabeer, 1996).

Self-Efficacy Influenced by Childhood Abuse

Self-efficacy is grounded in the attachment relationship with the primary caregiver. According to attachment theory, the quality of this attachment provides the "safe base" from which the child gains mastery experience. It has been the hypothesized as the primary source of efficacy beliefs (Ryan, Solberg, & Brown, 1996; Weinfield, Sroufe, Egeland, & Carlson, 1999). Children with secure attachments learn that they can get their needs met through their own efforts. In contrast, when children are abused or neglected, and their attachments are insecure, they grow up believing that their efforts are ineffective and they must rely on others who may or may not meet their needs (Weinfield et al., 1999).

In their study of children ages 8–12, Toth and Cicchetti (1996) found that maltreated children reported lower perceived competence than did their nonmaltreated peers. The construct was present on three different dimensions: scholastic competence, social acceptance, and behavioral conduct. The relationship with their mothers served to either buffer or exacerbate the difficulties these children encountered.

In a study of college students, parental childrearing style and family climate were related to self-efficacy *and* self-esteem. Affectionless parenting accounted for 13 percent of the variance in self-efficacy, self-esteem, and depression (Oliver & Paull, 1995).

Another recent study examined the effect of child abuse on health functioning and self-concept in a sample of adults (Sachs-Ericsson, Cromer, Hernandez, & Kendall-Tackett, 2009). Data were obtained from the Physical Health and Disability Study, which explored the impact of child abuse on current medical problems among older adults ($N = 1,460$). The researchers also examined the effects of self-efficacy on the abuse-health relationship. They found that childhood abuse was related to the number of current medical problems. It also related to lower self-efficacy, and self-efficacy explained, in part, the abuse-health relationship. However, health problems were not greater for abused individuals with lower self-efficacy compared to those with higher levels.

HIV-risky behavior is also related to self-efficacy. In a sample of 100 teens admitted to a psychiatric hospital, those who had been sexually abused (38 percent of the sample) had significantly lower self-efficacy concerning condom use; abuse history accounted for 16 percent of the variance in condom-use self-efficacy. The authors concluded that a history of sexual abuse impairs safe-sex decision-making ability and HIV-prevention communication (Brown, Kessel, Lourie, & Ford, 1997). These researchers found similar results in another group of teenage girls. In this study, girls who had been sexually abused showed significantly less condom self-efficacy and less knowledge of HIV. Not surprisingly, they also had significantly higher rates of

HIV infection (Brown, Lourie, Zlotnick, & Cohn, 2000). Self-efficacy is also a theme in revictimization. In a longitudinal study of eighth- and ninth-grade girls, Walsh and Foshee (1998) found that low self-efficacy predicted whether the girls had been forced into sexual activity in the six months between assessments.

Family dysfunction can even have an impact on students' ability to find jobs. According to Ryan et al. (1996), a dysfunctional family may block a student's opportunities for exploration and mastery. The family may not model functional coping in general, and family members may be excessively negative and discouraging. This can have an impact on self-efficacy in seeking a job (Ryan et al., 1996). In contrast, family support was related to stronger self-efficacy beliefs in a study of Latino college students' adjustment to college. Self-efficacy was related to stronger persistence of intentions and had an indirect association with better health (Torres & Solberg, 2001).

Health Effects of Self-Esteem/Self-Efficacy

Self-esteem and self-efficacy are both related to health. Self-efficacy, in particular, is a strong predictor of both health behavior and the use of strategies to avoid dangerous situations. For example, self-efficacy cognitions are important determinants for exercise and health-related behaviors. Self-efficacy is not concerned with the skills an individual has but rather with the judgments of what an individual can do with the skills he already possesses. People high in self-efficacy tend to approach more challenging tasks, put forth more effort, and persist longer in the face of aversive stimuli. In contrast, low self-efficacy persons tend to give up, attribute failure to some internal flaw of their own, and experience more anxiety and depression when faced with a difficult or aversive task (Bandura, 1999; Wallston, 2001).

Self-efficacy was related to health status is a study of 1,024 patients with coronary heart disease (Sarkar, Ali, & Whooley, 2007). The study examined cardiac self-efficacy, which they defined as patients' confidence in their ability to take care of their own health. The results indicated that after disease severity and depression were adjusted for, the lower the self-efficacy, the higher the overall rating of disease burden. Low self-efficacy was also related to more physical limitation, worse quality of life, and worse health overall.

Self-efficacy was found to be related to increased physical activity in a sample of 669 low-income, ethnic minority youth regardless of body mass index (BMI) (Kitzman-Ulrich, Wilson, Van Horn, & Lawman, 2010). It was related to physical activity for both boys and girls, regardless of BMI. In another study, it was related to dietary self-care in a sample of 237 people newly diagnosed with Type 2 diabetes (Nouwen et al., 2011).

In a study of undergraduates, those who considered themselves effective problem solvers reported fewer physical symptoms and were more likely to have an internal HLC than subjects who were not effective problem solvers (Elliot & Marmarosh, 1994). Self-efficacy significantly predicted survival in a study of patients with chronic obstructive pulmonary disease (Kaplan, Ries, Prewitt, & Eakin, 1994). And subjects with high self-efficacy had lower heart rates, systolic and diastolic blood pressure, and skin temperature in response to a stressor (Sanz & Villamarin, 2001). Self-efficacy can also influence adaptation to disability, compliance with treatment, and health behaviors. These studies are described next.

Compliance With Treatment

People high in self-efficacy are more likely to comply with treatment regimens. With some chronic conditions, compliance can mean the difference between life and death. For example, Type 2 diabetes is an illness with a strong behavioral component. Keeping blood sugar under control depends on patients' cooperation in maintaining their diet and exercise program and monitoring their blood sugar levels. In a study of adjustment to Type 2 diabetes, patients with high perceived control were significantly less likely to be depressed or anxious, had better blood glucose control, and had fewer microvascular complications, such as retinopathy, neuropathy, and kidney disease (Macrodimitris & Endler, 2001).

Self-efficacy was related to compliance with medication and exercise regimens for people with arthritis-related disability (Marks, 2001). In older adults, self-efficacy and affect at year 2 of a five-year follow-up of a physical exercise intervention predicted continued physical activity at year 5 (McAuley et al., 2007). Older patients who performed poorly on the cognitive tasks also reported low self-efficacy, more pain, and poorer mental health than did patients who performed well on cognitive tasks. In another study, patients with higher perceived competence were less depressed and reported greater life satisfaction than patients who reported lower perceived competence (Smith, Dobbins, & Wallston, 1991).

Affleck, Tennen, Pfeiffer, and Fifield (1987) assessed patients' beliefs about their control over daily symptoms, disease course, and medical care. For patients with rheumatoid arthritis, perceived control over medical care was associated with better mental health, regardless of the seriousness of their disease. For those with moderate-to-severe symptoms, perceived control over symptoms was associated with a more positive mood.

Self-efficacy is also related to recovery from orthopedic surgery. In a study of patients after joint-replacement surgery, researchers found that self-efficacy and presurgery goal importance at three months were independent predictors of disability at nine months, even after controlling for presurgery and three-month disability level (Orbell, Johnston, Rowley, Davey, & Espey, 2001).

For patients recovering from surgery, self-efficacy predicted recovery, even after controlling for prior health, functional limitations, sex and age, optimism, health value (the importance the person placed on their health), and perceived health competence (Waldrop, Lightsey, Ethington, Woemel, & Coke, 2001). Self-efficacy increased pain tolerance but did not influence pain perception in another study (Baker & Kirsch, 1991).

In HIV treatment, adherence to complex regimens is also vital to success. In a study of seventy-two women currently taking HIV medications, those with low self-esteem were significantly more likely to have missed at least one dose in the previous week (Kalichman et al., 2001). Another study found similar results (Catz, Kelly, Bogart, Benotsch, & McAuliffe, 2000). In this study, seventy-one men and women were on rigorous treatment regimens for HIV: Even a single lapse could diminish the effectiveness of the treatment. Yet fairly high percentages of patients had missed doses of medications: 31 percent had missed at least one dose in the preceding five days. Depression, low self-efficacy, and lack of social support were all related to poor treatment compliance.

In another study, problem-solving ability was related to health behavior. Those who had poor problem-solving skills consumed more alcohol over a two-week period and were more sedentary. However, problem solving was unrelated to smoking, illicit drug use, and exercise (Godshall & Elliot, 1997).

SUMMARY

Childhood abuse cuts to the core of a person's being and can shatter people's beliefs about who they are and how competent they are. If people perceive that they deserve abuse, and that are powerless to affect any positive change in their lives, they are less likely to behave in health-enhancing ways. And these beliefs can have serious and long-lasting effects on health. But beliefs about self are only half of the story. Childhood abuse can also affect beliefs about others, the focus of Chapter 7.

References

Abramson, L. Y., Seligman, M. E. P., & Teasdale, J. D. (1978). Learned helplessness in humans: Critique and reformulation. *Journal of Abnormal Psychology, 87*, 49–74.

Affleck, G., Tennen, H., Pfeiffer, C., & Fifield, J. (1987). Appraisals of control and predictability in adapting to chronic disease. *Journal of Personality and Social Psychology, 53*, 273–279.

Ali, A., Toner, B. B., Stuckless, N., Gallop, R., Diamant, N. E., Gould, M. I., et al. (2000). Emotional abuse, self-blame, and self-silencing in women with irritable bowel syndrome. *Psychosomatic Medicine, 62*, 76–82.

Andrews, B. (1997). Bodily shame in relation to abuse in childhood and bulimia: A preliminary investigation. *British Journal of Clinical Psychology, 36*, 41–49.

Andrews, B., Brewin, C. R., Rose, S., & Kirk, M. (2000). Predicting PTSD symptoms in victims of violent crime: The role of shame, anger, and childhood abuse. *Journal of Abnormal Psychology, 109*, 69–73.

Arata, C. M. (1999). Coping with rape: The roles of prior sexual abuse and attributions of blame. *Journal of Interpersonal Violence, 14*, 62–78.

Baker, S. L., & Kirsch, I. (1991). Cognitive mediators of pain perception and tolerance. *Journal of Personality and Social Psychology, 61*, 504–510.

Bandura, A. (1999). A sociocognitive analysis of substance abuse: A agentic perspective. *Psychological Science, 10*, 214–217.

Barker-Collo, S. L. (2001). Adult reports of child and adult attributions of blame for childhood sexual abuse: Predicting adult adjustment and suicidal behaviors in females. *Child Abuse and Neglect, 25*, 1329–1341.

Bennett, S. A., Beck, J. G., & Clapp, J. D. (2009). Understanding the relationship between posttraumatic stress disorder and trauma cognitions: The impact of thought control strategies. *Behaviour Research and Therapy, 47*, 1018–1023.

Berntsen, D., & Rubin, D. C. (2006). The centrality of event scale: A measure of integrating a trauma into one's identity and its relation to posttraumatic stress disorder symptoms. *Behavior Research and Therapy, 44*(2), 219–231.

Brayden, R. M., Deitrich-MacLean, G., Dietrich, M. S., Sherrod, K. B., & Altemeier, W. A. (1995). Evidence for specific effects of childhood sexual abuse on mental well-being and physical self-esteem. *Child Abuse and Neglect, 19*, 1255–1262.

Brewin, C. R., Andrews, B., & Rose, S. (2000). Fear, helplessness, and horror in posttraumatic stress disorder: Investigation DSM-IV criterion A2 in victims of violent crime. *Journal of Traumatic Stress, 13*, 499–509.

Brown, L. K., Kessel, S. M., Lourie, K. J., & Ford, H. H. (1997). Influence of sexual abuse on HIV-related attitudes and behaviors in adolescent psychiatric inpatients. *Journal of the American Academy of Child and Adolescent Psychiatry, 36*, 316–322.

Brown, L. K., Lourie, K. J., Zlotnick, C., & Cohn, J. (2000). Impact of sexual abuse on the HIV-risk-related behavior of adolescents in intensive psychiatric treatment. *American Journal of Psychiatry, 157*, 1413–1415.

Carey, T. C., Kempton, T. L., & Gemmill, W. D. (1996). The significance of emotions in the affective presentation of sexually abused girls. *Child Psychiatry and Human Development, 27*, 115–124.

Catz, S. L., Kelly, J. A., Bogart, L. M., Benotsch, E. G., & McAuliffe, T. L. (2000). Patterns, correlates, and barriers to medication adherence among persons prescribed new treatments for HIV disease. *Health Psychology, 19*, 124–133.

Chandy, J. M., Blum, R. W., & Resnick, M. D. (1996). Female adolescents with a history of sexual abuse: Risk, outcomes, and protective factors. *Journal of Interpersonal Violence, 11*, 503–518.

Conway, M., Mendelson, M., Giannopoulos, C., Csank, P. A. R., & Holm, S. L. (2004). Childhood and adult sexual abuse, rumination on sadness, and dysphoria. *Child Abuse and Neglect, 28*, 393–410.

Cutrona, C. E. (1983). Causal attributions and perinatal depression. *Journal of Abnormal Psychology, 92*, 161–172.

Danner, D. D., Snowdon, D. A., & Friesen, W. V. (2001). Positive emotions in early life and longevity: Findings from the Nun Study. *Journal of Personality and Social Psychology, 80*, 804–813.

Dickerson, S. S. (2011). Physiological responses to experiences of social pain. In G. MacDonald & L. A. Jensen-Campbell (Eds.), *Social pain: Neuropsychological and health implications of social loss and exclusion* (pp. 79–94). Washington, DC: American Psychological Association

Dickerson, S. S., Gruenewald, T. L., & Kemeny, M. E. (2004a). When the social self is threatened: Shame, physiology, and health. *Journal of Personality, 72*(6), 1191–1216.

Dickerson, S. S., Kemeny, M. E., Aziz, N., Kim, K. H., & Fahey, J. L. (2004b). Immunological effects of induced shame and guilt. *Psychosomatic Medicine, 66*, 124–131.

Elliot, T. R., & Marmarosh, C. L. (1994). Problem-solving appraisal, health complaints, and health-related expectancies. *Journal of Counseling and Development, 72*, 531–537.

Evans, S., Ferrando, S. J., Rabkin, J. G., & Fishman, B. (2000). Health locus of control, distress, and utilization of protease inhibitors among HIV-positive men. *Journal of Psychosomatic Research, 49*, 157–162.

Feiring, C., Rosenthal, S., & Taska, L. (2000). Stigmatization and the development of friendship and romantic relationships in adolescent victims of sexual abuse. *Child Maltreatment, 5*, 311–322.

Feiring, C., Taska, L., & Lewis, M. (1998). The role of shame and attributional style in children's and adolescents' adaptation to sexual abuse. *Child Maltreatment, 3*, 129–142.

Feiring, C., Taska, L., & Lewis, M. (2002). Adjustment following sexual abuse discovery: The role of shame and attributional style. *Developmental Psychology, 38*(1), 79–92.

Gibson, L. E., & Leitenberg, H. (2001). The impact of child sexual abuse and stigma on methods of coping with sexual assault among undergraduate women. *Child Abuse and Neglect, 25*, 1343–1361.

Gibson, R. L., & Hartshome, T. S. (1996). Childhood sexual abuse and adult loneliness and network orientation. *Child Abuse and Neglect, 20*, 1087–1093.

Godshall, F. J., & Elliot, T. R. (1997). Behavioral correlates of self-appraised problem-solving ability: Problem-solving skills and health-compromising behaviors. *Journal of Applied Social Psychology, 27*, 929–944.

Gold, E. R. (1986). Long-term effects of sexual victimization in childhood: An attributional approach. *Journal of Consulting and Clinical Psychology, 54*, 51–59.

Golding, J. M., Cooper, M. L., & George, L. K. (1997). Sexual assault history and health perceptions: Seven general population studies. *Health Psychology, 16*, 417–425.

Grossardt, B. R., Bower, J. H., Geda, Y. E., Colligan, R. C., & Rocca, W. A. (2009). Pessimistic, anxious, and depressive personality traits predict all-cause mortality: The Mayo Clinic Cohort Study of Personality and Aging. *Psychosomatic Medicine, 71*, 491–500.

Gutierres, S. E., & Todd, M. (1997). The impact of childhood abuse on treatment outcomes of substance users. *Professional Psychology: Research and Practice, 28*, 348–354.

Hoglund, C. L., & Nicholas, K. B. (1995). Shame, guilt, and anger in college students exposed to abusive family environments. *Journal of Family Violence, 10*, 141–157.

Hulme, P. A. (2000). Symptomatology and health care utilization of women primary care patients who experienced childhood sexual abuse. *Child Abuse and Neglect, 24*, 1471–1484.

Ikeda, A., Schwartz, J., Peters, J. L., Fang, S., Spiro, A., Sparrow, D., et al. (2011). Optimism in relation to inflammation and endothelial dysfunction in older men: The VA Normative Aging Study. *Psychosomatic Medicine, 73*, 664–671.

Kalichman, S. C., Rompa, D., DiFonzo, K., Simpson, D., Luke, W., Kyomugisha, F., et al. (2001). HIV treatment adherence in women living with HIV/AIDS: Research based on the Information-Motivation-Behavioral Skills model of health behavior. *Journal of the Association of Nurses in AIDS Care, 12*, 58–67.

Kaplan, G. A., & Camacho, T. (1983). Perceived health and mortality: A nine-year follow-up of the Human Population Laboratory cohort. *American Journal of Epidemiology, 11*, 292–304.

Kaplan, R. M., Ries, A. L., Prewitt, L. A., & Eakin, E. (1994). Self-efficacy expectations predict survival for patients with chronic obstructive pulmonary disease. *Health Psychology, 13*, 366–368.

Katerndahl, D. A. (1999). Illness attitudes and coping process in subjects with panic attacks. *Journal of Nervous and Mental Disease, 187*, 562–566.

Kendall-Tackett, K. A., Marshall, R., & Ness, K. E. (2000). Victimization, healthcare use and health maintenance. *Family Violence and Sexual Assault Bulletin, 16*, 18–21.

Kessler, B. L., & Bieschke, K. J. (1999). A retrospective analysis of shame, dissociation, and adult victimization in survivors of childhood sexual abuse. *Journal of Counseling Psychology, 46*, 335–341.

Kiecolt-Glaser, J. K., & Newton, T. L. (2001). Marriage and health: His and hers. *Psychological Bulletin, 127*, 472–503.

Kim, J., Talbot, N. L., & Cicchetti, D. (2009). Childhood abuse and current interpersonal conflict: The role of shame. *Child Abuse and Neglect, 33*, 362–371.

Kitzman-Ulrich, H., Wilson, D. K., Van Horn, M. L., & Lawman, H. G. (2010). Relationship of body mass index and psychosocial factors on physical activity in underserved adolescent boys and girls. *Health Psychology, 29*(5), 506–513.

Koss, M. P. (1990). The women's mental health research agenda: Violence against women. *American Psychologist, 45*, 374–380.

Kuyken, W., & Brewin, C. R. (1999). The relation of early abuse to cognition and coping in depression. *Cognitive Therapy and Research, 23*, 665–677.

Lancaster, S. L., Robriguez, B. F., & Weston, R. (2011). Path analytic examination of a cognitive model of PTSD. *Behaviour Research and Therapy, 49*, 194–201.

Liem, J. H., & Boudewyn, A. C. (1999). Contextualizing the effects of childhood sexual abuse on adult self- and social functioning: An attachment theory perspective. *Child Abuse and Neglect, 23*, 1141–1157.

Lopez, M. A., & Heffer, R. W. (1998). Self-concept and social competence of university student victims of childhood physical abuse. *Child Abuse and Neglect, 22*, 183–195.

Macrodimitris, S. D., & Endler, N. S. (2001). Coping, control, and adjustment in Type 2 diabetes. *Health Psychology, 20*(3), 208–216.

Marks, R. (2001). Efficacy theory and its utility in arthritis rehabilitation: Review and recommendations. *Disability and Rehabilitation: An International Multidisciplinary Journal, 23*, 271–280.

McAuley, E., Morris, K. S., Motl, R. W., Hu, L., Konopack, J. F., & Elavsky, S. (2007). Long-term follow-up of physical activity behavior in older adults. *Health Psychology, 26*(3), 375–380.

Messman-Moore, T. L., Coates, A. A., Gaffey, K. J., & Johnson, C. F. (2008). Sexuality, substance use, and susceptibility to victimization: Risk for rape and sexual coercion in a prospective study of college women. *Journal of Interpersonal Violence, 23*(12), 1730–1746.

Moeller, T. P., Bachman, G. A., & Moeller, J. R. (1993). The combined effects of physical, sexual and emotional abuse during childhood: Long-term health consequences for women. *Child Abuse and Neglect, 17*, 623–641.

Moore, S. A., Varra, A. A., Michael, S. T., & Simpson, T. L. (2010). Stress-related growth, positive reframing, and emotional processing in the prediction of post-trauma functioning among veterans in mental health treatment. *Psychological Trauma, 2*(2), 93–96.

Mossey, J. M., & Shapiro, E. (1982). Self-rated health: A predictor of mortality among the elderly. *American Journal of Public Health, 72*, 406–414.

Norman, P., Bennett, P., Smith, C., & Murphy, S. (1998). Health locus of control and health behaviour. *Journal of Health Psychology, 3*(2), 171–180.

Nouwen, A., Ford, T., Balan, A. T., Twisk, J., Ruggiero, L., & White, D. (2011). Longitudinal motivational predictors of dietary self-care and diabetes control in adults with newly diagnosed type 2 diabetes mellitus. *Health Psychology, 30*(6), 771–779.

Oliver, J. M., & Paull, J. C. (1995). Self-esteem and self-efficacy: Perceived parenting and family climate, and depression in university students. *Journal of Clinical Psychology, 51*, 467–481.

Orbell, S., Johnston, M., Rowley, D., Davey, P., & Espey, A. (2001). Self-efficacy and goal importance in the prediction of physical disability in people following hospitalization: A prospective study. *British Journal of Health Psychology, 6*, 25–41.

Ostrove, J. M., Adler, N. E., Kuppermann, M., & Washington, A. E. (2000). Objective and subjective assessments of socioeconomic status and their relationship to self-rated health in an ethnically diverse sample of pregnant women. *Health Psychology, 19*, 613–618.

Perrott, K., Morriss, E., Martin, J., & Romans, S. (1998). Cognitive coping styles of women sexually abused in childhood: A qualitative study. *Child Abuse and Neglect, 22*, 1135–1149.

Persons, E., Kershaw, T., Sikkema, K. J., & Hansen, N. B. (2010). The impact of shame on health-related quality of life among HIV-positive adults with a history of childhood sexual abuse. *AIDS Patient Care and STDs, 24*(9), 571–580.

Phanichrat, T., & Townshend, J. M. (2010). Coping strategies used by survivors of childhood sexual abuse on the journey to recovery. *Journal of Child Sexual Abuse, 19*, 62–78.

Robinaugh, D. J., & McNally, R. J. (2010). Autobiographical memory for shame or guilt providing events: Association with psychological symptoms. *Behaviour Research and Therapy, 48*, 646–652.

Robinaugh, D. J., & McNally, R. J. (2011). Trauma centrality and PTSD symptom severity in adult survivors of childhood sexual abuse. *Journal of Traumatic Stress, 24*(4), 483–486.

Rotheram-Borus, M. J., Mahler, K. A., Koopman, C., & Langabeer, K. (1996). Sexual abuse history and associated multiple risk behavior in adolescent runaways. *American Journal of Orthopsychiatry, 66*, 390–400.

Ryan, N. E., Solberg, V. S., & Brown, S. D. (1996). Family dysfunction, parental attachment, and career search self-efficacy among community college students. *Journal of Counseling Psychology, 43*, 84–89.

Sachs-Ericsson, N., Cromer, K., Hernandez, A., & Kendall-Tackett, K. A. (2009). Childhood abuse, health and pain-related problems: The role of psychiatric disorders and current life stress. *Journal of Trauma and Dissociation, 10*, 170–188.

Sanz, A., & Villamarin, F. (2001). The role of perceived control in physiological reactivity: Self-efficacy and incentive value as regulators of cardiovascular adjustment. *Biological Psychiatry, 56*,

219–246.

Sarkar, U., Ali, S., & Whooley, M. A. (2007). Self-efficacy and health status in patients with coronary heart disease: Findings from the Heart and Soul Study. *Psychosomatic Medicine, 69*, 306–312.

Scarinci, I. C., McDonald-Haile, J., Bradley, L. A., & Richter, J. E. (1994). Altered pain perception and psychosocial features among women with gastrointestinal disorders and history of abuse: A preliminary model. *American Journal of Medicine, 97*, 108–118.

Scheier, M. F., Matthews, K. A., Owens, J., Magovern, G. J., Lefebrvre, R. C., Abbott, R. A., et al. (1990). Dispositional optimism and recovery from coronary artery bypass surgery: The beneficial effects of physical and psychological well-being. *Journal of Personality and Social Psychology, 57*, 1024–1040.

Schnurr, P. P., & Spiro, A. (1999). Combat disorder, posttraumatic stress disorder symptoms and health behaviors as predictors of self-reported physical health in older veterans. *Journal of Nervous and Mental Disease, 187*, 353–359.

Schuck, A. M., & Widom, C. S. (2001). Childhood victimization and alcohol symptoms in females: Causal inferences and hypothesized mediators. *Child Abuse and Neglect, 25*, 1069–1092.

Schwarzer, R. (1999). Self-regulatory processes in the adoption and maintenance of health behaviors. *Journal of Health Psychology, 4*(2), 115–127.

Segerstrom, S. C., Taylor, S. E., Kemeny, M. E., & Fahey, J. L. (1998). Optimism is associated with mood, coping, and immune change in response to stress. *Journal of Personality and Social Psychology, 74*, 1646–1655.

Segerstrom, S., Taylor, S. E., Kemeny, M. E., Reed, G. M., & Visscher, B. R. (1996). Causal attributions predict rate of immune decline in HIV-seropositive gay men. *Health Psychology, 15*, 485–493.

Shah, R., & Waller, G. (2000). Parental style and vulnerability to depression: The role of core beliefs. *Journal of Nervous and Mental Disease, 188*, 19–25.

Simon, J. G., van de Mheen, H., Van der Meer, J. B., & Mackenbach, J. P. (2000). Socioeconomic differences in self-assessed health in a chronically ill population: The role of different health aspects. *Journal of Behavioral Medicine, 23*, 399–420.

Simoni, J. M., & Ng, M. T. (2002). Abuse, health locus of control, and perceived health among HIV-positive women. *Health Psychology, 21*, 89–93.

Smith, C. A., Dobbins, C. J., & Wallston, K. A. (1991). The mediational role of perceived competence in psychological adjustment to rheumatoid arthritis. *Journal of Applied Social Psychology, 21*, 1218–1247.

Snyder, C. R., Irving, L. M., & Anderson, J. R. (1991). Hope and health. In C. R. Snyder & D. R. Forsyth (Eds.), *Handbook of social and clinical psychology: The health perspective* (pp. 285–305). Elmsford, NY: Pergamon.

Street, A. E., & Arias, I. (2001). Psychological abuse and posttraumatic stress disorder in battered women: Examining the roles of shame and guilt. *Violence and Victims, 16*, 65–78.

Tafarodi, R. W., & Swann, W. B. (1995). Self-liking and self-competence as dimensions of global self-esteem: Initial validation of a measure. *Journal of Personality Assessment, 65*, 322–342.

Taylor, S. E., Kemeny, M. E., Reed, G. M., Bower, J. E., & Gruenewald, T. L. (2000). Psychological resources, positive illusions, and health. *American Psychologist, 55*, 99–109.

Torres, J. B., & Solberg, V. S. (2001). Role of self-efficacy, stress, social integration, and family support in Latino college student persistence and health. *Journal of Vocational Behavior, 59*, 53–63.

Toth, S. L., & Cicchetti, D. (1996). Patterns of relatedness, depressive symptomatology, and perceived competence in maltreated children. *Journal of Consulting and Clinical Psychology, 64*, 32–41.

Voisin, D. R. (2005). The relationship between violence exposure and HIV sexual risk behavior: Does gender matter? *American Journal of Orthopsychiatry, 75*(4), 497–506.

Waldrop, D., Lightsey, O. R., Ethington, C. A., Woemel, C. A., & Coke, A. L. (2001). Self-efficacy, optimism, health competence, and recovery from orthopedic surgery. *Journal of Counseling Psychology, 48*, 233–238.

Wallston, K. A. (2001). Conceptualization and operationalization of perceived control. In A. Baum, T. A. Revenson, & J. E. Singer (Eds.), *Handbook of health psychology* (pp. 49–59). Mahwah, NJ: Erlbaum.

Walsh, J. F., & Foshee, V. (1998). Self-efficacy, self-determination and victim blaming as predictors of adolescent sexual victimization. *Health Education Research, 13*, 139–144.

Warshaw, M. G., Fierman, E., Pratt, L., Hunt, M., Yonker, K. A., Massion, A. O., et al. (1993). Quality of life and dissociation in anxiety disorder patients with histories of trauma or PTSD. *American Journal of Psychiatry, 150*, 1512–1516.

Watari, K. F., & Brodbeck, C. (2000). Culture, health, and financial appraisals: Comparison of worry in older Japanese Americans and European Americans. *Journal of Clinical Geropsychology, 6*, 25–39.

Webb, M., Heisler, D., Call, S., Chickering, S. A., & Colburn, T. A. (2007). Shame, guilt, symptoms of depression, and reported history of psychological maltreatment. *Child Abuse and Neglect, 31*, 1143–1153.

Weinfield, N. S., Sroufe, L. A., Egeland, B., & Carlson, E. A. (1999). The nature of individual differences in infant-caregiver attachment. In J. Cassidy & P. R. Shaver (Eds.), *The handbook of attachment: Theory, research, and clinical applications* (pp. 68–88). New York: Guilford Press.

Weinstock, M. A., Rossi, J. S., Redding, C. A., Maddock, J. E., & Cottrill, S. D. (2000). Sun protection behaviors and stages of change for the primary prevention of skin cancers among beachgoers in southeastern New England. *Annals of Behavioral Medicine, 22*, 286–293.

Whiffen, V. E., & MacIntosh, H. B. (2005). Mediators of the link between childhood sexual abuse and emotional distress: A critical review. *Trauma, Violence, and Abuse, 6*(1), 24–39.

Wiest, M., Schuz, B., Webster, N., & Wurm, S. (2011). Subjective well-being and mortality revisited: Differential effects of cognitive and emotional facets of well-being on mortality. *Health Psychology, 30*(6), 728-735.

Xu, J., & Roberts, R. E. (2010). The power of positive emotions: It's a matter of life or death—subjective well-being and longevity over 28 years in a general population. *Health Psychology, 29*(1), 9–19.

Zinzow, H., Seth, P., Jackson, J., Niehaus, A., & Fitzgerald, M. (2010). Abuse and parental characteristics, attributions of blame, and psychological adjustment in adult survivors of child sexual abuse. *Journal of Child Sexual Abuse, 19*, 79–98.

Chapter 7

Cognitive Pathways II—Beliefs About Others

What we believe about other people affects our relationships and, ultimately, our health. Childhood abuse can distort adult survivors' views of others and convince abuse survivors that others mean them harm. It can also shape their religious beliefs and beliefs about God. This chapter discusses research on the impact of childhood abuse on beliefs about others, beginning with a description of the cognitive framework from attachment theory: the internal working model.

INTERNAL WORKING MODEL

The internal working model is the conceptual schema that frames perceptions about self and others and is related to people's beliefs about their personal power and how much they can do to help themselves. It is related to depression, health perception, and self-efficacy, and it is one mechanism by which attachment relationships remain stable over time (Liem & Boudewyn, 1999).

The internal working model is based on Bowlby's (1969, 1982) conceptualizations of attachment. When caregivers meet the needs of children with sensitivity and consistency, children develop a working model that says that people will accept and support them. In contrast, if caretakers respond to children's needs with rejection, children will develop working models that contain doubts and concerns about how others will treat them (Bretherton, 1992; Toth & Cicchetti, 1996).

The internal working model influences the aspects of interpersonal situations to which people pay attention, how they interpret the behaviors of others, and how they respond to their environment (Liem & Boudewyn, 1999). For example, if children believe that they can count on adults to be protective and nurturant, they are likely to seek help and support. Conversely, if children see themselves as powerless and incompetent, and see other people as untrustworthy, they are less likely to seek the help of others. These patterns carry over into adulthood in the form of insecure adult attachments and beliefs that lead to high-risk behaviors (Whiffen & MacIntosh, 2005). For example, when people are trying to cope with negative emotions and are feeling overwhelmed, they may utilize negative forms of coping, such as alcohol abuse, drugs, or self-destructive behaviors. Given that the abuse occurred many years before, the survivor may have thought that there is nothing that he or she could do except temporarily relieve the symptoms (Whiffen & MacIntosh, 2005). This type of negative coping can also increase the risk of revictimization.

Roemmele and Messman-Moore (2011) explored the impact of early maladaptive schemas. A schema is an organizing principle through which people make sense of their experiences. Maladaptive schemas may develop as a consequence of abuse and neglect, and they can result in a lifetime of self-defeating intrapersonal and interpersonal patterns. Roemmele and Messman-Moore examined the impact of other-directedness schemas that involved the tendency to pay excessive attention to others at the expense of one's own well-being. These schemas included subjugation (belief that one's own beliefs, wishes, and emotions were inferior to others and a willingness to sacrifice their own beliefs based on fear of negative reactions) and self-sacrifice (excessive drive to satisfy others at the expense of self). In their study of 653 female undergraduates, they discovered that physical, sexual, and emotional abuse were all related to early maladaptive schemas. They found that the defectiveness/shame and abandonment schemas were the most relevant to risky sexual behavior, in terms of both lifetime number of partners and frequency of risky sexual behavior with intimate and nonintimate partners. The impact of child abuse on sexual behavior is not limited to child sexual abuse (CSA); all types of maltreatment increase risk. The authors recommend that therapy designed to address the maladaptive schemas be introduced to help abuse survivors engage in healthy and safe sexual behavior.

Two related schemas that are common in abuse survivors include mistrust and hostility. Both are related to negative views of others and the assumption that others want to harm them.

HOSTILITY

Hostility includes interpersonal mistrust, suspiciousness, cynicism about human nature, and a tendency to interpret the actions of others as aggressive (Kubzansky & Kawachi, 2000; Lewis et al., 2009; Smith, 1992). Trait hostility increases physiological arousal because of the way hostile people interpret the world; they are more likely to perceive even neutral events in a negative way, responding strongly because they perceive interpersonal threat (Kiecolt-Glaser & Newton, 2001).

Hostility in Abuse Survivors

Abuse survivors tend to have higher levels of hostility than do their non-abused peers. In a study of undergraduates, students who reported family dysfunction had a negative or malevolent view of themselves and the world. Child abuse of all types was related to symptom distress, whereas parental alcoholism was not (Harter & Vanecek, 2000). A study of 294 newly abstinent cocaine/opiate-dependent patients (Roy, 2001) found a significant correlation between hostility and childhood maltreatment. Maltreatment included physical, sexual, and emotional abuse, as well as physical and emotional neglect. Adult survivors of child neglect also reported higher levels of hostility, anxiety, and paranoia (Gauthier, Stollak, Messe, & Aronoff, 1996) than subjects who were physically abused. The authors speculated that neglected subjects had more adjustment difficulties and trouble with relationships than physically abused subjects because of the chronicity of neglect (Gauthier et al., 1996).

Although not a study of abuse, another study found that trauma in general was also related to hostility. In a sample of ninety women veterans (Butterfield, Forneris, Feldman, & Beckham, 2000), women who had posttraumatic stress disorder (PTSD) reported significantly higher levels of hostility than did women without PTSD. PTSD was related to all measures of health, with poorer outcomes for women with PTSD even after controlling for age and education.

Health Effects of Hostility

Hostility is an understandable response in abuse survivors given their experiences. In the short term, it may have even proven adaptive, in that it allowed them to survive an abusive situation. However, the long-term effects are quite serious, especially their impact on physical health.

Cardiovascular Disease. Hostility has garnered a great deal of attention because of its link to cardiovascular disease, which is the leading cause of death in the United States for both men and women. People who are hostile and angry and have antagonistic social behavior are at increased risk for cardiovascular disease (Smith et al., 2007). In their review, Smith and Ruiz (2002) noted that people who are high in trait hostility are more prone to ischemia and constriction of the coronary arteries during mental stress. Trait hostility predicted new coronary events in previously healthy people. And for patients who already have coronary heart disease, hostility sped up progression of the disease.

Hostility can also exacerbate the cardiac symptoms of PSTD. In a sample of 101 women who completed twenty-four hours of ambulatory monitoring, researchers examined the impact of hostility and PTSD on ambulatory heart rate and blood pressure (Beckham, Flood, Dennis, & Calhoun, 2009). Women with PTSD had higher heart rates over time than did women in the comparison group. The authors found that there was an interaction between PTSD, hostile beliefs, and overt hostility for ambulatory heart rate. Increases in hostile beliefs were associated with greater increase in diastolic blood pressure in women with PTSD compared to control subjects. The authors concluded that PTSD might moderate the relationship between hostility and cardiovascular outcome.

Hostility and low life purpose were related to attenuated decline in nocturnal blood pressure (Mezick et al., 2010). Blood pressure normally drops at night. When the drop is attenuated, it predicts cardiovascular disease. In a study of 224 black and white men with a mean age of 60, hostility and low life purpose were related to this attenuated drop, after controlling for demographic characteristics, body mass index (BMI), and hypertensive status. Life purpose measures the degree to which one finds personal value and meaning in daily activities. High life purpose has a stress-buffering effect. Depression, anxiety, or optimism was not related to these changes. A longer sleep latency mediated these changes.

In a six-year follow-up of 444 African Americans with Type 1 diabetes, Roy, Janal, and Roy (2010) found that patients with a history of childhood trauma had significantly elevated risk for cardiovascular disease, coronary disease, and stroke. Each additional reported type of childhood trauma increased the risk by approximately one-third. Patients who reported three different types of childhood trauma had more than double the risk of cardiovascular disease compared to someone who had no childhood trauma.

A study of 149 postmenopausal women found that women with the highest rates of cynicism and anger suppression had the most coronary artery calcification progression over the three-year study period (Low, Matthews, Kuller, & Edmundowicz, 2011). Coronary artery calcification is measured by electron beam computed tomography (EBCT), and it significantly predicts future cardiovascular events. Contrary to their predictions, there was no significant relationship between positive psychosocial resources and coronary artery calcification.

According to a review, the link between coronary heart disease and hostility is more complex for women than it is for men (Low, Thurston, & Matthews, 2010). In this review, the authors found that hostile attitudes predicted clinical outcomes for black women and for women with preexisting coronary heart disease. Trait anger was associated with subclinical atherosclerosis.

Anger and intermittent explosive disorder was found to be related to nine of twelve health problems studied (McCloskey, Kleabir, Berman, Chen, & Coccaro, 2010). Intermittent explosive disorder is a psychiatric disorder used to classify individuals who engage in repeated acts of anger-based aggression that are disproportionate to provocation and are not due to substance abuse, medical conditions, or other psychological conditions. Health measures related to intermittent explosive disorder included coronary heart disease, hypertension, stroke, diabetes, arthritis, back and neck pain, ulcer, headaches, and other chronic pain. Interestingly, the strongest effects were not for cardiovascular symptoms but for chronic pain.

Diabetes and Metabolic Syndrome. Hostility is also related to increased risk of diabetes and metabolic syndrome, the precursor syndrome to Type 2 diabetes. In a sample of 1,081 older men, hostility was related several indices of metabolic syndrome (Niaura et al., 2000). Hostility score was positively associated with waist/hip ratio, BMI, total caloric intake, fasting insulin level, and serum triglycerides. It was inversely related to education and HDL cholesterol. The authors concluded that their results were consistent with previous studies indicating that hostility was associated with a pattern of obesity, central adiposity, and insulin levels.

Hostility also increased the risk of metabolic syndrome in teens. In a three-year follow-up of 134 white and African American adolescents, hostility at Time 1 predicted risk factors for metabolic syndrome at Time 2 (Raikkonen, Matthews, & Salomon, 2003). These risk factors were at the seventy-fifth percentile for age, gender, and race and included BMI, insulin resistance, a high ratio of triglycerides to HDL cholesterol, and mean arterial blood pressure.

Hostility was related to the amount of visceral fat in a sample 418 white and African-American women in Chicago (Lewis et al., 2009). Visceral fat is another risk factor for cardiovascular disease and is a symptom of metabolic syndrome. Overall, African Americans had higher levels of hostility than did whites. They also had more fat overall, as well as more visceral and more subcutaneous fat. Even with these ethnic-group differences, the association of hostility and visceral fat was significant for women of both races. Subcutaneous fat is not a risk factor for cardiovascular disease and had no relation to hostility.

Hostility and Pulmonary Function. In the CARDIA (Coronary Artery Risk Development in (Young) Adults) study of 4,629 young adults (ages 18–30), hostility was related to pulmonary function (Jackson, Kubzansky, Cohen, Jacobs, & Wright, 2007). Even small changes in pulmonary function are related to substantial decreases in health in later life. Two measures of pulmonary function were included: forced expiratory volume in 1 second (FEV1) and forced vital capacity (FVC). There was a highly significant inverse relationship between hostility and pulmonary function for each measure. For every standard deviation of increase in hostility there was a decrease in both FEV1 and FVC. The authors concluded that pulmonary function was inversely related to hostility across ethnic groups and gender, and the effects were independent of age, height, current socioeconomic status (SES), smoking, and asthma. Higher hostility predicts a more rapid decline in pulmonary function.

Hostility and Generalized Stress. Hostility also interacts with SES and allostatic load—the cumulative physiological cost of adaptation to stress. In this study, the sample included 818 men, ages 21–80 (Kubzansky, Kawachi, & Sparrow, 1999). The results indicated that high hostility and low education were both related to higher allostatic load. But the effects of education were mediated by hostility. Although HPA (hypothalamic-pituitary-adrenal) activation is essential for successful adaptation to short-term stress, long-term activation of HPA activity may lead to deleterious consequences for health, due to chronic elevations in glucocorticoid levels and associated increases in blood pressure, serum glucose, and lipid levels. Allostatic load affects wear and tear on the cardiovascular, endocrine, and metabolic systems, blood pressure, abdomen:hip ratio, HDL and total cholesterol levels, cortisol, and norepinephrine secretion. General hostility is a combination of cognitive, behavioral, and emotional aspects of hostility, and was strongly associated with allostatic load. People with a score in the top tertile had an 84 percent excess risk for high levels of allostatic load.

In a study of 268 people from Singapore, anger expression was related to reported stress (Diong & Bishop, 1999). High levels of anger expression were related to higher levels of stress and lower use of active coping. There was a direct negative relationship with psychosocial well-being. People with high levels of anger and hostility use less-effective coping strategies than did those lower in hostility. They tended to have a more cynical and threatening world view, leading to greater anger expression. When situations are perceived in threatening terms, the anger-prone person likely responds quickly and angrily. There is thus insufficient time to use problem-solving coping, which delays active coping methods. In summary, higher levels of anger expression are associated with higher levels of stress, which in turn are related to lower levels of physical well-being.

Hostility and Cognitive Functioning. Adult cognitive function can also be impaired by hostility. Barnes et al. (2009) studied 4,800 white and black adults, age 65 and older. They were assessed at three time points approximately three years apart. In this study, hostility at Time 1 was related to lower cognitive scores at Time 3, but hostility was not related to rate of decline. This relationship remained even after controlling for depressive symptoms, chronic health problems, neuroticism, or social or cognitive activity. The patterns were similar for white and black participants.

Hostility and Inflammation. As described in Chapter 2, unchecked inflammation can have a severe, negative impact on health. Unfortunately, hostility is one of the negative emotional states that increase inflammation and is a likely mediator between previous abuse and current health problems, particularly cardiovascular disease and metabolic syndrome.

Hostility was associated with higher levels of circulating the proinflammatory cytokines IL-1α, IL-1β, and IL-8 in 44 healthy, non-smoking, premenopausal women. The combination of depression and hostility was particularly harmful and increased levels of IL-1β, IL-8 and TNF-α (Suarez, Lewis, Krishnan, & Young, 2004). There was a dose-response effect: The more severe the depression and hostility, the greater the production of cytokines. A study with men had similar results (Suarez, 2003). The author noted that increased levels of IL-6 predicted both future risk of cardiac events and all-cause mortality. He hypothesized that IL-6 may mediate the relationship between hostility and these health problems.

Suarez (2006) studied 135 healthy patients (75 men, 60 women), with no symptoms of diabetes. He found that women with higher levels of depression and hostility, and who had a propensity to express anger, had higher levels of fasting insulin, glucose, and insulin resistance. These findings were not true for men and they were independent of other risk factors for metabolic syndrome including BMI, age, fasting triglycerides, exercise regularity, or ethnicity. The author indicated that these findings were significant since pre-study glucose levels were in the non-diabetic range. The author noted that inflammation, particularly elevated IL-6 and C-reactive protein, may mediate the relationship between depression and hostility and risk of Type 2 diabetes and cardiovascular disease, possibly because they increase insulin resistance.

A study of 6,814 healthy men and women found that participants with higher levels of cynical distrust, chronic stress, or depression had higher levels of inflammation (Ranjit et al., 2007). Inflammation measures included elevated C-reactive protein, IL-6, and fibrinogen. Chronic stress was associated with higher IL-6 and C-reactive protein, and depression was associated with higher IL-6.

Depression often co-occurs with hostility and depression and may moderate the relationship between hostility and inflammation (Stewart, Janicki-Deverts, Muldoon,

& Kamarck, 2008). In their study of 316 older adults, Stewart et al. (2008) examined depression, hostility, and inflammation (C-reactive protein and IL-6). They found that hostility augmented the inflammatory process, but only in the presence of depressive symptoms. These effects are described in more detail in Chapter 11.

Indirect Health Effect: Hostility and Social Relationships

Hostility also has indirect effects on health by impacting quality of relationships. Hostile persons can undermine relationships through their mistrustful thoughts and antagonistic actions and are more likely to have negative social relations with others (Smith & Ruiz, 2002). Hostile people are more likely to be socially isolated, to be insecure about the current relationships, and to perceive that others are making negative judgments about them.

The relation between social support and hostility is transactional; hostile persons undermine sources of support and foster conflicts through their mistrustful thoughts and antagonistic actions, and non-hostile people have more positive social relations with others (Smith & Ruiz, 2002). Not surprisingly, trait hostility has a serious impact on marriage and other important relationships. People who are high in hostility show more negative reactions to conflict. Hostility assessed early in a marriage predicted marital dissatisfaction several years later (Kiecolt-Glaser & Newton, 2001).

Vahtera, Kivimaki, Uutela, and Pentti (2000) studied the health effects of hostility in relation to life context and social relationships. The study included 757 municipal employees in Finland during two life contexts: a period of downsizing and after. Employees who were hostile had a 1.2- to 1.4-fold higher risk of sick leave than did non-hostile employees. Hostile people did not report lower levels of perceived social support or smaller social networks than did non-hostile people. However, hostile people were less able to take advantage of existing resources. If a hostile person had few psychosocial resources, he or she had a substantially increased risk of becoming sick when there was stress at work. In addition, even if a hostile person had a lot of psychosocial resources, it did not protect the individual from diseases. These findings did not vary by gender and were independent of health behaviors and biological risk factors. During downsizing, hostile people had a 50 percent higher risk of sick leave, and only strong spousal support protected the non-hostile employees from sickness. They concluded that risk of health problems related to hostility included heightened vulnerability in stressful conditions and an inability to benefit from existing psychosocial resources.

REJECTION SENSITIVITY

A construct related to mistrust and hostility is rejection sensitivity (RS). People incorporate their expectations of acceptance or rejection from others, and these beliefs shape relationships. When people expect others to reject them, they develop RS: the tendency to anxiously expect, readily perceive, and overreact to rejection (Downey, Freitas, Michaelis, & Khouri, 1998).

This sensitivity is formed through a series of steps. First, the person is rejected by significant others, leading him or her to develop rejection expectancies. Once these expectancies are activated, the person becomes more ready to perceive rejection. When the perceived rejection prompts an overreaction, the significant other may find this overreaction aversive and actually reject the person—thus rejection sensitivity becomes a self-fulfilling prophecy (Downey et al., 1998). Conversely, the rejection-sensitive person may become increasingly dissatisfied with relationships and may break up with partners as a preemptive strike to avoid rejection.

Perceptions of social threat help us understand how people defend themselves against it. People with anxious adult attachments evaluate social interaction as potentially threatening, consistent with being hypervigilant for rejection. Research suggests that defensive and hostile reactions that stem from this strategy often lead to self-fulfilling prophecies (MacDonald, Borsook, & Spielmann, 2011).

Rejection sensitivity has been linked to childhood rejection and abuse (Feldman & Downey, 1994). In a small sample of U.S. servicemen, Raczek (1992) noted a relationship between severe physical or sexual abuse and RS. Abuse was also related to avoidant and paranoid personality disorders, low self-esteem, shyness, extreme inhibition, and mistrust and suspiciousness toward others. However, even with all these difficulties, only a few became psychiatric patients. Another study found similar results. Adverse childhood experiences were associated with RS, as were avoidant personality disorder and pessimism (Meyer & Carver, 2000).

In another small sample, those who were high on RS were more likely to perceive intentional rejection in the ambiguous behaviors of others (Downey & Feldman, 1996). In this experiment, subjects were introduced to an opposite-sex confederate. After an initial pleasant interaction, the subjects were informed that the confederate did not want to continue. No other explanation was given. As predicted, the high-rejection-sensitive subjects were more likely to report feelings of rejection than low-rejection-sensitive subjects. Individuals in the high-rejection-sensitive group were also more likely to ruminate over what they had done to cause the confederate in the experiment to reject them. In contrast, those low in RS were not concerned about why the confederate did not return.

Recent research has found that there are neural differences in people who are rejection sensitive. In a series of studies, those who were rejection sensitive had greater activation of the anterior cingulate cortex when viewing pictures of disapproving facial expressions than those who were low in rejection sensitivity (Eisenberger, 2011). Interestingly, there was not increased activity in the amygdala and insula, which suggests that the anterior cingulate cortex, rather than the limbic system more generally, may be specifically responsive to cues of rejection.

Another type of response was to self-silence or to act ingratiatingly, both of which led to depression and diminished satisfaction with the relationship because conflicts never got constructively resolved (Downey et al., 1998). Downey and Feldman (1996) found that RS could predict how rejection-sensitive men and women would interpret insensitive behavior before a relationship even began.

Downey and Feldman (1996) also found that RS undermined romantic relationships. Rejection sensitivity led people to feel insecure about their relationships and to exaggerate their partners' dissatisfaction and desire to leave. The authors did not expect, but indeed found, that men and women acted out rejection-sensitive behaviors differently. Rejection-sensitive men's behavior became jealous and controlling, which was a risk factor for physical abuse within the relationship. Rejection-sensitive women reacted with hostility and diminished emotional support. Rumination fostered women's beliefs that their partners had given up on their relationships, and they were helpless to do anything about it. The women retaliated with anger and hostility.

Similarly, in a sample of 154 minority, low-income girls, Purdie and Downey (2000) found that those rated by peers and teachers as being highly sensitive to rejection at Time 1 were more likely to have relationship difficulties with boyfriends at Time 2. Specifically, RS predicted insecurity about boyfriends' commitment, and a willingness to do things they knew were wrong to maintain the relationship. Rejection sensitivity also predicted more physical aggression and nonphysical hostility during romantic conflicts.

Dating violence also appeared in a sample of rejection-sensitive men (Downey, Feldman, & Ayduk, 2000). Rejection-sensitive men may attempt to prevent anticipated rejection by lowering their investment in relationships. Or, they may become highly invested in relationships and may search for the unconditionally supportive partner. These men had a low threshold for perceiving rejection and were at increased risk for violence in the face of negative or ambiguous behavior from their partners.

One manifestation of RS is jealousy. Another study found a significant positive correlation between jealousy and physical abuse in couples, and jealousy and intrusiveness in separated couples. Jealousy was also related to borderline personality, fearful attachments, and symptoms of trauma (Dutton, Van Grinkel, & Landolt, 1996).

Whereas RS may originally develop to protect children from rejection, it becomes highly dysfunctional in the adult world. Indeed, it may undermine a person's chances of maintaining a close and satisfying relationship (Downey & Feldman, 1996). This pattern can also maintain a person's maladaptive beliefs and shape the interactions in future relationships. Downey and Feldman's findings seem especially true for women.

Rejection sensitivity has also been associated with depression. In a six-month longitudinal study of college women, those high in RS became more depressed when they experienced a partner-initiated breakup but not following a self-initiated or mutually initiated breakup. In contrast, rejection-sensitive women were not more likely to become depressed when they failed to achieve an academic goal. It seems that vulnerability to depression is domain specific to an important interpersonal relationship (Ayduk, Downey, & Minji, 2001).

Rejection sensitivity has also been associated with body dysmorphic disorder (Phillips, Nierenberg, Brendel, & Fava, 1996) and atypical depression (Derecho, Wetzler, McGinn, & Sanderson, 1996). Atypical depression is characterized by extreme sensitivity and emotional reactivity to perceived rejection. This type of depression is more common in women than in men (Downey & Feldman, 1996).

Hatzenbueler, Nolen-Hoeksema, and Erickson (2008) examined the impact of minority stress on gay men following the loss of their partner or close friend to AIDS (acquired immune deficiency syndrome) at one, six, thirteen, and eighteen months post-bereavement. Minority stress refers to stresses that are unique to minority group members. It is most frequently used to describe experiences of ethnic minorities, but can also be applied to sexual minorities. This includes objective discrimination events, expectations of rejection, and internalization of negative societal attitudes. One consequence of this is that individuals expect rejection and become hypervigilant to rejection cues. Some outcomes also include HIV (human immunodeficiency virus)-risk behaviors, substance abuse, and psychological distress. As hypothesized, minority stress significantly increased HIV-risk behaviors, substance abuse, and depressive symptoms.

BETRAYAL TRAUMA

DePrince and Freyd (2002) describe the role of cognitive appraisals and their role in trauma. The three beliefs examined are fear, shattered assumptions, and betrayal. Since the 1980s, conceptualizations of trauma have focused on fear. It is part of the diagnostic criteria for PTSD and is the response most frequently examined in PTSD onset, maintenance, and recovery. When individuals experience a traumatic event, they organize their lives around beliefs that stressful events are largely unpredictable. This increases their fear and chronic hyperarousal.

According to shattered assumptions, trauma attacks three basic assumptions: the world is benevolent, the world is meaningful, and the self is worthy. Traumatic events shatter these three assumptions. This theory shifted away from fear and emotion to cognitive appraisal.

In contrast is betrayal trauma theory. Betrayal trauma refers to traumas in which people are betrayed or violated in some way by individuals or institutions that they depend on for survival (Freyd, Klest, & Allard, 2005). It suggests that conscious appraisals of betrayal may be inhibited at the time of the trauma and as long as the victim is dependent on the perpetrator. Both shattered assumptions and betrayal trauma theory focus on the cognitive aspects of trauma. But betrayal trauma theory also includes the relational issues and social context. Betrayal trauma theory also postulates that dissociation is an important mechanism for keeping away threatening information in the wake of trauma (DePrince & Freyd, 2002). Betrayal trauma may not threaten death or injury, but it can be damaging to well-being, relationships, self-concept, and beliefs about others and the world. These experiences represent a mismatch between what should be and what is. Traumas with high levels of betrayal are more likely to result in depression, anxiety, and other symptoms compared to traumas with high physical threat but not betrayal (e.g., car accidents) (Freyd et al., 2005).

Betrayal trauma theory also includes the sociopolitical context in which trauma occurs. Current trauma can be exacerbated by cultural and intergenerational trauma, such as trauma history in Indian/Native American populations. It also could include disbelief, minimizing, or otherwise devaluing the individual's experience—and this can be another type of betrayal (DePrince & Freyd, 2002).

RELIGIOSITY

The final section of this chapter examines how religious beliefs can be influenced by victimization. Religiosity encompasses hope, finding meaning in suffering, forgiveness, and such existential questions as why God allows suffering or why God betrayed the individual. All these beliefs have a powerful impact on health.

According to a Gallup Poll (1995), 96 percent of Americans believe in God or a universal spirit, 42 percent attend a religious or worship service at least weekly, 67 percent are members of a local religious body, and 60 percent feel that religion is "very important" in their lives. Social science research indicates that active participation in religious activity is good for most people (Myers, 2000). Conversely, when children lack "cultural or religious anchors," they are more likely to be traumatized by negative events (Perry, 2001, p. 32). Bennett (1993) observes the following: "Faith is a source of discipline and power and meaning in the lives of the faithful of any major religious creed. It is a potent force in human existence. A shared faith binds people together in ways that cannot be duplicated by other means" (p. 741).

Impact of Past Abuse on Religious Faith

Unfortunately, religious faith can be influenced by past abuse. In a large national sample, Finkelhor, Hotaling, Lewis, and Smith (1989) found that sexual abuse survivors were significantly more likely to describe themselves as "nonpractitioners" of religion than were non-abused people. Men were less likely to be religious if their abuse experience included intercourse, or if their fathers were poorly educated. Women were less likely to be religious if they were younger when the abuse began, not close to their mother, if they lived with their mother only, or they reported an inadequate sex education. In speculating about their findings, Finkelhor et al. offered two possible explanations. The sexually abused men and women may have felt "different" from their peers and therefore concluded that they were unacceptable to God. Or, they may have been reluctant to believe in God once they experienced the world as a malevolent place.

In a study of sexually, physically, or emotionally abused men, abuse was found to have a negative impact on religiosity. The sample was a large group of veterans ($N =$ 1,207), 43 percent of whom had been abused. Sexual abuse was related to spiritual injury and less stability of spiritual behaviors. Surprisingly, all types of abuse were related to more frequent prayer and more spiritual experiences. A multivariate analysis revealed an overall small effect size of abuse on religion. The presence of abuse was more important than the type of abuse in these outcomes (Lawson, Drebing, Berg, Vincellette, & Penk, 1998).

Type of spiritual coping predicted level of current distress in a sample of 101 CSA survivors (Gall, 2006). Those who coped with their current life stress by being angry with God tended to have more depression. In contrast, those who relied more on spiritual coping that reflected a positive attitude toward God as a source of comfort and support experienced lower levels of anger and depression. For example, self-directed, active surrender and passive deferral all contributed to anxious mood. The self-directed construct assesses the use of individual initiative with no help from God. Active surrender assesses the active handing over of control to God. And passive deferral assesses the passive waiting for God to control the situation. Spiritual discontent contributed to depression and is related to expressing anger and dissatisfaction with God in relation to the stressor. Spiritual discontent was related to more distress, while spiritual support was related to less distress. Active surrender coping and religious forgiveness coping, such as seeking God's help to relinquish negative emotion, was associated with less depression. Spiritual support refers to the individual's search for reassurance from God's love. The author concludes that spirituality has relevance in the lives of adult survivors of childhood abuse. This seemed to especially be the case for survivors who have suffered more severe forms of abuse and who have achieved a lesser sense of personal resolution regarding their childhood abuse history.

A study of Mormon women (Pritt, 1998) compared 115 sexually abused Mormon women to 70 non-abused Mormon women. The sexually abused women had a significantly more negative concept of God, had a lower sense of spiritual well-being, and were more pessimistic than were the non-abused women.

For abused women with severe dissociative disorder, religion offered some healing aspects and some drawbacks (Bowman, 2000). The advantages included social support and connection with a benevolent parent-God. Other positives included rules to govern behavior, prohibitions against suicide, status as a child of God, existential meaning for suffering, and hope for justice. On the downside, abused dissociative patients had difficulties with institutionalized male dominance of women, male images of God, and the valuing of silent, submissive females. Other negatives included the church's lack of comfort with female anger, encouragement of premature forgiveness of the abuser, and attributing difficulties to demons. Overall, whether religion was helpful or harmful for survivors depended on the overall health of the church the survivor attended.

In summary, childhood abuse often has a negative impact on religiosity. This effect is often minimized in social science research because social scientists themselves are often low in religiosity. But a growing body of research indicates that low levels of religiosity can impair health. In contrast, positive religious experiences can be the means for both physical and mental healing.

Religion and Health

A number of studies have found a relationship between religious belief and health. In a meta-analysis of forty-two studies, McCullough, Hoyt, Larson, Koenig, and Thoresen (2000) found that religious involvement was significantly associated with lower mortality. Those with high religious involvement were more likely to be alive at follow-up than those with little or no involvement. Although the effect size was small across studies (.10), the authors still felt their findings had high practical significance given the importance of the criterion variable (death) and the number of people exposed to religion.

In a survey of ninety-nine patients with chronic health conditions in a primary care setting, 80 percent indicated that they have a daily spiritual experiences (McCauley, Tarpley, Haaz, & Bartlett, 2008). These patients were all over the age of 50. Daily spiritual experiences were more common in women than men. African-American women had the highest amount; white men had the lowest amount. After adjusting for age, race, sex, and comorbid conditions, daily spiritual experiences were associated with increased energy and less depression. Most of the patients in this study identified themselves as Christian. Many of the daily spiritual experiences were specifically cognitive. They included being thankful for blessings or touched by the beauty of creation. They also included a desire to be closer to God; learning to accept others even when they are wrong; finding strength or comfort in religion; accepting help from God or others; feeling God's presence, love, or guidance; experiencing deep inner peace; and experiencing joy when connecting lifts them out of daily concerns.

In a sample of 1,011 female teens who had been sexually abused, a "higher degree of religiosity" protected them against the adverse effects of abuse (Chandy, Blum, & Resnick, 1996a). Degree of religiosity and ability to discuss problems with friends and family both proved to be protective of health in another study of teens (Chandy,

Blum, & Resnick, 1996b). A study of ninth- to twelfth-graders revealed that teens who attended church regularly and viewed religion as having meaning in their lives were less likely to be depressed and had significantly lower scores on the Beck Depression Inventory (Wright, Frost, & Wisecarver, 1993). Finally, teens who identified themselves as religious, who reported that religion was important to them, and who felt a higher spiritual interconnectedness with friends were less likely to participate in voluntary sexual activity (Holder et al., 2000).

A study of 18,129 men and 21,205 women from twenty-two European countries found that less frequent attendance at religious services was related to poorer health for both men and women (Nicholson, Rose, & Bobak, 2010). The relationship was weaker between health and religious belief. The researchers found that those who never attended religious services but who prayed every day had the poorest self-reported health. And those who attended regularly but who never prayed had the best health. Self-assessed religiosity had only a weak association with health. The authors concluded that the social aspect of religious involvement may be the protective element, and emphasized the importance of using multidimensional measures of religious involvement.

In a thirty-year longitudinal study of adults in Alameda County, California, weekly religious attendance was related to better health (Strawbridge, Shema, Cohen, & Kaplan, 2001). For both men and women, weekly religious attendance resulted in less depression. It was also significantly associated with quitting smoking, becoming physically active, increasing the number of personal relationships, and getting married. The authors described how frequent attendance at religious services increases longevity by improving poor health behaviors, improving mental health and social relationships, and maintaining health behaviors that are already good.

Religiosity was related to longevity for women in another study (Clark, Friedman, & Martin, 1999). Religious women in their early 40s had a 16 percent lower risk of premature mortality than did those who were less religious. They had healthier behaviors, were more positive about their futures, and were happier than their nonreligious peers. The religious women were more involved in organizations, smoked less, and drank less alcohol. (For the men, there was only a slight relationship between religiosity and longevity.)

In a related study, Oman, Thoresen, and McMahon (1999) studied the health impact of volunteer work. In a longitudinal study of 1,972 older adults, those who volunteered in two or more organizations had a 63 percent lower mortality rate than did those who did not volunteer. Volunteering was slightly more protective for those with high religious involvement and higher levels of perceived social support.

In a sample of 271 patients diagnosed with clinical depression, religious belief was associated with lower levels of hopelessness and was indirectly related to lower levels of depression. Interestingly, there was not a similar relationship between lowered depression and religious behavior (Murphy et al., 2000). In a study of 232 elderly patients who had open-heart surgery, those who did not participate in a support group or did not have religious faith were three times more likely to die than those who participated in a group or had religious support (Oxman, Freeman, & Manheimer, 1996).

Even if not directly religious, people who are able to find meaning in stressful life events had better health. In a study of bereaved HIV-positive men, those who engaged in cognitive processing were more likely to find meaning in loss. The men who found meaning had less rapid declines in CD4 T cell levels, and lower rates of AIDS-related mortality. These findings occurred independent of health status at baseline, health behaviors, and other potential confounds (Bower, Kemeny, Taylor, & Fahey, 1998). Meaning seemed to offer men in this study a certain amount of biological protection. Not only did their CD4 levels remain stable, but they were also less likely to die during the follow-up period (Taylor, Kemeny, Reed, Bower, & Gruenewald, 2000). These results suggest that meaning, control, and optimism not only preserve mental health but may be protective of physical health as well.

Negative Religious Coping

When life is difficult, or when tragedy strikes, people may respond by becoming angry with God. This reaction is understandable. Unfortunately, it can have a negative impact on health. In patients who had strokes or spinal-cord injuries, negative religious coping, particularly anger at God, was related to less participation in the activities of daily living. This effect was above and beyond the effects of depression, social support, and demographic variables (Fitchett, Rybarczyk, DeMarco, & Nicholas, 1999).

A study of 200 undergraduates had a similar finding (Exline, Yali, & Lobel, 1999). Undergraduates who could not forgive God for some event or life circumstance had more anxious and depressed mood, and anger at God's contribution to mood was independent of forgiving oneself or forgiving others. For those who believed in God, being able to forgive God for a specific event resulted in lower levels of anxious or depressed mood. Views of God also had an impact on their feelings of depression or anxiety. If they felt alienated from God, or felt that they could not trust God, they were more likely to be depressed or anxious. The authors concluded that their findings indicated that lack of forgiveness toward God is a potent predictor of negative mental health.

Forgiveness

Another aspect of religiosity is forgiveness. Forgiveness is a specific component of many religions but can also happen in a secular context. Forgiveness is also highly relevant to abuse survivors. It can involve their forgiving themselves, the perpetrator, others who knew and did not act, and even God. Forgiveness is important in the healing process, and it can be beneficial to health. In contrast, unforgiveness mars relationships not only with the offender but with others as well. It affects cognitions and beliefs as the person who is not forgiving tends to ruminate on the offense. Finally, unforgiveness can influence the autonomic nervous system and lead to heightened arousal.

In one study, when undergraduates mentally rehearsed hurtful memories and grudges, it altered their physiology. Unforgiving thoughts prompted significantly higher corrugator (brow) electromyogram, skin conductance, and heart rate. These elevations persisted even during the recovery periods. In contrast, forgiving thoughts prompted greater perceived control and lower physiological stress responses (Witvliet, Ludwig, & Vander Laan, 2001).

Another study examined the relationship between forgiveness and general health in a sample of 324 undergraduates. Failure to forgive oneself was related to higher scores for men and women in neuroticism, depression, and anxiety. Failure to forgive others was related to higher depression for men and women, social introversion for men, and social dysfunction for women (Maltby, Macaskill, & Day, 2001).

In a randomized trial with 259 community men and women, Harris, Thoresen, McCullough, and Larson (1999) assigned volunteers to treatment or control conditions. Those in the treatment condition underwent a cognitive-behavioral intervention focused on forgiveness. Those in the treatment group had significantly lower levels of stress, anger, and somatization and greater optimism. The authors concluded that this intervention could prove effective in reducing anger as a coping style, reducing perceived stress and physical health symptoms. This may help reduce the allostatic load on the immune system and cardiovascular functioning and make dramatic improvements in daily living.

Forgiveness can also help abuse survivors. In a small group ($N = 12$) of incest survivors, half were randomly assigned to participate in a forgiveness intervention, and the others were put on a waiting list. The intervention focused on cognitive aspects of the offense and how to heal from it. At the end of the fourteen-month intervention, women in the intervention group were better on all measures for having participated in the intervention. They were able to forgive their abusers, had higher self-esteem and hope, and lowered depression and anxiety. Although the sample was small, the results show potential promise as an area of intervention with adult survivors (Freedman & Enright, 1996).

Hope

Hope is also related to both religiosity and health. According to Snyder, Irving, and Anderson (1991), hope comprises optimism, self-efficacy, and resourcefulness. Individuals high in hope are more likely to make positive appraisals and to see situations as challenges rather than threats (Snyder et al., 1991). Those who saw situations as challenges used more diverse coping strategies that included rational action, perseverance, positive thinking, intellectual denial, drawing strength from adversity, and humor.

Giving people hope could be one of the major roles of religious faith. In a survey conducted by *Family Circle* magazine after the September 11 terrorist attacks on the United States, for example, religious people were more optimistic and hopeful about the future. People who identified themselves as religious were more likely to believe that good triumphs over evil, that everything happens for a reason, and that love conquers all compared with people who were not religious ("Americans redefine 'religious,'" 2002).

In a study of 434 adults, three markers of endothelial dysfunction were measured: e-selectin, p-selectin, and soluble intercellular adhesion molecule-1 (sICAM-1), and compared with measures of hopelessness and depression (Phuong, Dowd, Ranjit, House, & Kaplan, 2010). Endothelial dysfunction is an important predictor of atherosclerosis. Selectins are involved in the first step of leukocyte adhesion at the site of injury, and soluble adhesion molecules reflect inflammation of the vessel wall and predict cardiovascular events in healthy populations.

People who felt hopeless had high levels of s-ICAM-1, even after researchers adjusted for systolic pressure, chronic health problems, smoking, and BMI. The relationship between hopelessness and e-selectin was weaker and only significant after other variables were held constant. There was no relationship between hopelessness and p-selectin. Both s-ICAM-1 and e-selectin are activated by the proinflammatory cytokines. P-selectin is not. Depressive symptoms also showed a positive relation with the three markers of endothelial dysfunction. The authors concluded that hopelessness may play a more direct role in the earlier stages of atherosclerosis than depressive symptoms, and may reflect a more chronic and permanent attribute than depression that influences physiological pathways over time (Phuong et al., 2010).

SUMMARY

Research indicates that religiosity is good for health and increasing longevity. These positive effects may be due to lesser involvement with harmful behaviors (such as smoking, substance abuse, and high-risk sexual activity), better social connections, increased hope, forgiveness, and finding meaning in suffering. In contrast, anger at God can lead to worse health outcomes. This chapter has described the impact of adult survivors' beliefs about others and how these beliefs can influence their health. Chapters 8 and 9 describe how social relationships are changed by abuse and can have a beneficial, or harmful, effect on health.

References

"Americans redefine 'religious.'" (2002, January 15). *Family Circle,* p. 58.

Ayduk, O., Downey, G., & Minji, K. (2001). Rejection sensitivity and depressive symptoms in women. *Personality and Social Psychology Bulletin, 27*, 868–877.

Barnes, L. L., Mendes de Leon, C. F., Bienias, J. L., Wilson, R. S., Everson-Rose, S. A., & Evans, D. (2009). Hostility and change in cognitive function over time in older blacks and whites. *Psychosomatic Medicine, 71*, 652–658.

Beckham, J. C., Flood, A. M., Dennis, M. F., & Calhoun, P. S. (2009). Ambulatory cardiovascular activity and hostility ratings in women with chronic posttraumatic stress disorder. *Biological Psychiatry, 65*(3), 268–272.

Bennett, W. J. (1993). *The book of virtues*. New York: Simon & Schuster.

Bower, J. E., Kemeny, M. E., Taylor, S. E., & Fahey, J. L. (1998). Cognitive processing, discovery of meaning, CD4 decline, and AIDs-related mortality among bereaved, HIV-seropositive men. *Journal of Consulting and Clinical Psychology, 66*, 979–986.

Bowlby, J. (1969). *Attachment and loss: Vol. 1. Attachment.* New York: Basic Books.

Bowlby, J. (1982). *Attachment and loss: Vol. 1. Attachment.* (2nd ed.). New York: Basic Books.

Bowman, E. S. (2000). The assets and liabilities of conservative religious faith for persons with servere dissociative disorder. *Journal of Psychology and Christianity, 19*, 122–148.

Bretherton, I. (1992). The origins of attachment theory: John Bowlby and Mary Ainsworth. *Developmental Psychopathology, 28*, 759–775.

Butterfield, M. I., Forneris, C. A., Feldman, M. E., & Beckham, J. C. (2000). Hostility and functional health status in women veterans with and without posttraumatic stress disorder: A preliminary study. *Journal of Traumatic Stress, 13* 735–741.

Chandy, J. M., Blum, R. W., & Resnick, M. D. (1996a). Female adolescents with a history of sexual abuse: Risk, outcomes, and protective factors. *Journal of Interpersonal Violence, 11*, 503–518.

Chandy, J. M., Blum, R. W., & Resnick, M. D. (1996b). History of sexual abuse and parental alcohol misuse: Risk, outcomes, and protective factors in adolescents. *Child and Adolescent Social Work Journal, 13*, 411–432.

Clark, K. M., Friedman, H. S., & Martin, L. R. (1999). A longitudinal study of religiosity and mortality risk. *Journal of Health Psychology, 4*, 381–391.

DePrince, A. P., & Freyd, J. J. (2002). The harm of trauma: Pathological fear, shattered assumptions, or betrayal? In J. Kauffman (Ed.), *Loss of the assumptive world: A theory of traumatic loss* (pp. 71–82). New York: Brunner-Routledge.

Derecho, C. N., Wetzler, S., McGinn, L. K., & Sanderson, W. C. (1996). Atypical depression among psychiatric inpatients: Clinical features and personality traits. *Journal of Affective Disorders, 39*, 55–59.

Diong, S.-M., & Bishop, G. D. (1999). Anger expression, coping styles, and well-being. *Journal of Health Psychology, 4*(1), 81–96.

Downey, G., & Feldman, S. (1996). Implications of rejection sensitivity for intimate relationships. *Journal of Personality and Social Psychology, 70*, 1327–1343.

Downey, G., Feldman, S., & Ayduk, O. (2000). Rejection sensitivity and male violence in romantic relationships. *Personal Relationships, 7*, 45–61.

Downey, G., Freitas, A. L., Michaelis, B., & Khouri, H. (1998). The self-fufilling prophecy in close relationships: Rejection sensitivity and rejection by romantic partners. *Journal of Personality and Social Psychology, 75*, 545–560.

Dutton, D. G., Van Grinkel, C., & Landolt, M. A. (1996). Jealousy, intimate abusiveness, and intrusiveness. *Journal of Family Violence, 11*(4), 411–423.

Eisenberger, N. I. (2011). The neural basis of social pain: Findings and implications. In G. MacDonald & L. A. Jensen-Campbell (Eds.), *Social pain: Neuropsychological and health implications of loss and exclusions* (pp. 53–78). Washington, DC: American Psychological Association.

Exline, J. J., Yali, A. M., & Lobel, M. (1999). When God disappoints: Difficulty forgiving God and its role in negative emotion. *Journal of Health Psychology, 4*(3), 365–379.

Feldman, S., & Downey, G. (1994). Rejection sensitivity as a mediator of the impact of childhood exposure to family violence on adult attachment behavior. *Development and Psychopathology, 6*, 231–247.

Finkelhor, D., Hotaling, G. T., Lewis, I. A., & Smith, C. (1989). Sexual abuse and its relationship to later sexual satisfaction, marital status, religion, and attitudes. *Journal of Interpersonal Violence, 4*, 379–399.

Fitchett, G., Rybarczyk, B. D., DeMarco, G. A., & Nicholas, J. J. (1999). The role of religion in medical rehabilitation outcomes: A longitudinal study. *Rehabilitation Psychology, 44*, 333–353.

Freedman, S. R., & Enright, R. D. (1996). Forgiveness as an intervention goal with incest survivors. *Journal of Consulting and Clinical Psychology, 64*, 983–992.

Freyd, J. J., Klest, B., & Allard, C. B. (2005). Betrayal trauma: Relationship to physical health, psychological distress, and a written disclosure intervention. *Journal of Trauma and Dissociation, 6*(3), 83–104.

Gall, T. L. (2006). Spirituality and coping with life stress among adult survivors of childhood sexual abuse. *Child Abuse and Neglect, 30*, 829–844.

Gallup Poll. (1995). *Public opinion in 1995*. Wilmington, DE: Scholarly Resources.

Gauthier, L., Stollak, G., Messe, L., & Aronoff, J. (1996). Recall of childhood neglect and physical abuse as differential predictors of current psychological functioning. *Child Abuse and Neglect, 20*, 549–559.

Harris, A. H. S., Thoresen, C. E., McCullough, M. E., & Larson, D. B. (1999). Spiritually and religiously oriented health interventions. *Journal of Health Psychology, 4*(3), 413–433.

Harter, S. L., & Vanecek, R. J. (2000). Cognitive assumptions and long-term distress in survivors of childhood abuse, parental alcoholism, and dysfunctional family environments. *Cognitive Therapy and Research, 24*, 445–472.

Hatzenbueler, M. L., Nolen-Hoeksema, S., & Erickson, S. J. (2008). Minority stress predictors of HIV risk behavior, substance use, and depressive symptoms: Results from a prospective study of bereaved gay men. *Health Psychology, 27*(4), 455–462.

Holder, D. W., Durant, R. H., Harris, T. L., Daniel, J. H., Obeidallah, D., & Goodman, E. (2000). The association between adolescent spirituality and voluntary sexual activity. *Journal of Adolescent Health, 26*, 295–302.

Jackson, B., Kubzansky, L. D., Cohen, S., Jacobs, D. R., & Wright, R. J. (2007). Does harboring hostility hurt? Associations between hostility and pulmonary function in the Coronary Artery Risk Development in (Young) Adults (CARDIA) Study. *Health Psychology, 26*(3), 333–340.

Kiecolt-Glaser, J. K., & Newton, T. L. (2001). Marriage and health: His and hers. *Psychological Bulletin, 127*, 472–503.

Kubzansky, L. D., & Kawachi, I. (2000). Going to the heart of the matter: Do negative emotions cause coronary heart disease? *Journal of Psychosomatic Research, 48*, 323–337.

Kubzansky, L. D., Kawachi, I., & Sparrow, D. (1999). Socioeconomic status, hostility, and risk factor clustering in the normative aging study: Any help from the concept of allostatic load? *Annals of Behavioral Medicine, 21*(4), 330–338.

Lawson, R., Drebing, C., Berg, G., Vincellette, A., & Penk, W. (1998). The long-term impact of child abuse on religious behavior and spirituality in men. *Child Abuse and Neglect, 22*, 369–380.

Lewis, T. T., Everson-Rose, S. A., Karavolos, K., Janssen, I., Wesley, D., & Powell, L. H. (2009). Hostility is associated with visceral, but not subcutaneous, fat in middle-aged African American and white women. *Psychosomatic Medicine, 71*, 733–740.

Liem, J. H., & Boudewyn, A. C. (1999). Contextualizing the effects of childhood sexual abuse on adult self- and social functioning: An attachment theory perspective. *Child Abuse and Neglect, 23*, 1141–1157.

Low, C. A., Matthews, K. A., Kuller, L. H., & Edmundowicz, D. (2011). Psychosocial predictors of coronary artery calcification progression in postmenopausal women. *Psychosomatic Medicine, 73*, 789–794.

Low, C. A., Thurston, R. C., & Matthews, K. A. (2010). Psychosocial factors in the development of heart disease in women: Current research and future directions. *Psychosomatic Medicine, 72*(9), 842–854.

MacDonald, G., Borsook, T. K., & Spielmann, S. (2011). Defensive avoidance of social pain via perceptions of social threat and reward. In G. MacDonald & L. A. Jensen-Campbell (Eds.), *Social pain: Neuropsychological and health implications of loss and exclusion* (pp. 141–160). Washington, DC: American Psychological Association.

Maltby, J., Macaskill, A., & Day, L. (2001). Failure to forgive self and others: A replication and extension of the relationship between forgiveness, personality, social desirability, and general health. *Personality and Individual Differences, 30*, 881–885.

McCauley, J., Tarpley, M. J., Haaz, S., & Bartlett, S. J. (2008). Daily spiritual experiences of older adults with and without arthritis and the relationship to health outcomes. *Arthritis Care and Research, 59*(1), 122–128.

McCloskey, M. S., Kleabir, K., Berman, M. E., Chen, E. Y., & Coccaro, E. F. (2010). Unhealthy aggression: Intermittent explosive disorder and adverse physical health outcomes. *Health Psychology, 29*(3), 324–332.

McCullough, M. E., Hoyt, W. T., Larson, D. B., Koenig, H. G., & Thoresen, C. E. (2000). Religious involvement and mortality: A meta-analytic review. *Psychological Bulletin, 19*, 211–222.

Meyer, B., & Carver, C. S. (2000). Negative childhood accounts, sensitivity and pessimism: A study of avoidant personality disorder features in college students. *Journal of Personality Disorders, 14*, 233–248.

Mezick, E. J., Matthews, K. A., Hall, M., Kamarck, T. W., Strollo, P. J., Buysse, D. J., et al. (2010). Low life purpose and high hostility are related to an attenuated decline in nocturnal blood pressure. *Health Psychology, 29*(2), 196–204.

Murphy, P. E., Ciarrocchi, J. W., Piedmont, R. L., Cheston, S., Peyrot, M., & Fitchett, G. (2000). The relation of religious belief and practices, depression, and hopelessness in persons with clinical depression. *Journal of Consulting and Clinical Psychology, 68*, 1102–1106.

Myers, D. G. (2000). The funds, friends, and faith of happy people. *American Psychologist, 55*, 56–67.

Niaura, R., Banks, S. M., Ward, K. D., Stoney, C. M., Spiro, A., 3rd, Aldwin, C. M., et al. (2000). Hostility and the metabolic syndrome in older males: the normative aging study. *Psychosomatic Medicine, 62*(1), 7–16.

Nicholson, A., Rose, R., & Bobak, M. (2010). Associations between different dimensions of religious involvement and self-rated health in diverse European populations. *Health Psychology, 29*(2), 227–235.

Oman, D., Thoresen, C. E., & McMahon, K. (1999). Volunteerism and mortality among community-dwelling elderly. *Journal of Health Psychology, 4*, 310–316.

Oxman, T. E., Freeman, D. H., & Manheimer, E. D. (1996). Lack of social participation or religious strength and comfort as risk factors for death after cardiac surgery in the elderly. *Psychosomatic Medicine, 57*, 5–15.

Perry, B. D. (2001). The neuroarcheology of childhood maltreatment: The neurodevelopmental costs of adverse chlidhood events. In K. Franey, R. Geffner & R. Falconer (Eds.), *The cost of child maltreatment: Who pays? We all do.* (pp. 15–37). San Diego: Family Violence & Sexual Assault Institute.

Phillips, K. A., Nierenberg, A. A., Brendel, G., & Fava, M. (1996). Prevalence and clinical features of body dysmorphic disorder in atypical major depression. *Journal of Nervous and Mental Disease, 184*, 125–129.

Phuong, D., Dowd, J. B., Ranjit, N., House, J. S., & Kaplan, G. A. (2010). Hopelessness, depression, and early markers of endothelial dysfunction in U.S. adults. *Psychosomatic Medicine, 72*, 613–619.

Pritt, A. F. (1998). Spiritual correlates of reported sexual abuse among Mormon women. *Journal for the Scientific Study of Religion, 37*, 273–285.

Purdie, V., & Downey, G. (2000). Rejection sensitivity and adolescent girls' vulnerability to relationship-centered difficulties. *Journal of Personality Disorders, 6*, 109–116.

Raczek, S. W. (1992). Childhood abuse and personality disorders. *Journal of Personality Disorders*, 6, 109–116.

Raikkonen, K., Matthews, K. A., & Salomon, K. (2003). Hostility predicts metabolic syndrome risk factors in children and adolescents. *Health Psychology, 22*, 279–286.

Ranjit, N., Diez-Roux, A. V., Shea, S., Cushman, M., Seeman, T., Jackson, S. A., et al. (2007). Psychosocial factors and inflammation in the Multi-Ethnic Study of Atherosclerosis. *Archives of Internal Medicine, 167*, 174–181.

Roemmele, M., & Messman-Moore, T. L. (2011). Child abuse, early maladaptive schemas, and risky sexual behavior in college women. *Journal of Child Sexual Abuse, 20*, 264–283.

Roy, A. (2001). Childhood trauma and hostility as an adult: Relevance to suicidal behavior. *Psychiatry Research, 102*, 97–101.

Roy, A., Janal, M. N., & Roy, M. (2010). Childhood trauma and prevalence of cardiovascular disease in patients with Type 1 diabetes. *Psychosomatic Medicine, 72*, 833–838.

Smith, T. W. (1992). Hostility and health: Current status of a psychosomatic hypothesis. *Health Psychology, 11*, 139–150.

Smith, T. W., & Ruiz, J. M. (2002). Psychosocial influences on the development and course of coronary heart disease: Current status and implications for research and practice. *Journal of Consulting and Clinical Psychology, 70*, 548–568.

Smith, T. W., Uchino, B. N., Berg, C. A., Florsheim, P., Pearce, G., Hawkins, M., et al. (2007). Hostile personality traits and coronary artery calcification in middle-aged and older married couples: Different effects for self-reports versus spouse ratings. *Psychosomatic Medicine, 69*, 441–448.

Snyder, C. R., Irving, L. M., & Anderson, J. R. (1991). Hope and health. In C. R. Snyder & D. R. Forsyth (Eds.), *Handbook of social and clinical psychology: The health perspective* (pp. 285–305). Elmsford, NY: Pergamon.

Stewart, J. C., Janicki-Deverts, D., Muldoon, M. F., & Kamarck, T. W. (2008). Depressive symptoms moderate the influence of hostility on serum Interleukin-6 and C-reactive protein. *Psychosomatic Medicine, 70*, 197–204.

Strawbridge, W. J., Shema, S. J., Cohen, R. D., & Kaplan, G. A. (2001). Religious attendance increases survival by improving and maintaining good health behavior, mental health, and social relationships. *Annals of Behavioral Medicine, 23*, 68–74.

Suarez, E. C. (2003). Joint effect of hostility and severity of depressive symptoms on plasma Interleukin-6 concentration. *Psychosomatic Medicine, 65*, 523–527.

Suarez, E. C. (2006). Sex differences in the relation of depressive symptoms, hostility, and anger expression to indices of glucose metabolism in nondiabetic adults. *Health Psychology, 25*, 484–492.

Suarez, E. C., Lewis, J. G., Krishnan, R. R., & Young, K. H. (2004). Enhanced expression of cytokines and chemokines by blood monocytes to in vitro lipopolysaccharide stimulation are associated with hostility and severity of depressive symptoms in healthy women. *Psychoneuroendocrinology, 29*, 1119–1128.

Taylor, S. E., Kemeny, M. E., Reed, G. M., Bower, J. E., & Gruenewald, T. L. (2000). Psychological resources, positive illusions, and health. *American Psychologist, 55*, 99–109.

Toth, S. L., & Cicchetti, D. (1996). Patterns of relatedness, depressive symptomatology, and perceived competence in maltreated children. *Journal of Consulting and Clinical Psychology, 64*, 32–41.

Vahtera, J., Kivimaki, M., Uutela, A., & Pentti, J. (2000). Hostility and ill health: Role of psychosocial resources in two contexts of working life. *Journal of Psychosomatic Research, 48*, 89–98.

Whiffen, V. E., & MacIntosh, H. B. (2005). Mediators of the link between childhood sexual abuse and emotional distress: A critical review. *Trauma, Violence, and Abuse, 6*(1), 24–39.

Witvliet, C. V., Ludwig, T. E., & Vander Laan, K. L. (2001). Granting forgiveness or harboring grudges: Implications for emotion, physiology, and health. *Psychological Science, 121*, 117–123.

Wright, L. S., Frost, C. J., & Wisecarver, S. (1993). Church attendance, meaningfulness of religion, and depressive symptomatology among adolescents. *Journal of Youth and Adolescence, 22*, 559–568.

Chapter 8

Social Pathways I—Social Networks, Support, and Relationships

> Our human ability to form social relationships and get along with others is essential to our well-being. And social connection has profound consequences for health. Being well integrated socially reduces all-cause age-adjusted mortality by a factor of twofold, about as much as having low cholesterol levels or being a nonsmoker. (Spiegel, 1999, p. 1328)

Social bonds are essential to our health. Eisenberger (2011) argues that over the course of our evolutionary history, avoiding social rejection and staying socially connected increased our chances of survival. Being part of a group provided resources, protection, and safety. The pain response to social rejection was thought to be adaptive in that it promotes social bonding. The separation-distress panic/grief system appears to be situated in similar areas of the brain across all mammals, an area called the anterior cingulate cortex (Panksepp, 2011). Recent neuroscience research has found that our bodies process threats to our relationships as threats to our survival (Jenson-Campbell & MacDonald, 2011).

Rejection or negative social evaluation is associated with increases in stress hormones, increased cardiovascular response, and greater proinflammatory cytokines. Social losses, emotional pain, grief, or loneliness shares the same neural pathways as physical pain (Eisenberger, 2011; Panksepp, 2011). Social losses during childhood are especially noxious and can predispose people to chronically elevated psychic pain, which predisposes them to depression for the rest of their lives.

Social pain and physical pain share some other commonalities. Treatments that help with social pain, such as SSRI (selective serotinin reuptake inhibitor) antidepressants, also decrease physical pain. Social support also helps lessen physical pain. In addition, treatments for physical pain, such as acetaminophen, actually lessen emotional pain (Eisenberger, 2011). These studies suggest that augmented sensitivity to one type of pain is related to augmented sensitivity to the other.

Situations that prolong social pain may have even longer-lasting consequences. For example, when people are exposed to chronic rejection or social evaluation, it activates the catecholamine, HPA (hypothalamic-pituitary-adrenal), and inflammatory systems, which increases allostatic load. This, in turn, has negative implications for health (Dickerson, 2011).

Unfortunately, the ability to form and maintain relationships is also affected by past abuse. Briere and Elliot (1994) reported that adult survivors of sexual abuse may have fewer friends, less interpersonal trust, less satisfaction in their relationships, and more maladaptive interpersonal patterns than do their non-abused counterparts.

Chapter 7 described how past abuse can affect people's beliefs about others. This chapter addresses how those beliefs play out in actual relationships through social isolation, marital disruptions, and insecure attachments.

ATTACHMENT THEORY REVISITED

Attachment theory has a lot to say about the quality of social relationships. A central tenet of attachment theory is that early attachment relationships form the prototype for other relationships throughout life. Chapter 7 described the cognitive aspect of attachment: the internal working model. The internal working model refers to the beliefs people have about others. These beliefs form the basis of attachment.

Child abuse can disrupt the normal process of trust and lead to an insecure attachment with the primary caregiver (Roche, Runtz, & Hunter, 1999). Insecurely attached children are more likely to become insecurely attached adults (Styron & Janoff-Bulman, 1997). Insecure attachments can cause difficulties throughout the lives of abuse survivors.

Insecure Adult Attachments

People with insecure attachments tend to distort general perceptions of threat in their environments. MacDonald, Borsook, and Spielmann (2011) described two types of insecure attachments. The first is the anxious attachment. This occurs when people strongly crave acceptance and validation from others. They tend to be chronically rejection sensitive and are hypervigilant for signs of rejection. In a study of 224 ethnically diverse college women, path analysis indicated that attachment anxiety partially mediated the link between intimate partner violence and posttraumatic symptoms. A similar pattern was seen for adolescent or adult sexual victimization and posttraumatic symptoms (Sandberg, Suess, & Heaton, 2010). Attachment security was not related to sequelae of noninterpersonal types of trauma (such as a serious car accident).

The other type of attachment is the avoidant attachment (MacDonald et al., 2011). People high in avoidant attachment tend to not value relationships highly and claim to prefer independence and self-reliance. This is a defensive response to fears of rejection. By perceiving that social situations lack any potential for meaningful connection, they reduce the possibility of social pain. They appear to minimize what they stand to lose in the loss of a close relationship rather than acknowledge that they are afraid they will be unliked. In the Sandberg et al. study (2010) cited previously, attachment avoidance did not mediate the relationship between interpersonal trauma and posttraumatic symptoms.

Dysfunctional Interpersonal Styles

Another way to examine relationship quality among abuse survivors is to examine interpersonal style. Interpersonal style refers to the way people relate to others. Some child maltreatment researchers feel that interpersonal style may be the mechanism that contributes to long-term effects (Toth & Cicchetti, 1996). Becker-Lausen and Mallon-Kraft (1997) characterize relationship dysfunction as the "pandemic" outcome of childhood sexual abuse, but these styles may be related to other forms of child maltreatment as well. And they show similarities with the types of insecure adult attachments described earlier.

Avoidant or Intrusive Styles. Adult survivors may adopt one of two interpersonal styles: avoidant or intrusive. The avoidant style is characterized by low interdependency, self-disclosure, and warmth. People with the avoidant style have few interpersonal ties and few friends. They are less likely to be married or involved in relationships with others.

The intrusive style is at the opposite end of the spectrum. People with an intrusive style have extreme needs for closeness. They exhibit excessive self-disclosure and their relationships are smotheringly warm. The intrusive style is overly demanding and controlling. Both the avoidant and intrusive styles are dysfunctional and are likely to result in loneliness (Becker-Lausen & Mallon-Kraft, 1997).

Relationship of Interpersonal Style to Health. Interpersonal style is also related to health. According to Helgeson and Fritz (1999), a healthy person balances between what they call "agency" and "communion." Agency refers to focus on self; communion involves caring for others. People who are psychologically healthy have relationships with others while still caring for themselves. This balance between agency and communion is also related to good physical health.

The two interpersonal styles related to poor health are unmitigated agency and unmitigated communion. These are the extremes of agency and communion. Unmitigated agency is the focus on self to the exclusion of others. Unmitigated communion is a focus on others to the exclusion of self.

People with this style have poorer adjustment to heart disease (Helgeson, 1993) and diabetes (Helgeson & Fritz, 1996). This style has also been associated with poor health behavior and failure to adhere to doctors' instructions in cardiac patients (Helgeson, 1993). In a study of cardiac patients (Helgeson & Fritz, 1999), unmitigated agency and unmitigated communion both predicted poor health outcomes. Both styles were related to hostility, and unmitigated communion was related to depression.

Unmitigated communion is similar to the intrusive style that Becker-Lausen and Mallon-Kraft (1997) described. There are two primary behavioral domains of this style: an overinvolvement with others and a negative view of self (Helgeson & Fritz, 1998). Development of this style seems to be at least partly related to a dysfunctional family or a poor family environment (Helgeson & Fritz, 1998), and this style is also much more common among women (Fritz & Helgeson, 1998). The following paragraphs discuss some of the characteristics of healthy (communion) and unhealthy (unmitigated communion) relationships with others.

The communion style is related to reciprocal relationships, while a hallmark of unmitigated communion is lack of social support. Men and women with the unmitigated communion (UC) style give lots of social support but rarely receive it from others. And they often feel coerced into providing support. In attempted to explain why this is so, Helgeson and Fritz (1998) offered a couple of possible explanations. People with a UC style may use "support" as a way to exercise control over the relationship. They may want to create a situation in which others depend on them, but they do not depend on others. And always being the support provider boosts their self-esteem. They may also avoid receiving support because they fear others will not be able to meet their needs. Thus they lower their expectations to avoid disappointment and rejection.

Attachment Difficulties in Abuse Survivors

Dysfunctional interpersonal styles can also affect attachment. Attachment difficulties appear early, even among school-age children. In a study of children ages 7–13, Lynch and Cicchetti (1991) found that maltreated children had more problems in their relationships than did their nonmaltreated peers, including their relationships with their mothers, teachers, peers, and best friends. The insecure attachments these children had as infants and toddlers became the "maladaptive pathways" to poor relationships in later childhood.

Styron and Janoff-Bulman (1997) examined the relationships between childhood abuse and adult relationships in a study of 879 college students. Using hierarchical linear regression, they found that abused students were less secure in their adult relationships than were their non-abused counterparts. Abused students were also more depressed and more likely to use destructive behaviors, such as insulting or hitting, during conflict.

In a study of the attachment style of 112 incest survivors, 14 percent described themselves as secure, 13 percent as preoccupied, 16 percent as dismissing, and 58 percent as fearful. In contrast, the normative non-abused sample was 49 percent secure, 12 percent preoccupied, 18 percent dismissing, and 21 percent fearful. Adult attachment style was not related to measures of depression or posttraumatic stress disorder (PTSD), but it was related to personality disorders (Alexander, 1993).

Sagi, van Ijzendorn, Joels, and Scharf (2002) further differentiated these types of insecure relationships in their sample of Holocaust survivors. Those with a preoccupied attachment style were concerned that others didn't value them the same way they valued others, but they strived for intimacy. Those with a dismissing style valued their strong, independent self while dismissing the need for intimacy with others. Those with a fearful attachment style were afraid of intimacy and afraid of being hurt by others. This is similar to the avoidant style. In contrast to the foregoing three styles, those with a secure attachment style had a positive view of themselves and others. They took comfort in the closeness of relationships without worrying about rejection or loneliness.

Using data from the National Comorbidity Survey Replication, McWilliams and Bailey (2010) examined the relationship between adult attachment and fifteen health conditions. They found that those with avoidant attachments were more likely to have conditions defined primarily by pain, such as frequent or severe headaches, arthritis, back, or neck pain. Anxious attachments were related to conditions involving the cardiovascular system, such as stroke, heart attack, and high blood pressure. These findings were still significant even after controlling for history of depression, anxiety, and substance abuse.

Similar findings have been noted among those who experienced loss during childhood. Thirty college students whose parent died while they were children were compared with thirty-one college students who had not experienced this type of loss (Luecken, 2000). The author also looked specifically at the care the child received after the loss, based on Bowlby's notion that post-loss care is a critical factor in how well the child adjusts (cited in Luecken, 2000). The results indicated that those who had experienced a loss and who had poor family relations after the loss had the worst symptoms overall. The combination of loss and poor family relations was associated with higher levels of depression and lower levels of social support than the other three groups (loss-good family relations; no loss-good family relations; no loss-poor family relations).

In a follow-up to the Harvard Mastery of Stress Study conducted in the 1950s, 91 percent of men who reported an estranged relationship with parents at Time 1 developed diseases in midlife (Time 2) that included coronary artery disease, hypertension, duodenal ulcer, and alcoholism. In contrast, only 45 percent of the group who reported a close relationship with parents at Time 1 had developed these diseases (Russek & Schwartz, 1997).

Child sexual abuse (CSA) survivors were more likely than a matched comparison group to report high levels of dysfunction in their families of origin (Mullen, Martin, Anderson, Romans, & Herbison, 1994). They were more likely to have been living in non-nuclear families, had parents who were separated, and had frequent changes of residence. Both their mothers and their fathers were more likely to have poor mental health, and the relationship between mother and father was likely to be poor as well. Their parents were likely to be low on care but high on control. And they were likely to have also been beaten during childhood. Over all, "the unholy trio of physical abuse, emotional deprivation, and sexual abuse tended to be found together. Physical beating in childhood were [sic] reported nearly 10 times as frequently by CSA victims, with 15% reporting such abuse" (p. 43).

QUALITY OF CURRENT PRIMARY INTIMATE RELATIONSHIP

Adult survivors are also at increased risk for difficulties in their adult partnerships. In an Australian study, sexual abuse survivors were more likely to be involved with alcoholic partners and to report dissatisfaction with their relationships. Interestingly, sexual abuse had no significant impact on perceived level of social support, having someone to confide in, or currently being in a relationship (Fleming, Mullen, Sibthorpe, & Bammer, 1999). CSA survivors whose abuse included intercourse were significantly less likely to be living with a partner but were more likely to have cohabited before the age of 20 in Mullen et al.'s (1994) comparison of 248 CSA survivors with a matched group of non-abused controls. Fifty-five percent of abuse survivors indicated that they were highly satisfied with their current relationship compared to 72 percent of the control group. Forty-six percent of the abuse survivors indicated that they could confide in their partners, compared to 62 percent of the control group, and only 23 percent of abuse survivors said that they had meaningful conversation with their partners.

In Mullen et al.'s (1994) study, abuse survivors were more likely to report that their partners were low on care and high on control. Abuse survivors were more likely to report that their partners did not provide emotional support but that they did receive emotional support from peers. They were as likely as the control group to confide in friends, siblings, or their own children as the non-abused group. The study described the relationship abuse survivors had with their partners as follows:

> Those reporting CSA were more likely to evince a general instability in close relationships, with a marked tendency to evaluate their current partner negatively. . . . This dissatisfaction with the quality of their closest relationship could relate to the actual behavior of those with whom they have an intimate relationship or could have its origins primarily in the attitudes and expectations of the subjects. (p. 44)

A study of 1,196 men and women (676 abused/neglected, and 520 controls) found that male and female abuse survivors reported higher rates of cohabitation, walking out on partnerships, and divorce than did the controls. Abused or neglected females were less likely than female controls to have positive perceptions of their current romantic partners, or to be sexually faithful (Colman & Widom, 2004). Contrary to their expectations, there was no significant difference in rates of marriage among neglected, sexually abused, or physically abuse men and women compared to the control group. But male and female victims were more likely to report that they were not currently involved in a relationship. Physical abuse, sexual abuse, and neglect all increased the risk for divorce, with the highest likelihood among the sexually abused males. The impact of maltreatment on current relationships did not differ by type of abuse.

In a longitudinal study from Avon, UK ($N = 8{,}292$) (Roberts, O'Connor, Dunn, Golding, & the ALSPAC Study Team, 2004), women who had been sexually abused were more likely than non-abused women to be single parents, cohabitating in their current relationships, or stepparents. They also reported less satisfaction with their current partners. In a community sample of 159 married men and women, Belt and Abidin (1996) examined the relationship between early parenting and the quality of their current marital relationship. For women, verbal abuse in childhood predicted marital conflict, whereas a caring relationship with their parents predicted a positive marital relationship. A different pattern emerged for men. None of the abuse variables were related to their current marital relationship, but parental overprotectiveness was related to current marital conflict.

Disclosure of Abuse to Partners

One aspect of having a close relationship with a partner is disclosing a history of abuse. Del Castillo and Wright (2009) conducted an interpretive phenomenological analysis of seven women's experiences of disclosure of CSA to their romantic partners. Analysis revealed ten themes. Disclosure can lead to relief and social support. It can also lead to increased distress. A romantic partner's positive attitude toward disclosure is related to adult health and fewer symptoms. Some participants indicated that being an abuse survivor was integral to their identities. Since CSA was part of "me," it also was part of "us."

Survivors went through three phases as they disclosed their abuse history. The first phase was struggling over whether they should divulge their experiences. Participants feared that they would be rejected and abandoned, and that their experiences would be minimized or misunderstood.

The second phase related to the experience of disclosing. Some experienced shame after disclosing when partners responded negatively to their disclosure. But most felt it necessary to explain why they were the way they were with their partners. And when disclosing, they often provided a "rough outline" rather than filling in all the details. They also carefully monitored the reaction during the disclosure, and whether it would change or color their partners' perceptions of them.

The final phase was dealing with the aftereffects of disclosure. Some partners reacted negatively, but most participants indicated that at least one romantic partner's response was important in their healing.

Single- vs. Dual-Trauma Couples

The difficulties that survivors experience with partners can be compounded when both partners are abuse or trauma survivors. Nelson et al. (2002) compared the experiences of single-trauma couples, where only one member has a trauma history, and dual-trauma couples, where both partners have a trauma history that resulted in similar effects for each. They conducted focus groups with trauma therapists who provided an initial framework for understanding the differences.

In couples where both have a trauma history, each member may seek a relationship with someone who has similar problems and coping style. Problems such as depression, poor self-esteem, isolation, and other symptoms may provide a common ground in their relationship. The problems of each may contribute to relationship problems and vice versa. Prior characteristics of both may exacerbate the problems they face as a couple.

Some issues for single-trauma couples include the possible inability of the nontraumatized partner to empathize, or secrecy surrounding the event. When traumatized people will not share what happened, the nontraumatized partner may try to rescue, or may be required to assume the "parental role" (or assume responsibility for family functioning). The trauma may also spill out onto other family members—for example, the children become parentified or start acting out.

In dual-trauma couples, issues of power and control become intensified as the couple may become highly dependent on each other. Power and control become dichotomized such that one partner has most of the power. Highly conflicted relationship dynamics can emerge, including extreme pursuer-distancer, which becomes more rigid in dual-trauma couples.

Competition between partners may emerge as each claims to have had the "worst" experience or disputes who is the "least traumatized," or healthier, partner. Both may exhibit trauma symptoms, which exacerbate any relationship problems. Dual-trauma couples may also present as preoccupied-dismissing couples, where one cannot get over it and the other claims it does not affect him or her. These couples may present as single-trauma couples. The preoccupied partner may be attempting to rescue the dismissing partner—taking on the traumas of both. The dismissing partner may assume an overfunctioning or extremely responsible role—taking on all the housework or financial provision.

Divorce

Divorce is common in the general population, but even more so for abuse survivors. Women with a history of CSA were significantly more likely to be divorced or separated than were their non-abused counterparts (Fleming et al., 1999). Felitti (1991) also found increased marital instability and divorce among patients who had been sexually abused in his sample of patients from a health maintenance organization (HMO). Similarly, Finkelhor, Hotaling, Lewis, and Smith (1989) found that men and women who had been sexually abused reported significantly more marital disruptions than did their non-abused counterparts. This was especially true for those whose abuse experience involved intercourse or occurred at an older age.

SOCIAL ISOLATION

Social isolation is also more common for abuse survivors. In a sample of university women, those who had been sexually abused reported that they were lonelier and less likely to utilize social support than women who had not been sexually abused. Among the sexually abused women, half were in treatment and half were not. The women in treatment were lonelier than the women not in treatment. However, those in treatment had also experienced more severe abuse overall (Gibson & Hartshome,

1996).

Another study found that relationship problems were common in a sample of sexual abuse survivors recruited from a primary care practice. For example, 24 percent of abuse survivors indicated that they had problems keeping friends and partners compared with 7 percent of the non-abused group (Hulme, 2000). Approximately half the women in a community sample of CSA survivors described themselves as socially isolated (Teegan, 1999). A sample of women in treatment for chronic headaches had similar findings (Domino & Haber, 1987). In this study, 78 percent of women who were physically or sexually abused were socially isolated compared to 38 percent of the non-abused group.

A similar pattern of problems in social relationships was found in families who were maltreating their children. Gaudin, Polansky, Kilpatrick, and Shilton (1993) compared neglectful, low-income mothers with those who were low-income but not neglectful. There were striking differences between the groups. The neglectful mothers were significantly lonelier and more socially isolated, they reported more depression, and averaged more than twice the number of stressful life events in the previous year. Mothers in the neglect group reported fewer social ties and had more people critical of them in their social networks. The authors recommended that case workers address loneliness and isolation in these families to help them cope with significant life stresses related to poverty, lack of access to health care, housing, and other support services.

HEALING VIA RELATIONSHIPS

As the above-cited studies indicate, relationships can be challenging for abuse survivors. They can also be significant sources of healing. In a qualitative study of sixteen male survivors of sexual abuse and multiple other types of abuse, Kia-Keating, Sorsoli, and Grossman (2010) found that positive adaptations to sexual abuse included engaging in safe relationships, belonging to a community of others with shared experiences, learning healthy ways of managing relationships, and achieving acceptance. The study was designed to explore how male survivors of sexual abuse learned to establish long-term relationships, negotiate intimacy, and disclose emotions. The narratives described relational challenges and relational recovery, which included growth and recovery across the lifespan. In childhood, relational challenges included isolation, inability to connect with caregivers, and a lack of predictable support. As adults, they reported less isolation than in their childhood. Relational recovery included finding safe relationships (including relationships with pets and gentle adults). Belonging and helping others occurred when the men connected with a community, particularly when the others had experienced hardship and relational difficulties (Kia-Keating, Sorsoli, & Grossman, 2010).

In a sample of 956 young adults, the impact of attachment and social support in predicting psychopathology was examined (McLewin & Muller, 2006). This sample included 294 participants with a history of physical abuse. The researchers found that attachment security with current partners, particularly when characterized by a positive view of self, strongly predicted lower levels of psychopathology for both abused and non-abused subjects. Psychopathology included depression, anxiety, dissociation, post-sexual abuse trauma, sleep disturbances, and sexual problems. They found that view of self was a stronger predictor of psychological health than view of other or social support, regardless of abuse history. Among the various types of maltreatment, psychological abuse emerged as being the strongest predictor of adult psychopathology.

Relationships and Resilience

Relationships during childhood and adolescence can even protect children from abuse and neglect within their families. In the Isle of Wight study, a two-year age-cohort study, subjects were enrolled from 1953 to 1955 and recontacted when they were 44 to 45 years old (Collishaw et al., 2007); 367 participated in the follow-up study. About 10 percent of the sample reported repeated or severe child physical or sexual abuse. This group showed high rates of adult psychopathology including major depression, suicidal behavior, substance abuse, and PTSD. Childhood abuse was strongly associated with an excess of other family adversities including parental divorce and discord, maternal psychiatric disorder, and childhood separation from parents. However, a substantial minority reported no mental health problems in adult life. Resilience was related to perceived parental care, adolescent peer relationships, quality of adult love relationships, and personality style.

Another study of resilience had a sample of 676 children with documented cases of maltreatment in the years 1967 to 1971 (DuMont, Widom, & Czaja, 2007). They were contacted again in 1995. Resiliency was measured via multiple domains: graduating from high school, no psychiatric diagnosis, no substance-abuse diagnosis, no official arrests, no self-reported violent behavior, no employment problems, never homeless, socially active, and resilient overall. Being female increased resiliency in both adolescence and young adulthood. Growing up in a stable living situation tripled resiliency in adolescence but not adulthood. Stressful life events and a supportive partner promoted resiliency in young adulthood.

Impact of Relationships on Health

Positive connections with other people are good for us, which has been demonstrated in a number of studies. People who report a greater number of social ties have better physical and mental health, and lower mortality rates than do people with few social ties (Seeman, 1996). Social ties are related to cognitive function. The longitudinal MacArthur Study of Successful Aging found that those who reported more emotional support at baseline had better cognitive function seven and a half years later than did subjects with less emotional support (Seeman, Lusignolo, Albert, & Berkman, 2001). These findings held true even after controlling for health status and sociodemographic, behavioral, and psychological factors—all of which are related to cognitive aging.

There are three possible mechanisms for these findings. One is that social support protects against heart disease, hypertension, and depression, all of which have been linked to cognitive decline. Second, support leads to lower physical reactivity, and higher reactivity has been linked to cognitive decline. Finally, support may keep people socially involved, thereby protecting against cognitive decline.

People without good social support were less likely to participate in health-promoting activities. A study of more than 5,000 male and female college students from sixteen European countries found that low social support was related to lack of physical activity, irregular sleep hours, and not using a seat belt (Allgower, Wardle, & Steptoe, 2001). Supportive relationships increase adherence to blood pressure regimens and reduce the probability of risky health habits including poor nutrition, substance abuse, and inadequate sleep (Kiecolt-Glaser & Newton, 2001).

Barth, Schneider, and von Kanel (2010) conducted a systematic review and meta-analysis of prospective studies that examined the impact of social support on the development of coronary heart disease. They found that there was some evidence to support the hypothesis that low functional support increases the incidence of coronary heart disease; low structural support did not. In prognostic studies, low functional support negatively affected cardiac and all-cause mortality and increased disease progression in patients who already had coronary heart disease. Functional support refers to the aid and encouragement that is provided by the social network and it includes various forms of support, such as instrumental support (help getting tasks done), financial, informational, appraisal (help in evaluating a situation), and emotional (feelings of being loved) support. In contrast, the relationship between structural support and cardiac risk remains unclear. Structural support included the network surrounding the individual, the number of interactions, frequency of contact, membership in groups, and marital status. The authors concluded that the perception of social support is important for the development of coronary heart disease and should be evaluated in patients with coronary heart disease and addressed prospectively in currently healthy patients.

Health Effects of Marriage and Marital Strife

Of all social relationships, marriage appears to have the strongest effect on health—for better or for worse.

Positive Effects of Good Marriages. Marriage seems particularly protective of men's health. In a review of the literature on marriage and health, Kiecolt-Glaser and Newton (2001) found that being married reduced premature mortality by 500 percent for men. For women, marriage reduced premature mortality by only 50 percent. This sex difference may be due to women's have larger social networks outside marriage than do men.

Kiecolt-Glaser and Newton (2001) concluded that marital happiness contributes to global happiness far more than any other variable, even more than friendships and satisfaction with work. Similarly, Myers (2000) found that married people had the lowest rates of depression. The groups with the highest percentage of depressed people were (in descending order) those who were divorced twice, those who cohabitate, and those who have divorced once. (Note: same-sex couples were not mentioned in this report; cohabitating couples were reported to have high rates of depression and also intimate partner violence.)

Sbarra (2009) examined the relationship between C-reactive protein (CRP) and marital status for 838 men (mean age = 69.5 years). Minor elevations in CRP are a nonspecific marker of systemic inflammation and predict future cardiovascular disease. Married men had the lowest, even after controlling for other risk factors. The amount of risk that was reduced was comparable to the effects of normal blood pressure, nonsmoking, or a lower body mass index (BMI). For these men, remaining married in late adulthood provided unique and robust protection against elevated CRP. These effects were not moderated by emotional distress. This study focused on men because the protective effect of marriage on health is stronger for men than it is for women. Women's health is more responsive to variations in marital quality than men's.

In data from the Framingham Offspring Study, married men were half as likely to die during the follow-up period as unmarried men (Eaker, Sullivan, Kelly-Hayes, D'Agostino, & Benjamin, 2007). The Framingham Offspring Study is the second generation of data collection from the Framingham Heart Study, a major study of cardiovascular disease, now following the second and third generations of study participants. The results were more complex for women. Marital status alone was not enough to prolong life; however, aspects of how women handled marital conflict were. Women who "self-silenced" in conflicts were four times more likely to die compared with those who did not. The findings were true even after adjusting for systolic blood pressure, age, BMI, cigarette smoking, diabetes, and cholesterol.

Negative Effects of Marital Strife. While the effects of marriage on health are generally good, ongoing marital strife is not. In fact, it increases the risk of heart disease, particularly for women. A review of the literature revealed that high-stress marriages can neutralize or lessen the effectiveness of vaccines, slow wound healing, and increase the risk of infectious disease (Kiecolt-Glaser & Newton, 2001). Marital conflicts were reliably related to higher blood pressure and have obvious negative influences on hypertension and cardiovascular disease. Cardiovascular reactivity (CVR) is considered the link between interpersonal reactions such as hostility, social isolation, and dominance and the subsequent development of cardiovascular disease. Some of these changes include enduring changes in heart rate and blood pressure (Miller, Smith, Turner, Guijarro, & Hallet, 1996).

A thirteen-year longitudinal study of married women found that women with poor-quality marriages had higher rates of several markers for cardiovascular disease: low HDL cholesterol, high triglycerides, and higher BMI, blood pressure, depression and anger (Gallo et al., 2003). In a study from Sweden, Orth-Gomer et al. (2000) followed 292 women for five years after a myocardial infarction. They found that women with high levels of marital strife were nearly three times more likely to have another heart attack, or other coronary event, as women who were married but not distressed. This relationship held even after adjusting for age, estrogen levels, education, and smoking. These findings are consistent with findings from neuropsychology research that indicates that women may be particularly sensitive to the effects of social pain and show signs of being more physiologically vulnerable (Dickerson, 2011).

In a study of 300 married couples (average age = 54.4), participants completed four measures of hostility (Smith et al., 2007). The participants had no previously diagnosed coronary artery disease. The measures were self-reports and spouse ratings of angry hostility (a tendency to experience anger) and antagonism, that included argumentative, mistrusting, and cold interpersonal behavior. Self-reports of hostility and antagonism were not related to coronary artery calcification. But spouse ratings of the person were. These findings were true for the older, but not middle-age subjects. These effects were also independent other demographic and psychosocial characteristics including socioeconomic status (SES), marital satisfaction, age, and gender. They were also independent of exercise, smoking, and alcohol use. The authors concluded that hostility was related to asymptomatic coronary artery disease, but that self-reports likely underestimated this variable.

Possible Explanations for Sex Differences in Reacting to Marital Strife. Smith, Gallo, Goble, Ngu, and Stark (1998) examined sex differences in cardiovascular reactivity. In looking at sixty couples in agreement versus disagreement conditions, men had increased cardiovascular reactivity to achievement challenges and women had increased cardiovascular reactivity to disagreement. In other words, women in the study reacted to potential threats in their relationships and men reacted to potential threats to their competence or dominance.

Newton and Sanford (2003) examined gender differences in responses to conflict and the influence of marital conflict structure. Marital conflict structure is who desires and requests change versus who responds to the change request. They studied forty-one married couples and found that spouses whose behavior was the most negative had the most pronounced diastolic blood pressure activity, but only when they were requesting change in their spouses. The authors noted that their findings are relevant to an emerging theme in the literature regarding gender differences in the psychophysiology of marital interaction. Wives' physiological responses during marital conflict show greater elevations than do those of their husbands. Part of this effect could be due to gender differences in wanting spouses to change, with wives desiring more change. These findings could also partially explain the consistent finding that marriage confers fewer health benefits for wives than for their husbands. Because wives typically desire more marital change, they may be repeatedly in the higher arousal position of seeking change, which over time stresses the cardiovascular system.

SOCIAL INTEGRATION VS. SOCIAL ISOLATION

Much of what we know about the health effects of social relationships comes from studying its absence, in the form of social isolation and low social integration. In elderly men, low social integration was associated with increased fibrinogen, even after adjusting for smoking, alcohol consumption, physical activity, BMI, age, race and education (Loucks, Berkman, Cruenewald, & Seeman, 2005). There was no relation between social integration and fibrinogen for women. This study included 800 high-functioning men and women (ages 70–79) who were part of the MacArthur Successful Aging Study. The researchers calculated social integration using marital status, number of contacts with family and friends, frequency of religious service attendance, and participation in volunteer organizations. Fibrinogen is a soluble protein that aids in clotting. Because it increases the speed of platelet aggregation and clotting, a high level of fibrinogen is a risk factor for cardiovascular disease and predicts cardiac events and strokes.

In a review of the literature, Myers (2000) described how people with five or more friends were significantly happier than people who have fewer than five friends. Socially isolated individuals are at increased risk for dying prematurely. Those with smaller or less diverse social networks, lower perceived social support, and less frequent interactions had an increased risk of cardiovascular disease and mortality. Size of social network may not vary between lonely and nonlonely individuals, but lonely people are more likely to rate their interactions more negatively (Thurston & Kubzansky, 2009). In a review of six major studies, House, Landis, and Umberson (1988) noted that social isolation is comparable to smoking, high blood pressure, and lack of physical activity in terms of mortality risk.

Smith and Ruiz (2002) also found in their review that people who are socially isolated, and who have low levels of perceived social support, are at increased risk for heart disease. A thirteen-year longitudinal study found that people who were depressed and socially isolated were four times more likely to have a heart attack than patients who were not depressed or isolated (Pratt et al., 1996). Social isolation is particularly harmful for patients who already have heart disease (Smith & Ruiz, 2002).

Social support and social integration also decreased health-compromising behaviors in a study of 193 adults over 14 consecutive nights (Cohen & Lemay, 2007). Social integration refers to the broad range of social relationships including close relationships and more distant ones, such as fellow workers, students, and volunteers. Participants who had more diverse social networks and interacted with more people smoked less and drank less alcohol than people who had lower levels of social integration. Contrary to predictions, social integration did not affect the between-subjects analysis. On the within-subjects analysis, people with more social integration had more positive affect.

Social isolation exacerbates other conditions. In a ten-year longitudinal study of depression, Moos and Cronkite (1999) found that those at highest risk for a chronic course of depression were those who did not socialize with friends outside the home and frequently coped with stressors by avoiding others. Singles were also more likely to experience dissociative symptoms following a car accident (Fullerton et al., 2000). And in a study of psychiatric emergency room patients, being single was associated with a greater incidence of violence against others and greater likelihood of past hospitalization (Briere, Woo, McRae, Foltz, & Sitzman, 1997).

In a sample of 783 middle-aged and older adults, social isolation increased levels of coronary artery calcification. Calcification is a potential marker for early atherosclerosis. The researchers found that 49 percent of subjects had calcification. The risk was higher in participants with diabetes mellitus, and men had higher levels of calcification than women. Social isolation (measured as being single or widowed) was related to calcification, even after adjusting for age, sex, systolic blood pressure, blood glucose, and LDL cholesterol. In contrast, health behaviors, socioeconomic status, and depression were not related to calcification (Kop et al., 2005). The authors proposed several possible mechanisms for this effect. Social isolation increases rates of serum norepinephrine and cortisol, and elevated heart rate. Therefore, isolation could induce sustained sympathetic hyperresponsiveness, which may promote vascular injury. Social isolation may also increase the risk of high-risk health behaviors, such as smoking and maintaining a high-fat diet.

Sex Differences in the Effects of Social Isolation

There appears to be a sex difference for the effects of living alone. In a study of 4,424 men and 4,380 women in Augsberg, Germany (ages 35–74), there were 402 cases of Type 2 diabetes that developed over the 10.9-year study period (Meisinger, Kandler, & Ladwig, 2009). Incident Type 2 diabetes was associated with living alone for men but not for women in the sample. This association held even after controlling for age, family history of diabetes, hypertension, dyslipidemia, physical activity, alcohol intake, and BMI. Inclusion of depression and education in the model had no impact on the relationship between living alone and diabetes for women, but it actually strengthened the relationship for men. The authors speculated that living alone was related to low social support for men, and that this lack of social support augmented the experience of stress. The combination of increased sympathetic nervous system and HPA axis activity may have increased plasma glucose and impaired glucose tolerance while upregulating inflammatory markers, such as IL-6 and C-reactive protein. These mechanisms may contribute to vascular endothelial dysfunction, development of hypertension, insulin resistance, glucose intolerance, and finally Type 2 diabetes.

Women are not totally immune to the lack of social support, however. Loneliness has been significantly associated with incident coronary heart disease for women but not for men in a nineteen-year longitudinal study with a community sample of 3,003 men and women (Thurston & Kubzansky, 2009). Loneliness was operationally defined as the perceived discrepancy between actual and desired social support, and was associated with younger age, unmarried status, less exercise, lower cholesterol, fewer friends and relatives, and higher depression. The relationship held even after controlling for age, race, education, income, marital status, hypertension, diabetes, cholesterol, physical activity, smoking, alcohol use, blood pressure, and BMI. Some possible mechanisms include upregulation of the HPA and inflammatory systems in lonely people, both of which have been implicated in the development of coronary heart disease.

Loneliness has also been found to increase the risk of metabolic syndrome in middle-age and older adults (Whisman, 2010). The sample included 3,211 adults, ages 52 to 79, living in England. Loneliness was particularly associated with waist circumference. Metabolic syndrome represents perhaps another path by which loneliness can increase cardiovascular risk.

Loneliness has also been associated with a number of other health outcomes in another study of 8,688 older adults in England (Shankar, McMunn, Banks, & Steptoe, 2011). This study found that social isolation and loneliness were associated with a greater risk of being inactive, smoking, and multiple health-risk behaviors. Social isolation was positively associated with increased blood pressure, C-reactive protein, and fibrinogen. The authors concluded that loneliness and social isolation impacts health through indirect factors, such as health-risk behaviors, and directly through apparently biological processes, such as the upregulation of the stress system.

A study of elderly men found that fibrinogen levels fall with increasing levels of social integration (Loucks et al., 2005). Interestingly, they found this effect even after controlling for other cardiovascular risk factors, but it was true only for men, not for women. Low social support predicted to the progression to AIDS (acquired immune deficiency virus) in a seven-year follow-up of eighty-two gay men with HIV (Leserman et al., 2000). Faster progression to AIDS was associated with stressful life events, coping by denial, higher cortisol, and lower cumulative satisfaction with social support. Tobacco use, risky sexual behavior, age, or education was not related to AIDS. The risk of AIDS almost doubled for every 1.5-unit decrease in cumulative average support.

Social Support Buffers Stress

One of chief benefits of social relationships is their ability to help people weather the storms of life. Social relationships can help people deal with physical symptoms, medical procedures, or traumatic events. In a study of patients undergoing kidney dialysis, "family expectation" was strongly correlated with depression, hopelessness, illness intrusiveness, and quality of life. When patients perceived more support from their families and medical staff, they reported less hopelessness and more optimism. Patients who felt that their families had unrealistic expectations about their abilities (i.e., expecting them to be able to do more than they felt they could) were more depressed, and experienced more hopelessness, illness intrusiveness, and poorer quality of life (Hatchett, Friend, Symister, & Wadhwa, 1997).

Age predicted increased systolic and diastolic blood pressure in a study of 67 men and women with normal blood pressure (Uchino, Holt-Lunstad, Uno, Betancourt, & Garvey, 1999). But the level of social support moderated the effects of age on blood pressure. Those with low social support showed age-related increases in blood pressure. In contrast, those with high levels of social support showed no age-related increases. The authors did caution that since their sample was mostly white, their findings may have limited generalizability to other ethnic groups.

Lower social support was related to increased levels of two measures of platelet aggregation and coagulability—D-dimer and fibrinogen—before and after acute stress in a sample of sixty-three nonsmoking, medication-free men (Wirtz, Redwine, Ehlert, & von Kanel, 2009). In addition, norepinephrine levels were elevated for men with lower social support. The association between low social support and inflammation held even after controlling for BMI, greater arterial pressure, age, and norepinephrine levels. Increased coagulability is a risk factor for both stroke and acute coronary events. For example, for each standard deviation increase in fibrinogen, there was an 84 percent increase in the five-year risk of ischemic heart disease. The authors concluded that their findings indicated that low social support was related to increased coagulation activity before and after acute stress.

Women with menstrual pain reported more disruptions in their social networks the previous year than did women with less pain (Alonso & Coe, 2001). Women who reported the loss of three or more support people in the previous year had the highest levels of pain. In a study of patients with rheumatoid arthritis, those with less social support had greater levels of emotional distress. In contrast, those with greater amounts of social support were buffered from the negative impact of stress (Affleck, Tennen, Urrows, & Higgins, 1994).

Positive ties to others and purposeful engagement in life were both related to lower levels of inflammation in another study (Friedman, Hayney, Love, Singer, & Ryff, 2007). This sample included 135 women ages 61 to 91. Regression analysis showed that plasma IL-6 levels were lower in women scoring higher on positive relationships. These findings are consistent with studies showing that social integration and social support predict reduced morbidity and mortality. In women scoring higher on purpose in life, levels of sIL-6R were lower, even after controlling for demographic and health factors that could account for the relationship. The inflammatory actions of IL-6 are amplified by sIL-6R, which forms a complex with IL-6 that prolongs biological activity and acts on cells not normally responsive to IL-6. Both IL-6 and sIL-6R are biological factors linked to age-related health outcomes.

In a review, Salovey, Rothman, Detweiler, and Steward (2000) noted that social support is related to lower mortality and greater resistance to communicable diseases. There is lower prevalence of coronary heart disease and faster recovery following surgery. When faced with stress, those with few social resources are more vulnerable to illness and mood disorders than people with good support.

Social support can also lessen cardiovascular reactivity to acute psychosocial stress. To test this hypothesis, Uchino and Garvey (1997) asked twenty-eight men and twenty-one women to make a speech and randomly assigned subjects to support-available or no-support-available conditions. People who believed that there was support available had lower systolic and diastolic blood pressure than those who believed they had no support.

A study of high-risk teens admitted to a psychiatric hospital indicated that social support was an effective buffer in some circumstances. The teens in this study had experienced or witnessed high levels of violence both in their families and in their communities. Social support shielded these teens from some of the effects of family violence. It did not appear to ameliorate the negative impact of community violence, however (Muller, Goebel-Fabbri, Diamond, & Dinklage, 2000).

Relational capabilities also predicted how well a woman coped with rape as an adult. Women who were high in PTSD and depression were also high on the alienation scale, insecure-attachment scale, egocentricity scale, and social-insecurity scale. They had problems with assertiveness, sociability, submission, and intimacy and indicated that they were too responsible and too controlling. The authors speculated that women who scored high on these scales would have trouble initiating and maintaining gratifying and reciprocal relationships (Regehr & Marziali, 1999).

Social support appeared to be especially important for people with lower incomes. Low-income individuals with social support had better cardiovascular health (i.e., high-density lipoproteins and lower mean arterial pressure) and natural-killer-cell activity than did low-income people without support. These findings did not occur for subjects with higher incomes (Vitaliano et al., 2001). Schollgen, Huxhold, Schuz, and Tesch-Romer (2011) had a similar finding in their study of 2,485 adults, ages 40 to 85, in Germany. They found that psychological resources, such as optimistic beliefs and social support, were important for all groups regardless of income. But they seemed to have the strongest beneficial effect among participants with fewer years of education and lower income than among the more highly educated and those with higher incomes.

Ethnic Group Differences in Social Support

Social support is important but may not be experienced equally by all ethnic groups. Cooper, Ziegler, Nelesen, and Dimsdale (2009) examined the relationship between blood pressure and social support for black and white adults. They found that as perceived social support increased, nocturnal dipping of blood pressure increased, with its associated lower risk of cardiovascular disease—for whites only. For black adults, social support not only did not decrease blood pressure but actually increased risk.

One possible reason for these paradoxical outcomes could be the way that blacks and whites experience social support. For example, if blacks' social interactions include negative outcomes, such as conflict, criticism, and excessive demands, they are more likely to experience social strain than social support. These stressful interactions may have increased blood pressure, which increases the risk of cardiovascular problems. The authors noted that their findings suggest that researchers need to consider more textured ways of examining social support and its links to cardiovascular outcomes.

In summary, social relationships can have a substantial impact on health. When relationships are positive, they buffer stress and help people cope more effectively with life. On the other hand, marital strife and social isolation can both be harmful.

Why Social Support Is Sometimes Stressful

Throughout this chapter, I have described the importance of social support to health and why abuse survivors sometimes have difficulty getting the support they need. As the discussion of unmitigated communion suggests, simply having people in one's life does not guarantee support. For people with low personal resources, relationships with others can actually create more stress by increasing emotional burden and contagion of stress from others. People who are overburdened and overstressed may withdraw from others so that they do not have to provide support. Unfortunately, people who adopt this interpersonal strategy are often the ones who most need help from others and are least likely to get it.

To examine this idea, Riley and Eckenrode (1986) randomly selected 356 low-income women from a neighborhood health clinic in Boston. They measured social support, and "personal resources," which consisted of financial and psychological resources related to effective coping. As predicted, social support actually increased negative affect for women with low resources. These women were at much higher risk from the "contagion of stress" phenomenon. "The low-resource women, when faced with many stressful events happening to others, are more distressed because they are less able to give the material and emotional support expected of them" (Riley & Eckenrode, 1986, p. 777). They concluded that a large social network was beneficial for high-resource women but was actually harmful for low-resource women.

SUMMARY

The studies reviewed in this chapter indicate that social support is generally important for good health. People involved in stressful or unbalanced relationships have worse health outcomes than do people with good support. Unfortunately, as the research has demonstrated, past abuse can set up relationship difficulties for people, which can then lead to poor health outcomes. Chapters 9 and 10 describe three more extreme aspects of failed social relationships: poverty, homelessness, and revictimization.

References

Affleck, G., Tennen, H., Urrows, S., & Higgins, P. (1994). Person and contextual features of daily stress reactivity: Individual difference in relations of undesirable daily events with mood disturbance and chronic pain intensity. *Journal of Personality and Social Psychology, 66*, 329–340.

Alexander, P. (1993). The differential effects of abuse characteristics and attachment in the prediction of long-term effects of sexual abuse. *Journal of Interpersonal Violence, 8*, 346–362.

Allgower, A., Wardle, J., & Steptoe, A. (2001). Depressive symptoms, social support, and personal health behaviors in young men and women. *Health Psychology, 20*(3), 223–227.

Alonso, C., & Coe, C. L. (2001). Disruptions of social relationships accentuate the association between emotional distress and menstrual pain in young women. *Health Psychology, 20*, 411–416.

Barth, J., Schneider, S., & von Kanel, R. (2010). Lack of social support in the etiology and the prognosis of coronary heart disease: A systematic review and meta-analysis. *Psychosomatic Medicine, 72*, 229–238.

Becker-Lausen, E., & Mallon-Kraft, S. (1997). Pandemic outcomes: the intimacy variable. In G. K. Kantor & J. S. Jasinski (Eds.), *Out of darkness: Current perspective on family violence* (pp. 49–57). Newbury Park, CA: Sage.

Belt, W., & Abidin, R. R. (1996). The relation of childhood abuse and early parenting experiences to current marital quality in a nonclinical sample. *Child Abuse and Neglect, 20*, 1019–1030.

Briere, J. N., & Elliot, D. M. (1994). Immediated and long-term impacts of child sexual abuse. *The Future of Children, 4*, 54–69.

Briere, J. N., Woo, R., McRae, B., Foltz, J., & Sitzman, R. (1997). Lifetime victimization history, demographics, and clinical status in female psychiatric emergency room patients. *Journal of Nervous and Mental Disease, 185*, 95–101.

Cohen, S., & Lemay, E. P. (2007). Why would social networks be linked to affect and health practices? *Health Psychology, 26*(4), 410–417.

Collishaw, S., Pickles, A., Messer, J., Rutter, M., Shearer, C., & Maughan, B. (2007). Resilience to adult psychopathology following childhood maltreatment: Evidence from a community sample. *Child Abuse and Neglect, 31*, 211–229.

Colman, R. A., & Widom, C. S. (2004). Childhood abuse and neglect and adult intimate relationships: A prospective study. *Child Abuse and Neglect, 28*, 1133–1151.

Cooper, D. C., Ziegler, M. G., Nelesen, R. A., & Dimsdale, J. E. (2009). Racial differences in the impact of social support on nocturnal blood pressure. *Psychosomatic Medicine, 71*, 524–531.

Del Castillo, D., & Wright, M. O. (2009). The perils and possibilities in disclosing childhood sexual abuse to a romantic partner. *Journal of Child Sexual Abuse, 18*, 386–404.

Dickerson, S. S. (2011). Physiological responses to experiences of social pain. In G. MacDonald & L. A. Jensen-Campbell (Eds.), *Social pain: Neuropsychological and health implications of social loss and exclusion* (pp. 79–94). Washington, DC: American Psychological Association.

Domino, J. V., & Haber, J. D. (1987). Prior physical and sexual abuse in women with chronic headache: Clinical correlates. *Headache, 27*, 310–314.

DuMont, K. A., Widom, C. S., & Czaja, S. J. (2007). Predictors of resilience in abused and neglected children grown-up: The role of individual and neighborhood characteristics. *Child Abuse and Neglect, 31*, 255–274.

Eaker, E. D., Sullivan, L. M., Kelly-Hayes, M., D'Agostino, R. B., & Benjamin, E. J. (2007). Marital status, marital strain, and risk of coronary heart disease or total mortality: The Framingham Offspring Study. *Psychosomatic Medicine, 69*, 509–513.

Eisenberger, N. I. (2011). The neural basis of social pain: Findings and implications. In G. MacDonald & L. A. Jensen-Campbell (Eds.), *Social pain: Neuropsychological and health implications of loss and exclusions* (pp. 53–78). Washington, DC: American Psychological Association.

Felitti, V. J. (1991). Long-term medical consequences of incest, rape, and molestation. *Southern Medical Journal, 84*, 328–331.

Finkelhor, D., Hotaling, G. T., Lewis, I. A., & Smith, C. (1989). Sexual abuse and its relationship to later sexual satisfaction, marital status, religion, and attitudes. *Journal of Interpersonal Violence, 4*, 379–399.

Fleming, J., Mullen, P. E., Sibthorpe, B., & Bammer, G. (1999). The long-term impact of childhood sexual abuse in Australian women. *Child Abuse and Neglect, 23*, 145–159.

Friedman, E. M., Hayney, M., Love, G. D., Singer, B. H., & Ryff, C. D. (2007). Plasma interleukin-6 and soluble IL-6 receptors are associated with psychological well-being in aging women. *Health Psychology, 6*(3), 305–313.

Fritz, H. L., & Helgeson, V. S. (1998). Distinctions of unmitigated communion from communion: Self-neglect and over-involvement with others. *Journal of Personality and Social Psychology, 75*, 121–140.

Fullerton, C. S., Ursano, R. J., Epstein, R. S., Crowley, R., Vance, K. L., Kao, T.-C., et al. (2000). Peritraumatic dissociation following motor vehicles accidents. *Journal of Nervous and Mental Disease, 188*, 267–272.

Gallo, L. C., Troxel, W. M., Matthews, K. A., & Kuller, L. H. (2003). Marital status and quality in middle-aged women: Associations with levels and trajectories of cardiovascular risk factors. *Health Psychology*, *22*, 453–463.

Gaudin, J. M., Polansky, N. A., Kilpatrick, A. C., & Shilton, P. (1993). Loneliness, depression, stress, and social supports in neglectful families. *American Journal of Orthopsychiatry, 63*, 597–605.

Gibson, R. L., & Hartshome, T. S. (1996). Childhood sexual abuse and adult loneliness and network orientation. *Child Abuse and Neglect, 20*, 1087–1093.

Hatchett, L., Friend, R., Symister, P., & Wadhwa, N. (1997). Interpersonal expectations, social support, and adjustment to chronic illness. *Journal of Personality and Social Psychology, 73*, 560–573.

Helgeson, V. S. (1993). Implications of agency and communion for patient and spouse adjustment to a first coronary event. *Journal of Personality and Social Psychology, 64*, 807–816.

Helgeson, V. S., & Fritz, H. L. (1996). Implications of unmitigated communion and communion for adolescent adjustment to Type 1 diabetes. *Women's Health: Research on Gender, Behavior, and Policy, 2*, 163–188.

Helgeson, V. S., & Fritz, H. L. (1998). A theory of unmitigated communion. *Personality and Social Psychology Review, 2*, 173–183.

Helgeson, V. S., & Fritz, H. L. (1999). Unmitigated agency and unmitigated communion: Distinctions from agency and communion. *Research in Personality, 33*, 131–158.

House, J. S., Landis, K. R., & Umberson, D. (1988). Social relationships and health. *Science, 241*, 540–545.

Hulme, P. A. (2000). Symptomatology and health care utilization of women primary care patients who experienced childhood sexual abuse. *Child Abuse and Neglect, 24*, 1471–1484.

Jenson-Campbell, L. A., & MacDonald, G. (2011). Introduction: Experiencing the ache of social injuries—an integrative approach to understanding social pain. In G. MacDonald & L. A. Jensen-Campbell (Eds.), *Social pain: Neuropsychological and health implications of loss and exclusion* (pp. 3–8). Washington, DC: American Psychological Association.

Kia-Keating, M., Sorsoli, L., & Grossman, F. K. (2010). Relational challenges and recovery processes in male survivors of childhood sexual abuse. *Journal of Interpersonal Violence, 25*(4), 666–683.

Kiecolt-Glaser, J. K., & Newton, T. L. (2001). Marriage and health: His and hers. *Psychological Bulletin, 127*, 472–503.

Kop, W. J., Berman, D. S., Gransar, H., Wong, N. D., Miranda-Peats, R., White, M. D., & et al. (2005). Social networks and coronary artery calcification in asymptomatic individuals. *Psychosomatic Medicine, 67*, 343–352.

Leserman, J., Petitto, J. M., Golden, R. N., Gaynes, B. N., Gu, H., Perkins, D. O., et al. (2000). Impact of stressful life events, depression, social support, coping, and cortisol on progression to AIDS. *American Journal of Psychiatry, 157*, 1221–1228.

Loucks, E. B., Berkman, L. F., Cruenewald, T. L., & Seeman, T. E. (2005). Social integration is associated with fibrinogen concentration in elderly men. *Psychosomatic Medicine, 67*, 353–358.

Luecken, L. J. (2000). Attachment and loss experiences during childhood are associated with adult hostility, depression, and social support. *Journal of Psychosomatic Research, 49*, 85–91.

Lynch, M., & Cicchetti, D. (1991). Patterns of relatedness in maltreated and nonmaltreated children: Connections among multiple representational models. *Development and Psychopathology, 3*, 207–226.

MacDonald, G., Borsook, T. K., & Spielmann, S. (2011). Defensive avoidance of social pain via perceptions of social threat and reward. In G. MacDonald & L. A. Jensen-Campbell (Eds.), *Social pain: Neuropsychological and health implications of loss and exclusion* (pp. 141–160). Washington, DC: American Psychological Association.

McLewin, L. A., & Muller, R. T. (2006). Attachment and social support in the prediction of psychopathology among young adults with and without a history of physical maltreatment. *Child Abuse and Neglect, 30*, 171–191.

McWilliams, L. A., & Bailey, S. J. (2010). Associations between adult attachment ratings and health conditions: Evidence from the National Comorbidity Survey Replication. *Health Psychology, 29*(4), 446–453.

Meisinger, C., Kandler, U., & Ladwig, K.-H. (2009). Living alone is associated with an increased risk of Type 2 diabetes mellitus in men but not women from the general population: The MONICA/KORA Augsburg Cohort Study. *Psychosomatic Medicine, 71*, 784–788.

Miller, T. Q., Smith, T. W., Turner, C. W., Guijarro, M. L., & Hallet, A. J. (1996). A meta-analytic review of research on hostility and physical health. *Psychological Bulletin, 119*, 322–348.

Moos, R. H., & Cronkite, R. C. (1999). Symptom-based predictors of a 10-year chronic course of treated depression. *Journal of Nervous and Mental Disease, 187*, 360–368.

Mullen, P. E., Martin, J. L., Anderson, J. C., Romans, S. E., & Herbison, G. P. (1994). The effect of child sexual abuse on social, interpersonal, and sexual function in adult life. *British Journal of Psychiatry, 165*, 35–47.

Muller, R. T., Goebel-Fabbri, A. E., Diamond, T., & Dinklage, D. (2000). Social support and the relationship between family and community violence exposure and psychopathology among high-risk adolescents. *Child Abuse and Neglect, 4*, 449–464.

Myers, D. G. (2000). The funds, friends, and faith of happy people. *American Psychologist, 55*, 56–67.

Nelson, E. C., Heath, A. C., Madden, P. A. F., Cooper, M. L., Dinwiddie, S., Bucholz, K. K., et al. (2002). Association between self-reported childhood sexual abuse and adverse psychosocial outcomes. *Archives of General Psychiatry, 59*(2), 139–145.

Newton, T. L., & Sanford, J. M. (2003). Conflict structure moderates associations between cardiovascular reactivity and negative marital interaction. *Health Psychology, 22*(3), 270–278.

Orth-Gomer, K., Wamala, S.P., Horsten, M., Schenk-Gustafsson, K., Schneiderman, N., & Mittleman, M. A. (2000). Marital stress worsens prognosis in women with coronary heart disease: The Stockholm Female Coronary Risk Study. *Journal of the American Medical Association, 284*, 3008–3014.

Panksepp, J. (2011). The neurobiology of social loss in animals: Some keys to the puzzle of psychic pain in humans. In G. MacDonald & L. A. Jensen-Campbell (Eds.), *Social pain: Neuropsychological and health implications of loss and exclusion* (pp. 11–51). Washington, DC: American Psychological Association.

Pratt, L. A., Ford, D. E., Crum, R. M., Armenian, H. K., Gallo, J. J., & Eaton, W. W. (1996). Depression, psychotropic medication, and risk of myocardial infarction: Prospective data from the Baltimore ECA follow-up. *Circulation, 94*, 3123–3129.

Regehr, C., & Marziali, E. (1999). Response to sexual assault: A relational perspective. *Journal of Nervous and Mental Disease, 187*, 618–623.

Riley, D., & Eckenrode, J. (1986). Social ties: Subgroup differences in costs and benefits. *Journal of Personality and Social Psychology, 51*, 770–778.

Roberts, R., O'Connor, T., Dunn, J., Golding, J., & the ALSPAC Study Team. (2004). The effects of child sexual abuse in later family life: Mental health, parenting and adjustment of offspring. *Child Abuse and Neglect, 28*, 525–545.

Roche, D. N., Runtz, M. G., & Hunter, M. A. (1999). Adult attachment: A mediator between child sexual abuse and later psychological adjustment. *Journal of Interpersonal Violence, 14*, 184–207.

Russek, L. G., & Schwartz, G. E. (1997). Feelings of parental caring predict health status in midlife: A 35-year follow up of the Harvard Mastery of Stress Study. *Journal of Behavioral Medicine, 20*, 1–13.

Sagi, A., van Ijzendoorn, M., Joels, T., & Scharf, M. (2002). Disorganized reasoning in Holocaust survivors. *American Journal of Orthopsychiatry, 72*(2), 194–203.

Salovey, P., Rothman, A. J., Detweiler, J. B., & Steward, W. T. (2000). Emotional states and physical health. *American Psychologist, 55*, 110–121.

Sandberg, D. A., Suess, E. A., & Heaton, J. L. (2010). Attachment anxiety as a mediator of the relationship between interpersonal trauma and posttraumatic symptomatology among college women. *Journal of Interpersonal Violence, 25*(1), 33–49.

Sbarra, D. A. (2009). Marriage protects men from clinically meaningful elevations in C-reactive protein: Results from the National Social Life, Health, and Aging Project (NSHAP). *Psychosomatic Medicine, 71*, 828–835.

Schollgen, I., Huxhold, O., Schuz, B., & Tesch-Romer, C. (2011). Resources for health: Differential effects of optimistic self-beliefs and social support according to socioeconomic status. *Health Psychology, 30*(3), 326–335.

Seeman, T. E. (1996). Social ties and health. *Annals of Epidemiology, 6*, 442–451.

Seeman, T. E., Lusignolo, T. M., Albert, M., & Berkman, L. (2001). Social relationships, social support, and patterns of cognitive aging in healthy, high-functioning older adults: MacArthur Studies of Successful Aging. *Health Psychology, 20*(4), 243–255.

Shankar, A., McMunn, A., Banks, J., & Steptoe, A. (2011). Loneliness, social isolation, and behavioral and biological health indicators in older adults. *Health Psychology, 30*(4), 377–385.

Smith, T. W., Gallo, L. C., Goble, L., Ngu, L. Q., & Stark, K. A. (1998). Agency, communion, and cardiovascular reactivity. *Health Psychology, 17*, 537–545.

Smith, T. W., & Ruiz, J. M. (2002). Psychosocial influences on the development and course of coronary heart disease: Current status and implications for research and practice. *Journal of Consulting and Clinical Psychology, 70*, 548–568.

Smith, T. W., Uchino, B. N., Berg, C. A., Florsheim, P., Pearce, G., Hawkins, M., et al. (2007). Hostile personality traits and coronary artery calcification in middle-aged and older married couples: Different effects for self-reports versus spouse ratings. *Psychosomatic Medicine, 69*, 441–448.

Spiegel, D. (1999). Healing words: Emotional expression and disease outcome. *Journal of the American Medical Association, 281*, 1328–1329.

Styron, T., & Janoff-Bulman, R. (1997). Childhood attachment and abuse: Long-term effects on adult attachment, depression, and conflict resolution. *Child Abuse and Neglect, 21*, 1015–1023.

Teegan, F. (1999). Childhood sexual abuse and long-term sequelae. In A. Maercker, M. Schutzwohl & Z. Solomon (Eds.), *Posttraumatic stress disorder: A lifespan developmental perspective* (pp. 97–112). Seattle, WA: Hogrefe & Huber.

Thurston, R. C., & Kubzansky, L. D. (2009). Women, loneliness, and incident coronary heart disease. *Psychosomatic Medicine, 71*(8), 836–842.

Toth, S. L., & Cicchetti, D. (1996). Patterns of relatedness, depressive symptomatology, and perceived competence in maltreated children. *Journal of Consulting and Clinical Psychology, 64*, 32–41.

Uchino, B. N., & Garvey, T. S. (1997). The availability of social support reduces cardiovascular reactivity to acute psychological stress. *Journal of Behavioral Medicine, 20*, 15–27.

Uchino, B. N., Holt-Lunstad, J., Uno, D., Betancourt, R., & Garvey, T. S. (1999). Social support and age-related differences in cardiovascular function: An examination of potential mediators. *Annals of Behavioral Medicine, 21*(2), 135–142.

Vitaliano, P. P., Scanlan, J. M., Zhang, J., Savage, M. V., Brummett, B., Barefoot, J., et al. (2001).

Are the salutogenic effects of social supports modified by income? A test of an "added value hypothesis." *Health Psychology, 20*(3), 155–165.

Whisman, M. A. (2010). Loneliness and the metabolic syndrome in a population-based sample of middle-aged and older adults. *Health Psychology, 29*(5), 550–554.

Wirtz, P. H., Redwine, L. S., Ehlert, U., & von Kanel, R. (2009). Independent association between lower level of social support and higher coagulation activity before and after acute psychosocial stress. *Psychosomatic Medicine, 71*, 30–37.

Chapter 9

Social Pathways II—Poverty and Homelessness

In the previous chapter, I discussed the importance of social ties in the maintenance of health. Unfortunately, difficulties in social relationships are common in abuse survivors. Poverty, homelessness, and revictimization are all extreme forms of failed social relationships. Each of these is more common in abuse survivors than in the general population and each can affect health.

SOCIOECONOMIC STATUS AND POVERTY

Socioeconomic status (SES) is a broad term that encompasses a person's or family's economic or financial health. SES has been measured in a variety of ways. Income, level of education, and occupation are all indices of SES. Sometimes these indices are used singly; other times they are combined for an overall measure of SES (Ostrove & Adler, 1998).

The Potential Impact of Childhood Abuse on SES

Adult survivors of childhood abuse are affected in both their level of lifetime income and their educational attainment. For example, in a study of gay and bisexual men, men who were sexually abused were more likely to have a lower income and to have completed less education (Jinich et al., 1998). In a sample from primary care, sexually abused women were more likely to use public aid and to have lower educational and occupational status than were women without a history of sexual abuse (Hulme, 2000).

Mullen, Martin, Anderson, Romans, and Herbison (1994) also found that sexual abuse survivors had a lower income than did a matched comparison group. The abuse survivors who experienced the most serious abuse had the lowest lifetime income. Their jobs were also significantly more likely to include unskilled labor despite education levels that were comparable to those of the non-abused group. And a recent study of 172 men and women from Victoria, Australia, found that 64 percent of child sexual abuse (CSA) survivors were unemployed at the time of the study, and 61 percent had completed high school or had fewer years of education (O'Leary, Coohey, & Easton, 2010).

Why would child maltreatment be related to lower income in adults? To consider SES, we must take a step back and examine how abuse and neglect affects school performance, learning disabilities, and behavior problems. School performance in the early years can have a direct and substantial impact on future education attainment and, ultimately, earning potential.

Difficulties in School

Abuse survivors often have had trouble in school. These difficulties can set the stage for later educational difficulties. Unfortunately, learning and social difficulties are apparent as early as preschool in abused children. Miller (1999) noted that child abuse can cause subtle brain damage that might not manifest itself immediately. For example, the temporal, occipital, and parietal lobes of the cerebral cortex are responsible for skills related to reading, math, writing, reasoning, and categorizing. These areas develop between the ages of 5 and 8 and, if damaged, can have a detrimental cognitive processing speed, memory, and psychomotor skill (Teicher, 2002).

In their longitudinal study of 267 high-risk mother-infant pairs, Egeland, Sroufe, and Erickson (1983) found that neglected children had more difficulty performing tasks at both 42 and 56 months than either the control group or other maltreated children. By the time these children were early school age, they had deficits in cognitive performance, academic achievement, behavior in the classroom, and social interactions. By second grade, all the neglected children were in special-education programs (Egeland, 1991).

Maltreated children continue to have difficulties in grades kindergarten through 12. A study on the effects of child maltreatment on school performance (Kendall-Tackett & Eckenrode, 1996) found that neglected children performed more poorly than did their nonmaltreated counterparts, having lower grades, more suspensions, more disciplinary referrals, and more grade repetitions, even when controlling for gender of child and SES. Neglect alone, and in combination with physical or sexual abuse, was related to lower grades and more suspensions. The combination of abuse and neglect had a particularly strong effect on the number of disciplinary referrals and grade repetitions. Abused/neglected students in middle school had the highest number of grade repetitions. The number of disciplinary referrals continued to increase through senior high for both neglected and abused/neglected students. Interestingly, the academic performance of all subjects dropped during middle school. Neglect alone, and in combination with abuse, exacerbated a decline in academic performance that occurs as children enter middle school.

Social and behavior problems can also be a sign of difficulties in school. In a study of youth ages 10–16, Boney-McCoy and Finkelhor (1995) noted that boys and girls who experienced victimization were also likely to have trouble in school. For example, girls who had been physically abused had a threefold increase in having trouble with their teachers compared with non-abused girls. Similarly, nonparental family violence was also associated with trouble with teachers for girls but not for boys. On the other hand, boys who had experienced attempted kidnapping were more likely to have trouble with teachers, but this was not true for girls.

Unfortunately, behavior problems in school do not bode well for a child's future. Hyperactivity, attention problems, larger family size, and lower SES predicted later substance abuse in a longitudinal study of young adults (Reinherz, Giaconia, Hauf, Wasserman, & Paradis, 2000). Behavioral outbursts in elementary school were also predictive of later difficulties in employment. In a twenty-eight-year longitudinal study of personality and social development in Finland, low control of emotions and aggression at age 8 predicted long-term unemployment in adulthood (Kokko, Pulkkinen, & Puustinen, 2000).

Learning Difficulties in Adults

Adults with a history of abuse often have learning difficulties that continue into adulthood. Sexually abused women in primary care reported having problems with learning, memory loss, episodes of their "mind going blank," and problems keeping their mind on what they were doing (Hulme, 2000). Learning disabilities were three and a half times more likely in women who had been sexually abused than in the women who had not been abused in another primary care sample (Springs & Friedrich, 1992).

Posttraumatic stress disorder (PTSD) can also create problems in learning and memory. Bremner et al. (1995) compared men and women with PTSD due to severe physical or sexual abuse to a non-abused sample without PTSD matched for age, gender, race, years of education, and years of alcohol abuse. Subjects with abuse-related PTSD had deficits in immediate and delayed recall, and percent of retention on the Wechsler Memory Scale (Logical Subscale). Deficits in short-term memory for the abused group were significantly correlated with severity of the abuse. But there were no differences in IQ or visual memory between the two groups.

Similar findings came from a study of neurological soft signs in chronic PTSD. Neurological soft signs refer to subtle abnormalities of language, motor coordination, perception, and other functions of the central nervous system. In this study, Gurvits et al. (2000) studied twenty-one female survivors of sexual abuse (twelve with PTSD, nine without) and thirty-eight male Vietnam War veterans (twenty-three with PTSD, fifteen without). For both sexual abuse survivors and veterans, those with PTSD had higher numbers of neurological soft signs than did subjects without PTSD. This difference could not be explained by either alcoholism or head injury. Overall, subjects with PTSD had lower IQ scores and reported more neurodevelopmental problems and more childhood attention deficit/hyperactivity disorder (ADHD). When looking specifically at the women who had been sexually abused, those with PTSD were significantly more likely to have had ADHD, motor hyperactivity, and learning problems, to have repeated grades in school, or to be left handed. Interestingly, except in the case of ADHD, no one in the non-PTSD group had these problems.

Lack of success in school can also be predictive of subsequent PTSD when exposed to traumatizing events. Looking back in the lives of Vietnam veterans, Watson, Davenport, Anderson, Mendez, and Gearhart (1998) found that veterans who developed PTSD were absent and tardy more in school and had lower grade point averages in secondary school than did veterans who did not develop PTSD. Many of the subjects in both groups were hospitalized for chemical dependency. The authors did not examine prior history of trauma that perhaps anteceded the poor grades.

People with PTSD may also have difficulties maintaining a job. In a community sample from Canada, men and women reported that PTSD interfered with their jobs, and there appears to have been a dose effect. Those with full PTSD reported more interference than those with partial PTSD. Those with partial PTSD reported more interference than those with no symptoms (Stein, Walker, Hazen, & Forde, 1997). Another study found that people with anxiety disorders were less likely to be working full time, and were more likely to be receiving public assistance or disability payments (Warshaw et al., 1993).

SES and Health

Income disparities in health are well known. Poor health has been related to both low income and low educational attainment. The death rates in one study were twice as high in those without adequate family income as those who have adequate income. Morbidity is also higher in low-income people. For example, 26 percent of people with income below $14,000 reported limitation of activity due to chronic conditions compared with only 9.2 percent of people with a family income of $50,000 or more (Ernster & Colford, 1998). Because childhood abuse can influence SES, it is one more way abuse can influence health.

Jokela, Elovainio, Singh-Manoux, and Kivimaki (2009) examined data from the U.S. National Longitudinal Study of Youth, a study of 11,321 men and women enrolled in the study at ages 16 to 23 and followed to ages 40 to 47. They examined the relation between IQ, SES, and early death and found that low IQ predicted early mortality in the United States but that this association was largely explained by SES. But IQ did not explain the health disparities that varied by SES. The results were independent of age, sex, baseline health limitation, and parental education and were the same for white, black, and Hispanic participants.

In a study of 3,554 young adults, ages 33–45, family environment was related to later-life SES and educational attainment (Loucks, Almeida, Taylor, & Matthews, 2011). Women from families designated as "risky" were significantly less likely to be married and had lower educational attainment. Risky families were characterized by cold and unaffectionate interactions, with conflict, aggression, neglect, and low nurturance. High family risk was related to low HDL ("good") cholesterol, smoking, body mass index (BMI), diabetes, depressive symptoms, anger expression, low social support, and ten-year coronary heart disease risk. For men, there was a similar pattern. Men from high-risk families were less likely to be married, had lower educational attainment, and lower family income. They also smoked, had more depressive symptoms, lower social support, more unemployment, and higher ten-year risk for coronary heart disease. The authors concluded that a negative family environment was positively associated with ten-year cardiovascular risk in young adults.

Income can also affect the experience of pain. In a study of 250 women with chronic pain diagnoses (osteoarthritis, fibromyalgia, or both), conditions of economic hardship and daily financial worries both increased daily pain (Rios & Zautra, 2011). Women with the highest levels of economic hardship reported more pain in response to daily financial worries than their counterparts with little or no financial hardship. Unemployed women who had high levels of financial worry also had high levels of pain. The authors noted that participating in the world of work was a psychological resource. Women who worked were less vulnerable to the relation between worry about finances and pain.

Unhealthy Behavior. Some economic disparities in health can be explained by the presence of health-compromising behavior. Poorer people tend to smoke more, eat less healthfully, and live in less healthy environments. For example, approximately 41 percent of males with a high school education or less smoke compared with 26 percent of males with more than a high school education. A similar pattern was found for females. Males and females with a high school education or less were significantly less likely to exercise and more likely to be overweight, chronic drinkers, drink and drive, and be irregular in their use of seatbelts. Only hypertension was more common in males with greater than a high school education (Ernster & Colford, 1998).

In another recent study that examined the links between low SES and cardiovascular disease, both poverty and low educational attainment were associated with elevated C-reactive protein (Kershaw, Mezuk, Abdou, Rafferty, & Jackson, 2010). These relations were explained primarily by higher levels of smoking and lower levels of exercise. In the model examining the impact of education, poor diet also emerged as a significant mediator. These behaviors accounted for 88 percent of the total effect of education on C-reactive protein, and 56 percent of the total effect of poverty on C-reactive protein. The authors stated that policymakers must also recognize that people in a low-income neighborhood may have a harder time practicing healthy behavior. There are frequently more fast-food restaurants, liquor stores, and billboards advertising cigarettes in low-income neighborhoods. Physical exercise and smoking cessation programs, along with healthy eating programs, are effective short-term targets for alleviating disparities due to SES.

Neighborhood Makes a Difference. A study that examined the role of neighborhood context in the accumulation of biological risk factors and racial/ethnic and socioeconomic disparities found that non-Hispanic blacks, Hispanics, and people with low or moderate education had significantly higher number of biological risks than other referent groups (King, Morenoff, & House, 2011). These markers included systolic and diastolic blood pressure, resting heart rate, hemoglobin A, C-reactive protein, waist size, and total and HDL cholesterol. There were disparities between black and white, and Hispanic and white, in cumulative biological risks, but this difference disappeared after accounting for neighborhood context. People living in more affluent neighborhoods had a lower number of biological risk factors. The authors explained their findings in the context of allostatic load, or the cumulative effect of prolonged exposure to stressors.

A fifty-nine-year longitudinal study from Scotland found that IQ at age 11 was related to health at age 70, in part because it helped explain the relation between SES and health (Johnson, Corley, Starr, & Deary, 2011). Age-11 IQ was related to neighborhood quality, which was correlated more with education and social class than with health behaviors and outcomes. It was also related to BMI, constraints on activities of daily living, anxiety and depression, number of diseases, physical activity, and smoking. More deprived childhood environments were associated with more smoking, diseases, anxiety, depression, and constraints of daily living in old age. They noted that childhood IQ may contribute directly to one's ability to obtain education and a safe and well-remunerated job. In turn, higher SES confers access to good environments with lower pollution and crime and better social services and support, which could reduce the amount of psychosocial stress.

Social Stratification and Cardiac Risk Factors. Where you fall on the social hierarchy also has an impact on your cardiovascular health. If men or women perceive that they have low social status—because of education, ethnicity, vocation, or income level—it raises risk of cardiovascular disease via several physiological mechanisms. Perceived social status also involves negative appraisals of what others think of them and triggers the inflammatory response. Unfortunately, there are discernible, physical sequelae associated with various measures of social status, socioeconomic status, and perceived discrimination.

Education, Income, and Inflammation. Friedman and Herd (2010) investigated the links between income, education, and three measures of inflammation (IL-6, C-reactive protein, and fibrinogen) using data from the MIDUS Study. The sample was 704 middle-age men and women from a population-based study. In multivariate analyses, only low income was related to increased inflammatory proteins. The inclusion of IL-6 in the equation eliminated the relation between C-reactive protein and fibrinogen to income. The authors noted that education is related to inflammation only because higher education lowers the likelihood of low income. These findings are not explained by demographic characteristics, health status, or health behavior. Further, the effects of C-reactive protein and fibrinogen are mediated by IL-6. IL-6 is an important driver of C-reactive protein and fibrinogen and so may not have an independent relationship with income or education. The authors concluded that inflammation may be an important mediator between social position and health outcomes.

In another study using the MIDUS data (Morozink, Friedman, Coe, & Ryff, 2010), greater educational attainment predicted lower levels of IL-6 independent of age and gender. This relationship was attenuated by health behaviors, BMI, waist-to-hip ratio, and chronic illnesses. Psychological well-being interacted with education and was particularly important for people with lower levels of education: Those with lower education but high psychological well-being had lower levels of IL-6. Elevated IL-6 levels predicted health problems ranging from cardiovascular disease to osteoporosis to Alzheimer's. The factors of well-being included autonomy, environmental mastery, personal growth, positive relations with others, purpose in life, and self-acceptance. Personal growth seemed particularly related to lower levels of IL-6.

Childhood IQ was also related to midlife inflammatory markers in a study from the United Kingdom (Calvin, Batty, Lowe, & Deary, 2011). This study included a sample of 9,377 men and women born in the United Kingdom in 1958. Inflammatory markers were collected at age 45. These were compared with cognitive tests at age 50 and IQ measured during childhood. Higher childhood intelligence test scores were significantly related to C-reactive protein, D-dimer, fibrinogen, and VWF antigen at age 45. Early life factors, including parental SES, accounted for 24–44 percent of these associations. Accounting for health behaviors, such as smoking, blood pressure, and BMI, largely attenuated the effects. The relationship between childhood intelligence and inflammatory markers in midlife is largely explained by health behaviors.

Another study examined the relationship between childhood IQ and current cardiovascular risk in 1,053 men and women from Scotland who were part of the Lothian Birth Cohort 1936 (Luciano, Marioni, Gow, Starr, & Deary, 2009). The researchers were interested in understanding the relationship between blood inflammatory markers, particularly C-reactive protein and fibrinogen, and cognitive ability in later life. The results indicated that there was a relationship between later cognitive ability and inflammation, with higher levels of C-reactive and fibrinogen protein related to lower cognitive ability. This association could be explained by childhood IQ, cardiovascular risk factors, or both. They indicated that lower IQ in childhood predicts later-life levels of inflammation.

Subjective Social Status. Subjective social status can also impact your health. If you feel that you are at or near the bottom, the effect is often negative. Low parental education level predicted metabolic and cardiovascular risk factors in 758 black and white high school students. This study tried to elucidate the physiological mechanisms by which social inequalities translate into health disparities among people with low income. Hyperinsulemia and insulin resistance are both related to diabetes and cardiovascular disease. Insulin is sensitive to signals along the HPA (hypothalamic-pituitary-adrenal) axis, and low social status appears to dysregulate the HPA axis. The authors hypothesized that cortisol and insulin are the primary hormonal factors regulating carbohydrate metabolism, inflammation, cholesterol metabolism, and adiposity, and that the chronic stress of low social status dysregulated these processes (Goodman, McEwen, Huang, Dolan, & Adler, 2005).

Low-status students had higher insulin levels, higher glucose, greater insulin resistance, higher LDL and lower HDL cholesterol, higher waist circumference, and higher BMI than high-status students (Goodman et al., 2005). However, low social status was not related to cortisol, fibrinogen, glycosylated hemoglobin, or triglycerides in the adjusted analysis. The authors concluded that low parental education was associated with multiple metabolic risks, suggesting an intergenerational transfer of risks for cardiovascular disease.

In a longitudinal study of 1,167 black and white adolescents, blacks and lower-SES youths had higher BMI and increased insulin resistance (Goodman, Daniels, & Dolan, 2007). Lower parental education, but not household income, was related to higher baseline insulin resistance and worsening insulin resistance over time. This effect was more pronounced for obese adolescents. They concluded that insulin resistance was especially difficult for obese teens from families with low parental education. These effects were independent of ethnicity.

Low SES was also related to increased sympathetic nervous system activity in a study of 672 participants, ages 18–30 (Janicki-Deverts et al., 2007). In this study, twelve-hour, overnight urine samples were analyzed for the catecholamines: norepinphrine and epinephrine. Participants also completed questionnaires that assessed demographic variables, health behavior, and psychosocial variables (such as perceived discrimination, negative support, and depression). The researchers measured SES by income, education, and occupation. Regardless of which measure of SES they used, those with higher SES had lower catacholamines. This effect was independent of race, age, and gender and was similar for blacks and whites. Two factors that mediated the effects were depressive symptoms and smoking.

Subjective social status was also examined in a community sample of 981 adults (ages = 30–54) (Manuck, Phillips, Gianaros, Flory, & Muldoon, 2010). The researchers were interested in the relation between subjective SES and metabolic syndrome. People who perceived themselves has having lower subjective SES had a larger waist circumference, increased blood pressure, increased serum triglycerides, higher fasting-insulin levels, higher insulin resistance, and lower HDL cholesterol. Subjective SES was also related to smoking and level of physical activity, but these behaviors did not appreciably reduce the associations between subjective SES and metabolic syndrome. The authors noted that a portion of subjective SES could contribute to disease via psychological stress.

Low social status was associated with vascular inflammation in a sample of 121 white and African-American men and women (Hong, Nelesen, Krohn, Mills, & Dimsdale, 2006). In this sample, researchers measured soluble intercellular adhesion molecule (sICAM) and endothelin-1 (ET-1). Both are measures of vascular inflammation and are correlated with elevated blood pressure. ICAM-1 is a membrane-bound adhesion molecule that if elevated in the vascular endothelium could lead to atherosclerosis. ET-1 is a vasoconstrictor peptide that is implicated in hypertension and vascular disease. Men and women in the lowest social class had the highest levels of sICAM and ET-1. Social status was calculated based on measures of occupation and education. These findings were independent of hypertension status and ethnicity, but were related to gender and health behaviors.

Low status also reflected affected level of C-reactive protein in a three-year longitudinal study of 188 middle-age and older adults, ages 52–70 (McDade, Hawkley, & Cacioppo, 2006). C-reactive protein (CRP) is an acute-phase protein that is produced in response to proinflammatory cytokines, such IL-1, IL-6, and TNF-α. Even slight elevations of C-reactive protein are predictive of cardiovascular disease. In this sample, African Americans, women, and those with lower education had the highest levels of CRP. However, ethnic-group differences disappeared once health behaviors were factored in. Waist circumference, latency to sleep, smoking, and perceived stress were independently associated with increased CRP. Men and women who took longer to get to sleep had higher levels of C-reactive protein. The authors concluded that psychosocial stress and health behaviors are both important determinants of systemic inflammation and increased cardiac risk.

Socioeconomic status also affects stress-hormone levels. Low SES was associated with higher basal cortisol levels and catecholamines in a sample of 193 black and white adults (Cohen, Doyle, & Baum, 2006). Elevated catecholamines are associated with several cardiac risk factors including increased blood pressure and heart rate, and abnormal cardiac rhythms, including ventricular arrhythmias. Cortisol is also a risk factor for cardiovascular disease and diabetes, partly because it facilitates central adiposity. The relationship between SES and cortisol and catecholamine levels was graded and independent of race, age, gender, and BMI. Low SES was associated with a higher likelihood of smoking and not eating breakfast and having a less diverse social network. These social variables appear to mediate the link between SES and norephinephrine, ephinephrine, and cortisol.

Chronic discrimination was related to coronary artery calcification in middle-age African-American women (Lewis et al., 2006). In this study, 181 middle-age African-American women were assessed once a year for five years. Discrimination was assessed at each time point, and coronary artery calcification was assessed at the fifth visit. The researchers found that chronic exposure to discrimination was significantly associated with coronary artery calcification, even after controlling for demographics, standard cardiac risk factors (total cholesterol, HDL cholesterol, systolic blood pressure, treatment for hypertension, and smoking), and BMI. Recent discrimination was only marginally associated with coronary artery calcification, and multiple forms of discrimination were more powerfully associated than racial discrimination alone. These effects were independent of both depression and hostility, so they could not be attributed to overall negative affect.

A study of forty-four women examined the impact of induced social status (Mendelson, Thurston, & Kubzansky, 2008). They randomly assigned women to either subordinate or dominant positions. The outcome variables were psychological distress and systolic and diastolic blood pressure. As predicted, induced lower social status produced increased negative affect and systolic blood pressure. The authors noted that their findings have implications for understanding the effects of SES.

Unemployment Impacts Health. Employment status has also been related to health. Men and women classified as "unable to work" because of long-term physical or mental disability had the highest relative risk for death (Sorlie, Backlund, & Keller, 1995). Similarly, Ostrove and Adler (1998) found that SES and labor-force participation predicted health, particularly for men: Employed men were in better health than those who were not. Within each labor-force group, health increases with increasing levels of income and education. For women, the relationship was more complex. There was an interaction between labor-force participation, income, and education in their impact on health. Both SES and labor-force participation were significantly related to self-rated health.

Summary

When combined with the effects of depression, PTSD, substance abuse, and smoking, SES is a powerful predictor of health status in abuse survivors. Abusive experiences and their sequelae may have already altered the immune and cardiovascular systems in such a way that there was a negative effect. Combine this with the effects of poverty and the mix is truly deadly. The following section describes the health impact of being at the very bottom of the economic food chain: the impact of abuse on homelessness.

HOMELESSNESS

A substantial percentage of homeless people have experienced violence or trauma. Women, in particular, seem to be especially vulnerable to homelessness due to physical or sexual abuse. These studies are discussed below.

History of Adverse Childhood Experiences in Homeless Men and Women

In a study of 7,222 homeless men and women with serious mental illness, 59 percent had been physically, sexually, or emotionally abused before age 18. When considering a subgroup of this sample that had three or more symptoms of conduct disorder, 72 percent had experienced parental abuse (Desai, Lam, & Rosenheck, 2000).

In another study, 144 adults were randomly sampled from three groups: currently homeless, previously (but not currently) homeless, and never-homeless poor (Toro et al., 1995). Homeless men and women were more likely to be recent victims of domestic violence, and men were significantly more likely to have been physically abused as children. The currently homeless were twice as likely as the never homeless to have a lifetime diagnosis of substance abuse. The currently homeless also had higher levels of self-reported psychological distress. Depression in this population may be due, in part, to the many traumas homeless people face both before and during their homelessness (Toro et al., 1995). A study comparing 220 homeless and 216 low-income housed mothers also showed high amounts of violence: 66 percent reported severe physical abuse in childhood, 42 percent reported childhood sexual abuse, and 61 percent reported severe violence by a male partner (Browne & Bassuk, 1997).

In a study of twenty homeless women, 33 percent had been battered, 50 percent had been physically abused as children, and 33 percent had been sexually abused (Redmond & Brackman, 1990). In a large sample of respondents in emergency shelters, researchers found twice as much sexual abuse and almost twice as much physical abuse among the homeless as among a comparison group of housed respondents on public assistance (Shinn, Knickman, & Weitzman, 1991).

Adverse childhood experiences also increased the risk of homelessness when previously homeless people were compared with a group whose members had never been homeless. Lack of parental care and physical abuse sharply increased the risk of homelessness. Sexual abuse was associated with a nonsignificant trend in homelessness. The combination of lack of care and either physical or sexual abuse dramatically increased the risk of homelessness compared to women who had had neither of these types of experiences (Herman, Susser, & Link, 1997).

Another study compared social support, adult victimization, and quality of childhood environment for low-income-housed and homeless women (Ingram, Corning, & Schmidt, 1996). In this study, the homeless women experienced significantly more types of aggressive sexual behavior than did the housed women. Forty-five percent of homeless women had been raped compared to (a still high) 33 percent of housed women. There were no significant differences in criminal victimization or sexual harassment, but the homeless women reported more problems at home growing up than did the housed women. For both groups, level of victimization was positively correlated with level of distress.

Even when comparing homeless women to women at risk for homelessness, the impact of past abuse is apparent. The homeless women experienced significantly more physical and sexual abuse. In addition, they reported more mental illness, more instability of employment and housing, more drug and alcohol problems, and fewer skills in interacting with others (Wagner & Perrine, 1994). In a study of periodically homeless, severely mentally ill women, the rate of violent assault and rape was high: 97 percent had been battered or raped. The risk of recurrent abuse was also high (Goodman, Dutton, & Harris, 1995). The authors concluded that the risk was so high as to make these horrific experiences seem almost normative.

Teens and Homelessness

Homelessness may begin during the teen years. A qualitative study of twenty-eight homeless youths found that family environment and abuse experiences were related to their homelessness (Ferguson, 2009). This study sought to address a limitation of previous studies that focused only on one type of abuse given the high occurrence of multiple types of abuse in the households of currently homeless youth. A comparative analysis was used to analyze transcripts. Themes that emerged included home instability, abandonment, and caregiver substance abuse. There was little structure provided by the parents as they themselves were struggling with mental illness, substance abuse, or homelessness. Many of the teens had experienced repeated incidents of abandonment by multiple caregivers. The youths described having little control over their environments. The study participants reported verbal, emotional, physical, and sexual abuse. Abuse-related subthemes included abuse in the family, caregiver abuse, rejection, and deprecation by caregivers. Deprecation included being told that they were "fat" or "stupid." The authors urged that practitioners address the multiple types of abuse present in the lives of homeless individuals rather than focusing on one specific type.

A qualitative study of 302 homeless young people (ages 12–20) were asked about their reasons for leaving home (Mallet & Rosenthal, 2009). Of the total, 103 cited a parent or stepparent's physical violence as the reason for leaving home. Females were more likely to be targeted by mothers, while males were more likely to be targeted by stepmothers. Reasons for the violent behavior included maternal personality characteristics (including substance abuse), issues with blended families, and the young people's own behavior. Most of the stories indicated that maternal violence was a common experience rather than a one-time occurrence. The majority did not attempt to return home again.

In a study of homeless and runaway adolescents, Whitbeck, Hoyt, and Ackley (1997) found that both teens and their parents reported significantly lower levels of parental monitoring and warmth and supportiveness and higher levels of parental rejection than did a comparison group of nonrunaway teens. Based on parental report, 33 percent of boys and 30 percent of girls had been hit with an object, 16 percent of boys and 10 percent of girls had been beaten with fists, and 23 percent of boys and 19 percent of girls had been threatened with a weapon. For sexual abuse, 18 percent of girls had been approached sexually by a caretaker and 15 percent had been sexually abused.

Bassuk and Rosenberg (1988) concluded that family violence creates social isolation that makes people more vulnerable to homelessness. Fragmentation of social networks and disruptions in familial supports were more common for women than for men (Milburn & D'Ercole, 1991). For example, foster care and other forms of separation from families were more common among homeless than among domiciled women. And for both women and men, high rates of childhood separation and lifetime physical or sexual assault were common.

Health Implications of Homelessness

There are many health problems associated with homelessness, including hunger and malnutrition, exposure to inclement weather, lack of medical care, lack of access to routine hygiene, and increased risk of physical injury. Homeless mentally ill veterans had significantly higher mortality rates than the U.S. general population. The rates were even higher for veterans who had medical problems at the beginning of the study, or who had a history of hospitalization for alcohol abuse (Kasprow & Rosenheck, 2000).

Homeless women are at increased risk for contracting HIV (human immunodeficiency virus) and other sexually transmitted diseases and are less likely to take precautions or seek medical care. In a study of 621 homeless women, women who received more social support, had more knowledge about AIDS (acquired immune deficiency syndrome), and used more problem-solving coping were more likely to be tested for AIDS and to return to receive the results of the test. Low self-esteem and self-worth and lack of social networks were common in this population. However, greater self-esteem and social support had significant indirect effects on HIV testing and return for results (Nyamathi, Stein, & Swanson, 2000).

Homeless persons are also at increased risk for substance abuse. McCarty, Argeriou, Huebner, and Lubran (1991) reported that substance abuse and homelessness have a bidirectional relationship: Substance abuse led to homelessness and homelessness led to substance abuse. Overall, they found that 30–40 percent of homeless people abuse alcohol, and 10–15 percent abuse drugs. The rates of alcohol abuse were higher among older men and American Indian men. Homeless alcoholics were twice as likely to suffer liver disease, seizure disorders, injuries, traumas, and nutritional deficiencies. They also had higher rates of drug abuse, mental illness, hypertension, pulmonary disease, and arterial disease.

Summary

A history of childhood abuse increases the risk of homelessness. Health problems for homeless people are myriad and include malnutrition, substance abuse, and increased risk of sexually transmitted diseases (STDs) and trauma.

Chapter 10 describes research that examines the relationship between a final type of social-network failure—revictimization, past abuse, and health.

References

Bassuk, E. L., & Rosenberg, L. (1988). Why does family homelessness occur? A case-control study. *American Journal of Public Health, 78*, 783–788.

Boney-McCoy, S., & Finkelhor, D. (1995). Psychological sequelae of violent victimization in a national youth sample. *Journal of Consulting and Clinical Psychology, 63*, 726–736.

Bremner, J. D., Randall, P., Scott, T. M., Capelli, S., R., D., McCarthy, G., & Charney, D. S. (1995). Deficits in short-term memory in adult survivors of childhood abuse. *Psychiatry Research, 59*, 97–107.

Browne, A., & Bassuk, S. S. (1997). Intimate violence in the lives of homeless and poor housed women: Prevalence and patterns in an ethnically diverse sample. *American Journal of Orthopsychiatry, 67*, 261–278.

Calvin, C. M., Batty, G. D., Lowe, G. D. O., & Deary, I. J. (2011). Childhood intelligence and midlife inflammatory and hemostatic biomarkers: The National Child Development Study (1958) Cohort. *Health Psychology, 30*(6), 710–718.

Cohen, S., Doyle, W. J., & Baum, A. (2006). Socioeconomic status is associated with stress hormones. *Psychosomatic Medicine, 68*, 414–420.

Desai, R. A., Lam, J., & Rosenheck, R. A. (2000). Childhood risk factors for criminal justice involvement in a sample of homeless people with serious mental illness. *Journal of Nervous and Mental Disease, 188*, 324–332.

Egeland, B. (1991). A longitudinal study of high-risk families: Issues and findings. In R. H. Starr & D. A. Wolfe (Eds.), *The effects of child abuse and neglect: Issues and research* (pp. 33–56). New York: Guilford Press.

Egeland, B., Sroufe, L. A., & Erickson, M. (1983). The developmental consequences of different patterns of maltreatment. *Child Abuse and Neglect, 7*, 459–469.

Ernster, V., & Colford, J. M. (1998). Host and disease: Influence of demographic and socioeconomic factors. In A. S. Fauci, E. Braunwald, K. J. Isselbacher, J. D. Wilson, J. Martin, D. L. Kasper, et al. (Eds.), *Harrison's principles of internal medicine* (14th ed.) (pp. 14–18). New York: McGraw-Hill.

Ferguson, K. M. (2009). Exploring family environment characteristics and multiple abuse experiences among homeless youth. *Journal of Interpersonal Violence, 24*(11), 1875–1891.

Friedman, E. M., & Herd, P. (2010). Income, education, and inflammation: Differential associations in a national probability sample (the MIDUS study). *Psychosomatic Medicine, 2*, 290–300.

Goodman, E., Daniëls, S. R., & Dolan, L. M. (2007). Socioeconomic disparities in insulin resistance: Results from the Princeton School District Study. *Psychosomatic Medicine, 69*, 61–67.

Goodman, E., McEwen, B. S., Huang, B., Dolan, L. M., & Adler, N. E. (2005). Social inequalities in biomarkers of cardiovascular risk in adolescence. *Psychosomatic Medicine, 67*, 9–15.

Goodman, L. A., Dutton, M. A., & Harris, M. (1995). Episodically homeless women with serious mental illness: Prevalence of physical and sexual assault. *American Journal of Orthopsychiatry, 65*, 468–478.

Gurvitz, T. V., Gilbertson, M. W., Lasko, N. B., Tarhan, A. S., Simeon, D., Macklin, M. L., et al. (2000). Neurologic soft signs in chronic posttraumatic stress disorder. *Archives of General Psychiatry, 7*, 181–186.

Herman, D. B., Susser, E. S., & Link, B. L. (1997). Adverse childhood experiences: Are they risk factors for adult homelessness? *American Journal of Public Health, 87*, 249–255.

Hong, S., Nelesen, R. A., Krohn, P. L., Mills, P. J., & Dimsdale, J. E. (2006). The association of social status and blood pressure with markers of vascular inflammation. *Psychosomatic Medicine, 68*, 517–523.

Hulme, P. A. (2000). Symptomatology and health care utilization of women primary care patients who experienced childhood sexual abuse. *Child Abuse and Neglect, 24*, 1471–1484.

Ingram, K. M., Corning, A. F., & Schmidt, L. D. (1996). The relationship of victimization experiences to psychological well-being among homeless women and low-income housed women. *Journal of Counseling Psychology, 43*, 218–227.

Janicki-Deverts, D., Cohen, S., Adler, N. E., Schwartz, J. E., Matthews, K. A., & Seeman, T. E. (2007). Socioeconomic status is related to urinary catecholamines in the Coronary Artery Risk Development in Young Adults (CARDIA) Study. *Psychosomatic Medicine, 69*, 514–520.

Jinich, S., Paul, J. P., Stall, R., Acree, M., Kegeles, S., Hoff, C., et al. (1998). Childhood sexual abuse and HIV risk-taking behavior among gay and bisexual men. *AIDS and Behavior, 2*, 41–51.

Johnson, W., Corley, J., Starr, J. M., & Deary, I. J. (2011). Psychological and physical health at age 70 in the Lothian Birth Cohort 1936: Links with early life IQ, SES, and current cognitive function and neighborhood environment. *Health Psychology, 30*(1), 1–11.

Jokela, M., Elovainio, M., Singh-Manoux, A., & Kivimaki, M. (2009). IQ, socioeconomic status, and early death: The U.S. National Longitudinal Survey of Youth. *Psychosomatic Medicine, 71*, 322–328.

Kasprow, W. J., & Rosenheck, R. (2000). Mortality among homeless and nonhomeless mentally ill veterans. *Journal of Nervous and Mental Disease, 188*, 141–147.

Kendall-Tackett, K. A., & Eckenrode, J. (1996). The effects of neglect on academic achievement and disciplinary problems: A developmental approach. *Child Abuse and Neglect, 20*, 161–169.

Kershaw, K. N., Mezuk, B., Abdou, C. M., Rafferty, J. A., & Jackson, J. S. (2010). Socioeconomic position, health behaviors, and C-reactive protein: A moderated-mediation analysis. *Health Psychology, 29*(3), 307–316.

King, K. E., Morenoff, J. D., & House, J. S. (2011). Neighborhood context and social disparities in cumulative biological risk factors. *Psychosomatic Medicine, 73*, 572–579.

Kokko, K., Pulkkinen, L., & Puustinen, M. (2000). Selection into long-term unemployment and its psychological consequences. *International Journal of Behavioral Development, 24*, 310–320.

Lewis, T. T., Everson-Rose, S. A., Powell, L. H., Matthews, K. A., Brown, C., Karavolos, K., et al. (2006). Chronic exposure to everyday discrimination and coronary artery calcification in African American women: The SWAN Heart Study. *Psychosomatic Medicine, 68*, 362–368.

Loucks, E. B., Almeida, N. D., Taylor, S. E., & Matthews, K. A. (2011). Childhood family psychosocial environment and coronary heart disease risk. *Psychosomatic Medicine, 73*, 563–571.

Luciano, M., Marioni, R. E., Gow, A. J., Starr, J. M., & Deary, I. J. (2009). Reverse causation in the association between C-reactive protein and fibrinogen levels and cognitive abilities in an aging sample. *Psychosomatic Medicine, 71*, 404–409.

Mallet, S., & Rosenthal, D. (2009). Physically violent mothers are a reason for young people's leaving home. *Journal of Interpersonal Violence, 24*(7), 1165–1174.

Manuck, S. B., Phillips, J. E., Gianaros, P. J., Flory, J. D., & Muldoon, M. F. (2010). Subjective socioeconomic status and presence of the metabolic syndrome in midlife community volunteers. *Psychosomatic Medicine, 72*, 35–45.

McCarty, D., Argeriou, M., Huebner, R. B., & Lubran, B. (1991). Alcoholism, drug abuse, and the homeless. *American Psychologist, 46*, 1161–1169.

McDade, T. W., Hawkley, L. C., & Cacioppo, J. T. (2006). Psychosocial and behavioral predictors of inflammation in middle-aged and older adults: The Chicago Health, Aging, and Social Relations Study. *Psychosomatic Medicine, 68*, 376–381.

Mendelson, T., Thurston, R. C., & Kubzansky, L. D. (2008). Affective and cardiovascular effects of experimentally induced social status. *Health Psychology, 27*(4), 482–489.

Milburn, N., & D'Ercole, A. (1991). Homeless women: Moving toward a comprehensive model. *American Psychologist, 46*, 1161–1169.

Miller, L. (1999). Child abuse brain injury: Clinical, neuropsychological, and forensic considerations. *Journal of Cognitive Rehabilitation, 17*(2), 10–19.

Morozink, J. A., Friedman, E. M., Coe, C. L., & Ryff, C. D. (2010). Socioeconomic and psychosocial predictors of interleukin-6 in the MIDUS National Sample. *Health Psychology, 29*(6), 626–635.

Mullen, P. E., Martin, J. L., Anderson, J. C., Romans, S.E., & Herbison, G. P. (1994). The effect of child sexual abuse on social, interpersonal, and sexual function in adult life. *British Journal of Psychiatry, 165*, 35–47.

Nyamathi, A. M., Stein, J. A., & Swanson, J. M. (2000). Personal, cognitive, behavioral, and demographic predictors of HIV testing and STDs in homeless women. *Journal of Behavioral Medicine, 23*, 123–147.

O'Leary, P., Coohey, C., & Easton, S. D. (2010). The effect of severe child sexual abuse and disclosure on mental health during adulthood. *Journal of Child Sexual Abuse, 19*, 275–289.

Ostrove, J. M., & Adler, N. E. (1998). The relationship of socioeconomic status, labor force participation, and health among men and women. *Journal of Health Psychology, 3*, 451–463.

Redmond, S. P., & Brackman, J. (1990). Homeless children and their caretakers. In J. Momeni (Ed.), *Homelessness in the United States* (Vol. 2, pp. 123–132). Westport, CT: Greenwood.

Reinherz, H. Z., Giaconia, R. M., Hauf, A. M. C., Wasserman, M. S., & Paradis, A. D. (2000). General and specific childhood risk factors for depression and drug disorders by early adulthood. *Journal of the American Academy of Child and Adolescent Psychiatry, 39*, 223–231.

Rios, R., & Zautra, A. J. (2011). Socioeconomic disparities in pain: The role of economic hardship and daily financial worry. *Health Psychology, 30*(1), 58–66.

Shinn, M., Knickman, J. R., & Weitzman, B. C. (1991). Social relationships and vulnerability to become homeless among poor families. *American Psychologist, 46*, 1180–1187.

Sorlie, P. D., Backlund, E., & Keller, J. B. (1995). U.S. mortality by economic, demographic, and social characteristics: The National Longitudinal Mortality Study. *American Journal of Public Health, 85*, 949–956.

Springs, F. E., & Friedrich, W. N. (1992). Health risk behaviors and medical sequelae of childhood sexual abuse. *Mayo Clinic Proceedings, 67*, 527–532.

Stein, M. B., Walker, J. R., Hazen, A. L., & Forde, D. R. (1997). Full and partial posttraumatic stress disorder: Findings from a community survey. *American Journal of Psychiatry, 154*, 1114–1119.

Teicher, M. H. (2002). Scars that won't heal: The neurobiology of child abuse. *Scientific American, 286*(3), 68–75.

Toro, P. A., Bellavia, C. W., Daeschler, C. V., Owens, B. J., Wall, D. D., Passero, J. M., et al. (1995). Distinguishing homelessness from poverty: A comparative study. *Journal of Consulting and Clinical Psychology, 63*, 280–289.

Wagner, J. K., & Perrine, R. M. (1994). Women at risk for homelessness: Comparison between housed and homeless women. *Psychological Reports, 75*, 1671–1678.

Warshaw, M. G., Fierman, E., Pratt, L., Hunt, M., Yonker, K. A., Massion, A. O., et al. (1993). Quality of life and dissociation in anxiety disorder patients with histories of trauma or PTSD. *American Journal of Psychiatry, 150*, 1512–1516.

Watson, C. G., Davenport, E., Anderson, P. E. D., Mendez, C. M., & Gearhart, L. P. (1998). The relationship between premilitary school record data and risk for posttraumatic stress disorder among Vietnam War veterans. *Journal of Nervous and Mental Disease, 186*, 338–344.

Whitbeck, L. B., Hoyt, D. R., & Ackley, K. A. (1997). Families of homeless and runaway adolescents: A comparison of parent/caretaker and adolescent perspectives on parenting, family violence, and adolescent conduct. *Child Abuse and Neglect, 21*, 517–528.

Chapter 10

Social Pathways III—Revictimization

It is one of the cruel twists of fate; without intervention, abused children are at increased risk of being revictimized throughout their lives. As I described in the previous chapter, a substantial proportion of men and women who become homeless do so because they are fleeing either an abusive partner or an abusive parent. Even if revictimization does not lead to homelessness, it has serious ramifications for the health and welfare of abuse survivors.

In a community sample of child sexual abuse (CSA) survivors, 41 percent had experienced sexual violence one or more times in relationships, at work, or in therapy (Teegan, 1999). Grauerholz's (2000) review indicated that anywhere from 32 percent to 82 percent of people who are sexually victimized as children are sexually revictimized as adults. Most previous research has focused on sexual abuse and sexual revictimization. But recent studies have found that child physical abuse and neglect can also increase risk of physical or sexual assault as adults. This chapter discusses the research on revictimization of abuse survivors, some theories for why it occurs, and its health implications.

REVICTIMIZATION DURING CHILDHOOD

Revictimization can begin during childhood. Two prospective studies of preschoolers revealed that harsh treatment early in life predicted peer victimization in elementary school. Children who were victimized by peers often came from homes characterized by harsh discipline, marital conflict, stress, abuse, and maternal hostility (Schwartz, Dodge, Pettit, & Bates, 2000). Children from these homes who were able to make friends, however, were less likely to be victimized by peers.

Early maltreatment also predicted both bullying and peer victimization in a study of 169 maltreated and 98 non-maltreated boys and girls. All types of maltreatment put children at risk for peer victimization. Bullying was especially common among children who were either physically or sexually abused. These findings were true for both boys and girls. Bullies and victims both had trouble with emotional regulation, and the study differentiated bullies and victims from children who were neither (Shields & Cicchetti, 2001).

Similarly, Bolger and Patterson (2001) found that maltreated children had a higher likelihood of rejection and maltreatment by peers than nonmaltreated children. In a prospective, longitudinal study of 107 maltreated children in grades 2–4 and a nonmaltreated comparison group, maltreated children were significantly more likely to be rejected by peers across multiple ages than were their nonmaltreated counterparts. The children's aggressive behavior accounted for a large part of the children's rejection. The children's social withdrawal was also related but did not account for the association between maltreatment and peer rejection. These results were true from elementary school through early adolescence, and for both boys and girls.

In a community sample of 2,000 boys and girls, prior victimization increased the risk of subsequent child sexual abuse (Boney-McCoy & Finkelhor, 1995). In addition, prior victimization exacerbated the impact of the current child sexual abuse and enhanced symptoms of posttraumatic stress disorder (PTSD). Prior victimization included physical assault by a family member, physical assault by a nonfamily member, attempted kidnapping, assault to the genitals (that was force, not sexual), and sexual abuse. Indirect victimization, or victimization of a family member, was also included. The authors stated that this risk is not simply an artifact of living in a dangerous situation or having a poor relationship with parents. Even peer or neighborhood violence increases the risk of sexual abuse. The explanation may lie in the cognitions of the individual (e.g., the tendency to consider oneself as "damaged goods," and not worthy of protection).

REVICTIMIZATION OF TEENS, COLLEGE STUDENTS, AND YOUNG ADULTS

Teens

Revictimization also occurs during adolescence and early adulthood and includes both physical and sexual abuse. A study of German adolescents (ages 17–20) indicated that young women who had been sexually abused were more likely to report unwanted sexual contacts as adolescents. The relationship between past abuse and current revictimization was mediated by a higher level of sexual activity among the abuse victims (Krahe, Scheinberger-Olwig, Waizenhofer, & Kolpin, 1999).

In a study from Quebec, Canada, of 917 teenage girls, Gagne, Lavoie, and Hebert (2005) found that 13–43 percent had experienced dating violence. Extrafamilial factors, especially being sexually harassed at school, were stronger risk factors for recent dating violence than were intrafamilal factors. Intrafamilial factors included parental violence, marital violence, and sexual abuse. Extrafamilial factors were verbal sexual harassment, extrafamilial sexual abuse, violent or victimized peers, previous dating violence, and community violence. They also found that girls in long-term relationships sustained more frequent physical and psychological violence than did girls victimized by multiple partners.

College Students and Young Adults

Messman-Moore and Brown (2004) studied the child abuse and adult rape histories of 925 college women. They found that 17 percent reported a history of any type of child maltreatment, 9 percent reported CSA, 4 percent reported child physical abuse, and 9 percent reported emotional abuse. Logistic regression indicated that a history of CSA almost doubled the risk for adult rape. The rates of adult rape varied widely depending on whether the individual had experienced zero, one, two, or three types of abuse: 14 percent of women who experienced zero types of child abuse were raped, 21 percent of women who experienced one type, 36 percent of women who experienced two types, and 43 percent of women who experienced all three types. The authors concluded that there are multiple pathways that lead to vulnerability to later sexual victimization.

In a national sample of college women (Koss & Dinero, 1989), 66 percent of women who had experienced rape or attempted rape had also been sexually abused as children. The risk was higher if there had been attempted or completed intercourse in childhood. In another study, sexually abused female undergraduates had increased risk of physical and psychological abuse in dating relationships but not increased risk of sexual coercion (Banyard, Arnold, & Smith, 2000).

In another college sample, 69 percent of women who were sexual abuse survivors had experienced some type of victimization in adulthood, compared to 42 percent of non-abused women. Adult victimization included unwanted sexual contact, sexual coercion, attempted rape, and rape (Kessler & Bieschke, 1999). Risk also varied by type of abuse. For women abused by peers during childhood, the odds ratios for adult victimization were as follows: 2.4 for sexual coercion, 6.7 for attempted rate, and 4.4 for rape. For incestuous abuse, the odds ratios were 5.6 for sexual coercion, 6.76 for attempted rape, and 9.35 for rape.

A study of 2,500 undergraduates found that exposure to violence in childhood predicted experiencing or perpetrating dating violence (Gover, Kaukinen, & Fox, 2008). More than 29 percent of the students had perpetrated physical dating violence and 22 percent had been victims. Those who had been abused, or had witnessed parental violence, were significantly more likely to have experienced or perpetrated violence in dating relationships. Of those abused during childhood, 38 percent perpetrated physical violence, compared to 25 percent of the non-abused group. Thirty-two percent of the abused group had been adult victims compared with 18 percent of the non-abused group. Those who witnessed either their fathers hitting their mothers, or their mothers hitting their fathers, were almost twice as likely to perpetrate or experience abuse. In this sample, females were more likely to perpetrate dating violence than males, but males and females were equally likely to be victimized.

Messman-Moore, Brown, and Koelsch (2005) examined the impact of victimization on both self-dysfunction and disturbed relatedness. Self-dysfunction includes maladaptive efforts to regulate affect, disturbances in intimate and sexual relationships, and disrupted sense of self. CSA may interfere with the development of self-concept and sexual identity. It may also distort basic beliefs about trust, safety, and control in significant relationships, which may lead to women being unable to protect themselves. They were more likely to put others' needs ahead of their own, to be overly nurturing, to have difficulty being assertive, and to be too responsible. In addition, revictimized women were more likely to assume that negative interpersonal relationships would continue from childhood into adulthood, and they anticipated that others would treat them in a hostile, controlling, and domineering manner. Those who were not revictimized did not make these assumptions.

A fifteen-year prospective, longitudinal study of female young adult reports of sexual victimization occurring after confirmed reports of CSA found that abused females were almost twice as likely to have been physically or sexually revictimized as females in the non-abused comparison group (Barnes et al., 2009). The revictimization of abused females was more likely to have been perpetrated by older, non-peers, and the revictimization was more likely characterized by physical injury than were victimizations reported by the comparison group.

Other forms of child abuse and neglect were also significantly related to risk of date rape, even when the risk associated with past sexual abuse was partialled out. Specifically, a negative or neglectful home environment was related to higher risk, as were reports of "unpredictable physical violence." Moreover, maltreatment was associated with dissociation, depression, and other trauma symptoms, including intrusive experiences, impaired self-reference, and tension-reduction behaviors (Sanders & Moore, 1999).

REVICTIMIZATION OF ADULTS

The risk of revictimization continues through adulthood. This finding was demonstrated in community, clinical, and ethnic-minority samples.

Community Samples

A sample of Australian women whose abuse included intercourse were four times more likely to have been battered and raped since age 16 than were women in the non-abused comparison group (Fleming, Mullen, Sibthorpe, & Bammer, 1999). Similarly, in a study of young women from New Zealand, those with a history of child sexual abuse had higher rates of sexual assault after age 16 (Fergusson, Horwood, & Lynskey, 1997).

In another community sample, 49 percent of women whose abuse included penetration had also been raped as adults (Parillo, Freeman, Collier, & Young, 2001). Parillo et al. speculated that childhood sexual abuse changes women's perceptions of sexuality and themselves as sexual beings. These women may feel that they do not deserve pleasure, do not cherish and respect their bodies, and therefore do not expect respect and care from others.

A study of 9,170 women and 7,823 men in Canada found that a history of CSA consistently predicted partner violence for women and men (Daigneault, Hebert, &

McDuff, 2009). Women in this sample who had histories of CSA had significantly higher rates of physical and sexual partner violence. The rates were especially high if the women were younger, in a recent relationship, or had any type of chronic condition that limited them. There were no significant differences between men and women on prevalence of child physical abuse or psychological intimate partner violence (IPV). For men, a history of CSA predicted more psychological or physical IPV than their non-abused counterparts.

Women who experienced both physical and sexual abuse had the highest rates of sexual and physical victimization as adults. Indeed, 77 percent of women who experienced both types of abuse also reported revictimization as adults, compared with 33 percent of those who reported sexual abuse alone, 50 percent of those who reported physical abuse alone, and 31 percent of those who reported no childhood abuse. The physically and sexually abused group also reported significantly higher rates of PTSD and trauma symptoms than did the non-abused group: 45 percent of those who experienced both types had a diagnosis of PTSD, compared with 15 percent of those who reported sexual abuse alone and 9 percent of those who reported physical abuse alone (Schaaf & McCanne, 1998).

A study of 555 adult female sexual assault survivors examined the effects of previous CSA, PTSD, drinking, and drug use in increasing the risk of revictimization (Ullman, Najdowski, & Filipas, 2009). Women with a history of CSA had more PTSD symptoms after the adult sexual assault. PTSD numbing symptoms directly predicted revictimization. Other PTSD symptoms, such as reexperiencing, avoidance, and arousal, were indirectly related to revictimization because of their relationship to problem drinking. The authors used a longitudinal design and path analysis, which allowed them to examine independent risk factors for revictimization.

Characteristics of sexual abuse also predicted sexual revictimization (Arata, 2000). Women were more likely to be revictimized if their experience of CSA included contact and intercourse or penetration. Women who were revictimized blamed themselves more and reported higher levels of PTSD and high-risk sexual behavior. A path model demonstrated that the relationship between revictimization and CSA was mediated by self-blame, PTSD, and consensual sexual activity.

In a study of men who have sex with men, Paul, Catania, Pollack, and Stall (2001) found that men with a history of sexual abuse were vulnerable to two types of revictimization: physical abuse by a partner in the past five years and sexual victimization, particularly if they had had two or more types of adverse childhood experiences. These experiences included parental substance abuse, parent-to-parent physical abuse, and parent-to-child physical abuse.

A study of ninety-eight low-income African-American women who had been abused as children found that neighborhood factors moderated the link between childhood emotional abuse and adult IPV (Obasaju, Palin, Jacobs, Anderson, & Kaslow, 2009). The neighborhood factors related to past and current abuse were perceived neighborhood disorder and community cohesion. Neighborhood disorder refers to physical elements, such as abandoned buildings and vandalism, and social conditions of a neighborhood. Neighborhoods high in disorder are marked by crime, noise, vandalism, drug use, and problems with neighborhoods. Community cohesion refers to how members of a community are interrelated, communicate, and provide support for one another. They found no relation between CSA and adult partner violence, contrary to previous studies. The results of this study highlight the need to consider the ecological context in which revictimization occurs, and that a woman's role in her neighborhood and community context plays a role in the likelihood that she will be abused as an adult.

Clinical Samples

Revictimization was also common in clinical populations of adult survivors. In a sample of poor urban women with severe mental illness, Goodman and Fallot (1998) found that early sexual abuse was related to adult sexual and physical assault, and childhood physical abuse was related to adult physical assault.

Among ninety-three adult women presenting at a psychiatric emergency department, victimization experiences were common: 84 percent had been assaulted as children or as adults. When comparing rates of revictimization for children who had been physically abused versus those who had been sexually abused, sexual abuse was related to attempted or completed rape and physical assault outside a sexual relationship but not battering within a sexual relationship. In contrast, childhood physical abuse was not related to any form of adult victimization (Briere, Woo, McRae, Foltz, & Sitzman, 1997).

In a study of 290 patients diagnosed with borderline personality disorder, almost half had been violently victimized as adults. Specifically, 33 percent had an abusive partner, 31 percent had been raped, 21 percent had been raped by a known perpetrator, 11 percent had been raped multiple times, and 19 percent had been both beaten and raped. Eighty-six percent of patients who had been assaulted or raped as adults had also been physically or sexually abused as children. However, only 50 percent of borderline patients with a history of childhood abuse reported that they were victimized as adults. Five types of experiences during childhood appeared to predict later victimization: physical neglect by a caretaker, emotional withdrawal by a caretaker, a caretaker's failure to provide needed protection, sexual abuse by a noncaretaker, and any type of sexual abuse (Zanarini et al., 1999).

PSYCHIATRIC DIAGNOSIS AND FAMILY DYSFUNCTION INCREASE RISK

Impact of Psychiatric Disorders

One possible risk factor for victimization is a history of psychiatric disorder. In a survey of a representative sample of 2,030 youth ages 2–17 and their parents, researchers found that psychiatric diagnosis was a risk factor for victimization (Cuevas, Finkelhor, Ormrod, & Turner, 2009). Using logistic regression, the researchers found that psychiatric diagnoses increased the risk for polyvictimization, conventional crime victimization, maltreatment, peer or sibling victimization, and witnessing crime. Psychiatric diagnoses did not increase the risk of sexual abuse. The authors recommended that clinicians broaden their assessment of victimization in the context of a comprehensive diagnostic and mental health assessment.

Messman-Moore et al. (2005) examined the role of posttraumatic stress symptoms and self-dysfunction as both consequences and predictors of sexual revictimization. Self-dysfunction refers to maladaptive efforts to regulate affect, disturbances in intimate and sexual relationships, and disrupted sense of self, all of which lead to increased risk of revictimization. Self-dysfunction may turn out to be more important to revictimization in that it affects social functioning and interpersonal behavior. Disturbed relatedness refers to self-concept, sexual identity, and distortion of basic beliefs about trust, safety, and control in significant relationships. For example, revictimized women with a history of CSA may assume that their negative interpersonal relationships from childhood carried over into their adult relationships versus women with a CSA history who were not revictimized as adults and did not carry over these beliefs from childhood.

Affect regulation and tension-reducing behavior can include binge eating, self-mutilation, substance abuse, and indiscriminate sexual activity that help the survivor cope with overwhelming affect (Messman-Moore et al., 2005). Impaired self-reference may interfere with a survivor's ability to separate herself from others and to have establish appropriate boundaries. Their sample included 339 female undergraduates. Consistent with previous studies, women with a history of child sexual assault were more likely to report an adult sexual assault during the nine-month study period, as were women with histories of adult sexual victimization. As predicted, both PTSD and self-dysregulation were related to a history of sexual victimization either as a child or an adult. Self-symptoms were associated with all three types of victimization (child, adult, and revictimization). The authors concluded that their findings suggested that prior child and adult victimization are directly and indirectly related to sexual revictimization.

Impact of Family of Origin

The family environment also affects risk of revictimization. Children who are sexually abused also often live in highly disorganized families that also have low levels of commitment, help, and support and high levels of conflict and aggression (Koverola, Proulx, Battle, & Hanna, 1996). Men and women who had been sexually victimized by multiple perpetrators had higher levels of dysfunction in their families of origin than did those victimized by only one perpetrator. The families of people with multiple victimizations were higher on conflict and lower on cohesion, intellectual-cultural orientation, and family fun than were families in which only one victimization occurred.

In another study comparing the experiences of men and women who had been victimized by one versus multiple perpetrators, Kellogg and Hoffman (1997) had similar findings. Men and women abused by multiple perpetrators had more family dysfunction than those abused by a single perpetrator. Dysfunction included victims being hit by a fist, one or more family members who abused substances, and at least one member of the family who had had a serious injury inflicted by another family member. Victims of multiple perpetrators were more likely to blame themselves and delay disclosure due to shame.

REVICTIMIZATION IN ETHNIC MINORITY POPULATIONS

Revictimization also cuts across ethnic lines. In a multiethnic sample of 243 women, 34 percent reported CSA and 24 percent had been raped as adults. The rates of CSA were similar for African-American and white women; Asian women and

Latinas had lower rates. Of women who reported rape, 65 percent had also been sexually abused. These women were three times more likely to be raped as adults than women without a history of sexual abuse. This finding held true for white and African-American women and Latinas but was not true for Asian women, who had the lowest rates of rape overall (Urquiza & Goodlin-Jones, 1994).

In a sample of 147 women, Fargo (2009) examined the direct and indirect pathways between child sexual abuse and adult sexual revictimization. Fifty-nine percent had been sexually abused, and 88 percent were African American. In this sample, 27 percent of adolescents and 42 percent of adults had experienced adult sexual victimization. Using structural equation modeling, Fargo found that the link between childhood abuse and adolescent revictimization was mediated by risk-taking behaviors. These behaviors included age at first alcohol use, illicit drug use, consensual sex, and whether the child had run away from home before the age of 18. The link between adolescent and adult sexual victimization is also indirect, mediated by high-risk sexual behavior, which included number of lifetime sexual partners, engaging in prostitution, and the woman's score on the "problematic sexual behaviors" scale of the Belief Inventory. Fargo also found that negative childhood family environment, including parental partner violence or mental illness, and child physical abuse also indirectly predicted sexual revictimization. The author concluded that the primary finding of his study was that revictimization depended on intervening experiences and risk factors, rather directly on prior experiences of sexual victimization.

Wyatt and Riederle (1994) found that sexually abused black and white women were significantly more likely to experience sexual harassment on the job than women who had not been abused. As a result of harassment, the sexually abused women were more likely to leave their jobs, become emotionally upset, or take legal action. Contact sexual abuse had a more negative impact on the emotional well-being of African-American women than repeat experiences of sexual violence.

Gilbert, El Bassel, Schilling, and Friedman (1997) examined the relationship between childhood abuse and domestic violence in a sample of predominantly minority women who were in a program of methadone maintenance. Women who were physically abused in childhood were nine times more likely to have also been abused by a spouse or boyfriend. Women who had been sexually abused in childhood were four times more likely to have also been domestically abused compared with methadone-maintained women who had not been abused in childhood.

THEORIES OF REVICTIMIZATION

As Koss (1990) has noted, "Repeated violent victimizations render women less skilled at self-protection, less sure of their own worth and personal boundaries, and more apt to accept victimization as a part of being female. Via these impacts, earlier victimization may increase the chances of future victimization" (pp. 376–377).

Many theories have been put forth as to why people who have experienced previous abuse are more vulnerable to revictimization (Krahe et al., 1999). One theory is that children who have been sexually abused may have acquired inappropriate repertoires of sexual behavior and may associate sexuality with pain. Rape or sexual victimization may be seen as the "normal" way men and women relate to each other (Grauerholz, 2000).

Revictimization may also be related to the greater number of sexual encounters that adult survivors have. Indiscriminant and frequent encounters may provide more opportunities for victimization. Sexually abused girls, for example, may learn that they are powerless and helpless in the face of sexual invasion, that there is no escape inside or outside the home, and indeed that the experience of victimization is part of being a girl (Draucker, 2001).

A negative family environment can drive children to leave home prematurely, putting them at risk for further victimization. Women with a sexual abuse history may feel powerless toward future sexual advances. They may also not know who they can trust and how to detect a dangerous situation. Each of these situations puts women at risk for future victimization (Schaaf & McCanne, 1998).

Noell, Rohde, Seeley, and Ochs (2001) used a "learned helplessness" model to explain revictimization among abuse survivors. In their study of homeless adolescent females, 38 percent had a history of child sexual abuse. The abuse survivors were significantly more likely to report recent sexual coercion. In the entire sample, those who reported sexual coercion within the past three months had more sexual partners and were more likely to have had a sexually transmitted disease with in the past six months (Noell et al., 2001). The authors pointed out that many assume high-risk sexual behaviors are voluntary. Their findings indicated that a large number of these behaviors are not. Sexual abuse survivors may adopt a repertoire of sexual behaviors that are not appropriate and may learn to associate sexuality with pain, punishment, or other negative consequences.

Role of Psychological Sequelae

Messman-Moore and Long (2003), in a review of the literature, examined the role of psychological sequelae in increasing vulnerability to revictimization in CSA survivors. The sequelae they considered were alcohol and drug use, sexual behavior, dissociation, posttraumatic symptomatology, poor risk recognition, and interpersonal difficulties. Only sexual behavior had any relationship to later victimization. The other factors provided limited or mixed support. Regarding alcohol's clear relationship to sexual victimization, what is less clear is whether alcohol connects prior abuse to current abuse. Further, the relationship between alcohol and adult victimization was mediated by sexual experience. CSA survivors reported more sexual experiences than did women without an abuse history. Child victimization increased the risk of adult sexual assault by five times. Alcohol increased the risk by two and a half times. Sexual behavior appears to increase risk, although it was unclear whether it was the number of consensual partners who increased risk (higher number increased risk) or the earlier age at first consensual intercourse.

Child maltreatment and loss may also create a climate that allows the child to be sexually exploited. In a study of 687 undergraduates, experiences of loss and maltreatment in early childhood increased the likelihood that these children would also experience CSA and sexual, physical, and emotional abuse as adults (Liem & Boudewyn, 1999). The greater the number of loss or maltreating experiences, the higher the likelihood of victimizing experiences in adulthood.

Finally, adult survivors' view of themselves can also be related to whether they are revictimized as adults. In one recent study, women who had a positive self-concept and a sense of mastery and who indicated that they had found meaning in the negative experiences lessened the negative impact of these prior traumatic events and lowered their risk of revictimization (Draucker, 2001).

Ecological Framework

Messman-Moore and Long (2003), in their review of literature, point out that current models for understanding revictimization are limited because they focus solely on victim characteristics or history without recognizing that revictimization would not occur were there not a perpetrator. Indeed, Messman-Moore and Long urge researchers and clinicians to recognize that revictimization is an intersection between victim vulnerability and perpetrators taking advantage of that vulnerability.

Instead of focusing on victim traits, Messman-Moore and Long (2003) suggest using an ecological framework, as illustrated in Figure 10.1. This could serve as an overarching framework that allows integration of research from various perspectives. An ecological perspective includes ontogenic developmental factors related to the initial victimization (such as the personal history, or psychological sequelae of previous abuse); microsystem factors (such as the context in which the abuse occurred, the victim's decreased ability to respond assertively); exosystem factors (lack of resources or alternatives, such as low socioeconomic status); and the macrosystem factors (such as cultural norms that support violence against women or blame the victim). Most current research focuses only on the first two factors—victim characteristics or psychological sequelae—and is therefore limited. This research does not consider microsystem factors, such as the perpetrator's perception of the victim as an easy target or cultural forces (such as patriarchy) that contribute to continued victimization of CSA survivors.

The microsystem risk includes both exposure risk (increased contract with perpetrators due to sexual activity and/or substance abuse) and psychological vulnerability (perpetrator identifies vulnerability due to dissociation, intoxication, or social vulnerability). Messman-Moore and Long suggested that instead of focusing on individual risk factors, clinicians and researchers should focus on mechanisms and processes.

Figure 10.1
Ecological Framework of Revictimization

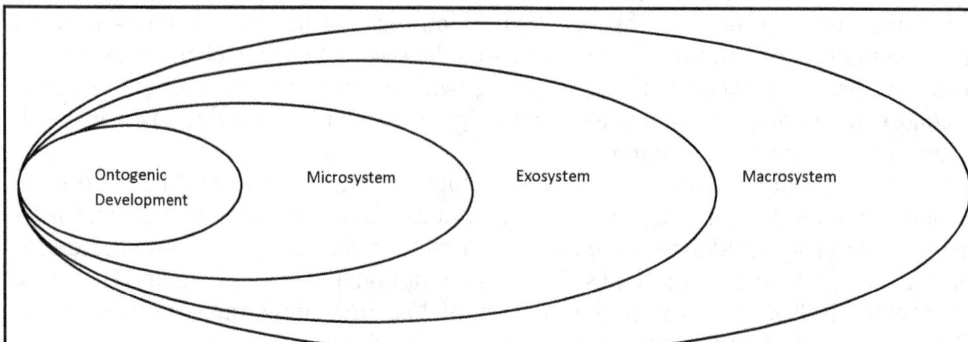

Adapted from Messman-Moore and Long (2003).

For example, alcohol abuse and dissociation are two distinct phenomena. But both act to increase vulnerability by leading to decreased awareness of surroundings and inability to respond to danger. Similarly, alcohol and sexual behavior are distinct but may share the same substrate that puts individuals at risk by putting them in contact with potential perpetrators. Thus factors that can increase risk include dissociation, substance abuse, interpersonal dysfunction, and sexual behaviors. These do not contradict each other but likely reflect different manifestations of the same underlying mechanism that increases their risk.

REVICTIMIZATION AND HEALTH

Not surprisingly, revictimization can have a serious long-term impact on health. Revictimization affects health through injury, and potential death, from each victimizing encounter. Revictimization also increases the risk of contracting any number of sexually transmitted diseases, including HIV (human immunodeficiency virus). In addition to frank injury, revictimization can lead to a state of chronic stress, where partners never know when violence might erupt. Chronic stress can elevate blood levels of triglycerides, free fatty acids, cholesterol, glucose, and insulin, all of which are related to cardiovascular disease and diabetes (Kendall-Tackett & Marshall, 1999; Lovallo, 1997). It can also lead survivors to self-medicate by abusing substances, bingeing and purging, self-mutilation, and smoking.

Peer victimization can affect the health of adolescents, whether they are bullies or victims. In a study of 819 Australian high school students (Rigby, 1998), respondents were asked to complete a survey in which they identified themselves as bullies, victims, bully/victims, or "other." Peer-victimized girls reported more emotional distress and adverse health outcomes, and both male and female victims had more somatic complaints, anxiety, social dysfunction, and depression than did the "other" group. Among the boys, bullies also consistently reported poorer health.

Rigby (1998) offered several possible explanations for these findings. Children who are victimized at school may find themselves in chronically stressful situations. They may experience frequent verbal or physical attacks and may be forced to endure these attacks without social support. Such situations may be difficult to control, and opportunities to escape are frequently unavailable. Moreover, it is often difficult for children to predict when these attacks are likely to occur. All the factors may heighten physiological arousal, which can impair the immune system and create a vulnerability to disease.

In adults, peer victimization, in the form of partner violence, can also dramatically increase the risk of health problems, often through comorbid psychiatric conditions. In a study of 941 young adults, researchers found that female victims of partner violence were at increased risk for mood disorders, eating disorders, substance abuse, and schizophrenia. Over half of the male perpetrators met criteria for anxiety disorder, substance use, and antisocial-personality disorder (Danielson, Moffitt, Caspi, & Silva, 1998). Revictimization may also increase that risk of subsequent PTSD (Arata, 1999). Women with repeated victimization experiences were more likely to have a lifetime diagnosis of PTSD. Age of onset of abuse and physical severity were both associated with the development of PTSD. PTSD is also related to a wide range of health conditions, including premature mortality.

SUMMARY OF THE SOCIAL EFFECTS OF ABUSE

Childhood abuse can create a lifetime of vulnerability to lower educational achievement, lower income, homelessness, and revictimization. All these situations can influence health in serious and negative ways. As the studies in this chapter indicate, revictimization is surprisingly common among abuse survivors and can compromise health in a number of serious ways. Working with abuse survivors to address the harmful behaviors and beliefs that increase their risk of revictimization will go a long way in terms of improving their health.

References

Arata, C. M. (1999). Coping with rape: The roles of prior sexual abuse and attributions of blame. *Journal of Interpersonal Violence, 14*, 62–78.

Arata, C. M. (2000). From child victim to adult victim: A model for predicting sexual revictimization. *Child Maltreatment, 5*, 28–38.

Banyard, V. L., Arnold, S., & Smith, J. (2000). Childhood sexual abuse and dating experiences of undergraduate students. *Child Maltreatment, 5*, 39–48.

Barnes, L. L., Mendes de Leon, C. F., Bienias, J. L., Wilson, R. S., Everson-Rose, S. A., & Evans, D. (2009). Hostility and change in cognitive function over time in older blacks and whites. *Psychosomatic Medicine, 71*, 652–658.

Bolger, K. E., & Patterson, C. J. (2001). Developmental pathways from child maltreatment to peer rejections. *Child Development, 72*(2), 549–568.

Boney-McCoy, S., & Finkelhor, D. (1995). Prior victimization: A risk factor for child sexual abuse and for PTSD-related symptomatology among sexually abused youth. *Child Abuse and Neglect, 19*, 1401–1421.

Briere, J. N., Woo, R., McRae, B., Foltz, J., & Sitzman, R. (1997). Lifetime victimization history, demographics, and clinical status in female psychiatric emergency room patients. *Journal of Nervous and Mental Disease, 185*, 95–101.

Cuevas, C. A., Finkelhor, D., Ormrod, R., & Turner, H. (2009). Psychiatric diagnosis as a risk marker for victimization in a national sample of children. *Journal of Interpersonal Violence, 24*(4), 636–652.

Daigneault, I., Hebert, M., & McDuff, P. (2009). Men's and women's childhood sexual abuse and victimization in adult partner relationships: A study of risk factors. *Child Abuse and Neglect, 33*, 638–647.

Danielson, K. K., Moffitt, T. E., Caspi, A., & Silva, P. A. (1998). Comorbidity between abuse of an adult and DSM III-R mental disorders: Evidence from an epidemiological study. *American Journal of Psychiatry, 155*, 131–133.

Draucker, C. B. (2001). Early family life and victimization in the lives of women. In K. Franey, R. Geffner & R. Falconer (Eds.), *The cost of child maltreatment: Who pays? We all do* (pp. 167–184). San Diego: Family Violence & Sexual Assault Institute.

Fargo, J. D. (2009). Pathways to adult sexual revictimization: Direct and indirect behavioral risk factors across the lifespan. *Journal of Interpersonal Violence, 24*(11), 1771–1791.

Fergusson, D. M., Horwood, L. J., & Lynskey, M. T. (1997). Childhood sexual abuse, adolescent sexual behaviors and sexual revictimization. *Child Abuse and Neglect, 21*, 789–803.

Fleming, J., Mullen, P. E., Sibthorpe, B., & Bammer, G. (1999). The long-term impact of childhood sexual abuse in Australian women. *Child Abuse and Neglect, 23*, 145–159.

Gagne, M.-H., Lavoie, F., & Hebert, M. (2005). Victimization during childhood and revictimization in dating relationships in adolescent girls. *Child Abuse and Neglect, 29*, 1155–1172.

Gilbert, L., El-Bassel, N., Schilling, R. F., & Friedman, E. (1997). Childhood abuse as a risk for partner abuse among women in methadone maintenance. *American Journal of Drug and Alcohol Abuse, 23*, 581–595.

Goodman, L. A., & Fallot, R. D. (1998). HIV risk behavior in poor urban women with serious mental disorders: Association with childhood physical and sexual abuse. *American Journal of Orthopsychiatry, 68*, 73–83.

Gover, A. R., Kaukinen, C., & Fox, K. A. (2008). The relationship between violence in the family of origin and dating violence among college students. *Journal of Interpersonal Violence, 23*(12), 1667–1693.

Grauerholz, L. (2000). An ecological approach to understanding sexual revictimization: Linking personal, interpersonal, and sociocultural factors and processes. *Child Maltreatment, 5*, 5–17.

Kellogg, N. D., & Hoffman, T. J. (1997). Child sexual revictimization by multiple perpetrators. *Child Abuse and Neglect, 21*, 953–964.

Kendall-Tackett, K. A., & Marshall, R. (1999). Victimization and diabetes: An exploratory study. *Child Abuse and Neglect, 23*, 593–596.

Kessler, B. L., & Bieschke, K. J. (1999). A retrospective analysis of shame, dissociation, and adult victimization in survivors of childhood sexual abuse. *Journal of Counseling Psychology, 46*, 335–341.

Koss, M. P. (1990). The women's mental health research agenda: Violence against women. *American Psychologist, 45*, 374–380.

Koss, M. P., & Dinero, T. E. (1989). Discriminant analysis of risk factors for sexual victimization among a national sample of college women. *Journal of Consulting and Clinical Psychology, 57*, 242–250.

Koverola, C., Proulx, J., Battle, P., & Hanna, C. (1996). Family functioning as predictors of distress in revictimized sexual abuse survivors. *Journal of Interpersonal Violence, 11*, 263–280.

Krahe, B., Scheinberger-Olwig, R., Waizenhofer, E., & Kolpin, S. (1999). Childhood sexual abuse and revictimization in adolescence. *Child Abuse and Neglect, 23*, 383–394.

Liem, J. H., & Boudewyn, A. C. (1999). Contextualizing the effects of childhood sexual abuse on adult self- and social functioning: An attachment theory perspective. *Child Abuse and Neglect, 23*, 1141–1157.

Lovallo, W. R. (1997). *Stress and health: Biological and psychological interactions*. Newbury Park, CA: Sage.

Messman-Moore, T. L., & Brown, A. L. (2004). Child maltreatment and perceived family environment as risk factors for adult rape: Is child sexual abuse the most salient experience? *Child Abuse and Neglect, 28*, 1019–1034.

Messman-Moore, T. L., Brown, A. L., & Koelsch, L. E. (2005). Posttraumatic symptoms and self-dysfunction as consequences and predictors of sexual revicitmization. *Journal of Traumatic Stress, 18*(3), 1–9.

Messman-Moore, T. L., & Long, P. J. (2003). The role of childhood sexual abuse sequelae in the sexual revictimization of women: An empirical review and theoretical reformulation. *Clinical Psychology Review, 23*, 537–571.

Noell, J., Rohde, P., Seeley, J., & Ochs, L. (2001). Childhood sexual abuse, adolescent sexual coercion, and sexually transmitted infection acquisition among homeless femal adolescents. *Child Abuse and Neglect, 25*, 137–148.

Obasaju, M. A., Palin, F. L., Jacobs, C., Anderson, P., & Kaslow, N. J. (2009). Won't you be my neighbor? Using an ecological approach to examine the impact of community on revictimization. *Journal of Interpersonal Violence, 24*(1), 38–53.

Parillo, K. M., Freeman, R. C., Collier, K., & Young, P. (2001). Association between early sexual abuse and adult HIV-risk sexual behaviors among community-recruited women. *Child Abuse and Neglect, 25*, 335–346.

Paul, J. P., Catania, J., Pollack, L., & Stall, R. (2001). Understanding childhood sexual abuse as a predictor of sexual risk-taking among men who have sex with men: The Urban Men's Health Study. *Child Abuse and Neglect, 25*, 557–584.

Rigby, K. (1998). The relationship between reported health and involvement in bully/victim problems among male and female secondary school children. *Journal of Health Psychology, 3*, 465–476.

Sanders, B., & Moore, D. L. (1999). Childhood maltreatment and date rape. *Journal of Interpersonal Violence, 14*, 115–124.

Schaaf, K. K., & McCanne, T. R. (1998). Relationship of childhood sexual, physical, and combined sexual and physical abuse to adult victimization and posttraumatic stress disorder. *Child Abuse and Neglect, 22*, 1119–1133.

Schwartz, D., Dodge, K. A., Pettit, G. S., & Bates, J. E. (2000). Friendship as a moderating factor in the pathway between early harsh home environment and later victimization in the peer group. *Developmental Psychology, 36*, 646–662.

Shields, A., & Cicchetti, D. (2001). Parental maltreatment and emotion dysregulation as risk factors in the pathway between early harsh home environment and later victimization. *Journal of Clinical Child Psychology, 30*, 349–363.

Teegan, F. (1999). Childhood sexual abuse and long-term sequelae. In A. Maercker, M. Schutzwohl & Z. Solomon (Eds.), *Posttraumatic stress disorder: A lifespan developmental perspective* (pp. 97–112. Seattle, WA: Hogrefe & Huber.

Ullman, S. E., Najdowski, C. J., & Filipas, H. H. (2009). Child sexual abuse, posttraumatic stress disorder, and substance use: Predictors of revictimization in adult sexual assault survivors. *Journal of Child Sexual Abuse, 18*, 367–385.

Urquiza, A. J., & Goodlin-Jones, B. L. (1994). Child sexual abuse and adult revictimization with women of color. *Violence and Victims, 9*, 223–265.

Wyatt, G. E., & Riederle, M. (1994). Sexual harassment and prior sexual trauma among African American and white American women. *Violence and Victims, 9*, 233–247.

Zanarini, M. C., Frankenburg, F. R., Reich, D., Marino, M. F., Haynes, M. C., & Gunderson, J. G. (1999). Violence in the lives of adult borderline patients. *Journal of Nervous and Mental Disease, 187*, 65–71.

Chapter 11

Emotional Pathways I—Depression

Depression is a common sequela of childhood abuse and a common reason why abuse survivors seek care. They may seek care in either primary care or outpatient settings, or they may seek inpatient care. In a study of ninety-three women presenting to psychiatric emergency departments, Briere, Woo, McRae, Foltz, and Sitzman (1997) found that 53 percent reported a history of child sexual abuse (CSA), 42 percent reported a history of childhood physical abuse, and 26 percent reported both types. CSA was the best predictor of later psychiatric problems. Briere and Elliot (1994) estimated that sexual abuse survivors have a four-times-greater lifetime risk for major depression compared with adults who have not been sexually abused. Depression is common among those who have experienced other types of maltreatment, as well.

Although researchers have found a wide range of psychiatric conditions related to past abuse, the two most common conditions in abuse survivors are depression and posttraumatic stress disorder (PTSD). We generally think of depression and PTSD as outcomes, which they are. But they are also both mechanisms that lead to poor overall health. Depression is the focus of this chapter.

DEPRESSION AND ABUSE SURVIVORS

Prevalence

Depression is characterized by sadness, insomnia, alterations in normal diurnal rhythms, difficulties in concentration, hopelessness, and guilt (Andreasen, 1997). Felitti (1991) found that 83 percent of sexually abused patients were depressed compared with 32 percent of the comparison group. Their symptoms included sleep disturbances, chronic fatigue, despondency, and frequent crying spells. The majority of the depressed patients had never been treated. In another primary care sample, women who had been sexually abused were significantly more likely to report feeling blue or depressed. Indeed, 65 percent were depressed compared with 35 percent of the non-abused group. An even higher percentage (68 percent) reported mood swings, compared with 29 percent of non-abused women. These same women were also more likely to report extreme anger and rage, fear of being alone, and spells of panic or terror, but a smaller percentage of women had these symptoms (Hulme, 2000).

In the Commonwealth Fund Adolescent Health Survey, physically and sexually abused girls were five times more likely to report depressive symptoms than were non-abused girls (Diaz, Simatov, & Rickert, 2000). In a primary care sample, 65 percent of sexually abused women reported feeling blue or depressed compared with 35 percent of non-abused women (Hulme, 2000). In a study of chronic pain in primary care patients, women with a history of child or domestic abuse were significantly more likely to be depressed than a matched group of non-abused women (Kendall-Tackett, Marshall, & Ness, 2003).

In a community sample from Ontario, Canada, Levitan et al. (1998) identified 653 people with major depression. For men and women, a history of physical or sexual abuse was associated with higher risk of depressive episodes with reverse neurovegetative symptoms (increased appetite, weight gain, and hypersomnia). There was also a strong relationship between physical abuse and mania.

Adolescents who had been raped in a nationally representative sample of French teens were significantly more likely to report that they "felt depressed" and "felt unhappy" than were their counterparts who had not been raped (Choquet, Darves-Bornoz, Ledoux, Manfredi, & Hassler, 1997). Similarly, in another sample of teens and young adults, those with a history of child maltreatment were three times more likely to be depressed or suicidal (Brown, Cohen, Johnson, & Smailes, 1999). Child maltreatment and loss before age 5 has also been causally linked to depression and low self-esteem in 687 undergraduates (Liem & Boudewyn, 1999). In a sample of 357 primiparous women, women who had been sexually abused as children were significantly more likely to be depressed during their pregnancies and to have been both physically and verbally abused before and during pregnancy (Benedict, Paine, Paine, Brandt, & Stallings, 1999). They were also more likely to have experienced negative life events, including death or illness of family members, financial problems, change in living arrangements or jobs, and "relationship issues," all within the past six months.

In a community sample of women, every woman whose sexual abuse involved penetration was depressed (Cheasty, Clare, & Collins, 1998). The lifetime prevalence of major depression was 86 percent in sexual abuse survivors with PTSD, and 29 percent of these women were currently depressed (Bremner et al., 1997). There also appears to be an additive effect of physical and sexual abuse in depression.

Exposure to parental violence has also been linked to major depression, conduct disorder, and anxiety disorders in a birth cohort sample of 18-year-olds from New Zealand. Of these three conditions, major depression was by far the most common. The higher the rates of parental violence, the higher the rates of major depression. The teens in this sample also had a high exposure to both sexual abuse and regular use of physical punishment (Fergusson & Horwood, 1998).

Co-Occurring Depression and Substance Abuse

Depression often co-occurs with substance abuse in abuse survivors. In a longitudinal study examining the impact of child maltreatment on subsequent development of alcohol problems, Schuck and Widom (2001) found that adult survivors were significantly more depressed than were their non-abused counterparts. Depression also played a mediating role in subsequent development of alcohol abuse. In a study of U.S. teenage girls (Rao, Daley, & Hammen, 2000), the co-occurrence of substance abuse disorder and major depression was high, with both occurring at approximately the same time. In this sample, substance abuse predicted major depression, but major depression did not predict substance abuse.

A history of childhood abuse was also related to participation in a drug treatment program. For women in treatment, a history of sexual abuse was associated with depression, anxiety, suicidal ideation, suicide attempts, and PTSD, but there were milder effects for child physical abuse. For men, on the other hand, only anxiety was associated with sexual abuse. But physical abuse was associated with depression, anxiety, suicidal ideation, and PTSD (Gil-Rivas, Fiorentine, Anglin, & Taylor, 1997). Sexual abuse was also related to a longer duration of depression in another study but not related to suicidal attempts (Zlotnick, Mattia, & Zimmerman, 2001).

Is Child Sexual Abuse Uniquely Harmful?

In looking at the impact of childhood abuse, an intriguing question arises. Is there something more inherently harmful about CSA that makes adult survivors more likely to experience depression as adults? Three studies have examined this issue specifically.

The first was a prospective study of girls removed from their home for abuse or neglect. One group was removed for confirmed sexual abuse. The second group was removed for physical neglect, absence of the mother, or household disorganization. Upon follow-up, a third group of women who had not been abused or removed from their homes was added. The researchers found that as adults, the women who had been sexually abused had significantly more depressive symptoms than either of the comparison groups (Bagley & McDonald, 1984).

The second study considered whether sexual abuse survivors were a distinct subgroup among depression patients (Gladstone, Parker, Wilhelm, & Mitchell, 1999). This study examined 269 outpatients with major depression, 46 of whom had histories of CSA. Those with a sexual abuse history had more self-reported depression, personality dysfunctions, and more overall adversity in childhood. Sexual abuse was also related to adult self-destructiveness. Sexual abuse was not a direct cause of depression in childhood, but it was associated with a greater chance of a dysfunctional home environment, having a borderline personality style, and experiencing depression in adulthood.

Zuravin and Fontanella (1999) compared the effects of sexual abuse to other types of maltreatment and family dysfunction. They examined data from 513 low-income women, 105 of whom were sexually abused, and considered depression and eleven other markers of family dysfunction, including four other types of maltreatment (verbal abuse, emotional neglect, physical abuse, and physical neglect). Their results indicated that women who had experienced CSA were three times more likely to be depressed than non-abused women in their sample. CSA made an independent contribution to the variance in depression that was over and above that of other adverse events in childhood.

In summary, the results from two of these three studies suggest that sexual abuse survivors are uniquely vulnerable to depression. This conclusion is tentative, however, because of the difficulties in teasing these relationships apart. CSA often co-occurs with other types of family pathology. Future studies may find that severity or timing of the experience may indeed prove to be more relevant than type of abuse.

THE BIOLOGY OF DEPRESSION

Abuse survivors may be more prone to depression because abusive experiences changed their physiology. Aversive experiences change neural circuitry and affect several key areas of the brain, including the amygdala, thalamus, hippocampus, and cerebral cortex (Andreasen, 1997). Abuse survivors may also have an activated inflammatory response system, which is related to both depression and increased vulnerability to disease (Danese et al., 2009; Danese, Pariante, Caspi, Taylor, & Poulton, 2007). These findings are described in more detail below.

Inflammation and Depression

Researchers have extensively documented the role of inflammation in depression (Kendall-Tackett, 2010; Maes, 2001; Maes et al., 2009b; Miller, 1998; Robles, Glaser, & Kiecolt-Glaser, 2005). This research is key to understanding how child maltreatment can influence adult health. Elevated levels of proinflammatory cytokines increase the risk of depression. And depression causes an elevation in proinflammatory cytokines. Proinflammatory cytokines are messenger molecules of the immune system that cause inflammation (see Chapter 2). The ones most frequently identified in depression research are interleukin 1β (IL-1β), interleukin-6 (IL-6), and tumor necrosis factor-α (TNF-α). C-reactive protein is an acute-phase reactant that is released by the liver in response to elevated levels of proinflammatory cytokines. It too is a measure of inflammation. Maes (2001) describes the relationships between inflammation and depression as follows:

> The discovery that psychological stress can induce the production of proin-

> flammatory cytokines has important implications for human psychopathology and, in particular, for the etiology of major depression. Psychological stressors, such as negative life events, are emphasized in the etiology of depression. Thus psychosocial and environmental stressors play a role as direct precipitants of major depression or they function as vulnerability factors which predispose humans to develop major depression. Major depression is accompanied by activation of the inflammatory response system (IRS) with, among other things, an increased production of proinflammatory cytokines, such as IL-1β, IL-6, TNF-α and IFN-γ, signs of monocytic- and T-cell activation and an acute-phase response. (p. 193)

The net result of these findings is that our bodies "translate" physical and psychological stress into inflammation, and it underlies all the other risk factors for depression. Inflammation is not simply a risk factor; it is the risk factor for depression, the one that ties the others together (Kendall-Tackett, 2007). Two studies have found an increase in inflammation in abuse survivors twenty years (Danese et al., 2007) and thirty-two years (Danese et al., 2009) after the abuse occurred.

Even within non-abused samples, there is a strong relationship between depression and inflammation, with important implications for health. For example, in a study of men and women at risk for heart disease ($N = 68$), Taylor et al. (2006) compared psychophysiological and cortisol reactions of depressed and nondepressed patients to psychological stress. The mean age of the patients was 62 years old, and all had risk factors for heart disease. Depressed patients had elevated C-reactive protein compared to the controls. The depressed patients also had abnormally low cortisol levels in response to stress, and a lower respiratory sinus arrhythmia.

In a sample of 129 patients with heart failure, soluble TNF-α levels were significantly higher in depressed versus non-depressed patients (Moorman et al., 2007). These findings were also true for the subgroup of patients who were no longer depressed, but were on antidepressant medications. These findings suggest that medications were treating depression, but not adequately reversing inflammation. There were no significant differences between the depressed and non-depressed groups in IL-1β or IL-6.

A review of 136 articles examined the relationship between depression and C-reactive protein, IL-6, IL-1, and IL-1ra (Howren, Lamkin, & Suls, 2009). They found that each inflammatory marker was positively associated with depression. The strongest associations were with populations of clinically depressed people. But they noted a similar, though weaker, relation in community samples. They also noted that there were three causal pathways: depression to inflammation, inflammation to depression, and a bidirectional relationship.

A population study of 6,005 men and women over age 30 from Finland found similar results (Elovainio et al., 2009). They found that C-reactive protein was related to depression for men, but not for women. The authors speculated that estrogen may be protecting women from the inflammatory processes during depression.

Another study of patients older than 65 years found that depression was related to both inflammation and coagulation factors (Kop et al., 2002). This study included 4,268 patients who were free of cardiovascular disease (mean age = 72.4 years). Depressed men and women had several measures of inflammation including elevated

C-reactive protein, elevated white blood cell count, and increased coaguability, which included elevated fibrinogen and factor VIIc. Exhaustion was related to both inflammation and coagulation markers, especially for men. Exhausted men had significantly a higher C-reactive protein levels. It was also related to higher albumin and fibrinogen, and higher white blood cell count. Proinflammatory markers were more robustly related to exhaustion than to depression. The authors concluded that depression and exhaustion were both associated with low-grade inflammation and elevated coagulation factors.

One of the more intriguing aspects of this research is that it becomes an organizing framework for understanding treatment. All effective treatments for depression are specifically anti-inflammatory. This includes medications, psychotherapy, exercise, and even social support (Kendall-Tackett, 2010; Maes et al., 2009a).

Depression and HPA Alterations

Vulnerability to depression may also come about because of abuse-related changes in the hypothalamic-pituitary-adrenal (HPA) axis. In a review of the literature examining the link between childhood sexual abuse and depression in women, Weiss, Longhurst, and Mazure (1999) noted that early stressors produce long-term dysregulation in the HPA axis, including hypersecretion of corticotropin-releasing hormone (CRH). These stressors can create a lifelong vulnerability to depression in adulthood. Depressed people, especially those with major depressive disorder, often have elevated cortisol levels and less diurnal variation in cortisol, indicating alterations in the HPA system. Elevated cortisol levels can lead to a breakdown of serotonin.

This observation has been confirmed by Heim et al. (2000). Their study compared four groups of women: those with no history of childhood abuse or psychiatric disorder, those with a current diagnosis of major depression who were physically or sexually abused as children, abuse survivors who were not currently depressed, and those who were depressed but had no history of childhood abuse. The authors measured ACTH (adrenocorticotropic hormone) and cortisol levels, and heart rate responsiveness to a standardized laboratory stressor. Women abused as children had increased responsiveness to stress compared with controls, and increased ACTH concentrations compared with controls and non-abused depressed women.

Elevated levels of cortisol, particularly if it is elevated over a sustained period, can produce immune suppression, cardiovascular dysfunctions, and even death of certain cell populations (Campeau, Day, Helmreich, Kollack-Walker, & Watson, 1998). Increased levels of cortisol can lead to difficulties with the hippocampus. McEwen (1999) noted that chronically high levels of cortisol can atrophy pyramidal neurons of the hippocampus. After prolonged or severe stress, these neurons may actually die. Depressed patients, even formerly depressed patients, had smaller hippocampal volume than did patients who were not depressed. The decrease in volume ranged from 12 percent in the right hippocampus to 19 percent in the left hippocampus (Sapolsky, 2000).

The effects of childhood abuse and current major depression were particularly strong. The women who were currently depressed and who had a history of abuse had a sixfold greater ACTH response to stress than did age-matched controls. Minutes after the stress, the abused women with major depression also had higher cortisol levels than all the other groups (Heim et al., 2000). Finally, abused women with major depression exhibited significantly higher heart rate responses than the controls. The authors interpreted their findings as indicating a hyperreactivity of the HPA in abuse survivors, and this may have contributed to their vulnerability to adult depression. In the abuse survivors without depression, there appears to be a different mechanism at work. These women had increased ACTH concentrations but normal cortisol responses. The depressed non-abused women showed normal stress reactivity.

HPA abnormality is also used to explain somatic symptoms that accompany depression, including gastrointestinal, gynecological, urological, cardiovascular, endocrinological, musculoskeletal, and immune system disturbances. Although the mechanism for these somatic complaints is not well understood, some postulate that changes in hypothalamic and pituitary function, as well as changes in the adrenal medulla, are responsible. Indeed, all types of antidepressants improve HPA function in both human and animal studies (Plotsky, Owens, & Nemeroff, 1998).

DEPRESSION AND COGNITIVE PROCESSES

Gibb et al. (2001), in their study of 297 adults, examined the cognitive processes involved in depression for adult survivors of childhood abuse. They examined the role of hopelessness and dysfunctional self-schema as two possible mechanisms by which abuse experiences become translated to depression. They included three different types of maltreatment: physical abuse, sexual abuse, and emotional abuse. They did not find a significant relationship between sexual abuse and participants' cognitive style. Further, they did not find a relationship between physical or sexual abuse and average levels of hopelessness or diagnoses of either endogenous or hopelessness depression. Only childhood emotional abuse was related to hopelessness and depression.

Another study of 201 undergraduates found that survivors of childhood sexual abuse were more likely to ruminate on sadness, which increased their vulnerability to depression, than were their non-abused counterparts (Conway, Mendelson, Giannopoulos, Csank, & Holm, 2004). Rumination on sadness includes thoughts regarding the antecedents, nature, and consequences of one's current affective state. It is not goal-directed and does not lead to plans for remedial action. It is a solitary, negative activity and is intrusive. Interestingly, the ruminations were not regarding their prior sexual abuse, but they could be triggered by a wide range of current circumstances. Rumination on sadness is significant in that it may lead sad people to become more dysphoric or depressed. It can also interfere with goal-directed behavior that could attenuate or remedy the immediate problem causing the distress, and it makes it more difficult for people to address their own distress in a more constructive way. The authors indicated that cognitive-behavioral techniques would likely prove beneficial in helping abuse survivors with ruminative thoughts since the goal of cognitive therapy was to help clients identify, evaluate, and respond to persistent thoughts in a more adaptive way.

HOW DEPRESSION INFLUENCES HEALTH

Depression has a profound and devastating impact on health, and its effects are myriad. In the Global Burden of Disease Study, major depression was the fourth most common cause of early death and disability throughout the world, and second only to coronary artery disease in industrialized countries (Murray & Lopez, 1997). A number of health problems have been associated with depression including coronary heart disease, myocardial infarction, chronic pain syndromes, premature aging, impaired immune function, impaired wound healing, Alzheimer's disease, and even premature mortality (Howren et al., 2009; Kiecolt-Glaser & Glaser, 2002; Kiecolt-Glaser et al., 2005; Mykletun et al., 2009; Wilson, Finch, & Cohen, 2002). All of these have been linked to increased inflammation.

In a study of veterans ($N = 35{,}715$), patients who had a history of depression without PTSD were at increased risk of death over the two-year study period, while those who had PTSD but not depression were not at increased risk (Kinder et al., 2008). The researchers found that patients with depression were more likely to smoke and abuse substances and to have a history of other medical conditions including cancer, lung disease, heart disease, pneumonia, and stroke. Depression also affects pain perception. In a study of patients with rheumatoid arthritis (RA), those who had had an episode of major depression, but who were not currently depressed, had more pain from RA than those who did not (Fifield, Tennen, Reisine, & McQuillan, 1998).

Depression and Cardiovascular Health

Most of the research on depression and health has examined the link between depression and cardiovascular disease. Depression is a robust risk factor for cardiovascular disease, and even minor symptoms increase risk (Davidson, Rieckmann, & Lesperance, 2004; Frasure-Smith & Lesperance, 2005; Rutledge et al., 2006). Specifically, depression leads to poor treatment adherence, more frequent and earlier hospital readmissions, and higher rates of behavioral cardiac risk factors including smoking, obesity, and lack of exercise. It also increases the risk of cardiovascular events and mortality following a cardiac event (Davidson et al., 2004; Rutledge et al., 2006).

A large population study in Norway ($N = 61{,}349$) found that case-level depression was associated with increased mortality at a level comparable to smoking (Mykletun et al., 2009). This relationship was only partially explained by confounding factors, such as somatic symptoms, physical impairments, physical activity, smoking, alcohol problems, educational level and socioeconomic status (SES), blood pressure, cholesterol, and body mass index (BMI). The effect was stronger for younger participants. Oddly, comorbid anxiety reduced mortality compared to depression alone. But the relation of anxiety to mortality was U-shaped, with increased mortality in the highest and lowest quartiles.

Depression predicted cardiac symptoms in a sample of 750 women middle-age women with suspected myocardial ischemia. As part of the study, these women underwent an exam that included depression measures, coronary angiogram, ischemia testing, and a coronary disease risk factor assessment (Rutledge et al., 2006). These women were followed for 2.3 years and monitored for cardiac events. Both treatment for depression and current depression severity were related to cardiac symptoms and outcomes. Depressed women had more chest tightness, left-arm pain, angina during sleep, knife-like pain, and use of nitroglycerin. Depression severity increased mortality risk over the course of the follow-up. Each point increase on the Beck Depression Inventory was associated with a 3 percent increase in mortality risk even after adjusting for age, disease severity, and other coronary artery disease risk factors. History of treatment for depression was related to increased risk for hospitalization, but also to less severe coronary artery disease from angiogram and lower likelihood of a positive ischemia test.

In a prospective study of 457 acute coronary syndrome patients, researchers examined the link between depression and mortality above and beyond the effect of known prognostic indicators (Kronish, Rieckmann, Schwartz, Schwartz, & Davidson, 2009). They discovered the depression did increase mortality independent of known prognosticators, including smoking, hypercholesterolemia, hypertension, and diabetes.

In a ten-year longitudinal study of 309 patients who had coronary artery bypass surgery, the overall mortality rate was 37.9 percent, with 20 percent due to cardiac causes (Connerney, Sloan, Shapiro, Bagiella, & Seckman, 2010). Patients who met the criteria for major depressive disorder in the hospital had an almost twofold increased risk for cardiac mortality in the ten years postsurgery. The authors concluded that depression was significantly associated with elevated cardiac mortality ten years after coronary bypass surgery.

Depression that develops after a cardiac event is also predictive of cardiac events post-myocardial infarction. In a recent review of psychosocial factors in the development of heart disease in women (Low, Thurston, & Matthews, 2010), Low and colleagues noted that depression, anxiety disorders, anger suppression, and relationship-related stress were associated with increased risk of coronary heart disease. The strongest relationship between depression and heart disease is found when depression is severe and chronic. Supportive relationships lower risk, and general anxiety, hostility, and work-related stress were less consistently related to heart disease relative to men. They also noted that psychological interventions for depression have not benefited women with regard to cardiovascular outcomes.

Another study (Carney et al., 2009) compared three groups of patients recovering from myocardial infarction (MI): those with no history of depression ($n = 408$), those with an initial episode of depression post-MI ($n = 370$), and those with recurrent depression ($n = 550$). The researchers followed these patients for approximately twenty-nine months. They found that both initial episode and recurrent depression decreased survival time. But the patients with the poorest survival rates were those who had an initial episode of depression following their MI: 18.4 percent died by follow-up (all-cause mortality), compared with 11.8 percent of those with recurrent depression, and 3.4 percent for those with no history of depression. The patients with initial depression did not have more severe coronary heart disease than the other two groups, so that possible explanation does not account for these findings.

In a study of elderly patients, eighteen patients with chronic heart failure and major depression were compared with sixteen patients with heart failure and no depression and thirteen healthy controls (Andrei et al., 2007). Patients with chronic heart failure and major depression had significantly higher C-reactive protein levels than the healthy controls. The C-reactive protein levels of the nondepressed heart patients were elevated compared to the healthy controls, but not significantly so. There were no differences in TNF-α or IL-6 between the groups.

Why might the inflammation associated with depression increase the risk of heart disease? Kop and Gottdiener (2005) hypothesized that depression in early adulthood may actually promote vascular injury, and that the immune system may increase further early-stage cardiovascular disease by encouraging lipid and macrophage deposits. For people with preexisting cardiovascular disease, the chronic inflammation associated with depression can reduce the stability of plaque, which can lead to acute cardiac episodes.

Depression, Metabolic Syndrome, and Obesity

Depressed people are also at risk for other health conditions in addition to heart disease. Depression increases the risk of obesity, metabolic syndrome, and diabetes. A study of 6,820 men and 3,346 women from London found that people with mental disorders of all types, as measured by the General Health Questionnaire, had an excess risk of obesity, and this difference did not vary by race or gender (Kivimaki et al., 2009). Obesity increased with age across the sample, with 6 percent obese at age 40 and 35 percent obese at age 70. The authors found that the link between obesity and mental disorders increases with age.

A recent meta-analysis of fifteen prospective, cohort studies ($N = 58{,}745$) found a reciprocal relationship between depression and obesity (Luppino et al., 2010). The authors found that being overweight or obese at baseline increased the risk of onset of depression, with a stronger relationship among American versus European subjects. Obese persons had a 55 percent increased risk of developing depression over time, and depressed persons had a 58 percent increased risk of becoming obese. To explain their findings, they hypothesized that obesity can be seen as an inflammatory state. Weight gain activates inflammatory pathways, and inflammation causes depression. Because inflammation is involved in both depression and obesity, they speculated that it could be the mediator between obesity and depression.

Along these same lines, a prospective study of 496 adolescent girls from Austin, Texas, found that obesity—but not overweight—status was associated with future depressive symptoms (Boutelle, Hannan, Fulkerson, Crow, & Stice, 2010). This study considered whether obesity could be a trigger for depression. It demonstrated that obesity is a risk factor for depressive symptoms, but not for clinical depression. A study from Finland had similar findings (Elovainio et al., 2010). In this study of 824 young adults, participants whose triglyceride levels increased over time were more likely to be depressed as adults. This relationship persisted even after accounting for various risk factors. Also, a higher childhood BMI and a greater change in BMI from childhood to adulthood also predicted depressive symptoms.

In a study of 409 middle-age women, 45 percent of whom were black, depressive symptoms were related to increased visceral fat, a symptom of metabolic syndrome (Everson-Rose et al., 2009). Visceral fat, that is fat around the abdomen and internal organs, is more metabolically active and confers greater cardiovascular risk than subcutaneous fat. The researchers found that depressed women had 24.5 percent more visceral fat than women who were not depressed, or only mildly depressed. There were no differences for blacks and whites. The findings were strongest for women who were overweight or obese. The authors speculated that the mechanism by which depression contributes to visceral fat may be due to either inflammation or an excess of cortisol due to HPA axis activation.

A study of 652 women who had received coronary angiography explored the links between depression and symptoms of metabolic syndrome (Vaccarino et al., 2008). Women who had had both prior episodes of depression and current depressive symptoms had an 80 percent higher odds for metabolic syndrome compared to women with no depression. The number of metabolic symptoms increased across the categories of depression (no depression, 1 type, 2 types). Triglyceride levels and waist circumference had the strongest relation to depression. Over the 5.9-year follow-up, women who experienced both types of depression had 2.6 times higher risk of cardiovascular disease. Both depression and metabolic syndrome were significant predictors for cardiovascular disease.

Depression prospectively predicted metabolic syndrome in a study from the Pittsburgh cohort of the SWAN (Study of Women's Health Across the Nation) study, a seven-year longitudinal study of women in midlife (Goldbacher, Bromberger, & Matthews, 2009). This study found that in women who were free of metabolic syndrome at the outset of the study, a lifetime history of major depression, or a current major depressive episode at baseline, was significantly associated with developing metabolic syndrome at follow-up. Lifetime alcohol abuse at baseline also predicted metabolic syndrome and attenuated the effect of depression. The authors concluded that depression is a significant predictor of the onset of metabolic syndrome, and that targeting depression may prevent the development of metabolic syndrome.

Depressive symptoms also increased the risk of Type 2 diabetes in a sample from the English Longitudinal Study of Aging, a study of 6,111 community-dwelling, middle-age and older adults (Demakakos, Pierce, & Hardy, 2010). These findings were true even after accounting for many factors that impact diabetes risk: age, marital status, education, socioeconomic status, BMI, cardiovascular, psychiatric comorbidities, and health behaviors. The authors noted that the risk associated with depression was comparable to risk associated with lack of exercise.

In patients who already have diabetes, depression is related to increased mortality, and people with diabetes are twice as likely to experience depression compared with the general population. In a cohort of 4,184 patients with Type 2 diabetes, 12.9 percent of patients with no depression died compared with 17.8 percent of patients with depression (Lin et al., 2009). Forty-three percent of the deaths were due to cardiovascular disease, 27 percent were due to cancer, and the remaining 31 percent were due to a range of other conditions including infections, dementia, renal failure, and chronic obstructive pulmonary disease (COPD). After adjusting for demographic characteristics, depression was related only to all-cause mortality.

Depression and Health Behaviors

Depression is also related to health behaviors. In a review of the literature, negative emotions were correlated with poor eating habits, use of tobacco, and abuse of alcohol and drugs. People may use these harmful behaviors as a way to cope with negative emotions (Salovey, Rothman, Detweiler, & Steward, 2000). Even chocolate consumption increases when people are depressed, unfortunately without alleviating symptoms. Indeed, the increase in chocolate consumption often adds guilt feelings to already negative emotions.

In a study of more than 5,000 male and female college students, depression was associated with lack of physical activity, not eating breakfast, irregular sleep hours, and not using a seatbelt in men and women. In addition, depression was associated with smoking, not eating fruit, and not using sunscreen in women (Allgower, Wardle, & Steptoe, 2001). Depression has been shown to have a direct and significant impact on nicotine dependence in a study of male and female college students who smoke (Ong & Walsh, 2001). And depressed elderly patients were less likely to comply with treatment following a heart attack (Carney, Freedland, Eisen, Rich, & Jaffe, 1995).

Depression and Increased Vulnerability

Depression is associated with less support and more problems in social relationships (Wade & Kendler, 2000). The association was strongest for the more intimate social relationships, such as spouse and relatives. A prior incident of major depression significantly predicted who would develop peritraumatic dissociative symptoms (a precursor of PTSD) following a car accident (Fullerton et al., 2000). There were no significant findings for presence of a previous traumatic event. The authors speculated that because major depression is comorbid with PTSD, peritraumatic dissociation may be part of the neurobiological link between PTSD and depression.

In a thirty-five-year follow-up of 113 men, there was an attempt to determine whether depression could cause negative life events. The authors looked at two types of negative life events: "independent life events"—those that occurred without the subject's complicity (e.g., death of a family member, wife or child's medical condition, and mental or drug problems)—and "dependent life events"—those events that occurred with the men's involvement (e.g., marital separation or divorce and legal or employment difficulties). Because of the longitudinal nature of the data collection, the authors were able to determine whether events occurred before or after an episode of depression.

Dependent life events were significantly related to depression, whereas independent life events were only marginally so. After their first episode of depression, events more likely to occur for depressed men were separation, financial problems, being fired, unemployment, and legal difficulties. Depression appears to create a "domino effect" of negative events and had a major impact on their lives. These negative life events contributed to the chronicity of depression (Cui & Vaillant, 1997). Depression could also influence health through employment problems, and disruptions in relationships.

SUMMARY

Depression is common in abuse survivors. It can lead to serious health consequences, including conditions with high rates of mortality, such as heart disease and diabetes. Chapter 12 describes PTSD, another common sequela of childhood abuse that is often comorbid with depression. It too can have a serious impact on health.

References

Allgower, A., Wardle, J., & Steptoe, A. (2001). Depressive symptoms, social support, and personal health behaviors in young men and women. *Health Psychology, 20*(3), 223–227.

Andreasen, N. C. (1997). Linking mind and brain in the study of mental illness: A project for a scientific psychopathology. *Science, 275*, 1586–1593.

Andrei, A. M., Fraguas, R., Jr., Telles, R. M., Alves, T. C., Strunz, C. M., Nussbacher, A., et al. (2007). Major depressive disorder and inflammatory markers in elderly patients with heart failure. *Psychosomatics, 48*(4), 319–324.

Bagley, C., & McDonald, M. (1984). Adult mental health sequels of child sexual abuse, physical abuse and neglect in maternally separated children. *Canadian Journal of Community Mental Health, 3*, 15–26.

Benedict, M. I., Paine, L. L., Paine, L. A., Brandt, D., & Stallings, R. (1999). The associations of childhood sexual abuse with depressive symptoms during pregnancy, and selected pregnancy outcomes. *Child Abuse and Neglect, 23*, 659–670.

Boutelle, K. N., Hannan, P., Fulkerson, J. A., Crow, S. J., & Stice, E. (2010). Obesity as a prospective predictor of depression in adolescent females. *Health Psychology, 29*(3), 293–298.

Bremner, J. D., Randall, P., Vermetten, E., Staib, L., Bronen, R. A., Mazure, C. M., et al. (1997). Magnetic resonance imaging-based measurements of hippocampal volume in posttraumatic stress disorder related to childhood physical and sexual abuse: A preliminary report. *Biological Psychiatry, 41*, 23–32.

Briere, J. N., & Elliot, D. M. (1994). Immediated and long-term impacts of child sexual abuse. *The Future of Children, 4*, 54–69.

Briere, J. N., Woo, R., McRae, B., Foltz, J., & Sitzman, R. (1997). Lifetime victimization history, demographics, and clinical status in female psychiatric emergency room patients. *Journal of Nervous and Mental Disease, 185*, 95–101.

Brown, J., Cohen, P., Johnson, J. G., & Smailes, E. M. (1999). Childhood abuse and neglect: Specificity of effects on adolescent and young adult depression and suicidality. *Journal of the American Academy of Child and Adolescent Psychiatry, 38*, 1490–1496.

Campeau, S., Day, H. E. W., Helmreich, D. L., Kollack-Walker, S., & Watson, S. J. (1998). Principles of psychoneuroendocrinology. *Psychiatric Clinics of North America, 21*, 259–275.

Carney, R. M., Freedland, K. E., Eisen, S. A., Rich, M. W., & Jaffe, A. S. (1995). Major depression and medication adherence in elderly patients with coronary artery disease. *Health Psychology, 14*, 88–90.

Carney, R. M., Freedland, K. E., Steinmeyer, B., Blumenthal, J. A., DeJonge, P., Davidson, K. W., et al. (2009). History of depression and survival after acute myocardial infarction. *Psychosomatic Medicine, 71*, 253–259.

Cheasty, M., Clare, A. W., & Collins, C. (1998). Relation between sexual abuse in childhood and adult depression: Case-control study. *British Medical Journal, 316*, 198–201.

Choquet, M., Darves-Bornoz, J.-M., Ledoux, S., Manfredi, R., & Hassler, C. (1997). Self-reported health and behavioral problems among adolescent victims of rape in France: Results of a cross-sectional survey. *Child Abuse and Neglect, 21*, 823–832.

Connerney, I., Sloan, R. P., Shapiro, P. A., Bagiella, E., & Seckman, C. (2010). Depression is associated with increased mortality 10 years after coronary artery bypass surgery. *Psychosomatic Medicine, 72*(9).

Conway, M., Mendelson, M., Giannopoulos, C., Csank, P. A. R., & Holm, S. L. (2004). Childhood and adult sexual abuse, rumination on sadness, and dysphoria. *Child Abuse and Neglect, 28*, 393–410.

Cui, X.-J., & Vaillant, G. E. (1997). Does depression generate negative life events? *Journal of Nervous and Mental Disease, 185*, 145–150.

Danese, A., Moffitt, T. E., Harrington, H., Milne, B. J., Polanczyk, G., Pariante, C. M., et al. (2009). Adverse childhood experiences and adult risk factors for age-related disease: Depression, inflammation, and clustering of metabolic risk factors. *Archives of Pediatric & Adolescent Medicine, 163*(12), 1135–1143.

Danese, A., Pariante, C. M., Caspi, A., Taylor, A., & Poulton, R. (2007). Childhood maltreatment predicts adult inflammation in a life-course study. *Proceedings of the National Academy of Sciences USA, 104*(4), 1319–1324.

Davidson, K. W., Rieckmann, N., & Lesperance, F. (2004). Psychological theories of depression: Potential application for the prevention of acute coronary syndrome recurrence. *Psychosomatic Medicine, 66*, 165–173.

Demakakos, P., Pierce, M. B., & Hardy, R. (2010). Depressive symptoms and risk of Type 2 diabetes in a national sample of middle-aged and older adults. *Diabetes Care, 33*, 792–797.

Diaz, A., Simatov, E., & Rickert, V. I. (2000). The independent and combined effects of physical and sexual abuse on health. Results from a national survey. *Journal of Pediatric and Adolescent Gynecology, 13*, 89.

Elovainio, M., Aalto, A.-M., Kivimaki, M., Pirkola, S., Sundvall, J., Lonnqvist, J., et al. (2009). Depression and C-reactive protein: Population-based Health 2000 Study. *Psychosomatic Medicine, 71*, 423–430.

Elovainio, M., Pulkki-Raback, L., Kivimaki, M., Jokela, M., Viikari, J. S., Raitakari, O. T., et al. (2010). Lipid trajectories as predictors of depressive symptoms: The Young Finns study. *Health Psychology, 29*(3), 237–245.

Everson-Rose, S. A., Lewis, T. T., Karavolos, K., Dugan, S. A., Wesley, D., & Powell, L. H. (2009). Depressive symptoms and increased visceral fat in middle-aged women. *Psychosomatic Medicine, 71*, 410–416.

Felitti, V. J. (1991). Long-term medical consequences of incest, rape, and molestation. *Southern Medical Journal, 84*, 328–331.

Fergusson, D. M., & Horwood, L. J. (1998). Exposure to interparental violence in childhood and psychosocial adjustment in young adulthood. *Child Abuse and Neglect, 22*, 339–357.

Fifield, J., Tennen, H., Reisine, S., & McQuillan, J. (1998). Depression and the long-term risk of pain, fatigue, and disability in patients with rheumatoid arthritis. *Arthritis and Rheumatism, 41*, 1851–1857.

Frasure-Smith, N., & Lesperance, F. (2005). Reflections on depression as a cardiac risk factor. *Psychosomatic Medicine, 67*, S19–S25.

Fullerton, C. S., Ursano, R. J., Epstein, R. S., Crowley, R., Vance, K. L., Kao, T.-C., et al. (2000). Peritraumatic dissociation following motor vehicles accidents. *Journal of Nervous and Mental Disease, 188*, 267–272.

Gibb, B. E., Alloy, L. B., Abramson, L. Y., Rose, D. T., Whitehouse, W. G., Donovan, P., et al.. (2001). History of childhood maltreatment, negative cognitive styles, and episodes of depression in adulthood. *Cognitive Therapy and Research, 25*(4), 425–446.

Gil-Rivas, V., Fiorentine, R., Anglin, M. D., & Taylor, E. (1997). Sexual and physical abuse: Do they compromise drug treatment outcomes? *Journal of Substance Abuse Treatment, 14*, 351–358.

Gladstone, G., Parker, G., Wilhelm, K., & Mitchell, P. (1999). Characteristics of depressed patients who report childhood sexual abuse. *American Journal of Psychiatry, 156*, 431–437.

Goldbacher, E. M., Bromberger, J., & Matthews, K. A. (2009). Lifetime history of major depression predicts the development of the metabolic syndrome in middle-aged women. *Psychosomatic Medicine, 71*, 266–272.

Heim, C., Newport, D. J., Heit, S., Graham, Y. P., Wilcox, M., Bonsall, R., et al. (2000). Pituitary-adrenal and autonomic responses to stress in women after sexual and physical abuse in childhood. *Journal of the American Medical Association 284*, 592–597.

Howren, M. B., Lamkin, D. M., & Suls, J. (2009). Associations of depression with C-Reactive protein, IL-1, and IL-6: A meta-analysis. *Psychosomatic Medicine, 71*, 171–186.

Hulme, P. A. (2000). Symptomatology and health care utilization of women primary care patients who experienced childhood sexual abuse. *Child Abuse and Neglect, 24*, 1471–1484.

Kendall–Tackett, K. A. (2007). A new paradigm for depression in new mothers: The central role of inflammation and how breastfeeding and anti-inflammatory treatments protect mental health. *International Breastfeeding Journal, 2*(6). Available online at: *http://www.international breastfeedingjournal.com/contents/2/1/6.*

Kendall–Tackett, K. A. (Ed.). (2010). *The psychoneuroimmunology of chronic disease*. Washington, DC: American Psychological Association.

Kendall-Tackett, K. A., Marshall, R., & Ness, K. E. (2003). Chronic pain syndromes and violence against women. *Women and Therapy, 26*, 45–56.

Kiecolt-Glaser, J. K., & Glaser, R. (2002). Depression and immune function: Central pathways to morbidity and mortality. *Journal of Psychosomatic Research, 53*, 873–876.

Kiecolt-Glaser, J. K., Loving, T. J., Stowell, J. R., Malarky, W. B., Lemeshow, S., Dickinson, S. L., & Glaser, R. (2005). Hostile marital interactions, proinflammatory cytokine production, and wound healing. *Archives of General Psychiatry, 62*, 1377–1384.

Kinder, L. S., Bradley, K. A., Katon, W. J., Ludman, E. J., McDonnell, M. B., & Bryson, C. L. (2008). Depression, posttraumatic stress disorder, and mortality. *Psychosomatic Medicine, 70*, 20–26.

Kivimaki, M., Batty, G. D., Singh-Manoux, A., Nabi, H., Sabia, S., Tabak, A. G., et al. (2009). Association between common mental disorder and obesity over the adult life course. *British Journal of Psychiatry, 195*, 149–155.

Kop, W. J., & Gottdiener, J. S. (2005). The role of immune system parameters in the relationship between depression and coronary artery disease. *Psychosomatic Medicine, 67*, S37–S41.

Kop, W. J., Gottdiener, J. S., Tangen, C. M., Fried, L. P., McBurnie, M. A., Walston, J., et al. (2002). Inflammation and coagulation factors in persons > 65 years of age with symptoms of depression but without evidence of myocardial ischemia. *American Journal of Cardiology, 89*(4), 419–424.

Kronish, I. M., Rieckmann, N., Schwartz, J. E., Schwartz, D. R., & Davidson, K. W. (2009). Is depression after an acute coronary syndrome simply a marker of known prognostic factors for mortality? *Psychosomatic Medicine, 71*, 697–703.

Levitan, R. D., Parikh, S. V., Lesage, A. D., Hegadoren, K. M., Adams, M., Kennedy, S. H., et al. (1998). Major depression in individuals with a history of childhood physical or sexual abuse: Relationship to neurovegative features, mania, and gender. *American Journal of Psychiatry, 155*, 1746–1752.

Liem, J. H., & Boudewyn, A. C. (1999). Contextualizing the effects of childhood sexual abuse on adult self- and social functioning: An attachment theory perspective. *Child Abuse and Neglect, 23*, 1141–1157.

Lin, E. H. B., Heckbert, S. R., Rutter, C. M., Katon, W. J., Ciechanowski, P., Ludman, E. J., et al. (2009). Depression and increased mortality in diabetes: Unexpected causes of death. *Annals of Family Medicine, 7*(5), 414–421.

Low, C. A., Thurston, R. C., & Matthews, K. A. (2010). Psychosoical faxtors in the development of heart disease in women: Current research and future directions. *Psychosomatic Medicine, 72*(9), 842–854.

Luppino, F. S., deWit, L. M., Bouvy, P. F., Stijnen, T., Cuijpers, P., Penninx, B. W. J. H., et al. (2010). Overweight, obesity, and depression: A systematic review and meta-analysis of longitudinal studies. *Archives of General Psychiatry, 67*(3), 220–229.

Maes, M. (2001). Psychological stress and the inflammatory response system. *Clinical Science, 101*, 193–194.

Maes, M., Christophe, A., Bosmans, E., Lin, A., & Neels, H. (2000). In humans, serum polyunsaturated fatty acid levels predict the response of proinflammatory cytokines to psychologic stress. *Biological Psychiatry, 47*, 910–920.

Maes, M., Yirmyia, R., Noraberg, J., Brene, S., Hibblen, J., Perini, G., et al. (2009a). The inflammatory & neurodegenerative (I&ND) hypothesis of depression: Leads for future research and new drug development. *Metabolic Brain Disease, 24*, 27–53.

Maes, M., Yirmyia, R., Noraberg, J., Brene, S., Hibblen, J., Perini, G., et al. (2009b). The inflammatory & neurodegenerative hypothesis of depression: Leads for future research and new drug developments in depression. *Metabolic Brain Disease, 24*, 27–53.

McEwen, B. (1999). Development of the cerebral cortex: XIII Stress and brain development: II. *Journal of the American Academy of Child and Adolescent Psychiatry, 38*, 101–103.

Miller, A. H. (1998). Neuroendocrine and immune system interactions in stress and depression. *Psychiatric Clinics of North America, 21*, 443–463.

Moorman, A. J., Mozaffarian, D., Wilkinson, C. W., Lawler, R. L., McDonald, G. B., Crane, B. A., et al. (2007). In patients with heart failure elevated soluble TNF-receptor 1 is associated with higher risk of depression. *Journal of Cardiac Failure, 13*(9), 738–743.

Murray, C. J. L., & Lopez, A. D. (1997). Global mortality, disability, and the contribution of risk factors: Global Burden of Disease Study. *Lancet, 349*, 1436–1442.

Mykletun, A., Bjerkeset, O., Overland, S., Prince, M., Dewey, M., & Stewart, R. (2009). Levels of anxiety and depression as predictors of mortality: The HUNT study. *British Journal of Psychiatry, 195*, 118–125.

Ong, A. D., & Walsh, D. A. (2001). Nicotine dependence, depression, and the moderating role of goal cognitions. *Psychology of Addictive Behaviors, 25*, 252–254.

Plotsky, P. M., Owens, M. J., & Nemeroff, C. B. (1998). Psychoneuroendocrinology of depression: Hypothalamic-pituitary-adrenal axis. *Psychiatric Clinics of North America, 21*, 293–307.

Rao, U., Daley, S. E., & Hammen, C. (2000). Relationship between depression and substance use disorder in adolescent women during the transition to adulthood. *Journal of the American Academy of Child and Adolescent Psychiatry, 39*, 215–222.

Robles, T. F., Glaser, R., & Kiecolt-Glaser, J. K. (2005). Out of balance: A new look at chronic stress, depression, and immunity. *Current Directions in Psychological Science, 14*, 111–115.

Rutledge, T., Reis, S. E., Olson, M., Owens, J., Kelsey, S. F., Pepine, C. J., et al.. (2006). Depression is associated with cardiac symptoms, mortality risk, and hospitalization among women with suspected coronary disease: the NHLBI-sponsored WISE study. *Psychosomatic Medicine, 68*(2), 217–223.

Salovey, P., Rothman, A. J., Detweiler, J. B., & Steward, W. T. (2000). Emotional states and physical health. *American Psychologist, 55*, 110–121.

Sapolsky, R. M. (2000). Glucocorticoids and hippocampal atrophy in neuropsychiatric disorders. *Archives of General Psychiatry, 57*, 925–935.

Schuck, A. M., & Widom, C. S. (2001). Childhood victimization and alcohol symptoms in females: Causal inferences and hypothesized mediators. *Child Abuse and Neglect, 25*, 1069–1092.

Taylor, C. B., Conrad, A., Wilhelm, F. H., Neri, E., DeLorenzo, A., Kramer, M. A., et al. (2006). Psychophysiological and cortisol responses to psychological stress in depressed and nondepressed older men and women with elevated cardiovascular disease risk. *Psychosomatic Medicine, 68*(4), 538–546.

Vaccarino, V., McClure, C., Johnson, D., Sheps, D. S., Bittner, V., Rutledge, T., et al. (2008). Depression, the metabolic syndrome and cardiovascular risk. *Psychosomatic Medicine, 70*, 40–48.

Wade, T. D., & Kendler, K. S. (2000). The relationship between social support and major depression: Cross-sectional, longitudinal, and genetic perspectives. *Journal of Nervous and Mental Disease, 188*, 251–258.

Weiss, E. L., Longhurst, J. G., & Mazure, C. M. (1999). Childhoood sexual abuse as a risk factor for depression in women: Psychosocial and neurobiological correlates. *American Journal of Psychiatry, 156*, 816–828.

Wilson, C. J., Finch, C. E., & Cohen, H. J. (2002). Cytokines and cognition—The case for a head-to-toe inflammatory paradigm. *Journal of the American Geriatrics Society, 50*, 2041–2056.

Zlotnick, C., Mattia, J., & Zimmerman, M. (2001). Clinical features of survivors of sexual abuse with major depression. *Child Abuse and Neglect, 25*, 357–367.

Zuravin, S. J., & Fontanella, C. (1999). The relationship between child sexual abuse and major depression among low-income women: A function of growing up experiences? *Child Maltreatment, 4*, 3–12.

Chapter 12

Emotional Pathways II—Posttraumatic Stress Disorder

People who experience psychological trauma, either as children or adults, may manifest symptoms of posttraumatic stress disorder (PTSD). PTSD is a common, but not universal, response to stress and is one type of potential reaction that includes major depression and somatic complaints (Yehuda, 1998). Initially, PTSD was proposed as a normative response to extreme stress. In fact, research has demonstrated that only a small minority of individuals exposed to traumatic events develop PTSD (Heim & Nemeroff, 2009). That raises many issues about why some people are vulnerable to this condition while others can experience extreme stress and not develop PTSD. PTSD was originally formulated to describe reactions of men who had been in combat. It has been applied to trauma associated with childhood abuse.

PTSD IN ABUSE SURVIVORS

While not all survivors of childhood abuse develop PTSD, many do. In addition, childhood victimization can increase one's vulnerability to developing PTSD when exposed to a subsequent life stressor.

Studies With Children

In a study of children exposed to chronic or single-incident trauma, McCloskey and Walker (2000) found that approximately 25 percent met the diagnostic criteria for PTSD. Death or illness of someone close to the child was the event most likely to lead to PTSD. Both child physical abuse and observing partner violence were also frequent causes of PTSD. Children who were physically abused were twice as likely to have PTSD as children who witnessed abuse of their mothers. Children with a history of abuse were not more likely to develop PTSD when exposed to a subsequent stressor. However, the authors speculated that this group of children had experienced so much violence and abuse that one more incident was unlikely to add to their symptoms.

A sample of 157 help-seeking children, ages 8–17, found that witnessing domestic violence, physical abuse, and sexual abuse were each significantly associated with PTSD (Luthra et al., 2009). Other trauma exposures were not related to PTSD. These included witnessing or being the victim of a crime and exposure to accidents, fire, or disaster. The authors concluded that type of trauma exposure is related to child PTSD. Their findings underscore the importance of interpersonal violence in the etiology of PTSD.

A recent study of twenty sexually abused children in Turkey found that 35 percent met the criteria for PTSD at their first assessment, 10 percent for general anxiety disorder, and 10 percent for major depression (Ozbaran et al., 2009). There were no significant associations between the diagnoses and demographic characteristics, type or duration of abuse. Two years later, the children no longer met criteria for PTSD, generalized anxiety disorder, or major depression. All the children had been treated during the two years between assessments. The children no longer met diagnostic criteria, but they still showed a significant number of behavior problems, such as attentional problems, aggressiveness, social withdrawal, and somatization.

In a randomized, representative study of youth ages 10–16, sexual assault that occurred between the two interviews was significantly related to both depression and PTSD symptoms (Boney-McCoy & Finkelhor, 1996). Because of the prospective nature of the design, the authors felt a causal link could be made between victimization and the subsequent development of depression and PTSD. Another analysis with the same sample also found high levels of PTSD, sadness, and school difficulties from other forms of victimization, including nonfamily assaults involving weapons or physical injury, assaults by parents, violence to the genitals, and attempted kidnappings (Boney-McCoy & Finkelhor, 1995).

In a study of 100 consecutive referrals to an inner-city child and adolescent psychiatry clinic, fifty-nine reported trauma exposure (Silva et al., 2000). Of the fifty-nine children, twenty-two met full criteria for PTSD, 32 percent had some symptoms, and 46 percent had no symptoms. Two types of family violence predicted PTSD: witnessing domestic violence and being physically abused. There were no differences in subjects' age, gender, and ethnicity that were associated with the severity of the reaction to a traumatic event, but higher IQ seemed to protect children and adolescents from PTSD.

A study of hospitalized teens found that 93 percent had experienced at least one traumatic event, and 32 percent met the criteria for PTSD. Of the patients with PTSD,

69 percent had been sexually abused and 28 percent had been physically abused (Lipschitz, Winegar, Hartmick, Foote, & Southwick, 1999). The traumatic events included being a victim or witness of community violence, a witness of domestic violence, or a victim of physical or sexual abuse. Multiple traumas were common. Of the whole sample, 76 percent had experienced two types of trauma, 23 percent three types of trauma, and 16 percent four or more types of trauma.

Studies With Adults

A study of 221 female veterans who were receiving primary care found that childhood emotional abuse was associated with poorer role-physical functioning, increased bodily pain, and greater odds of using pain medication in the past six months (Lang et al., 2006). Sexual abuse was significantly associated with the number of visits to primary care, but with less utilization. Women who were emotionally abused had the most emotional distress about somatic symptoms and highest number of visits to health care providers. These effects were above and beyond the contribution of physical or sexual abuse. PTSD mediated the relationship between childhood abuse and adult health outcomes.

A study of medical students from Sri Lanka also showed increased PTSD among those students who witnessed parental violence or experienced parental violence (Haj-Yahia, Tishby, & deZoysa, 2009). The more severe their experiences, the more severe their PTSD symptoms. There was also an association between participants' perceptions of their family environment and levels of PTSD: The more support the participants experienced in their families, the lower their levels of PTSD. In contrast, when the family was perceived as dysfunctional and rejecting, levels of PTSD were higher.

A sample of 172 child sexual abuse (CSA) survivors in their 30s and 40s from Victoria, Australia, examined a list of trauma-related symptoms, such as guilt, sadness, grief, helplessness, emotional numbness, depression, anxiety, panic attacks, fears and phobias, dissociation, and a sense of vulnerability (O'Leary, Coohey, & Easton, 2010). The authors found that the more severe the abuse, the higher the number of mental health symptoms. If the abuse was of high frequency and long duration, if the abuser also assaulted or injured the child, if there was more than one abuser, or if the abuser was a family member, participants reported a higher number of symptoms. There was no increase for a younger age of onset. Participants who told someone at the time of the abuse had more symptoms. The authors speculated that this may reflect an inadequate response from the people to whom they disclosed. Only 11 percent of participants discussed their abuse with someone within in a year after the abuse. These participants reported fewer symptoms.

Another Australian study found that 95 percent of a sample of forty CSA survivors had posttraumatic stress symptoms that were clinically significant (Shakespeare-Finch & De Dassel, 2009). This study also examined posttraumatic growth. Posttraumatic growth is one step beyond successful coping; it is the actual perception of benefits from the traumatic event. Some of these benefits included increased appreciation of life and positive spiritual changes. Participants in this study also indicated that they had experienced posttraumatic growth at rates comparable to other trauma samples.

A study of 467 female college undergraduates examined the impact of childhood physical and sexual abuse, peritraumatic dissociation, and adult victimization (Hetzel & McCanne, 2005). The research indicated that the young women who experienced both childhood physical and sexual abuse or sexual abuse only had higher rates of PTSD than those who experienced physical abuse only or no abuse. The women in the child abuse groups were more likely to be sexually victimized as adults than women in the no-abuse group. Across all groups, peritraumatic dissociation rates were associated with both higher levels of PTSD and adult sexual or physical revictimization.

The impact of multiple types of child maltreatment was studied in a sample of 100 women recruited from a gynecological treatment center for low-income women (Vranceanu, Hobfoll, & Johnson, 2007). The researchers examined a model whereby abuse led to lack of social support and an impaired response to stress, which increased the risk of PTSD. Within their sample, maltreatment was common: 85 percent reported experiencing at least one type of abuse. The researchers found that child maltreatment was highly related to adult stress, but stress was not directly predictive of PTSD. They suggested that perhaps stress acts indirectly through women's deteriorating social support resources. This suggests that maltreatment not only impairs women's ability to develop necessary social support structures but also makes them more vulnerable to stressors and additional losses, which could place excessive demands on their social networks and further erode their sources of support.

A study of sixty outpatients in a Victims of Violence program in São Paulo, Brazil found that the relative risk of having severe PTSD symptoms was ten times higher in patients reporting sexual abuse after age 12 than in those reporting sexual abuse before age 12 (Schoedl et al., 2010). All the patients had a PTSD diagnosis, and 92 percent had comorbid major depression. Many had also endured other types of violent victimization; 48 percent had been sexually abused. The authors concluded that sexual abuse at different stages may lead to distinct psychiatric symptoms in adults.

Lindberg and Distad (1985) examined the relationship between PTSD and symptoms that led survivors to seek treatment. A significant number of people in their sample manifested symptoms of PTSD, including flashbacks and intrusive memories. Approximately one-third experienced dissociative reactions. In another study, 51 percent of 105 female psychiatric inpatients had a history of sexual abuse. Among the abuse survivors, 66 percent met the diagnostic criteria for PTSD (Craine, Henson, Colliver, & MacLean, 1988). Women whose sexual abuse experience included intercourse were much more likely to have severe symptoms of PTSD, even after controlling for overall level of psychopathology in another study (Briggs & Joyce, 1997).

Approximately 6 percent of a large community sample of adults in New Zealand reported "frequently" experiencing three or more dissociative symptoms. Among the dissociative group, the rate of child sexual abuse was two and a half times higher, child physical abuse was five times higher, and current psychiatric disorder was four times higher than the rest of the sample (Mulder, Beautrais, Joyce, & Fergusson, 1998). Dissociative symptoms were also likely in abuse survivors who presented at a university psychiatric outpatient clinic. Interestingly, women with the highest scores on the Dissociative Experiences Scale were those who reported physical abuse, followed by those who reported CSA and those who reported emotional abuse (Pribor, Yutzy, Dean, & Wetzel, 1993).

THE PHYSIOLOGY OF PTSD

The findings of the aforementioned studies indicate that PTSD is a common sequela of childhood abuse. Even if children or adults do not meet full criteria for PTSD, they may have symptoms, and these can have a detrimental effect on health. PTSD is also associated with increased levels of inflammation.

Inflammation and PTSD

In a German community sample of 3,049 adults, 55 had diagnoses of PTSD (Spitzer et al., 2010). Participants with PTSD were twice as likely to have C-reactive protein levels higher than 3mg/L (considered high-risk for cardiovascular disease), even after accounting for other risk factors such as body mass index (BMI), blood pressure, lipid profiles, exercise, alcohol, and other trauma exposure. The authors noted that this is likely one pathway by which PTSD can lead to poor cardiovascular and metabolic health.

In a study of intimate partner violence (IPV), sixty-two women who had been in abusive relationships eight to eleven years ago were compared with non-abused women (Woods et al., 2005). The researchers found that interferon-γ (IFN-γ) levels, were significantly higher in abused versus non-abused women, and in women with current PTSD symptoms versus women without PTSD. Fifty-two percent of women in the IPV group reported depression, and 39 percent had high levels of PTSD symptoms. These findings also demonstrated the lingering health effects of intimate partner violence in women who had previously experienced violence yet were still manifesting significant physical symptomotology.

Inflammatory markers were also altered in a study of rape (Groer, Thomas, Evans, Helton, & Weldon, 2006). In this study, fifteen women who had been raped were compared with sixteen women who had not been sexually assaulted. Women who had been raped were assessed twenty-four to seventy-two hours after their assault. The findings revealed that women who had been sexually assaulted had higher cytotoxic cells and proinflammatory biomarkers twenty-four to seventy-two hours after their assaults than the control group. Specifically, the sexually assaulted women had higher ACTH (adrenocorticotropic hormone), C-reactive protein, IL-6, IL-10, IFN-γ than did women in the control group, which represents some specific alterations in innate and adaptive immunity.

Dysregulation of Cortisol and Norepinephrine

The endocrinology of PTSD has been the focus of a number orf studies (Bremner, 1999, 2005; Yehuda, 1999). Researchers initially thought that the biology of PTSD would be similar to that of depression. What emerged instead was a distinct and qualitatively different set of abnormalities in PTSD (Yehuda et al., 1996). PTSD, particularly chronic PTSD, appears to be a dysregulation of a normal stress response. In a normal response, cortisol and norepinephrine operate in concert. In PTSD, they operate separately (Bremner, 1999). In some cases, people with PTSD have abnormally low levels of cortisol, abnormally high levels of norepinephrine, and a progressive sensitization of the entire HPA (hypothalamic-pituitary-adrenal) axis. In other cases, cortisol levels are high (Yehuda, 1999; Yehuda et al., 1996).

One role of cortisol is to contain the other stress hormones. However, people with abnormally low levels of cortisol cannot contain these other reactions (Bremner, 2005; Yehuda, 1999). An overactive sympathetic nervous system may ultimately lead to PTSD because cortisol fails to control this response. The separate actions of these two hormones has led some researchers to speculate that each may be involved in different aspects of PTSD symptomatology (Yehuda, Resnick, Schmeider, Yang, & Pitman, 1998b). High levels of norepinephrine are thought to be the result of a lowered activation threshold of the locus coereulus (Bremner, 2005; Miller, 2000), and have been linked to intrusive thoughts and more severe PTSD symptoms (Lemieux & Coe, 1995). Low levels of cortisol will also fail to curb the inflammatory response (Kendall-Tackett, 2010).

Low cortisol levels immediately after a stressful event predicted the risk of developing PTSD from the current stressor (Yehuda, McFarlane, & Shalev, 1998a). Women with a history of either physical or sexual assault had significantly lower cortisol response to a current rape than women who did not have such a history (Resnick, Yehuda, Pitman, & Foy, 1995). In an effort to refine these results, the authors, using a subgroup from the original study, examined the relationship between past abuse, rape characteristics, and levels of cortisol and MHPG (3-Methoxy-4-hydroxyphenylglycol, a metabolite of norepinephrine). They found that cortisol was related to a prior history of rape or assault, but not with either rape or symptom severity. In contrast, MHPG was associated with rape severity and symptoms of avoidance, but not related to prior history. The results of this study provided further evidence that prior traumatization may have affected the coordination between HPA and catecholamine systems (Yehuda et al., 1998b).

Effects of PTSD on the Brain

Children with histories of child maltreatment have demonstratively different brains than children without such a history (Dallam, 2001; DeBellis, 2011). For example, the anterior cingulate cortex differs between maltreated children with PTSD and healthy comparison children in a study of eleven children and teens with PTSD and eleven comparison children (DeBellis, Keshvan, Spencer, & Hall, 2000). The results of that study suggested neuronal loss in the maltreated children, which could contribute to the pathophysiology PTSD and other impairments in psychosocial and cognitive functioning.

In another study, the left hemispheres of maltreated children had fewer nerve connections between nerve cells than those of nonmaltreated children (Ito, Teicher, Glod, & Ackerman, 1998). MRIs have revealed that children with a severe history of physical or sexual abuse have lower brain volumes than matched controls. This lower brain volume is associated with age of onset and duration of the abuse, and the severity of current dissociative and PTSD symptoms (DeBellis, 2011; DeBellis et al., 1999).

Brain abnormalities have also been noted in adults with PTSD. In one study (Bremner et al., 1995), adult survivors of physical and sexual abuse had significant problems with short-term memory. These deficits correlated with the severity of the abuse experienced. The parts of the brain involved in learning and memory are the amygdala, locus coeruleus, hippocampus, and sensory cortex (Bremner, 2005). The hippocampus is the brain structure involved in learning and memory, and seems to be easily damaged by an abnormal stress response (Bremner, 2005; DeBellis, 2011).

The amygdala seems to be a particularly important structure in memories associated with PTSD. Of particular interest are the N-methyl-D-aspartate (NMDA) receptors on the amygdala. These appear to be involved in the formation and retrieval of traumatic memories because NMDA antagonists can be applied to the amygdala and prevent the development of fear-conditioning responses (Bremner, 2005; Miller, 2000).

Patients with histories of severe physical or sexual abuse were compared to a similar-age control group. All the abused patients met the criteria for PTSD. MRIs (magnetic resonance imaging) demonstrated that those with PTSD had 12 percent smaller hippocampal volume relative to controls, even after controlling for age, sex, race, handedness, years of education, socioeconomic status (SES), body size, and years of alcohol abuse. There was no difference in the volume of the comparison structures: amygdala, caudate, and temporal lobe (Bremner et al., 1997).

Another study had similar findings. Twenty-one women who reported severe sexual victimization were compared with a group of twenty-one healthy control women with no history of sexual abuse. They were matched for age, education, height, weight, BMI, and intellectual functioning. Seventy-one percent of women in the sexual abuse group met criteria for PTSD and 71 percent met the criteria for dissociative disorder. Thirteen subjects had both PTSD and dissociative disorder. The results revealed that sexually abused women had significantly reduced left-sided hippocampal volume than women without such a history. The right side was also smaller, but not significantly so. Atrophy of the left hippocampus was highly correlated with severity of dissociative symptoms but not with memory function. The authors observed that reduced hippocampal size may be a result of the traumatic events or a risk factor for developing psychiatric symptoms in the wake of traumatic events (Stein, Koverola, Hanna, Torchina, & McClarty, 1997).

HOW PTSD AFFECTS HEALTH

Recent studies have found that health problems, disability, and suicidal behavior were more common in men and women with PTSD than their counterparts without PTSD. For example, analyzing data from the Canadian Community Health Survey (N = 36,984), 1 percent (N = 478) had a formal diagnosis of PTSD from a health care provider (Sareen et al., 2007). Participants with PTSD had significantly higher levels of many types of illnesses including cardiovascular disease (hypertension and heart disease), respiratory diseases (asthma and chronic obstructive pulmonary disease), chronic pain syndromes (fibromyalgia, arthritis, migraine), gastrointestinal illnesses (ulcerative colitis and ulcers), and cancer. PTSD was strongly associated with chronic fatigue syndrome and multiple-chemical sensitivity. Contrary to previous studies, there was no significant difference in rates of diabetes. PTSD was also associated with suicide attempts, poor quality of life, and short- and long-term disability. The authors concluded that these effects were above and beyond the effects of depression or other mental disorders and were the unique contribution of PTSD.

PTSD following a man-made disaster showed similar health effects (Dirkzwager, van der Velden, Grievink, & Yzermans, 2007). In this study, 896 survivors of a man-made disaster were surveyed at three weeks and eighteen months after the disaster. These data were combined with health data one year before the disaster and four years after. (The disaster was an explosion of a fireworks depot that killed 23 people, injured 1,000, and forced the evacuation of 1,200 people). The authors found that PTSD increased the rates of physician-reported vascular, musculoskeletal, and dermatological problems. These problems appeared even after controlling for previous health problem, smoking, and demographic characteristics.

Spitzer et al. (2009) studied three groups of adults living in the community (N = 3,171): people who had no trauma exposure; those with a trauma history but no PTSD; and those with PTSD on a series of health measures. They found that those with a trauma history were at higher risk for angina and heart failure, stroke, renal disease, bronchitis, asthma, and polyarthritis than those without a trauma history. Those with PTSD were also at risk for angina, heart failure, bronchitis, asthma, liver, and peripheral artery disease, even after controlling for SES, age, smoking, BMI, blood pressure, depression, and alcohol use. The traumas the participants experienced included life-threatening illness, serious accident, rape, CSA, unexpected death of a loved one, combat, torture, and natural disasters. The authors concluded that there was strong evidence to support the supposition that PTSD increases the risk for both cardiovascular and pulmonary diseases.

A study of a nationally representative sample of 34,653 adults in the United States examined the associations between lifetime trauma exposures, PTSD, PTSD symptoms, and past-year medical conditions (Pietrzak, Goldstein, Southwick, & Grant, 2011). Participants with full or partial PTSD were more likely to be women, previously married, with less than a high school education, and lower household incomes. Participants with full-criteria PTSD reported higher rates of diabetes, noncirrhotic liver disease, angina pectoris, tachycardia, hypercholesterolemia, other heart disease, stomach ulcer, HIV, gastritis, and arthritis than did those without PTSD. Those with PTSD symptoms but who did not meet full criteria reported more past-year angina pertoris, tachycardia, and arthritis than those who did not have PTSD. The authors concluded that greater lifetime trauma exposure and PTSD are associated with numerous medical conditions, many of which are stress-related and chronic.

Findings From Studies on the Effect of Combat Exposure

Much of what we know about the health effects of PTSD comes from studies of combat veterans. Shalev, Bleich, and Ursano (1990) found that combat-exposed veterans with PTSD reported significantly more health symptoms than did combat veterans without PTSD. These participants reported significantly more cardiovascular symptoms, including palpitations, chest pains, shortness of breath, vertigo, cold sweating, and weakness (Shalev et al., 1990). They were also more likely to report neurological symptoms and significantly more subjective hearing loss (although audiological tests revealed no significant differences). Interestingly, they found no significant differences in actual health on most of the indices. The authors concluded that the overreporting of symptoms may be due to heightened physiological arousal or attentiveness to health problems.

In a study of Vietnam veterans, 83 percent were currently depressed. Those with PTSD reported twice as many health problems, health complaints, and total illnesses as those without PTSD, even after controlling for confounding factors (Beckham et al., 1998). The more severe the PTSD, the worse their self-reported and physician-rated health.

Another study of Vietnam combat veterans found that chronic PTSD was associated with both drug and alcohol dependence, major depression, and several types of anxiety disorders. Interestingly, except for cocaine (which increases symptoms of hyperarousal), the veterans reported that the alcohol and drugs improved their symptoms of PTSD (Bremner, Southwick, Darnell, & Charney, 1996). In a sample of 921 male veterans ages 50–85, combat exposure combined with PTSD was related to poorer health. Combat exposure had an only indirect effect on health, but PTSD had a direct effect as determined by path analysis. These findings were not explained by harmful health behaviors. Indeed, PTSD alone appears to have a detrimental effect on health (Schnurr & Spiro, 1999).

Not surprisingly, given the aforementioned findings, people with PTSD use more health care services. In a study of women seeking health care at Veterans Administration facilities (N = 2,578), 33 percent (N = 858) screened positive for PTSD (Dobie et al., 2006). The women with PTSD had more outpatient visits to the emergency department, primary care, medical or surgery subspecialties, ancillary services, and diagnostic tests. They had higher rates of hospitalizations and surgical procedures. The mean number of days in the hospital for a year was 43.4 for women with PTSD and 17 for women without PTSD. Women with PTSD were significantly younger than women without, were significantly less likely to be married, were more likely to have a service-related disability, to have chronic pain (e.g., irritable bowel syndrome and fibromyalgia), or to be obese. They were also more likely to smoke, abuse alcohol, and be depressed. Indeed, 75 percent of women with PTSD also screened positive for depression.

PTSD and Comorbidity

PTSD has been described as a highly comorbid disorder and is likely to co-occur with depression and anxiety disorders, alcohol abuse, smoking, and drug abuse, all of which have a negative impact on health (Perkonigg & Wittchen, 1999). In considering this comorbidity, Miller (2000) notes: "PTSD is so frequently comorbid with other disorders . . . that 'pure' chronic PTSD would seem to be the exception, not the rule" (p. 29).

Comorbid substance abuse appears to be particularly common. For example, PTSD was recently found to be the mediator between childhood rape and alcohol use in a sample of adult women (Epstein, Saunders, Kilpatrick, & Resnick, 1998). Using path analysis, the authors evaluated the mediating role of PTSD on alcohol use. They found that childhood rape doubled the number of alcohol-abuse symptoms that women experienced. Cross-validation results demonstrated significant pathways connecting childhood rape to PTSD symptoms and PTSD symptoms to alcohol use. The authors suggested that there may be some "third factor" at work in these situations. For example, women raped as children may view the world as a dangerous place that is uncontrollable, unpredictable, and hostile. Alcohol may provide these women with a way to cope, albeit a dysfunctional one.

In another study of 801 mothers of low-birthweight infants, Breslau, Davis, Peterson, and Schultz (1997) found that PTSD dramatically increased the risk for first-time major depressive disorder and alcohol abuse. In addition, preexisting major depression increased the risk for PTSD in the wake of trauma-producing events and even increased their risk of exposure to traumatic events. Among psychiatric inpatients, males with PTSD were significantly more likely to have eating, anxiety, and somatization disorders. Both males and females were also more likely to have attempted suicide, and to have more symptoms of depression and dissociation (Lipschitz et al., 1999).

PTSD and Sleep Quality

PTSD also affects the quality of sleep. Intrusive thoughts may manifest as disturbing dreams. Even though sleep disturbances in PTSD have been observed clinically, relatively few studies have examined the sleep patterns of those with PTSD. In one study, female sexual assault survivors with PTSD had severe sleep disturbances that were equal to or greater than those of people with insomnia or depression. The women with PTSD especially had problems with insomnia and chronic nightmares. Other problems included sleep latency, sleep efficiency, and use of sleep medication (Krakow, Tandberg, Sandoval, Cutchen, & Schrader, 1998). Chapter 3 describes other studies on PTSD and sleep. Abuse survivors often have poor patterns of sleep which can affect their health in a wide variety of ways.

PTSD and Health in Aging Trauma Survivors

Something that has not really been examined in adult survivors of childhood abuse, but should be, is what happens when they age. Some fascinating research has come from a study of aging Holocaust survivors in Israel (Solomon & Ginzburg, 1999). Researchers had an opportunity to compare a cohort of Holocaust survivors to a age-matched group that did not go through the Holocaust. Initially, the Holocaust survivors functioned well. They were encouraged to put their traumatic pasts behind them and focus on building a new nation. Problems did not appear until these Holocaust survivors hit the milestones of middle and old age. For example, retirement was more difficult for Holocaust survivors. It entailed a loss of routine, self-esteem, status, and social interaction. Further, it removed the daily "busy-ness" that acted like a shield against traumatic memories. Other triggers to traumatic events included loss of parents, children leaving home, and increasing medical disability.

Holocaust survivors also had a difficult time when they become ill. Hospitalization or entering a nursing home were potent triggers to past memories of traumatic events. Serious illnesses, such as cancer, were experienced more intensely in survivors than in their non-traumatized counterparts. Aspects of these experiences that may have triggered PTSD included loss of control, being told what to do by authority figures whom they did not trust, sharing quarters with strangers, and exposures to smells and sounds that may have reminded them of their previous experiences. And, sadly, these survivors tended to have more illnesses than similar-age Israelis without traumatic pasts. These results suggest some fruitful areas of study with adult survivors of childhood abuse.

SUMMARY

Depression and PTSD are common symptoms among abuse survivors. They also influence health via physiological, behavioral, and social pathways. The study of the relationship of past abuse to PTSD and depression is still in its infancy. Yehuda (1998) noted that PTSD is something that researchers can describe but not fully explain. The same could also be said for depression. As research progresses in this field, we may be able to answer these questions more thoroughly. In the meantime, we can observe that both have a significant impact on health.

References

Beckham, J. C., Moore, S. D., Feldman, M. E., Hertzberg, M. A., Kirby, A. C., & Fairbank, J. A. (1998). Health status, somatization, and severity of post-traumatic stress disorder. *American Journal of Psychiatry, 155*, 1565–1569.

Boney-McCoy, S., & Finkelhor, D. (1995). Psychological sequelae of violent victimization in a national youth sample. *Journal of Consulting and Clinical Psychology, 63*, 726–736.

Boney-McCoy, S., & Finkelhor, D. (1996). Is youth victimization related to trauma symptoms and depression after controlling for prior symptoms and family relationships? A longitudinal, prospective study. *Journal of Consulting and Clinical Psychology, 64*, 1406–1461.

Bremner, J. D. (1999). Does stress damage the brain? *Biological Psychiatry, 45*, 797–805.

Bremner, J. D. (2005). The neurobiology of childhood sexual abuse in women with posttraumatic stress disorder. In K. A. Kendall-Tackett (Ed.), *Handbook of women, stress, and trauma* (pp. 181–206). New York: Brunner-Routledge.

Bremner, J. D., Randall, P., Scott, T. M., Capelli, S., R., D., McCarthy, G., & Charney, D. S. (1995). Deficits in short-term memory in adult survivors of childhood abuse. *Psychiatry Research, 59*, 97–107.

Bremner, J. D., Randall, P., Vermetten, E., Staib, L., Bronen, R. A., Mazure, C. M., et al. (1997). Magnetic resonance imaging-based measurements of hippocampal volume in posttraumatic stress disorder related to childhood physical and sexual abuse: A preliminary report. *Biological Psychiatry, 41*, 23–32.

Bremner, J. D., Southwick, S. M., Darnell, A., & Charney, D. S. (1996). Chronic PTSD in Vietnam combat veterans: Course of illness and substance abuse. *American Journal of Psychiatry, 153*, 369–375.

Breslau, N., Davis, G. C., Peterson, E. L., & Schultz, L. (1997). Psychiatric sequelae of posttraumatic stress disorder in women. *Archives of General Psychiatry, 54*, 81–87.

Briggs, L., & Joyce, P. R. (1997). What determines post-traumatic stress disorder symptomatology for survivors of childhood sexual abuse? *Child Abuse and Neglect, 21*, 575–582.

Craine, L., Henson, C., Colliver, J., & MacLean, D. (1988). Prevalence of a history of sexual abuse among female psychiatric patients in a state hospital system. *Hospital and Community Psychiatry, 39*, 300–304.

Dallam, S. J. (2001). The hidden effects of childhood maltreatment on adult health. In K. Franey, R. Geffner & R. Falconer (Eds.), *The cost of child maltreatment: Who pays? We all do* (pp. 1–14). San Diego: Family Violence & Sexual Assault Institute.

DeBellis, M. D. (2011). Neurodevelopmental biology associated with childhood sexual abuse. *Journal of Child Sexual Abuse, 20*, 548–587.

DeBellis, M. D., Keshavan, M. S., Clark, D. B., Casey, B. J., Giedd, J. N., Boring, A. M., et al. (1999). A. E. Bennett Research Award. Developmental traumatology, Part II: Brain development. *Biological Psychiatry, 45*, 1271–1284.

DeBellis, M. D., Keshvan, M. S., Spencer, S., & Hall, J. (2000). N-acetylaspartate concentrations in the anterior cingulate of maltreated children and adolescents with PTSD. *American Journal of Psychiatry, 157*, 1175–1177.

Dirkzwager, A. J., van der Velden, P. G., Grievink, L., & Yzermans, C. J. (2007). Disaster-related posttraumatic stress disorder and physical health. *Psychosomatic Medicine, 69*(5), 435–440.

Dobie, D. J., Maynard, C., Kivlahan, D. R., Johnson, K. M., Simpson, T., David, A. C., & Bradley, K. (2006). Posttraumatic stress disorder screening status is associated with increased VA medical and surgical utilization in women. *Journal of General Internal Medicine, 21*(Suppl. 3), S58–S64.

Epstein, J. N., Saunders, B. E., Kilpatrick, D. G., & Resnick, H. S. (1998). PTSD as a mediator between childhood rape and alcohol use in adult women. *Child Abuse and Neglect, 22*, 223–234.

Groer, M. W., Thomas, S. P., Evans, G. W., Helton, S., & Weldon, A. (2006). Inflammatory effects and immune system correlates of rape. *Violence and Victims, 21*(6), 796–808.

Haj-Yahia, M., Tishby, O., & deZoysa, P. (2009). Posttraumatic stress disorder among Sri Lankan university students as a consequence of their exposure to family violence. *Journal of Interpersonal Violence, 24*(12), 2018–2038.

Heim, C., & Nemeroff, C. B. (2009). Neurobiology of posttraumatic stress disorder. *CNS Spectrums, 14*(1 Suppl. 1), 13–24.

Hetzel, M. D., & McCanne, T. R. (2005). The roles of peritraumatic dissociation, child physical abuse, and child sexual abuse in the development of posttraumatic stress disorder and adult victimization. *Child Abuse and Neglect, 29*, 915–930.

Ito, Y., Teicher, M. H., Glod, C. A., & Ackerman, E. (1998). Preliminary evidence for aberrant corticol development in abused children: A quantitative EEG study. *Journal of Neuropsychiatry and Clinical Neurosciences, 10*, 298–307.

Kendall-Tackett, K. A. (Ed.). (2010). *The psychoneuroimmunology of chronic disease*. Washington, DC: American Psychological Association.

Krakow, B., Tandberg, D., Sandoval, D., Cutchen, L., & Schrader, R. (1998). Severity of sleep disturbances in sexual assault survivors. *Sleep, 21*(Suppl.), 150.

Lang, A. J., Laffaye, C., Satz, L. E., McQuaid, J. R., Malcarne, V. L., Dreselhaus, T. R., et al. (2006). Relationships among childhood maltreatment, PTSD, and health in female veterans with a history of child maltreatment. *Child Abuse and Neglect, 30*, 1281–1292.

Lemieux, A. M., & Coe, C. L. (1995). Abuse-related posttraumatic stress disorder: Evidence for chronic neuroendocrine activation in women. *Psychosomatic Medicine, 57*, 105–115.

Lindberg, F. H., & Distad, I. J. (1985). Post-traumatic stress disorders in women who experienced childhood incest. *Child Abuse and Neglect, 9*, 329–345.

Lipschitz, D. S., Winegar, R. K., Hartmick, E., Foote, B., & Southwick, S. M. (1999). Posttraumatic stress disorder in hospitalized adolescents: Psychiatric comorbidity and clinical correlates. *Journal of the American Academy of Child and Adolescent Psychiatry, 38*, 385–392.

Luthra, R., Abramowitz, R., Greenberg, R., Schoor, A., Newcorn, J., Schmeidler, J., et al. (2009). Relationship between type of trauma exposure and posttraumatic stress disorder among urban children and adolescents. *Journal of Interpersonal Violence, 24*(11), 1919–1927.

McCloskey, L. A., & Walker, M. (2000). Posttraumatic stress in children exposed to family violence. *Journal of the American Academy of Child and Adolescent Psychiatry, 39*, 108–115.

Miller, L. (2000). Neurosensitization: A model for persistent disability in chronic pain, depression, and posttraumatic stress disorder following injury. *NeuroRehabilitation, 14*, 25–32.

Mulder, R. T., Beautrais, A. L., Joyce, P. R., & Fergusson, D. M. (1998). Relationship between dissociation, childhood sexual abuse, childhood physical abuse, and mental illness in a general population sample. *American Journal of Psychiatry, 155*, 806–811.

O'Leary, P., Coohey, C., & Easton, S. D. (2010). The effect of severe child sexual abuse and disclosure on mental health during adulthood. *Journal of Child Sexual Abuse, 19*, 275–289.

Ozbaran, B., Erermis, S., Bukusoglu, N., Bildik, T., Tamar, M., Ercan, E. S., et al. (2009). Social and emotional outcomes of child sexual abuse: A clinical sample in Turkey. *Journal of Interpersonal Violence, 24*(9), 1478–1493.

Perkonigg, A., & Wittchen, H.-U. (1999). Prevalence and co-morbidity of traumatic events and posttraumatic stress disorder in adolescents and young adults. In A. Maercker, M. Schutzwohl & Z. Solomon (Eds.), *Posttraumatic stress disorder: A lifespan developmental perspective* (pp. 113–136). Seattle, WA: Hogrefe & Huber.

Pietrzak, R. H., Goldstein, R. B., Southwick, S. M., & Grant, B. F. (2011). Medical comorbidity of full and partial posttraumatic stress disorder in U.S. adults: Results from wave 2 of the National Epidemiologic Survey on Alcohol and Related Conditions. *Psychosomatic Medicine, 73*, 697–707.

Pribor, E. F., Yutzy, S. H., Dean, J. T., & Wetzel, R. D. (1993). Briquet's syndrome, dissociation, and abuse. *American Journal of Psychiatry, 150*, 1507–1511.

Resnick, H. S., Yehuda, R., Pitman, R. K., & Foy, D. W. (1995). Effect of previous trauma on acute plasma cortisol level following rape. *American Journal of Psychiatry, 152*, 1675–1677.

Sareen, J., Cox, B. J., Stein, M. B., Afifi, T. O., Fleet, C., & Asmundson, G. J. (2007). Physical and mental comorbidity, disability, and suicidal behavior associated with posttraumatic stress disorder in a large community sample. *Psychosomatic Medicine, 69*(3), 242–248.

Schnurr, P. P., & Spiro, A. (1999). Combat disorder, posttraumatic stress disorder symptoms and health behaviors as predictors of self-reported physical health in older veterans. *Journal of Nervous and Mental Disease, 187*, 353–359.

Schoedl, A. F., Costa, M. C. P., Mari, J. J., Mello, M. F., Tyrka, A. R., Carpenter, L. L., et al. (2010). The clinical correlates of reported childhood sexual abuse: An association between age at trauma onset and severity of depression and PTSD in adults. *Journal of Child Sexual Abuse, 19*, 156–170.

Shakespeare-Finch, J., & De Dassel, T. (2009). Exploring posttraumatic outcomes as a function of childhood sexual abuse. *Journal of Child Sexual Abuse, 18*, 623–640.

Shalev, A. Y., Bleich, A., & Ursano, R. J. (1990). Posttraumatic stress disorder: Somatic comorbidity and effort tolerance. *Psychosomatics, 31*, 197–203.

Silva, R. R., Alpert, M., Munoz, D. M., Singh, S., Matzner, F., & Dummit, S. (2000). Stress and vulnerability to posttraumatic stress disorder in children and adolescents. *American Journal of Psychiatry, 157*, 1229–1235.

Solomon, Z., & Ginzburg, K. (1999). Aging in the shadow of war. In A. Maercker, M. Schutzwohl, & Z. Solomon (Eds.), *Posttraumatic stress disorder: A lifespan developmental perspective* (pp. 137–154). Seattle: Hogrefe & Huber.

Spitzer, C., Barnow, S., Volzke, H., John, U., Freyberger, H. J., & Grabe, H. J. (2009). Trauma, posttraumatic stress disorder, and physical illness: Findings from the general population. *Psychosomatic Medicine, 71*(9), 1012–1017.

Spitzer, C., Barnow, S., Volzke, H., Wallaschotski, H., John, U., Freyberger, H. J., et al. (2010). Association of posttraumatic stress disorder with low-grade elevation of C-reactive protein: Evidence from the general population. *Journal of Psychiatric Research, 44*(1), 15–21.

Stein, M. B., Koverola, C., Hanna, C., Torchina, M. G., & McClarty, B. (1997). Hippocampal volume in women victimized by childhood sexual abuse. *Psychological Medicine, 27*, 951–959.

Vranceanu, A.-M., Hobfoll, S. E., & Johnson, R. J. (2007). Child multi-type maltreatment and associated depression and PTSD symptoms: The role of social support and stress. *Child Abuse and Neglect, 31*, 71–84.

Woods, A. B., Page, G. G., O'Campo, P., Pugh, L. C., Ford, D., & Campbell, J. C. (2005). The mediation effect of posttraumatic stress disorder symptoms on the relationship of intimate partner violence and IFN-gamma levels. *American Journal of Community Psychology, 36*(1–2), 159–175.

Yehuda, R. (1998). Psychoneuroendocrinology of post–traumatic stress disorder. *Psychiatric Clinics of North America, 21*, 359–379.

Yehuda, R. (1999). Biological factors associated with susceptibility to posttraumatic stress disorder. *Canadian Journal of Psychiatry, 44*, 34–39.

Yehuda, R., Levengood, R. A., Schmeider, J., Wilson, S., Guo, L. S., & Gerber, D. (1996). Increased pituitary activation following metyrapone administration in posttraumatic stress disorder. *Psychoneuroendocrinology, 21*, 1–16.

Yehuda, R., McFarlane, A. C., & Shalev, A. Y. (1998a). Predicting the development of posttraumatic stress disorder from the acute resposne to a traumatic event. *Biological Psychiatry, 44*, 1305–1313.

Yehuda, R., Resnick, H. S., Schmeidler, J., Yang, R.-K., & Pitman, R. K. (1998b). Predictors of cortisol and 3-methoxy-4-hydroxyphenylglycol responses in the acute aftermath of rape. *Biological Psychiatry, 43*, 855–859.

Chapter 13

Individual Differences in the Expression of Symptoms

Every child responds differently to traumatic events; there is no one pattern of response that every child follows (Wright, Master, & Hubbard, 1997). But, we can make some reasoned predictions about which children will fare better than others. Perry (2001) says that three factors influence how children will respond to traumatic events: characteristics of the child, characteristics of the traumatic event, and characteristics of the family or social system. Yehuda et al. (1996) have also found that a biological response to stress depends on an interaction of several factors: nature of the stressor (type, chronicity, severity, controllability, and predictability), prior vulnerabilities (e.g., previous stress history, genetic and social vulnerabilities), and the current family environment. This chapter describes some of the abuse and child and family characteristics that influence how children respond to maltreatment and how symptomatic they become.

TIMING OF ABUSE, BRAIN MATURATION, AND APPRAISAL OF EVENTS

Timing of Abuse

The timing of maltreatment in children's lives can explain the range of symptoms seen in abuse survivors (Lazarus & Folkman, 1984). As discussed in Chapter 2, the development of the brain is sequential and hierarchical. If abuse or neglect occurs during the time a portion of the brain is developing, maltreatment may adversely affect its development. Although many assume that abuse that occurs at an earlier age is automatically more harmful than abuse that occurs later, there is no linear relationship between age and vulnerability to abusive experiences (Maccoby, 1983). Rather, each stage of development has its own vulnerabilities and protections. By understanding the normal processes of brain and cognitive development, we can make reasonable predictions about how the brain is affected.

Brain Maturation

The human brain is at its most vulnerable in the first five years of life (Perry, Pollard, Blakley, Baker, & Vigilante, 1995; Rutter & Rutter, 1993). During this time, many maturational events take place. The main structure of the brain is formed, followed by the development of nerve cells. After the nerve cells are formed, they migrate to their final destination within the brain. Simultaneous to these processes, the neuronal network in the brain is increasing in complexity and number of synapses. Finally, selective cell death acts as a pruning and fine-tuning process.

Alterations in the brain can take many forms. Early damage may lead to overall problems and a general lowering of intelligence. Studies of children raised by depressed mothers provide an example of this phenomenon. Depression affects the quality of the mother-infant relationship, and poor mother-infant interactions have been observed to be stressful for infants (Cicchetti & Toth, 1998), even resulting in EEG abnormalities (Jones, Field, Fox, Lundy, & Devalos, 1997). Children raised with chronically depressed mothers have been found to perform poorly in school (Radke-Yarrow, 1998) and may be at risk for developing depression as they mature (Cicchetti & Toth, 1998).

Abuse or neglect in early childhood might also damage the limbic system, which can result in lifelong difficulties in social relationships and memory and learning. For example, a child neglected for the first three years of life and then adopted into a caring family may still have problems with attachment, intimacy, and social interactions—functions that depend on the healthy development of the limbic system. Early abuse may also damage the cortex, but this damage may not be obvious for several years until the area becomes fully functional (Perry, 2001; Perry & Pollard, 1998).

Later development depends on the development of lower brain regions that take place early in the process. Therefore, assessing specific damage can also be difficult. As described in Chapter 2, the same part of the brain may serve different functions at different phases of development because of cell migration and the changing organization pattern of nerve cells. The effects of early damage on the brain thus may not appear until several years after the damage occurs. These delayed effects may also account for different symptoms at different ages and for children who are asymptomatic at their original assessment (Kendall-Tackett, Williams, & Finkelhor, 1993; Rutter & Rutter, 1993). Although the brain is more vulnerable in the first five years, symptoms may be more pronounced if abuse takes place at a later age because the brain is not as able to have other sections take over for the damaged portion (Bremner et al., 1997).

Critical Periods of Brain Development. The developing brain has critical periods—that is, times at which certain experiences must occur or the opportunity to learn is lost. Abuse that happens during critical periods can be especially devastating. For example, primary language must be learned before puberty or the opportunity is lost forever. Critical periods can be disrupted by either neglect (i.e., failure to provide needed stimulation or experience) or abuse, which overactivates the neural systems and floods the brain with extremes of experience (Perry, 2001; Perry et al., 1995). When children experience chaotic or unpredictable input, the brain reflects such input by showing dysregulation or dysynchrony (Perry, 2001). These can result in compromised function in such far-reaching areas as humor, empathy, attachment, and regulation of affect.

Sensitization Revisited. Early trauma, in particular, may make children hypersensitive to stimuli. Early onset of trauma may render an adult particularly vulnerable to posttraumatic flashbacks, physiological arousal, and kinesthetic memories of the abuse (van der Kolk, 1994). In a study of seventy-seven female victims of child sexual abuse (ages 6–16), early age of onset was associated with dissociative and "hyperactive" behavior, bizarre destructive behaviors, and anxious depression (Trickett, Reiffman, Horowitz, & Putnam, 1997).

Perry et al. (1995) also noted that sensitization can lead to hyperarousal or dissociation. Children sensitized to hyperarousal tend to act out and exhibit hyperactivity, behavioral impulsivity, sleep problems, and oppositional activity. In contrast, those sensitized to a dissociative state tend to "freeze" when confronted with an anxiety-producing stressor. Age of onset can be related to the types of symptoms that are likely to manifest. For children who are younger when the abuse begins, a fight-or-flight response is unlikely to be helpful. Instead, these children may dissociate as the only way of coping with the current situation. In dissociation, there is increased activity of dopaminergic systems, which modulate endogenous opioids that mediate pain and alter perception of painful stimuli.

Appraisal of Events

Appraisal is also crucial in terms of understanding the appearance of symptoms. The cognitive ability to evaluate events is key in the body's response to threat. Cortisol is not released until the event is perceived as noxious (Lovallo, 1997). Interestingly, appraisal is even a factor in animals. In a review of animal studies,

Campeau et al. (1998) noted that apparent cognitions are important in how stress manifests as symptoms: "Even in the presence of the same physical stimuli. . . . their impact upon the HPA axis can lead to different outcomes. . . . The effect of challenging situations on endocrine functioning is intricately associated with the perception and evaluation of these situations" (p. 272).

The cognitive ability to evaluate or consider the motives of the abuser, or to even realize that abuse is not part of everyone's life experience, is not likely to occur until children have gained the ability to "decenter" their thinking—around ages 5–7. Decentering is the ability to take into account more than one perspective. Especially with sexual abuse, young children may be protected by their naiveté when the abuse is not physically painful. (Even infants and young children can understand that a physically painful event is noxious.) Because of cognitive development and the appraisal process, children are also vulnerable after age 5 (Finkelhor & Kendall-Tackett, 1997).

CHARACTERISTICS OF THE ABUSE

Specific aspects of the abuse experience itself can influence how people react. Some people have more symptoms because their experiences were more severe. Abuse can vary by the identity of the perpetrators, severity of the abusive acts, duration and frequency, and use of force. Studying the characteristics of abuse demonstrates the complexity of its effects. For almost any statement made, exceptions occur. To further complicate matters, many of these factors are related to each other. For example, a perpetrator who is a family member will have more access to a child and for a longer time. Thus the identity of the perpetrator is often related to the duration of the abuse. Severity of the abusive acts is often related to the duration of the abuse as well, with more severe acts occurring over time. However, many one-time assaults are rapes or brutal beatings. In other words, instead of abuse that becomes gradually more severe over time, the first contact is very severe. This section describes factors affecting overall severity of the abuse experience.

Identity of the Perpetrator

In general, abuse will be more harmful if the abuser is someone the child knows and trusts and the abuse violates that trust (Finkelhor, 1987; Freyd, Klest, & Allard, 2005). This is reflected in the difference in the percentage of abuse by parent figures in clinical versus nonclinical samples. (Presumably, more harmful abuse occurred among people who are seeking treatment.) For sexual abuse, abuse by parent figures ranges from 16 percent in nonclinical samples to as high as 62 percent in clinical samples (Berliner & Elliot, 1996; Kendall-Tackett & Simon, 1987). However, abuse by family members is not necessarily always more harmful. The child's emotional attachment to the perpetrator and sense of betrayal can be more important predictors of harm than strict familial relationships (Finkelhor, 1987).

Severity of Abusive Acts

Defining severity of abusive acts continues to be challenging. Some people are more seriously affected by abuse because their experiences were more severe. This seems to be especially the case for defining severity of child sexual abuse (CSA). One study of 275 CSA survivors attempted to address the issue of severity (Young, Riggs, & Robinson, 2011). They performed an exploratory factor analysis and produced seven factors:

1. Less intrusive forms of CSA, such as kissing or sexual invitations;
2. More intrusive forms, such as oral, anal, or vaginal penetration;
3. Humiliation and fear;
4. CSA involving photography;
5. Familiarity with the perpetrator;
6. Physical force/rape; and
7. Active digital penetration.

The authors concluded that physical intrusiveness, which is often the most common measure of severity, had little to do with critical factors, such as humiliation, fear, and association with the perpetrator. Therefore, physical intrusiveness appears to be an inadequate stand-alone measure of severity.

In a review, Leserman, Toomey, and Drossman (1995) found that severe physical or sexual abuse was related to worse outcomes. In a sample of 252 women from a primary care practice with "unexplained" physical symptoms, researchers found a strong association between severity of sexual abuse and degree of impairment in health-related quality of life. These findings held true even after controlling for current psychiatric diagnosis (Dickinson, deGruy, Dickinson, & Candib, 1999). Similarly, women who had been raped or had experienced life-threatening physical abuse had worse overall health than did women whose abuse experiences were less severe. Interestingly, patients whose abuse first occurred in childhood did not have worse health outcomes than those whose abuse first occurred as adults (Leserman et al., 1996).

In studies of fibromyalgia, severity of abuse was also related to more severe manifestations of symptoms. For example, contact abuse and multiple abusive events led to increased severity of symptoms (Boisset-Pioro, Esdaile, & Fitzcharles, 1995). Further, there appeared to be an additive effect; the most severe manifestations of musculoskeletal pain were experienced by those who experienced both physical and sexual abuse, or those whose abuse occurred during both childhood and adulthood (Boisset-Pioro et al., 1995; Taylor, Trotter, & Csuka, 1995).

In contrast, a study of forty-five sexual abuse survivors hospitalized for bulimia found no significant differences in the severity of depression or eating disorders based on the characteristics of the abuse. There were no differences in intrafamilial versus extrafamilial abuse, force versus no force, one versus multiple incidents, early abuse versus abuse that happened after age 14, disclosed versus nondisclosed abuse, and the combination of physical and sexual abuse versus sexual abuse alone. However, the subjects in this study were already at the high end of severity for their eating disorder. It may be that there was little variability in their abuse experiences or in the severity of their eating disorder.

Duration and Force

Abuse that occurs often and lasts for years will typically be more harmful than abuse that happened only sporadically, and over less time. The exception is the one-time violent assault (Kendall-Tackett et al., 1993). Not surprisingly, use of force has been shown to increase the severity of reaction to sexual abuse (Elwell & Ephross, 1987). Force may be more likely in stranger and/or one-time assaults, but this is not always true (Kendall-Tackett et al., 1993). Although all sexual abuse is, by definition, nonconsensual, sometimes the abuser uses trickery or mental coercion, rather than force, to gain compliance. In other situations, the abuser hits, assaults, or physically restrains his victim. Victims who experience this type of abuse are more likely to have more symptoms.

ETHNIC GROUP DIFFERENCES IN HOW ABUSE IS EXPERIENCED

Abuse experiences also vary by ethnicity. No clear patterns have emerged to date, and the studies discussed in this section were all of sexual abuse. But they demonstrated differences in risk by ethnic group and meaning of the abuse when experienced in various cultures. Asian children tended to be older at the onset of victimization than their non-Asian counterparts, while African-American children tended to be younger at onset of victimization than either Asians or whites (Berliner & Elliot, 1996). The overall rates of sexual abuse were lowest for Asian women but high for Hispanic women when reported retrospectively (Russell, 1984). In a sample of 582 Southwestern American Indians, rates of sexual abuse were high, especially for females. Forty-nine percent of females and 14 percent of males reported a history of sexual abuse; 78 percent percent reported intrafamilial abuse (Robin, Chester, Rasmussen, Jaranson, & Goldman, 1997).

African Americans had approximately the same rates of victimization as did white children but were more likely to experience penetration as part of their abuse experiences (Wyatt, 1985; Wyatt, Guthrie, & Notgrass, 1992). Moreover, Wyatt (1985) found a difference between the age of onset for blacks and whites, but the age for both ethnic groups was prepubescent. Abuse of white girls was likely to start between 6 and 8 years of age, while abuse of black girls was likely to start between 9 and 12 years of age. Another ethnic group difference appeared in rates of revictimization. In a sample drawn from a community college, black women who were sexually abused in childhood were more likely to be raped as adults than their white, Latina, or Asian counterparts (Urquiza & Goodlin-Jones, 1994).

In a community sample of Latina women, 35 percent reported some form of sexual abuse in child or adulthood (Ulibarri, Ulloa, & Camacho, 2009). They identified themselves as being either Mexican or Mexican American and were living in San Diego County, California. They ranged in age from 18 to 34 years. The perpetrators were family members in 31 percent of the cases, and 52 percent were boyfriends, friends, or acquaintances. Forty-four percent had not disclosed their abuse to anyone. Of those who reported rape, when it was before the age of 13, it was more likely to have been to a friend rather than a parent. After age 13, it was more likely to have been a family member. After disclosure, 75 percent reported that they received support and that was most often from family members, consistent with the cultural value of families in Hispanic communities, which provides an important role in social support.

Mennen (1995) found no overall effect of ethnicity on the severity of symptoms manifested by Latinas, African-American girls, or white girls, but they did find that ethnicity and type of abuse together influenced severity of symptoms. Latinas whose abuse included penetration had more anxiety and depression than did African-American or white girls. The author felt this symptom was due to the emphasis in Latin communities on purity and virginity. When virginity is lost, the trauma of sexual abuse is compounded because the Latinas believed that they were no longer suitable marriage partners.

Some recent studies suggest that there might also be some differences in susceptibility to the effects of stress, trauma, and abuse based on ethnicity.

In a study comparing black and Hispanic pregnant women, researchers found a difference in the effects of cumulative stress of HPA (hypothalamic-pituitary-adrenal) functioning, particularly on the diurnal pattern of cortisol secretion (Suglia et al., 2010). They found that Hispanic women were more likely to report lower cumulative stress, while black women were more likely to report moderate or high amounts of cumulative stress. The stressors included intimate partner violence (IPV), discrimination, negative life events, and community violence. Among the black women, cumulative stress was related to lower morning cortisol levels, including a flatter bedtime rhythm than it was with Hispanic women. This pattern is characteristic of people with posttraumatic stress disorder (PTSD) or who have been exposed to violence. These findings suggest that the combination of cumulative stress and disrupted HPA functioning varies by ethnic group, and this could have some implications for racial disparities in prematurity and other infant health outcomes.

A follow-up from participants in the CARDIA (Coronary Artery Risk Development in (Young) Adults) study found an ethnic group difference in the impact of depressive symptoms on levels of C-reactive protein (CRP) five years later (Deverts et al., 2010). This sample included 2,544 men and women, ages 33–45, 42 percent of whom were black. They found that the five-year increase in CRP based on depressive symptoms was found for blacks but not for whites. This was a prospective analysis and they found that depressive symptoms preceded increases in CRP, but CRP did not precede depressive symptoms. The authors concluded that depression may be linked more closely to inflammation in blacks than in whites.

There may be other ethnic group differences between blacks and whites in the way they experience trauma. One study considered the impact of trauma on nocturnal blood pressure dipping (Mellman, Brown, Jenifer, Hipolito, & Randall, 2009). In normal sleep, blood pressure shows a pattern of dipping during the night. When blood pressure does not show the pattern of dipping (nondipping), it is associated with hypertension. In a sample of thirty young adult blacks, there was a significant association between lifetime full and subthreshold PTSD and blood pressure nondipping. Nondipping was also correlated with lifetime and current PTSD severity. The authors concluded that this might be one link between PTSD and cardiovascular morbidity, especially since racial differences have been demonstrated in previous studies with blacks being more likely to show a pattern of nondipping.

Another study found a relationship between early-life adversity and inflammation for blacks but not for whites (Slopen et al., 2010). This study included 177 black men and women, and 822 whites, ages 35–86. They used a composite measure of early-life adversities that included stressful events during childhood (parental unemployment, being sent away from home for doing something wrong, school failure, parental drug or alcohol, move to a new town more than two times), self-rated relationship with parents, and frequency of verbal and physical abuse by parents. There were five measures of inflammation: CRP, IL-6, fibrinogen, E-selectin, and sICAM-1. The researchers found significant interactions by race for each measure of inflammation. Early-life adversities predicted higher levels of inflammation for blacks but not for whites. One theory for these findings is accelerated biological aging associated with racial health disparities. An implication of this notion is that physiological aging is accelerated in contexts of high exposure to adversity. One possible explanation is that blacks in this sample, who were chronologically younger, were on an accelerated course of disease progression relative to whites.

On the other hand, these ethnic group differences have not been consistently found. In a study comparing black and white men and women (age 30–65 years), white women were the only group that showed a relationship between depression and CRP. Overall, the black men had higher depression scores on the Beck Depression Inventory than did white men. And there was a significant race-sex-depression interactions: White women with mild-to-severe depression had higher CRP compared with those who had lower levels of depression. There was no difference in the level of CRP for white men or black men or women. The relationship for white women was eliminated once metabolic factors were added to the model, suggesting that metabolic risk factors possibly mediate the relationship between depression and inflammation.

Another study suggests possible mechanisms accounting for ethnic differences in health. In this study of 296 older African Americans (mean age = 73), self-reported experiences of discrimination were associated with elevated CRP levels (Lewis, Aiello, Leurgans, Kelly, & Barnes, 2010). This association remained even after controlling for depression, smoking and chronic health conditions, such as heart disease, diabetes, and hypertension. The results were attenuated when body mass index (BMI) was added to the model. But there was still an association.

CRP has been consistently related to depression, hostility, and chronic stress, and it tends to be higher in African Americans. The authors hypothesized a relationship between CRP and discrimination based on the well-established relationship between CRP and depression and depression and discrimination. Some of the questions included:

- Are you treated with less courtesy than other people?
- Are you treated with less respect than other people?
- Do you receive poorer service than other people at restaurants or stores?
- Do people act as if they think you are not smart?

The authors found that it wasn't necessary for these behaviors to be based on race or ethnic group per se, but that people in this sample felt that they were being discriminated against, and this perception led to an increase in CRP (Lewis et al., 2010).

SEX DIFFERENCES AND SYMPTOMATOLOGY

Rates and Type of Victimization

Sex of subject also influences rate and type of victimization and subsequent symptoms. A recent survey of the victimization experiences of 2,030 children ages 2 to 17, showed developmental patterns that varied by gender (Finkelhor, Ormrod, & Turner, 2009). Peer assaults increased in adolescence for boys but not for girls. Child maltreatment and sexual victimization increased in adolescence for girls but not for boys. Boys were more likely to have experienced multiple types of victimization—an experience Finkelhor et al. refers to as polyvictimization. Injurious victimization for boys is continuous from ages 6–9 to ages 10–13, and then again for ages 14–17. For girls, the rate of injurious victimization was approximately equal for younger ages, and then sharply increased for 14- to 17-year-olds. Sexual victimization for 14- to 17-year-olds was more common for girls than it was for boys. Physical and emotional abuse, and neglect also increased sharply for girls 14 to 17 years of age.

Sex Differences in Sequelae

The sex difference in depression is well established: Women have twice the lifetime rate (Weiss, Longhurst, & Mazure, 1999). Women also appear to be more vulnerable to PTSD in the wake of traumatic events than are males (Perry, 2001). This is interesting as most of the original work on PTSD was conducted on male combat veterans.

In one large study, 1,007 community subjects were assessed for psychiatric disorders and were then reassessed three and five years later. The men and women had experienced the same number of traumatic events, but more women had PTSD. Some of this difference was accounted for by preexisting anxiety or depressive disorders. Interestingly, the sex differences were more pronounced when the exposure to traumatic events occurred during childhood (Breslau, Davis, Andreski, & Peterson, 1997).

In a community sample from Canada, Stein, Walker, Hazen, and Forde (1997) examined the prevalence of trauma-producing events in the lives of men and women. They also found a substantial sex difference in the manifestation of PTSD. The respondents in their sample with current full or partial PTSD were overwhelmingly female—82 percent. Partial PTSD was defined as lacking some symptoms for a full diagnosis, but still exhibiting clinically relevant symptoms of distress.

A study of hospitalized adolescents also revealed a sex difference in PTSD. In this study, 93 percent of the sample had been exposed to at least one traumatic event. There were differences in the rates of trauma exposure for males versus females. Females in this study were more likely to have been sexually abused than males (77 percent vs. 33 percent, respectively) and were more likely to have witnessed family violence (67 percent vs. 32 percent). There were no other differences in the rates at which the other traumas were experienced or in the total number of traumas experienced between males and females. However, patients with PTSD were more likely to be female than male (43 percent vs. 20 percent). These findings were true even though there were no other significant differences in age, ethnicity, religion, parental marital status, family income, or household composition. The sample was mostly low-income, inner-city youth of African-American or Latino ethnicity (Lipschitz, Winegar, Hartmick, Foote, & Southwick, 1999).

In discussing this difference in women's vulnerability, Yehuda (1999) noted that, at this point, we really do not know whether this sex difference has to do with biological differences between men and women (e.g., possibly hormonal differences) or whether women are simply have more traumatic experiences.

QUALITY OF THE FAMILY OF ORIGIN

Researchers continue to debate whether abuse and neglect lead to symptoms or are simply markers for a general level of family pathology (Kendall-Tackett et al., 1993). The evidence so far indicates that family dysfunction appears to compound the traumatic symptoms of childhood abuse but does not fully explain them. Children who have experienced trauma were more vulnerable if their caregivers had also been traumatized; there was continuing threat and disruption to family; the family was chaotic, overwhelmed, or physically isolated; or the caregivers were distant (Perry, 2001). Children with secure attachments fare better when faced with traumatic events than do children who were raised with severe abuse or neglect (van der Kolk & Fisler, 1994).

The combination of family characteristics and severity of sexual abuse has been found to predict both social isolation and adjustment difficulties whereas abuse alone did not (Harter, Alexander, & Neimeyer, 1988). Early family characteristics were also predictive of pervasive disturbances of self in incest survivors, but the characteristics of the abuse itself were more predictive of depression in adults (Alexander, 1993). This section summarizes several studies that have attempted to tease apart the effects of maltreatment from the effects of family pathology.

Independent Effects of Abuse vs. Family Dysfunction

One review described eight studies that examined the relationship between family dysfunction, sexual abuse, and depression. Four of these studies found that there was a positive relationship between family dysfunction and CSA. The markers of family dysfunction included physical punishment, lack of parental warmth, and early parental separation. Indeed, these poor parenting experiences are also associated with depression, even in the absence of sexual abuse. However, in the four studies that controlled for family dysfunction and poor parenting, there was still a relationship between sexual abuse and later depression (Weiss et al., 1999).

Another study examined the relative impact of maltreatment, family environment, socioeconomic status (SES), and other factors on children's functioning at school (Herrenkohl, Herrenkohl, Rupert, Egolf, & Lutz, 1995). This study included a sample of physically abused and neglected children and a comparison group of nonmaltreated children. The children were assessed during preschool and at school age. Teachers' ratings sorted them into high, medium, and low functioning. A discriminant function analysis indicated that family environment was the best predictor of behavioral functioning. Maltreatment also predicted functioning but was less powerful. The family environment variable included SES, with more positive family interactions associated with a higher SES. Mothers' interaction behavior was also included, particularly the degree of rejection, hostility, and control. Mothers' positive interaction was also important. Physical health of the child (more physical problems were related to poorer functioning) and the presence of a male head of household who was the child's natural father were also both associated with better behavioral functioning.

In a sample of homeless adolescents, Ryan, Kilmer, Cauce, Watanabe, and Hoyt (2000) considered the unique contribution of all types of maltreatment and family environment to current pathology. They found that the teens with a history of physical and sexual abuse had the most severe symptoms and were at the greatest risk for revictimization. When comparing the relative contribution of family environment versus abuse, they found that abuse history was more predictive of internalizing symptoms and family characteristics were more predictive of externalizing symptoms. The mother's drug use distinguished between the abused and non-abused groups.

Brock, Mintz, and Good (1997) examined a group of sexual abuse survivors that is rarely considered: abuse survivors from functional families. They found that only the abused women from dysfunctional families stood apart on anxiety, depression, and interpersonal problems. There were no significant differences between the other groups (non-abused/dysfunctional, abused/functional, non-abused/functional). The authors cautioned that we should not assume that all families of abuse survivors are dysfunctional. And survivors from dysfunctional families tend to have the highest levels of emotional distress overall.

Family Dysfunction Compounds Effects of Abuse

Sexual abuse often occurs in conjunction with other forms of family dysfunction. In a study of teens in treatment for substance abuse, those who had been sexually abused had a greater incidence of physical abuse and parental substance abuse (Blood & Cornwall, 1996). A study of 1,959 teens revealed that those at highest risk for substance abuse had been sexually abused and had parents who abused substances. The combination was a much better predictor than either of these risk factors alone. Moreover, teens with both risk factors also had higher rates of suicide risk, disordered eating, and high-risk sexual behaviors (Chandy, Blum, & Resnick, 1996b). Other factors that increased the likelihood of a negative outcome included subject's depression, perceived substance abuse in school, and worries about the family financial security. In another large sample ($N = 1{,}011$) of sexually abused teens, mothers' use of alcohol and family stressor events in the past year were both risk factors for adverse outcomes for the girls (Chandy, Blum, & Resnick, 1996a). On the other hand, caring from adults, the presence of a school nurse or clinic, and living with both biological parents both proved to be protective factors against adverse outcomes.

Family dysfunction and abuse were also related to dissociative symptoms in psychiatric inpatients (Draijer & Langeland, 1999). Dissociative symptoms were highest for those who reported physical and sexual abuse and maternal dysfunction. The authors concluded that dissociation is related to both trauma and maternal neglect.

Another sample of psychiatric inpatients had similar findings. There were 358 patients diagnosed with borderline personality disorder (BPD), 91 percent of whom had been abused and 92 percent of whom had been neglected. Compared to the patients with other personality disorders ($N = 108$), those with BPD were significantly more likely to report that their caretaker emotionally withdrew from them, treated them inconsistently, denied their thoughts and feelings, placed them in the role of parent, and failed to protect them. Patients with both BPD and a history of sexual abuse were significantly more likely to report the other types of abuse and neglect (Zanarini et al., 1997).

In a study of early-onset dysthymic disorder (DD), researchers noted that DD was significantly associated with mood and personality disorders in first-degree relatives and with high levels of childhood adversity. There was also a strong relationship between parental personality disorder and a negative childhood home environment.

Both mothers and fathers with mood and/or personality disorders were more likely to physically and sexually abuse their children (Lizardi & Klein, 2000).

Family Dysfunction Also Increases the Risk of Abuse

Family dysfunction also put children at risk for sexual abuse. Alexander (1992) argued that sexual abuse is often preceded by an insecure attachment. Dynamics in abusive families, including role reversal, rejection, and unresolved trauma, are similar to those found in families with insecure attachments. A birth cohort study in New Zealand bore out this finding. Researchers found that the higher the level of family dysfunction, the higher the risk for being sexually abused. Females were at highest risk. Family characteristics associated with risk included parental alcoholism, high levels of marital conflict, low parental attachment, and high levels of parental overprotection (Fergusson, Lynskey, & Horwood, 1996). Families with the highest violence levels were also low SES (39 percent), in the lowest quartile of family income (44 percent), and at the lowest quartile of average family living standards (56 percent). They had young mothers (23 percent), who lacked formal educational qualifications (67 percent). These families had more than two changes of parents (66 percent); had a history of parental criminality (43 percent), parental alcoholism (43 percent), or drug use (30 percent); and were in the highest quartile of stressful family life events (63 percent) (Fergusson & Horwood, 1998).

In a national random survey of youth (ages 10–16), Boney-McCoy and Finkelhor (1996) found that quality of the parent-child relationship put subjects at risk for both victimization and later developing of symptoms in response to their victimization experiences. The authors described how previous studies that found the effects of childhood abuse disappear once they have controlled for family level of pathology may, in fact, have "overcontrolled" and thus eliminated any true association between victimization and subsequent symptoms.

From these studies, it appears that family function is an important component but cannot fully explain symptoms associated with child maltreatment. Physical abuse, sexual abuse, and neglect all appear to be related to symptoms. Family dysfunction compounds these affects and, indeed, appears to put children at risk for future victimization.

SUMMARY

The effects of abuse are not uniform. Many aspects of abuse can be related to increased symptomatology in adult survivors. Each of these factors can help explain why two people can experience abuse and yet react so differently.

Chapters 14 and 15 describe one of the most common outcomes of childhood abuse: chronic pain.

References

Alexander, P. (1992). Application of attachment theory to the study of sexual abuse. *Journal of Consulting and Clinical Psychology, 60*, 185–195.

Alexander, P. (1993). The differential effects of abuse characteristics and attachment in the prediction of long-term effects of sexual abuse. *Journal of Interpersonal Violence, 8*, 346–362.

Berliner, L., & Elliot, D. M. (1996). Sexual abuse of children. In J. Briere, L. Berliner, C. J. Bulkley, & T. Reid (Eds.), *The APSAC handbook on child maltreatment* (pp. 51–71). Newbury Park, CA: Sage.

Blood, L., & Cornwall, A. (1996). Childhood sexual victimization as a factor in the treatment of substance misusing adolescents. *Substance Use and Misuse, 31*, 1015–1039.

Boisset-Pioro, M. H., Esdaile, J. M., & Fitzcharles, M.-A. (1995). Sexual and physical abuse in women with fibromyalgia syndrome. *Arthritis and Rheumatism, 38*, 235–241.

Boney-McCoy, S., & Finkelhor, D. (1996). Is youth victimization related to trauma symptoms and depression after controlling for prior symptoms and family relationships? A longitudinal, prospective study. *Journal of Consulting and Clinical Psychology, 64*, 1406–1461.

Bremner, J. D., Randall, P., Vermetten, E., Staib, L., Bronen, R. A., Mazure, C. M., et al. (1997). Magnetic resonance imaging-based measurements of hippocampal volume in posttraumatic stress disorder related to childhood physical and sexual abuse: A preliminary report. *Biological Psychiatry, 41*, 23–32.

Breslau, N., Davis, G. C., Andreski, P., & Peterson, E. L. (1997). Sex differences in posttraumatic stress disorder. *Archives of General Psychiatry, 54*, 1044–1048.

Brock, K. J., Mintz, L. B., & Good, G. E. (1997). Differences among sexually abused and nonabused women from functional and dysfunctional families. *Journal of Counseling Psychology, 44*, 425–432.

Campeau, S., Day, H. E. W., Helmreich, D. L., Kollack-Walker, S., & Watson, S. J. (1998). Principles of psychoneuroendocrinology. *Psychiatric Clinics of North America, 21*, 259–275.

Chandy, J. M., Blum, R. W., & Resnick, M. D. (1996a). Female adolescents with a history of sexual abuse: Risk, outcomes, and protective factors. *Journal of Interpersonal Violence, 11*, 503–518.

Chandy, J. M., Blum, R. W., & Resnick, M. D. (1996b). History of sexual abuse and parental alcohol misuse: Risk, outcomes, and protective factors in adolescents. *Child and Adolescent Social Work Journal, 13*, 411–432.

Cicchetti, D., & Toth, S. L. (1998). The development of depression in children and adolescents. *American Psychologist, 53*, 221–241.

Deverts, D. J., Cohen, S., DiLillo, V. G., Lewis, C. E., Kiefe, C., Whooley, M. A., et al. (2010). Depressive symptoms, race, and circulating C-reactive protein: The Coronary Artery Risk Development in Young Adults (CARDIA) Study. *Psychosomatic Medicine, 72*, 734–741.

Dickinson, L. M., deGruy, F. V., Dickinson, W. P., & Candib, L. M. (1999). Health-related quality of life and symptom profiles of female survivors of sexual abuse. *Archives of Family Medicine, 8*, 35–43.

Draijer, N., & Langeland, W. (1999). Childhood trauma and perceived parental dysfunction in the etiology of dissociative symptoms in psychiatric inpatients. *American Journal of Psychiatry, 156*, 379–385.

Elwell, M. E., & Ephross, P. H. (1987). Initial reactions of sexually abused children. *Social Casework: Journal of Contemporary Social Work, 68*, 109–116.

Fergusson, D. M., & Horwood, L. J. (1998). Exposure to interparental violence in childhood and psychosocial adjustment in young adulthood. *Child Abuse and Neglect, 22*, 339–357.

Fergusson, D. M., Lynskey, M. T., & Horwood, L. J. (1996). Childhood sexual abuse and psychiatric disorder in young adulthood: I. Prevalence of sexual ause and factors associated with sexual abuse. *Journal of the American Academy of Child and Adolescent Psychiatry, 35*, 1355–1364.

Finkelhor, D. (1987). The trauma of child sexual abuse: Two models. *Journal of Interpersonal Violence, 2*, 348–366.

Finkelhor, D., & Kendall-Tackett, K. A. (1997). A developmental perspective on the childhood impact of crime, abuse, and violent victimization. In D. Cicchetti & S. L. Toth (Eds.), *Rochester symposium on developmental psychopathology: Developmental perspectives on trauma* (Vol. 8) (pp. 1–32). Rochester, NY: University of Rochester Press.

Finkelhor, D., Ormrod, R. K., & Turner, H. A. (2009). The developmental epidemiology of childhood victimization. *Journal of Interpersonal Violence, 24*(5), 711–731.

Freyd, J. J., Klest, B., & Allard, C. B. (2005). Betrayal trauma: Relationship to physical health, psychological distress, and a written disclosure intervention. *Journal of Trauma and Dissociation, 6*(3), 83–104.

Harter, S., Alexander, P., & Neimeyer, R. (1988). Long-term effects of incestuous child abuse in college women: Social adjustments, social cognitions, and family characteristiscs. *Journal of Consulting and Clinical Psychology, 56*, 5–8.

Herrenkohl, E. C., Herrenkohl, R. C., Rupert, L. J., Egolf, B. P., & Lutz, G. (1995). Risk factors for behavioral dysfunction: The relative impact of maltreatment, SES, physical health problems, cognitive ability, and quality of parent-child interaction. *Child Abuse and Neglect, 19*, 191–203.

Jones, N., Field, T., Fox, N., Lundy, B., & Devalos, M. (1997). EEG activation in one-month-old infants of depressed mothers. *Development & Psychopathology, 9*, 491–505.

Kendall-Tackett, K. A., & Simon, A. F. (1987). Perpetrators and their acts: Data from 265 adults molested as children. *Child Abuse and Neglect, 11*, 237–245.

Kendall-Tackett, K. A., Williams, L. M., & Finkelhor, D. (1993). The impact of sexual abuse on children: A review and synthesis of recent empirical studies. *Psychological Bulletin, 113*, 164–180.

Lazarus, R. S., & Folkman, S. (1984). *Stress, appraisal, and coping*. New York: Springer.

Leserman, J., Drossman, D. A., Li, Z., Toomey, T. C., Nachman, G., & Glogau, L. (1996). Sexual and physical abuse history in gastroenterology practice: How types of abuse impact health status. *Psychosomatic Medicine, 58*, 4–15.

Leserman, J., Toomey, T. C., & Drossman, D. A. (1995). Medical consequences of sexual and physical abuse in women. *Humane Medicine, 11*, 23–28.

Lewis, T. T., Aiello, A. E., Leurgans, S., Kelly, J., & Barnes, L. L. (2010). Self-reported experiences of everyday discrimination are associated with elevated C-reactive protein levels in older African-American adults. *Brain, Behavior and Immunity, 24*(3), 438–443.

Lipschitz, D. S., Winegar, R. K., Hartmick, E., Foote, B., & Southwick, S. M. (1999). Posttraumatic stress disorder in hospitalized adolescents: Psychiatric comorbidity and clinical correlates. *Journal of the American Academy of Child and Adolescent Psychiatry, 38*, 385–392.

Lizardi, H., & Klein, D. N. (2000). Parental psychopathology and reports of the childhood home environment in adults with early-onset dysthymic disorder. *Journal of Nervous and Mental Disease, 188*, 63–70.

Lovallo, W. R. (1997). *Stress and health: Biological and psychological interactions*. Newbury Park, CA: Sage.

Maccoby, E. (1983). Social-emotional development and response to stressors. In N. Garmezy & M.

Rutter (Eds.), *Stress, coping, and development in children* (pp. 217–234). New York: McGraw-Hill.

Mellman, T. A., Brown, D. D., Jenifer, E. S., Hipolito, M. M. S., & Randall, O. S. (2009). Posttraumatic stress disorder and nocturnal blood pressure dipping in young adult African Americans. *Psychosomatic Medicine, 71*, 627–630.

Mennen, F. E. (1995). The relationship of race/ethnicity to symptoms of childhood sexual abuse. *Child Abuse and Neglect, 19*, 115–124.

Perry, B. D. (2001). The neuroarcheology of childhood maltreatment: The neurodevelopmental costs of adverse childhood events. In K. Franey, R. Geffner & R. Falconer (Eds.), *The cost of child maltreatment: Who pays? We all do* (pp. 15–37). San Diego: Family Violence & Sexual Assault Institute.

Perry, B. D., & Pollard, R. (1998). Homeostasis, stress, trauma, and adaptation: A neurodevelopmental view of childhood trauma. *Child and Adolescent Psychiatric Clinics of North America, 7*, 33–51.

Perry, B. D., Pollard, R., Blakley, T. L., Baker, W. L., & Vigilante, D. (1995). Childhood trauma, the neurobiology of adaptation, and "use-dependent" development of the brain: How "states" become "traits." *Infant Mental Health Journal, 16*, 271–291.

Radke-Yarrow, M. (1998). *Children of depressed mothers: From early childhood to maturity*. New York: Cambridge University Press.

Robin, R. W., Chester, B., Rasmussen, J. K., Jaranson, J. M., & Goldman, D. (1997). Prevalence, characteristics, and impact of childhood sexual abuse in a Southwestern American Indian tribe. *Child Abuse and Neglect, 21*, 769–787.

Russell, D. E. H. (1984). The prevalence and eriousness of incestuous abuse: Stepfathers vs. biological fathers. *Child Abuse and Neglect, 8*, 15–22.

Rutter, M., & Rutter, M. (1993). *Developing minds: Challenge and continuity across the life span.* New York: Basic Books.

Ryan, K. D., Kilmer, R. P., Cauce, A. M., Watanabe, H., & Hoyt, D. R. (2000). Psychological consequences of child maltreatment in homeless adolescents: Untangling the unique effects of maltreatment and family environment. *Child Abuse and Neglect, 24*, 333–352.

Slopen, N., Lewis, T. T., Gruenewald, T. L., Mujahid, M. S., Ryff, C. D., Albert, M. A., & Williams, D. R. (2010). Early life adversity and inflammation in African Americans and whites in midlife in the United States Survey. *Psychosomatic Medicine, 72*, 694–701.

Stein, M. B., Walker, J. R., Hazen, A. L., & Forde, D. R. (1997). Full and partial posttraumatic stress disorder: Findings from a community survey. *American Journal of Psychiatry, 154*, 1114–1119.

Suglia, S. F., Staudenmayer, J., Cohen, S., Enlow, M. B., Rich-Edwards, J. W., & Wright, R. (2010). Cumulative stress and cortisol disruption among black and Hispanic pregnant women in an urban cohort. *Psychological Trauma, 2*(4), 326–334.

Taylor, M. L., Trotter, D. R., & Csuka, M. E. (1995). The prevalence of sexual abuse in women with fibromyalgia. *Arthritis and Rheumatism, 38*, 229–234.

Trickett, P. K., Reiffman, A., Horowitz, L. A., & Putnam, F. W. (1997). Characteristics of sexual abuse trauma and the prediction of developmental outcomes. In D. Cicchetti & S. L. Toth (Eds.), *Rochester symposium on developmental psychopathology: Developmental perspectives on trauma* (Vol. 8, pp. 289–314). Rochester, NY: University of Rochester Press.

Ulibarri, M. D., Ulloa, E. C., & Camacho, L. (2009). Prevalence of sexually abusive experiences in childhood and adolescence among a community sample of Latinas: A descriptive study. *Journal of Child Sexual Abuse, 18*, 405–421.

Urquiza, A. J., & Goodlin-Jones, B. L. (1994). Child sexual abuse and adult revictimization with women of color. *Violence and Victims, 9*, 223–265.

van der Kolk, B. A. (1994). The body keeps score: Memory and the evolving psychobiology of posttraumatic stress. *Harvard Review of Psychiatry, 1*, 223–232.

van der Kolk, B. A., & Fisler, R. (1994). Childhood abuse and neglect and loss of self-regulation.

Bulletin of the Menninger Clinic, 58, 145–168.

Weiss, E. L., Longhurst, J. G., & Mazure, C. M. (1999). Childhoood sexual abuse as a risk factor for depression in women: Psychosocial and neurobiological correlates. *American Journal of Psychiatry, 156*, 816–828.

Wright, M. O., Master, A. S., & Hubbard, J. J. (1997). Long-term effects of massive trauma: Developmental and psychobiological perspectives. In D. Cicchetti & S. L. Toth (Eds.), *Rocheter symposium on developmental psychopathology: Developmental perspectives on trauma* (Vol. 8, pp. 181–225). Rochester, NY: University of Rochester Press.

Wyatt, G. E. (1985). The sexual abuse of Afro-American and white-American women in childhood. *Child Abuse and Neglect, 9*, 507–519.

Wyatt, G. E., Guthrie, D., & Notgrass, C. M. (1992). Differential effects of women's child sexual abuse and subsequent sexual revictimization. *Journal of Consulting and Clinical Psychology, 60*, 167–173.

Yehuda, R. (1999). Biological factors associated with susceptibility to posttraumatic stress disorder. *Canadian Journal of Psychiatry, 44*, 34–39.

Yehuda, R., Levengood, R. A., Schmeider, J., Wilson, S., Guo, L. S., & Gerber, D. (1996). Increased pituitary activation following metyrapone administration in posttraumatic stress disorder. *Psychoneuroendocrinology, 21*, 1–16.

Young, T. L., Riggs, M., & Robinson, J. L. (2011). Childhood sexual abuse severity reconsidered: A factor structure of CSA characteristics. *Journal of Child Sexual Abuse, 20*, 373–395.

Zanarini, M. C., Williams, A. A., Lewis, R. E., Reich, R. B., Vera, S. C., Marino, M. F., et al. (1997). Reported pathological childhood experiences associated with the development of borderline personality disorder. *American Journal of Psychiatry, 154*, 1101–1106.

Chapter 14

Pain I—Overview of Chronic Pain in Abuse Survivors

Chronic pain is perhaps the most common symptom reported by adult survivors of childhood abuse. Three studies of childhood sexual abuse found that it was associated with increased levels of several types of pain. For example, in a community sample of adults in Germany, Austria, and Switzerland, "almost all" female sexual abuse survivors reported pain symptoms and other somatic complaints, making pain more common than even depression (Teegan, 1999).

A more recent review in the *Journal of the American Medical Association* included twenty-three studies, with 4,640 patients, and found that a history of child sexual abuse (CSA) was associated with a number of somatic disorders (Paras et al., 2009).

The researchers found that there was a significant association between history of sexual abuse and lifetime diagnosis of functional gastrointestinal (GI) disorders, nonspecific chronic pain, psychogenic seizures, and chronic pelvic pain. They did not find a significant relation between CSA and fibromyalgia, obesity, or headache. However, when CSA included rape, there was a significant relationship between CSA and three pain syndromes: fibromyalgia, chronic pelvic pain, and functional GI disorders.

A sample of 163 psychiatric patients, age 50 and older, with primary mood disorders had similar findings (Talbot et al., 2009). The researchers found that severe childhood sexual abuse was associated with higher cumulative medical illness burden, worse physical functioning, and greater bodily pain. They calculated that severe CSA was comparable to adding eight years of chronological age for illness burden and twenty years of chronological age for activities-of-daily-living impairment and bodily pain. The authors noted that the impact of CSA is profound, even in later life. They recommended early identification of these patients to target interventions to prevent or decelerate the progression of morbidity in this high-risk group.

Generally speaking, pain is common in women. A recent study of 1,647 gynecology patients found that 29 percent reported moderate, severe, or very severe bodily pain of all types in the past four weeks. Ten percent reported both pain and depression (Poleshuck et al., 2009); 13 percent of these women also reported physical or sexual abuse in the past year.

Chronic pain can also account high rates of health care use among abuse survivors. According to Marcus (2000), patients with chronic pain are five times more likely to use health care services than people without chronic pain. In another study of women in a support group for sexual abuse survivors, 69 percent reported at least one chronic pain syndrome compared with 43 percent of the comparison group. In addition, abused women had significantly more painful body areas, more diffuse pain, and more diagnoses of fibromyalgia (Finestone et al., 2000).

This chapter provides an overview of chronic pain among abuse survivors. It highlights some of the controversies about pain as a sequela of abuse and outlines some of the biological alterations that may be related to pain in abuse survivors. Chapter 15 goes on to describe five chronic-pain syndromes that can occur subsequent to childhood abuse.

THE ENIGMA OF CHRONIC PAIN

Chronic pain can begin with or without an injury. The patient goes through a cycle of pain that no one can explain or treat. The pain continues and treatment regimens fail. The patient starts withdrawing from others. Pain becomes the focus of the patient's life as the patient becomes more and more disabled (Miller, 2000).

Difficulties in Diagnosis and Treatment

To practitioners, chronic pain is a diagnostic enigma. There are frequently no laboratory or radiological findings that verify its existence, and the amount of pain patients experience seems far above the "appropriate" amount given the patient's condition. Practitioners often become frustrated with chronic pain patients (Fields & Martin, 1998): "Managing patients with chronic pain is intellectually and emotionally challenging. The patient's problem is often difficult to diagnose: such patients are demanding of the physician's time and often appear emotionally distraught" (p. 56).

Chronic pain is challenging in a number of ways (Bennett, 1996). First, pain is a subjective experience, and it is often interpreted in an emotional context. It is difficult for an outsider to quantify or fully comprehend the patient's experience. Second, practitioners cannot explain chronic pain in terms of classic models of disease that say that pain is due to tissue damage. In most cases of chronic pain, there is little or no verifiable physical evidence to support a patient's story. Finally, pain-related disability stems from a complex interplay of experiences, past and present, socioeconomic status, education, social support, personal values, fatigue, and ethnic background (with some ethnic groups tending to be more "stoic" about pain than others).

Functional vs. Organic Conditions

Chronic pain conditions are often functional rather than organic. There are no lab tests for functional illnesses, and diagnoses must be made solely on patient history. This fact alone makes practitioners leery. Gershon (1998) describes the difficulties patients face when speaking to doctors about functional disorders: "Physicians become angry. Patients who present themselves to doctors with problems that are insoluble are perceived as threatening and are often dismissed as mentally unbalanced, with the epithet 'crocks' whispered behind their backs" (p. xiv).

The nebulous nature of chronic pain can create an atmosphere of mistrust between doctor and patient that prevents them from working together.

The Pain-Abuse Connection

There is a great deal of circumstantial evidence connecting chronic pain to childhood abuse. A high percentage of abuse survivors report pain, and a high percentage of chronic pain patients are abuse survivors. For example, Wolfe (1997) states that fibromyalgia is "obviously associated with trauma" (p. 1248). However, no one has been able to firmly establish whether trauma causes chronic pain, or whether both are the result of some third condition, such as sleep problems.

Past abuse is often the "missing piece" in refractory pain (Leserman & Drossman, 1995). Drossman (1995) noted that abuse history has been associated with poorer adjustment to illness, greater symptom severity, and higher rates of health care use. "I have noted that many of the patients with refractory GI illness had experienced physical or sexual abuse" (p. 90), and only 17 percent of patients in his study had even shared their abuse history with their doctors. This is unfortunate, as health care providers who know that past abuse is a factor in a particular patient's history may be able to address this issue directly, thereby reducing symptoms.

Past abuse has been related to chronic or recurring headaches, pelvic pain, back pain, and pain syndromes, such as irritable bowel syndrome and fibromyalgia (Kendall-Tackett, Marshall, & Ness, 2003). Sachs-Ericsson, Kendall-Tackett, and Hernandez (2007), using data from the National Comorbidity Survey, found that participants with a history of either intimate partner violence or childhood physical or sexual abuse were more likely to report pain when describing their current health symptoms.

Patients with chronic pain often have marked physiological abnormalities in brain structure and function that appears when using technology such as PET (positron emission tomography) scans, CT (computed tomography) scans, and MRIs (magnetic resonance imaging) of the brain (Bremner, 2005). A recent study not specifically on abuse survivors, but relevant to them, examined the role of self-concealment in pain (Uysal & Lu, 2011). The researchers defined self-concealment as the tendency to hide negative or distressing personal information from others and noted that it had three characteristics: It is private and personal, consciously accessible, and actively kept hidden. They examined the relationship of self-concealment to pain in two samples: a healthy group of volunteers and patients with chronic pain. They found that self-concealment was associated with higher levels of pain in both healthy and chronic pain patients.

PSYCHIATRIC COMORBIDITY IN PAIN PATIENTS

Pain rarely travels alone; it is often accompanied by psychiatric conditions. Chronic pain patients often have high rates of psychiatric comorbidity, and pain in psychiatric patients is associated with more severe depression, depression of longer duration, poorer clinical outcome, earlier relapse, and higher health care costs (Vaccarino, Sills, Evans, & Kalali, 2009). In a study of 2,191 patients with major depression, comorbid pain was common (Vaccarino et al., 2009). Depressed patients were more likely to report headache, pain in the lower back, neck pain, pain in the joints, soreness in the muscles, pain in the heart or chest, or pain or cramps in the abdomen. Only 25 percent of these patients reported no pain symptoms: 18 percent reported one symptom, and 57 percent reported from two to seven pain symptoms. Headache was the most common symptom, reported by 40 percent of the patients.

Teasing apart pain and these psychiatric symptoms is an ongoing challenge for both researchers and clinicians. Some do not even try, and assume that the presence of psychiatric symptoms indicates that the pain is purely psychosomatic (Gordon, 1997). Miller (2000) found that "[a] common diagnostic association occurs between depression and chronic pain. In many cases, no 'legitimate' medical explanation for pain can be discovered and patients make the rounds from clinician to clinician until they are eventually shunted into the mental health system" (p. 27).

Chronic, unexplained pain was also related to high rates of depression in a study of 3,189 patients with unexplained chronic pain (Aguera, Failde, Cervilla, Diaz-Fernandez, & Mico, 2010). The average duration of pain was 30.8 months, and the most common locations were the neck and back. Thirty-eight percent knew the origin of their pain, but the intensity of their pain was not fully explained by this cause. Depressed pain patients had more visits to their primary health care provider in the previous six weeks than pain patients who were not depressed, and they were more likely to have seen a specialist in the previous six weeks. Women in their sample were more susceptible to depression than men.

Patients are also in a Catch-22 when it comes to reporting symptoms. They may need to be vigilant to certain symptoms that could indicate the onset of a more serious condition. However, at some point, the daily monitoring of symptoms needs to stop so they can get on with their lives. Patients may also hesitate to tell their doctors about co-occurring depression or other psychiatric conditions for fear that the physical symptoms may be downplayed or considered only manifestations of a psychiatric condition.

Explanations for Psychiatric Diagnoses in Functional Illness

As described earlier, many of the pain syndromes that are more common in abuse survivors are functional. Psychiatric comorbidity is common in patients with functional disorders, including irritable bowel syndrome (IBS) and fibromyalgia. The most common symptoms are major depression, substance abuse, and anxiety disorders.

Many explanations have been offered for why patients with functional illnesses are depressed, anxious, or have other psychiatric conditions. Psychiatric symptoms may have existed before the pain symptoms, they may both may have been caused by a common neurobiolgical mechanism (Malt, Berle, Olafsson, Lund, & Ursin, 2000), or the psychiatric condition may be reactive and could have developed as a response to living in pain (Domino & Haber, 1987). In a study of fibromyalgia, the number of comorbidities was the best predictor of both health care costs and use. Half of the patients in this study were not satisfied with their health, and 59 percent of these patients rated their health as fair or poor (Wolfe, Russell, Vipraio, Ross, & Anderson, 1997).

The psychiatric conditions may be what compelled the patients to seek treatment, or those in treatment may have had a more serious manifestation of the condition that both distressed them and compelled them to seek treatment (Aaron et al., 1996). Indeed, chronic pain disrupts normal life, changing normal routines, self-perceptions, and interaction with others (Loren, 1998). Chronic pain can limit participation in activities of daily living and make daily routines more difficult. Loss of independence can contribute to depression, as can feelings of not being able to contribute to the family.

Psychiatric comorbidity might also be a function of severity of the abuse experience. Walker, Katon, Roy-Byrne, Jemelka, and Russo (1993) found high levels of psychiatric comorbidity among the pain patients who had experienced severe lifetime abuse when compared with patients who had experienced no abuse or milder forms of abuse.

Genetic factors may further complicate the picture. Patients with co-occurring fibromyalgia and depression often have family histories of both depression and alcoholism (Hudson & Pope, 1989; Katz & Kravitz, 1996). Hudson, Goldenberg, Pope, Keck, and Schlesinger (1992) found similar results. First-degree relatives were likely to suffer from major mood disorders, alcohol abuse or dependence, and migraines. Indeed, sixteen of the thirty-one probands of fibromyalgia patients (52 percent) had at least one first-degree relative with a major mood disorder.

Pain and Inflammation

Pain is also related to higher levels of inflammation. The relationship between pain and inflammation appears to be bidirectional: pain is related to inflammation, and inflammation is related to pain. When a man or woman experiences pain, stress hormones and levels of proinflammatory cytokines increase. Cytokines are stimulated by substance P. Substance P is the neuropeptide that is high in the cerebral spinal fluid of pain patients. High levels of Substance P increase inflammation via high levels of proinflammatory cytokines. High levels of inflammation, in turn, increase pain by increasing prostaglandin synthesis, which increases pain (Geracioti et al., 2006).

In one study, patients with major depression or posttraumatic stress disorder (PTSD) were compared to healthy controls ($N = 101$). The patients with depression or PTSD had significantly elevated levels of substance P in their cerebrospinal fluid. Moreover, the levels of substance P rose significantly when the patients were stressed in the laboratory. The authors concluded that substance P was related to both depression and PTSD and responded to acute stress (Geracioti et al., 2006).

In a randomized study of postoperative pain, three methods of pain relief were included in the trial (Beilin et al., 2003). All the patients were having elective lower abdominal surgery. The first type of pain relief was opiates on demand. The second was patient-controlled analgesia. The third was patient-controlled epidural analgesia, an approach that combines opiates with local anesthesia, which is opiate sparing. The local anesthesia is anti-inflammatory, which may contribute to its pain-reducing effects. The researchers found that pain intensity was lowest in the epidural group. There were higher levels of IL-1β and IL-6 in the on-demand opiates and patient-controlled analgesia than in the epidural group. The researchers argued that proinflammatory cytokines mediate hyperalgesia, including the upregulation of Cox-2, and increased production of substance P and nerve growth factor. Nociception (pain) and proinflammatory cytokines are mutually upregulatory; because of the feedback cascade between nociception and proinflammatory cytokines, pain increases inflammation and inflammation increases pain. Under certain circumstances, central pain sensitization can lead to the development of chronic or neuropathic pain.

Chronic Pain vs. Somatization

Another issue to consider is role of somatization in chronic pain. Somatization is a psychiatric diagnosis for somatic complaints that cannot be verified in terms of conventionally defined medical conditions and often co-occurs with depression and anxiety (Dallam, 2001; Drossman, Talley, Leserman, Olden, & Barreiro, 1995). Some speculate on whether somatization is a catch-all diagnosis for pain that physicians cannot explain, as Gershon (1998) describes:

> If a lesion in the gut is obvious, doctors become sympathetic, grant a patient the right to be in pain, and seek to alleviate the problem. If no lesion is detected, enteric pain tends to be belittled and blamed on neurotic thought processes. . . . The fact that doctors do not yet always know why it occurs is no reason either to dismiss its severity or to attribute the pain to what substitutes in the modern world for a supernatural cause, psychoneurosis. (pp. 178–179)

Pain researchers are split on whether abuse survivors are experiencing "actual" pain or somatizing. For example, in three studies of fibromyalgia, there are widely different percentages of patients diagnosed with somatization. In one study, only 14–23 percent had a formal diagnosis of somatization (Bennett, 1996). In the second study, there were more diagnoses of somatization in patients with fibromyalgia (FM or

FMS) compared to people with fibromyalgia who were not in treatment (Aaron et al., 1996). However, in another study, no fibromyalgia patients met the criteria for somatization (Hudson et al., 1992), and indeed, the authors were concerned that FMS patients would be misdiagnosed as somatizers.

In an editorial on fibromyalgia, Hadler (1997) states that the very process of diagnosing a patient with this condition can magnify symptoms and is counterproductive to patient coping because it "fosters a life of somatizing. When it comes to disability determination, anyone who has to prove he or she is ill will be rendered more ill in the proving. When a physician participates in the process, it becomes worse than counterproductive, it becomes iatrogenic" (p. 1251).

Abuse survivors often receive a diagnosis of somatization. In one study, women were screened into the study if they indicated that over the past year they had been to a medical doctor for a problem without an apparent physical explanation. All types of child maltreatment (physical, sexual, and/or emotional) were highly significantly correlated with a diagnosis of somatization, as was sexual abuse/assault as adults. Of 100 women who had been diagnosed with somatization, 90 percent reported some type of abuse, and 80 percent reported sexual assault as either children or adults (Pribor, Yutzy, Dean, & Wetzel, 1993).

Treatment Impact of Somatization

Patients with somatization used more health care services. In a study of 1,000 primary care patients from four sites, Kroenke et al. (1997) found that patients with major depression or multisomatoform disorder had approximately seven sick days and .35 visits to the emergency room in the previous three months. They noted that doctors described 54 percent of patients with multi-somatoform disorder, 56 percent of patients with panic disorder, and 40 percent of patients with dysthymia as "difficult."

Psychological factors also complicate treatment. Patients with chronic pain may be incensed when a practitioner suggests that their symptoms have a psychological basis, or even a psychological component. Patients may also be unwilling to disclose depression or other psychological difficulties because they fear their symptoms will not be taken seriously. Unfortunately, this fear may lead them to reject any form of psychological intervention that could actually be helpful. Patients may find themselves trapped in a cycle of hyperattention to physical symptoms, disability, increased health care costs, and general dissatisfaction with their health and health care (Leserman & Drossman, 1995).

CATASTROPHIZING: COGNITIVE PROCESSES IN PAIN

Cognitions about pain can influence patients' emotional and behavioral response to physical symptoms. Individuals with chronic pain syndromes may misinterpret minor physical symptoms as signs of serious disease. This increases pain, anxiety, and disability and becomes a vicious cycle. Appraisals of their pain can also result in avoidance of activities, social withdrawal, disruptions in work, and physical and psychological disability (Shelby et al., 2009).

One important type of cognition is pain catastrophizing. This is a tendency to exaggerate the threat value of pain sensations, ruminate on them, and feel helpless when experiencing them. Some items include the following: "It's awful and I feel that it overwhelms me," "I wonder whether something serious will happen," "I become afraid that the pain will get worse," and "I keep thinking about how much it hurts." Catastrophizing includes feelings of helplessness, and a generally pessimistic orientation (Edwards, Bingham, Bathon, & Haythornthwaite, 2006; Shelby et al., 2009).

In a review of the literature on the impact of catastrophizing on patients with arthritis, fibromyalgia, and other rheumatic diseases, the researchers found that catastrophizing was positively related to reported pain severity, affective distress, muscle and joint tenderness, pain-related disability, poor outcomes of pain treatment, and possibly to an increase in inflammatory disease activity (Edwards et al., 2006). For example, catastrophizing was found to be prospectively related to increased erythrocyte sedimentation rate (ESR), a measure of systemic inflammation. Catastrophizing was related to more severe and widespread pain, and more emotional disturbance. It may also be related to increased sensitivity of the central nervous system. These effects persist even after controlling for depression. They noted that catastrophizing was an important target for both psychosocial and pharmacologic treatment of pain.

In a neuroimaging study of patients with FMS, researchers found that fibromyalgia patients displayed greater catastrophizing behavior in general, but not during the anticipation of the experimental pain (Burgmer et al., 2011). Furthermore, there were differences between the FMS patients and healthy controls on activation of the periaqueductal gray, dorsolateral prefrontal cortex, and the posterior parietal cortex. The authors concluded that these functional changes are related to the context of stimulus presentation may contribute to central sensitization in FMS.

Another recent study included patients with noncardiac chest pain (Shelby et al., 2009). In this study of ninety-seven patients, researchers examined the contributions of chest pain and anxiety to disability via catastrophizing. Using path models, they found that chest pain and anxiety accounted for 46 percent of the variance in pain castrophizing, and that both chest pain and trait anxiety demonstrated significant indirect relationships with psychosocial disability via pain catastrophizing. The authors recommended that clinicians address catastrophizing in order to improve functioning in patients with noncardiac chest pain.

POSSIBLE MECHANISMS BY WHICH CATASTROPHIZING AFFECTS PAIN

In their review, Edwards et al. (2006) hypothesized about several possible mechanisms by which catastrophizing could increase pain.

- *Catastrophizing interferes with pain coping and beneficial health behaviors.* People high in catastrophizing cognitions are less likely to use other pain management techniques, such as distraction, relaxation, or exercise. In addition, helplessness correlates with adherence to treatment regimens.
- *Catastrophizing increases attention to pain.* Catastrophizing causes patient to focus selectively and intensely on pain-related stimuli.
- *Catastrophizing amplifies pain processing in the central nervous system.* Recent brain imagining studies have found that high catastrophizers

showed enhanced activity in parts of the brain involved in affective processing of pain, such as the anterior cingulate cortex and insular cortex.

- *Catastrophizing has a maladaptive impact on the social environment.* Others may reinforce experiences of pain, thus amplifying it. Or they may withdraw and offer less support. Both could increase the experience of pain.

Interventions, such as cognitive-behavioral therapy, may help to address these cognitions, thereby decreasing the experience of pain.

NEUROLOGICAL MECHANISMS IN PAIN

Research in neuroscience is opening a whole new world in terms of understanding chronic pain. This research may soon reveal how traumatic events can alter the way bodily sensations are perceived, and why abuse survivors seem prone to chronic pain. These same processes might also explain depression, PTSD, and other psychiatric conditions. Rather than one causing the other, they might all be the result of alterations in the neural substrate.

This section provides an overview of neuroscience theory and research involving chronic pain in trauma survivors. This discussion is brief and meant to provide an introduction to the concepts. Some specifics of research findings are presented in the next chapter as they pertain to headache, pelvic pain, fibromyalgia, and IBS.

Brain Structures in Pain

Brain structures that are involved in pain include the hypothalamus, midbrain, medulla, and amygdala (Fields & Martin, 1998; Garcia-Campayo, Fayed, Serrano-Blanco, & Roca, 2009; Price, 2000). Miller (2000) noted that chronic pain starts in the thalamus. Two structures called the cingulum bundle and fornix connect the anterior thalamic nuclei to the cingulate cortex, hippocampus, and mammillary bodies. More recent research in neuroscience has identified that the dorsolateral prefrontal, insular, rostal, anterior cingulate, premotor, and parietal cortices are involved in mild pain (Garcia-Campayo et al., 2009)

Pain endured over time involves the prefrontal cortex in reflection and rumination over the future implications of a persistent pain condition (Garcia-Campayo et al., 2009). The anterior cingulate cortex receives multiple inputs, and it is closely associated with pain unpleasantness that provides interactions with the prefrontal cortex. The anterior cingulate cortex plays a key role in pain perception (Price, 2000).

On functional MRI, patients with pain disorder responded to induced pain with hypoactivation of the ventromedial prefrontal/orbitofrontal cortex, and hyperactivation fo the amygdala, parahippocampal gyrus, and anterior insula. The finding of altered cerebral processing of inducted pain supports the hypothesis of dysfunctional pain processing (Garcia-Campayo et al., 2009).

Changes in the Pain Threshold

Some people have a higher tolerance for pain than others. In making these comparisons, we speak of the pain threshold. Threshold refers to the magnitude of sensation necessary for it to be perceived. A touch or bodily sensation can be pleasant, neutral, or painful. Traumatic events can lower pain thresholds so that even mild sensations are perceived as painful.

When describing the process of sensitization, Fields and Martin (1998) noted that "when intense, repeated, or prolonged stimuli are applied in the presence of damaged tissue or inflammation, the threshold for activating primary afferent nociceptors is lowered and the frequency of firing is higher for all stimulus intensities" (p. 53).

Some consider this hypersensitivity a major evolutionary advantage, in that it makes an individual more aware of potential danger. However, the increased pain that accompanies hypersensitivity makes day-to-day living difficult for people who have experienced violence (Woolf & Salter, 2000).

Hyperarousal was noted in a study of women with a history of childhood maltreatment who had one of two types of chronic pain: fibromyalgia or osteoarthritis (Nicholson, Davis, Kruszewski, & Zautra, 2010). In this study, women reporting more severe maltreatment had higher cortisol levels throughout the day. Sexual and emotional abuse were the forms of maltreatment most closely linked to cortisol levels. PTSD, depression, or daily affect did not mediate the link between maltreatment and cortisol. Women reporting the most severe sexual abuse had not only higher cortisol levels but also flatter diurnal slopes, meaning that levels did not dip significantly over a twenty-four-hour period. The authors noted that their findings support a link between abuse and long-term changes in the activation of the hypothalamic-pituitary-adrenal (HPA) axis.

Another way to describe the lowered pain threshold is secondary hyperalgesia. In primary hyperalgesia, pain perception stems directly from nociceptor (i.e., painful) stimulation due to injured tissue. In secondary hyperalgesia, pain exists without injured tissues; even light touches are perceived as painful (Bennett, 1996). Prolonged sensory disturbances reduce the pain threshold, and the net result is that the neurons fire at low levels.

Secondary Hyperalgesia

Secondary hyperalgesia results from a synergism between the neuropeptide substance P and N-methyl D-aspartate (NMDA) receptors (Bennett, 1996; Crofford, 2007; Woolf & Salter, 2000). The fact that there have been increased levels of substance P in patients with fibromyalgia is consistent with this theory of pain (Russell et al., 1994). Nerve damage changes receptors and transmitters, and can trigger a cascade of changes in the central nervous system (CNS). There is increasing evidence that chronic pain syndromes that have been called "functional" in the past may be the result of HPA dysfunction similar to that found in PTSD and depression (Dallam, 2001; Heim, Ehlert, Hanker, & Hellhammer, 1998).

Central Sensitization

Central sensitization is another key concept (Marcus, 2000; Woolf & Salter, 2000). Central sensitization explains why pain that starts in one specific area of the body can "spread" to other areas—even when there has been no tissue damage in those areas (Crofford, 2007). This process is called "wind-up" and is similar to the phenomenon known as "kindling" in depression (Crofford, 2007; Miller, 2000). It can occur as an immediate or delayed phenomenon resulting in widespread pain.

Therefore, pain hypersensitivity and functional changes within the CNS are expressions of neuronal plasticity (Bennett, 1996). Pain is not a passive consequence of the transfer of a sensory input to a pain center in the brain. Rather, it is an active and transactional process that is partly generated in the periphery, and partly in the CNS, by the changes made via plasticity (Crofford, 2007; Woolf & Salter, 2000).

WHAT WE KNOW ABOUT PAIN AND ABUSE

This chapter has reported the results of numerous studies that described why there is a probable link between chronic pain and past abuse. But differences may be present even before abuse survivors become patients. In comparing a small sample of college women with a history of sexual abuse and those with no history, the women who had been sexually abused showed significantly more physical symptoms than did the non-abused women in the five days prior to a highly stressful day. The daily hassles included everything from the weather to employers, intimacy, and car maintenance. Physical symptoms included gynecological symptoms, sleeping problems, headaches, muscular and other types of pain, and respiratory symptoms (Thakkar & McCanne, 2000).

In considering all the evidence together, what have we learned? With all that has been written about the link between chronic pain and childhood abuse, we can make a few generalizations.

Pain Syndromes Co-Occur

The studies reviewed in this chapter and Chapter 15 demonstrate that pain is common among abuse survivors. Although some studies started with a focus on one type of pain, researchers found that different types of pain often co-occur. For example, one study found that 70 percent of the FMS patients also had IBS, and 65 percent of the IBS patients had FMS compared with 12 percent of controls (Veale, Kavanagh, Fielding, & Fitzgerald, 1991). Sufferers of both syndromes also have other types of pain.

Golding (1994) found that chronic pain in sexual assault survivors was not limited to the pelvis. In her sample, those with a lifetime history of sexual assault were significantly more likely to report a wide range of chronic pain. Reproductive or sexual symptoms were no more consistently associated with sexual assault history than with GI pain or cardiopulmonary or neurological symptoms. She noted that the focus on pelvic pain is limited.

Similarly, in our study of chronic pain in women from a primary care practice, we combined six pain symptoms into a measure of self-reported pain and compared women who had experienced child or domestic abuse with those who had not reported such a history. The symptoms included abdominal pain, pain or stiffness in joints or muscles, pain during urination, arthritis, back pain, and severe headaches. Women who reported either physical or sexual abuse in childhood, or domestic abuse as adults, reported significantly more pain symptoms than women in the control group, but no one type was particularly common. There was no significant difference between women who had experienced domestic abuse versus child abuse alone. These findings held true even after controlling for depression (Kendall-Tackett et al., 2003).

Pain Syndromes Have Commonalities

A broader view also encourages us to consider what the various pain syndromes have in common. For example, people with FMS, IBS, and migraine headaches have lower pain thresholds and increased sensitivity to both pain and environmental stresses than do their healthy counterparts (Hassinger, Semenchuck, & O'Brien, 1999; Levy, Cain, Jarrett, & Heitkemper, 1997; Silverman et al., 1997; Wolfe et al., 1997). Research on IBS and FMS suggest that a common mechanism, such as a generalized disorder of smooth muscle, could account for the wide range of pain symptoms, including dysmenorrhea and migraine (Veale et al., 1991).

Still No Proof That Abuse *Causes* Chronic Pain

Earlier in this chapter, I indicated that the link between childhood abuse and chronic pain was circumstantial. A prospective study failed to find a relationship between pain and childhood victimization (Raphael, Widom, & Lange, 2001). In this study, children were identified as having confirmed maltreatment. They were matched with non-abused children of the same age, ethnicity, and sex. These children were located twenty years later and asked about their lives. It is the only prospective study of pain in adult survivors.

Using this prospective approach, the authors failed to find a relationship (Raphael et al., 2001). However, they also used a retrospective approach and asked subjects about their abuse experiences. In this case, there was a strong finding of chronic pain symptoms among those with a history of abuse. The authors did not explain why they had a difference but merely noted that it existed. The problem is that they had a surprisingly high number of abuse survivors in their "non-abused" control group. So comparison between abused and non-abused participants are not nearly as clear as we might expect (Kendall-Tackett & Becker-Blease, 2004).

Interestingly, these same authors had similar findings for substance abuse (Widom, Weiler, & Cottler, 1999). The substance abuse study also had prospective and retrospective data, and the researchers came up with contradictory findings. Prospectively, there was no significant relationship between abuse and neglect, and substance abuse. However, the retrospective accounts found that child victimization of all types was significantly related to substance abuse (Kendall-Tackett & Becker-Blease, 2004; Widom, Weiler, & Cottler, 1999).

SUMMARY

The research reviewed in this chapter looked at some possible mechanisms by which abuse in childhood could lead to chronic pain in adults. In the next chapter, I describe research on five chronic pain conditions that are more common among abuse survivors than among the general public.

References

Aaron, L. A., Bradley, L. A., Alarcon, G. S., Alexander, R. W., Triana-Alexander, M., Martin, M. Y., et al. (1996). Psychiatric diagnoses in patients with fibromyalgia are related to health care-seeking behavior rather than illness. *Arthritis and Rheumatism, 39*, 436–445.

Aguera, L., Failde, I., Cervilla, J. A., Diaz-Fernandez, P., & Mico, J. A. (2010). Medically unexplained pain complaints are associated with underlying unrecognized mood disorders in primary care. *BMC Family Practice, 11*, 17.

Beilin, B., Shavit, Y., Trabekin, E., Mordashev, B., Mayburd, E., Zeidel, A., et al. (2003). The effects of postoperative pain management on immune response to surgery. *Anesthesia and Analgesia, 97*, 822–827.

Bennett, R. M. (1996). Fibromyalgia and the disability dilemma: A new era in understanding a complex, multidimensional pain syndrome. *Arthritis and Rheumatism, 39*, 1627–1634.

Bremner, J. D. (2005). The neurobiology of childhood sexual abuse in women with posttraumatic stress disorder. In K. A. Kendall-Tackett (Ed.), *Handbook of women, stress, and trauma* (pp. 181–206). New York: Brunner-Routledge.

Burgmer, M., Petzke, F., Giesecke, T., Gaubitz, M., Heuft, G., & Pfleiderer, B. (2011). Cerebral activatioin and catastrophizing during pain anticipation in patients with fibromyalgia. *Psychosomatic Medicine, 73*, 751–759.

Crofford, L. J. (2007). Violence, stress, and somatic syndromes. *Trauma, Violence, and Abuse, 8*(3), 299–313.

Dallam, S. J. (2001). The hidden effects of childhood maltreatment on adult health. In K. Franey, R. Geffner & R. Falconer (Eds.), *The cost of child maltreatment: Who pays? We all do* (pp. 1–14). San Diego: Family Violence & Sexual Assault Institute.

Domino, J. V., & Haber, J. D. (1987). Prior physical and sexual abuse in women with chronic headache: Clinical correlates. *Headache, 27*, 310–314.

Drossman, D. A. (1995). Sexual and physical abuse and gastrointestinal illness. *Scandinavian Journal of Gastroenterology, 30*(Suppl.), 90–96.

Drossman, D. A., Talley, N. J., Leserman, J., Olden, K. W., & Barreiro, M. A. (1995). Sexual and physical abuse and gastrointestinal illness: Review and recommendations. *Annals of Internal Medicine, 123*, 782–794.

Edwards, R. R., Bingham, C. O., Bathon, J., & Haythornthwaite, J. A. (2006). Catastrophizing and pain in arthritis, fibromyalgia, and other rheumatic diseases. *Arthritis Care and Research, 55*(2), 325–332.

Fields, H. L., & Martin, J. B. (1998). Pain: Pathophysiology and management. In A. S. Fauci, E. Braunwald, K. J. Isselbacher, J. D. Wilson, J. B. Martin, D. L. Kasper, et al. (Eds.), *Harrison's priniciples of internal medicine* (14th ed.) (pp. 53–58). New York: McGraw-Hill.

Finestone, H. M., Stenn, P., Davies, F., Stalker, C., Fry, R., & Koumanis, J. (2000). Chronic pain and health care utilization in women with a history of childhood sexual abuse. *Child Abuse and Neglect, 24*, 547–556.

Garcia-Campayo, J., Fayed, N., Serrano-Blanco, A., & Roca, M. (2009). Brain dysfunction behind functional symptoms: Neuroimaging and somatoform, conversive, and dissociative disorders. *Current Opinions in Psychiatry, 22*, 224–231.

Geracioti, T. D. J., Carpenter, L. L., Owens, M. J., Baker, D. G., Ekhator, N. N., Horn, P. S., et al. (2006). Elevated cerebrospinal fluid substance P concentrations in posttraumatic stress disorder and major depression. *American Journal of Psychiatry, 63*, 637–643.

Gershon, M. D. (1998). *The second brain.* New York: Harper.

Golding, J. M. (1994). Sexual assault history and physical health in randomly selected Los Angeles women. *Health Psychology, 13*, 130–138.

Gordon, D. A. (1997). Fibromyalgia: Out of control? *Journal of Rheumatology, 24*, 1247.

Hadler, N. M. (1997). Fibromyalgia: La maladie est mort. Vive la maladie! *Journal of Rheumatology, 24*, 1250–1252.

Hassinger, H. J., Semenchuck, E. M., & O'Brien, W. H. (1999). Appraisal and coping responses to pain and stress in migraine headache sufferers. *Journal of Behavioral Medicine, 22*, 327–340.

Heim, C., Ehlert, U., Hanker, J. P., & Hellhammer, D. H. (1998). Abuse-related posttraumatic stress disorder and alterations of the hypothalamic-pituitary-adrenal axis in women with chronic pelvic pain. *Psychosomatic Medicine, 60*, 309–318.

Hudson, J. L., Goldenberg, D. L., Pope, H. G., & Schlesinger, L. (1992). Comorbidity of fibromyalgia with medical and psychiatric disorders. *American Journal of Medicine, 92*, 363–367.

Hudson, J. L., & Pope, H. G. (1989). Fibromyalgia and psychopathology: Is fibromyalgia a form of "affective spectrum disorder"? *Journal of Rheumatology, 16*(Suppl. 19), 15–22.

Katz, R. S., & Kravitz, H. M. (1996). Fibromyalgia, depression, and alcoholism: A family history study. *Journal of Rheumatology, 23*, 149–154.

Kendall-Tackett, K. A., & Becker-Blease, K. (2004). Why we need retrospective findings in child maltreatment research. *Child Abuse and Neglect, 28*, 723–727.

Kendall-Tackett, K. A., Marshall, R., & Ness, K. E. (2003). Chronic pain syndromes and violence against women. *Women and Therapy, 26*, 45–56.

Kroenke, K., Spitzer, R. L., DeGruy, F. V., Hahn, S. R., Linzer, M., Williams, J. B., et al. (1997). Multisomatoform disorder: An alternative to undifferentiated somatoform disorder for the somatizing patient in primary care. *Archives of General Psychiatry, 54*, 352–358.

Leserman, J., & Drossman, D. A. (1995). Sexual and physical abuse history and medical practice. *General Hospital Psychiatry, 17*, 71–74.

Levy, R. L., Cain, K. C., Jarrett, M., & Heitkemper, M. M. (1997). The relationship between daily life stress and gastrointestinal symptoms in women with irritable bowel syndrome. *Journal of Behavioral Medicine, 20*, 177–193.

Loren, B. (1998). The intimate relationship between chronic pain and depression. In M. Forster, B. Loren, C. Potter, S. Rosloff, S. VonTobel, & B. Voss (Eds.), *Phillips Graduate Institute 1998 progress journal* (pp. 3–10). Available online at: *www.pgi.edu.*

Malt, E. A., Berle, J. E., Olafsson, S., Lund, A., & Ursin, H. (2000). Fibromyalgia is associated with panic disorder and functional dyspepsia with mood disorders: A study of women with random sample population controls. *Journal of Psychosomatic Research, 49*, 285–289.

Marcus, D. A. (2000). Treatment of nonmalignant chronic pain. *American Family Physician, 61*, 1331–1338.

Miller, L. (2000). Neurosensitization: A model for persistent disability in chronic pain, depression, and posttraumatic stress disorder following injury. *NeuroReabilitation, 14*, 25–32.

Nicholson, N. A., Davis, M. C., Kruszewski, D., & Zautra, A. J. (2010). Childhood maltreatment and diurnal cortisol patterns in women with chronic pain. *Psychosomatic Medicine, 72*, 471–480.

Paras, M. L., Murad, M. H., Chen, L. P., Goranson, E. N., Sattler, A. L., Colbenson, K. M., et al. (2009). Sexual abuse and lifetime diagnosis of somatic disorders: A systematic review and meta-analysis. *Journal of the American Medical Association, 302*(5), 550–561.

Poleshuck, E. L., Bair, M. J., Kroenke, K., Watts, A., Tu, X., & Giles, D. E. (2009). Pain and depression in gynecology patients. *Psychosomatics, 50*, 270–276.

Pribor, E. F., Yutzy, S. H., Dean, J. T., & Wetzel, R. D. (1993). Briquet's syndrome, dissociation, and abuse. *American Journal of Psychiatry, 150*, 1507–1511.

Price, D. D. (2000). Psychological and neural mechanisms of the affective mechanisms of the affective dimension of pain. *Science, 288*, 1769–1772.

Raphael, K. G., Widom, C. S., & Lange, G. (2001). Childhood victimization and pain in adulthood: A prospective investigation. *Pain, 92*, 283–293.

Russell, I. J., Orr, M. D., Littman, B., Vipraio, G. A., Alboukrek, D., Michalek, J. E., et al. (1994). Elevated cerebrospinal fluid levels of substance P in patients with the fibromyalgia syndrome. *Arthritis and Rheumatism, 37*, 1593–1601.

Sachs-Ericsson, N., Kendall-Tackett, K. A., & Hernandez, A. (2007). Childhood abuse, chronic pain, and depression in the National Comorbidity Survey. *Child Abuse and Neglect, 31*, 531–547.

Shelby, R. A., Somers, T. J., Keefe, F. J., Silva, S. G., McKee, D. C., She, L., et al. (2009). Pain catastrophizing in patients with noncardiac chest pain: Relationships with pain, anxiety, and disability. *Psychosomatic Medicine, 71*(8), 861–868.

Silverman, D. H. S., Munakata, J. A., Ennes, H., Mandelkern, M. A., Hoh, C. K., & Mayer, E. A. (1997). Regional cerebral activity in normal and pathological perception of visceral pain. *Gastroenterology, 112*, 64–72.

Talbot, N. L., Chapman, B., Conwell, Y., McCollumn, K., Franus, N., Cotescu, S., et al. (2009). Childhood sexual abuse is associated with physical illness burden and functioning in psychiatric patients 50 years of age or older. *Psychosomatic Medicine, 71*, 417–422.

Teegan, F. (1999). Childhood sexual abuse and long-term sequelae. In A. Maercker, M. Schutzwohl, & Z. Solomon (Eds.), *Posttraumatic stress disorder: A lifespan developmental perspective* (pp. 97–112). Seattle, WA: Hogrefe & Huber.

Thakkar, R. R., & McCanne, T. R. (2000). The effects of daily stressors on physical health in women with and without a childhood history of sexual abuse. *Child Abuse and Neglect, 24*, 209–221.

Uysal, A., & Lu, Q. (2011). Is self-concealment associated with acute and chronic pain? *Health Psychology, 30*(5), 606–614.

Vaccarino, A. L., Sills, T. L., Evans, K. R., & Kalali, A. H. (2009). Multiple pain complaints in patients with major depressive disorder. *Psychosomatic Medicine, 71*, 159–162.

Veale, D., Kavanagh, G., Fielding, J. F., & Fitzgerald, O. (1991). Primary fibromyalgia and the irritable bowel syndrome: Different expressions of a common pathogenetic process. *British Journal of Rheumatology, 30*, 220–222.

Walker, E., Katon, W., Roy-Byrne, P., Jemelka, R., & Russo, J. (1993). Histories of sexual victimization in patients with irritable bowel syndrome or inflammatory bowel disease. *American Journal of Psychiatry, 150*, 1502–1506.

Widom, C. S., Weiler, B. L., & Cottler, L. B. (1999). Childhood victimization and drug abuse: A comparison of prospective and retrospective findings. *Journal of Consulting and Clinical Psychology, 67*, 867–880.

Wolfe, F. (1997). The fibromyalgia problem. *Journal of Rheumatology, 24*, 1247–1249.

Wolfe, F., Russell, I. J., Vipraio, G., Ross, K., & Anderson, J. (1997). Serotonin levels, pain thresholds, and fibromyalgia symptoms in the general population. *Journal of Rheumatology, 24*, 555–559.

Woolf, C. J., & Salter, M. W. (2000). Neuronal plasticity: Increasing the gain in pain. *Science, 288*, 1765–1768.

Chapter 15

Pain II—Chronic Pain Syndromes in Adult Survivors of Childhood Abuse

In the previous chapter, I described possible mechanisms by which past abuse could lead to chronic pain in adults. This chapter examines the relationship between childhood abuse and five chronic pain syndromes: headache, back pain, pelvic pain, fibromyalgia, and irritable bowel syndrome. When describing these specific condistions, we also revisit some of the physical processes described in the previous chapter, such as neuronal plasticity, secondary hyperalgesia, inflammation, substance P, and hypothalamic-pituitary-adrenal (HPA) alterations.

BACK PAIN

Back pain is common in the general population, and it is the most common cause of disability in patients under age 45. The annual estimated cost of back pain is $30 billion, with an additional loss of $100–$200 billion per year in decreased wages and productivity (Committee on Advancing Pain Research, Care and Education & Institute of Medicine, 2011). Twenty-six percent of Americans have experienced low back pain at least one day in the past three months.

It is also more common in abuse survivors. Hulme (2000) found that sexual abuse survivors were significantly more likely to report back pain and soreness in their muscles than were their non-abused counterparts. Similarly, Golding (1994) found that women who had been sexually assaulted had significantly more back pain than non-assaulted comparison women.

Childhood abuse has even been related to the success of surgery for back pain. In a study of spine surgery, patients were asked about five types of childhood adversity: sexual abuse, physical abuse, emotional abuse, parental substance abuse, and abandonment. Those reporting three or more types of abuse had a surgery failure rate of 85 percent, compared with a 5 percent failure rate among those with no history of trauma (Schofferman, Anderson, Hinds, Smith, & White, 1992).

HEADACHES

Headaches are also common for both men and women, and they cost approximately $14 billion per year, of which only $1 billion is for health care costs. Acute headaches account for more than 2.1 million visits annually to U.S. emergency departments. Five percent of American women ages 18–65 experience fifteen headaches or more per year (Committee on Advancing Pain Research, Care and Education, & Institute of Medicine, 2011). Approximately 45 million people each year suffer from headaches severe enough that they need to be treated by a doctor. Headache is one of the most common causes of outpatient physician visits (Golding, 1999).

Headaches have also been found to be more common in people who have been abused than in non-abused people (Domino & Haber, 1987; Felitti, 1991; Golding, 1999). Women who experienced severe physical or sexual abuse reported significantly more headaches, muscle aches, and pain in their eyes and ears than did their non-abused counterparts (Leserman, Li, Drossman, & Hu, 1998).

In another study, 62 percent of women in the abused group reported having a headache every day compared with 33 percent of the non-abused group. Ninety percent of abused women's headaches were precipitated by stressful life events compared with 43 percent of the non-abused women, possibly indicating hyperreactive stress response (Domino & Haber, 1987).

A meta-analysis of five studies with community samples ($N = 7{,}502$) found that headaches are related to past sexual assault (Golding, 1999). The odds of chronic headaches were higher for sexual assault that occurred in childhood than sexual assault that occurred in adulthood. These findings held true even when controlling for ethnicity and gender. Interestingly, the association of headache and sexual assault was stronger for adult men (especially Latino and European-American men) than it was for women. In Hulme's (2000) primary care sample, however, there was no significant difference among abused and non-abused women in incidence of migraines and other headaches.

PELVIC PAIN AND OTHER GYNECOLOGICAL CONDITIONS

Chronic pelvic pain is noncyclic pain, with a duration of six months or longer, that is localized to the pelvis, anterior abdominal wall at or below the umbilicus and that is sufficient to cause functional disability or lead to medical care (Agency for

Healthcare Research and Quality, 2011). It accounts for 10–40 percent of outpatient visits to gynecologists, at least one-third of diagnostic laparoscopies performed on women, and 15 percent of hysterectomies (Agency for Healthcare Research and Quality, 2011; Kuligowska, Deeds, & Lu, 2005; Latthe, Mignini, Gray, Hills, & Khan, 2006; Walling et al., 1994). Pelvic pain costs $14 billion per year in lost productivity, and $12.8 million per year in potentially unnecessary medical care (Kuligowska et al., 2005).

Chronic pelvic pain was one of the first types of pain found to be more common among abuse survivors. The Agency for Healthcare Research and Quality (2011) lists physical or sexual abuse as risk factors for chronic pelvic pain. One of the original studies to link sexual abuse and pelvic pain found high amounts of pelvic pain in patients with borderline personality syndrome (Gross, Doerr, Caldirola, Guzinkski, & Ripley, 1980). The authors noted that many of the women had histories of incest and broken families, and they were surprised by the relationship between past abuse and pelvic pain. The authors offered an explanation with a psychoanalytic spin:

> Since incest in this population was frequent, it may be that the pelvic pain was a result of early sexual "acting out" to solve pregenital needs with subsequent development of guilt, denial, and pain. The pain may function to fulfill a masochistic wish for punishment. It is likely that pain occurred often with the incest incident and that the recurrence of the pelvic pain may be a result of revived incestuous fantasies with accompanying pain and guilt. Dyspareunia was a frequent finding in our patients. This too may be a result of traumatic sexual acts. (Gross et al., 1980, p. 94)

Another study (Harrop-Griffiths et al., 1988) compared twenty-five women with chronic pelvic pain to a group of thirty women who had laparoscopic exams for tubal sterilization or infertility. Patients in the pelvic-pain group were significantly more likely to have been victims of either childhood (64 percent vs. 7 percent) or adult sexual abuse (48 percent vs. 13 percent) than the comparison group. There was a high incidence of depression in the abused group and adult sexual dysfunction (52 percent vs. 2 percent). There were no significant differences in degree or type of pelvic disease between women with pelvic pain and women in the comparison group. The women with chronic pelvic pain were significantly younger, were less likely to be married, and had significantly lower occupational status than did women in the control group. Twenty-eight percent (vs. 3 percent) indicated that they had been "sickly their entire life" (Harrop-Griffiths et al., 1988).

Walling et al. (1994) compared three groups: women with chronic pelvic pain, women with chronic headaches, and women with no pain. Women with chronic pelvic pain had a higher lifetime prevalence of sexual abuse involving penetration than either the headache or pain-free group, and they had a higher prevalence of physical abuse as both children and adults. Women who were physically abused without sexual abuse had more global pain (i.e., both headache and pelvic pain), whereas the pain of women who were sexually abused only was localized in the pelvis.

In a study of sixty-seven female veterans, researchers compared the range and severity of distress and pain during pelvic exams for women with and without a history of sexual violence (Weitlauf et al., 2008). An astonishing 77 percent of women in the sample reported a history of sexual violence. Would posttraumatic stress syndrome (PTSD) account for additional variance in pain above and beyond that accounted for by sexual violence? Women with both a history of sexual violence and PTSD had the highest levels of distress, followed by the women who had experienced sexual violence but did not have PTSD. Both groups were significantly higher on distress than non-abused women without a history of PTSD. Women with a history of sexual violence were more likely to report pain, but PTSD was not linked to increased pain. The overall level of pain women reported was low in comparison to their distress. The researchers recommend that clinicians who administer pelvic exams anticipate, prevent, and actively manage distress when it does occur. They also recommended that practitioners explain the procedure to the patient, avoid rushing her, and assure her that the exam can be stopped at any time.

In a sample of 2,133 women with PTSD and 14,948 comparison women receiving Medicaid in Michigan, researchers found that PTSD was associated with increased risk of endometriosis and dyspareunia (Seng, Clark, McCarthy, & Ronis, 2006). Other pain syndromes were also related to PTSD. When PTSD was not comorbid with depression, the odds ratios ranged from 1.9 for fibromyalgia to 4.3 for irritable bowel syndrome. When there was comorbid depression, dissociation, or borderline personality syndrome, risk increased in a dose-response pattern.

In a review of the literature that included 122 studies, authors examined fifty-four risk factors for dysmenorrhea, fourteen risk factors for dyspareunia, and forty-eight risk factors for noncyclical pelvic pain (Latthe et al., 2006). They found that dysmenorrhea was associated with sexual abuse, age younger than 30, low body mass index (BMI), smoking, earlier menarche, longer cycles, heavy menstrual flow, nulliparity, premenstrual syndrome, sterilization, pelvic inflammatory disease, and psychological symptoms. Dypareunia (painful intercourse) was associated with sexual abuse, menopause, pelvic inflammatory disease, anxiety, and depression. Noncyclical pelvic pain was associated with childhood physical or sexual abuse, drug and alcohol abuse, miscarriage, heavy menstrual flow, pelvic inflammatory disease, previous caesarean section, pelvic pathology, and psychological comorbidity.

In addition, Latthe et al. (2006) found that child sexual abuse and adult sexual assault increased the risk of dysmenorrhea. However, depression, anxiety, and particularly somatization had a much stronger influence. The findings for dyspareunia were similar. Dyspareunia was more than two and a half times more likely for sexual abuse survivors than for non-abused women. But anxiety tripled the risk, and risk was more than seven times higher for women who were depressed. For noncyclical pelvic pain, both childhood physical and sexual abuse increased risk, but adult sexual abuse more than tripled the risk. Other adverse childhood experiences, such as an unsatisfactory relationship with their mothers or spouses, parental divorce, or disturbed pregnancy elevated risk by three to five times. PTSD quintupled the risk. These findings suggest that direct effects of abuse or adverse childhood experiences increase pain. But indirect factors, such as depression, PTSD, or anxiety, also contribute to the increased risk for pelvic pain in abuse survivors.

Another recent study (Girdler et al., 2007) examined whether a woman's history of abuse increased her risk of premenstrual dysphoric disorder (PMDD). This study included a sample of twenty-five women with PMDD and forty-two controls. The researchers found that a higher proportion of abuse survivors had PMDD compared to non-abused women. All abused women, regardless of PMDD status, had lower plasma norepinephrine, higher heart rate, and lower plasma cortisol at rest and during stress. Women with abuse histories reported more severe daily physical and emotional symptoms. The authors concluded that abused women showed a persistent dysregulation of the stress response. This difference could not be accounted for by current psychiatric illness or use of medications. For women with abuse histories and PMDD, there was an even increased vulnerability.

To date, the majority of studies have examined the effects of abuse on pelvic pain in women. However, one study examined chronic prostatitis and pelvic pain in men. The constellation of symptoms included infection or inflammation of the prostrate and/or spasm of the pelvic floor muscles. Symptoms included pain or discomfort in the perineum or on ejaculation or lower urinary-tract symptoms. The multi-ethnic sample was of 2,301 men, ages 30 to 79 (Hu, Link, McNaughton-Collins, Barry, & McKinlay, 2007). The researchers found that men who reported sexual, physical, or emotional abuse had increased odds of chronic prostatitis and chronic pelvic pain. Men who experienced two or more types of abuse were at increased risk, suggesting a cumulative effect.

FIBROMYALGIA SYNDROME

Fibromyalgia syndrome (FMS) is chronic pain syndrome characterized by widespread musculoskeletal pain, decreased pain threshold, sleep disturbance, and psychological distress. The prevalence is 2 percent of the U.S. population—approximately 5 million adults. Patients with fibromyalgia missed seventeen days of work per year compared with six days per year for someone without fibromyalgia. The total costs annual costs of fibromyalgia are $5,945 per person, or an astonishing $300 billion. Patients with fibromyalgia as their primary diagnosis account for 14–20 percent of patients in rheumatology practices (Centers for Disease Control and Prevention, 2011).

Fibromyalgia used to be assessed with tender points on the body in all four body quadrants. These criteria have recently changed. The current American College of Rheumatology diagnostic criteria call for an assessment of widespread pain. Pain must be present in at least seven of nineteen possible body points in the past week, and there must be a symptom severity score of 5 or more. Alternatively, fibromyalgia can be diagnosed with three to six possible body points and a symptom severity of 9 or more. Symptom severity includes rating of fatigue (scored 0–3), waking unrefreshed (0–3), and cognitive symptoms, such as poor memory or "fog" (0–3). In addition, the pain cannot be explained by any other physical condition (Wolfe et al., 2010).

Pain symptoms of fibromyalgia are not the result of injury or disease but a central progress that leads to greater reactivity to pain. Poor sleep promotes hypersensitization to a wide range of affective stimuli, and greater reactivity to events by impeding recovery from stressful or painful events (Hamilton et al., 2008). In one brain-imaging study, patients with fibromyalgia had accelerated age-related changes in the brain regions that functionally link to core symptoms of the disorder, including depression and chronic widespread pain (Garcia-Campayo, Fayed, Serrano-Blanco, & Roca, 2009).

Effects of Past Abuse in Development of FMS

Several studies have examined the effects of past abuse on the development of FMS. Van Houdenhove, Luyten, and van den Eede (2008) found that 64 percent of patients in a group for FMS or chronic fatigue syndrome had at least one type of either child or adult trauma. More concerning was that 39 percent of the group reported abuse during childhood and as adults, indicating a lifelong pattern of abuse. Sachs-Ericsson, Kendall-Tackett, and Hernandez (2007), using data from the National Comorbidity Survey, noted that subjects with a history of either physical or sexual child abuse or intimate partner violence were more likely to report pain when describing their current health symptoms.

In another study, forty women with FMS were compared to forty-two women with no history of connective tissue disease or other medical problems (Taylor, Trotter, & Csuka, 1995). Sixty-five percent of women with FMS reported a history of sexual abuse, compared with 52 percent of the controls, which did not differ significantly. Abuse history was related to a more severe manifestation of symptoms, however. When abused FMS patients were compared with non-abused FMS patients, the abused patients reported poorer general health, less energy, and lower levels of social and recreational activity than did their non-abused counterparts. Sexual abuse was also associated with functional disability. Overall, sexually abused FMS patients reported significantly more symptoms and pain than did non-abused FMS patients (Taylor et al., 1995).

Boisset-Pioro, Esdaile, and Fitzcharles (1995) compared 83 FMS patients with 161 rheumatology patients who did not have FMS but had another rheumatological condition. Fifty-three percent of the FMS patients reported a history of abuse (both physical and sexual), compared with 42 percent of non-FMS patients, with no significant difference. Despite the lack of significant differences between patient groups, some interesting differences appeared when the authors looked at the specific type of abuse involved. FMS patients were significantly different from non-FMS patients if there was sexual abuse during childhood, if there was sexual abuse during both childhood and adulthood, if the abuse was contact abuse, or if there were multiple events. All these indices indicate increasing severity of the abuse experiences. The results for physical abuse appeared even more strongly. FMS patients were significantly more likely to report physical abuse in childhood and adulthood, or in combination with sexual abuse, than were the non-FMS patients. The authors also noted that FMS has some similarities to PTSD, including sleep disorders and an association with depression. In addition, substance abuse, alcohol abuse, and eating disorders were more common in the women with fibromyalgia.

The results of the Taylor et al. (1995) and Boisset-Pioro et al. (1995) studies indicate that past abuse can influence the severity of FMS symptoms. Both of these studies, however, have a peculiarity that limits the application of their findings. The two studies included both contact and noncontact abuse in their definitions of sexual abuse—everything from unwanted exposure of sexual parts to forced penetration.

This same group of questions was used in other abuse/pain studies by Scarinci, McDonald-Haile, Bradley, and Richter (1994) and Drossman et al. (1990). But in later studies, Drossman et al. discovered that only contact sexual abuse made any difference in terms of health (Leserman et al., 1996). They therefore excluded noncontact abuse from subsequent analyses. Once they did this, there were large effects of physical and sexual abuse on current health (Drossman, Whitehead, & Camilleri, 1997; Leserman et al., 1997).

The inclusion of noncontact abuse also accounts for the high incidence of abuse survivors in the FMS and non-FMS groups. A more typical incidence of contact child sexual abuse is much lower, approximately 20 percent across studies (Gorey & Leslie, 1997), or approximately 17 percent of women and 0 percent of men in a normative sample from primary care (Greenwood, Tangalos, & Maruta, 1990). Nevertheless, the findings of Taylor et al. and Boisset-Pioro et al. suggest that past abuse can heighten the sensation of pain in vulnerable individuals.

Another study (McBeth, MacFarlane, Benjamin, Morris, & Silman, 1999) with a community sample indicated that childhood adversity, including child abuse, parental loss, illness of a family member, and parental drug overdose, was associated with a significantly higher tender-point count than subjects without this history. The tender-point count was also related to low levels of self-care, more somatic symptoms, high levels of fatigue, and increased medical care usage. The physicians of these patients also recorded a greater number of symptoms of unknown origin.

Aaron et al. (1997) compared fibromyalgia patients and a community sample of men and women who were not in treatment but met the old American College of Rheumatology (ACR) criteria for fibromyalgia. They found that 54 percent of the patient group had been physically or sexually abused, compared with 36 percent of the nonpatient group. The primary focus of the study was whether people with fibromyalgia were more likely to report an emotional or physical trauma as precipitating their illness. Emotional trauma was more likely to precipitate FMS in the patient group than in the nonpatient group, even after controlling for previous physical and sexual abuse, demographics, and pain duration. Although abuse was not the primary focus, these findings at least raise the possibility that prior abuse made the subjects more vulnerable to the effects of current emotional stressors.

Pathophysiology of Fibromyalgia

One theory for the pathogenesis of FMS is that prolonged emotional stress, infection, or physical trauma combine with a genetic predisposition to influence neuroendocrine function and neurotransmitter levels, particularly serotonin and substance P levels (Bradley & Alarcon, 1997; Centers for Disease Control and Prevention, 2011). This theory has inherent appeal. Many FMS sufferers can point to a specific traumatic event (e.g., a car accident, an infection, or a severe life stress) as the precipitant of their illness. Other studies indicate that patients with FMS differ in key ways from healthy controls. For example, serotonin levels are abnormal among patients with FMS.

Wolfe, Russell, Vipraio, Ross, and Anderson (1997) noted that patients with FMS have low levels of serotonin and the serotonin metabolite 5-HIAA in the cerebral spinal fluid. Although the FMS patients had lower levels of serotonin overall, serotonin levels did not correlate with any clinical manifestations of pain. They were, however, significantly related to both depression and tender-point count (Wolfe et al., 1997).

Patients with FMS also show blunted or reduced cortisol levels, and this could be due to HPA dysfunction due to early or severe stress exposure (van Houdenhove et al., 2008). Van Houdenhove et al. noted that many of their patients, who had either FMS or chronic fatigue syndrome, remained entangled in burdensome, threatening, or chaotic family environments. This entanglement in "risky families" started in early childhood. They noted that this often led to lower optimism, more worrying and catastrophizing, less social support, as well as more depression and PTSD, leaving them with few resources with which to cope with their illness and disability.

Patients diagnosed with FMS also have higher levels of the neuropeptide substance P. In a study of thirty-two FMS patients compared with thirty healthy controls, those with FMS had three times higher levels of substance P in their cerebral spinal fluid than did the healthy controls (Russell et al., 1994). Substance P levels were weakly correlated with tender-point count, however. Consistent with other studies, patients with fibromyalgia had significantly higher levels of anxiety and depression, pain and stiffness, and lower pain thresholds than healthy controls. Substance P has a role in the transmission of pain from the periphery to the central nervous system (CNS).

Women with fibromyalgia had abnormalities in their pattern of blood flow to parts of the brain associated with pain perception (Mountz et al., 1995). Seven women with fibromyalgia were compared with seven healthy controls on resting state cerebral blood flood measured by computerized tomography (CT) scan. They were assessed for tender-point count and pain thresholds. As predicted, women with fibromyalgia had significantly impaired blood flow to the left and right hemithalami, and the right and left heads of the caudate nucleus. They had significantly lower blood flow to the cortex and significantly lower pain thresholds. The authors concluded that fibromyalgia may represent a functional abnormality within the CNS.

Researchers have noted abnormal HPA-axis function among patients with FMS. Crofford et al. (1994) compared twelve women with FMS to ten healthy controls. They found several indices of disturbed HPA function, including significantly lower twenty-four-hour urinary-free cortisol levels, significantly elevated evening total and free cortisol (demonstrating an abnormal pattern of fluctuations over the day), and hyporesponsiveness of the adrenal gland. The authors were uncertain as to the meaning of their findings with regard to clinical manifestations of FMS, but they point out that low levels of glucocorticoids may influence the perception of pain. HPA disturbances may also have an influence on levels of serotonin.

Another recent study had somewhat more ambiguous findings. This study compared women with chronic pelvic pain (n = 18), fibromyalgia (n = 17), and healthy controls (n = 24) on measures of HPA responses to stress and adrenocorticotropic hormone (ACTH) stimulation (Wingenfeld et al., 2008). They found that women with chronic pelvic pain had normal HPA responses to stress and ACTH. Women with fibromyalgia had reduced total cortisol release. The women with fibromyalgia had significantly higher levels of fatigue, cardiovascular symptoms, pain, and total symptoms than did women with chronic pelvic pain and healthy control women. They also reported significantly higher physical and mental fatigue.

Sleep Problems in Fibromyalgia

Sleep problems are also common in patients with fibromyalgia. In patients with FMS, deep, delta-stage sleep is interrupted by faster alpha waves that are superimposed on the delta sleep. This interruption of deep sleep appears to be related to the pain associated with FMS. When the delta sleep of healthy volunteers was interrupted, they too exhibited increases in muscle tenderness (Bradley & Alarcon, 1997). Lack of sleep can also interfere with the ability to cope with pain during the day because of daytime sleepiness (Lewin & Dahl, 1999).

One study took a more in-depth look at the sleep of patients with fibromyalgia. In examining the sleep of forty patients with FMS and forty-three healthy controls, Roizenblatt, Moldofsky, Benedito-Silva, and Tufik (2001) found three distinct patterns of alpha-wave activity in sleep. The first is phasic alpha, in which there is an episodic occurrence of alpha waves during delta activity. The second is tonic alpha sleep, where alpha is continuously present during non-REM (rapid eye movement) sleep, not only during delta sleep. The third pattern is low alpha activity.

The phasic-alpha pattern was the most common pattern for FMS patients (50 percent) compared to only 7 percent of the controls. In contrast, the low-alpha pattern was the most common for the controls (83 percent) compared to 30 percent of the patients with FMS. The phasic pattern was associated with longer-lasting pain symptoms and poor sleep. The patients with phasic sleep exhibited less total sleep time than the other two groups, lower sleep efficiency, and less slow-wave sleep than patients with tonic-alpha sleep. The phasic-alpha pattern was also associated with subjective ratings of pain, an increase in tender-point count, and correlated better with clinical manifestations of FMS. Traumatic events may create changes in sleep such that abuse survivors manifest more phasic-alpha sleep (Roizenblatt, Moldofsky, Benedito-Silva, & Tufik, 2001).

Sleep problems also appear to be long lasting. In a ten-year longitudinal study of FMS patients, Kennedy and Felson (1996) found that 55 percent of patients reported moderate-to-severe pain, 48 percent reported sleep difficulties, and 59 percent reported extreme fatigue. However, even with reports of these types of symptoms, 66 percent indicated that they felt a little or a lot better since they were first diagnosed, and 55 percent said they felt well or very well overall. Interestingly, despite findings from other studies on high health care utilization, 48 percent indicated that they had not seen a doctor in the previous year.

IRRITABLE BOWEL SYNDROME

Irritable bowel syndrome (IBS) is a functional disorder of the lower gastrointestinal (GI) tract whose pathogenesis is currently unknown. IBS affects more than 20 million people in the United States, or approximately 10–20 percent of the U.S. population (Freeman, 2010; Silverman et al., 1997; Subramani & Janowitz, 1991). IBS accounts for approximately 12 percent of primary-care patients and 28 percent of gastroenterology patients. Costs associated with IBS are estimated as $1.7–$10 billion in direct medical costs, and an additional $20 billion in indirect costs (Freeman, 2010).

Of all pain syndromes described in the literature, the link between childhood abuse and IBS has been studied the most. Major life stress, including abuse, can strongly influence the treatment outcome of IBS (American Gastroenterological Association, 2002; Freeman, 2010). Traditionally, IBS is a diagnosis of exclusion, made after ruling out possible organic causes of the symptoms. IBS is diagnosed using the "Rome III criteria." Symptoms include abdominal pain or cramping; abnormal stool frequency for at least three days per month for six months; straining; urgency; passage of mucus; and bloating or abdominal distention. The symptoms can be continuous or recurrent, and must be present for at least three months (Freeman, 2010; Longstreth et al., 2006; Rey & Talley, 2009).

IBS affects predominantly women, and its sufferers tend to have high levels of psychiatric comorbidity (Blanchard, 1993; Freeman, 2010; Whitehead & Crowell, 1991). There are generally two patterns of presentation: diarrhea without abdominal pain and alternating diarrhea and constipation with abdominal pain (Subramani & Janowitz, 1991), although these categories are controversial because they vary so much between countries even when applying the same diagnostic criteria (Rey & Talley, 2009).

Four factors have been associated with care-seeking behavior in patients with IBS. Women are more likely to seek care, as are older patients. There has been no consistent finding for socioeconomic status (SES) or education level. Severity of pain is the best predictor of health care seeking, but additional symptoms, such as blood in stools, can also increase care seeking. Psychological factors tend to drive health care seeking in general and may be incidental to IBS symptoms (Rey & Talley, 2009).

Childhood Abuse, IBS, and Other Functional GI Illnesses

Consistent with findings on other chronic pain syndromes, a relatively high percentage of people with IBS have a history of either physical or sexual abuse. As Leserman and Drossman (2007) noted, patients with a history of physical or sexual abuse in childhood, or intimate partner violence as adults, have one and a half to two times the risk of having a functional GI disorder. In a recent review, Rey and Talley (2009) noted that a history childhood abuse, particularly sexual abuse, has been associated with IBS. The findings have been mixed for community samples. Abuse in adulthood and other types of childhood adversity, such as preterm delivery, also increase the risk for IBS.

Walker, Kahn, Roy-Byrne, Jemelka, and Russo (1993) administered structured interviews to twenty-eight patients with IBS and nineteen patients with inflammatory bowel disease (IBD). Sexual victimization was much more common among the IBS patients compared to those who had IBD. Patients with IBS had higher rates of severe lifetime sexual trauma (32 percent vs. 0 percent), severe child sexual abuse (11 percent vs. 0 percent), and "any" lifetime sexual victimization (54 percent vs. 5 percent). The authors noted that those patients with both chronic pelvic pain and IBS had the most psychological distress and the most functional disability compared with women with either complaint alone. The authors attributed these findings to an overall pattern of somatization.

IBS, heartburn, and dyspepsia (upper GI pain) have been significantly related to sexual, verbal, and emotional abuse in both child and adulthood. Abused patients were twice as likely to have IBS as those who were not abused. Patients who reported abuse both in adulthood and in childhood were three times as likely to have IBS. Forty-percent of subjects reporting a peptic ulcer reported some type of abuse, with 37 percent of the total reporting past sexual abuse. The odds of having an ulcer were not significantly different based on abuse history, however (Talley, Fett, Zinsmeister, & Melton, 1994).

All these functional diseases were related to marital disruptions, lack of satisfaction with social support, poorer quality of life, and lower educational level after controlling for age and sex. In a large outpatient study of patients with GI conditions ($N = 997$), 22 percent of those with functional bowel disease reported some type of abuse, compared with 16 percent of those with organic disease. This was not a significant difference. Those who had experienced all three types of abuse (physical, sexual, and emotional) had the greatest odds for IBS symptoms, however (Talley, Fett, & Zinsmeister, 1995).

In another study of functional and organic GI illness, Ali et al. (2000) found that women with functional GI illness were significantly more likely to have been raped than women with organic GI illness (34 percent vs. 10 percent). For physical abuse, 18 percent of women with functional illness reported having been repeatedly hit, kicked, or beaten compared with 10 percent of women with organic illness.

In a study of 206 patients in a university-based gastroenterology practice, 44 percent related a history of physical or sexual abuse in childhood or later in life (Drossman et al., 1990). All but one of the physically abused patients had also been sexually abused, and half of the subjects abused as children were also abused as adults. Patients with functional disorders (including IBS) were more likely to report a history of threatened sex, incest or forced intercourse, and frequent physical abuse. One fMRI (functional magnetic imaging resonance) study found that a history of physical or sexual abuse enhanced the effect of induced pain on the activation of the dorsal cingulate cortex. Patients with IBS and abuse histories reported more pain, and greater activation of the pain centers in the brain (Garcia-Campayo et al., 2009).

Drossman and colleagues (Drossman, Li, Leserman, Toomey, & Hu, 1996; Leserman et al., 1996) compared health status for women with functional versus organic diagnoses and histories of abuse. There was a high percentage of abuse in the total study sample (60 percent). For women with a functional diagnosis, the total was 67 percent, and for women with an organic condition, the total was 56 percent. This was an only marginally significant difference. The patients with histories of severe abuse (i.e., rape and life-threatening injuries) had more functional than organic illnesses. The functional conditions included esophageal pain, dyspepsia (upper abdominal pain), IBS, and functional abdominal pain. The organic illnesses included ulcerative colitis, Crohn's disease, liver disease, pancreatic/biliary disease, and "other" organic disease. Interestingly, the highest percentages of abuse survivors were for functional abdominal pain (84 percent) and liver disease (72 percent). Liver disease included cirrhosis and chronic hepatitis B and C. All could be a result of high-risk health behaviors (alcohol abuse, unsafe sex, sharing needles), which might partially explain why there is a high percentage of abuse survivors in this group.

Another study found that a history of childhood sexual and physical abuse was related to functional dyspepsia (Van Oudenhove et al., 2011). Functional dyspepsia is defined as the presence of symptoms that originate in the gastroduodenal region in the absence of any organic, systemic, or metabolic disease likely to explain the symptoms. Some characteristics include gastric hypersensitivity, impaired accommodation, and delayed gastric emptying. The researchers found that age, sexual abuse history, physical abuse history, and somatization were independently related to gastric discomfort threshold. Physical abuse history and somatization were independently related to gastric emptying. None of the factors were related to gastric accommodation of a meal. The authors concluded that the mechanisms underlying these relationships remain to be determined, but that the autonomic nervous system, HPA axis, and immune systems may be involved.

Overall, abused patients had significantly worse health status than did their non-abused counterparts (Drossman et al., 1996). They had more pain, bed disability days, psychological distress, and highly impaired daily function than did other patients with GI conditions. Drossman et al. (2000) followed a group of 174 women who had been referred to a GI clinic for a period of twelve months. The researchers had baseline information on the initial diagnosis (functional vs. organic), neuroticism score, history of sexual or physical abuse, and scores on two measures of coping. Half of their subjects had been physically or sexually abused, and 14 percent had experienced severe abuse. Patients with poor health status had less education, a functional GI diagnosis, a higher neuroticism score, and more severe abuse. Patients who were "profoundly pessimistic" about their illnesses had poorer outcomes, and these effects were enhanced if the patient had a history of abuse. Abuse history and maladaptive coping were the two most important predictors of health outcome.

GI symptoms have also been found in studies that include children. In a study of 845 who were part of the LONGSCAN study, children were observed from ages 4 to 12 (van Tilburg et al., 2010). At age 12, children reported GI symptoms. Lifetime Child Protective Services (CPS) allegations were associated with abdominal pain at age 12. Sexual abuse preceded or coincided with abdominal pain in 91 percent of the cases. Also, self-reports of psychological, physical, or sexual abuse were significantly associated with both abdominal pain and nausea or vomiting. Girls were significantly more likely to report abdominal symptoms than boys.

Scarinci et al. (1994) drew a sample of fifty patients with one of three pain syndromes: thirteen with gastroesophogeal reflux disease (GERD), twenty-six with non-cardiac chest pain (NCCP), and eleven with IBS. Fifty-six percent of the sample reported a history of physical or sexual abuse. A higher percentage of abused patients occurred among those with GERD (92 percent) and IBS (82 percent) compared to those with NCCP (27 percent). Relative to the non-abused patients, abused patients had significantly lower pain threshold levels in response to finger pressure and significantly lower cognitive standards for judging stimuli as noxious. These results held even after controlling for psychiatric disturbance.

Some Theories of IBS

Because IBS is functional, occurs mostly in women, and tends to co-occur with psychiatric illness, some have considered it predominantly a psychological problem (Blanchard, 1993; Whitehead & Crowell, 1991). However, as with FMS, some intriguing neuroendocrine and cerebral abnormalities have been observed. There are several possible mechanisms for the connection between abuse and GI illness (Leserman & Drossman, 2007). First, there is greater autonomic reactivity to physical and psychological stressors. Second, increased visceral hypersensitivity and lowered pain threshold means that ordinary sensations get perceived as painful. Third, there appears to be altered stress reactivity via the HPA axis, which increases cortisol and proinflammatory cytokines, which increases visceral hypersensitivity.

However, Wingate (1991) noted that the association between chronic abdominal pain and psychoneurosis is not clear-cut: "Although there is an association with psychoneurotic disorder, the association is by no means close, and apparently it [IBS] is not primarily a psychiatric illness, even though it may carry the risk of some secondary psychiatric morbidity" (p. 357).

More recent research has highlighted the significant comorbidity of functional GI disorders and psychiatric conditions, such as depression or PTSD (Leserman & Drossman, 2007), but this does not mean that IBS is a predominantly psychiatric condition.

Two lines of research raise the possibility that there is something going on that is beyond a purely psychiatric explanation. The first is the increasing evidence that people with IBS physiologically experience bodily sensations, including pain, differently. The second is that IBS (and pelvic pain for that matter) co-occurs with pain that has nothing to do with the genitals or abdomen.

For example, women with IBS are more sensitive to daily stressors, and this reaction could manifest as GI symptoms. Levy, Cain, Jarrett, and Heitkemper (1997) compared symptoms and daily stresses among three groups of female subjects: twenty-six IBS patients, twenty-six women who had IBS symptoms but were not patients (nonpatients), and twenty-six controls. Not surprisingly, IBS patients and nonpatients showed higher levels of gastrointestinal symptoms than the controls. In addition, there was a significant and positive relationship between daily stress and symptoms in both patient and nonpatient groups, suggesting increased sensitivity to life stressors among those with IBS.

The second line of research has to do with a portion of the brain involved in processing of painful stimuli: the anterior cingulate cortex (ACC).

The Anterior Cingulate Cortex and Pain. The ACC is the region of the brain of particular interest when discussing pain regulation, the stress response, and functional pain disorders (Leserman & Drossman, 2007). This area processes information on stimulus intensity, emotion, mood, and attention. It is also involved in unpleasant affect and autonomic responses.

There are two subregions of the ACC. The first is the anterior perigenual ACC (pACC). This region is linked to emotions and may be activated or inactivated with pain. It has connections to the amygdala and contains endogenous opioids (Leserman & Drossman, 2007).

The second region is the mid-cingulate cortex. A subregion of that is the anterior mid-cingulate cortex of the ACC (aMCC). The aMCC is linked with attention, decision making, and premotor activities associated with a visceral response. Activation of the aMCC is associated with high levels of fear. With visceral pain, there may be an increase in activity of the pACC associated with emotional distress, and an increase in activity of the aMCC where pain is coupled with fear (Leserman & Drossman, 2007).

Hypersensitivity has also been related to cerebral activity. In this study, six IBS patients were compared with six healthy controls in their perception of painful stimuli. Researchers noted that cerebral blood flow associated with painful stimuli was different for the two groups using positron emission tomography (PET) scans (Silverman et al., 1997). Following delivery of a painful stimuli, the healthy subjects in one study had activity of the ACC. Because the pain occurred midline (in the center of the body), it activated both the right and left ACC. The patients with IBS, on the other hand, had an aberrant brain activation pattern, with activation of the left prefrontal cortex and no activity of the ACC.

The ACC is associated with active opiate binding and is part of a CNS response to incoming or anticipated pain (Toner, Segal, Emmott, & Myran, 2000). The lack of response of the ACC represents a failure of the pain modulation system that would normally control the release of endorphins. Because endorphins are not released, patients are more susceptible to the effects of painful stimuli. The prefrontal cortex is associated with both hypervigilance and anxiety. Activation of the prefrontal cortex shows an exaggerated vigilance in anticipation of pain (Silverman et al., 1997; Toner, Segal, Emmott, & Myran, 2000). Cognitive-behavioral techniques are thought to increase activation of the ACC and decrease activation in the prefrontal cortex.

The Enteric Nervous System. A final possible explanation for pain in IBS is the designation, by some researchers, of three nervous systems: sympathetic, parasympathetic, and enteric (Gershon, 1998). The enteric nervous system is the nervous system in the gut. Amazingly, the enteric nervous system can act independently of the other nervous systems and can activate effectors all by itself. Moreover, serotonin is manufactured and stored in the bowel, and is prefentially located on enteric nerves. Serotonin "exerts the same effect on the bowel as does the stimulation of enteric nerves" (Gershon, 1998, p. 41).

This line of research raises some intriguing questions relevant to abuse survivors. Namely, what is the impact of traumatic events on the enteric nervous system? Earlier, I referenced research on fibromyalgia that found abnormally low levels of serotonin related to sleep and pain difficulties. What is the relationship between trauma and levels of serotonin in the gut? How is the sensation of pain in the gut influenced by changes in serotonin levels? What is the relationship between the enteric nervous system and the central nervous system? Given what we know about visceral hypersensitivity, these questions should be considered in future research. Leserman and Drossman (2007) describe how the link between abuse and GI pain are related to a variety of neural and humoral pathways, and that abuse can influence GI reactivity directly or through psychological comorbidity. A framework that includes discussion of an enteric nervous system may help us to more fully understand why abuse experiences can increase abdominal and gastrointestinal pain.

SUMMARY

There is increasing evidence that past abuse is related to chronic pain. In the wake of traumatic events, the body learns to hyperrespond to stimuli, increasing the experience of pain. Treatment of pain in abuse survivors should include ways to help the body "unlearn" its dysfunctional way of handling current stressors. Relaxation techniques and biofeedback are two techniques that teach patients to be more aware of their bodies and how they work and some of the early warning signs of impending pain.

Another approach involves educating patients who have been through traumatic events about the source of their pain. This approach can be empowering and validating, letting patients know that their pain is not "all in their heads." Cognitive therapy can also help in pain reduction. Learning to recognize the cognitive distortions that often accompany chronic pain (e.g., that pain means something is "seriously wrong") is an important step toward effective pain management. Practitioners should continue to occasionally check for underlying illness. But for patients, learning that their chronic pain exists independent of an underlying illness can slow the cycle of multiple doctors' appointments, surgeries, and treatments.

Once adult survivors learn how their abuse experiences may have altered their sense of pain, they are in a position to do something about it. Relaxation techniques, biofeedback, education, and cognitive therapy can be combined with medications, physical therapy, and lifestyle changes. This multifaceted, mind-body approach can help adult survivors manage pain, one of the most difficult symptoms of past abuse, and move toward healing their lives.

References

Aaron, L. A., Bradley, L. A., Alarcon, G. A., Triana-Alexander, M., Alexander, R. W., Martin, M. Y., et al. (1997). Perceived physical and emotional trauma as precipitating events in fibromyalgia. *Arthritis and Rheumatism, 40*, 453–460.

Agency for Healthcare Research and Quality. (2011). Chronic pelvic pain. Available online at: *http://www.guideline.gov/content.aspx?id=10940.*

Ali, A., Toner, B. B., Stuckless, N., Gallop, R., Diamant, N. E., Gould, M. I., et al. (2000). Emotional abuse, self-blame, and self-silencing in women with irritable bowel syndrome. *Psychosomatic Medicine, 62*, 76–82.

American Gastroenterological Association. (2002). American Gastroenterological Association medical position statement: Irritable bowel syndrome. *Gastroenterology, 123*(6), 2105–2107.

Blanchard, E. B. (1993). Irritable bowel syndrome. In R. J. Gatchel & E. B. Blanchard (Eds.), *Psychophysiological disorders: Research and clinical applications* (pp. 23–62). Washington, DC: American Psychological Association.

Boisset-Pioro, M. H., Esdaile, J. M., & Fitzcharles, M.-A. (1995). Sexual and physical abuse in women with fibromyalgia syndrome. *Arthritis and Rheumatism, 38*, 235–241.

Bradley, L. A., & Alarcon, G. S. (1997). Fibromyalgia. In W. J. Koopman (Ed.), *Arthritis & allied conditions* (Vol. 2, 13th ed.) (pp. 1619–1640). Baltimore, MD: Williams & Wilkins.

Centers for Disease Control and Prevention. (2011). Fibromyalgia. Available online at: *http://www.cdc.gov/arthritis/basics/fibromyalgia.htm.*

Committee on Advancing Pain Research, Care and Education, & Institute of Medicine. (2011). *Relieving pain in America*. Washington, DC: National Academies Press.

Crofford, L. J., Pillemer, S. R., Kalogeras, K. T., Cash, J. M., Michelson, D., Kling, M. A., et al. (1994). Hypothalamic-pituitary-adrenal axis perturbations in patients with fibromyalgia. *Arthritis and Rheumatism, 37*, 1583–1592.

Domino, J. V., & Haber, J. D. (1987). Prior physical and sexual abuse in women with chronic headache: Clinical correlates. *Headache, 27*, 310–314.

Drossman, D. A., Leserman, J., Li, Z., Keefe, F., Hu, Y. J. B., Toomey, T. C., & Mitchell, C. M.

(2000). Effects of coping on health outcomes among women with gastrointestinal disorders. *Psychosomatic Medicine, 62*, 309–317.

Drossman, D. A., Leserman, J., Nachman, G., Li, Z., Gluck, H., Toomey, T. C., et al. (1990). Sexual and physical abuse in women with functional or organic gastrointestinal disorders. *Annals of Internal Medicine, 113*, 828–833.

Drossman, D. A., Li, Z., Leserman, J., Toomey, T. C., & Hu, Y. J. B. (1996). Health status by gastrointestinal diagnosis and abuse history. *Gastroenterology, 110*, 999–1007.

Drossman, D. A., Whitehead, W. E., & Camilleri, M. (1997). Irritable bowel syndrome: A technical review for practice guideline development. *Gastroenterology, 112*, 2120–2137.

Felitti, V. J. (1991). Long-term medical consequences of incest, rape, and molestation. *Southern Medical Journal, 84*, 328–331.

Freeman, K. (2010). Irritable bowel syndrome. Available online at: *http://www.clevelandclinicmeded.com/medicalpubs/diseasemanagement/gastroenterology/irritable-bowel-syndrome/#s0015.*

Garcia-Campayo, J., Fayed, N., Serrano-Blanco, A., & Roca, M. (2009). Brain dysfunction behind functional symptoms: Neuroimaging and somatoform, conversive, and dissociative disorders. *Current Opinions in Psychiatry, 22*, 224–231.

Gershon, M. D. (1998). *The second brain*. New York: Harper.

Girdler, S. S., Leserman, J., Bunevicius, R., Klatzkin, R., Pedersen, C. A., & Light, K. C. (2007). Persistant alterations in biological profiles in women with abuse histories: Influence of premenstrual dysphoric disorder. *Health Psychology, 26*(2), 210–213.

Golding, J. M. (1994). Sexual assault history and physical health in randomly selected Los Angeles women. *Health Psychology, 13*, 130–138.

Golding, J. M. (1999). Sexual assault history and headache: Five general population studies. *Journal of Nervous and Mental Disease, 187*, 624–629.

Gorey, K. M., & Leslie, D. R. (1997). The prevalence of child sexual abuse: Integrative review adjustment for potential response and measurement biases. *Child Abuse and Neglect, 21*(4), 391–398.

Greenwood, C. L., Tangalos, E. G., & Maruta, T. (1990). Prevalence of sexual abuse, physical abuse, and concurrent traumatic life events in a general medical population. *Mayo Clinic Proceedings, 65*, 1067–1071.

Gross, R. J., Doerr, H., Caldirola, D., Guzinkski, G. M., & Ripley, H. S. (1980). Borderline syndrome and incest in chronic pelvic pain patients. *International Journal of Psychiatry in Medicine, 10*, 79–96.

Hamilton, N. A., Affleck, G., Tennen, H., Karlson, C., Luxton, D., Preacher, K. J., & Templin, J. L. (2008). Fibromyalgia: The role of sleep in affect and in negative event reactivity and recovery. *Health Psychology, 27*(4), 490–494.

Harrop-Griffiths, J., Katon, W., Walker, E., Holm, L., Russo, J., & Hickok, L. (1988). The association between chronic pelvic pain, psychiatric diagnoses, and childhood sexual abuse. *Obstetrics and Gynecology, 71*, 589–593.

Hu, J. C., Link, C. L., McNaughton-Collins, M., Barry, M. J., & McKinlay, J. B. (2007). The association of abuse and symptoms suggestive of chronic prostatitis/chronic pelvic pain syndrome: Results from the Boston Area Community Health Survey. *Journal of General Internal Medicine, 22*(11), 1532–1537.

Hulme, P. A. (2000). Symptomatology and health care utilization of women primary care patients who experienced childhood sexual abuse. *Child Abuse and Neglect, 24*, 1471–1484.

Kennedy, M., & Felson, D. T. (1996). A prospective long-term study of fibromyalgia syndrome. *Arthritis and Rheumatism, 39*, 682–685.

Kuligowska, E., Deeds, L., & Lu, K. (2005). Pelvic pain: Overlooked and underdiagnosed gynecologic conditions. *RadioGraphics, 25*, 3–20.

Latthe, P., Mignini, L., Gray, R., Hills, R., & Khan, K. (2006). Factors predisposing women to chronic pelvic pain: Systematic review. *British Medical Journal, 332*, 749–755.

Leserman, J., & Drossman, D. A. (2007). Relationship of abuse history to functional gastrointestinal disorders and symptoms: Some possible mediating mechanisms. *Trauma, Violence, and Abuse, 8*(3), 331–343.

Leserman, J., Drossman, D. A., Li, Z., Toomey, T. C., Nachman, G., & Glogau, L. (1996). Sexual and physical abuse history in gastroenterology practice: How types of abuse impact health status. *Psychosomatic Medicine, 58*, 4–15.

Leserman, J., Li, Z., Drossman, D. A., & Hu, Y. J. B. (1998). Selected symptoms associated with sexual and physical abuse history among female patients with gastrointestinal disorders: The impact on subsequent health care visits. *Psychological Medicine, 28*, 417–425.

Leserman, J., Li, Z., Drossman, D. A., Toomey, T. C., Nachman, G., & Glogau, L. (1997). Impact of sexual and physical abuse dimensions on health status: Development of an abuse severity measure. *Psychosomatic Medicine, 59*, 152–160.

Levy, R. L., Cain, K. C., Jarrett, M., & Heitkemper, M. M. (1997). The relationship between daily life stress and gastrointestinal symptoms in women with irritiable bowel syndrome. *Journal of Behavioral Medicine, 20*, 177–193.

Lewin, D. S., & Dahl, R. E. (1999). Importance of sleep in the mangement of pediatric pain. *Journal of Behavioral and Developmental Pediatrics, 20*, 244–252.

Longstreth, G. F., Thompson, W. G., Chey, W. D., Houghton, L. A., Mearin, F., & Spiller, R. C. (2006). Functional bowel disorders. *Gastroenterology, 130*, 1480–1491.

McBeth, J., MacFarlane, G. J., Benjamin, S., Morris, S., & Silman, A. J. (1999). The association between tender points, psychological distress, and adverse childhood experiences: A community-based sample. *Arthritis and Rheumatism, 42*, 1397–1404.

Mountz, J. M., Bradley, L. A., Modell, J. G., Alexander, R. W., Triana-Alexander, M., Aaron, L. A., et al. (1995). Fibromyalgia in women: Abnormalities of regional cerebral blood flow in the thalamus and the caudate nucleus are associated with low pain threshold levels. *Arthritis and Rheumatism, 7*, 926–938.

Rey, E., & Talley, N. J. (2009). Irritable bowel syndrome: Novel views on the epidemiology and potential risk factors. *Digestive and Liver Disease, 41*, 772–780.

Roizenblatt, S., Moldofsky, H., Benedito-Silva, A. A., & Tufik, S. (2001). Alpha sleep characteristics in fibromyalgia. *Arthritis and Rheumatism, 44*, 222–230.

Russell, I. J., Orr, M. D., Littman, B., Vipraio, G. A., Alboukrek, D., Michalek, J. E., et al. (1994). Elevated cerebrospinal fluid levels of substance P in patients with the fibromyalgia syndrome. *Arthritis and Rheumatism, 37*, 1593–1601.

Sachs-Ericsson, N., Kendall-Tackett, K. A., & Hernandez, A. (2007). Childhood abuse, chronic pain, and depression in the National Comorbidity Survey. *Child Abuse and Neglect, 31*, 531–547.

Scarinci, I. C., McDonald-Haile, J., Bradley, L. A., & Richter, J. E. (1994). Altered pain perception and psychosocial features among women with gastrointestinal disorders and history of abuse: A preliminary model. *American Journal of Medicine, 97*, 108–118.

Schofferman, J., Anderson, D., Hinds, R., Smith, G., & White, A. (1992). Childhood psychological trauma correlates with unsuccessful lumbar spine surgery. *Spine, 17*, S1381–S1384.

Seng, J. S., Clark, M. K., McCarthy, A. M., & Ronis, D. L. (2006). PTSD and physical comorbidity among women receiving Medicaid: Results from service-use data. *Journal of Traumatic Stress, 19*(1), 45–56.

Silverman, D. H. S., Munakata, J. A., Ennes, H., Mandelkern, M. A., Hoh, C. K., & Mayer, E. A. (1997). Regional cerebral activity in normal and pathological perception of visceral pain. *Gastroenterology, 112*, 64–72.

Subramani, K., & Janowitz, H. D. (1991). The irritable bowel syndrome: A continuing dilemma. *Gastroenterology Clinics of North America, 20*, 363–367.

Talley, N. J., Fett, S. L., & Zinsmeister, A. R. (1995). Self-reported abuse and gastrointestinal disease in outpatients: Association with irritable bowel-type symptoms. *American Journal of Gastroenterology, 90*, 366–371.

Talley, N. J., Fett, S. L., Zinsmeister, A. R., & Melton, L. J. (1994). Gastrointestinal tract symptoms and self-reported abuse: A population-based study. *Gastroenterology, 107*, 1040–1049.

Taylor, M. L., Trotter, D. R., & Csuka, M. E. (1995). The prevalence of sexual abuse in women with fibromyalgia. *Arthritis and Rheumatism, 38*, 229–234.

Toner, B. B., Segal, Z. V., Emmott, S. D., & Myran, D. (2000). *Cognitive-behavioral treatment of irritable bowel syndrome: The brain-gut connection*. New York: Guilford Press.

van Houdenhove, B., Luyten, P., & van den Eede, F. (2008). Early life stress in chronic pain and fatigue syndromes: Prevalence, consequences, and etio-pathogenic pathways. *Family and Intimate Partner Quarterly, 1*(2), 101–114.

Van Oudenhove, L., Vandernberghe, J., Vos, R., Fischler, B., Demyttenaere, K., & Tack, J. (2011). Abuse history, depression, and somatization are associated with gastric sensitivity and gastric emptying in functional dyspepsia. *Psychosomatic Medicine, 73*, 648–655.

van Tilburg, M. A. L., Runyan, D., Zolotor, A. J., Graham, J. C., Dubowitz, H., Litrownik, A. J., et al. (2010). Unexplained gastrointestinal symptoms after abuse in a prospective study of children at risk for abuse and neglect. *Annals of Family Medicine, 8*(2), 134–140.

Walker, E., Katon, W., Roy-Byrne, P., Jemelka, R., & Russo, J. (1993). Histories of sexual victimization in patients with irritable bowel syndrome or inflammatory bowel disease. *American Journal of Psychiatry, 150*, 1502–1506.

Walling, M. K., Reiter, R. C., O'Hara, M. W., Milburn, A. K., Lilly, G., & Vincent, S. D. (1994). Abuse history and chronic pain in women: I. Prevalences of sexual abuse and physical abuse. *Obstetrics and Gynecology, 84*, 193–199.

Weitlauf, J. C., Finney, J. W., Ruzek, J. I., Lee, T. T., Thailkill, A., Jones, S., et al. (2008). Distress and pain during pelvic examinations: Effect of sexual violence. *Obstetrics and Gynecology, 112*(6), 1343–1350.

Whitehead, W. E., & Crowell, M. D. (1991). Psychologic considerations in the irritable bowel syndrome. *Gastroenterology Clinics of North America, 20*, 249–267.

Wingate, D. L. (1991). The irritable bowel syndrome. *Gastroenterology Clinics of North America, 20*, 351–361.

Wingenfeld, K., Heim, C., Schmidt, I., Wagner, D., Meinlschmidt, G., & Hellhammer, D. H. (2008). HPA axis reactivity and lymphocyte glucocorticoid sensitivity in fibromyalgia syndrome and chronic pelvic pain. *Psychosomatic Medicine, 70*, 65–72.

Wolfe, F., Clauw, D. J., Fitzcharles, M.-A., Goldenberg, D. L., Katz, R. S., Mease, P., et al. (2010). The American College of Rheumatology preliminary diagnostic criteria for fibromyalgia and measurement of symptom severity. *Arthritis Care and Research, 62*(5), 600–610.

Wolfe, F., Russell, I. J., Vipraio, G., Ross, K., & Anderson, J. (1997). Serotonin levels, pain thresholds, and fibromyalgia symptoms in the general population. *Journal of Rheumatology, 24*, 555–559.

Chapter 16

Perinatal Effects of Childhood Abuse

Women's health care providers are beginning to perceive that violence in the lives of girls and women is a common reality. It is time to consider systematically that perhaps some of the problems clients face in childbearing may not be only pregnancy-related—they may also be trauma-related. Research is needed on the impacts of childhood sexual abuse on childbearing, including physiologic studies of PTSD in women and its potential alterations to pregnancy processes. (Seng & Hassinger, 1998, p. 293)

Abusive experiences, both past and present, can influence women throughout pregnancy and postpartum. Although an important topic, much of what we know is still preliminary. However, even with a relatively limited literature, researchers have begun to document how violence influences women's health throughout the childbearing year. This chapter focuses on what we know so far.

PREGNANCY

The impact of childhood maltreatment on childbearing actually predates pregnancy. As I described in Chapter 5, abuse survivors of all types are more likely to engage in high-risk sexual activity than are their nonmaltreated peers (Hulme, 2000; Raj, Silverman, & Amaro, 2000; Springs & Friedrich, 1992). Women who have been sexually abused are more likely to engage in consensual sexual activity at an earlier age, have more lifetime sexual partners, and participate in high-risk sexual activity including not using condoms or contraceptives (Raj et al., 2000; Stock, Bell, Boyer, & Connell, 1997). High-risk sexual activity increases the risk for unplanned pregnancies among teens (Raj et al., 2000; Springs & Friedrich, 1992) and adults (Prentice, Lu, Lange, & Halfon, 2002). In a nationally representative U.S. sample of mothers of children under age 3 ($N = 1{,}220$), women with a history of child sexual abuse were more likely to have both an unwanted pregnancy and late prenatal care (Prentice et al., 2002).

However, even though high-risk sexual activity increases the risk of unplanned pregnancy, not all unplanned pregnancies are due to previous abuse—even among teens. A recent study of 252 pregnant teens from Montreal found that 79 percent had no reported history of sexual or physical abuse. However, 21 percent reported multiple forms of past abuse. Sexual abuse did increase the risk of depression during pregnancy (Romano, Zoccolillo, & Paquette, 2006).

Prenatal Depression and PTSD: The Impact of Abuse Sequelae on Pregnancy

Previous abuse can lead to high-risk activities, which lead to pregnancy. But even when a woman is in a stable, non-abusive relationship and intentionally plans a pregnancy, past abuse has the potential to impact the health of both the women and their babies. Common sequelae of abuse, such as depression, anxiety, and posttraumatic stress disorder (PTSD), can all have an impact on pregnancy. One possible effect is prenatal depression, which can increase the risk of birth complications.

Prenatal Depression. A study from Boston compared the pregnancy experiences of 2,128 women from the suburbs to 1,509 women from urban community health centers (Rich-Edwards et al., 2011). They found that women from the urban community centers had twice the rate of depression in pregnancy (22 percent) compared with women from the suburban centers (11 percent). In both samples, lifetime physical or sexual abuse was an independent predictor of prenatal depression. There was a stronger association between prenatal depression abuse in adulthood versus abuse in childhood. The authors concluded that physical and sexual abuse histories were positively associated with prenatal depression in two economically diverse populations.

A prospective study of 959 women in Hong Kong found that depression in the third trimester was associated with increased use of interventions during labor, such as epidural anesthesia, higher rates of cesarean sections and instrumental vaginal deliveries, and more infant admissions to neonatal intensive care units (NICUs). These effects were still present even after controlling for pregnancy complications, showing an independent effect of depression (Chung, Lau, Yip, Chiu, & Less, 2001).

A longitudinal study of 200 pregnant women examined the relationship between depressive symptoms and health-related quality of life throughout pregnancy and after delivery (Setse et al., 2009). The rates of depression were 15 percent during the first trimester, 14 percent during the second, 30 percent during the third trimester, and 9 percent postpartum. Using eight domains from the Medical Outcomes Study, they found that depression affected women's social functioning, vitality, and Role-Emotional. Vitality measures fatigue or energy. Role-Emotional assesses problems with activities because of health problems. Social functioning measures limitations in social activities because of physical or emotional problems.

Prepregnancy depression has also been examined in relation to preterm birth in a study of 555 women enrolled in the CARDIA (Coronary Artery Risk Development in (Young) Adults) study (Gavin, Chae, Mustillo, & Kiefe, 2009). The researchers examined the associations of race, prepregnancy depressive mood, and preterm birth for both black and white women. They found that black women had significantly higher levels of prepregnancy depressive mood than did white women. After adjusting for covariates, black women had 2.7 times the odds of preterm birth compared to whites, but when higher depressive mood was added to the model, higher depressive mood was associated with increased risk for preterm birth, and the effect of race was attenuated. The authors hypothesized that the stress hormone CRH (corticotropin-releasing hormone) may have a role a early labor. CRH is present in the human placenta and plays a central role in initiating and coordinating endocrine events associated with delivery. CRH tends to be elevated in depression. And placental CRH is sensitive to stress. The authors concluded that depressive mood is a risk factor for preterm birth for both black and white women.

Preterm Birth and Depression. Preterm birth is one of our most pressing public health concerns, and it is specifically related to infant mortality. Also, there are substantial ethnic group differences, with black women almost three times more likely to deliver a baby before thirty-two weeks than non-Hispanic white women. This has direct implications for infant survival, and it is specifically related to increased infant mortality among black infants (Gavin et al., 2009). Socioeconomic status does not entirely account for these differences.

There is also evidence that prenatal stress, anxiety, or depression influences the outcome of human pregnancies. For example, in a prospective study of 681 pregnant women from France, women who were depressed had almost triple the rate of preterm birth compared to nondepressed women, Odds Ratio (OR) = 3.3, 95 percent Confidence Interval (CI) = 1.2-9.2, even after controlling for possible confounding variables (Dayan et al., 2006). All the women enrolled in the study were considered low risk for preterm birth and were enrolled at twenty to twenty-eight weeks gestation. There were some differences between the depressed and nondepressed women. The depressed women had a lower level of education, were more likely to be victims of partner violence, were more frequently hospitalized during the second trimester, and more frequently attended a high stress prenatal visit at enrollment in the study. The factors were controlled for in the analyses. The authors concluded that prenatal depression is significantly associated with spontaneous preterm birth even in a population of women receiving early and regular prenatal care.

A population study of 101,042 pregnancies, from a national pregnancy registry in Denmark, found that life stress and "emotional symptoms" were associated with a shorter length of gestation and increased offspring body weight, body length, abdominal circumference, and head circumference (Tegethoff, Greene, Olsen, Meyer, & Meinlschmidt, 2010). Emotional symptoms alone were related to shorter offspring. Mothers answered questions on the life stress inventory, which includes burdens in major areas of life such as finances, housing, work, relationships, pregnancy, and health. They also answered questions about "emotional symptoms" including anxiety and "nervousness."

Prenatal Anxiety, PTSD, and Birth Complications. Depression is not the only sequel of abuse that can lead to complications for mother and baby. A study of 1,820 women in Baltimore found that those who had high levels of pregnancy-related anxiety had higher rates of preterm birth than those with low pregnancy-related anxiety (Orr, Reiter, Blazer, & James, 2007). They used six items from the Prenatal Social Environment Inventory that asked specifically about pregnancy-related anxiety. These items asked if the women were worried or had concerns about the health of the baby, labor and delivery, or nausea with the current pregnancy. Women received a score of 1 for each affirmative answer, so scores could rank from 0 to 6. Twenty-eight percent had a score of 4 or greater and were considered the group with high amounts of pregnancy-related anxiety. The association between anxiety and preterm birth remained even after controlling for other risk factors for preterm birth, such as prior poor pregnancy outcome, low body mass index (BMI), bleeding, smoking, and race.

Seng et al. (2001) compared 455 pregnant women with PTSD to 638 pregnant women without PTSD. They found that women with PTSD had significantly higher odds ratios for ectopic pregnancy, spontaneous abortion, hyperemesis, preterm contractions, and excessive fetal growth. While not specifically addressing childhood abuse, these studies nevertheless provide us with a glimpse of some possible health problems abuse survivors with PTSD may encounter antenatally.

A history of abuse also impacts women's antenatal health through their behaviors. In a study from Norway, 56 percent of women who reported childhood sexual abuse smoked during pregnancy compared to 31 percent of nonabused women. Abuse survivors also reported more health problems during pregnancy and used more health care services than did their nonabused counterparts (Grimstad & Schei, 1999).

Inflammation and Negative Emotional States During Pregnancy

One possible explanation for why depression and other negative mental states might lead to preterm birth, in particular, has to do with an upregulation of the inflammatory response system. Of particular interest is the role of cytokines in the maintenance of pregnancy (Coussons-Read, Okun, Schmitt, & Giese, 2005). Pro-inflammatory cytokines are chiefly known for their role in protecting against infection and healing wounds. However, IL-6, IL-8, and TNF-alpha are also involved in ripening the cervix in preparation for labor. If the in utero environment is high in these levels due to prenatal depression, stress, anxiety, or PTSD, the mother's body may be mistakenly signaling that it is time to have the baby—even if it is too early. In Coussons-Read et al.'s study of twenty-four pregnant women, they found that high prenatal stress was associated with high IL-6 and TNF-α levels. In addition, the placenta produces large amounts of CRH, so pregnant women have high blood levels of cortisol. Cortisol is a major regulator of the inflammatory state, and may play a role in keeping pregnancy associated inflammation in check (Mastorakos & Ilias, 2003).

A study of sixty pregnant women, 57 percent of whom were African American, found that prenatal depression was related to significantly higher levels of IL-6 and marginally significant levels of TNF-α (Christian, Franco, Glaser, & Iams, 2009). This study examined the relationship between perceived stress, depression, and serum inflammatory markers. The majority of the sample was low-socioeconomic status (SES). The association was for depression only, not for stress, and remained even after controlling for prepregnancy BMI. The authors concluded that their findings are consistent with the contention that depressive symptoms may contribute to negative perinatal outcomes via inflammatory pathways.

Another study from Greece had similar findings (Boufidou et al., 2009). This study included fifty-six pregnant women. At delivery, blood samples were taken and a sample of cerebral spinal fluid collected while administering epidural analgesia. They found that TNF-α and IL-6 levels in the cerebral spinal fluid were related to depressive mood during the first four days and a six weeks postpartum. Serum TNF-α levels were also associated with depressive mood at four days postpartum. They speculated that postpartum mood disorders may be due to a rebound effect of the immune system in the immediate postpartum.

A recent study of 145 pregnant women from a clinic that serves primarily low-income, high-psychosocial-risk mothers examined the link between psychiatric symptoms and proinflammatory cytokines during pregnancy (Blackmore et al., 2011). They found that levels of IL-6 and TNF-± were consistent throughout the pregnancy. A mother's history of trauma was associated with significantly higher TNF-α, controlling for potentially psychosocial and obstetric factors. Contrary to previous studies, neither psychiatric symptoms nor proinflammatory cytokines predicted birth weight, gestational age, or obstetric complications. They concluded that trauma was related to persistently elevated TNF-α, but that inflammation was not related to depression or anxiety in pregnant women.

Impact of Maternal Prenatal Stress on Infants

When mothers experience severe stress during pregnancy, their infants might also be affected. One recent study recruited twenty-three mothers in the first or second trimester and followed them until their babies were six months of age (Enlow et al., 2009). They assessed mothers' self-reported lifetime exposure to trauma, perinatal traumatic stress, and current symptoms of PTSD. They videotaped the mother-infant dyad in the still-faced mother paradigm, which includes baseline, stressor, and recovery phases. In this paradigm, mothers are asked to maintain a still face and not to respond to their infants' social cues. The infants try to engage their mothers and become increasingly upset when they cannot. This paradigm is an analog to the way depressed mothers interact with their babies. The researchers found that infants of mothers with low exposure to trauma and perinatal traumatic distress showed the normal pattern of increases in distress and cardiorespiratory activation when their mothers did not respond to them, and decreases in stress when their mothers started to respond normally again.

In contrast, infants of mothers with multiple traumas and elevated perinatal traumatic stress showed similar patterns of distress when their mothers did not respond. Their distress did not lessen when the mothers started behaving normally. In fact, mothers with the highest levels of trauma had infants whose heart rate and behavioral distress increased from stressor to recovery (Enlow et al., 2009). The infants categorized as "highly distressed" during the reunion, and who did not return to the nondistressed state by the end of the episode, had mothers with significantly higher levels of trauma than mothers of infants who did not exhibit high distress levels. Infants' birthweight, gestational age, and age at the time of assessment were not associated with maternal trauma. These findings demonstrate that maternal lifetime trauma exposure was associated with disrupted infant cardiorespiratory regulation. These findings support the concept of perinatal programming, and the researchers noted maternal trauma's potential role in health outcomes.

In the wake of 9/11, researchers examined the impact of mothers' PTSD severity and cortisol levels following direct exposure to the World Trade Center collapse on infants' behavior at 9 months of age (Brand, Engel, Canfield, & Yehuda, 2006). This sample included ninety-eight pregnant women directly exposed to the World Trade Center collapse. They found that mothers who developed PTSD in response to 9/11 had lower morning and evening salivary cortisol levels compared with mothers who did not develop PTSD. Mothers with low morning cortisol levels had infants who became highly distressed in response to loud noises, new foods, and unfamiliar people.

A study in the Netherlands of 8,052 women found that babies born to women with high depressive symptoms had increased risk of being small for gestational age (SGA) or having a low Apgar score (Goedhart et al., 2010). A population study of 1,501,894 singletons born in Denmark from 1979 to 2004 found that maternal bereavement (particularly loss of a child) during pregnancy, or one year before pregnancy, was related to increased incidence of cerebral palsy in the children (Li et al., 2009).

Another study from the Netherlands examined the relationship between maternal psychopathology in pregnancy and two months postpartum, and its impact on infant heart rate variability at fourteen months in 528 infants (Dierckx et al., 2009). The researchers found that a maternal history of a psychiatric disorder was associated with higher mean heart rate in the infant. Maternal anxiety and depression postpartum were related to infant heart rate, such that higher maternal distress was associated with higher infant heart rate. Infant temperament did not mediate the association between maternal psychopathology and infant autonomic functioning. Severity of maternal symptoms was also related to heart rate, with more severe symptoms related to a higher mean heart rate. Interestingly, maternal lifetime psychiatric diagnosis and postpartum psychiatric symptoms were related to higher infant heart rate, but prenatal affective symptoms were not.

In a review of the literature (Field, Diego, & Hernandez-Reif, 2006), prenatal depression was noted to have numerous effects on the fetus and newborn. The authors noted that the fetuses of depressed mothers had elevated fetal activity, slowed prenatal growth, and increased rates of prematurity and low birthweight. Newborns born to mothers who were depressed during pregnancy had elevated cortisol, lower levels of dopamine and serotonin, greater relative right frontal EEG activation (a pattern present in chronically depressed adults), and lower vagal tone. Lower vagal tone may reflect dysregulation of the autonomic nervous system. They noted that maternal elevated prenatal cortisol was the strongest predictor of neonatal outcomes. Infants with mothers with high cortisol levels showed more crying, fussing, and negative facial expressions, and their mothers were more likely to rate their infants' temperament as "difficult." The researchers concluded that prenatal depression may affect fetal growth through complex pathways involving both the HPA (hypothalamic-pituitary-adrenal) axis and the sympathetic nervous system. CRH levels may also be involved as they restrict blood vessels and could restrict oxygen and nutrient flow to the fetus, resulting in slowed infant growth.

Summary

A history of childhood abuse can increase women's health problems during pregnancy. Common sequelae of past abuse can lead to pregnancy complications and an increased number of interventions during labor, demonstrating that the effects of abuse can last long after the abuse has ended. These complications can also affect babies after birth and increase women's risk of difficulties during the postpartum period, which is the focus of the next section.

POSTPARTUM IMPLICATIONS

Women with a history of childhood abuse or current partner abuse are at risk for postpartum mental health problems (Kendall-Tackett, 2005, 2010). Unfortunately, neither pregnancy nor the postpartum period offers protection from current abuse. To date, no specific pattern has emerged regarding whether pregnancy or postpartum is the time of highest risk.

Risk of Current Intimate Partner Violence

Three recent large, population-based studies found that many women are beaten during pregnancy and the postpartum period. In a Chinese study that included thirty-two communities, 8.5 percent of women were beaten before pregnancy, 3.6 percent during pregnancy, and 7.4 percent after pregnancy (Guo, Wu, Qu, & Yan, 2004). A study from Hong Kong of 3,245 pregnant women found that 9 percent had been beaten while pregnant (Chan et al., 2009). In-law conflict was the strongest predictor of abuse during pregnancy.

In North Carolina, 6.9 percent were beaten before pregnancy, 6.1 percent during pregnancy, and 3.2 percent postpartum (n = 2,648) (Martin, Mackie, Kupper, Buescher, & Moracco, 2001). Finally, in Bristol Avon, UK (n = 7,591), 5 percent were beaten during pregnancy and 11 percent postpartum (Bowen, Heron, Waylen, Wolke, & Team, 2005). At this point, it is difficult to know whether pregnancy versus postpartum period puts women more at risk, as these studies offer conflicting findings. The differences in these results may be due to different subgroups of abusers within the samples. Abuse during pregnancy is especially dangerous and is a risk factor for lethal abuse (Campbell & Kendall-Tackett, 2005). Samples with a higher percentage of women abused during pregnancy may have had a higher proportion of these more dangerous perpetrators.

A study of 157 women who had either sought shelter for partner violence or were in counseling for it found that motherhood increased the risk for longer duration of physical, psychological, and sexual partner violence, even when controlling for confounding variables (Vatnar & Bjorkly, 2010). Physical and psychological intimate partner violence (IPV) increased during pregnancy. In short, having children gave no protection against IPV severity, injury, frequency, or mortal danger. In addition, having children may be a risk factor for post-separation IPV.

A study of 570 teen mothers showed the continuity between antenatal and postpartum violence. The prevalence of IPV was highest at three months postpartum (21 percent) and lowest at twenty-four months (13 percent). Seventy-five percent of mothers beaten during pregnancy were also beaten during their first two years postpartum. And 78 percent who experienced IPV at three months postpartum had not reported IPV during their pregnancy (Harrykissoon, Rickert, & Wiemann, 2002).

Lutz (2005) also described the continuity between past and present violence in her qualitative study of twelve women who were survivors of IPV during at least one childbearing cycle. Among these women, depression, PTSD, and anxiety were common. The study participants reported many types of violence during their lives: child physical, emotional, and sexual abuse; neglect; parental IPV and substance abuse; current IPV; adult sexual assault; and community violence. The women experienced each exposure to violence as influencing and flowing into the next. They viewed IPV during childbearing as just part of the continuum of abusive experiences in their lives.

Impact of Past or Current Abuse on Postpartum Depression

Past or current abuse can also increase the risk of postpartum depression (Kendall-Tackett, 2010). A study of 200 Canadian women at eight to ten weeks postpartum found that women with a history of childhood abuse were more likely to experience both depression and physical health symptoms in the postpartum period (Ansara et al., 2005). A three-year follow-up of forty-five Australian mothers with postpartum major depressive disorder found that half had a history of child sexual abuse. The sexually abused women had significantly higher depression and anxiety scores, and greater life stresses compared to the non-abused depressed women. Moreover, the sexually abused women had less improvement in their symptoms over time (Buist & Janson, 2001).

A study of teen mothers from Australia found that 21 percent reported a history of physical abuse and 9 percent reported sexual abuse before the age of 16 (Gilson & Lancaster, 2008). Both physical and sexual abuse were related to depression and anxiety postpartum, but not during pregnancy. The authors noted that the difficulties of parenting during adolescence may be compounded for teen mothers with a history of child maltreatment. They were more likely to suffer from depression and anxiety, and this may impair their ability to function as parents.

A sample of forty-four mothers were assessed during pregnancy, and thirty-two of these mothers were assessed at one year postpartum (Lang, Rodgers, & Lebeck, 2006). Women who reported childhood sexual abuse or emotional neglect were more likely to have symptoms of psychopathology during pregnancy. Sexual abuse was related to more depression and anxiety during pregnancy. Child maltreatment predicted drug use during pregnancy. Emotional neglect was related to more state anxiety during both pregnancy and postpartum, and the women were more likely to have experienced multiple types of abuse and/or severe abuse. The women who reported emotional neglect, physical abuse, and neglect had poorer maternal outcomes at one year postpartum. They noted that psychopathology peaks during the last trimester of pregnancy and the first four months postpartum.

In another sample of fifty-three low-income single mothers, childhood abuse and low self-esteem predicted depressive symptoms, and these symptoms influenced women's reactions to their babies (Lutenbacher, 2002). Everyday stressors, when combined with depression, predicted higher levels of anger in the mothers. But current partner abuse was the best predictor of the mothers' overall abusive parenting attitudes (measured by the Adult-Adolescent Parenting Inventory), and more parent-child role reversal.

A history of childhood sexual abuse can also predict birth-related and postpartum posttraumatic stress (Lev-Wiesel, Daphna-Tekoah, & Hallak, 2009). In a sample of 837 women from Israel, women were assessed mid-pregnancy, and again at two and six months postpartum. Three groups were represented in the sample: those who had experienced child sexual abuse (CSA), women who had survived other types of trauma, and women with no trauma exposure. The researchers found that CSA increased the intrusion and arousal symptoms following childbirth, but not the overall PTSD score. However, CSA survivors had the highest PTSD scores of the three groups. The authors concluded that CSA has an even greater negative effect on women than other types of traumas that may be present in a population of pregnant women.

Inflammation in the Postpartum Period

Depression, anxiety, and other negative mental states upregulate the stress and inflammatory response systems. In a recent review, Kendall-Tackett (2007) found that inflammation is related to all the major risk factors for postpartum depression. These include maternal stress, pain, fatigue and sleep deprivation, and trauma. Since the levels of proinflammatory cytokines rise during the last trimester of pregnancy, and remain elevated postpartum, the addition of these outside stressors can increase inflammation to the point that is causes depression. Indeed, inflammation is not a risk factor for depression. It is the risk factor for depression in new mothers because it underlies all the others (Corwin & Pajer, 2008; Kendall-Tackett, 2010).

Maes et al. (2000) also noted that inflammation in the postpartum period was related to postpartum depression and anxiety. One study found that postpartum women are generally higher in the cytokines IL-6, IL-6R, and IL-IRA than before delivery. Another study compared anxiety scores of first-time mothers and women who have had more han one child and found higher levels of anxiety in first-time mothers (Maes, Bosmans, & Ombelet, 2004). They noted that depression and anxiety are associated with activation of the inflammatory response system. In addition, they noted that because proinflammatory cytokines, such as IL-1, IL-6 and TNF-α, may induce depression and anxiety, increased proinflammatory activity in the postpartum period may have caused higher anxiety levels.

These findings suggest that women with abuse histories are at higher risk for depression in the postpartum period. Trauma survivors often have a hyperreactive stress response and a more rapid inflammatory response to current stressors. This increases their risk of depression postpartum because cytokine levels are already elevated. Current stressors are additive and can push these levels into the depression range. Interestingly, breastfeeding can downregulate that response and actually lowers the risk of depression and anxiety, yet it is often overlooked as a factor that protects maternal mental health. Breastfeeding is far more than a way to feed a baby. Rather, it is a way to counter some of the harmful effects of abuse (Dennis & McQueen, 2009; Groer & Kendall-Tackett, 2011).

BREASTFEEDING

Breastfeeding is a major facet of the postpartum experience. At the present time, there are few studies on how abuse influences women's breastfeeding experiences (but some are in progress). But what we know so far suggests that it is highly relevant to abuse survivors, and that if these mothers decide to breastfeed, they should be strongly supported.

Breastfeeding and the Sexual Abuse Survivor

Currently, three studies consider the impact of sexual abuse on breastfeeding. Benedict, Paine and Paine (1994) looked at 360 primiparous women in the Baltimore area. The sample was predominantly African American and low-income. Of these women, 12 percent were sexual abuse survivors. Contrary to popular belief, a higher percentage of sexual abuse survivors (54 percent) indicated an intention to breastfeed than did their non-abused counterparts (41 percent).

Prentice et al. (2002) had similar findings with a very different population of mothers. Their study included a nationally representative sample of 1,220 mothers with children younger than age 3. Of these women, 7 percent indicated that they were survivors of sexual abuse. As with the previous study, women who had been sexually abused were twice as likely to initiate breastfeeding (OR = 2.58) as their non-abused counterparts.

A more recent study of seventy-eight Mexican-American teen mothers, ages 15 to 19, found that 31 percent had a history of childhood sexual abuse (Bowman, Ryberg, & Becker, 2009). There was no correlation between CSA history and intimate-parenting anxiety. Intimate-parenting anxiety is anxiety about parenting tasks, such as bathing, dressing, diapering, hugging, and kissing. There was no difference prevalence of breast- and formula-feeding between CSA survivors and non-abused mothers.

As hopeful as these findings are, there are significant gaps in what we know about survivors' breastfeeding experiences. For example, we don't know how many of these mothers are able to breastfeed, or even what barriers they might face. From clinical observation, we know that these mothers sometimes encounter substantial difficulties.

Some of these problems may be due to the impact of their abuse experiences on their cortisol levels. Cortisol levels can have an impact on breastfeeding in the early days after birth. A recent study from Guatemala indicated that women who had abnormally high levels of cortisol after birth had a delayed onset of Lactogenesis II, the time when women's milk "comes in" at three to four days postpartum (Grajeda & Perez-Escamilla, 2002). A delayed milk supply at this critical time can cause women to falsely conclude that they cannot produce enough and they may quit breastfeeding. Without proactive lactation management, these women may find it difficult to establish successful breastfeeding.

In addition, breastfeeding protects mothers' mental health because breastfeeding mothers get more sleep and report less daytime fatigue or better subjective well-being than mixed- or formula-feeding mothers (Kendall-Tackett, Cong, & Hale, 2011). Breastfeeding has these protective effects because it specifically downregulates the stress response and lowers inflammation, particularly C-reactive protein and IL-6 (Groer & Kendall-Tackett, 2011)

Current Partner Violence and Breastfeeding

Mothers in currently abusive relationships may face additional challenges. A recent review of ninety-four studies on the impact of childhood exposure to parental IPV asked whether women abused by their partners are less likely to breastfeed (Bair-Merritt, Blackstone, & Feudtner, 2006). The authors concluded that there was insufficient evidence to draw a conclusion; only one study had addressed this issue and found no difference between abused and non-abused women in initiation or duration of breastfeeding. This study included a sample of 212 women recruited from a WIC (Women, Infants, & Children)[1] population (Bullock, Libbus, & Sable, 2001). Approximately 52 percent of the women had a history of abuse, and 13 percent had been hit in the past year. Among the women currently being abused, the number of women who breastfed ($n = 11$) was almost identical to the number of women who bottle fed ($n = 10$). The authors found no relationship between past or current abuse and feeding choice. The same proportion of abused and non-abused women breastfed their infants.

Current Abuse and Barriers to Breastfeeding

As hopeful as the previously cited findings are, they have not been replicated and the actual sample was quite small. From the broader breastfeeding literature, we can surmise that women involved in currently abusive relationships are likely to face significant barriers to breastfeeding. Research has identified several barriers to breastfeeding that are all more common in women in currently abusive relationships. For example, women who smoke, either in general or during pregnancy, are more likely to stop breastfeeding (Amir & Donath, 2002; Heck, Schoendorf, Chavez, & Braveman, 2003). And women who are being abused may smoke as a way to relieve stress. Similarly, women with short postpartum hospital stays are also more likely to stop breastfeeding (Heck et al., 2003). And, it is likely that women with abusive partners are more likely to have short stays since their partners probably do not want them to remain in the hospital where someone could possibly detect abuse.

Women who have low birthweight babies (Heck et al., 2003) or babies admitted to the Special Care Nursery or NICU are also likely to stop breastfeeding. Premature delivery or other complications may come about as a result of abuse to the mother or the chronic stress of being in an abusive relationship (Scott, Binns, Graham, & Oddy, 2006). Finally, women whose husbands or partners do not support breastfeeding are more likely to stop. An abusive husband or partner may be more likely to consider his partner's breasts to be "his" and not for the baby (Kong & Lee, 2004; Scott et al., 2006).

Health Effects of Not Breastfeeding

Although cessation of breastfeeding is understandable in abuse survivors, there are health consequences of breastfeeding cessation for both mother and baby. According to the U.S. Surgeon General, babies fed formula during the first year of life have a higher incidence of a number of diseases including pneumonia and bronchitis, diarrhea and other digestive illnesses, ear infections, urinary tract infections, meningitis, and SIDS (sudden infant death syndrome) (U.S. Department of Health and Human Services, 2011). Examining research worldwide, Jones et al. (2003) concluded that exclusive breastfeeding for six months could prevent 13 percent of child deaths—or prevent the deaths of 1.3 million children annually.

Breastfeeding is important for the mothers' health as well. A number of recent studies have found that women lower their lifetime risk of cardiovascular disease, metabolic syndrome, and diabetes when they breastfeed. And these effects continue into middle and old age (Schwartz et al., 2009; Stuebe & Rich-Edwards, 2009). Some of these effects are likely due to a permanent downregulation of the stress response, which results in lower risk of disease. Given abuse survivors' propensity for these illnesses, breastfeeding can be especially important in this population.

Breastfeeding also helps mothers immediately in terms of getting more sleep. In our study of 6,410 mothers with infants 0 to 12 months of age, mothers who were exclusively breastfeeding reported sleeping longer each night and taking fewer minutes to fall asleep than mothers who were either mixed feeding or exclusive-formula feeding (Kendall-Tackett et al., 2011). Both total sleep time and minutes to fall asleep (sleep latency) are predictive of depression. In addition, exclusively breastfeeding mothers reported less daily fatigue, more energy, and more subjective well-being than did their mixed- or formula-feeding counterparts. And they had significantly lower reports of depressed mood, anhedonia, and depression on the Patient Health Questionnaire-2 (PHQ-2).

Summary

Past or current abuse can lead to breastfeeding cessation, which increases the risk of illness in both babies and mothers. However, even though women often face significant obstacles to breastfeeding, some still manage to breastfeed their babies, which has a positive effect on both infant and maternal health. Breastfeeding may prove to be especially important for this population of mothers because of its effects on long-term health.

ABUSE HISTORY AND PARENTING DIFFICULTIES

What happens when abuse survivors have children of their own? A history of childhood abuse can make parenting difficult. Current partner violence compounds these effects. Parenting difficulties can starting during infancy and continue as the child grows. Women who have been abused as children or adults may have problematic relationships with their children, which can add to their life stress and compromise the health of both mother and child.

In a study from Scotland, women with a history of childhood sexual abuse were more anxious about the intimate aspects of caring for their own babies including activities such as diapering (Douglas, 2000). These mothers were more worried that their normal parenting behaviors were inappropriate—or that others would see them that way. Finally, they reported more parenting stress than their non-abused counterparts. Non-abused mothers were more likely to describe their own parents as caring than mothers in the sexual-abuse group. Women in the sexual abuse group seemed to have few, if any, internal working models of appropriate, loving parent/child physical intimacy. The author suggested that peer support with non-abused mothers can be helpful, as it provides a forum for mothers to discuss their feelings, which might reduce their anxiety and permit great physical and emotional closeness between mother and child.

Impact of Maternal Depression

Some of the difficulties abused mothers face are due to depression (Dubowitz et al., 2001). Dubowitz and colleagues found that when mothers have experienced multiple types of abuse, they are more likely to be depressed. They also used harsher discipline and had more problems with their children. When mothers had been both physically and sexually abused as children, they had more difficulties than those who suffered only one type of abuse. The authors speculated that abused mothers may be less attentive to their children and less emotionally available. These mothers may also have less tolerance for the day-to-day stresses of parenting and be more inclined to view their children's behaviors as problematic. The authors concluded that a mother's history of victimization appears to be highly prevalent in high-risk samples. About half of the mothers victimized in childhood were also victimized as adults.

Another study compared 107 pregnant women with a CSA history to 156 non-abused pregnant women recruited from a prenatal clinic prior to birth (Schuetze & Das Eiden, 2005). The mothers were interviewed prenatally and when their babies were 2 to 4 years old. At Time 2, the researchers found that the CSA mothers were more likely to use punitive discipline and have a negative perception of their children if they were depressed or their current partner was violent. Once maternal depression and current partner violence were added to the model, the relationship between CSA and parenting outcomes was no longer significant. These finding suggest that the relationship between CSA and parenting problems is indirect rather than direct. They noted that mental health services for CSA survivors should consider adding a preventative element designed to help women avoid abusive partnerships, which in turn may lessen and even eliminate any potential adverse parenting issues associated with CSA.

Using data from the Avon Longitudinal Study of Parents and Children (ALSPAC), researchers explored the links between childhood sexual abuse before the age of 13, later maternal mental health, family organization, parenting behaviors, and adjustment in offspring (Roberts, O'Connor, Dunn, Golding, & the ALSPAC Study Team, 2004). This sample included 8,292 families in an ongoing study of women and their families in Avon, England. After adjusting for other childhood adversity, mothers' history of childhood sexual abuse was associated with a range of outcomes in adulthood, including poorer psychological well-being, teenage parenting, parenting problems, and adjustment problems in their offspring. The CSA mothers were also significantly more likely to report experiencing physical and emotional cruelty during childhood.

The children of abused mothers had more conduct problems, peer problems, and emotional problems than did children of non-abused mothers. The results of regression analyses suggest that the relationship between CSA and later parent-child problems are largely due to the effects of CSA on mother's mental health (Roberts et al., 2004). If the mother was well adjusted, the child was well adjusted. If, on the other hand, the mother was poorly adjusted, so was the child. Both maternal depression and anxiety exerted independent effects on children's adjustment.

A large-scale, community-based study of American Indians ($N = 3{,}084$) (Libby, Orton, Beals, Buchwald, & Manson, 2008) examined the relationship between abuse, reported parenting satisfaction, and parenting-role impairment. Contrary to earlier studies, it was substance abuse—not depression—that mediated the relationship between childhood abuse and subsequent impaired parenting. For members of the Northern Plains tribe, lifetime substance abuse fully mediated the relationship between physical abuse and both parenting satisfaction and parenting-role impairment. There were only partial mediation between childhood sexual abuse and parenting-role impairment in the Southwest tribe. In both tribes, lifetime depression was not related to impaired parenting. Social support enhanced parenting satisfaction, while negative support reduced satisfaction and impaired parenting.

A history of childhood abuse and current partner violence can both increase the risk of mothers abusing their children. A study of fifty-three low-income, single mothers found that there was a high prevalence of abuse, depressive symptoms, and abusive parenting attitudes within their sample (Lutenbacher, 2002). Both current partner violence and childhood physical abuse predicted higher everyday stressors, which predicted lower maternal self-esteem. A history of childhood abuse and low self-esteem predicted more depressive symptoms, which in turn led to more state anger. The combination of everyday stressors and depression predicted more trait anger. But current partner violence was the best predictor of overall abusive attitudes and more parent-child role reversal.

Although the majority of research on child dysfunction focuses on mothers, fathers' mental health also plays a part. In a recent analysis of the Medical Expenditure Panel Survey, a representative sample of 21,993 U.S. children, depression in fathers was associated with increased behavioral and emotional problems in the children and adolescents (Weitzman, Rosenthal, & Liu, 2011). The effect of mothers' depression was actually stronger than the effect of fathers' depression. But the strongest negative effects for children were when both mother and father were depressed.

Ability to Deal With Parenting Stress

Handling infant crying is one of the challenges faced by new parents. A study of eighty-four parents from the general population were assessed regarding their interpretations, feelings, and behaviors following exposure to a two-minute videotaped segment of a crying infant (Crouch, Skowronski, Milner, & Harris, 2008). The researchers were interested in whether child abuse risk and hostility led to more negative interpretations of infant crying. As predicted, the parents rated high on abuse potential were more likely to rate the infant crying negatively and report higher feelings of hostility while watching the video than parents rated as low on abuse potential. Even among low-risk parents, crying produced more hostility than watching a video with a quiet baby. Parents who were primed with hostile words prior to exposure reported increased hostility relative to other conditions. Hostile priming was also modestly associated with excessive use of force in the hand grip task among parents rated as having high abuse potential. The authors noted that while crying may be viewed as an adaptive activity that allows infants to signal distress and enlist assistance, it may also elicit a hostile and aggressive response by increasing parental negativity and hostility.

A study comparing 670 non-abusing families with 166 abusive families found similar results (Gracia & Musitu, 2003). The families in this sample were Colombian and Spanish. The authors found that in both cultures abusive parents showed lower levels of community integration, participation in social activities, and use of formal and informal organizations than parents who were providing adequate care for their children. The abusive parents tended to be more socially isolated and negative in their attitudes toward their community and neighborhood.

In a sample of 483 mothers receiving public assistance (predominantly African American), the investigator sought to understand the impact of childhood sexual abuse after controlling for the effects of other childhood adversities (Barrett, 2009). Sexual abuse survivors reported significantly lower rates of parental warmth, higher rates of psychological aggression, and more frequent use of corporal punishment than non-abused mothers. There was no significant difference in parenting stress compared to the women in this sample without a CSA history. However, this entire sample was likely under considerable stress. The effects of CSA became nonsignificant when other forms of childhood adversity were considered. The other maternal factors included childhood physical abuse, observing domestic violence, child neglect, living apart from one or both parents during childhood, and childhood poverty, all of which predicted current parenting behavior. Barrett also noted that this study did not include any of the adult stressors that these women were facing, including simultaneous forms of oppression based on race, class, and gender, and that the more proximal stressors, such as what was happening to them now, probably exerted a stronger impact on their parenting behaviors.

INTERVENTIONS TO IMPROVE PARENTING

Abuse survivors face a number of difficulties when it comes to bearing and caring for their own children. Even with this rather bleak picture, there are two interventions that counter some of these effects: nurse home visitation and breastfeeding.

Home Visiting

A nineteen-year follow-up of families that participated in a home visiting program when their children were infants suggests that home visiting is an effective intervention for high-risk families (Eckenrode et al., 2010). The women enrolled in the original study were young, unmarried, and low income. For their offspring, home visiting decreased the number of girls who had been arrested and convicted. They also had fewer lifetime arrests than offspring in the other groups. Nurse-home-visited girls had fewer children and less Medicaid usage than did their comparison group counterparts. There were fewer effects for boys.

In an evaluation of a home visiting program in Oahu, Hawaii, mothers with an infant at high risk for child maltreatment were provided with home visits for the first three years of their children's lives (Bair-Merritt et al., 2010). During the program's implementation, mothers reported lower rates of both physical partner victimization and perpetration. During the long-term follow-up, overall IPV victimization and perpetration decreased, but this group did not significantly differ from the comparison group. Overall, early childhood home visitation appears to be a promising strategy for reducing partner violence in high-risk families.

Breastfeeding as a Preventive Strategy for Child Abuse

Several recent studies have found that breastfeeding is a surprisingly effective intervention for decreasing maternal depression, promoting mother-infant bonding, and decreasing the risk of child maltreatment. In a fifteen-year cohort study of 7,223 Australian mother-infant pairs, 512 cases of substantiated maltreatment occurred (4.3 percent of the cohort) (Strathearn, Mamun, Najman, & O'Callaghan, 2009). Breastfeeding significantly decreased the risk of maternal-perpetrated child maltreatment. Non-breastfed infants were 2.6 times more likely to have been abused by their mothers. The risk of neglect was even more striking. For infants who were breastfed for four months or longer, the odds ratio of being neglected was 1.0. If they were breastfed for less than four months, the odds ratio was 2.3. And if they were not breastfed at all, the odds ratio of neglect was 3.8. The mothers were the most frequently identified perpetrators of neglect, emotional abuse, and physical abuse. The biological fathers were the most common perpetrators of sexual abuse. The authors noted that the abuse-lowering effects of breastfeeding may be due to oxytocin release, which reduces anxiety, elevates mood, increases maternal responsiveness, lowers maternal stress, and increases attachment. They noted that also there are many causes of child abuse and neglect, that promoting breastfeeding may be a relatively simple and cost-effective means of strengthening the relationship between mother and child.

Another Australian study found that breastfeeding improves children's mental health at every time point in a fourteen-year longitudinal study of 2,900 pregnant women in Western Australia (Oddy et al., 2009). The children were assessed at 2, 6, 8, 10, and 14 years of age. Longer duration of breastfeeding was associated with better child mental health at every assessment, and there was a dose-response effect: the longer the duration of breastfeeding, the better the children's mental health. The most striking data were comparing children who never breastfed with those who breastfed for twelve months or longer. At every assessment point, the breastfed children had significantly lower scores on the Child Behavior Checklist (high scores mean more pathology).

One possible reason for breastfeeding's protective effect is that breastfeeding mothers have lower rates of depression. In a qualitative review of forty-nine studies, breastfeeding mothers had lower rates of depression than mothers who bottle fed (Dennis & McQueen, 2009). Breastfeeding specifically downregulates the stress response and decreases the inflammatory response, and by doing so, protects maternal mental health (Groer, Davis, & Hemphill, 2002; Groer & Kendall-Tackett, 2011).

Breastfeeding also protects babies whose mothers are depressed from the harmful effects of maternal depression. Since abuse survivors are at high risk for depression, this study is of special interest. Jones, McFall, and Diego (2004) compared the infants of four groups of women: depressed mothers who were either breast or bottle feeding and nondepressed mothers who were either breast or bottle feeding. The outcome measure was the babies' electroencephalogram (EEG) patterns, looking specifically for right-frontal asymmetry. Right-frontal asymmetry is a pattern that is also found in chronically depressed adults. When the researchers compared the babies of the depressed and nondepressed mothers, they found that babies of depressed/nonbreastfeeding mothers had the abnormal pattern of right-frontal asymmetry, but that the babies of depressed/breastfeeding mothers had normal EEGs.

In contrast, the infants of the depressed/breastfeeding mothers had patterns that were indistinguishable from the babies of nondepressed women. In other words, breastfeeding protected these babies from the effects of maternal depression. The authors explained these findings by noting that the depressed/breastfeeding mothers did not disengage from their babies but continued to look at, touch and stroke their babies because these behaviors are built in to the breastfeeding relationship. In contrast, when mothers use a bottle to feed their babies, they do not have to even hold their babies, making it easier for them to disengage. This disengagement can lead to the symptoms that babies typically exhibit when their mothers are depressed (Jones et al., 2004).

CONCLUSIONS

Although data are limited on the impact of abuse on women's perinatal health, we do know that women who experienced past or current abuse are at increased risk for depression, PTSD, and physical health consequences antenatally and postpartum. Breastfeeding has health implications for women and their babies, but there can be significant barriers to breastfeeding that need to be addressed.

As bleak as this situation might first appear, there are some hopeful signs. Not all women who have experienced past abuse become depressed, end up in unsupportive or abusive relationships, or have difficult relationships with their children. In fact, the majority do not. And even in the face of significant barriers, women who have experienced violence are breastfeeding their babies. These hopeful signs offer us at least a glimpse of what the perinatal experiences of all abuse survivors could be like. And improving the antenatal and postpartum experiences of women with a history of violence is a goal worth pursuing.

Endnote

1. WIC is a U.S. supplemental feeding program for women, infants and children.

References

Amir, L. H., & Donath, S. M. (2002). Does maternal smoking have a negative physiological effect on breastfeeding? The epidemiological evidence. *Birth, 29*, 112–123.

Ansara, D., Cohen, M. M., Gallop, R., Kung, R., Kung, R., & Schei, B. (2005). Predictors of women's physical health problems after childbirth. *Journal of Psychosomatic Obstetrics and Gynecology, 26*, 115–125.

Bair-Merritt, M. H., Blackstone, M., & Feudtner, C. (2006). Physical health outcomes of childhood exposure to intimate partner violence: A systematic review. *Pediatrics, 117*, 278–290.

Bair-Merritt, M. H., Jennings, J. R., Chen, R., Burrell, L., McFarlane, E., Fuddy, L., et al. (2010). Reducing maternal intimate partner violence after the birth of a child. *Archives of Pediatric and Adolescent Medicine, 164*(1), 16–23.

Barrett, B. (2009). The impact of childhood sexual abuse and other forms of childhood adversity on adulthood parenting. *Journal of Child Sexual Abuse, 18*, 489–512.

Benedict, M. I., Paine, L., & Paine, L. (1994). *Long-term effects of child sexual abuse on functioning in pregnancy and pregnancy outcomes (Final Report).* Washington, DC: National Center of Child Abuse & Neglect.

Blackmore, E. R., Moynihan, J. A., Rubinow, D. R., Pressman, E. K., Gilchrist, M., & O'Connor, T. G. (2011). Psychiatric symptoms and proinflammatory cytokines in pregnancy. *Psychosomatic Medicine, 73*, 656–663.

Boufidou, F., Lambrinoudaki, I., Argeitis, J., Zervas, I. M., Pliatsika, P., Leonardou, A. A., et al. (2009). CSF and plasma cytokines at delivery and postpartum mood disorders. *Journal of Affective Disorders, 115*, 287–292.

Bowen, E., Heron, J., Waylen, A., Wolke, D., & Team, A. S. (2005). Domestic violence risk during and after pregnancy: Findings from a British longitudinal study. *British Journal of Obstetrics and Gynecology, 112*(8), 1083–1089.

Bowman, K. G., Ryberg, J. W., & Becker, H. (2009). Examining the relationship between a childhood history of sexual abuse and later dissociation, breast-feeding practices, and parenting anxiety. *Journal of Interpersonal Violence, 24*(8), 1304–1317.

Brand, S. R., Engel, S. M., Canfield, R. L., & Yehuda, R. (2006). The effect of maternal PTSD following in utero trauma exposure on behavior and temperament in the 9-month-old infant. *Annals of the New York Academy of Sciences, 1071*, 454–458.

Buist, A., & Janson, H. (2001). Childhood sexual abuse, parenting, and postpartum depression: A 3-year follow-up study. *Child Abuse and Neglect, 25*, 909–921.

Bullock, L. F., Libbus, M. K., & Sable, M. R. (2001). Battering and breastfeeding in a WIC population. *Canadian Journal of Nursing Research, 32*, 43–56.

Campbell, J. C., & Kendall-Tackett, K. A. (2005). Intimate partner violence: Implications for women's physical and mental health. In K. A. Kendall-Tackett (Ed.), *Handbook for women, stress, and trauma* (pp. 123–140). New York: Brunner-Routledge.

Chan, K. L., Tiwari, A., Fong, D. Y. T., Leug, W. C., Brownridge, D. A., & Ho, P. C. (2009). Correlates of in-law conflict and intimate partner violence against Chinese pregnant women in Hong Kong. *Journal of Interpersonal Violence, 24*(1), 97–110.

Christian, L. M., Franco, A., Glaser, R., & Iams, J. D. (2009). Depressive symptoms are associated with elevated serum proinflammatory cytokines among pregnant women. *Brain, Behavior and Immunity, 23*, 75–754.

Chung, T. K., Lau, T. K., Yip, A. S., Chiu, H. F., & Less, D. T. (2001). Antepartum depressive symptomatology is associated with adverse obstetric and neonatal outcomes. *Psychosomatic Medicine, 63*, 830–834.

Corwin, E. J., & Pajer, K. (2008). The psychoneuroimmunology of postpartum depression. *Journal of Women's Health, 17*(9), 1529–1534.

Coussons-Read, M. E., Okun, M. L., Schmitt, M. P., & Giese, S. (2005). Prenatal stress alters cytokine levels in a manner that may endanger human pregnancy. *Psychosomatic Medicine, 67*, 625–631.

Crouch, J. L., Skowronski, J. J., Milner, J. S., & Harris, B. (2008). Parental responses to infant crying: The influence of child physical abuse risk and hostile priming. *Child Abuse and Neglect, 32*, 702–710.

Dayan, J. Creveuil, C., Marks, M. N., Conroy, S. Herlicoviez, M., Dreyfus, M., et al. (2006). Prenatal depression, prenatal anxiety, and spontaneous preterm birth: A prospective cohort study among women with early and regular care. *Psychosomatic Medicine, 68*, 938–946.

Dennis, C.-L., & McQueen, K. (2009). The relationship between infant-feeding outcomes and postpartum depression: A qualitative systematic review. *Pediatrics, 123*, e736–e751.

Dierckx, B., Tulen, J. H. M., van den Berg, M. P., Tharner, A., Jaddoe, V. W., Moll, H. A., et al. (2009). Maternal psychopathology influences infant heart rate variability: Generation R Study. *Psychosomatic Medicine, 71*, 313–321.

Douglas, A. R. (2000). Reported anxieties concerning intimate parenting in women sexually abused as children. *Child Abuse and Neglect, 24*(3), 425–434.

Dubowitz, H., Black, M. M., Kerr, M. A., Hussey, J. M., Morrel, T. M., Everson, M. D., et al. (2001). Type and timing of mothers' victimization: Effects on mothers and children. *Pediatrics, 107*, 728–735.

Eckenrode, J., Campa, M., Luckey, D. W., Henderson, C. R., Cole, R., Kitzman, H., et al. (2010). Long-term effects of prenatal and infancy nurse home visitation on the life course of youths. *Archives of Pediatric and Adolescent Medicine, 164*(1), 9–15.

Enlow, M. B., Kullowatz, A., Staudenmayer, J., Spasojevic, J., Ritz, T., & Wright, R. J. (2009). Associations of maternal lifetime trauma and perinatal traumatic stress symptoms with infant cardiorespiratory reactivity to psychological challenge. *Psychosomatic Medicine, 71*, 607–614.

Field, T., Diego, M., & Hernandez-Reif, M. (2006). Prenatal depression effects on the fetus and newborn: A review. *Infant Behavior and Development, 29*, 445–455.

Gavin, A. R., Chae, D. H., Mustillo, S., & Kiefe, C. I. (2009). Prepregnancy depressive mood and preterm birth in black and white women: Findings from the CARDIA Study. *Journal of Women's Health, 18*(6), 803–811.

Gilson, K. J., & Lancaster, S. (2008). Childhood sexual abuse in pregnant and parenting adolescents. *Child Abuse and Neglect, 32*, 869–877.

Goedhart, G., Snijders, A. C., Hesselink, A. E., van Poppel, M. N., Bonsel, G. J., & Vridkotte, T. G. M. (2010). Maternal depressive symptoms in relation to perinatal mortality and morbidity: Results from a large multiethnic cohort study. *Psychosomatic Medicine, 72*, 769–776.

Gracia, E., & Musitu, G. (2003). Social isolation from communities and child maltreatment: A cross-cultural comparison. *Child Abuse and Neglect, 27*, 153–168.

Grajeda, R., & Perez-Escamilla, R. (2002). Stress during labor and delivery is associated with delayed onset of lactation among urban Guatemalan women. *Journal of Nutrition, 132*, 3055–3060.

Grimstad, H., & Schei, B. (1999). Pregnancy and delivery for women with a history of child sexual abuse. *Child Abuse and Neglect, 23*, 81–90.

Groer, M. W., Davis, M. W., & Hemphill, J. (2002). Postpartum stress: Current concepts and the possible protective role of breastfeeding. *Journal of Obstetric, Gynecologic, and Neonatal Nursing, 31*(4), 411–417.

Groer, M. W., & Kendall-Tackett, K. A. (2011). *How breastfeeding protects women's health throughout the lifespan: The psychoneuroimmunology of human lactation*. Amarillo, TX: Hale.

Guo, S. F., Wu, J. L., Qu, C. Y., & Yan, R. Y. (2004). Physical and sexual abuse of women before, during and after pregnancy. *International Journal of Gynaecology and Obstetrics, 84*(3), 281–286.

Harrykissoon, S. D., Rickert, V. I., & Wiemann, C. M. (2002). Prevalence and patterns of intimate partner violence among adolescent mothers during the postpartum period. *Archives of Pediatric and Adolescent Medicine, 156*(4), 325–330.

Heck, K. E., Schoendorf, K. C., Chavez, G. F., & Braveman, P. (2003). Does postpartum length of stay affect breastfeeding duration? A population-based study. *Birth, 30*, 153–159.

Hulme, P. A. (2000). Symptomatology and health care utilization of women primary care patients who experienced childhood sexual abuse. *Child Abuse and Neglect, 24*, 1471–1484.

Jones, G. R., Steketee, W., Black, R. E., Bhutta, Z. A., Morris, S. S., & Bellagio Child Survival Study Group. (2003). How many child deaths can we prevent this year? *Lancet, 362*, 65–71.

Jones, N. A., McFall, B. A., & Diego, M. A. (2004). Patterns of brain electrical activity in infants of depressed mothers who breastfeed and bottle feed: The mediating role of infant temperament. *Biological Psychology, 67*, 103–124.

Kendall-Tackett, K. A. (2005). Trauma associated with perinatal events: Birth experience, prematurity, and childbearing loss. In K. A. Kendall-Tackett (Ed.), *Handbook of women, stress, and trauma* (pp. 53–74). New York: Brunner-Routledge.

Kendall-Tackett, K. A. (2007). A new paradigm for depression in new mothers: The central role of inflammation and how breastfeeding and anti-inflammatory treatments protect maternal mental health. *International Breastfeeding Journal, 2*(6). Available online at: *http://www.international breastfeedingjournal.com/content/2/1/6.*

Kendall-Tackett, K. A. (2010). *Depression in new mothers: Causes, consequences and treatment options* (2nd ed.). London: Routledge.e.

Kendall-Tackett, K. A., Cong, Z., & Hale, T. W. (2011). The effect of feeding method on sleep duration, maternal well-being, and postpartum depression. *Clinical Lactation, 2*(2), 22–26.

Kong, S. K., & Lee, D. T. (2004). Factors influencing decision to breastfeed. *Journal of Advanced Nursing, 46*, 369–379.

Lang, A. J., Rodgers, C. S., & Lebeck, M. M. (2006). Associations between maternal childhood maltreatment and psychopathology and aggression during pregnancy and postpartum. *Child Abuse and Neglect, 30*, 17–25.

Lev-Wiesel, R., Daphna-Tekoah, S., & Hallak, M. (2009). Childhood sexual abuse as a predictor of birth-related posttraumatic stress and postpartum posttraumatic stress. *Child Abuse and Neglect, 33*, 877–887.

Li, J., Vestergaard, M., Obel, C., Precht, D. H., Christensen, J., Lu, M., et al. (2009). Prenatal stress and cerebral palsy: A nationwide cohort study in Denmark. *Psychosomatic Medicine, 71*, 615–618.

Libby, A. M., Orton, H. D., Beals, J., Buchwald, D., & Manson, S. M. (2008). Childhood abuse and later parenting outcomes in two American Indian tribes. *Child Abuse and Neglect, 32*, 195–211.

Lutenbacher, M. (2002). Relationship between psychosocial factors and abusive parenting attitudes in low-income single mothers. *Nursing Research, 51*(3), 158–167.

Lutz, K. F. (2005). Abuse experiences, perceptions, and associated decisions during the childbearing cycle. *Western Journal of Nursing, 27*, 802–824

Maes, M., Bosmans, E., & Ombelet, W. (2004). In the puerperium, primiparae exhibit higher levels of anxiety and serum peptidase activity and greater immune responses than multiparae. *Journal of Clinical Psychiatry, 65*(1), 71–76.

Maes, M., Lin, A., Ombelet, W., Stevens, K., Kenis, G., DeJongh, R., et al. (2000). Immune activation in the early puerperium is related to postpartum anxiety and depressive symptoms. *Psychoneuroendocrinology, 25*, 121–137.

Martin, S. L., Mackie, L., Kupper, L. L., Buescher, P. A., & Moracco, K. E. (2001). Physical abuse of women before, during, and after pregnancy. *Journal of the American Medical Association, 285*(12), 1581–1584.

Mastorakos, G., & Ilias, I. (2003). Maternal and fetal hypothalamic-pituitary-adrenal axes during pregnancy and postpartum. *Annals of the New York Academy of Sciences, 997*, 136–149.

Oddy, W. H., Kendall, G. E., Li, J., Jacoby, P., Robinson, M., de Klerk, N. H., et al. (2009). The long-term effects of breastfeeding on child and adolescent mental health: A pregnancy cohort study followed for 14 years. *Journal of Pediatrics, 156*(4), 568–574.

Orr, S. T., Reiter, J. P., Blazer, D. G., & James, S. A. (2007). Maternal prenatal pregnancy-related anxiety and spontaneous preterm birth in Baltimore, Maryland. *Psychosomatic Medicine, 69*, 566–570.

Prentice, J. C., Lu, M. C., Lange, L., & Halfon, N. (2002). The association between reported childhood sexual abuse and breastfeeding initiation. *Journal of Human Lactation, 18*, 291–226.

Raj, A., Silverman, J. G., & Amaro, H. (2000). The relationship between sexual abuse and sexual risk among high school students: Findings form the 1997 Massachusetts Youth Risk Behavior Survey. *Maternal and Child Health Journal, 4*, 125–134.

Rich-Edwards, J. W., James-Todd, T., Mohllajee, A., Kleinman, K., Burke, A., Gillman, M. W., et al. (2011). Lifetime maternal experiences of abuse and risk of pre-natal depression in two demographically distinct populations in Boston. *International Journal of Epidemiology, 40*(2), 375–384.

Roberts, R., O'Connor, T., Dunn, J., Golding, J., & the ALSPAC Study Team. (2004). The effects of child sexual abuse in later family life: Mental health, parenting and adjustment of offspring. *Child Abuse and Neglect, 28*, 525–545.

Romano, E., Zoccolillo, M., & Paquette, D. (2006). Histories of child maltreatment and psychiatric disorder in pregnant adolescents. *Journal of the American Academy of Child and Adolescent Psychiatry, 45*(3), 329–336.

Schuetze, P., & Das Eiden, R. (2005). The relationship between sexual abuse during childhood and parenting outcomes: Modeling direct and indirect pathways. *Child Abuse and Neglect, 29*, 645–659.

Schwartz, E. B., Ray, R. M., Stuebe, A. M., Allison, M. A., Ness, R. B., Freiberg, M. S., et al. (2009). Duration of lactation and risk factors for maternal cardiovascular disease. *Obstetrics & Gynecology, 113*(5), 974–982.

Scott, J. A., Binns, C. W., Graham, K. I., & Oddy, W. H. (2006). Temporal changes in the determinants of breastfeeding initiation. *Birth, 33*, 37–45.

Seng, J. S., & Hassinger, J. A. (1998). Relationship strategies and interdisciplinary collaboration: Improving maternity care with survivors of childhood sexual abuse. *Journal of Nurse-Midwifery, 43*(4), 287–295.

Seng, J. S., Oakley, D. J., Sampselle, C. M., Killion, C., Graham-Bermann, S., & Liberzon, I. (2001). Posttraumatic stress disorder and pregnancy complications. *Obstetrics and Gynecology, 97*, 17–22.

Setse, R., Grogan, R., Pham, L., Cooper, L. A., Strobino, D., Powe, N. R., et al. (2009). Longitudinal study of depressive symptoms and health-related quality of life during pregnancy and after delivery: The Health Status in Pregnancy (HIP) Study. *Maternal Child Health Journal, 13*, 577–587.

Springs, F. E., & Friedrich, W. N. (1992). Health risk behaviors and medical sequelae of childhood sexual abuse. *Mayo Clinic Proceedings, 67*, 527–532.

Stock, J. L., Bell, M. A., Boyer, D. K., & Connell, F. A. (1997). Adolescent pregnancy and sexual risk-taking among sexually abused girls. *Family Planning Perspective, 29*, 200–203, 227.

Strathearn, L., Mamun, A. A., Najman, J. M., & O'Callaghan, M. J. (2009). Does breastfeeding protect against substantiated child abuse and neglect? A 15-year cohort study. *Pediatrics, 123*(2), 483–493.

Stuebe, A. M., & Rich-Edwards, J. W. (2009). The reset hypothesis: Lactation and maternal metabolism. *American Journal of Perinatology, 26*(1), 81–88.

Tegethoff, M., Greene, N., Olsen, J., Meyer, A. H., & Meinlschmidt, G. (2010). Maternal psychosocial adversity during pregnancy is associated with length of gestation and offspring size at birth: Evidence from a population-based cohort study. *Psychosomatic Medicine, 72*, 419–426.

U.S. Department of Health and Human Services. (2011). The Surgeon General's call to action to support breastfeeding. Washington, DC: Author.

Vatnar, S. K. B., & Bjorkly, S. (2010). Does it make any difference if she is a mother? An interactional perspective on intimate partner violence with a focus on motherhood and pregnancy. *Journal of Interpersonal Violence, 25*(1), 94–110.

Weitzman, M., Rosenthal, D. G., & Liu, Y.-H. (2011). Paternal depressive symptoms and child behavioral or emotional problems in the United States. *Pediatrics, 128*(6), 1126–1134.

Chapter 17

Clinical Approaches to Abuse Survivors in Health Care Settings

> Despite the high prevalence of sexual and physical abuse in women, physicians rarely identify these experiences in their patients; it seems essential in medical practice that physicians elicit such a history. (Leserman, Toomey, & Drossman, 1995, p. 23)

All health care providers periodically see patients who are difficult to treat and do not respond to typical treatment protocols. Many of these patients are abuse survivors. Even though past abuse is related to many chronic conditions, health care providers rarely ask about it, and patients do not tend to offer this information. In one study, fewer than 2 percent of sexual abuse survivors in a rural family practice had discussed their abuse with their physician, despite having many health symptoms (Springs & Friedrich, 1992). When health care professionals do not recognize the impact of past abuse on their patients, they perpetuate the secrecy and shame of that experience and expose patients to unnecessary and costly procedures. Despite high use of health care services, abuse survivors often have a difficult time in health care settings. Many procedures designed to collect necessary health information can feel demeaning, or even traumatizing (Schachter, Stalker, & Teram, 2001).

There are some hopeful signs that this might be changing, but there is still a way to go. In a community survey of sixty-one child sexual abuse (CSA) survivors from Auckland, New Zealand, ages 22 to 65, 69 percent had disclosed their abuse history to health care professionals, but only 23 percent indicated that a health care provider had asked them about past abuse (McGregor, Julich, Glover, & Gautam, 2010). Female providers were more likely to be rated as very or somewhat helpful than male providers, and participants were more likely to disclose to female providers. Twenty-four percent said that disclosing to a male provider was "very unhelpful" compared to only 10 percent of who disclosed to a female. Seventy-two percent disclosed to a general practitioner. Of those who had not disclosed, about half indicated that they would have liked to disclose but had not been asked. Some participants who did not disclose mentioned embarrassment, shame, or unworthiness, and they feared that the provider would not be able to help. Further, most suggested routine questioning about CSA. The majority of participants indicated that they feared exams and medical procedures, and 64 percent said that this fear had stopped them from attending routine health checks.

This chapter suggests effective approaches to dealing with patients who have been abused. The main focus is how to provide treatment while caring for patients' emotional needs. I highlight aspects of medical situations that are potentially traumatizing and indicate how to assess patients for current safety.

WHEN TO SUSPECT PAST ABUSE

Some patients choose not to reveal their history of abuse, even when asked. However, some specific signs can indicate past abuse (Drossman, 1995; Schachter et al., 2001; Schulman, 2010). These signs fall into four general categories. It is important to keep in mind that not everyone with these symptoms is an abuse survivor, but these symptoms can at least raise abuse as a possible issue.

- *Psychological issues.* Patients who are mistrustful of others or have difficulty relinquishing control may have been abused, as may patients who act helpless and dependent or who report feelings of guilt and shame.
- *Medical disorders.* Some medical conditions may also be red flags for past abuse. Chronic refractory pain is one condition. The presence of depression or posttraumatic stress disorder (PTSD) is another. Patients with eating disorders, sexual dysfunctions, or sexually transmitted diseases may have also been abused. These disorders can also occur in people who are not abuse survivors, but their presence indicates that abuse is a possibility.
- *Patients' behaviors in medical settings.* Another possible indicator is use of health care services. A patient who makes frequent and excessive use of diagnostic procedures, treatments, and surgeries may be an abuse survivor. However, many patients with chronic illnesses who are not abuse survivors also have high patterns of health care use. So this information must be considered alongside the other health care data. High use of services is one indicator, but avoidance is another. Frequent cancellations or appointment changes may indicate past abuse.
- *Illness behaviors.* Illness behaviors include the degree and manner to which symptoms are reported (e.g., frequency, severity, and description). Patients who have been abused may have a level of disability that is disproportionate to the clinical data. They may want their health care providers to assume responsibility for their illness. These patients may also strenuously deny the role of psychogenic factors and refuse to comply with treatment. Again, these characteristics may also appear in people who have not been abused, but abuse is a possibility.

HOW TO INQUIRE ABOUT PAST ABUSE

Once a clinician suspects that past abuse may be an issue, he or she can take a number of specific steps. Men and women will not reveal abuse if they do not feel safe and respected (Schachter et al., 2001). Taking time to get to know the patient and to establish rapport is an essential first step. Once rapport is established, the patient may volunteer this information. Clinicians can look for natural windows of opportunity when they can indicate that they are receptive to discussing the patient's past experiences. Having information in the waiting area and exam rooms about the effects of past abuse can also open conversations on this topic. The clinician might begin by talking generally about how trauma is frequently part of the history of people who have chronic pain, for example. The clinician may tell the patient that many types of trauma—including childhood abuse, loss of a parent, car accidents, or serious illnesses during childhood—can be related to health problems. This information often opens the door to future discussion. If a patient suggests that things were "difficult" in his or her childhood, clinicians can ask questions to encourage the patient to elaborate. Open-ended questions are frequently helpful.

Drossman (1997) suggests that health care providers prepare for possible revelations of abuse by having referral sources in place and knowing where to send patients. He recommends that health care providers continue providing care for patients who reveal childhood abuse. If care is discontinued, patients may assume that the clinician is rejecting them because of their "secret."

Clinicians should take care to ask about past abuse in private, in a setting in which there will be no interruptions. If a patient denies the abuse but the clinician suspects otherwise, the clinician should simply mentally note his or her suspicion and leave the option open for future discussion. If the patient becomes uncomfortable, the clinician can end the discussion but remain open to talking about it another day. Many abuse survivors honestly do not see any connection between what happened in childhood and their current health. A strenuous insistence on the clinician's part can leave the impression that the patient's health problems are not seen as "real," or that the clinician is somehow blaming the patient for his or her current health problems.

Routine Screening

Organizations such as UN Women, the United Nations Entity for Gender Equality and the Empowerment of Women recommend routine screening for family violence (see *http://www.endvawnow.org/en/articles/667-consider-routine-screening.html*), even when a patient is not showing signs of abuse. Such organizations note that without routine screening, providers only identify a fraction of women with histories of abuse. They also note that universal screening ensures that a minimum standard is met for safety and quality of care.

Questions about past and current abuse can be part of a review of systems or can be asked while taking a social or sexual history. Abuse can be asked about when women are contemplating pregnancy, are currently pregnant, or if they report a recent change in family relationships (e.g., recently married or divorced). After an initial screening, periodic screening is helpful. The goal of finding out about past abuse is to provide safe and appropriate care in health care settings. It is also to assess current safety, documenting past or current abuse, providing treatment for medical or mental health conditions, and being a conduit to other resources in the community.

A Safe Passage (*http://www.asafepassage.info/screening.shtml#routine*), a website for abuse survivors during the childbearing years, recommends that before you ask about abuse, you let your patient or client know the following:

- You ask all your clients these questions;
- You care about your client and want to make sure she has the care and support she needs;
- Many women live with abuse and are afraid to tell;
- Her information will be kept confidential except in certain circumstances (and what those circumstances are); and
- She has the right not to answer at the present time but you would be available at a future time should she wish to speak with you.

Clinician Concerns When Screening

Health care providers may be uncomfortable eliciting information about traumatic experiences and providing emotional support. In an era of managed care, a practitioner may feel pressured to move patients through the system and not feel able to take the time to learn about patients' past experiences. Patients' stories of abuse can also remind practitioners of their own abusive experiences and can make them want to distance themselves. Though these reactions are understandable, health care providers should not deal with their own discomfort by distancing themselves from, or pathologizing, the patient. This distancing can mimic the dynamics of the abuse experience and can also be traumatizing. Health care providers might also go too far the other way and become too involved. This approach compromises the patient's autonomy and can lead to professional burnout.

A Safe Passage encourages professionals to ask themselves the following questions before talking with clients or patients about abuse.

- Do I have professional guidelines to follow?
- Do I have the skills and resources to respond to a disclosure?
- Do I have the time to provide support?
- Could the answer help me to provide her with better support or services?
- What obstacles prevent me from asking/responding?
- Are there any foreseeable negative consequences for my client/patient for which I do not feel I could provide assistance (in the form of safety planning, referrals)?

If you have answered "no" to any of these questions, it could indicate that you need additional information or training so that you can meet the needs of abuse survivors in your practice.

WHY ABUSE SURVIVORS MAY DENY ABUSE

Even when directly asked, some patients will deny past abuse. Some will deny it because it never happened. But some will deny it even when it did happen. There are a variety of reasons why an abuse survivor might deny past abuse.

Trust Issues

Patients may not admit to a history of abuse on the practitioner's first attempt to elicit such information. As discussed previously, abuse survivors are often mistrustful of others. The practitioner may have to demonstrate that he or she will preserve the patient's confidentiality. When asking for this difficult information, it might be helpful to indicate why it is needed and how it will be used. Some survivors are concerned that their employers will find out via their health insurance company. Although we all hope that medical records are confidential, leaks do occur. Before asking about this type of information, think through what will be done with it. Will people at the health insurance company or the patient's company have access to it? A violation of a trust or confidence can be highly damaging to patients who already have difficulties trusting others. Practitioners must proceed with caution.

Fears About How You Will Respond

Another factor is whether abuse survivors feel a practitioner can handle the information. Though it is perfectly normal to react with horror at the news some patients share, it is important that the professional stay in control. It is appropriate to say, "That must have been awful for you." But if the practitioner reacts strongly, patients will stop sharing. Because I am a family-violence researcher, people frequently share their stories with me. I have found, over the years, that people often send up "trial balloons" that hint at an abusive past to see how I handle the information. Sometimes when I suspect past abuse, I make a general statement about the impact of traumatic events on health. That often opens the discussion.

In considering whether to ask, the practitioner should honestly assess whether he or she can handle this information. Not everyone can. Someone who is going to be upset in front of the patient or have trouble relating to a patient who reveals this information probably should not ask in the first place. The clinician does not always need to know for sure. Sometimes a practitioner can have a working hypothesis and proceed "as if" the patient were an abuse survivor. It is not necessary to know for certain in order to devise a treatment plan.

Possible Amnesia

Another reason patients deny abuse is that they honestly do not remember their abuse experiences. Amnesia for abuse-related events is common. Williams (1994) conducted a prospective study of adult survivors who had been treated in an emergency room of a large urban hospital during the 1970s. All had documented cases of sexual abuse. When she recontacted these women twenty years later, she found that 38 percent had experienced full or partial amnesia regarding their abuse experiences. Subjects in this study were willing to share information about drug abuse, criminal behavior, prostitution, pregnancies, and abortions. It is unlikely that they were simply withholding information about their past sexual abuse.

RESPONDING WHEN PATIENTS SHARE ABUSE HISTORY

If patients indicate that they have been abused, acknowledge that you know that this information was difficult to share and validate the patient's experiences. You can let your patient know that past abuse is fairly common and it can have an impact on health. You can also ask patients if they would like information on referral sources.

Once a patient's past abuse is known, the clinician must note it on patient medical records, assess the patient's current safety, and, if appropriate, report and warn. These tasks and obligations are described next.

Charting Abuse Information

If patients reveal past or current abuse, clinicians must document it in their medical records. This revelation, along with relevant observations and laboratory results, should all be recorded. Health care providers may be held liable for failure to recognize and respond to ongoing abuse. Reports should be factual, using phrases such as "patient reports history of child physical abuse" or "patient reports childhood sexual abuse." If there are physical injuries or scarring, the practitioner must document these, as well, describing the location and type of injury. The practitioner should document whether this injury was ever treated and when treatment took place. Practitioners may also inquire about past illnesses, including a history of childhood sexually transmitted diseases (STDs), urinary tract infections, or fractures that support claims of abuse. Abuse and its sequelae should be listed on the master problem list for each patient.

If injuries are current, the practitioner should document them by type, severity, and location. A body map is helpful, as are photographs (with the patient's written permission). The clinician should also record what the patient says about these injuries. Particularly with ongoing abuse, medical records may be used in court proceedings.

Maintaining Confidentiality

Documenting family violence in medical records should be relatively straightforward. However, ethical issues arise because of third-party reimbursement and the use of electronic medical records. Confidentiality becomes an issue when information about past abuse can be accessed by health insurers, employers, and family members or via the Internet. Clinicians should not include any abuse information on forms to employers, and they should make sure that only authorized people have access to patient records.

The American Psychiatric Association (APA) has also indicated that because there is a growing vulnerability of medical records, practitioners need to be circumspect about what they record. The APA recommends not writing anything that would expose patients to a breach of privacy and confidentiality, and recording only factual and descriptive information—not anything related to process or content of what was said or practitioners' personal observations of patients (American Psychiatric Association, 2002).

Assessing Current Patient Safety

Unfortunately, the risk of ongoing abuse is high among survivors of childhood abuse. Clinicians therefore may find that such patients are currently in abusive relationships. It is essential to talk to patients when they are alone, and not in the presence of partners, family members, friends, personal assistants, or nonofficial translators. Before asking patients whether they are in abusive relationships, the clinicians must make clear any limits to confidentiality including mandatory reporting of partner, elder, or child abuse.

Indications of current abuse include presentation at an emergency department or in primary care with an injury that does not look as if it could have been caused in the way that was described. Also of concern are injuries during pregnancy, patients who come for treatment one or two days after receiving an injury, or patients who have several different injuries in various stages of healing. Other symptoms of current abuse include repeat emergency department or primary care visits, unexplained somatic complaints, drug overdoses, suicide attempts, or self-mutilation. Finally, health care providers should question ongoing abuse if the patient is accompanied to the visit by an overly attentive or aggressive partner.

If it is determined that domestic violence is occurring, the clinician's top consideration is for the safety of the patient. Referrals should be made to community resources, such as battered women's shelters, support groups, legal assistance, or mental health professionals for individual or group psychotherapy. The clinician should offer patients a chance to use the telephone even before they leave the office or the hospital (Campbell & Kendall-Tackett, 2005). Medication may be necessary, too, but health care providers should be cautious in their choice; medications that impair patients' ability to accurately assess their safety and act protectively should be prescribed with extreme care, including many of the tranquilizers that are often prescribed (Hastings & Kaufman, 2004).

Clinicians must also assess the safety needs of older patients. Elderly patients may be currently abused by their spouses, caregivers, or adult children. Each state has its own requirements for reporting elder abuse, so it behooves the practitioner to become familiar with state laws. Adult survivors of childhood abuse are at increased risk of revictimization throughout their lives. But elder abuse is frequently overlooked in health care settings.

Other Legal Obligations

Health care providers who learn of ongoing family violence have other specific legal responsibilities. These include the duty to report and the duty to warn.

Duty to Report. All states require that health care providers report cases of ongoing child abuse. A report may be necessary if an adult survivor has minor children and is involved with an abusive partner. Adult survivors may also be abusive or neglectful if they are incapacitated due to mental illness or substance abuse.

Similarly, health care providers are also mandated to report elder abuse in most states. The abuse survivor may be either victim or perpetrator. Finally, many states have a law requiring physicians to report injuries that come about via the use of deadly weapons; thus, even if the abuse is not specifically covered under mandated reporting laws (e.g., domestic violence), it would have to be reported if it involved a weapon.

Duty to Warn. Health care providers have a legal obligation to report a patient's intention to harm a third party, although states vary in their definitions of the scope of this duty. This duty might involve encouraging patients to turn in weapons, using medication to lessen homicidal ideations, and possibly hospitalizing patients.

Because these actions breach patient confidentiality, patients should be informed of this ahead of time.

TREATING WITHOUT TRAUMATIZING: APPROACHES TO PATIENTS IN MEDICAL SETTINGS

Once it has been determined that a patient is an abuse survivor, the next step is to provide health care services in a way that does not cause additional trauma. To anticipate and avoid some common problems, it is helpful for the practitioner to see procedures from the patient's perspective. Many medical procedures involve authority figures touching, manipulating, and invading body parts. These procedures can be especially difficult for sexual abuse survivors because the dynamic is similar to their abuse. Procedures such as general anesthesia, muscle paralysis, confinement, immobilization (e.g., for an MRI), or insertion of catheters can be difficult for abuse survivors (Hastings & Kaufman, 2004; Schachter et al., 2001).

Invasive procedures such as breast exams and mammograms, pelvic exams, pap smears, catheterization, or rectal exams can trigger flashbacks. Dental exams have even been shown to increase anxiety among abuse survivors. Disrobing and lying supine on an exam table can cause difficulties. Pain syndromes, which are common among abuse survivors, may lead to even more invasive procedures. For example, a vaginal ultrasound or uterine biopsy may be necessary for a woman with chronic pelvic pain. She may also require gynecological surgery. For patients with lower abdominal pain, colonoscopies, sigmoidoscopies, and barium enemas might be part of the diagnostic workup. Hospitalization can also be intimidating, as is lack of control of basic bodily functions and a parade of caregivers who are strangers. Seclusion and lack of privacy can also cause problems (Hastings & Kaufman, 2004; Schachter et al., 2001).

Because abuse-survivor patients have been disempowered by their previous experiences, clinicians will want to empower them as much as possible. Following are some specific suggestions about ways to make patients feel more comfortable during exams and procedures:

- *Talk to patients before any procedure and warn them about what to expect.* This is a good practice for any patient, but it is especially helpful for abuse survivors. If it is an emergency, you may have to talk as you go. Patients will feel better about a procedure if they had a say in whether it was performed. If there was no time in the midst of an emergency, the practitioner should talk to the patient about it once the danger has passed. In the hospital, the practitioner should keep the number of caregivers to a minimum, provide explanation and advance warnings for each procedure, and introduce all team members to the patient.
- *Ask permission before touching patients.* Again, this is always a good idea with any patient, but it is especially important for abuse survivors. It is particularly important when touching "private" body parts such as the breasts, genitals, or rectum. But a touch anywhere without permission is likely to feel invasive. Some practitioners have also found that it is helpful to have patients assist by putting their hands over the physician's to guide to exam.
- *If you know the patient is an abuse survivor, ask what he or she normally*

does to cope. A particular patient with whom you are working may already have a way to cope with things that are reminders of abusive experiences. Such patients may distract themselves, practice relaxation techniques, or listen to music. You should give patients permission and encouragement to use whatever technique they need to cope with the present examinations and procedures. Also, you must realize that some standard "stress reduction" techniques, such as hypnosis or guided relaxation, may actually increase stress in abuse survivors, because patients feel they are losing control of their bodies.

- *Allow patients to have emotional support during exams or procedures.* Abuse survivors might cope better if they have a support person with them during a procedure. You should offer this option but not force it. A "support" person that the patient does not want could actually make the patient feel more exposed in an already vulnerable situation.
- *Warn about any procedure that is likely to be painful.* You must be truthful when describing the amount of pain you expect patients to feel. Also, you must bear in mind that many abuse survivors have lowered pain thresholds; something you would not expect to be painful might in fact be painful for the patient.
- *Allow ample time for exams.* If you know, or suspect, that a particular patient is an abuse survivor, you should be sure to allow extra time for examinations. That time will be necessary to explain everything thoroughly and to allow the patient breaks. If you are hurried or rushed, you may be tempted to dispense with parts of the exam that take extra time (such as explaining things). The patient may leave the office feeling revictimized by his or her medical experiences.
- *"Check in" with the patient from time to time.* As you proceed through an exam or procedure, you should periodically check in with patients to make sure they are okay or to see if they need a break. It might take several appointments before a procedure can be completed.
- *Be aware of situations that make patients feel vulnerable.* As described previously, some specific types of procedures or examinations may make abuse survivors feel vulnerable. If at all possible, you should discuss these procedures with your patients, let the patients know why the procedure is necessary, or describe other options. Some patients may be fine with various procedures; others may have a hard time.
- *Patients are likely to feel vulnerable when unclothed, or when lying flat on their backs.* You should try to minimize this position as much as possible. If part of the exam can be done while a patient is sitting up, you should do as much as you can from this position. Also, you should try to keep patients' exposure of their bodies to a minimum as such exposure can dramatically increase vulnerability.

Chances are these procedures are already part of the way most clinicians approach patients. But I reiterate them here because a reminder is often helpful when working with a vulnerable population (Hastings & Kaufman, 2004; Schachter et al., 2001).

Using a Medical/Mental Health Team Approach to Care

Treatment for adult survivors typically involves mental health services that are delivered separately from medical services. Such an approach is generally inadequate. Considering the comorbidity of physical and mental health concerns, the most effective treatment plans are those that address both. The mental health professional should be considered an integral part of the treatment team for the patient's overall care.

How the practitioner presents the mental health component of care will influence the patient's willingness to accept it. When presenting this option, the practitioner should frame it in such a way that the patient sees that it is part of the treatment plan. The practitioner should explain how past abuse can influence current functioning. Patients are much more likely to accept a recommendation if the mental health provider is someone the practitioner personally knows, and if the practitioner is going to be involved in their ongoing care (Drossman, 1995).

A mental health intervention does not mean that the patient is "crazy." The practitioner must let the patient know that he or she is suggesting such an intervention so the patient can break the cycle of depression, psychological distress, painful symptoms, and other chronic conditions (Drossman, Talley, Leserman, Olden, & Barreiro, 1995). Improvement in psychological distress can help patients make a better overall adjustment to illness. If patients do not want to use mental health care services, however, Drossman suggests that the practitioner continue normal care.

Finding Clinicians in the Community

To begin a team approach to treatment, it is important to locate other clinicians who can participate. To compile of a list of mental health providers with experience in treating family violence, begin by contacting local victim advocacy groups, including battered women's shelters, rape crisis centers, and family-violence hotlines. State psychological associations also generally keep a list of clinicians who treat trauma. Before adding someone to a list, it is best to make contact and find out what types of clients the referral accepts, whether the referral is willing to accept new patients, and the type of payment the referral requires. This can be particularly important for survivors who require low-cost options. If possible, offer patients more than one option so they can select a mental health provider with whom they are comfortable and have rapport.

Identifying Comorbid Psychological Conditions

One important role of mental health providers is to identify psychiatric conditions that might be hampering medical treatment, such as depression, anxiety, PTSD, eating disorders, and substance abuse. The mental health provider can also ask about a history of abuse if the medical provider has not already done so, or can confirm a history of abuse that the doctor has already identified. The mental health practitioner can also gather more information about these experiences, and this history can become the focus rather than simply one part of a medical history. However, patients should not be forced or coerced into dealing with abuse issues until they are ready to so. If patients are not ready to confront their abusive pasts, mental health providers can still help them cope with their current situation and illness.

Ideally, there should be ongoing collaboration between the health care provider and mental health provider as to the best way to approach and treat a particular patient. This might lead to adding psychopharmacological treatments to the plan and/or specific psychological interventions, such as cognitive therapy, to address maladaptive health beliefs. When psychological disturbance is extreme, the mental health practitioner may assume the primary treatment role for this patient, but the medical care provider should continue to be involved (Drossman et al., 1995).

Using Support Groups

Support groups are another important adjunct to treatment for abuse survivors. Depending on which need is more pressing, patients may attend groups addressing survivor issues and substance abuse recovery or specifically addressing their illness. The one caveat is that the groups must be formatted so that they focus on positive coping and do not just dwell on the negative aspects of the survivor's conditions or life. Negativity in groups is contagious, and members can often leave feeling worse than they did before they arrived.

CLINICIAN SELF-CARE

Self-care is critical when one works with traumatized patients. The sheer needs of these patients can become overwhelming, and burnout rates are high. You might also be dealing with your own history of abuse, and working with adult survivors makes these memories more salient. There are two specific occupational hazards in working with trauma survivors: vicarious traumatization and countertransference.

Vicarious Traumatization

The phenomenon of vicarious traumatization is well documented in children of Holocaust survivors (Levav, Kohn, & Schwartz, 1998; Yehuda, Schmeidler, Giller, Siever, & Binder-Brynes, 1998) and children of American Indians (Braveheart & BeBruyn, 1998). These children often develop PTSD simply by hearing about the experiences of their parents.

Vicarious traumatization can also happen to clinicians who work with adult survivors. When patients recount the circumstances leading to their trauma, it is not unusual for a clinician to experience intense emotions. You may feel guilt that you have not been through the horrific events patients describe (Friedman, 2001). You may also feel a sense of powerlessness that you were unable to protect a patient even when you rationally know that you could never have done so (e.g., the event took place long before you knew the patient).

Although it is natural to feel bad about what one's patients have gone through, it gets to be a problem when you begin to have symptoms of PTSD yourself. For example, you might start experiencing intrusive thoughts, nightmares about your patient's experiences, or emotional numbing. All these experiences can cloud professional judgment to such an extent that you try to "rescue" your patients or avoid the patients' references to their traumas, which can lead to severe personal distress (DeAngelis, 2002; Friedman, 2001).

Vicarious traumatization appears to be relatively common among those who work with abuse survivors. In a national study of 1,000 women psychotherapists, those with the highest levels of exposure to sexual abuse material had the highest levels of trauma symptoms. However, spirituality offered some protection. When the subjects had a spiritual life, they seemed to do well even when exposed to abuse histories of their patients. The clinicians who saw the highest numbers of abuse survivors also reported the highest levels of spiritual well-being (Brady, Guy, Poelstra, & Brokaw, 1999).

Countertransference

Countertransference is a psychoanalytic term that has relevance to trauma work. It happens when a patient's story triggers memories of abuse in the clinician. Vicarious traumatization can occur in the absence of previous trauma; countertransference draws on a clinician's traumatic past. Countertransference is more likely to occur when patients reveal histories similar to the clinician's own story (Friedman, 2001).

Abuse histories are fairly common in both mental health and medical providers and are often found in those who work with either victims or perpetrators of abuse. For example, in a survey of 645 professionals who conduct sexual abuse evaluations, 17 percent reported a history of sexual abuse, and 7 percent reported a history of physical abuse (Nuttal & Jackson, 1994).

In another study of 501 clinicians, Little and Hamby (1996) found that 32 percent reported a history of child sexual abuse. Therapists who had been sexually abused reported more difficulties with countertransference and boundary issues. However, gender differences were a stronger source of variance than past abuse. Female clinicians were more likely to report that sexual abuse was more difficult to treat, that they screened regularly for sexual abuse in their patients, and that they used more coping strategies in their work than did male clinicians.

In a sample of 150 clinicians working with sex offenders, 37 percent of females and 27 percent of males had a history of child sexual abuse (Hilton, Jennings, Drugge, & Stephens, 1995). Interestingly, those clinicians with a history of sexual abuse reported that either it had no impact on their work or its effects were positive. The authors offered one possible explanation for their finding: The overall abuse experiences of most of their subjects were relatively mild.

Finally, a study of 323 nurses revealed that 13 percent had a history of CSA. In comparing the work of abused and non-abused nurses, there were no significant differences between the two groups on whether they thought patients should be screened for past abuse (most thought nurses should screen) and whether they thought patients would be upset if they asked the patients about past abuse (slightly over half thought that these questions would upset patients). Past history did seem to influence the nurses' level of comfort in talking about abuse with patients. Twenty-three percent of the abused nurses and 34 percent of the non-abused nurses felt "extremely comfortable" listening to patients' stories of abuse. On the other end, 9.5 percent of abused nurses and 3.6 percent of non-abused nurses reported that they would be "extremely uncomfortable" talking to patients about abuse. For the nurses who were moderately comfortable, there were no differences between the abused and non-abused groups. The nurses who thought that all patients should be screened offered the following caveats: The nurse needs to be skilled in knowing how to ask and must have the resources in place to respond to any needs that should arise (Gallop, McKeever, Toner, Lancee, & Lueck, 1995).

Some Warning Signs of Possible Burnout

Some signs that may indicate that you are overinvolved with others include fatigue, resentment, strained relationships with others, irritability, feeling coerced or obligated to help, or feeling self-important (i.e., that you are the only one who can help with this problem, this patient, or this type of patient).

You must also pay attention to your beliefs about helping. The research of Helgeson and Fritz (1998), described in Chapter 8 of this volume, has relevance to professional burnout. Of particular interest is the construct of unmitigated communion (UC). People with this interpersonal style tend not to have reciprocal relationships and are too involved in the needs of others. In many caretaking situations, it is appropriate for the clinician to be the one giving. However, it is of concern when all the clinician's relationships are this way. If you are the one at work, in the family, and in your circle of friends who takes care of everyone's needs, you may be at risk for burning out. Here are some beliefs that might be problematic for such clinicians. These are the characteristics of the UC style (Helgeson & Fritz, 1998):

- *Attachments.* The clinician has a hard time connecting with others, fears abandonment, and does not feel sure that people love him or her.
- *Relationships.* The clinician has a negative view of him- or herself or others, feels that others perceive him or her negatively, or does not enjoy helping people but feels coerced into it.
- *Social support.* The clinician lacks genuine support, is always the one to give support and never receives it, or likes the sense of control he or she has by being the "support provider."
- *Motivations for helping.* The clinician is motivated to help others so that people will think well of him or her rather than because he or she has a genuine concern for the well-being of others.

Although most practitioners experience these thoughts from time to time, such thoughts become problematic when they are predominant beliefs. A clinician may not even be aware that he or she is thinking this way, but it can be damaging nonetheless in both the clinician's professional life, and his or her personal life. Adult survivors may be especially prone to these beliefs. But once they recognize these beliefs, they can address them.

Professional Self-Care

Given the inherent difficulties in working with abuse survivors, taking care of yourself is absolutely essential. Without self-care, you, your patients, and your family all suffer. Vicarious traumatization and countertransference can impair both professional judgment and personal mental health. Friedman (2001) describes how clinicians may find themselves trapped in a vicious cycle of increasing symptoms and increasing ineffectiveness with clients, which leads them to plunge themselves into their work further. Some specific suggestions for breaking this cycle are described here.

Recognize the Occupational Hazards. The first step to breaking the vicious cycle is to recognize that there are unique hazards associated with working with adult survivors and other traumatized patients. This may also involve recognizing one's own vulnerability and acknowledging, perhaps for the first time, one's own history of childhood abuse. This history can eventually make you more effective in your work. But it also brings with it an increased vulnerability.

Take Steps to Counter Vicarious Traumatization and Countertransference. Once you recognize your vulnerability, you must take specific steps to counter it. Here are some ideas to help (Friedman, 2001):

- *Don't go it alone.* Clinical work is often a solitary activity, even when you share office space with others. Acknowledge that some patients require more care than one clinician can offer. This can include having regular supervision if you are in training. Peer support is also important as you work with challenging patients. A team approach also works well in this regard. Make relationships with family and friends a priority, and nurture these relationships. If a patient's story is stirring up memories in you, don't be afraid to seek counseling yourself.
- *Limit your involvement.* An important type of self-care is learning not to carry your patients' concerns once you leave the office. Keep firm boundaries between your work and home life. For example, you may resolve to leave your briefcase in your office, or not to think about clients once you are on your way home. This way you can continue to be connected and caring in the office while minimizing the emotional toll of this type of caring. Another strategy is to limit the number of trauma cases you see. Try to balance out your caseload with less severely affected patients.
- *Take care of your body.* This final strategy applies to anyone doing stress-

ful work, but it is especially important for you—take care of your body. This means getting enough sleep, eating nutritious foods, exercising, connecting with others, and maintaining a spiritual life. Taking care of your body might mean taking a walk in the middle of the day, getting a massage, or making a date with a friend. If you want your patients to live balanced lives, you are going to have to model that for them.

Summary

There are some unique aspects to working with traumatized patients that make it easy to get overwhelmed. It is important that you do not isolate yourself, that you connect with others, and that you make time for activities away from work. If you are going to be available to your patients, you must take time to refresh, refuel, and restore balance. In this way, you can continue to be a healthy helper.

CONCLUSIONS

Past and current abuse can lead to serious health consequences. Medical care providers can take some specific steps to make it safe for adult survivors in their practice. A team approach is the most effective for helping abuse survivors with health problems, and it can keep the medical care provider from shouldering the load alone. The next three chapters describe protocols for clinical management of three conditions that often present in health care settings: depression, PTSD, and chronic pain.

References

American Psychiatric Association. (2002). *Documentation of psychotherapy by psychiatrists* (Resource Document). Available online at: *http://www.americanmentalhealth.com/media/pdf/200202apaonnotes.pdf.*

Brady, J. L., Guy, J. D., Poelstra, P. L., & Brokaw, B. F. (1999). Vicarious traumatization, spirituality, and the treatment of sexual abuse survivors: A national survey of women psychotherapists. *Professional Psychology: Research and Practice, 30*, 386–393.

Braveheart, M. Y. H., & BeBruyn, L. M. (1998). The American Indian holocaust: Healing historical unresolved grief. *American Indian and Alaska Native Mental Health Research, 8*, 60–82.

Campbell, J. C., & Kendall-Tackett, K. A. (2005). Intimate partner violence: Implications for women's physical and mental health. In K. A. Kendall-Tackett (Ed.), *Handbook for women, stress, and trauma* (pp. 123–140). New York: Brunner-Routledge.

DeAngelis, T. (2002, July-August). Normalizing practitioners' stress. *Monitor on Psychology*, pp. 62–64.

Drossman, D. A. (1995). Sexual and physical abuse and gastrointestinal illness. *Scandinavian Journal of Gastroenterology, 30*(Suppl.), 90–96.

Drossman, D. A. (1997). Irritable bowel syndrome and sexual/physical abuse history. *European Journal of Gastroenterology and Hepatology, 9*, 327–330.

Drossman, D. A., Talley, N. J., Leserman, J., Olden, K. W., & Barreiro, M. A. (1995). Sexual and physical abuse and gastrointestinal illness: Review and recommendations. *Annals of Internal Medicine, 123*, 782–794.

Friedman, M. J. (2001). *Posttraumatic stress disorder: The latest assessment and treatment strategies*. Kansas City, MO: Compact Clinicals.

Gallop, R., McKeever, P., Toner, B., Lancee, W., & Lueck, M. (1995). Inquiring about childhood sexual abuse as part of the nursing history: Opinions of abuse and nonabused nurses. *Archives of Psychiatric Nursing, 9*, 146–151.

Hastings, D. P., & Kaufman, G. K. (2004). Screening for family violence in perioperative settings. In K. A. Kendall-Tackett (Ed.), *Health consequences of abuse in the family* (pp. 33–44). Washington, DC: American Psychological Association.

Helgeson, V. S., & Fritz, H. L. (1998). A theory of unmitigated communion. *Personality and Social Psychology Review, 2*, 173–183.

Hilton, N. Z., Jennings, K. T., Drugge, J., & Stephens, J. (1995). Childhood sexual abuse among clinicians working with sex offenders. *Journal of Interpersonal Violence, 10*, 525–532.

Leserman, J., Toomey, T. C., & Drossman, D. A. (1995). Medical consequences of sexual and physical abuse in women. *Humane Medicine, 11*, 23–28.

Levav, I., Kohn, R., & Schwartz, S. (1998). The psychiatric after-effects of the Holocaust on the second generation. *Psychological Medicine, 28*, 755–760.

Little, L., & Hamby, S. (1996). Impact of a clinician's sexual abuse history, gender, and theoretical orientation on treatment issues related to childhood sexual abuse. *Professional Psychology: Research and Practice, 27*, 617–625.

McGregor, K., Julich, S., Glover, M., & Gautam, J. (2010). Health professionals' responses to disclosure of child sexual abuse history: Female child sexual abuse survivors' experiences. *Journal of Child Sexual Abuse, 19*, 239–254.

Nuttal, R., & Jackson, H. (1994). Personal history of childhood abuse among clinicians. *Child Abuse and Neglect, 18*, 455–472.

Schachter, C., Stalker, C., & Teram, E. (2001). *Handbook on sensitive practice for health professionals: Lessons from women survivors of childhood sexual abuse.* Ottawa, Ontario: Health Canada, Family Violence Prevention Unit.

Schulman, E. (2010, June). Abuse screening should be part of the neurology exam. *World Neurology*, p. 4.

Springs, F. E., & Friedrich, W. N. (1992). Health risk behaviors and medical sequelae of childhood sexual abuse. *Mayo Clinic Proceedings, 67*, 527–532.

Williams, L. M. (1994). Recall of childhood trauma: A prospective study of women's memories of child sexual abuse. *Journal of Consulting and Clinical Psychology, 62*, 1167–1176.

Yehuda, R., Schmeidler, J., Giller, E. L., Siever, L. J., & Binder-Brynes, K. (1998). Relationship between posttraumatic stress disorder characteristics of Holocaust survivors and their adult offspring. *American Journal of Psychiatry, 155*, 841–843.

Chapter 18

Clinical Management of Depression in Health Care Settings

Depression is one of the most common symptoms experienced by people who have suffered childhood abuse, and it can have a significant impact on health. As discussed in Chapter 11, depression influences compliance with treatment and increases the likelihood of other complications. It also co-occurs with conditions such as post-traumatic stress disorder (PTSD) and chronic pain. Unlike substance abuse, eating disorders, and PTSD, mild to moderate depression can be managed in primary care or a general medical setting. (In cases of severe depression, specialized care, or even hospitalization, may be necessary.) A treatment plan for adult survivors of childhood abuse should include assessment and management of depression.

ASSESSMENT OF PATIENTS FOR DEPRESSION

One of the first steps for the primary care physician or other health care provider is to assess new patients, or patients who have not been seen for a while, for possible depression. This can be tricky. Depression is often masked in its presentation. Patients may deny that they are depressed, or they may not even realize it themselves. Fatigue, irritability, somatic complaints, anxiety, and frequent doctors' visits may be the only presenting symptoms. This is especially true for patients presenting with comorbid physical health complaints (Institute for Clinical Systems Improvement, 2000). Following are some guidelines for assessing patients for depression in health care settings. After determining that a patient is depressed, the primary care clinician may refer the patient to a mental health provider or manage the depression in the health care setting. The health care provider might also collaborate with a mental health provider for a more comprehensive approach. (See Appendix 18.1 for additional resources for depression.)

Depressive Symptoms

Patients may have symptoms of depression without meeting criteria for major depression. Following are some general questions that can be used as an initial screen for depression. Patients who are having difficulty in one or more of these areas may need further screening.

- Have you had any difficulty sleeping?
- Have you been more tired or less active than usual?
- Have you felt more stressed than usual?
- Have you been less interested in interacting with others, including your partner, friends, or children?

Diagnostic Criteria for Major Depression

Major depression is a more serious manifestation of depressive symptoms. Following are the specific criteria for diagnosing major depression according to the

the fourth edition, text revision of the *Diagnostic and Statistical Manual of Mental Disorders* (DSM-IV-TR; American Psychiatric Association, 2000). For a diagnosis of major depression, patients must have at least five of the following symptoms during the same two-week period:

1. Depressed mood most of the day;
2. Anhedonia most of the day;
3. Significant weight loss when not dieting, or weight gain, or change in appetite;
4. Insomnia or hypersomnia;
5. Activity disturbance, psychomotor agitation or retardation;
6. Abnormal fatigue or loss of energy;
7. Feelings of worthlessness or excessive guilt;
8. Diminished ability to think or concentrate or make decisions; and
9. Recurrent thoughts of death, or recurrent suicidal ideation, with or without a specific plan.

Someone who meets the criteria for major depression will need specialized care. One important consideration is the severity of the current episode. In attempting to evaluate severity of the current episode, there are three factors to consider: duration, intensity of symptoms, and level of impairment. Two weeks of symptoms is the cut-off for determining whether presenting symptoms are depression or a more transitory condition. Intensity of the symptoms and level of impairment can also provide a good indication of whether aggressive treatment is warranted. If patients suddenly stop paying attention to personal grooming, cannot manage their households, or have days when they cannot get out of bed, the depressive episode should be considered severe.

RISK FACTORS FOR DEPRESSION

Not every patient, or even every abuse survivor, is equally at risk. Certain factors put patients at higher risk for depression; the presence of these risk factors should at least raise the possibility that depression could be an issue. Some common risk factors are described next. Past history can also provide valuable information about which treatments worked and which were not effective.

Psychiatric and Physical Comorbidity

Another factor to consider in the management of depression is whether it is occurring in conjunction with another condition. Substance abuse, PTSD, and anxiety disorders all tend to co-occur with depression, and all are common among adult survivors of childhood abuse.

Similarly, patients who are depressed may also be coping with physical conditions that have depression as a possible symptom. These conditions include chronic pain, diabetes, cancer, cardiovascular disease, thyroid disease, and autoimmune disease. Medication for these conditions can also cause depression.

Assessing Active Substance Abuse

Another key consideration is whether patients are actively abusing alcohol or drugs. As discussed in Chapter 4, abuse survivors are at increased risk for substance abuse. Because active substance abuse complicates treatment for depression, when it is detected, patients should be referred to a substance abuse treatment program. The following are some screening questions for possible substance abuse (Institute for Clinical Systems Improvement, 2000).

- Have you ever felt you ought to cut down on your drinking or drug use?
- Have you ever had people annoy you by criticizing your drinking or drug use?
- Have you ever felt bad or guilty about your drinking or drug use?
- Have you ever had a drink or used drugs first thing in the morning to steady your nerves or get rid of a hangover or to get the day started?

If a patient says yes to two or more of these questions, make a referral to a substance abuse program for further evaluation.

Assessing Suicide Risk

Suicide risk is always an important consideration when working with people who are depressed. As described in Chapter 5, abuse survivors, particularly sexual abuse survivors, are at increased risk for suicide. In the list that follows, the Institute for Clinical Systems Improvement (2000) cites some specific signs that may indicate increased suicide risk:

- Previous history of suicide attempts;
- Suicidal ideation, particularly with specific suicide plans;
- Substance abuse or dependency;
- Personality disorder;
- Family history of suicide;
- Single marital status;
- Recent death of a loved one;
- Recent divorce or separation;
- Insomnia;
- Panic attacks;

- Diminished concentration; and
- Severe anhedonia or hopelessness.

Even when these signs are present, it is difficult to predict suicide. Clinicians must be sure to document the assessment of suicide risk in patient records. The presence of even one of these risk factors may call for a more specialized consult, and patients exhibiting these symptoms should be closely monitored. Patients at high risk for suicide may need to be hospitalized.

Assessing the Need for Psychiatric Hospitalization

Hospitalization may be necessary when severe symptoms are present. Particularly troubling are signs that patients plan to harm themselves or others. When making a decision about whether psychiatric hospitalization is necessary, consider the following questions:

- Does the patient have suicidal thoughts or plans?
- Do you fear for the patient's safety?
- Does the patient have plans to assault or kill another person?
- Is there psychotic thinking?
- Has the patient lost the ability to care for him- or herself?

An answer of "yes" to one or more of these questions could indicate the need for hospitalization. Any concerns about the safety of the patient or others should be noted in the medical record, as well as any follow-up steps taken.

TREATMENT WITH ANTIDEPRESSANT MEDICATIONS

A variety of modalities are useful in the treatment of depression, including antidepressant medications, cognitive therapy, and some alternative approaches using herbal antidepressants, exercise, and supplements. Often, a combination of modalities is the most effective, especially for refractory depression or recurring episodes of major depression. This section summarizes treatments with antidepressant medications.

Medications for depression are often the first line of treatment offered to patients in a health care setting. Antidepressant medications are generally necessary for the treatment of major depression but may be used for mild and moderate depression as well. Medications can be combined with other treatment modalities.

Some patients resist the idea of taking medications for depression. When deciding whether patients should be on medication, the clinician should consider the severity of the depression and the types of symptoms the patient has. Medications are especially helpful in treating the following symptoms: sleep disturbance, especially early-morning awakening, frequent awakenings, decreased sleep efficiency, or hypersomnia; appetite disturbance, eating too much or too little; fatigue; decreased sex drive;

diurnal variations in mood (e.g., feeling worse in the morning); restlessness, agitation, or psychomotor retardation; impaired concentration and forgetfulness; and "pronounced anhedonia"—or the inability to experience pleasure (Preston & Johnson, 2009). If depression is severe and/or patients have these types of symptoms, medications are probably the best approach.

Major Types of Antidepressants

The three major types of antidepressants are described in this section. All work to increase the amount of neurotransmitters serotonin, norepinephrine, or dopamine available in the brain.

Tricyclics. Tricyclic antidepressants (TCAs) are the oldest, and least expensive, of the antidepressants. They have a solid track record of effectiveness and include medications such as Pamelor (Nortiptyline), and Elavil (Amitriptyline). They are effective, but tend to have side effects that people do not like, such as dry mouth and constipation. Patient compliance is often a problem with TCAs. Once they start to feel better, they may choose to discontinue the medications. And that can negatively affect their treatment.

There are also some contraindications for these medications. For example, TCAs should not be used on patients with comorbid coronary artery disease. Lesperance and Frasure-Smith (2000) outline three reasons for this: TCAs have antiarrhythmic properties similar to quinidine and moricizine; TCAs may contribute to postural hypotension, which may be a problem for patients taking other medications to regulate their blood pressure; and the side effect profile may be unacceptable for patients already on other medications.

TCAs have another serious drawback that must be considered: the risk of suicide. Tricyclics can be lethal in too large a dose. If these medications are used, patients must be closely monitored and not be given sufficient medication in each prescription period to provide the means for them to kill themselves. Preston and Johnson (2009) recommend avoiding TCAs and monoamine oxidase inhibitors (MAOIs) for patients with high suicide risk.

Selective Serotonin Reuptake Inhibitors. Selective serotonin reuptake inhibitors (SSRIs) are the a newer class of antidepressants, and they include such well-known medications as fluoxetine (Prozac), sertraline (Zoloft), paroxetine (Paxil), and citalopram (Celexa). As their name implies, they work specifically on serotonin receptors. While these medications still have side effects, they have fewer than the other antidepressants, and their dosing schedule is less complex. Many patients experience sexual side effects, particularly inorgasmia, and may stop taking their medications because of them. SSRIs are effective for approximately 80 percent of patients, but they do not work for everyone. If patients do not respond to one type of SSRI, another should be tried (Institute for Clinical Systems Improvement, 2000; Preston & Johnson, 2009).

Because SSRIs have the potential for interacting with other medications, a careful history of other medications (prescription and over-the-counter) should always be taken. SSRIs can be dangerous if taken with MAOIs, nonsedating antihistamines (e.g., Hismanal), TCAs, and lithium because the SSRIs may increase levels of each.

Problems can also occur if SSRIs are taken with carbamazepine and St. John's Wort (Preston & Johnson, 2009). Even with their drawbacks, SSRIs work and can be an effective tool in the arsenal of treatments for depression.

MAO Inhibitors. MAOIs are also very effective, but they have fallen out of favor because of the strict dietary restrictions associated with their use. MAOIs include phenelzine (Nardil), isocarboxazid (Marplan), and tranylcypromine (Parnate). When taking these medications, patients cannot eat or drink anything with tyramine. Tyramine is by-product of bacterial fermentation, and is common in foods such as red wine and cheese. When these foods are consumed with an MAOI, hypertensive crisis or even death can occur. They are not widely used in the United States, but they may be prescribed if other types have failed. They are also effective in the treatment of atypical depression (Institute for Clinical Systems Improvement, 2000). These medications are enjoying a renaissance of use, however, because if the dietary restrictions are observed, they are safer than TCAs and have fewer side effects (Preston & Johnson, 2009).

Phases of Depression Management With Medication

Management of depression with medication has three main phases (Lesperance & Frasure-Smith, 2000).

Acute Phase. The acute phase occurs during the first six to twelve weeks of the depressive episode. This begins with the first dose and lasts until the patient is asymptomatic (Preston & Johnson, 2009). The objectives during this stage are to rapidly reduce symptoms of depression and monitor patients for the risk of suicide. It is important to evaluate whether the antidepressant prescribed is effective. If it is not, there are two possible explanations: The dose is inadequate or treatment has not been sufficiently lengthy for an adequate response (Institute for Clinical Systems Improvement, 2000). Assessments should include an evaluation of symptoms, work or school productivity, and whether interpersonal relationships have improved.

In this phase, it is also important to talk to patients about what they should expect from medications. Patients who are adequately educated are more likely to comply with treatments because they understand side effects, and have realistic expectations about what medication will do. Preston and Johnson (2009) recommend that the following be part of educating patients about medication use:

1. Medications may take ten to twenty-one days before patients notice a difference in symptoms.
2. When symptoms do improve, it is likely that they will be the ones with a biological basis, such as sleep disturbance. Medications may not help with more psychologically based symptoms such as self-esteem.
3. Treatment is working when patients are sleeping better, have less daytime fatigue, and have some improvement in emotional control.
4. There may be side effects, but these can be managed.
5. The total length of time to be on antidepressants varies for each individual.

6. Antidepressants are not addictive.
7. Do not drink alcohol while on antidepressants as it can block their effectiveness.
8. Never discontinue "cold turkey," as this can cause withdrawal symptoms.
9. Two strategies always improve depression: exercise and reduction of substances that impair sleep, such as caffeine or alcohol.

Continuation Phase. The continuation phase lasts from four to nine months. The objective during this phase is to prevent a relapse of symptoms, which can occur if treatment is terminated during this time (Lesperance & Frasure-Smith, 2000). If symptoms have not improved, or if the patient has relapsed, it is appropriate to reevaluate both the diagnosis and patient compliance. Are there comorbid conditions (especially substance abuse) that are keeping treatments from being effective? Is the medication effective for the patient or should another be tried? Is the patient complying with treatment and taking the medications at the appropriate intervals?

Depression can co-occur with other problems, which may influence the choice of medication. If a patient is not responding well to a treatment regimen, it could be that conditions co-occurring with depression are masking any progress that the patient may be making. Preston and Johnson (2009) recommend the following medications for patients with co-occurring depression and panic attacks: phenelzine, imipramine (Tofranil), fluoxetine, and paroxetine. For patients with chronic pain and depression, they recommend amitriptyline or doxepin (Sinequan).

A larger dose may be needed in some cases, or the patient may need to be on the medication for a longer period. Preston and Johnson (2009) noted that the most common mistake that family physicians make is undermedicating. Generally, the length of an adequate trial is four to six weeks. If the medication is not effective after that time, another medication should be considered. Or, an additional medication could be added to the regimen (Institute for Clinical Systems Improvement, 2000).

Maintenance Phase. This phase should be initiated for patients who have had multiple episodes of depression, who have particularly severe or difficult-to-treat episodes, and are therefore at high risk of recurrence. This phase may be for life in some patients.

COGNITIVE-BEHAVIORAL THERAPY

Addressing Distortions in Thinking

Cognitive-behavioral therapy (CBT) is a highly effective treatment for depression, anxiety, and a host of other conditions. Its central premise is that depression is caused by distortions in thinking. CBT is not replacing negative thoughts with "happy" ones. Rather, it helps patients to identify patterns of negative thoughts and then to judge whether these thoughts are true. CBT helps patients identify distortions in their thinking and replace them with more accurate (and less self-defeating) cognitions (Rupke, Blecke, & Renfrow, 2006).

As described previously (see Chapters 6 and 7), abuse survivors often have cognitive distortions about their own powerlessness, and about the motives and intentions of others. Abuse survivors manifest a wide range of beliefs and strategies to cope with past abuse. In a qualitative analysis of forty interviews with sexual abuse survivors, the authors identified six coping styles that the women manifested (Perrott, Morriss, Martin, & Romans, 1998). These strategies ranged from deliberately suppressing their past experiences to working through them. Some survivors made a conscious effort to "forget" the experiences or put them in the past, while others minimized the experiences' impact on their lives. Some survivors coped by talking to partners and/or mental health professionals or by reading self-help books. Other survivors spoke of their experiences to no one. Strategies that involved survivors processing abuse experiences were more effective than those that suppressed or ignored such experiences.

Efficacy of CBT for Abuse Survivors

Given the number of beliefs about self and others that are affected by past abuse, therapy designed to address these beliefs can be positive. Gorey, Richter, and Snider (2001) studied the effects of group intervention on a sample of sexual abuse survivors. They were compared with a similar group of survivors who were on a waiting list for group therapy. The intervention targeted three specific constructs: inappropriate guilt, hopelessness, and isolation. After completing the fifteen-week group, survivors were significantly less likely to feel guilty or ashamed or to blame themselves for their abuse experiences. They were less likely to feel alone or socially isolated, and they were more likely to feel hopeful about the future and their own ability to do something positive for themselves than survivors who were still on the waiting list.

Self-efficacy beliefs were addressed in a program designed to prevent sexual revictimization in a group of sixty-six women who had been sexually assaulted as teens or adults. Women who participated in the prevention group displayed significant improvement in psychological adjustment and self-efficacy (Marx, Calhoun, Wilson, & Meyerson, 2000). A cognitive approach to therapeutic interventions appears to have had the greatest impact on women's self-efficacy beliefs and personal control. In a group of chemically dependent women, those receiving a cognitive intervention had significant improvement in self-efficacy compared with women who received an experiential approach (Washington, 2001).

In another study, researchers described treatment goals for women who had been sexually abused. These goals included helping women see connections between their past abuse and current behavior, assign appropriate guilt to the perpetrators, develop a positive and healthy sexual identity and attitude toward sex, and ultimately to adopt safer and self-protective sexual practices to limit their exposure to HIV (human immunodeficiency virus) (Parillo, Freeman, Collier, & Young, 2001).

Cognitive approaches may not be appropriate for all abuse survivors, however. If there is hyperactivation of the hypothalamic-pituitary-adrenal (HPA) axis, response to psychotherapy is less effective. In a study of twenty-nine hospitalized patients (Thase et al., 1996), patients with increased levels of urinary-free cortisol responded less to cognitive-behavioral approaches than did those with normal cortisol levels at baseline. Because abnormal HPA activation is an issue among adult survivors, it bears a closer look. Hypercortisolemia is associated with a number of somatic symptoms of depression including anhedonia, weight loss, early-morning waking, electroencephalogram (EEG) sleep abnormalities, and psychomotor disturbance. Hypercortisolemia may cause impaired cognitive function, which may have made it difficult for patients to participate in cognitive therapy. The authors felt that somatic interventions, such as antidepressants and electroconvulsive therapy (ECT), may be necessary in such cases to help "turn down" the HPA function directly.

ALTERNATIVE TREATMENT APPROACHES

Alternative medicine is increasingly popular with the general public, and abuse survivors may want to give some of these techniques a try to help manage their depression. Most are effective for mild-to-moderate depression. Abuse survivors, particularly those who experienced severe abuse, may also require medication to alleviate the symptoms of depression.

But these alternative approaches are good adjuncts to traditional treatments with antidepressants and therapy, and they may be part of an adult survivor's plan to improve overall wellness.

There are other reasons why alternative therapies may appeal to abuse survivors more than traditional forms of treatment:

- With alternative treatments, patients have more control over their own treatment; most of what they need can be purchased over the counter and taken when and where they need it.
- Abuse survivors often have difficulties with authority figures, and practitioners of Western medicine may be perceived as such—another person "in charge" of their bodies. In contrast, practitioners of alternative medicine may encourage more of a team approach to their treatment. Of course, there are many exceptions to these generalizations. But it is helpful to look at this issue from the patient's perspective.
- Alternative medical practitioners often take a more holistic view of health than Western practitioners, and may include more emotional support and a careful medical history as part of their treatment.
- For many chronic conditions, particularly chronic pain syndromes, medications alone are rarely sufficient. Alternative approaches are often tried after patients have had an inadequate benefit from Western medicine.

When talking to a patient, it is important to find out what other types of approaches the patient has been trying. It is particularly important to find out what supplements and herbs a patient may be taking because of potential drug interactions. Most people who consult alternative practitioners do not share this information with their medical practitioners. The clinician will have to ask.

Supplements

Taking vitamin and mineral supplements will not "cure" depression. But supplements are helpful in forming a foundation for good mental health, and they may allow the body to cure itself. People who are depressed are frequently low in B vitamins, and omega-3 fatty acids (especially EPA). Following is a list of supplements that are helpful in depression:

- Omega-3 fatty acids (1,000 mg EPA);
- B-complex;
- B6 (75 mg);
- B12 (100 mcg);
- Folic acid (400 mcg); and
- Choline (150 to 500 mg).

Exercise

Exercise is also effective in alleviating symptoms of depression in both healthy and clinical populations (Blumenthal et al., 2007; Brosse, Sheets, Lett, & Blumenthal, 2002), and it was as effective as sertraline in two randomized clinical trials (Babyak et al., 2000; Blumenthal et al., 2007). Exercise can also be an important adjunct to other treatments; it has the added benefit of improving patients' overall level of fitness. In one study (Kull, 2002), women who were physically active had better mental health, less depression, and better general health. Even low-level physical activity was associated with better mental health.

St. John's Wort

St. John's Wort (SJW) is the most widely used antidepressant in the world. SJW is generally safe, but it can interact with a number of types of prescription medications (Kendall-Tackett, 2010). It has been shown to be as effective as antidepressants in numerous clinical trials, with fewer side effects (Lecrubier, Clerc, Didi, & Kieser, 2002; Van Gurp, Meterissian, Haiek, McCusker, & Bellavance, 2002). SJW takes about four to six weeks to alleviate depression.

Herbal antidepressants have been enjoying a surge of popularity in the United States. Many people are attracted to them because they are natural, frequently cheaper than prescription medications, and generally have fewer side effects. People also like being able to take these without a prescription, thereby exercising more control over their own mental health. (Many physicians are uncomfortable with patients self-medicating, however.) Bear in mind that, natural or not, these substances are medications, and they should be used judiciously.

ANTIDEPRESSANT USE IN PREGNANT AND BREASTFEEDING WOMEN

As described in Chapter 16, abuse survivors are at high risk of depression while pregnant or breastfeeding. A question that often arises is whether it is safe to treat depression in this population, particularly with antidepressants. It frequently comes down to a risk-benefit analysis. Does the risk associated with treatment outweigh the possible benefits? Proponents of antidepressants point out, correctly, that depression during pregnancy is also risky and can lead to premature delivery and other complications. But there are risks associated with antidepressant use during pregnancy, so we cannot be cavalier about these. Finally, it is important to remember that there are risks associated with *not* treating depression.

Medications mothers take are transferred to their infants differently depending on whether mothers take them while pregnant or while breastfeeding. Following is a brief overview of antidepressant transfer to infants during pregnancy and via breast milk, focusing on SSRIs. Researchers know a fair amount about how these medications affect infants after exposure in utero and via breastfeeding. This is a summary of a much larger literature. But it provides a starting place for understanding what we know about medication use in pregnant and postpartum women.

Medication Transfer in Pregnant Women—In Utero Exposure

During pregnancy, medications transfer to babies via the placenta and amniotic fluid. The amount transferred via the placenta is significant and can equal the mother's dose. But medications differ in terms of how much they transfer, and using a medication that transfers in smaller amounts is one strategy for selecting a medication to use during pregnancy. For example, in a study of thirty-eight pregnant women who were taking SSRIs, antidepressant and metabolite concentrations were found in 87 percent of umbilical cord samples. The mean serum ratios ranged from 0.29 to 0.89. The lowest ratios were for sertraline (Zoloft) and paroxetine (Paxil), and the highest for citalopram (Celexa) and fluoxetine (Prozac) (Hendrick et al., 2003).

Risk of Birth Defects. With regard to SSRIs causing birth defects if administered during pregnancy, the Sloane Epidemiology Center Birth Defects Study recently confirmed that that the overall risk of having a child affected by SSRI use was only 0.2 percent (Louik, Lin, Werler, Hernandez-Diaz, & Mitchell, 2007). They did note increased risk of three birth defects with SSRI use in the first trimester: omphalocele and septal defects with sertraline and the heart defect right ventricular outflow tract obstruction with paroxetine. But only 2–5 percent of infants with these defects were exposed to SSRIs.

Discontinuation Syndrome. In neonates, third-trimester exposure can lead to "discontinuation" syndrome due to SSRI withdrawal. Discontinuation syndrome includes acrocynaosis, tachypnea, temperature instability, irritability, and elevated drug levels (Hale, Kendall-Tackett, Cong, Votta, & McCurdy, 2010; Oberlander et al., 2004). Fortunately, these symptoms are generally mild and self-limiting, and they can be managed with supportive care. Severe symptoms are rare, and no reported neonatal deaths have occurred that are attributable to in utero SSRI exposure. Discontinuation syndrome can be distressing to both mothers and babies, but the symptoms are self-limiting, last for twenty-four to forty-eight hours, and do not require further treatment.

Research from our lab also suggests that mothers who continue on the medication while breastfeeding can ease discontinuation symptoms in their infants.

Exposure of Infants via Breast Milk

Infants can also be exposed to maternal medications via breast milk, but the amount of exposure is substantially less than in utero exposure. Some medications are better than others in terms of amount of exposure the infant receives. A recent meta-analysis of sixty-seven studies of antidepressant levels in breastfeeding infants pooled data from 337 research cases, including 238 infants (Weissman et al., 2004). The researchers had access to data on fifteen different antidepressants and their major metabolites. They found that antidepressants were detectable in the breast milk for all the antidepressants they studied. Fluoxetine produced the highest proportion of elevated infant levels and the highest mean infant level (Weissman et al., 2004). Citalopram was also relatively high. Only one infant across studies had an elevated paroxetine level, and that infant had also been exposed prenatally. All other infant paroxetine levels were zero, and this included three infants with prenatal exposure. Maternal dose was highly correlated with infant plasma level for citalopram. The correlation was weak for sertraline. And maternal dose did not predict infant level for fluoxetine, nortriptyline, or paroxetine. Compared with other antidepressants, fluoxetine was more likely to accumulate in breastfeeding infants.

With regard to long-term effects, the authors noted that low or undetectable infant plasma concentrations alone cannot reassure us that the antidepressant will have no effect on the rapidly developing brain and that chronic, low-dose exposure poses a risk. However, they noted that the studies with asymptomatic infants are reassuring. Moreover, they noted that although antenatal exposure differs from exposure via breastfeeding, the antenatal data suggest little or no long-term effects on developmental outcomes. They noted that we must factor in whether there was prenatal exposure as that provides a "loading dose" that far exceeds any exposure from breast milk and can thus distort findings regarding exposure via breast milk (Weissman et al., 2004).

In summary, Weissman et al. noted that breastfeeding infants' exposure to paroxetine, sertraline, and nortriptyline are unlikely to have detectable or elevated plasma drug levels. In contrast, infants exposed to fluoxetine had higher medication levels, especially if they had also been exposed prenatally. Citalopram may lead to elevated levels in some infants, but more data are needed. Although these appear safe for the majority of babies, some adverse effects have been identified through case studies. Therefore, breastfeeding mothers should be advised to watch for any possible signs of adverse reactions including irritability, poor feeding, or uneasy sleep. Premature babies or others with impaired metabolic efficiency should especially be monitored for adverse effects (Weissman et al., 2004).

Summary

Antidepressant medications are not the only option for treating depression. But for individual mothers, they may be the best or most realistic choice. Although there is some risk associated with antidepressant use, the risk of untreated depression may be even greater. All risks and benefits must be carefully weighed for each mother.

CONCLUSIONS

Many adult survivors of childhood abuse suffer from depression. Fortunately, there are a variety of effective treatments. It sometimes is necessary to try a number of different approaches before finding the right combination, but recovery is possible, even when depression is severe. Treating depression will also lower their risk of health problems, such as cardiovascular disease, diabetes, and other illnesses associated with depression.

References

American Psychiatric Association. (2000). *Diagnostic and statistical manual of mental disorders* (4th ed., text rev.). Washington, DC: Author.

Babyak, M., Blumenthal, J. A., Herman, S., Khatri, P., Doraiswamy, M., Moore, K., et al. (2000). Exercise treatment for major depression: Maintenance of therapeutic benefit at 10 months. *Psychosomatic Medicine, 62*, 633–638.

Blumenthal, J. A., Babyak, M. A., Doraiswamy, P. M., Watkins, L., Hoffman, B. M., Barbour, K. A., et al. (2007). Exercise and pharmacotherapy in the treatment of major depressive disorder. *Psychosomatic Medicine, 69*, 587–596.

Brosse, A. L., Sheets, E. S., Lett, M. S., & Blumenthal, J. A. (2002). Exercise and the treatment of clinical depression in adults: Recent findings and future directions. *Sports Medicine, 32*, 741–760.

Gorey, K. M., Richter, N. L., & Snider, E. (2001). Guilt, isolation, and hopelessness among female survivors of childhood sexual abuse: Effectiveness of group work intervention. *Child Abuse and Neglect, 25*, 347–355.

Hale, T. W., Kendall-Tackett, K. A., Cong, Z., Votta, R., & McCurdy, F. (2010). Discontinuation syndrome in newborns whose mothers took antidepressants while pregnant or breastfeeding. *Breastfeeding Medicine, 5*(6), 283–288.

Hendrick, V., Stowe, Z. N., Altshuler, L. L., Hwang, S., Lee, E., & Haynes, D. (2003). Placental passage of antidepressant medications. *American Journal of Psychiatry, 160*(5), 993–996.

Institute for Clinical Systems Improvement. (2000). *Health care guidelines: Major depression in specialty care in adults*. Retrieved from *www.icsi.org*.

Kendall-Tackett, K. A. (2010). *Depression in new mothers: Causes, consequences and treatment options* (2nd ed.). London: Routledge.

Kull, M. (2002). The relationships between physical activity, health status, and psychological well-being of fertility-aged women. *Scandinavian Journal of Medicine and Science of Sports, 12*, 241–247.

Lecrubier, Y., Clerc, G., Didi, R., & Kieser, M. (2002). Efficacy of St. John's wort extract WS 5570 in major depression: A double-blind, placebo-controlled trial. *American Journal of Psychiatry, 159*, 1361–1366.

Lesperance, F., & Frasure-Smith, N. (2000). Depression in patients with cardiac disease: A practical review. *Journal of Psychosomatic Research, 48*, 379–391.

Louik, C., Lin, A. E., Werler, M. M., Hernandez-Diaz, S., & Mitchell, A. A. (2007). First-trimester use of selective serotonin-reuptake inhibitors and the risk of birth defects. *New England Journal of Medicine, 356*, 2675–2683.

Marx, B. P., Calhoun, K. S., Wilson, A. E., & Meyerson, L. A. (2000). Sexual revictimization prevention: An outcome evaluation. *Journal of Consulting and Clinical Psychology, 69*(1), 25–32.

Oberlander, T. F., Misri, S., Fitzgerald, C. E., Kostaras, X., Rurak, D., & Riggs, W. (2004).

Pharmacologic factors associated with transient neonatal symptoms following prenatal psychotropic medication exposure. *Journal of Clinical Psychiatry, 65*(2), 230–237.

Parillo, K. M., Freeman, R. C., Collier, K., & Young, P. (2001). Association between early sexual abuse and adult HIV-risk sexual behaviors among community-recruited women. *Child Abuse and Neglect, 25*, 335–346.

Perrott, K., Morriss, E., Martin, J., & Romans, S. (1998). Cognitive coping styles of women sexually abused in childhood: A qualitative study. *Child Abuse and Neglect, 22*, 1135–1149.

Preston, J., & Johnson, J. (2009). *Clinical psychopharmacology made ridiculously simple* (6th ed.). Miami, FL: MedMaster.

Rupke, S. J., Blecke, D., & Renfrow, M. (2006). Cognitive therapy for depression. *American Family Physician, 73*, 83–86.

Thase, M. E., Dube, S., Bowler, K., Howland, R. H., Myers, J. E., Friedman, E., et al. (1996). Hypothalamic-pituitary-adrenocortical activity and response to cognitive behavior therapy in unmedicated, hospitalized depressed patients. *American Journal of Psychiatry, 153*, 886–891.

Van Gurp, G., Meterissian, G. B., Haiek, L. N., McCusker, J., & Bellavance, F. (2002). St. John's wort or sertraline?: Randomized controlled trial in primary care. *Canadian Family Physician, 48*, 905–912.

Washington, O. G. M. (2001). Using brief therapeutic interventions to create change in self-efficacy and personal control of chemically dependent women. *Archives of Psychiatric Nursing, 15*, 32–40.

Weissman, A. M., Levy, B. T., Hartz, A. J., Bentler, S., Donohue, M., Ellingrod, V. L., et al. (2004). Pooled analysis of antidepressant levels in lactating mothers, breast milk, and nursing infants. *American Journal of Psychiatry, 161*(6), 1066–1078.

Appendix 18.1
Online Resources for Depression

Mayo Clinic
http://www.mayoclinic.com/health/depression/DS00175

The Mayo Clinic offers a comprehensive approach to depression via their online depression self-manager. This includes an assessment for depression, a program to create a depression manager (integrating psychological, medical, and alternative treatments), and a guide to self-care for patients with depression that includes links to support organizations.

National Alliance on Mental Illness (NAMI)
http://www.nami.org/template.cfm?section=Depression

NAMI is a national patient advocacy group for those suffering with serious mental illness. They offer education, support, and referrals to nationwide support groups. They also offer services for families of those with depression, bipolar disorder, dissociative disorders, eating disorders attention deficit hyperactivity disorder, post-traumatic stress disorder, and several other conditions.

Depression and Bipolar Support Alliance
http://www.ndmda.org/depression.html

The NDMDA has recently changed its name to the Depression and Bipolar Support Alliance. It provides information for patients on depression, bipolar disorder, and other types of mood disorders.

Pfizer
http://www.phqscreeners.com/

Pzifer Pharmaceuticals offers a link for depression screening tools that can be used in a primary care setting. This site offers a variety of tools to promote women's health including news alerts and an online library to research health concerns.

Screening for Mental Health, Inc.
http://www.nmisp.org/

Doctor's offices and mental health professionals can sign up to screen for psychiatric conditions. Registered sites receive instruments for screening for depression, PTSD, and other mental illnesses.

Chapter 19

Clinical Management of Posttraumatic Stress Disorder

Posttraumatic stress disorder (PTSD) is a common symptom of childhood abuse, and it can also have a negative impact on health. This chapter provides a brief overview of the assessment and treatment of PTSD. Treatment can take place in a general medical setting, but medical management typically occurs alongside psychotherapy. Even if a practitioner does not provide psychotherapy, it is helpful to understand these techniques to more effectively collaborate with mental health providers. Treatment begins with diagnosis.

DIAGNOSIS OF PTSD

As with depression, the first step in management of PTSD is making a diagnosis. A diagnosis can be difficult to make in a medical setting, but screening questions can help a clinician to decide whether a more in-depth evaluation would be helpful.

Initial Screening

Lange, Lange, and Cabaltica (2000) recommend using the following screening questions in a primary care medical setting:

- Have you ever been physically attacked or assaulted?
- Have you ever had a severe accident?
- Have you ever been in a war or disaster?

These questions are for traumatic events in general, but they can be useful for adult survivors. They may also reveal that a patient has experienced multiple traumatic events. Lange et al. (2000) recommend the use of this screening approach anytime a patient has symptoms of depression or anxiety. Another question they recommend for determining whether a patient has experienced childhood abuse is the following:

- Many people continue to think about frightening aspects of their childhood? Do you?

If you want to ask in more detail about Adverse Childhood Experiences, you can ask questions from the Adverse Childhood Experiences Study (Centers for Disease Control and Prevention, 2010):

☐ **Abuse**

○ ***Emotional Abuse***

- Did a parent or other adult often or very often swear at you, insult you, or put you down?
- Did a parent sometimes, often, or very often act in a way that made you think that you might be physically hurt?

○ ***Physical Abuse***

- Were you sometimes, often, or very often pushed, grabbed, slapped, or having something thrown at you?
- Did you ever get hit so hard that you had marks or were injured?

○ ***Sexual Abuse***

- Did an adult or person at least five years older ever touch or fondle you in a sexual way, or have you touch his or her body in a sexual way?
- Did that person attempt oral, anal, or vaginal intercourse with you?
- Did that person actually have oral, anal, or vaginal intercourse with you?

☐ **Neglect**

○ ***Emotional Neglect***

- Did someone in your family make you feel special or loved?
- Was your family a source of strength, support, and protection?

○ ***Physical Neglect***

- Did you have enough to eat?
- Did your parents' drinking interfere with your care?
- Did you have to wear dirty clothes?
- Was there was someone to take you to the doctor?

☐ **Household Dysfunction**

○ ***Mother Treated Violently***

- Was your mother or stepmother sometimes, often, or very often pushed, grabbed, or slapped?
- Did she have something thrown at her?
- Was she sometimes, often, or very often kicked, bitten, hit with a fist, or hit with something hard?
- Was she ever repeatedly hit over at least a few minutes?
- Was she ever threatened or hurt by a knife or gun?

○ ***Household Substance Abuse***

- Did you live with anyone who was a problem drinker or alcoholic?
- Did you live with anyone who used street drugs?

○ ***Household Mental Illness***

- Was a household member depressed or mentally ill?
- Did a household member attempt suicide?

○ ***Parental Separation or Divorce***

- Were your parents ever separated or divorced?

○ ***Incarcerated Household Member***

- Did a household member ever go to prison?

Although some patients may respond directly to these questions, others may not. Patients may not talk about traumatic events for a number of reasons. They may feel ashamed or embarrassed, especially if they have experienced sexual abuse or assault. Symptoms of PTSD can also wax and wane. You may be asking at a time when symptoms were not posing a problem for the patient, or when numbness or avoidance were the most common manifestation. Finally, PTSD can be latent. Other symptoms such as job difficulties, substance abuse, or problems in relationships might be present, obscuring symptoms of PTSD. It is often challenging to look beyond the presenting problem to the PTSD that is underlying it.

Diagnostic Criteria for PTSD

Screening questions can indicate that patients have experienced traumatic events. However, a formal diagnosis of PTSD is more exacting. According to criteria found in the fourth edition, text revision of *Diagnostic and Statistical Manual of Mental Disorders* (DSM-IV-TR; American Psychiatric Association, 2000), a diagnosis requires a discernible traumatic event, and the victim's response must have included fear, helplessness, or horror. (If the event occurred during childhood, this response may have been disorganized or agitated behavior.) In addition, there must be symptoms in each of the following clusters:

- *Reexperiencing the trauma.* Frequent reexperiencing of the event via nightmares or intrusive thoughts;
- *Avoidance and numbing.* Numbing or lack of responsiveness to or avoidance of current events that remind patients of their trauma; and
- *Hyperarousal.* Persistent symptoms of increased arousal including jumpiness, sleep disturbances, or poor concentration. (Weathers, Keane, & Foa, 2009)

PTSD is acute if the symptoms have been present for less than three months and chronic if the symptoms have been present for three months or more. The onset of PTSD is considered "delayed" if it occurs six months or more after the initial stressor.

Even if patients do not meet full diagnostic criteria for PTSD, they may have PTSD symptoms that can be troublesome. Indeed, Briere and Elliot (1994) note: "Although most child sexual abuse victims do not meet full diagnostic criteria for PTSD, more than 80 percent are reported to have some 'post-traumatic' symptoms" (p. 56).

To make a formal diagnosis, the practitioner may need to refer patients to a clinician who specializes in trauma work. However, it is possible to make a reasonable hypothesis about whether such follow-up is warranted. Lange et al. (2000) suggest that clinicians use the mnemonic DREAM for remembering the diagnostic criteria:

D: is for *detachment* from the event or a more general emotional numbing.

R: is for *reexperiencing* the event. This can be through flashbacks, dreams or intrusive thoughts.

E: is for the *event* itself. Was it sufficient to produce trauma?

A: is for *avoidance*. This may manifest as avoidance of people, places, or things that remind them of the event, or avoiding any thoughts of the event.

M: is for *month*. Symptoms have lasted for at least one month.

Complex PTSD

Complex PTSD is a relatively new diagnosis that is not part of the DSM-IV-TR criteria but is listed as an associated feature of PTSD (Courtois, 2010). Proponents of complex PTSD view this diagnosis as a way to differentiate between patients who have experienced more neutral one-time traumas, such as natural disasters, from patients who have endured ongoing, chronic, and cumulative forms of family trauma, such as childhood or domestic abuse (Courtois, 2010; van der Kolk, 2002; Weathers, et al., 2009). Complex PTSD also applies to people in slave labor camps, abusive hostage situations, or religious cults. Note that many of these symptoms have been described in previous chapters as occurring in survivors of childhood abuse (Courtois, 2010).

- *Behaviors.* Self-destructive behavior, difficulty modulating sexual involvements, excessive risk taking.
- *Cognitions.* Alterations in self-perception including a sense of ineffectiveness (low self-efficacy) or being permanently damaged, suicidal preoccupations, guilt and sense of responsibility (self-blame), shame, a sense that no one can understand, minimizing traumatic effects, despair and hopelessness, loss of previously sustaining beliefs.
- *Emotions.* Affect dysregulation.
- *Social.* Inability to trust, being revictimized, and victimizing others. (Weathers et al., 2009)

Patients with complex PTSD often have difficulties in their relationships with their care providers. These patients may overreact to minor frustrations, and they appear manipulative, difficult, and ungrateful. When faced with real violations, they may dissociate and become paralyzed (van der Kolk, 2002). This interpersonal style can make them more vulnerable to revictimization. Fortunately, most care providers will not take advantage of this vulnerability; unfortunately, some will. Recall Teegen's (1999) findings that 41 percent of a community sample of female sexual abuse survivors had experienced sexual violence one or more times in relationships, at work, or in therapy.

The diagnosis of complex PTSD is not without controversy, however. Some have pointed out that patients who have a diagnosis of complex PTSD have already met criteria for PTSD, and that an additional diagnosis really adds nothing to the picture. It for this reason that complex PTSD was not included in DSM-IV (Friedman, 2001). In contrast, van der Kolk (2002) states that patients with complex PTSD do not respond to standard treatment for PTSD, and indeed, these standard treatments may be harmful. In addition, these patients often have trouble functioning in everyday life and may need assistance with developing coping resources so they can process their traumatic pasts and cope with their current lives. van der Kolk (2002) insists that therapists who do not understand the intricacies of complex PTSD may inadvertently retraumatize these patients.

TREATMENT, GENERALLY

Treatment for PTSD involves a combination of patient education, peer counseling, medications, and psychotherapy. In their book on psychopharmacology, Preston and Johnson (2009) state that the "treatment of choice" for PTSD is psychotherapy (p. 55). Medications can be useful for managing certain symptoms of PTSD, such as hyperarousal or sleep difficulties, and can be used to treat co-occurring depression, anxiety, or other conditions. Patient education and peer counseling provide support and encourage self-care. The combination of all these modalities provides the best overall care, and each is described in this section. Treatment approaches described in this chapter are for adults, consistent with the focus of the book.

Before Treatment Begins

Friedman, Cohen, Foa, and Keane (2009) recommend that diagnosis and careful evaluation precede treatment. First, there must be a formal diagnosis of PTSD and any comorbid conditions. Second, there should be a determination of the most disturbing problem. This may not be the PTSD diagnosis, but it could be something related (e.g., marriage breakup, violence, or depression). The patient's resources and deficiencies should be evaluated. Finally, there should be an evaluation of the patient's motivation to commit to the prescribed course of treatment. Friedman et al. (2009) stated that "Indeed, engaging patients with PTSD in the therapeutic process (or in complying with prescribed medication) is a first and critical stage of the treatment" (p. 620).

Choosing a Treatment Modality

There are currently no clear guidelines for choosing one treatment modality over another, but efficacy should be the first consideration. If efficacy is not at the core, the fundamental principle of treatment is violated (Friedman et al., 2009). Friedman et al. (2009) recommend some other criteria for choosing a treatment for PTSD (p. 362). These criteria include the following:

- Expected efficacy for amelioration of PTSD severity;
- Associated disorders and problems;

- Difficulties, side effects, and negative effects;
- Acceptability and consent;
- Cultural appropriateness;
- Length, cost, and availability of resources;
- Legal, administrative, and forensic implications; and
- Accessibility and acceptability to the family.

TREATMENT MODALITIES

Patient Education

The goal of patient education is to help patients learn the name of their condition, the symptoms, and the rationale for common forms of treatments. Education can be the first component of a treatment plan. It can reassure patients that they are not going "crazy," which many actually fear, and lets them know that they are not alone. The key elements of patient education are described below (Friedman, 2001). Group psychotherapy can also be a useful adjunctive treatment (Friedman et al., 2009).

Normalization. Normalization lets patients know that their symptoms are similar to those experienced by millions of people who have been through traumatic events. This can create a profound sense of relief. Patients learn that there is no stigma to this condition, nor is it a result of their "weakness." Rather, normalization communicates that PTSD is a common human response to trauma.

Removing Self-Blame and Self-Doubt. Many survivors of traumatic events blame themselves for being in harm's way and are ashamed that they did not take some kind of heroic steps to avoid the trauma or get out of the dangerous circumstance. Education can help patients realize that they did the best they could under the circumstances and with the information that was available. Patient education can also help patients evaluate how realistic their heroic fantasies are, and that the "failure" to act was due to the overwhelming nature of the event itself.

Correcting Misunderstandings. Patient education, and education of family members and friends, can help people understand the patient's behaviors in terms of PTSD. Behaviors that seem strange or upsetting can be explained when seen through the patient's experiences. This can help those in a patient's support network to work with, rather than against, treatment goals.

Clinician Credibility. Finally, patient education can help establish clinicians as knowledgeable about PTSD and understanding of what the patients are experiencing, which helps in enlisting patients' cooperation in treatment and can facilitate the development of trust.

The Efficacy of Patient Education. At this point, there has been no study of patient education alone in the treatment of PTSD. This is because education is never used alone. It is always an adjunct to other treatment modalities (Friedman, 2001). However, most clinicians agree that it is an important component of any type of therapeutic approach.

Peer Counseling

Peer counseling uses an approach similar to that of Alcoholic Anonymous; that is, everyone involved in the group has had personal experience with PTSD and wants to take more control over his or her life. Other examples of peer counseling are battered women's shelters and rape crisis centers. The relationships in the peer group are egalitarian, and there is no authority figure, or professional, who leads the group. Peer counselors often serve as role models for new clients and demonstrate that it is possible to move beyond traumatic experiences and do something positive with their lives (Friedman, 2001).

Peer counseling has really not been studied for its effectiveness because the very nature of the peer group (open only to those who have had a traumatic experience) tends to limit professional involvement. However, there is anecdotal and clinical information that indicates that these groups can have a positive effect on participants and can be a useful component of treatment (Friedman, 2001).

Psychotherapy

When people are traumatized, they develop a conditioned response that pairs the traumatic event with certain environmental cues (e.g., sights, sounds, and smells) and bodily sensations (e.g., pain). Traumatized people also develop beliefs associated with the trauma, such as that they are helpless and vulnerable and people in the world are out to harm them. This is known as fear conditioning. In psychotherapy for PTSD, there are two specific goals. The first is to unlearn the conditioned response to cues that trigger PTSD symptoms. The second is to address cognitions about themselves and others that accompany PTSD.

As described earlier, psychotherapy is generally the treatment of choice for people with PTSD (Friedman et al., 2009; Preston & Johnson, 2009). There are many types of psychotherapy available, and most of these require specialized training. However, even if a professional does not practice psychotherapy, it is helpful to know about the particular methods used to treat PTSD. Two of the most effective individual treatments are cognitive-behavioral therapy and eye-movement desensitization and reprocessing. These techniques are described in this section.

Cognitive-Behavioral Therapy. In the wake of traumatic events, the body and mind become conditioned to respond to certain stimuli in a fearful way, and to maintain maladaptive beliefs. Cognitive-behavioral therapy (CBT) is designed to counteract conditioned fear responses and to normalize abnormal thoughts, behaviors, and feelings of patients with PTSD. CBT is the most studied intervention for PTSD, and all clinical guidelines recognize its effectiveness as a treatment modality (Friedman et al., 2009). There are several types of CBT; some are more effective than others. Three popular forms of CBT are exposure therapy, cognitive therapy, and stress-inoculation training.

Exposure Therapy. Exposure therapy is specifically designed to alleviate the conditioned emotional response of the traumatic event to traumatic stimuli. After a traumatic event, patients naturally tend to avoid any memories of it, or any stimuli that reminds them of their trauma. However, when patients avoid processing their trauma, this avoidance inhibits their recovery. Exposure therapy forces trauma survivors to confront these memories, thereby lessening their hold on patients (Foa & Cahill, 2002).

Exposure therapy begins when patients are asked to imagine the traumatic event. Patients who have experienced multiple or continuous traumatic events (such as childhood abuse) are asked to imagine the worst event that they can remember completely. Patients are asked to describe what happened and their thoughts and feelings that occurred during the trauma repeatedly in a single session (Foa & Cahill, 2002). During their narratives, patients are asked to report their level of distress every ten minutes. Initially, most patients are highly distressed. However, as they repeat their stories, their level of distress tends to decrease. If treatment has been successful, patients can confront their traumatic pasts without triggering PTSD symptoms, especially intrusive thoughts or hyperarousal. It also helps patients to not generalize their anxiety to other situations that are actually safe but appear similar to the dangerous situation they were in.

Exposure therapy helps patients master their fears and counters the belief that they are weak or incompetent (Foa & Cahill, 2002). This form of treatment is highly effective and has had higher rates of success than supportive counseling (Foa & Cahill, 2002; Friedman, 2001). However, van der Kolk (2002) cautions that too much exposure to traumatic memories can backfire and actually precipitate PTSD symptoms such as hyperarousal and sensitization. It is important that exposure to the traumatic event not reactivate full-blown symptoms of "pain, dissociation, and helplessness. . . . [but] instead should help patients to be fully present in the here and now without the residual dissociation and/or hyperarousal characteristic of PTSD" (p. 149).

Cognitive Therapy. As described in earlier chapters, cognitive therapy addresses distortions in thinking. Adult survivors often see the world as a dangerous place and see themselves as helpless (Foa & Cahill, 2002; Friedman, 2001). Unfortunately, these beliefs can become a self-fulfilling prophecy; a survivor who feels helpless is at increased risk for repeated victimization. Also, mistrustful beliefs about others can disrupt social relationships and have a negative impact on health.

The goal of cognitive therapy is to help patients identify these automatic thoughts and replace them with more accurate ones (Foa & Cahill, 2002). This form of therapy is also highly effective in reducing symptoms of PTSD (Friedman, 2001).

Stress-Inoculation Training. Stress-inoculation training (SIT) uses a combination of methods to help survivors cope with anxiety, trauma-related stimuli, and threatening situations. SIT is based on social-learning theory, which states that traumatic events create behavioral, social, and cognitive fear responses. SIT uses classical conditioning techniques to overcome the pairing of fear with neutral stimuli and teach techniques that can reduce fear (Foa & Cahill, 2002). It includes relaxation techniques, biofeedback, cognitive restructuring, and assertiveness training to help patients deal more effectively in social relationships (Friedman, 2001).

Though relaxation techniques alone have not been effective in dealing with PTSD symptoms, they are helpful in combination with these other techniques. SIT is as effective as exposure therapy for reducing PTSD symptoms, and these improvements last over time (Friedman, 2001).

Eye-Movement Desensitization and Reprocessing. Eye-movement desensitization and reprocessing (EMDR) is another treatment that has proven effective for many patients, and most (but not all) clinical practice guidelines consider it an evidence-based treatment for PTSD (Friedman et al., 2009). It is based on the hypothesis that saccadic eye movements can reprogram the brain, and therefore can be used to help alleviate the emotional impact of trauma. (Saccadic eye movements are those quick eye movements that jump from one fixation point to another.)

During EMDR treatment, patients imagine a traumatic memory, or any negative emotions associated with that memory. Then patients are asked to articulate a belief that is incompatible with their previous memory (e.g., concerning their personal worth). While patients are remembering this event, they are asked use their eyes to follow the clinician's fingers, which are making rapid movements. During treatment, patients are asked to rate the strength of both the traumatic memory and the counteracting positive beliefs (Friedman, 2001).

Studies have demonstrated that this method of treatment is effective and has superior results to psychodynamic or supportive therapies. In examining the results of a number of different studies, 50–70 percent of patients no longer met criteria for PTSD after receiving EMDR treatment. In contrast, only 20–50 percent of patients who received supportive therapy no longer met PTSD criteria (Friedman, 2001). However, studies on the efficacy of EMDR have some methodological limitations, including non-blind evaluations, lack of pretreatment diagnosis via a valid measure, and small sample sizes. Nevertheless, initial data suggest that this is a promising approach for the treatment of chronic PTSD (Foa & Cahill, 2002).

Van der Kolk (2002) states that EMDR has several important advantages over exposure therapy in the treatment of PTSD. First, EMDR is easier to "dose" than exposure therapy, in that patients are asked to indicate the moment they have an emotional response to the memory and "stay there" to process the memory using eye movements. Because patients control the amount of exposure, they do not get the extremes of arousal that are possible with exposure therapy. The second advantage is that patients do not have to describe their thoughts to clinicians but are only asked to report on changes in emotional arousal and somatic sensations. This can be especially helpful if traumatic memories are accompanied by guilt and shame, which is frequently the case. Finally, EMDR can allow treatment to proceed in cases in which patients have no words or cannot articulate what happened to them.

Interestingly, the exact mechanism for how these changes are brought about remains unclear. The eye movements do not appear to have any impact on results when treatment is offered with or without eye movements (Friedman, 2001; van der Kolk, 2002). Some have hypothesized that the reason this treatment works has to do with its impact on underlying cognitions, making it a form of cognitive-behavioral therapy. Proponents of EMDR strongly disagree (Friedman, 2001).

The Efficacy of Psychotherapy. Overall, it appears that CBT is the most effective treatment for PTSD. Of the forms of cognitive-behavioral therapy, exposure therapy has the best empirical support (Foa & Cahill, 2002; Friedman et al., 2009). EMDR is also effective in treating all three clusters of symptoms and can be a useful addition to treatment regimens (Friedman, 2001). SIT has also proven effective for the treatment of rape-related PTSD. Interestingly, combining psychotherapy treatments does not increase their effectiveness and may actually lessen the effectiveness of the individual treatment (Foa & Cahill, 2002). Exposure therapy appears to be most effective for those with low levels of functioning before beginning treatment, whereas SIT is helpful for patients with high levels of anxiety (Foa & Cahill, 2002). However, van der Kolk (2002) cautions that, particularly in the case of complex PTSD, there are still many questions about what is the optimal treatment. He states that what appears to be most important is to give patients a sense of mastery that will allow them to live in the present rather than the past, and to no longer be held captive by their memories.

Medications

Medications are another form of treatment for PTSD and can be an important adjunct to psychotherapy, peer support, and patient education. Medications can significantly reduce symptoms of PTSD. But there is no medication so far that was developed with the unique pathophysiology of PTSD in mind. At the present time, remission rates from medications alone are far less than they are with cognitive-behavioral therapy. Nevertheless, some medications are useful in managing symptoms or comorbid disorders (Friedman et al., 2009).

Empirical support for medication use is limited. Mellman (2002) describes a number of issues that make clinical research difficult to conduct with PTSD patients. One problem is that research designs often exclude patients with comorbid conditions. But because PTSD tends to be highly comorbid, patients who end up in clinical trials often bear little resemblance to patients we are likely to see in clinical practice. In addition, patients in clinical trials are often taking only one medication, whereas it is common to combine medications in clinical practice, and there is little research that documents the efficacy of combined medications. Finally, there is little research that documents the efficacy or provides clinical guidelines for combining medication and psychotherapy, even though the combination of medication and psychotherapy is one of the most common forms of treatment. Are these effective together? Does the combination detract from either form of treatment? At what point in the treatment should medications be introduced? These are questions that have not yet been addressed by controlled clinical trials. Nor have there been empirical studies that can guide treatment decisions about how to combine these treatments and in what order or sequence.

In the absence of empirically based guidelines, three clinical criteria can be used to make judgments about when to use medications (Mellman, 2002). First, there should be an explicit rationale for the use of each medication. Second, medications can augment psychotherapy when there has been an unacceptable level of response to psychotherapy alone, or when symptoms persist after psychotherapy. Third, medications may also be tried when comorbid symptoms are so prominent that they are limiting the effectiveness of psychotherapy, or keeping patients from participating in psychotherapy at all. However, Mellman (2002) cautions that medications cannot be presented to patients in such a way that they appear as an afterthought because patients are less likely to comply if they view medications as simply add-ons. Following are the most common types of medications used to treat PTSD.

Antidepressants. Antidepressants are a key part of treatment of PTSD in that they address not only PTSD symptoms but also comorbid depression and obsessive-compulsive disorder (OCD). The best evidence supports the use of selective serotonin reuptake inhibitors (SSRIs) and serotonin/norepinephrine reuptake inhibitors (SNRIs) as first-line drugs for PTSD (International Society for Traumatic Stress Studies, 2009).

Selective Serotonin Reuptake Inhibitors. SSRIs address all three classes of symptoms: intrusive thoughts, avoidance and numbing, and hyperarousal (Friedman, 2001). Of the SSRIs, fluoxetine (Prozac) and sertraline (Zoloft) have been most successful, although higher doses may be required for the treatment of PTSD than for the treatment of depression (Preston & Johnson, 2001).

SSRIs and SNRIs also treat depression, panic disorder, and OCD (Friedman, 2001). For patients with comorbid alcoholism, sertraline reduces the amount of alcohol consumed. Fluvoxamine (Luvox) can help with both obsessional thoughts and insomnia (Lange, et al., 2000).

These medications have some significant side effects, however, that patients often find intolerable, including insomnia, restlessness, nausea, decreased appetite, nervousness, and anxiety. Some of the most troubling symptoms are the sexual side effects, which include decreased libido, sexual dysfunction, and anorgasmia (Friedman, 2001). Some of these side effects can be managed with the addition of other medications to the regimen.

Tricyclic Antidepressants. According to Sutherland and Davidson (1994), the tricyclic antidepressants (TCAs) imipramine (Tofranil), desipramine (Norpramin), and amitriptyline (Elavil) have an established track record of efficacy in the treatment of PTSD. However, Lange et al. (2000) noted that these medications have minimal effects on arousal or avoidance symptoms, and therefore they recommend the SSRIs over the TCAs.

TCAs reduce intrusive thoughts and recollections. They also treat any co-occurring depression, produce an overall improvement in symptoms, and may help with panic symptoms. Imipramine and amitriptyline have been shown to be moderately effective. Desipramine has not proven effective (International Society for Traumatic Stress Studies, 2009). However, their side effects (such as dry mouth, rapid pulse, blurred vision, constipation, and daytime sedation) may lead to low compliance with treatment (Friedman, 2001).

Monoamine Oxidase Inhibitors (MAOIs). MAOIs are another class of antidepressants that includes phenelzine (Nardil) and tranylcypromine (Parnate). These medications are helpful in managing symptoms of reexperiencing, avoidance, and insomnia. They can also reduce the number of nightmares that patients experience. However, these medications are not widely used in the United States because they have strict dietary limitations. Patients cannot consume anything with tyramine, which is found in many aged foods, including cheese and wine, or any alcohol or illegal drugs.

MAOIs can also have dangerous interactions with other prescription medications including SSRIs. Given the high rate of comorbid substance abuse in patients with PTSD, these medications are often contraindicated for this population. But they may be tried if other medications have failed to bring relief in symptoms (International Society for Traumatic Stress Studies, 2009; Lange et al., 2000).

Benzodiazepines. Benzodiazepines have a long history of use among patients with PTSD. However, they are contraindicated for PTSD because of the potential for addiction, the possible exacerbation of depressive symptoms, and possible excessive daytime sedation (International Society for Traumatic Stress Studies, 2009).

Antiadrenergic Agents. Antidrenergic agents work by blocking norepinephrine receptors and include clonidine (Catapres), guanfacine (Tenex), and propranolol (Inderal). They are frequently prescribed to control hypertension, but in patients with PTSD, they also control symptoms of arousal, reexperiencing, and possibly dissociative states (International Society for Traumatic Stress Studies, 2009). Prazosin reduces traumatic nightmares, and possibly overall PTSD symptom severity. Propranolol has shown promise as a treatment for children, and could be used as a prophylactic agent to prevent later symptoms of PTSD (International Society for Traumatic Stress Studies, 2009).

These medications also have some significant side effects. They may cause dangerous decreases in blood pressure. Propranolol may also produce depressive symptoms, especially psychomotor slowing; thus they are contraindicated in patients with comorbid depression (Friedman, 2001).

Anticonvulsants. Anticonvulsants are another category of medications used in the treatment of PTSD. They do not have empirical support from randomized clinical trials testing their efficacy with PTSD (Bisson, 2002), but they do have a history of clinical use. They are not recommended for PTSD at this time (International Society for Traumatic Stress Studies, 2009).

Atypical Antipsychotics. Atypical antipsychotics can be used to augment SSRIs if patients are having a partial response. They can also be used with other treatment-refractory patients (International Society for Traumatic Stress Studies, 2009).

Phases of Treatment With Medications

Management of symptoms of PTSD with medications has several phases that begin with selecting the appropriate medication regimen and continue as long as there are symptoms.

Selection of a Medication Regimen. When first considering medications for a patient with PTSD, Lange et al. (2000) and Friedman (2001) recommend starting with a trial of SSRIs, since they address the broadest range of symptoms. If insomnia is a problem, trazodone can be added to the regimen. Hyperarousal can be treated with clonidine. The combination of the three medications (SSRIs, trazodone, and clonidine) can alleviate the majority of symptoms for many patients with PTSD.

For patients who cannot tolerate SSRIs, Friedman (2001) recommends a trial of TCAs because these are safer to administer than MAOIs. Beyond these recommendations, guidelines are unclear as to which medications might be most helpful. In this case, it is helpful to consider comorbid symptoms. Friedman makes recommendations for five types of symptoms:

- *For irritability, aggressiveness, mood lability, impulsivity, or suicidal behavior.* SSRIs are most effective for these types of symptoms.
- *For hyperreactivity or excessive arousal.* SSRIs supplemented with clonidine, guanfacine, or propranolol are often helpful. The clinician will know within two weeks whether these adrenergic medications are going to be effective. Most medications take at least eight weeks before their effectiveness can be evaluated.
- *For aggression, lability, or impulsivity.* The anticonvulsants are often helpful.
- *For comorbid major depression.* Use an SSRI, TCA, or MAOI. Avoid propranolol because it can produce symptoms of depression.
- *For comorbid substance abuse.* Sertraline has been shown to reduce both symptoms of PTSD and alcohol consumption. Avoid MAOIs because there are dangerous interactions between these medications and common substances of abuse including alcohol and cocaine.

Initial Management With Medications. After deciding on a medication regimen, the next goal is stabilization (Sutherland & Davidson, 1994). PTSD symptoms do not remit easily, and it can be eight to ten weeks before patients notice any difference in symptoms. During this stage, frequent contact should be made with the patient, and an anti-anxiety medication may be temporarily added to reduce symptoms.

Maintenance. The next phase is maintenance. This stage can last anywhere from one year to indefinitely. The need for changes in the medication regimen may vary by whether patients are in psychotherapy and how they are dealing with traumatic material. Exploring new areas of their traumatic pasts may lead to an exacerbation in symptoms. In this case, an increased dose of medication is required to keep symptoms under control. By reducing the symptoms that patients are experiencing, they can continue in therapy working through these issues.

Long-Term Stabilization. Once symptoms have been stabilized long term, you might consider the discontinuation of medication. This should not be done while the patient is still undergoing psychotherapy and uncovering traumatic material unless the patient demonstrates an ability to handle these thoughts and feelings without medication. A slow taper is the most appropriate method for reducing or discontinuing medications. This gives you a chance to monitor for the return of PTSD or symptoms of drug withdrawal (Sutherland & Davidson, 1994).

If the patient starts experiencing symptoms again, medication can be restarted or continued. Even when patients have completely weaned off of medications, they may require a brief course when they face a significant life stressor such as an illness or death in the family, birth of a child, or a major social disruption such as a move or marital breakup.

SUMMARY

PTSD is a complex web of physiological, behavioral, social, and cognitive sequelae. Treatment approaches mirror this complexity. As with many other aspects of health and wellness, a holistic approach is likely to yield the best results. And clinicians are more likely to be successful if they work with a team that can provide social support, patient education, psychotherapy, life skills training, and medications. Although chronic PTSD can be difficult to treat, particularly if it is related to long-term and severe abuse, it is possible to improve symptoms and help survivors regain their lost sense of efficacy,

References

American Psychiatric Association. (2000). *Diagnostic and statistical manual of mental disorders* (4th ed., text rev.). Washington, DC: Author.

Bisson, J. (2002). Posttraumatic stress disorder. In S. Barton (Ed.), *Clinical evidence: Mental health* (pp. 120-126). London: BMJ.

Briere, J. N., & Elliot, D. M. (1994). Immediated and long-term impacts of child sexual abuse. *The Future of Children, 4*, 54-69.

Centers for Disease Control and Prevention. (2010). *Adverse childhood experiences: Data and statistics.* Available online at: *http://www.cdc.gov/ace/prevalence.htm#ACED.*

Courtois, C. (2010). *Healing the incest wound: Adult survivors in therapy* (2nd ed.). New York: W.W. Norton.

Foa, E. B., & Cahill, S. P. (2002). Specialized treatment for PTSD: Matching survivors to the appropriate modality. In R. Yehuda (Ed.), *Treating trauma survivors with PTSD* (pp. 43–62). Washington, DC: American Psychiatric Association Press.

Friedman, M. J. (2001). *Posttraumatic stress disorder: The latest assessment and treatment strategies*. Kansas City, MO: Compact Clinicals.

Friedman, M. J., Cohen, J. A., Foa, E. B., & Keane, T. M. (2009). Integration and summary. In E. B. Foa, T. M. Keane, M. J. Friedman & J. A. Cohen (Eds.), *Effective treatments for PTSD: Practice guidelines from the International Society for Traumatic Stress Studies* (pp. 617–642). New York: Guilford Press.

International Society for Traumatic Stress Studies. (Ed.). (2009). *Effective treatments for PTSD: Psychopharmacology for adults (Guideline 6)*. New York: Guilford Press.

Lange, J. T., Lange, C. L., & Cabaltica, R. B. G. (2000). Primary care treatment of posttraumatic stress disorder. *American Family Physician, 62*, 1035–1040, 1046.

Mellman, T. A. (2002). Rationale and role for medication in the comprehensive treatment of PTSD. In R. Yehuda (Ed.), *Treating trauma survivors with PTSD* (pp. 63–74). Washington, DC: American Psychiatric Association Press.

Preston, J., & Johnson, J. (2009). *Clinical psychopharmacology made ridiculously simple* (6th ed.). Miami, FL: MedMaster.

Sutherland, S. M., & Davidson, J. R. T. (1994). Pharmacotherapy for posttraumatic stress disorder. *Psychiatric Clinics of North America, 17*, 409–423.

Teegen, F. (1999). Childhood sexual abuse and long-term sequelae. In A. Maercker, M. Schutzwohl, & Z. Solomon (Eds.), *Posttraumatic stress disorder: A lifespan developmental perspective* (pp. 97–112). Seattle, WA: Hogrefe & Huber.

van der Kolk, B. A. (2002). Assessment and treatment of complex PTSD. In R. Yehuda (Ed.), *Treating trauma survivors with PTSD* (pp. 127–156). Washington, DC: American Psychiatric Association Press.

Weathers, F. W., Keane, T. M., & Foa, E. B. (2009). Diagnosis and treatment of adults. In E. B. Foa, T. M. Keane, M. J. Friedman, & J. A. Cohen (Eds.), *Effective treatments for PTSD: Practice guidelines from the International Society for Traumatic Stress Studies* (2nd ed.) (pp. 23–61). New York: Guilford Press.

Appendix 19.1
Online Resources for Posttraumatic Stress Disorder

National Center for PTSD
www.ncptsd.org

The National Center for PTSD offers a great deal of information on PTSD, including full-text research and clinical articles and information on assessment tools and how to order them. This is an outstanding site with a wealth of information.

The American Psychological Association Division of Trauma Psychology
www.apatraumadivision.org

The Division of Trauma Psychology is the official trauma group within the American Psychological Association. This division publishes the journal *Psychological Trauma* and a quarterly newsletter with short articles. The newsletter is available on its site. Nonpsychologists can join under Professional Affiliate status, and there is a special rate for students.

International Society for Traumatic Stress Studies
www.istss.org

The International Society for Traumatic Stress Studies is the premier multidisciplinary professional organization for those interested in traumatic stress. Its site provides links to articles, resources, and patient information. ISTSS publishes *Journal of Traumatic Stress.*

AtHealth.com
www.athealth.com

AtHealth.com offers links to full-text articles for practitioners on a variety of topics related to PTSD, including treatment of PTSD in primary care and treatment guidelines for children with PTSD. AtHealth.com also offers a free e-mail subscription to its newsletters on various aspects of mental health and patient fact sheets on a wide variety of conditions.

National Alliance on Mental Illness
www.nami.org

NAMI has links to expert guidelines on the treatment of PTSD, including the full-text Expert Consensus Guidelines on the Treatment of PTSD. NAMI is a national patient advocacy group for those suffering with serious mental illness. It offers education, support, and referrals to nationwide support groups. NAMI also offers services for families of those with depression, bipolar disorder, dissociative disorders, eating disorders, attention deficit/hyperactivity disorder, PTSD, and several other conditions. This is an outstanding site.

The Trauma Center
www.traumacenter.org

The Trauma Center is a treatment faculty for psychological trauma in Massachusetts under the directorship of Dr. Bessel van der Kolk. The Trauma Center offers a variety of trauma articles online It has also put together a package of reasonably priced assessment tools for various types of trauma, including complex PTSD. These instruments can be ordered through the Trauma Center's web site.

Chapter 20

Basic Pain Management in a Health Care Setting

Chronic pain is a complex interplay between physical, psychological, cognitive, and behavioral factors (Toner, Segal, Emmott, & Myran, 2000). As described in Chapters 14 and 15, chronic pain is a part of life for many adult survivors. It is not unusual for survivors to have one or several chronic pain symptoms, and these symptoms may be difficult to treat. This chapter outlines the basics of pain management that can take place in a health care setting and discusses difficulties in treating chronic pain, clinicians' beliefs about it, and the range of treatment modalities.

It is important to be realistic about pain management. Chronic pain is rarely completely eliminated. Patients who expect to be pain free will be frustrated and disappointed. However, it is possible to improve daily pain levels, as well as the frequency, severity, and duration of flares of painful symptoms. In so doing, many patients can resume their normal lives (Marcus, 2000). (For a list of resources for pain management, see Appendix 20.1.)

WHY PAIN IS DIFFICULT TO TREAT

Pain is subjective by its very nature and can only be measured indirectly, which presents a challenge for many clinicians. Moreover, pain severity is only weakly associated with self-reported disability or underlying physical impairment. Disability due to pain is also highly subjective. It can be explained by both psychosocial and biomedical factors. And, indeed, psychological factors are often more important than physical factors in the prediction of future disability, especially beliefs, appraisals, and coping strategies (Main, Richards, & Fortune, 2000). Zatura (1998) makes a similar observation. In cases of rheumatoid and osteoarthritis, only 15–20 percent of levels of pain and limitation of activity can be predicted from physical findings such as joint swelling and x-rays of damaged joints.

MANAGEMENT OF CHRONIC PAIN

Chronic pain is best managed using a biopsychosocial approach. Psychological and social factors influence the impact of disabling conditions, levels of distress, and patient outcomes. How people perceive their illness can have a great impact on their adjustment to it (Main et al., 2000).

Assessment

Assessment of chronic pain is challenging, but it is the first step in pain management. According to Weisberg and Clavel (1999), several factors should be taken into consideration. First, of course, the clinician must assess the initial pain complaint. Next, the clinician should chronicle previous attempts at treatment, as well as the patient's prior history of use of medical services. Then, any comorbid psychiatric and physical symptoms should be assessed, especially the presence of other pain syndromes. Patients should be asked about what exacerbates or relieves their symptoms.

Treatment Team

Treatment of complex chronic pain is best handled by a team of health care providers. Chronic pain treatment involves weekly to monthly visits for a period of six to twelve months. The clinician must allow sufficient time with these patients to hear their concerns and educate them about their condition. Patients with chronic pain may also call frequently for reassurance. The team approach helps prevent provider burnout because there are others involved in patient care (American Pain Foundation, 2008; Weisberg & Clavel, 1999).

Weisberg and Clavel (1999) recommend that the following list of professionals be involved in the treatment of chronic pain:

- A physician specializing in chronic pain. This physician can be from a variety of specialties including internal medicine, family practice, anesthesiology, neurology, or rehabilitation medicine.
- A clinical health psychologist.
- A physical therapist.

Other specialists may be added to the team as needed and may include a dentist, allergist, or psychiatrist. Depending on the primary pain syndrome, a gastroenterologist, rheumatologist, or gynecologist can also be added to the team. The goal for the team is to promote gradual change in patients that moves them toward compliance with treatment, self-efficacy, self-responsibility, and self-care.

Barriers to Treatment

Even with a team approach, some patients do not seem to get better. In such cases, it can be helpful to determine whether there are any barriers to treatment present. These barriers include substance abuse, psychological disorders, and overwhelming life stresses above and beyond the pain syndrome. Two other barriers are ongoing litigation and lack of motivation to change (Weisberg & Clavel, 1999).

Not surprisingly, many abuse survivors have complex chronic pain, which is more difficult to treat. Factors that distinguish between simple and complex pain are some of the very things described in previous chapters as being more common in abuse survivors. These factors are multiple pain syndromes and medical problems, pain duration of longer than six months, frequent health care visits and medication use, significant lifestyle disturbance, significant deconditioning, and a history of multiple treatment failures (Weisberg & Clavel, 1999).

Even when these barriers are present, there are effective techniques for pain management. The next section describes the two major types of treatment modalities available to pain patients: pharmacological and nonpharmacological. Both are necessary to effectively treat chronic pain.

PHARMACOLOGICAL TREATMENT OF CHRONIC PAIN

Medications are a significant part of the treatment of patients with chronic pain. Medication provides baseline pain relief, enabling patients to participate in self-care and rehabilitation (Weisberg & Clavel, 1999). Medications for chronic pain fall into three basic classes.

Nonsteroidal Anti-Inflammatory Drugs

Nonsteroidal anti-inflammatory drugs (NSAIDs) are a widely used class of medications in the treatment of pain (American Chronic Pain Association, 2012). They are available in both over-the-counter and prescription strengths and work by blocking the action of the COX-2 enzyme. Traditional NSAIDs also block the production of COX-1, which protects the mucous lining of the stomach. Not surprisingly, a major side effect of these medications is gastrointestinal bleeding. The newer NSAIDs work selectively on the COX-2 enzyme, and they are theoretically gentler on the stomach than older NSAIDs.

On the downside, NSAIDs have a ceiling effect and only are effective for mild to moderate pain. Side effects of these medications also limit how long they can be used. Ulcers occur in 2–4 percent of NSAID users, and as many as 2 patients per 1,000 can develop end-stage renal disease after daily use of NSAIDs for five years or more (Marcus, 2000). The newer COX-2 inhibitors are also expensive because generic equivalents are not yet available. Some insurers refuse to pay for these more expensive medications. And the long-term safety of these new medications has not yet been demonstrated.

Narcotics

Narcotics, or opioids, are an important type of medication in the management of both acute and chronic pain (American Chronic Pain Association, 2012). They bind to the opioid receptors in the brain. For chronic pain, long-acting narcotics are frequently used. Long-acting narcotics last for eight to ten hours and include methadone, morphine sulfate continuous (MS contin), long-acting oxycodone (Oxycontin), and fentanyl (Duragesic). These will not create a "high" when used in the recommended dose. Short-acting drugs typically last four hours, are used for acute pain (such as postsurgical pain), and include Vicodin and Percocet (Allen, 1996).

With narcotics, there is always the concern about addiction, and given the tendency toward addiction in some adult survivors, this concern is realistic. There have also been some high-profile cases of people abusing pain medications, such as Vicodin and Oxycontin. This tendency toward addiction does not completely rule out the use of such medications, but they should be used cautiously in patients who have a history of substance abuse or addictive behavior (American Chronic Pain Association, 2012; Marcus, 2000; Schneider, 2001). Addiction in chronic pain patients is rare, but it does occur. Some behaviors that indicate possible addiction are ongoing abuse of other substances, forging prescriptions, getting medications from other sources, multiple incidents of prescription loss, and unsanctioned increase in dose.

Medication contracts are often helpful for patients taking narcotics. A medication contract describes the specific regimen in detail, including dose and timing of medications. Patients agree to adhere to the recommended course of treatment, take medications at the intervals the doctor recommends (e.g., twice a day), not hoard medication, seek medication from other sources, or increase their dose without approval.

Timed doses are also important when using potentially addictive medications (Schneider, 2001). Patients using this method take medications continuously rather than waiting until they feel pain. If patients wait for symptoms, they start "chasing pain" and may require a larger dose to get it back under control. Schneider also stresses the importance of adequate pain medication so that patients are not compelled to "drug seek" because their medication dose is inadequate to control their symptoms. He encourages staff to maintain open communication with patients so that they know when a patient is being inadequately medicated. Finally, he recommends that practitioners use long-acting pain medication for the scheduled medication regimens and short-acting medications for breakthrough pain.

Antidepressant Medications

Antidepressants are an important class of drugs to treat chronic pain (American Chronic Pain Association, 2012). The doses are substantially lower than those prescribed for depression (approximately one-third to one-half), and antidepressants work faster for pain than they do for depression. Antidepressants do not work equally well for different kinds of pain. They are more effective with conditions such as headache, fibromyalgia, and neuropathic pain. They are less effective with pain due to injury (American Chronic Pain Association, 2012).

Two possible explanations have been offered for why antidepressants are effective for pain management:

1. Antidepressants increase the levels of the neurotransmitters norepinephrine and serotonin, which increase pain control. Medications that increase norepinephrine appear to more effective in controlling pain (American Chronic Pain Association, 2012).
2. Antidepressants stabilize sleep. Sleep disturbances are common in pain patients, and lack of sufficient stage 4 sleep has also been found to increase pain.

There are three major classes of antidepressants found to be effective in pain management: tricyclics, selective serotonin reuptake inhibitors (SSRIs), and selective norepinephrine reuptake inhibitors (SNRIs). Tricyclics are an older class of medication and include amitriptyline (Elavil), imipramine (Tofranil), desipramine (Norpramin), and nortriptyline (Pamelor). Their side effects include dry mouth, weight gain, and sedation. Of these, Elavil is the most effective for the treatment of pain, but it also is the most sedating and has the most side effects. Pamelor and Norpramin have fewer side effects but are also less effective (Schneider, 2001). Tricyclics in dosages between 75 and 200 mg per day can be expected to relieve pain in 55–67 percent of patients (American Chronic Pain Association, 2012; Marcus, 2000).

The SSRIs are newer medications with dosing regimens that are less complicated. They also have a better side effect profile, but they do have side effects, the most notorious of which are sexual. Some patients become agitated on these medications, and the medications can cause insomnia. On the other hand, for patients with overwhelming fatigue, these medications can provide a needed "boost." This class includes fluoxetine (Prozac), sertraline (Zoloft), paroxetine (Paxil), and citalopram (Celexa).

The third class of medications is the mixed SNRIs. The SNRIs commonly used in pain management include duloxetine, venlafaxine, milnacipran, and buproprion. All have been shown to treat various pain syndromes, including fibromyalgia and diabetic peripheral neuropathy (American Chronic Pain Association, 2012).

NONPHARMACOLOGICAL MANAGEMENT OF CHRONIC PAIN

Because medications alone are rarely sufficient, it is necessary to approach pain with mind-body techniques, and that includes nonpharmacological techniques for pain management. These can be used in conjunction with pain medications and give patients control over their pain, allowing them to function well.

Abuse survivors often have altered neural responses that make them hypersensitive to bodily sensations. Because of hyperalgesia (see Chapters 2 and 14), what began as pain in one part of the body may have spread due to sensitization of the central nervous system. Exercise and psychological treatment can retrain the nervous system to establish more normal neural connections (Marcus, 2000).

According to the American Pain Foundation (2008), non-drug treatments also allow patients to take an active role in managing their pain. This improves patient satisfaction. They reduce pain and manage related symptoms, such as depression or anxiety, fatigue, and insomnia. They enhance the effectiveness of medications, reduce health care costs, improve functioning and ability to perform activities of daily living, and enhance wellness and quality of life.

Relaxation and Rehabilitative Techniques

Stress can make pain more intense. It starts a cycle of tensing to guard against pain, increasing pain, and more tensing to guard against it. One way to counter pain of this type is to manage stress. Relaxation techniques decrease overall arousal of the sympathetic nervous system and decrease muscle tension (American Pain Foundation, 2008; Catalano & Hardin, 1996; Schneider, 2001). Some of the basic components of relaxation techniques include focusing, passive attitude, and receptiveness to unfamiliar experiences. A few of these techniques are described below.

For certain types of pain conditions, this exercise may not be appropriate because tensing muscles may actually increase the level of pain. If that happens, another technique should be tried (Schneider, 2001). Further, relaxation techniques may increase anxiety in abuse survivors. Because their level of autonomic arousal increases, they may find that their pain symptoms also increase (Weisberg & Clavel, 1999).

In the case of chronic headaches, for example, patients are instructed in how to "move warmth" from the painful part of their body (e.g., their head) to another part of their body, such as their hands. A machine provides feedback to let them know when they are having the desired reaction. Soon patients can create these responses without the machine (Catalano & Hardin, 1996). This technique is especially helpful for patients who do not believe that they are tense or who have not been successful with traditional relaxation approaches. Rehabilitative techniques may include exercise, heat or cold therapy, stretching, and physical therapy (American Pain Foundation, 2008). These are also effective in chronic pain management.

Cognitive Aspects of Pain Management

Patient beliefs are an important component of the pain experience (Main et al., 2000). If patients believe that their pain indicates that something is seriously wrong, their experience of that pain is going to be worse. They may become hypervigilant to bodily sensations, which increases anxiety, which in turn heightens the sensation of pain. It becomes a vicious cycle of pain, hypervigilance, beliefs that something has been overlooked, and an increased experience of pain. The combination of self-scrutiny and physiological arousal heightens already painful stimuli (Toner et al., 2000). Several techniques aimed at addressing patient beliefs are described next.

Patient Education. Patient education is an important component of pain management—especially for patients who have experienced traumatic events. Education can be empowering and validating, letting patients know that their pain is not "all in their heads." Patient education can also enhance self-responsibility and self-efficacy by involving patients in their own treatment plans. It can improve patient compliance, and improve their satisfaction and involvement with treatment. It can also lessen their defensiveness and need to "prove" that they are really in pain (Weisberg & Clavel, 1999).

A component of patient education is the therapeutic relationship. It can be healing for patients to enter a partnership with their health care providers, especially if the providers identify and respond to patients' concerns about their condition. Continuity of care is also important so that patients do not feel abandoned by their health care providers (Whitehead & Crowell, 1991).

Pain Diary. A pain diary is another helpful self-management tool for chronic pain patients. In the pain diary, patients record time of day, what activity they were participating in, how they felt, and what their level of pain was (usually a number from 1 to 10). The purpose of the pain diary is twofold: It provides evidence for patients that their level of pain varies throughout the day, and it helps them identify what activities might trigger pain. Patients should keep these for a couple of weeks, and may start keeping them again if there has been a substantial change in their daily activities and/or their level of pain.

Activity Pacing. Another helpful self-management tool is activity pacing. This helps patients learn to break the activity-pain cycle. As described in previous chapters, abuse survivors are often poor at caring for themselves. They may not take the time needed to ensure that they have adequate rest and relaxation during the day, and may "always" be working. This is especially true for women, particularly those with the unmitigated communion style. And this flurry of activity is associated with increased pain (Schneider, 2001).

In activity pacing, patients learn the utility of prophylactic rest. At first, patients learn to balance half an hour of activity with half an hour of rest. As pain decreases, patients can gradually increase the amount of activity while maintaining the amount of rest. This technique can also help patients identify tasks they can do while resting, thereby increasing their productivity and the amount they are able to accomplish.

Pleasant-Activity Scheduling. One of the difficulties of living with chronic pain relates to things that pain patients can no longer do. When they focus on what they can't do, they are likely to experience frustration, guilt, sadness, or anger. They may feel "worthless" since they can no longer maintain the level of activity they were used to.

What is often helpful is to get patients to refocus on what they still can do. There may even be some new activities in which patients can participate. This is not to deny the feelings of loss that often accompany chronic pain. Rather, it is a technique to keep the patients from dwelling on these losses. It encourages patients to focus on the more positive aspects of their lives and to set reasonable goals for themselves about what they can do (Schneider, 2001).

Addressing Beliefs About Pain. One factor driving the continued use of health care services is the belief that there is something more seriously wrong. It is best to devise a plan that periodically checks for other conditions while holding the number of invasive procedures to a minimum. The health care team should come up with a treatment plan that shows how various other conditions have been considered and then ruled out so that patients can see that something has not been overlooked.

Reframing or Cognitive Restructuring. People's beliefs about their pain can influence how they cope. Negative beliefs can aggravate pain, increase a sense of helplessness, and lead to depression. One of the principle goals of reframing is to help patients identify negative self-talk. Negative self-talk can include cognitions such as "why is this happening to me?" or "there's nothing I can do to recover from this." Catalano and Hardin (1996) describe some other types of negative thinking associated with chronic pain: "I'll never get better," "This is going to get worse and worse until I go crazy," and "I'll never be able to enjoy life again" (p. 68).

Other types of negative thoughts that increase the experience of pain include blaming others or themselves for their pain (e.g., patients might blame their boss for not being more understanding about their situation) or blaming themselves for being a "burden" on others. Catastrophizing, another type of dysfunctional thinking, involves considering the worst possible outcome and acting as if it is already true—for example, a headache means a brain tumor, gastrointestinal pain means colon cancer, chest pain means open-heart surgery (Catalano & Hardin, 1996; Edwards, Bingham, Bathon, & Haythornthwaite, 2006; Shelby et al., 2009).

Also unhelpful are "control fallacies"; patients see themselves in the hands of powerful others (see Chapter 6 on health locus of control), not in control of their own health, and indeed as hopeless victims of their pain.

A final type of negative thinking is entitlement fallacy. The entitlement fallacy has to do with patients' belief that they are entitled to a pain-free life, that they should not have to suffer or be limited in any way. When they have limitations, they begin to feel "cheated" out of the life they feel they deserve. This type of focus keeps people from thinking about the many things that they can still do and, more important, what they can do to cope with pain.

Interventions can reverse negative thoughts, helping patients to view the situation as controllable and to develop a more effective coping strategy. Self-efficacy beliefs are good predictors of compliance with treatment and, as described earlier, are something that is often difficult for child abuse survivors.

Approaches that used a combination of cognitive techniques were effective in one study of refractory irritable bowel syndrome (IBS). In this study, patients were assigned to either a treatment group or a waiting list. The treatment included patient education, homework focused on cognitive changes, support from other patients, and progressive muscle relaxation. Patients who were in the treatment group had a significant reduction in their IBS symptoms compared with patients on the waiting list. The patients improved in frequency and severity of symptoms but also had improvements in their avoidance behaviors and use of positive coping strategies (van Dulmen, Fennis, & Bleijenberg, 1996).

Physical Treatments

Physical treatments are another important component in the treatment of chronic pain and include physical therapy, chiropractic care, and acupuncture. These treatments are discussed below.

Physical Therapy. Some patients may not do well in physical therapy, however. Patients who do not have a clear diagnosis often have a hard time and may inadvertently cause more damage. Those with low self-efficacy, who feel that nothing they do will make any difference in their pain levels, and those who were in poor physical condition before they started therapy may also fail to benefit (American Pain Foundation, 2008; Schneider, 2001).

Chiropractic and Acupuncture. Chiropractic and acupuncture are two of the most popular alternative treatments for pain. Chiropractic involves making adjustments to subtle dislocations (sublaxations) of the spine. There is growing evidence that chiropractic is effective for both neck and back pain, with some limited success in carpal tunnel syndrome (Bronfort, Assendelft, Evans, Mass & Bouter, 2001; Nyiendo, Maas, Goldberg, & Sexton, 2001). Acupuncture with its roots in traditional Chinese medicine, is an ancient form of healing. Acupuncture involves the placing of sterile needles along meridians in the body to unblock "chi," or the body's life force. Although it is difficult to conduct controlled studies on acupuncture (i.e., to use "sham" acupuncture, not along meridians), initial results have found that acupuncture along meridians appears to be more effective than sham acupuncture in the treatment of arthritis pain. It appears to be helpful in treating other chronic conditions as well, and many patients have had success with this approach (Imich et al., 2002; Targino et al., 2002).

These two types of treatment are increasingly popular with the general public. Many pain patients seek out these forms of treatment because they perceive that practitioners of chiropractic and acupuncture are less hurried and have a more holistic approach than their regular medical doctors. They are also perceived as more gentle, with fewer side effects (American Pain Foundation, 2008).

PRACTITIONER MISBELIEFS ABOUT CHRONIC PAIN

Patients are not the only ones who need to pay attention to their beliefs. Clinicians may approach chronic pain patients with beliefs that are not accurate or helpful (Toner et al., 2000). These beliefs can hamper relationships between health care providers and patients. It is important for clinicians to be aware of misconceptions that they might have when working with pain patients. Common erroneous beliefs are described as follows:

- *Pain is primarily a psychiatric disorder.* Pain has a great deal of psychiatric comorbidity associated with it, as discussed earlier in this book. Chronic pain often responds well to antidepressant medication, although usually at a dose that is lower than that used to treat depression. Although it is important to acknowledge that pain carries with it a high degree of psychiatric comorbidity, there is little or no evidence that depression, anxiety, or other psychiatric conditions cause pain.

- *Severe pain always has a discernible organic cause.* Not necessarily. Because of hyperalgesia and sensitization of the central nervous system, pain may not have an obvious cause. Indeed, sometimes people with functional pain conditions have more severe pain than those with a condition that is primarily organic. It is important for practitioners to realize that pain can be quite real without any evidence that shows up in traditional laboratory tests or radiological measures.
- *Patients benefit from the "sick role."* The idea of secondary gain (i.e., that patients have something to get from being sick) has been seriously tossed around as a cause of chronic pain. No doubt, there are situations in which this happens, but to approach all patients with this idea is to sow the seeds of mistrust on both sides. Practitioners are put in the role of investigating whether patients are "really" sick, and patients are put in the role of proving it. When patients feel they must prove that they are sick, it tends to heighten the hyperarousal symptoms doctors are trying to control.

In describing patients with IBS, Toner et al. (2000) noted that they generally do not want to be ill and do not take any pleasure from having a chronic condition. A chronic condition may mean some financial benefit, but usually not. Pain may be able to get patients out of situations in which they did not want to be. But this is not the case for everyone and should not be an assumption.

Patients with chronic pain can be difficult. People with chronic pain syndromes are often perceived to be difficult by the very people whose help they seek (Toner et al., 2000). Toner reframes these thoughts and asks clinicians to remember that pain patients are dealing with difficult conditions that are stigmatized and trivialized. Other health care providers may tell them that they "do not believe in" IBS or fibromyalgia. They may need to continually prove their illness to people in their lives. This can make anyone crabby. Although it is appropriate to place some boundaries on patient behavior (i.e., it is not all right to yell or swear), you must approach all these interactions recognizing that chronic pain is difficult or hard to manage.

SOME FINAL SUGGESTIONS FOR CLINICIANS

Drossman (1995), one of the world's leading experts on IBS, offers specific suggestions to practitioners. Though he was mainly concerned with IBS, his suggestions have relevance to other pain conditions as well.

- *Avoid searching for unlikely organic diseases.* Adult survivors often undergo multiple diagnostic procedures in order to locate the source of their pain. After ruling out possible organic conditions, it is important for the clinician to stop searching. This means to stop performing tests after a reasonable amount of time, or performing them at longer intervals.

- *Avoid dogma.* Because we are unclear of the pathogenesis of most chronic pain syndromes, avoid acting as if there is a clear answer. Whatever explanation is offered, the patient will know someone else who has been offered a different explanation.
- *Avoid ineffective therapy.* Treatment should be tailored to the patient's individual symptoms. The same regimen will not be valid for every patient.
- *Allay fears of cancer and other serious conditions.* Patients with functional diseases often have great fears of more serious illnesses lurking in their bodies. Cancer is often a very big concern in patients with gastrointestinal symptoms, headaches, or pelvic pain. To allay fears of cancer, you may have to offer tests to patients that you feel are unnecessary, but these tests could be important to patients in helping them cope with their symptoms.

SUMMARY

For most of the chronic pain syndromes described in Chapters 14 and 15, there is no cure. The clinician's goals are to manage symptoms, help patients cope with a chronic condition, help patients identify triggers to episodes of illness, and realistically plan for how long symptoms will last. Although functional disease is not generally a harbinger of more serious illness, the symptoms will most likely persist or come and go with some regularity. Symptom control depends on a plan between patients and their health care providers that is tailored to their individual needs. These individual plans help patients cope with a minimal disruption of their daily lives (Toner et al., 2000).

References

Allen, R. W. (1996). Medication and pain management. In E. M. Catalano & K. N. Hardin (Eds.), *The chronic pain control workbook* (2nd ed.) (pp. 141–158). Oakland, CA: New Harbinger.

American Chronic Pain Association. (2012). *ACPA resource guide to chronic pain medication and treatment.* Retrieved from *http://www.theacpa.org/uploads/ACPA_Resource_Guide_2012_Final%20010912.pdf.*

American Pain Foundation. (2008). *Integrative medicine: Non-drug treatment options for pain management.* Retrieved from *http://www.painfoundation.org/learn/publications/files/IntegrativeMedicine.pdf.*

Bronfort, G., Assendelft, W. J., Evans, R., Mass, M., & Bouter, L, (2001). Efficacy of spine manipulation for chronic headache: A systematic review. *Journal of Manipulation and Physiological Therapy*, *24*, 457–460.

Catalano, E. M., & Hardin, K. N. (1996). *The chronic pain control workbook* (2nd ed.). Oakland, CA: New Harbinger.

Drossman, D. A. (1995). Sexual and physical abuse and gastrointestinal illness. *Scandinavian Journal of Gastroenterology, 30*(Suppl.), 90–96.

Edwards, R. R., Bingham, C. O., Bathon, J., & Haythornthwaite, J. A. (2006). Catastrophizing and pain in arthritis, fibromyalgia, and other rheumatic diseases. *Arthritis Care and Research, 55*(2), 325–332.

Imich, D., Behrens, N., Gleditsch, J., Stor, W., Schreiber, M., Schops, P., et al. (2002). Immediate effects of dry needling and acupuncture at distant points in chronic neck pain: Results of a randomized, double-blind, sham-controlled crossover trial. *Pain, 99*, 83–98.

Main, C. J., Richards, H. L., & Fortune, D. G. (2000). Why put new wine in old bottles: The need for a biopsychosocial approach to the assessment, treatment, and understanding of unexplained and explained symptoms in medicine. *Journal of Psychosomatic Research, 48*, 511–514.

Marcus, D. A. (2000). Treatment of nonmalignant chronic pain. *American Family Physician, 61*, 1331–1338.

Nyiendo, J., Maas, M., Goldberg, B., & Sexton, G. (2001). Pain, disability, and satisfaction outcomes and predictors of outcomes: A practice-based study of chronic low back pain patients attending primary care and chiropractic physicians. *Journal of Manipulation and Physiological Therapy, 24*, 433–439.

Schneider, M. S. (2001). *Pain: Perception and management*. Mountain View, CA: Cortext.

Shelby, R. A., Somers, T. J., Keefe, F. J., Silva, S. G., McKee, D. C., She, L., et al. (2009). Pain catastrophizing in patients with noncardiac chest pain: Relationships with pain, anxiety, and disability. *Psychosomatic Medicine, 71*(8), 861–868.

Targino, R. A., Imamura, M., Kaziyama, M. M., Souza, L. P., Hsing, W. T., & Imamura, S. T. (2002). Pain treatment with acupuncture for patients with fibromyalgia. *Current Pain and Headache Report, 6*, 379–383.

Toner, B. B., Segal, Z. V., Emmott, S. D., & Myran, D. (2000). *Cognitive-behavioral treatment of irritable bowel syndrome: The brain-gut connection*. New York: Guilford Press.

van Dulmen, A. M., Fennis, J. F. M., & Bleijenberg, G. (1996). Cognitive-behavioral group therapy for irritable bowel syndrome: Effects and long-term follow-up. *Psychosomatic Medicine, 58*, 508–514.

Weisberg, M. B., & Clavel, A. L. (1999). Why is chronic pain so difficult to treat? Psychological considerations from simple to complex care. *Postgraduate Medicine, 106*, 141–164.

Whitehead, W. E., & Crowell, M. D. (1991). Psychologic considerations in the irritable bowel syndrome. *Gastroenterology Clinics of North America, 20*, 249–267.

Zatura, A. (1998). Individual differences in response to pharmacological treatments: The role of psychosocial factors. *The Health Psychologist, 20*, 10–11.

Appendix 20.1
Online Resources for Pain

The American Pain Foundation
http://www.painfoundation.org/

The web site of the American Pain Foundation is for patients with chronic pain. The organization provides encouragement, support, and advocacy for patients with pain. Its web site has downloadable articles on a wide variety of pain conditions and management techniques. It also has a public policy branch and hosts online chats on various topics.

American Academy of Pain Management
http://www.aapainmanage.org/

The American Academy of Pain Management is a professional organization dedicated to multidisciplinary pain management. It offers information sheets for both professionals and patients, a listing of pain management specialists, and accreditation for pain specialists.

American Academy of Pain Medicine
http://www.painmed.org/

The American Academy of Pain Medicine is a professional organization for physicians who treat pain. Membership provides a journal and newsletter. The web site has downloadable copies of its newsletter Pain Medicine Network.

The American Chronic Pain Association
http://www.theacpa.org/

The American Chronic Pain Association is for patients and professionals who treat chronic pain. Its web site offers a link to the free full-text document *Medication and Chronic Pain* (2002).

American Pain Society
http://www.ampainsoc.org/about/

The American Pain Society is a multidisciplinary professional society that includes basic and clinical scientists, clinicians, and policy analysts. It offers a free e-newsletter, and a variety of other services to members.

The National Institute of Neurological Disorders and Stroke
*http://www.ninds.nih.gov/health_and_medical/disorders/chronic_pain.*htm

NINDS is a National Institute of Health that fosters and supports research on neurological disorders and stroke. They have articles on various types of chronic pain and links to other sites.

Pain.com
http://www.pain.com/

Pain.com is an online source for professional and patient information on all types of pain. A pain assessment tool is available online, as are articles, an online pain journal, and free continuing medical education materials on pain-related topics for physicians.

Epilogue

"Health" is a complex web of behaviors, thoughts, emotions, and social connections. All these not only influence each other but ultimately influence health as well. Abuse can influence health at any, or all, of these junctures. These experiences vary for each individual patient.

Abuse survivors are more likely to have long medical histories and vague symptoms that come and go. They are simultaneously overtreated and undertreated. They have many surgeries, procedures, and medical tests while failing to get relief from their symptoms. Patients and doctors are often frustrated.

To improve health outcomes for adult survivors of abuse, we must consider and address each of the ways victimization can influence health. For example, admonitions to abstain from smoking or substance abuse are likely to be unsuccessful until the patient addresses and resolves the traumatic events that are driving these harmful activities. Admonitions to exercise will not be helpful if the patient believes that nothing he or she does makes any difference. Telling a patient to "lose weight" is likely to fail if the patient has no ability to make and keep friends and eats when lonely or stressed out.

THE IMPORTANCE OF SELF CARE

I cannot leave this book without providing some caution about the necessity of self-care. Patients who have been through a lot can become some of your most challenging patients. It is easy to either withdraw or become overly involved. Neither of these approaches is ideal. It is important for clinicians to reach out to these patients with compassion but to realize that a health care provider cannot meet all needs. This is where a team approach is valuable. It is also important for professionals who work with adult survivors to have a source of emotional support. Asking about abuse will make clinicians privy to some terrible secrets. A clinician who carries the load alone runs the risk of vicarious traumatization and eventual burnout. Finally, learning about patients' abusive experiences may bring up issues from your own past. It is important to have a safe place to vent and process these feelings—for your benefit and the patients' benefit. (For some guidelines on clinician self-care, see Chapter 17.)

THE CHALLENGE OF TREATING ABUSE SURVIVORS

What are the long-term health effects of childhood abuse? It is a question that many in the last two decades have begun to ask. Throughout this book, I have described results from recent research studies and explored the reasons why abuse makes people sick. This research is both fascinating and eye-opening. But we must always remember that behind the numbers are real people who need our help. Returning to the patient I described in Chapter 1, Felitti (2001) lists the patient's current medical problems as follows.

- Childhood sexual abuse;

- Chronic depression;
- Morbid obesity;
- Diabetes mellitus;
- Hypertension;
- Coronary artery disease;
- Macular degeneration; and
- Psoriasis.

This is a challenging list of problems—ones that will not easily remit. But what choice do we have? To ignore these problems is to sentence this woman to a life of illness and incapacity. Eventually, these problems will kill her. In contrast, addressing these health issues with compassion and a team approach can increase the quality of her life, and may even increase longevity. The patients who at first seem most challenging are likely to be those who most benefit from your expertise.

Felitti challenges professionals who work in health care settings to step up to the plate and intervene on behalf of these patients. To do so, we must address childhood abuse and the health problems it can cause.

> Which diagnostic choice shall we make? Who shall make it? And if not now, when? (Felitti, 2001, p. 4)

The time is now.

— Kathleen Kendall-Tackett

Reference

Felitti, V. J. (2001). Reverse alchemy in childhood: Turning gold into lead. *Health Alert*, *8*, 1–4.

Appendix A

Bibliography

Aaron, L. A., Bradley, L. A., Alarcon, G. S., Alexander, R. W., Triana-Alexander, M., Martin, M. Y., et al. (1996). Psychiatric diagnoses in patients with fibromyalgia are related to health care-seeking behavior rather than illness. *Arthritis and Rheumatism, 39*, 436–445.

Aaron, L. A., Bradley, L. A., Alarcon, G. A., Triana-Alexander, M., Alexander, R. W., Martin, M. Y., et al. (1997). Perceived physical and emotional trauma as precipitating events in fibromyalgia. *Arthritis and Rheumatism, 40*, 453–460.

Abramson, L. Y., Seligman, M. E. P., & Teasdale, J. D. (1978). Learned helplessness in humans: Critique and reformulation. *Journal of Abnormal Psychology, 87*, 49–74.

Ackard, D. M., Neumark-Sztainer, D., Hannan, P. J., French, S., & Story, M. (2001). Binge and purge behavior among adolescents: Associations with sexual and physical abuse in a nationally representative sample: The Commonwealth Fund Survey. *Child Abuse and Neglect, 25*, 771–785.

Affleck, G., Tennen, H., Pfeiffer, C., & Fifield, J. (1987). Appraisals of control and predictability in adapting to chronic disease. *Journal of Personality and Social Psychology, 53*, 273–279.

Affleck, G., Tennen, H., Urrows, S., & Higgins, P. (1994). Person and contextual features of daily stress reactivity: Individual difference in relations of undesirable daily events with mood disturbance and chronic pain intensity. *Journal of Personality and Social Psychology, 66*, 329–340.

Agency for Healthcare Research and Quality. (2011). Chronic pelvic pain. Available online at: *http://www.guideline.gov/content.aspx?id=10940.*

Aguera, L., Failde, I., Cervilla, J. A., Diaz-Fernandez, P., & Mico, J. A. (2010). Medically unexplained pain complaints are associated with underlying unrecognized mood disorders in primary care. *BMC Family Practice, 11*, 17.

Alexander, P. (1992). Application of attachment theory to the study of sexual abuse. *Journal of Consulting and Clinical Psychology, 60*, 185–195.

Alexander, P. (1993). The differential effects of abuse characteristics and attachment in the prediction of long-term effects of sexual abuse. *Journal of Interpersonal Violence, 8*, 346–362.

Ali, A., Toner, B. B., Stuckless, N., Gallop, R., Diamant, N. E., Gould, M. I., et al. (2000). Emotional abuse, self-blame, and self-silencing in women with irritable bowel syndrome. *Psychosomatic Medicine, 62*, 76–82.

Allen, R. W. (1996). Medication and pain management. In E. M. Catalano & K. N. Hardin (Eds.), *The chronic pain control workbook* (2nd ed.) (pp. 141–158). Oakland, CA: New Harbinger.

Allgower, A., Wardle, J., & Steptoe, A. (2001). Depressive symptoms, social support, and personal health behaviors in young men and women. *Health Psychology, 20*(3), 223–227.

Alonso, C., & Coe, C. L. (2001). Disruptions of social relationships accentuate the association between emotional distress and menstrual pain in young women. *Health Psychology, 20*, 411–416.

American Chronic Pain Association. (2012). *ACPA resource guide to chronic pain medication and treatment.* Retrieved from *http://www.theacpa.org/uploads/ACPA_Resource_Guide_2012_Final%20010912.pdf.*

American Gastroenterological Association. (2002). American Gastroenterological Association medical position statement: Irritable bowel syndrome. *Gastroenterology, 123*(6), 2105–2107.

American Pain Foundation. (2008). *Integrative medicine: Non-drug treatment options for pain management.* Retrieved from *http://www.painfoundation.org/learn/publications/files/IntegrativeMedicine.pdf.*

American Psychiatric Association. (1994). *Diagnostic and statistical manual of mental disorders* (4th ed.). Washington, DC: Author.

American Psychiatric Association. (2000). *Diagnostic and statistical manual of mental disorders* (4th ed., text rev.). Washington, DC: Author.

American Psychiatric Association. (2002). *Documentation of psychotherapy by psychiatrists* (Resource Document). Available online at: *http://www.americanmentalhealth.com/media/pdf/200202apaonnotes.pdf.*

"Americans redefine 'religious.'" (2002, January 15). *Family Circle,* p. 58.

Amir, L. H., & Donath, S. M. (2002). Does maternal smoking have a negative physiological effect on breastfeeding? The epidemiological evidence. *Birth, 29*, 112–123.

Anda, R. F., Croft, J. B., Felitti, V. J., Nordenberg, D., Giles, W. H., Williamson, D. F., et al. (1999). Adverse childhood experiences and smoking during during adolescence and adulthood. *Journal of the American Medical Association, 282*, 1652–1658.

Anderson, B. L., Kiecolt-Glaser, J. K., & Glaser, R. (1994). A biobehavioral model of cancer stress and disease course. *American Psychologist, 49*, 389–404.

Andreasen, N. C. (1997). Linking mind and brain in the study of mental illness: A project for a scientific psychopathology. *Science, 275*, 1586–1593.

Andrei, A. M., Fraguas, R., Jr., Telles, R. M., Alves, T. C., Strunz, C. M., Nussbacher, A., et al. (2007). Major depressive disorder and inflammatory markers in elderly patients with heart failure. *Psychosomatics, 48*(4), 319–324.

Andrews, B. (1997). Bodily shame in relation to abuse in childhood and bulimia: A preliminary investigation. *British Journal of Clinical Psychology, 36*, 41–49.

Andrews, B., Brewin, C. R., Rose, S., & Kirk, M. (2000). Predicting PTSD symptoms in victims of violent crime: The role of shame, anger, and childhood abuse. *Journal of Abnormal Psychology, 109*, 69–73.

Ansara, D., Cohen, M. M., Gallop, R., Kung, R., Kung, R., & Schei, B. (2005). Predictors of women's physical health problems after childbirth. *Journal of Psychosomatic Obstetrics and Gynecology, 26*, 115–125.

Appels, A., Golombeck, B., Gorgels, A., de Vreede, J., & van Bruekelen, G. (2000). Behavioral risk factors of sudden cardiac arrest. *Journal of Psychosomatic Research, 48*, 463–469.

Arata, C. M. (1999). Coping with rape: The roles of prior sexual abuse and attributions of blame. *Journal of Interpersonal Violence, 14*, 62–78.

Arnold, R. P., Rogers, D., & Cook, D. A. G. (1990). Medical problems of adults who were sexually abused in childhood. *British Medical Journal, 300*, 705–708.

Arata, C. M. (2000). From child victim to adult victim: A model for predicting sexual revictimization. *Child Maltreatment, 5*, 28–38.

Ayduk, O., Downey, G., & Minji, K. (2001). Rejection sensitivity and depressive symptoms in women. *Personality and Social Psychology Bulletin, 27*, 868–877.

Babyak, M., Blumenthal, J. A., Herman, S., Khatri, P., Doraiswamy, M., Moore, K., et al. (2000). Exercise treatment for major depression: Maintenance of therapeutic benefit at 10 months. *Psychosomatic Medicine, 62*, 633–638.

Bagley, C., & McDonald, M. (1984). Adult mental health sequels of child sexual abuse, physical abuse and neglect in maternally separated children. *Canadian Journal of Community Mental Health, 3*, 15–26.

Bair-Merritt, M. H., Blackstone, M., & Feudtner, C. (2006). Physical health outcomes of childhood exposure to intimate partner violence: A systematic review. *Pediatrics, 117*, 278–290.

Bair-Merritt, M. H., Jennings, J. R., Chen, R., Burrell, L., McFarlane, E., Fuddy, L., et al. (2010). Reducing maternal intimate partner violence after the birth of a child. *Archives of Pediatric and Adolescent Medicine, 164*(1), 16–23.

Baker, S. L., & Kirsch, I. (1991). Cognitive mediators of pain perception and tolerance. *Journal of Personality and Social Psychology, 61*, 504–510.

Bandura, A. (1999). A sociocognitive analysis of substance abuse: A agentic perspective. *Psychological Science, 10*, 214–217.

Banyard, V. L., Arnold, S., & Smith, J. (2000). Childhood sexual abuse and dating experiences of undergraduate students. *Child Maltreatment, 5*, 39–48.

Banyard, V. L., Edwards, V. J., & Kendall-Tackett, K. A. (Eds.). (2009). *Trauma and physical health: Understanding the effects of extreme stress and of psychological harm*. London: Routledge.

Barker-Collo, S. L. (2001). Adult reports of child and adult attributions of blame for childhood sexual abuse: Predicting adult adjustment and suicidal behaviors in females. *Child Abuse and Neglect, 25*, 1329–1341.

Barnes, L. L., Mendes de Leon, C. F., Bienias, J. L., Wilson, R. S., Everson-Rose, S. A., & Evans, D. (2009). Hostility and change in cognitive function over time in older blacks and whites. *Psychosomatic Medicine, 71*, 652–658.

Baron, K. G., Smith, T. W., Czajkowski, L. A., Gunn, H. E., & Jones, C. R. (2009). Relationship quality and CPAP adherence in patients with obstructive sleep apnea. *Behavioral Sleep Medicine, 7*(1), 22–36.

Barrett, B. (2009). The impact of childhood sexual abuse and other forms of childhood adversity on adulthood parenting. *Journal of Child Sexual Abuse, 18*, 489–512.

Barth, J., Schneider, S., & von Kanel, R. (2010). Lack of social support in the etiology and the prognosis of coronary heart disease: A systematic review and meta-analysis. *Psychosomatic Medicine, 72*, 229–238.

Bartholow, B. N., Doll, L. S., Joy, D., Douglas, J. M., Bolan, G., Harrison, J. S., et al. (1994). Emotional, behavioral, and HIV risks associated with sexual abuse among adult homosexual and bisexual men. *Child Abuse and Neglect, 18*, 747–761.

Bassuk, E. L., & Rosenberg, L. (1988). Why does family homelessness occur? A case-control study. *American Journal of Public Health, 78*, 783–788.

Batten, S. V., Aslan, M., Maciejewski, P. K., & Mazure, C. M. (2004). Childhood maltreatment as a risk factor for adult cardiovascular disease and depression. *Journal of Clinical Psychiatry, 65*, 249–254.

Bartholow, B. N., Doll, L. S., Joy, D., Douglas, J. M., Bolan, G., Harrison, J. S., et al. (1994). Emotional, behavioral, and HIV risks associated with sexual abuse among adult homosexual and bisexual men. *Child Abuse and Neglect, 18*, 747–761.

Bear, M. F., Connors, B. W., & Paradiso, M. A. (1996). *Neuroscience: Exploring the brain*. Baltimore, MD: Williams & Wilkins.

Beatty, D. L., Hall, M. H., Kamarck, T. W., Buysse, D. J., Owens, J. F., Reis, S. E., et al. (2011). Unfair treatment is associated with poor sleep in African American and Caucasian adults: Pittsburgh SleepSCORE Project. *Health Psychology, 30*(3), 351–359.

Becker, N., Bondegaard, T. A., Olsen, A. K., Sjogren, P., Bech, P., & Eriksen, J. (1997). Pain epidemiology and health-related quality of life in chronic non-malignant pain patients referred to a Danish multi-disciplinary pain center. *Pain, 73*, 393–400.

Becker-Lausen, E., & Mallon-Kraft, S. (1997). Pandemic outcomes: the intimacy variable. In G. K. Kantor & J. S. Jasinski (Eds.), *Out of darkness: Current perspective on family violence* (pp. 49–57). Newbury Park, CA: Sage.

Beckham, J. C., Flood, A. M., Dennis, M. F., & Calhoun, P. S. (2009). Ambulatory cardiovascular activity and hostility ratings in women with chronic posttraumatic stress disorder. *Biological Psychiatry, 65*(3), 268–272.

Beckham, J. C., Moore, S. D., Feldman, M. E., Hertzberg, M. A., Kirby, A. C., & Fairbank, J. A. (1998). Health status, somatization, and severity of post-traumatic stress disorder. *American Journal of Psychiatry, 155*, 1565–1569.

Beilin, B., Shavit, Y., Trabekin, E., Mordashev, B., Mayburd, E., Zeidel, A., et al. (2003). The effects of postoperative pain management on immune response to surgery. *Anesthesia and Analgesia, 97*, 822–827.

Belleville, G., Guay, S., & Marchand, A. (2009). Impact of sleep disturbances on PTSD symptoms and perceived health. *Journal of Nervous and Mental Disease, 197*(2), 126–132.

Belt, W., & Abidin, R. R. (1996). The relation of childhood abuse and early parenting experiences to current marital quality in a nonclinical sample. *Child Abuse and Neglect, 20*, 1019–1030.

Benedict, M. I., Paine, L., & Paine, L. (1994). *Long-term effects of child sexual abuse on functioning in pregnancy and pregnancy outcomes (Final Report)*. Washington, DC: National Center of Child Abuse & Neglect.

Benedict, M. I., Paine, L. L., Paine, L. A., Brandt, D., & Stallings, R. (1999). The associations of childhood sexual abuse with depressive symptoms during pregnancy, and selected pregnancy outcomes. *Child Abuse and Neglect, 23*, 659–670.

Bennett, R. M. (1996). Fibromyalgia and the disability dilemma: A new era in understanding a complex, multidimensional pain syndrome. *Arthritis and Rheumatism, 39*, 1627–1634.

Bennett, S. A., Beck, J. G., & Clapp, J. D. (2009). Understanding the relationship between posttraumatic stress disorder and trauma cognitions: The impact of thought control strategies. *Behaviour Research and Therapy, 47*, 1018–1023.

Bennett, W. J. (1993). *The book of virtues*. New York: Simon & Schuster.

Berliner, L., & Elliot, D. M. (1996). Sexual abuse of children. In J. Briere, L. Berliner, C. J. Bulkley, & T. Reid (Eds.), *The APSAC handbook on child maltreatment* (pp. 51–71). Newbury Park, CA: Sage.

Berntsen, D., & Rubin, D. C. (2006). The centrality of event scale: A measure of integrating a trauma into one's identity and its relation to posttraumatic stress disorder symptoms. *Behavior Research and Therapy, 44*(2), 219–231.

Bisson, J. (2002). Posttraumatic stress disorder. In S. Barton (Ed.), *Clinical evidence: Mental health* (pp. 120–126). London: BMJ.

Blackmore, E. R., Moynihan, J. A., Rubinow, D. R., Pressman, E. K., Gilchrist, M., & O'Connor, T. G. (2011). Psychiatric symptoms and proinflammatory cytokines in pregnancy. *Psychosomatic Medicine, 73*, 656–663.

Blanchard, E. B. (1993). Irritable bowel syndrome. In R. J. Gatchel & E. B. Blanchard (Eds.), *Psychophysiological disorders: Research and clinical applications* (pp. 23–62). Washington, DC: American Psychological Association.

Blood, L., & Cornwall, A. (1996). Childhood sexual victimization as a factor in the treatment of substance misusing adolescents. *Substance Use and Misuse, 31*, 1015–1039.

Blumenthal, J. A., Babyak, M. A., Doraiswamy, P. M., Watkins, L., Hoffman, B. M., Barbour, K. A., et al. (2007). Exercise and pharmacotherapy in the treatment of major depressive disorder. *Psychosomatic Medicine, 69*, 587–596.

Boden, J. M., Fergusson, D. M., & Horwood, L. J. (2009). Experience of sexual abuse in childhood and abortion in adolescence and early adulthood. *Child Abuse and Neglect, 33*, 870–876.

Boisset-Pioro, M. H., Esdaile, J. M., & Fitzcharles, M.-A. (1995). Sexual and physical abuse in women with fibromyalgia syndrome. *Arthritis and Rheumatism, 38*, 235–241.

Bolger, K. E., & Patterson, C. J. (2001). Developmental pathways from child maltreatment to peer rejections. *Child Development, 72*(2), 549–568.

Boney-McCoy, S., & Finkelhor, D. (1995). Prior victimization: A risk factor for child sexual abuse and for PTSD-related symptomatology among sexually abused youth. *Child Abuse and Neglect, 19*, 1401–1421.

Boney-McCoy, S., & Finkelhor, D. (1995). Psychological sequelae of violent victimization in a national youth sample. *Journal of Consulting and Clinical Psychology, 63*, 726–736.

Boney-McCoy, S., & Finkelhor, D. (1996). Is youth victimization related to trauma symptoms and depression after controlling for prior symptoms and family relationships? A longitudinal, prospective study. *Journal of Consulting and Clinical Psychology, 64*, 1406–1461.

Bonomi, A. E., Cannon, E. A., Anderson, M. L., & Rivara, F. P. (2008). Association between self-reported health and physical and/or sexual abuse experienced before age 18. *Child Abuse and Neglect, 32*, 693–701.

Boufidou, F., Lambrinoudaki, I., Argeitis, J., Zervas, I. M., Pliatsika, P., Leonardou, A. A., et al. (2009). CSF and plasma cytokines at delivery and postpartum mood disorders. *Journal of Affective Disorders, 115*, 287–292.

Boutelle, K. N., Hannan, P., Fulkerson, J. A., Crow, S. J., & Stice, E. (2010). Obesity as a prospective predictor of depression in adolescent females. *Health Psychology, 29*(3), 293–298.

Bowen, E., Heron, J., Waylen, A., Wolke, D., & Team, A. S. (2005). Domestic violence risk during and after pregnancy: Findings from a British longitudinal study. *British Journal of Obstetrics and Gynecology, 112*(8), 1083–1089.

Bower, J. E., Kemeny, M. E., Taylor, S. E., & Fahey, J. L. (1998). Cognitive processing, discovery of meaning, CD4 decline, and AIDs-related mortality among bereaved, HIV-seropositive men. *Journal of Consulting and Clinical Psychology, 66*, 979–986.

Bowlby, J. (1969). *Attachment and loss: Vol. 1. Attachment.* New York: Basic Books.

Bowlby, J. (1982). *Attachment and loss: Vol. 1. Attachment.* (2nd ed.). New York: Basic Books.

Bowman, E. S. (2000). The assets and liabilities of conservative religious faith for persons with servere dissociative disorder. *Journal of Psychology and Christianity, 19*, 122–148.

Bowman, K. G., Ryberg, J. W., & Becker, H. (2009). Examining the relationship between a childhood history of sexual abuse and later dissociation, breast-feeding practices, and parenting anxiety. *Journal of Interpersonal Violence, 24*(8), 1304–1317.

Bradley, L. A., & Alarcon, G. S. (1997). Fibromyalgia. In W. J. Koopman (Ed.), *Arthritis & allied conditions* (Vol. 2, 13th ed.) (pp. 1619–1640). Baltimore, MD: Williams & Wilkins.

Brady, J. L., Guy, J. D., Poelstra, P. L., & Brokaw, B. F. (1999). Vicarious traumatization, spirituality, and the treatment of sexual abuse survivors: A national survey of women psychotherapists. *Professional Psychology: Research and Practice, 30*, 386–393.

Brand, S. R., Engel, S. M., Canfield, R. L., & Yehuda, R. (2006). The effect of maternal PTSD following in utero trauma exposure on behavior and temperament in the 9-month-old infant. *Annals of the New York Academy of Sciences, 1071*, 454–458.

Braveheart, M. Y. H., & BeBruyn, L. M. (1998). The American Indian holocaust: Healing historical unresolved grief. *American Indian and Alaska Native Mental Health Research, 8*, 60–82.

Brayden, R. M., Deitrich-MacLean, G., Dietrich, M. S., Sherrod, K. B., & Altemeier, W. A. (1995). Evidence for specific effects of childhood sexual abuse on mental well-being and physical self-esteem. *Child Abuse and Neglect, 19*, 1255–1262.

Bremner, J. D. (1999). Does stress damage the brain? *Biological Psychiatry, 45*, 797–805.

Bremner, J. D. (2005). The neurobiology of childhood sexual abuse in women with posttraumatic stress disorder. In K. A. Kendall-Tackett (Ed.), *Handbook of women, stress, and trauma* (pp. 181–206). New York: Brunner-Routledge.

Bremner, J. D., Randall, P., Scott, T. M., Capelli, S., R., D., McCarthy, G., & Charney, D. S. (1995). Deficits in short-term memory in adult survivors of childhood abuse. *Psychiatry Research, 59*, 97–107.

Bremner, J. D., Randall, P., Vermetten, E., Staib, L., Bronen, R. A., Mazure, C. M., et al. (1997). Magnetic resonance imaging-based measurements of hippocampal volume in posttraumatic stress disorder related to childhood physical and sexual abuse: A preliminary report. *Biological Psychiatry, 41*, 23–32.

Bremner, J. D., Southwick, S. M., Darnell, A., & Charney, D. S. (1996). Chronic PTSD in Vietnam combat veterans: Course of illness and substance abuse. *American Journal of Psychiatry, 153*, 369–375.

Bremner, J. D., Southwick, S. M., Johnson, D. R., Yehuda, R., & Charney, D. S. (1993). Childhood physical abuse and combat-related posttraumatic stress disorder in Vietnam veterans. *American Journal of Psychiatry, 150*, 235–239.

Breslau, N., Davis, G. C., Andreski, P., & Peterson, E. L. (1997). Sex differences in posttraumatic stress disorder. *Archives of General Psychiatry, 54*, 1044–1048.

Breslau, N., Davis, G. C., Peterson, E. L., & Schultz, L. (1997). Psychiatric sequelae of posttraumatic stress disorder in women. *Archives of General Psychiatry, 54*, 81–87.

Bretherton, I. (1992). The origins of attachment theory: John Bowlby and Mary Ainsworth. *Developmental Psychopathology, 28*, 759–775.

Brewin, C. R., Andrews, B., & Rose, S. (2000). Fear, helplessness, and horror in posttraumatic stress disorder: Investigation DSM-IV criterion A2 in victims of violent crime. *Journal of Traumatic Stress, 13*, 499–509.

Briere, J. N., & Elliot, D. M. (1994).

Immediated and long-term impacts of child sexual abuse. *The Future of Children, 4*, 54–69.

Briere, J. N., & Runtz, M. (1987). Post sexual abuse trauma: Data and implications for clinical practice. *Journal of Interpersonal Violence, 2*, 367–379.

Briere, J. N., Woo, R., McRae, B., Foltz, J., & Sitzman, R. (1997). Lifetime victimization history, demographics, and clinical status in female psychiatric emergency room patients. *Journal of Nervous and Mental Disease, 185*, 95–101.

Briere, J. N., & Zaidi, L. Y. (1989). Sexual abuse history and sequelae in female psychiatric emergency room patients. *American Journal of Psychiatry, 146*, 1602–1606.

Briggs, L., & Joyce, P. R. (1997). What determines post-traumatic stress disorder symptomatology for survivors of childhood sexual abuse? *Child Abuse and Neglect, 21*, 575–582.

Brock, K. J., Mintz, L. B., & Good, G. E. (1997). Differences among sexually abused and nonabused women from functional and dysfunctional families. *Journal of Counseling Psychology, 44*, 425–432.

Bronfort, G., Assendelft, W. J., Evans, R., Mass, M., & Bouter, L, (2001). Efficacy of spine manipulation for chronic headache: A systematic review. *Journal of Manipulation and Physiological Therapy, 24*, 457–460.

Brosse, A. L., Sheets, E. S., Lett, M. S., & Blumenthal, J. A. (2002). Exercise and the treatment of clinical depression in adults: Recent findings and future directions. *Sports Medicine, 32*, 741–760.

Brown, J., Cohen, P., Johnson, J. G., & Smailes, E. M. (1999). Childhood abuse and neglect: Specificity of effects on adolescent and young adult depression and suicidality. *Journal of the American Academy of Child and Adolescent Psychiatry, 38*, 1490–1496.

Brown, L. K., Kessel, S. M., Lourie, K. J., & Ford, H. H. (1997). Influence of sexual abuse on HIV-related attitudes and behaviors in adolescent psychiatric inpatients. *Journal of the American Academy of Child and Adolescent Psychiatry, 36*, 316–322.

Brown, L. K., Lourie, K. J., Zlotnick, C., & Cohn, J. (2000). Impact of sexual abuse on the HIV-risk-related behavior of adolescents in intensive psychiatric treatment. *American Journal of Psychiatry, 157*, 1413–1415.

Browne, A., & Bassuk, S. S. (1997). Intimate violence in the lives of homeless and poor housed women: Prevalence and patterns in an ethnically diverse sample. *American Journal of Orthopsychiatry, 67*, 261–278.

Brownlee, S., & Schrof, J. M. (1997). The quality of mercy. *U.S. News & World Report, March 17*, 54–67.

Bryant, S. L., & Range, L. M. (1997). Type and severity of child abuse and college students' lifetime suicidality. *Child Abuse and Neglect, 21*, 1169–1176.

Buist, A., & Janson, H. (2001). Childhood sexual abuse, parenting, and postpartum depression: A 3-year follow-up study. *Child Abuse and Neglect, 25*, 909–921.

Bullock, L. F., Libbus, M. K., & Sable, M. R. (2001). Battering and breastfeeding in a WIC population. *Canadian Journal of Nursing Research, 32*, 43–56.

Burgmer, M., Petzke, F., Giesecke, T., Gaubitz, M., Heuft, G., & Pfleiderer, B. (2011). Cerebral activatioin and catastrophizing during pain anticipation in patients with fibromyalgia. *Psychosomatic Medicine, 73*, 751–759.

Butterfield, M. I., Forneris, C. A., Feldman, M. E., & Beckham, J. C. (2000). Hostility and functional health status in women veterans with and without posttraumatic stress disorder: A preliminary study. *Journal of Traumatic Stress, 13* 735–741.

Buysse, D. J., Angst, J., Gamma, A., Ajdacic, V., Eich, D., & Rossler, W. (2008).

Prevalence, course, and comorbidity of insomnia and depression in young adults. *Sleep, 31*(4), 473–480.

Calvin, C. M., Batty, G. D., Lowe, G. D. O., & Deary, I. J. (2011). Childhood intelligence and midlife inflammatory and hemostatic biomarkers: The National Child Development Study (1958) Cohort. *Health Psychology, 30*(6), 710–718.

Campbell, J. C., & Kendall-Tackett, K. A. (2005). Intimate partner violence: Implications for women's physical and mental health. In K. A. Kendall-Tackett (Ed.), *Handbook for women, stress, and trauma* (pp. 123–140). New York: Brunner-Routledge.

Campeau, S., Day, H. E. W., Helmreich, D. L., Kollack-Walker, S., & Watson, S. J. (1998). Principles of psychoneuroendocrinology. *Psychiatric Clinics of North America, 21*, 259–275.

Cappuccio, F. P., Taggart, F. M., Kandala, N. B., Currie, A., Peile, E., Stranges, S., et al. (2008). Meta-analysis of short sleep duration and obesity in children and adults. *Sleep, 31*(5), 19–26.

Carey, T. C., Kempton, T. L., & Gemmill, W. D. (1996). The significance of emotions in the affective presentation of sexually abused girls. *Child Psychiatry and Human Development, 27*, 115–124.

Carmichael, C. L., & Reis, H. T. (2005). Attachment, sleep quality, and depressed affect. *Health Psychology, 24*, 526–531.

Carney, R. M., Freedland, K. E., Eisen, S. A., Rich, M. W., & Jaffe, A. S. (1995). Major depression and medication adherence in elderly patients with coronary artery disease. *Health Psychology, 14*, 88–90.

Carney, R. M., Freedland, K. E., Steinmeyer, B., Blumenthal, J. A., DeJonge, P., Davidson, K. W., et al. (2009). History of depression and survival after acute myocardial infarction. *Psychosomatic Medicine, 71*, 253–259.

Cartwright, R. (2008). Sleeping together: A pilot study of the effects of shared sleeping on adherence to CPAP treatment in obstructive sleep apnea. *Journal of Clinical Sleep Medicine, 4*(2), 123–127.

Caska, C. M., Hendrickson, B. E., Wong, M. H., Ali, S., Neylan, T. C., & Whooley, M. A. (2009). Anger expression and sleep quality in patients with coronary heart disease: Findings from the Heart and Soul Study. *Psychosomatic Medicine, 71*, 280–285.

Catalano, E. M., & Hardin, K. N. (1996). *The chronic pain control workbook* (2nd ed.). Oakland, CA: New Harbinger.

Catz, S. L., Kelly, J. A., Bogart, L. M., Benotsch, E. G., & McAuliffe, T. L. (2000). Patterns, correlates, and barriers to medication adherence among persons prescribed new treatments for HIV disease. *Health Psychology, 19*, 124–133.

Centers for Disease Control and Prevention. (2002). *Targeting tobacco use: The nation's leading cause of death*. Atlanta: Author.

Centers for Disease Control and Prevention. (2010). *Adverse childhood experiences: Data and statistics.* Available online at: *http://www.cdc.gov/ace/prevalence.htm#ACED.*

Centers for Disease Control and Prevention. (2011). Fibromyalgia. Available online at: *http://www.cdc.gov/arthritis/basics/fibromyalgia.htm.*

Chan, K. L., Tiwari, A., Fong, D. Y. T., Leug, W. C., Brownridge, D. A., & Ho, P. C. (2009). Correlates of in-law conflict and intimate partner violence against Chinese pregnant women in Hong Kong. *Journal of Interpersonal Violence, 24*(1), 97–110.

Chandy, J. M., Blum, R. W., & Resnick, M. D. (1996). Female adolescents with a history of sexual abuse: Risk, outcomes, and protective factors. *Journal of Interpersonal Violence, 11*, 503–518.

Chandy, J. M., Blum, R. W., & Resnick,

M. D. (1996). History of sexual abuse and parental alcohol misuse: Risk, outcomes, and protective factors in adolescents. *Child and Adolescent Social Work Journal, 13*, 411–432.

Cheasty, M., Clare, A. W., & Collins, C. (1998). Relation between sexual abuse in childhood and adult depression: Case-control study. *British Medical Journal, 316*, 198–201.

Choquet, M., Darves-Bornoz, J.-M., Ledoux, S., Manfredi, R., & Hassler, C. (1997). Self-reported health and behavioral problems among adolescent victims of rape in France: Results of a cross-sectional survey. *Child Abuse and Neglect, 21*, 823–832.

Christian, L. M., Franco, A., Glaser, R., & Iams, J. D. (2009). Depressive symptoms are associated with elevated serum proinflammatory cytokines among pregnant women. *Brain, Behavior and Immunity, 23*, 75–754.

Chung, T. K., Lau, T. K., Yip, A. S., Chiu, H. F., & Less, D. T. (2001). Antepartum depressive symptomatology is associated with adverse obstetric and neonatal outcomes. *Psychosomatic Medicine, 63*, 830–834.

Cicchetti, D., & Toth, S. L. (1998). The development of depression in children and adolescents. *American Psychologist, 53*, 221–241.

Clark, D. B., Lesnick, L., & Hegedus, A. M. (1997). Traumas and other adverse life events in adolescents with alcohol abuse and dependence. *Journal of the American Academy of Child and Adolescent Psychiatry, 36*, 1744–1751.

Clark, K. M., Friedman, H. S., & Martin, L. R. (1999). A longitudinal study of religiosity and mortality risk. *Journal of Health Psychology, 4*, 381–391.

Clum, G. A., Nishith, P., & Resick, P. A. (2001). Trauma-related sleep disturbance and self-reported physical health symptoms in treatment-seeking female rape victims. *Journal of Nervous and Mental Disease, 189*, 618–622.

Cohen, S., Doyle, W. J., & Baum, A. (2006). Socioeconomic status is associated with stress hormones. *Psychosomatic Medicine, 68*, 414–420.

Cohen, S., & Lemay, E. P. (2007). Why would social networks be linked to affect and health practices? *Health Psychology, 26*(4), 410–417.

Collishaw, S., Pickles, A., Messer, J., Rutter, M., Shearer, C., & Maughan, B. (2007). Resilience to adult psychopathology following childhood maltreatment: Evidence from a community sample. *Child Abuse and Neglect, 31*, 211–229.

Colman, R. A., & Widom, C. S. (2004). Childhood abuse and neglect and adult intimate relationships: A prospective study. *Child Abuse and Neglect, 28*, 1133–1151.

Committee on Advancing Pain Research, Care and Education & Institute of Medicine. (2011). *Relieving pain in America*. Washington, DC: National Academies Press.

Connelly, M. T., & Inni, T. S. (1998). Principles of disease prevention. In A. S. Fauci, E. Braunwald, K. J. Isselbacher, J. D. Wilson, J. B. Martin, D. L. Kasper, et al. (Eds.), *Harrison's principles of internal medicine* (14th ed., pp. 46–48). New York: Mc-Graw-Hill.

Connerney, I., Sloan, R. P., Shapiro, P. A., Bagiella, E., & Seckman, C. (2010). Depression is associated with increased mortality 10 years after coronary artery bypass surgery. *Psychosomatic Medicine, 72*(9).

Conroy, E., Degenhardt, L., Mattick, R. P., & Nelson, E. C. (2009). Child maltreatment as a risk factor for opioid dependence: Comparison of family characteristics and type and severity of child maltreatment with a matched control group. *Child Abuse and Neglect, 33*, 343–352.

Conway, M., Mendelson, M., Giannopoulos, C., Csank, P. A. R., & Holm, S. L. (2004). Childhood and adult sexual abuse, rumination on sadness, and dysphoria. *Child Abuse and Neglect, 28*, 393–410.

Cooper, D. C., Ziegler, M. G., Nelesen, R. A., & Dimsdale, J. E. (2009). Racial differences in the impact of social support on nocturnal blood pressure. *Psychosomatic Medicine, 71*, 524–531.

Corwin, E. J., & Pajer, K. (2008). The psychoneuroimmunology of postpartum depression. *Journal of Women's Health, 17*(9), 1529–1534.

Courtois, C. (2010). *Healing the incest wound: Adult survivors in therapy* (2nd ed.). New York: W.W. Norton.

Coussons-Read, M. E., Okun, M. L., Schmitt, M. P., & Giese, S. (2005). Prenatal stress alters cytokine levels in a manner that may endanger human pregnancy. *Psychosomatic Medicine, 67*, 625–631.

Craine, L., Henson, C., Colliver, J., & MacLean, D. (1988). Prevalence of a history of sexual abuse among female psychiatric patients in a state hospital system. *Hospital and Community Psychiatry, 39*, 300–304.

Crepaz, N., & Marks, G. (2001). Are negative affective states associated with HIV sexual risk behaviors? A meta-analytic review. *Health Psychology, 20*(4), 291–299.

Crofford, L. J. (2007). Violence, stress, and somatic syndromes. *Trauma, Violence, and Abuse, 8*(3), 299–313.

Crofford, L. J., Pillemer, S. R., Kalogeras, K. T., Cash, J. M., Michelson, D., Kling, M. A., et al. (1994). Hypothalamic-pituitary-adrenal axis perturbations in patients with fibromyalgia. *Arthritis and Rheumatism, 37*, 1583–1592.

Crouch, J. L., Skowronski, J. J., Milner, J. S., & Harris, B. (2008). Parental responses to infant crying: The influence of child physical abuse risk and hostile priming. *Child Abuse and Neglect, 32*, 702–710.

Cuevas, C. A., Finkelhor, D., Ormrod, R., & Turner, H. (2009). Psychiatric diagnosis as a risk marker for victimization in a national sample of children. *Journal of Interpersonal Violence, 24*(4), 636–652.

Cui, X.-J., & Vaillant, G. E. (1997). Does depression generate negative life events? *Journal of Nervous and Mental Disease, 185*, 145–150.

Cunningham, J., Pearce, T., & Pearce, P. (1988). Childhood sexual abuse and medical complaints in adult women. *Journal of Interpersonal Violence, 3*, 131–144.

Cutrona, C. E. (1983). Causal attributions and perinatal depression. *Journal of Abnormal Psychology, 92*, 161–172.

Daigneault, I., Hebert, M., & McDuff, P. (2009). Men's and women's childhood sexual abuse and victimization in adult partner relationships: A study of risk factors. *Child Abuse and Neglect, 33*, 638–647.

Dallam, S. J. (2001). The hidden effects of childhood maltreatment on adult health. In K. Franey, R. Geffner & R. Falconer (Eds.), *The cost of child maltreatment: Who pays? We all do.* (pp. 1–14). San Diego: Family Violence & Sexual Assault Institute.

Danese, A., Moffitt, T. E., Harrington, H., Milne, B. J., Polanczyk, G., Pariante, C. M., et al. (2009). Adverse childhood experiences and adult risk factors for age-related disease: Depression, inflammation, and clustering of metabolic risk markers. *Archives of Pediatric and Adolescent Medicine, 163*(12), 1135–1143.

Danese, A., Pariante, C. M., Caspi, A., Taylor, A., & Poulton, R. (2007). Childhood maltreatment predicts adult inflammation in a life-course study. *Proceedings of the National Academy of Sciences USA, 104*(4), 1319–1324.

Danaei, G., Ding, E. L., Mozaffarian, D., Taylor, B., Rehm, J., Murray, C. J. L., et al. (2009). The preventable causes of death in the United States: Comparative risk assessment of dietary, lifestyle, and metabolic risk factors. *PLoS Medicine, 6*(4), e1000058.

Danielson, K. K., Moffitt, T. E., Caspi, A., & Silva, P. A. (1998). Comorbidity between abuse of an adult and DSM III-R mental disorders: Evidence from an epidemiological study. *American Journal of Psychiatry, 155*, 131–133.

Danner, D. D., Snowdon, D. A., & Friesen, W. V. (2001). Positive emotions in early life and longevity: Findings from the Nun Study. *Journal of Personality and Social Psychology, 80*, 804–813.

Davidson, K. W., Rieckmann, N., & Lesperance, F. (2004). Psychological theories of depression: Potential application for the prevention of acute coronary syndrome recurrence. *Psychosomatic Medicine, 66*, 165–173.

Davidson, R. J. (2000). Affective style, psychopathology, and resilience: Brain mechanisms and plasticity. *American Psychologist, 55*, 1193–1214.

Dayan, J. Creveuil, C., Marks, M. N., Conroy, S. Herlicoviez, M., Dreyfus, M., et al. (2006). Prenatal depression, prenatal anxiety, and spontaneous preterm birth: A prospective cohort study among women with early and regular care. *Psychosomatic Medicine, 68*, 938–946.

DeAngelis, T. (2002, July-August). Normalizing practitioners' stress. *Monitor on Psychology*, pp. 62–64.

DeAngelis, T. (2002). Promising treatments for anorexia and bulimia. *Monitor on Psychology, 33*, 38–41.

DeBellis, M. D. (2011). Neurodevelopmental biology associated with childhood sexual abuse. *Journal of Child Sexual Abuse, 20*, 548–587.

DeBellis, M. D., Keshavan, M. S., Clark, D. B., Casey, B. J., Giedd, J. N., Boring, A. M., et al. (1999). A. E. Bennett Research Award. Developmental traumatology, Part II: Brain development. *Biological Psychiatry, 45*, 1271–1284.

DeBellis, M. D., Keshvan, M. S., Spencer, S., & Hall, J. (2000). N-acetylaspartate concentrations in the anterior cingulate of maltreated children and adolescents with PTSD. *American Journal of Psychiatry, 157*, 1175–1177.

Del Castillo, D., & Wright, M. O. (2009). The perils and possibilities in disclosing childhood sexual abuse to a romantic partner. *Journal of Child Sexual Abuse, 18*, 386–404.

Demakakos, P., Pierce, M. B., & Hardy, R. (2010). Depressive symptoms and risk of Type 2 diabetes in a national sample of middle-aged and older adults. *Diabetes Care, 33*, 792–797.

Dennis, C.-L., Janssen, P. A., & Singer, J. (2004). Identifying women at-risk for postpartum depression in the immediate postpartum period. *Acta Psychiatrica Scandanavica, 110*, 338–346.

Dennis, C.-L., & McQueen, K. (2009). The relationship between infant-feeding outcomes and postpartum depression: A qualitative systematic review. *Pediatrics, 123*, e736–e751.

DePrince, A. P., & Freyd, J. J. (2002). The harm of trauma: Pathological fear, shattered assumptions, or betrayal? In J. Kauffman (Ed.), *Loss of the assumptive world: A theory of traumatic loss* (pp. 71–82). New York: Brunner-Routledge.

Derecho, C. N., Wetzler, S., McGinn, L. K., & Sanderson, W. C. (1996). Atypical depression among psychiatric inpatients: Clinical features and personality traits. *Journal of Affective Disorders, 39*, 55–59.

Desai, R. A., Lam, J., & Rosenheck, R. A. (2000). Childhood risk factors for criminal justice involvement in a sample of homeless people with serious mental illness. *Journal of Nervous and Mental Disease, 188*, 324–332.

Deverts, D. J., Cohen, S., DiLillo, V. G., Lewis, C. E., Kiefe, C., Whooley, M. A., et al. (2010). Depressive symptoms, race, and circulating C-reactive protein: The Coronary Artery Risk Development in Young Adults (CARDIA) Study. *Psychosomatic Medicine, 72*, 734–741.

DeWit, D. J., MacDonald, K., & Offord, D. R. (1999). Childhood stress and symptoms of drug dependence in adolescence and early adulthood. *American Journal of Orthopsychiatry, 69*, 61–72.

Diaz, A., Simatov, E., & Rickert, V. I. (2000). The independent and combined effects of physical and sexual abuse on health. Results from a national survey. *Journal of Pediatric and Adolescent Gynecology, 13*, 89.

Dickerson, S. S. (2011). Physiological responses to experiences of social pain. In G. MacDonald & L. A. Jensen-Campbell (Eds.), *Social pain: Neuropsychological and health implications of social loss and exclusion* (pp. 79–94). Washington, DC: American Psychological Association.

Dickerson, S. S., Gruenewald, T. L., & Kemeny, M. E. (2004a). When the social self is threatened: Shame, physiology, and health. *Journal of Personality, 72*(6), 1191–1216.

Dickerson, S. S., Kemeny, M. E., Aziz, N., Kim, K. H., & Fahey, J. L. (2004b). Immunological effects of induced shame and guilt. *Psychosomatic Medicine, 66*, 124–131.

Dickinson, L. M., deGruy, F. V., Dickinson, W. P., & Candib, L. M. (1999). Health-related quality of life and symptom profiles of female survivors of sexual abuse. *Archives of Family Medicine, 8*, 35–43.

Dierckx, B., Tulen, J. H. M., van den Berg, M. P., Tharner, A., Jaddoe, V. W., Moll, H. A., et al. (2009). Maternal psychopathology influences infant heart rate variability: Generation R Study. *Psychosomatic Medicine, 71*, 313–321.

Diong, S.-M., & Bishop, G. D. (1999). Anger expression, coping styles, and well-being. *Journal of Health Psychology, 4*(1), 81–96.

Dirkzwager, A. J., van der Velden, P. G., Grievink, L., & Yzermans, C. J. (2007). Disaster-related posttraumatic stress disorder and physical health. *Psychosomatic Medicine, 69*(5), 435–440.

Dobie, D. J., Maynard, C., Kivlahan, D. R., Johnson, K. M., Simpson, T., David, A. C., & Bradley, K. (2006). Posttraumatic stress disorder screening status is associated with increased VA medical and surgical utilization in women. *Journal of General Internal Medicine, 21*(Suppl. 3), S58–S64.

Domino, J. V., & Haber, J. D. (1987). Prior physical and sexual abuse in women with chronic headache: Clinical correlates. *Headache, 27*, 310–314.

Dong, M., Anda, R. F., Felitti, V. J., Dube, S. R., Williamson, D. F., Thompson, T. J., et al. (2004). The interrelatedness of multiple forms of childhood abuse, neglect, and household dysfunction. *Child Abuse and Neglect, 28*(7), 771–784.

Douglas, A. R. (2000). Reported anxieties concerning intimate parenting in women sexually abused as children. *Child Abuse and Neglect, 24*(3), 425–434.

Downey, G., & Feldman, S. (1996). Implications of rejection sensitivity for intimate relationships. *Journal of Personality and Social Psychology, 70*, 1327–1343.

Downey, G., Feldman, S., & Ayduk, O. (2000). Rejection sensitivity and male violence in romantic relationships. *Personal Relationships, 7*, 45–61.

Downey, G., Freitas, A. L., Michaelis, B., & Khouri, H. (1998). The self-fufilling prophecy in close relationships: Rejection sensitivity and rejection by romantic partners. *Journal of Personality and Social Psychology, 75*, 545–560.

Draijer, N., & Langeland, W. (1999). Childhood trauma and perceived parental dysfunction in the etiology of dissociative symptoms in psychiatric inpatients. *American Journal of Psychiatry, 156*, 379–385.

Draucker, C. B. (2001). Early family life and victimization in the lives of women. In K. Franey, R. Geffner & R. Falconer (Eds.), *The cost of child maltreatment: Who pays? We all do* (pp. 167–184). San Diego: Family Violence & Sexual Assault Institute.

Drossman, D. A. (1995). Sexual and physical abuse and gastrointestinal illness. *Scandinavian Journal of Gastroenterology, 30*(Suppl.), 90–96.

Drossman, D. A. (1997). Irritable bowel syndrome and sexual/physical abuse history. *European Journal of Gastroenterology and Hepatology, 9*, 327–330.

Drossman, D. A., Leserman, J., Li, Z., Keefe, F., Hu, Y. J. B., Toomey, T. C., & Mitchell, C. M. (2000). Effects of coping on health outcomes among women with gastrointestinal disorders. *Psychosomatic Medicine, 62*, 309–317.

Drossman, D. A., Leserman, J., Nachman, G., Li, Z., Gluck, H., Toomey, T. C., et al. (1990). Sexual and physical abuse in women with functional or organic gastrointestinal disorders. *Annals of Internal Medicine, 113*, 828–833.

Drossman, D. A., Li, Z., Leserman, J., Toomey, T. C., & Hu, Y. J. B. (1996). Health status by gastrointestinal diagnosis and abuse history. *Gastroenterology, 110*, 999–1007.

Drossman, D. A., Talley, N. J., Leserman, J., Olden, K. W., & Barreiro, M. A. (1995). Sexual and physical abuse and gastrointestinal illness: Review and recommendations. *Annals of Internal Medicine, 123*, 782–794.

Drossman, D. A., Whitehead, W. E., & Camilleri, M. (1997). Irritable bowel syndrome: A technical review for practice guideline development. *Gastroenterology, 112*, 2120–2137.

Druss, B. G., Rohbaugh, R. M., & Rosenheck, R. A. (1999). Depressive symptoms and health care costs in older medical patients. *American Journal of Psychiatry, 156*, 477–479.

Dube, S. R., Fairweather, D., Pearson, W. S., Felitti, V. J., Anda, R. F., & Croft, J. B. (2009). Cumulative childhood stress and autoimmune diseases in adults. *Psychosomatic Medicine, 71*(2), 243–250.

Dubowitz, H., Black, M. M., Kerr, M. A., Hussey, J. M., Morrel, T. M., Everson, M. D., et al. (2001). Type and timing of mothers' victimization: Effects on mothers and children. *Pediatrics, 107*, 728–735.

DuMont, K. A., Widom, C. S., & Czaja, S. J. (2007). Predictors of resilience in abused and neglected children grown-up: The role of individual and neighborhood characteristics. *Child Abuse and Neglect, 31*, 255–274.

Dunai, A., Keszei, A. P., Kopp, M. S., Shapiro, C. M., & Mucsi, I. (2008). Cardiovascular disease and health-care utilization in snorers: A population survey. *Sleep, 31*(3), 411–416.

Duncan, S. C., Strycker, L. A., & Duncan, T. E. (1999). Exploring associations in developmental trends of adolescent substance use and risky sexual behavior in a high-risk population. *Journal of Behavioral Medicine, 22*, 21–34.

Dutton, D. G., Van Grinkel, C., & Landolt, M. A. (1996). Jealousy, intimate abusiveness, and intrusiveness. *Journal of Family Violence, 11*(4), 411–423.

Eaker, E. D., Sullivan, L. M., Kelly-Hayes, M., D'Agostino, R. B., & Benjamin, E. J. (2007). Marital status, marital strain, and risk of coronary heart disease or total mortality: The Framingham Offspring Study. *Psychosomatic Medicine, 69*, 509–513.

Eckenrode, J., Campa, M., Luckey, D. W.,

Henderson, C. R., Cole, R., Kitzman, H., et al. (2010). Long-term effects of prenatal and infancy nurse home visitation on the life course of youths. *Archives of Pediatric and Adolescent Medicine, 164*(1), 9–15.

Edwards, R. R., Bingham, C. O., Bathon, J., & Haythornthwaite, J. A. (2006). Catastrophizing and pain in arthritis, fibromyalgia, and other rheumatic diseases. *Arthritis Care and Research, 55*(2), 325–332.

Egeland, B. (1991). A longitudinal study of high-risk families: Issues and findings. In R. H. Starr & D. A. Wolfe (Eds.), *The effects of child abuse and neglect: Issues and research* (pp. 33–56). New York: Guilford Press.

Egeland, B., Sroufe, L. A., & Erickson, M. (1983). The developmental consequences of different patterns of maltreatment. *Child Abuse and Neglect, 7*, 459–469.

Einvik, G., Hrubos-Strom, H., Ranby, A., Hordhus, I. H., Somers, V. K., Omland, T., et al. (2011). Major depressive disorder, anxiety disorders, and cardiac biomarkers in subjects at high risk of obstructive sleep apnea. *Psychosomatic Medicine, 73*, 378–384.

Eisenberger, N. I. (2011). The neural basis of social pain: Findings and implications. In G. MacDonald & L. A. Jensen-Campbell (Eds.), *Social pain: Neuropsychological and health implications of loss and exclusions* (pp. 53–78). Washington, DC: American Psychological Association.

Elliot, T. R., & Marmarosh, C. L. (1994). Problem-solving appraisal, health complaints, and health-related expectancies. *Journal of Counseling and Development, 72*, 531–537.

Elovainio, M., Aalto, A.-M., Kivimaki, M., Pirkola, S., Sundvall, J., Lonnqvist, J., et al. (2009). Depression and C-reactive protein: Population-based Health 2000 Study. *Psychosomatic Medicine, 71*, 423–430.

Elovainio, M., Pulkki-Raback, L., Kivimaki, M., Jokela, M., Viikari, J. S., Raitakari, O. T., et al. (2010). Lipid trajectories as predictors of depressive symptoms: The Young Finns study. *Health Psychology, 29*(3), 237–245.

Elwell, M. E., & Ephross, P. H. (1987). Initial reactions of sexually abused children. *Social Casework: Journal of Contemporary Social Work, 68*, 109–116.

Enlow, M. B., Kullowatz, A., Staudenmayer, J., Spasojevic, J., Ritz, T., & Wright, R. J. (2009). Associations of maternal lifetime trauma and perinatal traumatic stress symptoms with infant cardiorespiratory reactivity to psychological challenge. *Psychosomatic Medicine, 71*, 607–614.

Epstein, J. N., Saunders, B. E., Kilpatrick, D. G., & Resnick, H. S. (1998). PTSD as a mediator between childhood rape and alcohol use in adult women. *Child Abuse and Neglect, 22*, 223–234.

Ernster, V., & Colford, J. M. (1998). Host and disease: Influence of demographic and socioeconomic factors. In A. S. Fauci, E. Braunwald, K. J. Isselbacher, J. D. Wilson, J. Martin, D. L. Kasper, et al. (Eds.), *Harrison's principles of internal medicine* (14th ed.) (pp. 14–18). New York: McGraw-Hill.

Evans, S., Ferrando, S. J., Rabkin, J. G., & Fishman, B. (2000). Health locus of control, distress, and utilization of protease inhibitors among HIV-positive men. *Journal of Psychosomatic Research, 49*, 157–162.

Everson-Rose, S. A., Lewis, T. T., Karavolos, K., Dugan, S. A., Wesley, D., & Powell, L. H. (2009). Depressive symptoms and increased visceral fat in middle-aged women. *Psychosomatic Medicine, 71*, 410–416.

Exline, J. J., Yali, A. M., & Lobel, M. (1999). When God disappoints: Difficulty forgiving God and its role in negative emotion. *Journal of Health Psychology, 4*(3), 365–379.

Fargo, J. D. (2009). Pathways to adult sexual

revictimization: Direct and indirect behavioral risk factors across the lifespan. *Journal of Interpersonal Violence, 24*(11), 1771–1791.

Feiring, C., Rosenthal, S., & Taska, L. (2000). Stigmatization and the development of friendship and romantic relationships in adolescent victims of sexual abuse. *Child Maltreatment, 5*, 311–322.

Feiring, C., Taska, L., & Lewis, M. (1998). The role of shame and attributional style in children's and adolescents' adaptation to sexual abuse. *Child Maltreatment, 3*, 129–142.

Feiring, C., Taska, L., & Lewis, M. (2002). Adjustment following sexual abuse discovery: The role of shame and attributional style. *Developmental Psychology, 38*(1), 79–92.

Feldman, S., & Downey, G. (1994). Rejection sensitivity as a mediator of the impact of childhood exposure to family violence on adult attachment behavior. *Development and Psychopathology, 6*, 231–247.

Felitti, V. J. (1991). Long-term medical consequences of incest, rape, and molestation. *Southern Medical Journal, 84*, 328–331.

Felitti, V. J. (2001). Reverse alchemy in childhood: Turning gold into lead. *Health Alert, 8*, 1–4.

Felitti, V. J. (1991). Long-term medical consequences of incest, rape, and molestation. *Southern Medical Journal, 84*, 328–331.

Felitti, V. J. (2001). Reverse alchemy in childhood: Turning gold into lead. *Health Alert, 8*, 1–4.

Felitti, V. J., Anda, R. F., Nordenberg, D., Williamson, D. F., Spitz, A. M., Edwards, V., et al. (1998). Relationship of childhood abuse and household dysfunction to many of the leading causes of death in adults. The Adverse Childhood Experiences (ACE) Study. *American Journal of Preventive Medicine, 14*(4), 245–258.

Ferguson, K. M. (2009). Exploring family environment characteristics and multiple abuse experiences among homeless youth. *Journal of Interpersonal Violence, 24*(11), 1875–1891.

Fergusson, D. M., & Horwood, L. J. (1998). Exposure to interparental violence in childhood and psychosocial adjustment in young adulthood. *Child Abuse and Neglect, 22*, 339–357.

Fergusson, D. M., Boden, J. M., & Horwood, L. J. (2008). Exposure to childhood sexual and physical abuse and adjustment in early adulthood. *Child Abuse and Neglect, 32*, 607–619.

Fergusson, D. M., & Horwood, L. J. (1998). Exposure to interparental violence in childhood and psychosocial adjustment in young adulthood. *Child Abuse and Neglect, 22*, 339–357.

Fergusson, D. M., Horwood, L. J., & Lynskey, M. T. (1997). Childhood sexual abuse, adolescent sexual behaviors and sexual revictimization. *Child Abuse and Neglect, 21*, 789–803.

Fergusson, D. M., & Lynskey, M. T. (1997). Physical punishment/maltreatment during childhood and adjustment in young adulthood. *Child Abuse and Neglect, 21*, 617–630.

Fergusson, D. M., Lynskey, M. T., & Horwood, L. J. (1996). Childhood sexual abuse and psychiatric disorder in young adulthood: I. Prevalence of sexual ause and factors associated with sexual abuse. *Journal of the American Academy of Child and Adolescent Psychiatry, 35*, 1355–1364.

Fernandez-Mendoza, J., Vela-Bueno, A., Vgontzas, A. N., Ramos-Platon, M. J., Olavarrieta-Bernardino, S., Bixler, E. O., et al. (2010). Cognitive-emotional hyperarousal as a premorbid characteristic of individuals vulnerable to insomnia. *Psychosomatic Medicine, 72*, 397–403.

Field, T., Diego, M., & Hernandez-Reif, M. (2006). Prenatal depression effects on the fetus and newborn: A review. *Infant Behavior and Development, 29*, 445–455.

Fields, H. L., & Martin, J. B. (1998). Pain: Pathophysiology and management. In A. S. Fauci, E. Braunwald, K. J. Isselbacher, J. D. Wilson, J. B. Martin, D. L. Kasper, et al. (Eds.), *Harrison's priniciples of internal medicine* (14th ed.) (pp. 53–58). New York: McGraw-Hill.

Fifield, J., Tennen, H., Reisine, S., & McQuillan, J. (1998). Depression and the long-term risk of pain, fatigue, and disability in patients with rheumatoid arthritis. *Arthritis and Rheumatism, 41*, 1851–1857.

Finestone, H. M., Stenn, P., Davies, F., Stalker, C., Fry, R., & Koumanis, J. (2000). Chronic pain and health care utilization in women with a history of childhood sexual abuse. *Child Abuse and Neglect, 24*, 547–556.

Finkelhor, D. (1987). The trauma of child sexual abuse: Two models. *Journal of Interpersonal Violence, 2*, 348–366.

Finkelhor, D., & Browne, A. (1985). The traumatic impact of child sexual abuse: A conceptualization. *American Journal of Orthopsychiatry, 55*, 530–541.

Finkelhor, D., Hotaling, G. T., Lewis, I. A., & Smith, C. (1989). Sexual abuse and its relationship to later sexual satisfaction, marital status, religion, and attitudes. *Journal of Interpersonal Violence, 4*, 379–399.

Finkelhor, D., & Kendall-Tackett, K. A. (1997). A developmental perspective on the childhood impact of crime, abuse, and violent victimization. In D. Cicchetti & S. L. Toth (Eds.), *Rochester symposium on developmental psychopathology: Developmental perspectives on trauma* (Vol. 8) (pp. 1–32). Rochester, NY: University of Rochester Press.

Finkelhor, D., Ormrod, R. K., & Turner, H. A. (2009). The developmental epidemiology of childhood victimization. *Journal of Interpersonal Violence, 24*(5), 711–731.

Finkelhor, D., Ormrod, R. K., & Turner, H. A. (2009). Lifetime assessment of poly-victimization in a national sample of children and youth. *Child Abuse and Neglect, 33*, 403–411.

Fitchett, G., Rybarczyk, B. D., DeMarco, G. A., & Nicholas, J. J. (1999). The role of religion in medical rehabilitation outcomes: A longitudinal study. *Rehabilitation Psychology, 44*, 333–353.

Fleming, J., Mullen, P. E., Sibthorpe, B., & Bammer, G. (1999). The long-term impact of childhood sexual abuse in Australian women. *Child Abuse and Neglect, 23*, 145–159.

Foa, E. B., & Cahill, S. P. (2002). Specialized treatment for PTSD: Matching survivors to the appropriate modality. In R. Yehuda (Ed.), *Treating trauma survivors with PTSD* (pp. 43-62). Washington, DC: American Psychiatric Association Press.

Frasure-Smith, N., & Lesperance, F. (2005). Reflections on depression as a cardiac risk factor. *Psychosomatic Medicine, 67*, S19–S25.

Franzen, P. L., Gianaros, P. J., Marsland, A. L., Hall, M. H., Siegle, G. J., Dahl, R. E., et al. (2011). Cardiovascular reactivity to acute psychological stress following sleep deprivation. *Psychosomatic Medicine, 73*, 679–682.

Freedman, S. R., & Enright, R. D. (1996). Forgiveness as an intervention goal with incest survivors. *Journal of Consulting and Clinical Psychology, 64*, 983–992.

Freeman, K. (2010). Irritable bowel syndrome. Available online at: *http://www.clevelandclinicmeded.com/medicalpubs/diseasemanagement/gastroenterology/irritable-bowel-syndrome/#s0015.*

Freyd, J. J., Klest, B., & Allard, C. B. (2005). Betrayal trauma: Relationship to physical health, psychological distress, and a written disclosure intervention. *Journal of Trauma and Dissociation, 6*(3), 83–104.

Friedman, E. M., Hayney, M., Love, G. D., Singer, B. H., & Ryff, C. D. (2007). Plasma interleukin-6 and soluble IL-6 receptors are associated with psychological well-being in aging women. *Health Psychology, 6*(3), 305–313.

Friedman, E. M., & Herd, P. (2010). Income, education, and inflammation: Differential associations in a national probability sample (the MIDUS study). *Psychosomatic Medicine, 2*, 290–300.

Friedman, M. J. (2001). *Posttraumatic stress disorder: The latest assessment and treatment strategies*. Kansas City, MO: Compact Clinicals.

Friedman, M. J., Cohen, J. A., Foa, E. B., & Keane, T. M. (2009). Integration and summary. In E. B. Foa, T. M. Keane, M. J. Friedman, & J. A. Cohen (Eds.), *Effective treatments for PTSD: Practice guidelines from the International Society for Traumatic Stress Studies* (pp. 617–642). New York: Guilford Press.

Fritz, H. L., & Helgeson, V. S. (1998). Distinctions of unmitigated communion from communion: Self-neglect and over-involvement with others. *Journal of Personality and Social Psychology, 75*, 121–140.

Fullerton, C. S., Ursano, R. J., Epstein, R. S., Crowley, R., Vance, K. L., Kao, T.-C., et al. (2000). Peritraumatic dissociation following motor vehicles accidents. *Journal of Nervous and Mental Disease, 188*, 267–272.

Gagne, M.-H., Lavoie, F., & Hebert, M. (2005). Victimization during childhood and revictimization in dating relationships in adolescent girls. *Child Abuse and Neglect, 29*, 1155–1172.

Gall, T. L. (2006). Spirituality and coping with life stress among adult survivors of childhood sexual abuse. *Child Abuse and Neglect, 30*, 829–844.

Gallo, L. C., Troxel, W. M., Matthews, K. A., & Kuller, L. H. (2003). Marital status and quality in middle-aged women: Associations with levels and trajectories of cardiovascular risk factors. *Health Psychology, 22*, 453–463.

Gallop, R., McKeever, P., Toner, B., Lancee, W., & Lueck, M. (1995). Inquiring about childhood sexual abuse as part of the nursing history: Opinions of abuse and nonabused nurses. *Archives of Psychiatric Nursing, 9*, 146–151.

Gallup Poll. (1995). *Public opinion in 1995*. Wilmington, DE: Scholarly Resources.

Garcia-Campayo, J., Fayed, N., Serrano-Blanco, A., & Roca, M. (2009). Brain dysfunction behind functional symptoms: Neuroimaging and somatoform, conversive, and dissociative disorders. *Current Opinions in Psychiatry, 22*, 224–231.

Gaudin, J. M., Polansky, N. A., Kilpatrick, A. C., & Shilton, P. (1993). Loneliness, depression, stress, and social supports in neglectful families. *American Journal of Orthopsychiatry, 63*, 597–605.

Gauthier, L., Stollak, G., Messe, L., & Aronoff, J. (1996). Recall of childhood neglect and physical abuse as differential predictors of current psychological functioning. *Child Abuse and Neglect, 20*, 549–559.

Gavin, A. R., Chae, D. H., Mustillo, S., & Kiefe, C. I. (2009). Prepregnancy depressive mood and preterm birth in black and white women: Findings from the CARDIA Study. *Journal of Women's Health, 18*(6), 803–811.

Geracioti, T. D. J., Carpenter, L. L., Owens, M. J., Baker, D. G., Ekhator, N. N., Horn, P. S., et al. (2006). Elevated cerebrospinal fluid substance P concentrations in posttraumatic stress disorder and major depression. *American Journal of Psychiatry, 63*, 637–643.

Gershon, M. D. (1998). *The second brain*. New York: Harper.

Gibb, B. E., Alloy, L. B., Abramson, L. Y., Rose, D. T., Whitehouse, W. G., Donovan, P., et al.. (2001). History of childhood maltreatment, negative cognitive styles, and episodes of depression in adulthood. *Cognitive Therapy and Research, 25*(4), 425–446.

Gibson, L. E., & Leitenberg, H. (2001). The impact of child sexual abuse and stigma on methods of coping with sexual assault among undergraduate women. *Child Abuse and Neglect, 25*, 1343–1361.

Gibson, R. L., & Hartshome, T. S. (1996). Childhood sexual abuse and adult loneliness and network orientation. *Child Abuse and Neglect, 20*, 1087–1093.

Gilbert, L., El-Bassel, N., Schilling, R. F., & Friedman, E. (1997). Childhood abuse as a risk for partner abuse among women in methadone maintenance. *American Journal of Drug and Alcohol Abuse, 23*, 581–595.

Gil-Rivas, V., Fiorentine, R., Anglin, M. D., & Taylor, E. (1997). Sexual and physical abuse: Do they compromise drug treatment outcomes? *Journal of Substance Abuse Treatment, 14*, 351–358.

Gilson, K. J., & Lancaster, S. (2008). Childhood sexual abuse in pregnant and parenting adolescents. *Child Abuse and Neglect, 32*, 869–877.

Girdler, S. S., Leserman, J., Bunevicius, R., Klatzkin, R., Pedersen, C. A., & Light, K. C. (2007). Persistant alterations in biological profiles in women with abuse histories: Influence of premenstrual dysphoric disorder. *Health Psychology, 26*(2), 210–213.

Gladstone, G., Parker, G., Wilhelm, K., & Mitchell, P. (1999). Characteristics of depressed patients who report childhood sexual abuse. *American Journal of Psychiatry, 156*, 431–437.

Godshall, F. J., & Elliot, T. R. (1997). Behavioral correlates of self-appraised problem-solving ability: Problem-solving skills and health-compromising behaviors. *Journal of Applied Social Psychology, 27*, 929–944.

Goedhart, G., Snijders, A. C., Hesselink, A. E., van Poppel, M. N., Bonsel, G. J., & Vridkotte, T. G. M. (2010). Maternal depressive symptoms in relation to perinatal mortality and morbidity: Results from a large multiethnic cohort study. *Psychosomatic Medicine, 72*, 769–776.

Gold, E. R. (1986). Long-term effects of sexual victimization in childhood: An attributional approach. *Journal of Consulting and Clinical Psychology, 54*, 51–59.

Goldbacher, E. M., Bromberger, J., & Matthews, K. A. (2009). Lifetime history of major depression predicts the development of the metabolic syndrome in middle-aged women. *Psychosomatic Medicine, 71*, 266–272.

Golding, J. M. (1994). Sexual assault history and physical health in randomly selected Los Angeles women. *Health Psychology, 13*, 130–138.

Golding, J. M. (1999). Sexual assault history and headache: Five general population studies. *Journal of Nervous and Mental Disease, 187*, 624–629.

Golding, J. M., Cooper, M. L., & George, L. K. (1997). Sexual assault history and health perceptions: Seven general population studies. *Health Psychology, 16*, 417–425.

Goodman, E., Daniels, S. R., & Dolan, L. M. (2007). Socioeconomic disparities in insulin resistance: Results from the Princeton School District Study. *Psychosomatic Medicine, 69*, 61–67.

Goodman, E., McEwen, B. S., Huang, B., Dolan, L. M., & Adler, N. E. (2005). Social inequalities in biomarkers of cardiovascular risk in adolescence. *Psychosomatic Medicine, 67*, 9–15.

Goodman, L. A., Dutton, M. A., & Harris,

M. (1995). Episodically homeless women with serious mental illness: Prevalence of physical and sexual assault. *American Journal of Orthopsychiatry, 65*, 468–478.

Goodman, L. A., & Fallot, R. D. (1998). HIV risk behavior in poor urban women with serious mental disorders: Association with childhood physical and sexual abuse. *American Journal of Orthopsychiatry, 68*, 73–83.

Gordon, D. A. (1997). Fibromyalgia: Out of control? *Journal of Rheumatology, 24*, 1247.

Gorey, K. M., & Leslie, D. R. (1997). The prevalence of child sexual abuse: Integrative review adjustment for potential response and measurement biases. *Child Abuse and Neglect, 21*(4), 391–398.

Gorey, K. M., Richter, N. L., & Snider, E. (2001). Guilt, isolation, and hopelessness among female survivors of childhood sexual abuse: Effectiveness of group work intervention. *Child Abuse and Neglect, 25*, 347–355.

Gover, A. R., Kaukinen, C., & Fox, K. A. (2008). The relationship between violence in the family of origin and dating violence among college students. *Journal of Interpersonal Violence, 23*(12), 1667–1693.

Gracia, E., & Musitu, G. (2003). Social isolation from communities and child maltreatment: A cross-cultural comparison. *Child Abuse and Neglect, 27*, 153–168.

Grajeda, R., & Perez-Escamilla, R. (2002). Stress during labor and delivery is associated with delayed onset of lactation among urban Guatemalan women. *Journal of Nutrition, 132*, 3055–3060.

Grauerholz, L. (2000). An ecological approach to understanding sexual revictimization: Linking personal, interpersonal, and sociocultural factors and processes. *Child Maltreatment, 5*, 5–17.

Green, B. L., Kaltman, S., Frank, L., Glennie, M., Subramanian, A., Fritts-Wilson, M., et al. (2011). Primary care providers' experiences with trauma patients: A qualitative study. *Psychological Trauma, 3*(1), 37–41.

Greenberg, P. E., Sisitsky, T., Kessler, R. C., Finkelstein, S. N., Berndt, E. R., Davidson, J. R. T., et al. (1999). The economic burden of anxiety disorders in the 1990s. *Journal of Clinical Psychology, 60*, 427–435.

Greenwood, C. L., Tangalos, E. G., & Maruta, T. (1990). Prevalence of sexual abuse, physical abuse, and concurrent traumatic life events in a general medical population. *Mayo Clinic Proceedings, 65*, 1067–1071.

Grimstad, H., & Schei, B. (1999). Pregnancy and delivery for women with a history of child sexual abuse. *Child Abuse and Neglect, 23,* 81–90.

Groer, M. W., Davis, M. W., & Hemphill, J. (2002). Postpartum stress: Current concepts and the possible protective role of breast-feeding. *Journal of Obstetric, Gynecologic, and Neonatal Nursing, 31*(4), 411–417.

Groer, M. W., & Kendall-Tackett, K. A. (2011). *How breastfeeding protects women's health throughout the lifespan: The psychoneuroimmunology of human lactation*. Amarillo, TX: Hale.

Groër, M. W., Davis, M. W., Smith, K. W., Casey, K., Kramer, V., & Bukovsky, E. (2005). Immunity, inflammation and infection in post-partum breast and formula feeders. *American Journal of Reproductive Immunology, 54*, 222–231.

Groer, M. W., Thomas, S. P., Evans, G. W., Helton, S., & Weldon, A. (2006). Inflammatory effects and immune system correlates of rape. *Violence and Victims, 21*(6), 796–808.

Gross, R. J., Doerr, H., Caldirola, D., Guzinkski, G. M., & Ripley, H. S. (1980). Borderline syndrome and incest in chronic pelvic pain patients. *International Journal of Psychiatry in Medicine, 10*, 79–96.

Grossardt, B. R., Bower, J. H., Geda, Y. E., Colligan, R. C., & Rocca, W. A. (2009). Pessimistic, anxious, and depressive personality traits predict all-cause mortality: The Mayo Clinic Cohort Study of Personality and Aging. *Psychosomatic Medicine, 71*, 491–500.

Gurvitz, T. V., Gilbertson, M. W., Lasko, N. B., Tarhan, A. S., Simeon, D., Macklin, M. L., et al. (2000). Neurologic soft signs in chronic posttraumatic stress disorder. *Archives of General Psychiatry, 7*, 181–186.

Guo, S. F., Wu, J. L., Qu, C. Y., & Yan, R. Y. (2004). Physical and sexual abuse of women before, during and after pregnancy. *International Journal of Gynaecology and Obstetrics, 84*(3), 281–286.

Gutierres, S. E., & Todd, M. (1997). The impact of childhood abuse on treatment outcomes of substance users. *Professional Psychology: Research and Practice, 28*, 348–354.

Hadler, N. M. (1997). Fibromyalgia: La maladie est mort. Vive la maladie! *Journal of Rheumatology, 24*, 1250–1252.

Haj-Yahia, M., Tishby, O., & deZoysa, P. (2009). Posttraumatic stress disorder among Sri Lankan university students as a consequence of their exposure to family violence. *Journal of Interpersonal Violence, 24*(12), 2018–2038.

Hale, T. W., Kendall-Tackett, K. A., Cong, Z., Votta, R., & McCurdy, F. (2010). Discontinuation syndrome in newborns whose mothers took antidepressants while pregnant or breastfeeding. *Breastfeeding Medicine, 5*(6), 283–288.

Hall, J. M. (1996). Pervasive effects of childhood sexual abuse in lesbians' recovery from alcohol problems. *Substance Use and Misuse, 31*, 225–239.

Hall, M., Buysse, D. J., Nowell, P. D., Nofzinger, E. A., Houck, P., Reynolds, C. F., et al. (2000). Symptoms of stress and depression as correlates of sleep in primary insomnia. *Psychosomatic Medicine, 62*, 227–230.

Hall, M. H., Muldoon, M. F., Jennings, J. R., Buysse, D. J., Flory, J. D., & Manuck, S. B. (2008). Self-reported sleep duration is associated with the metabolic syndrome in midlife adults. *Sleep, 31*(5), 635–643.

Hamilton, N. A., Affleck, G., Tennen, H., Karlson, C., Luxton, D., Preacher, K. J., et al. (2008). Fibromyalgia: The role of sleep in affect and in negative event reactivity and recovery. *Health Psychology, 27*(4), 490–494.

Hamilton, N. A., Affleck, G., Tennen, H., Karlson, C., Luxton, D., Preacher, K. J., & Templin, J. L. (2008). Fibromyalgia: The role of sleep in affect and in negative event reactivity and recovery. *Health Psychology, 27*(4), 490–494.

Hamilton, N. A., Catley, D., & Karlson, C. (2007). Sleep and the affective response to stress and pain. *Health Psychology, 26*(3), 288–295.

Hanson, M. D., & Chen, E. (2010). Daily stress, cortisol, and sleep: The moderating role of childhood psychosocial environments. *Health Psychology, 29*(4), 394–402.

Harris, A. H. S., Thoresen, C. E., McCullough, M. E., & Larson, D. B. (1999). Spiritually and religiously oriented health interventions. *Journal of Health Psychology, 4*(3), 413–433.

Harrison, P. A., Fulkerson, J. A., & Beebe, T. J. (1997). Multiple substance use among adolescent physical and sexual abuse victims. *Child Abuse and Neglect, 21*, 529–539.

Harrop-Griffiths, J., Katon, W., Walker, E., Holm, L., Russo, J., & Hickok, L. (1988). The association between chronic pelvic pain, psychiatric diagnoses, and childhood sexual abuse. *Obstetrics and Gynecology, 71*, 589–593.

Harrykissoon, S. D., Rickert, V. I., &

Wiemann, C. M. (2002). Prevalence and patterns of intimate partner violence among adolescent mothers during the postpartum period. *Archives of Pediatric and Adolescent Medicine, 156*(4), 325–330.

Harter, S., Alexander, P., & Neimeyer, R. (1988). Long-term effects of incestuous child abuse in college women: Social adjustments, social cognitions, and family characteristiscs. *Journal of Consulting and Clinical Psychology, 56*, 5–8.

Harter, S. L., & Vanecek, R. J. (2000). Cognitive assumptions and long-term distress in survivors of childhood abuse, parental alcoholism, and dysfunctional family environments. *Cognitive Therapy and Research, 24*, 445–472.

Hassinger, H. J., Semenchuck, E. M., & O'Brien, W. H. (1999). Appraisal and coping responses to pain and stress in migraine headache sufferers. *Journal of Behavioral Medicine, 22*, 327–340.

Hastings, D. P., & Kaufman, G. K. (2004). Screening for family violence in perioperative settings. In K. A. Kendall-Tackett (Ed.), *Health consequences of abuse in the family* (pp. 33–44). Washington, DC: American Psychological Association.

Hatchett, L., Friend, R., Symister, P., & Wadhwa, N. (1997). Interpersonal expectations, social support, and adjustment to chronic illness. *Journal of Personality and Social Psychology, 73*, 560–573.

Hatzenbueler, M. L., Nolen-Hoeksema, S., & Erickson, S. J. (2008). Minority stress predictors of HIV risk behavior, substance use, and depressive symptoms: Results from a prospective study of bereaved gay men. *Health Psychology, 27*(4), 455–462.

Hawkley, L. C., Preacher, K. J., & Cacioppo, J. T. (2010). Loneliness impairs daytime functioning but not sleep duration. *Health Psychology, 29*(2), 124–129.

Hazen, A. L., Connelly, C. D., Roesch, S. C., Hough, R. L., & Landsverk, J. A. (2009). Child maltreatment profiles and adjustment problems in high-risk adolescents. *Journal of Interpersonal Violence, 24*(2), 361–378.

Heck, K. E., Schoendorf, K. C., Chavez, G. F., & Braveman, P. (2003). Does postpartum length of stay affect breastfeeding duration? A population-based study. *Birth, 30*, 153–159.

Heffernan, K. (1998). Bulimia nervosa. In E. A. Blechman & K. D. Brownell (Eds.), *Behavioral medicine & women: A comprehensive handbook* (pp. 358–363). New York: Guilford Press.

Heim, C., & Nemeroff, C. B. (2009). Neurobiology of posttraumatic stress disorder. *CNS Spectrums, 14*(1 Suppl. 1), 13–24.

Heim, C., Ehlert, U., Hanker, J. P., & Hellhammer, D. H. (1998). Abuse-related posttraumatic stress disorder and alterations of the hypothalamic-pituitary-adrenal axis in women with chronic pelvic pain. *Psychosomatic Medicine, 60*, 309–318.

Heim, C., Newport, D. J., Heit, S., Graham, Y. P., Wilcox, M., Bonsall, R., et al. (2000). Pituitary-adrenal and autonomic responses to stress in women after sexual and physical abuse in childhood. *Journal of the American Medical Association 284*, 592–597.

Helgeson, V. S. (1993). Implications of agency and communion for patient and spouse adjustment to a first coronary event. *Journal of Personality and Social Psychology, 64*, 807–816.

Helgeson, V. S., & Fritz, H. L. (1996). Implications of unmitigated communion and communion for adolescent adjustment to Type 1 diabetes. *Women's Health: Research on Gender, Behavior, and Policy, 2*, 163–188.

Helgeson, V. S., & Fritz, H. L. (1998). A theory of unmitigated communion. *Personality and Social Psychology Review, 2*, 173–183.

Helgeson, V. S., & Fritz, H. L. (1999).

Unmitigated agency and unmitigated communion: Distinctions from agency and communion. *Research in Personality, 33*, 131–158.

Hendrick, V., Stowe, Z. N., Altshuler, L. L., Hwang, S., Lee, E., & Haynes, D. (2003). Placental passage of antidepressant medications. *American Journal of Psychiatry, 160*(5), 993–996.

Herman, D. B., Susser, E. S., & Link, B. L. (1997). Adverse childhood experiences: Are they risk factors for adult homelessness? *American Journal of Public Health, 87*, 249–255.

Herrenkohl, E. C., Herrenkohl, R. C., Rupert, L. J., Egolf, B. P., & Lutz, G. (1995). Risk factors for behavioral dysfunction: The relative impact of maltreatment, SES, physical health problems, cognitive ability, and quality of parent-child interaction. *Child Abuse and Neglect, 19*, 191–203.

Hetzel, M. D., & McCanne, T. R. (2005). The roles of peritraumatic dissociation, child physical abuse, and child sexual abuse in the development of posttraumatic stress disorder and adult victimization. *Child Abuse and Neglect, 29*, 915–930.

Hofer, M. A. (1996). On the nature and consequences of early loss. *Psychosomatic Medicine, 58*, 570–586.

Hilton, N. Z., Jennings, K. T., Drugge, J., & Stephens, J. (1995). Childhood sexual abuse among clinicians working with sex offenders. *Journal of Interpersonal Violence, 10*, 525–532.

Hoglund, C. L., & Nicholas, K. B. (1995). Shame, guilt, and anger in college students exposed to abusive family environments. *Journal of Family Violence, 10*, 141–157.

Holder, D. W., Durant, R. H., Harris, T. L., Daniel, J. H., Obeidallah, D., & Goodman, E. (2000). The association between adolescent spirituality and voluntary sexual activity. *Journal of Adolescent Health, 26*, 295–302.

Holzer, S. R., Uppala, S., Wonderlich, S. A., Crosby, R. D., & Simonich, H. (2008). Mediational significance of PTSD in the relationship of sexual trauma and eating disorders. *Child Abuse and Neglect, 32*, 561–566.

Hong, S., Nelesen, R. A., Krohn, P. L., Mills, P. J., & Dimsdale, J. E. (2006). The association of social status and blood pressure with markers of vascular inflammation. *Psychosomatic Medicine, 68*, 517–523.

House, J. S., Landis, K. R., & Umberson, D. (1988). Social relationships and health. *Science, 241*, 540–545.

Howren, M. B., Lamkin, D. M., & Suls, J. (2009). Associations of depression with C-Reactive protein, IL-1, and IL-6: A meta-analysis. *Psychosomatic Medicine, 71*, 171–186.

Hu, J. C., Link, C. L., McNaughton-Collins, M., Barry, M. J., & McKinlay, J. B. (2007). The association of abuse and symptoms suggestive of chronic prostatitis/chronic pelvic pain syndrome: Results from the Boston Area Community Health Survey. *Journal of General Internal Medicine, 22*(11), 1532–1537.

Hudson, J. L., Goldenberg, D. L., Pope, H. G., & Schlesinger, L. (1992). Comorbidity of fibromyalgia with medical and psychiatric disorders. *American Journal of Medicine, 92*, 363–367.

Hudson, J. L., & Pope, H. G. (1989). Fibromyalgia and psychopathology: Is fibromyalgia a form of "affective spectrum disorder"? *Journal of Rheumatology, 16*(Suppl. 19), 15–22.

Hulme, P. A. (2000). Symptomatology and health care utilization of women primary care patients who experienced childhood sexual abuse. *Child Abuse and Neglect, 24*, 1471–1484.

Humphreys, J. C., Lee, K. A., Neylan, T. C., & Marmar, C. R. (1999). Sleep patterns of sheltered battered women. *Journal of Nursing Scholarship, 31*, 139–143.

Ikeda, A., Schwartz, J., Peters, J. L., Fang, S., Spiro, A., Sparrow, D., et al. (2011). Optimism in relation to inflammation and endothelial dysfunction in older men: The VA Normative Aging Study. *Psychosomatic Medicine, 73*, 664–671.

Ingram, K. M., Corning, A. F., & Schmidt, L. D. (1996). The relationship of victimization experiences to psychological well-being among homeless women and low-income housed women. *Journal of Counseling Psychology, 43*, 218–227.

Imich, D., Behrens, N., Gleditsch, J., Stor, W., Schreiber, M., Schops, P., et al. (2002). Immediate effects of dry needling and acupuncture at distant points in chronic neck pain: Results of a randomized, double-blind, sham-controlled crossover trial. *Pain, 99*, 83–98.

Institute for Clinical Systems Improvement. (2000). *Health care guidelines: Major depression in specialty care in adults*. Retrieved from *www.icsi.org*.

International Society for Traumatic Stress Studies. (Ed.). (2009). *Effective treatments for PTSD: Psychopharmacology for adults (Guideline 6)*. New York: Guilford Press.

Ito, Y., Teicher, M. H., Glod, C. A., & Ackerman, E. (1998). Preliminary evidence for aberrant corticol development in abused children: A quantitative EEG study. *Journal of Neuropsychiatry and Clinical Neurosciences, 10*, 298–307.

Jackson, B., Kubzansky, L. D., Cohen, S., Jacobs, D. R., & Wright, R. J. (2007). Does harboring hostility hurt? Associations between hostility and pulmonary function in the Coronary Artery Risk Development in (Young) Adults (CARDIA) Study. *Health Psychology, 26*(3), 333–340.

Janicki-Deverts, D., Cohen, S., Adler, N. E., Schwartz, J. E., Matthews, K. A., & Seeman, T. E. (2007). Socioeconomic status is related to urinary catecholamines in the Coronary Artery Risk Development in Young Adults (CARDIA) Study. *Psychosomatic Medicine, 69*, 514–520.

Jarvis, T. J., & Copeland, J. (1997). Child sexual abuse as a predictor of psychiatric co-morbidity and its implications for drug and alcohol treatment. *Drug and Alcohol Dependence, 49*, 61–69.

Jasinski, J. S., Williams, L. M., & Siegel, J. A. (2000). Childhood physical and sexual abuse as risk factors for heavy drinking among African American women: A prospective study. *Child Abuse and Neglect, 24*, 1061–1071.

Jenson-Campbell, L. A., & MacDonald, G. (2011). Introduction: Experiencing the ache of social injuries—an integrative approach to understanding social pain. In G. MacDonald & L. A. Jensen-Campbell (Eds.), *Social pain: Neuropsychological and health implications of loss and exclusion* (pp. 3–8). Washington, DC: American Psychological Association.

Jimerson, D. C., Wolfe, B. E., Metzger, E. D., Finkelstein, D. M., Cooper, T. B., & Levine, J. M. (1997). Decreased serotonin function in bulimia nervose. *Archives of General Psychiatry, 54*, 529–534.

Jinich, S., Paul, J. P., Stall, R., Acree, M., Kegeles, S., Hoff, C., et al. (1998). Childhood sexual abuse and HIV risk-taking behavior among gay and bisexual men. *AIDS and Behavior, 2*, 41–51.

Johnson, W., Corley, J., Starr, J. M., & Deary, I. J. (2011). Psychological and physical health at age 70 in the Lothian Birth Cohort 1936: Links with early life IQ, SES, and current cognitive function and neighborhood environment. *Health Psychology, 30*(1), 1–11.

Jokela, M., Elovainio, M., Singh-Manoux, A., & Kivimaki, M. (2009). IQ, socioeconomic status, and early death: The U.S. National Longitudinal Survey of Youth. *Psychosomatic Medicine, 71*, 322–328.

Jones, G. R., Steketee, W., Black, R. E., Bhutta, Z. A., Morris, S. S., & Bellagio Child Survival Study Group. (2003). How many child deaths can we prevent this year? *Lancet, 362*, 65–71.

Jones, N., Field, T., Fox, N., Lundy, B., & Devalos, M. (1997). EEG activation in one-month-old infants of depressed mothers. *Development & Psychopathology, 9*, 491–505.

Jones, N. A., McFall, B. A., & Diego, M. A. (2004). Patterns of brain electrical activity in infants of depressed mothers who breastfeed and bottle feed: The mediating role of infant temperament. *Biological Psychology, 67*, 103–124.

Kalichman, S. C., Rompa, D., DiFonzo, K., Simpson, D., Luke, W., Kyomugisha, F., et al. (2001). HIV treatment adherence in women living with HIV/AIDS: Research based on the Information-Motivation-Behavioral Skills model of health behavior. *Journal of the Association of Nurses in AIDS Care, 12*, 58–67.

Kaplan, G. A., & Camacho, T. (1983). Perceived health and mortality: A nine-year follow-up of the Human Population Laboratory cohort. *American Journal of Epidemiology, 11*, 292–304.

Kaplan, R. M., Ries, A. L., Prewitt, L. A., & Eakin, E. (1994). Self-efficacy expectations predict survival for patients with chronic obstructive pulmonary disease. *Health Psychology, 13*, 366–368.

Kaplan, S. J., Pelcovitz, D., Salzinger, S., & Weiner, M. (1998). Adolescent physical abuse: Risk for adolescent psychiatric disorders. *American Journal of Psychiatry, 155*, 954–959.

Kasprow, W. J., & Rosenheck, R. (2000). Mortality among homeless and nonhomeless mentally ill veterans. *Journal of Nervous and Mental Disease, 188*, 141–147.

Katerndahl, D. A. (1999). Illness attitudes and coping process in subjects with panic attacks. *Journal of Nervous and Mental Disease, 187*, 562–566.

Katz, R. S., & Kravitz, H. M. (1996). Fibromyalgia, depression, and alcoholism: A family history study. *Journal of Rheumatology, 23*, 149–154.

Kaufman, J., Birmaher, B., Perel, J., Dahl, R. E., Moreci, P., Nelson, B., et al. (1997). The corticotropin-releasing hormone challenge in depressed abuse, depressed nonabused, and normal control children. *Biological Psychiatry, 42*, 669–679.

Kellogg, N. D., & Hoffman, T. J. (1997). Child sexual revictimization by multiple perpetrators. *Child Abuse and Neglect, 21*, 953–964.

Kendall-Tackett, K. A. (Ed.). (2004). *Health consequences of abuse in the family: A clinical guide for evidence-based practice.* Washington, DC: American Psychological Association.

Kendall-Tackett, K. A. (2005). Trauma associated with perinatal events: Birth experience, prematurity, and childbearing loss. In K. A. Kendall-Tackett (Ed.), *Handbook of women, stress, and trauma* (pp. 53–74). New York: Brunner-Routledge.

Kendall-Tackett, K. A. (Ed.). (2005). *Handbook of women, stress and trauma.* New York: Brunner-Routledge.

Kendall-Tackett, K. A. (2007). A new paradigm for depression in new mothers: The central role of inflammation and how breastfeeding and anti-inflammatory treatments protect maternal mental health. *International Breastfeeding Journal, 2*(6). Available online at: *http://www.internationalbreastfeedingjournal.com/content/2/1/6).*

Kendall-Tackett, K. A. (2009). Psychological trauma and physical health: A psychoneuro-immunology approach to etiology of negative health effects and possible interventions. *Psychological Trauma, 1*(1), 35–48.

Kendall-Tackett, K. A. (2010). *Depression in new mothers: Causes, consequences and treatment options* (2nd ed.). London: Routledge.

Kendall-Tackett, K. A. (Ed.). (2010). *The psychoneuroimmunology of chronic disease.* Washington, DC: American Psychological Association.

Kendall-Tackett, K. A., & Becker-Blease, K. (2004). Why we need retrospective findings in child maltreatment research. *Child Abuse and Neglect, 28*, 723–727.

Kendall-Tackett, K. A., Cong, Z., & Hale, T. W. (2011). The effect of feeding method on sleep duration, maternal well-being, and postpartum depression. *Clinical Lactation, 2*(2), 22–26.

Kendall-Tackett, K. A., & Eckenrode, J. (1996). The effects of neglect on academic achievement and disciplinary problems: A developmental approach. *Child Abuse and Neglect, 20*, 161–169.

Kendall-Tackett, K. A., & Klest, B. (Eds.). (2010). *Trauma, dissociation and health.* London: Routledge.

Kendall-Tackett, K. A., & Marshall, R. (1999). Victimization and diabetes: An exploratory study. *Child Abuse and Neglect, 23*, 593–596.

Kendall-Tackett, K. A., Marshall, R., & Ness, K. E. (2000). Victimization, healthcare use and health maintenance. *Family Violence and Sexual Assault Bulletin, 16*, 18–21.

Kendall-Tackett, K. A., Marshall, R., & Ness, K. E. (2003). Chronic pain syndromes and violence against women. *Women and Therapy, 26*, 45–56.

Kendall-Tackett, K. A., & Simon, A. F. (1987). Perpetrators and their acts: Data from 265 adults molested as children. *Child Abuse and Neglect, 11*, 237–245.

Kendall-Tackett, K. A., Williams, L. M., & Finkelhor, D. (1993). The impact of sexual abuse on children: A review and synthesis of recent empirical studies. *Psychological Bulletin, 113*, 164–180.

Kendler, K. S., Bulik, C. M., Silberg, J., Hettema, J. M., Myers, J., & Prescott, C. A. (2000). Childhood sexual abuse and adult psychiatric and substance use disorders in women. *Archives of General Psychiatry, 57*, 953–959.

Kennedy, M., & Felson, D. T. (1996). A prospective long-term study of fibromyalgia syndrome. *Arthritis and Rheumatism, 39*, 682–685.

Kershaw, K. N., Mezuk, B., Abdou, C. M., Rafferty, J. A., & Jackson, J. S. (2010). Socioeconomic position, health behaviors, and C-reactive protein: A moderated-mediation analysis. *Health Psychology, 29*(3), 307–316.

Kessler, B. L., & Bieschke, K. J. (1999). A retrospective analysis of shame, dissociation, and adult victimization in survivors of childhood sexual abuse. *Journal of Counseling Psychology, 46*, 335–341.

Kia-Keating, M., Sorsoli, L., & Grossman, F. K. (2010). Relational challenges and recovery processes in male survivors of childhood sexual abuse. *Journal of Interpersonal Violence, 25*(4), 666–683.

Kiecolt-Glaser, J. K., & Glaser, R. (2002). Depression and immune function: Central pathways to morbidity and mortality. *Journal of Psychosomatic Research, 53*, 873–876.

Kiecolt-Glaser, J. K., Loving, T. J., Stowell, J. R., Malarky, W. B., Lemeshow, S., Dickinson, S. L., & Glaser, R. (2005). Hostile marital interactions, proinflammatory cytokine production, and wound healing. *Archives of General Psychiatry, 62*, 1377–1384.

Kiecolt-Glaser, J. K., & Newton, T. L. (2001). Marriage and health: His and hers. *Psychological Bulletin, 127*, 472–503.

Kiecolt-Glaser, J. K., Preacher, K. J., MacCallum, R. C., Atkinson, C., Malarkey, W. B., & Glaser, R. (2003). Chronic stress and age-related increases in the proinflammatory cytokine IL-6. *Proceedings of the National Academy of Sciences USA, 100*(15), 9090–9095.

Kim, J., Talbot, N. L., & Cicchetti, D. (2009). Childhood abuse and current interpersonal conflict: The role of shame. *Child Abuse and Neglect, 33*, 362–371.

Kimerling, R., Ouimette, P. C., Cronkite, R. C., & Moos, R. H. (1999). Depression and outpatient medical utilization: A naturalistic 10-year follow-up. *Annals of Behavioral Medicine, 21*(4), 317–321.

Kinder, L. S., Bradley, K. A., Katon, W. J., Ludman, E. J., McDonnell, M. B., & Bryson, C. L. (2008). Depression, posttraumatic stress disorder, and mortality. *Psychosomatic Medicine, 70*, 20–26.

King, D. W., King, L. A., & Foy, D. W. (1996). Prewar factors in combat-related posttraumatic stress disorder: Structual equation modeling with a national sample of female and male Vietnam veterans. *Journal of Consulting & Clinical Psychology, 64*, 520–531.

King, K. E., Morenoff, J. D., & House, J. S. (2011). Neighborhood context and social disparities in cumulative biological risk factors. *Psychosomatic Medicine, 73*, 572–579.

King, T. K., Clark, M. M., & Pera, V. (1996). History of sexual abuse and obesity treatment outcome. *Addictive Behaviors, 21*, 283–290.

Kinzl, J. F., & Biebl, W. (1997). Sexual abuse in people with alcohol problems. *British Journal of Psychiatry, 170*, 193.

Kinzl, J. F., Traweger, C., Guenther, V., & Biebl, W. (1994). Family background and sexual abuse associated with eating disorders. *American Journal of Psychiatry, 151*, 1127–1131.

Kitzman-Ulrich, H., Wilson, D. K., Van Horn, M. L., & Lawman, H. G. (2010). Relationship of body mass index and psychosocial factors on physical activity in underserved adolescent boys and girls. *Health Psychology, 29*(5), 506–513.

Kivimaki, M., Batty, G. D., Singh-Manoux, A., Nabi, H., Sabia, S., Tabak, A. G., et al. (2009). Association between common mental disorder and obesity over the adult life course. *British Journal of Psychiatry, 195*, 149–155.

Klein, H., Elifson, K. W., & Sterk, C. E. (2007). Childhood neglect and adulthood involvement in HIV-related risk behaviors. *Child Abuse and Neglect, 31*(1), 39–53.

Kokko, K., Pulkkinen, L., & Puustinen, M. (2000). Selection into long-term unemployment and its psychological consequences. *International Journal of Behavioral Development, 24*, 310–320.

Koob, G. F., & LeMoal, M. (1997). Drug abuse: Hedonic homeostatic dysregulation. *Science, 278*, 52–57.

Kong, S. K., & Lee, D. T. (2004). Factors influencing decision to breastfeed. *Journal of Advanced Nursing, 46*, 369–379.

Kop, W. J., Berman, D. S., Gransar, H., Wong, N. D., Miranda-Peats, R., White, M. D., & et al. (2005). Social networks and coronary artery calcification in asymptomatic individuals. *Psychosomatic Medicine, 67*, 343–352.

Kop, W. J., & Gottdiener, J. S. (2005). The role of immune system parameters in the relationship between depression and coronary artery disease. *Psychosomatic Medicine, 67*, S37–S41.

Kop, W. J., Gottdiener, J. S., Tangen, C. M., Fried, L. P., McBurnie, M. A., Walston, J., et al. (2002). Inflammation and coagulation factors in persons > 65 years of age with symptoms of depression but without evidence of myocardial ischemia. *American Journal of Cardiology, 89*(4), 419–424.

Koss, M. P. (1990). The women's mental health research agenda: Violence against women. *American Psychologist, 45*, 374–380.

Koss, M. P., & Dinero, T. E. (1989). Discriminant analysis of risk factors for sexual victimization among a national sample of college women. *Journal of Consulting and Clinical Psychology, 57*, 242–250.

Koss, M. P., Koss, P. G., & Woodruff, M. S. (1991). Deleterious effects of criminal victimization on women's health and medical utilization. *Archives of Internal Medicine, 151*, 342–347.

Koverola, C., Proulx, J., Battle, P., & Hanna, C. (1996). Family functioning as predictors of distress in revictimized sexual abuse survivors. *Journal of Interpersonal Violence, 11*, 263–280.

Krahe, B., Scheinberger-Olwig, R., Waizenhofer, E., & Kolpin, S. (1999). Childhood sexual abuse and revictimization in adolescence. *Child Abuse and Neglect, 23*, 383–394.

Krakow, B., Artar, A., Warner, T. D., Melendez, D., Johnston, L., Hollifield, M., et al. (2000a). Sleep disorder, depression, and suicidality in female sexual assault survivors. *Crisis, 21*, 163–170.

Krakow, B., Lowry, C., Germain, A., Gaddy, L., Hollifield, M., Koss, M., et al. (2000b). A retrospective study on improvements in nightmares and post-traumatic stress disorder following treatment for co-morbid sleep-disordered breathing. *Journal of Psychosomatic Research, 49*(5), 291–298.

Krakow, B., Tandberg, D., Sandoval, D., Cutchen, L., & Schrader, R. (1998). Severity of sleep disturbances in sexual assault survivors. *Sleep, 21*(Suppl.), 150.

Kroenke, K., Spitzer, R. L., DeGruy, F. V., Hahn, S. R., Linzer, M., Williams, J. B., et al. (1997). Multisomatoform disorder: An alternative to undifferentiated somatoform disorder for the somatizing patient in primary care. *Archives of General Psychiatry, 54*, 352–358.

Kronish, I. M., Rieckmann, N., Schwartz, J. E., Schwartz, D. R., & Davidson, K. W. (2009). Is depression after an acute coronary syndrome simply a marker of known prognostic factors for mortality? *Psychosomatic Medicine, 71*, 697–703.

Kubzansky, L. D., & Kawachi, I. (2000). Going to the heart of the matter: Do negative emotions cause coronary heart disease? *Journal of Psychosomatic Research, 48*, 323–337.

Kubzansky, L. D., Kawachi, I., & Sparrow, D. (1999). Socioeconomic status, hostility, and risk factor clustering in the normative aging study: Any help from the concept of allostatic load? *Annals of Behavioral Medicine, 21*(4), 330–338.

Kuligowska, E., Deeds, L., & Lu, K. (2005). Pelvic pain: Overlooked and underdiagnosed gynecologic conditions. *RadioGraphics, 25*, 3–20.

Kull, M. (2002). The relationships between physical activity, health status, and psychological well-being of fertility-aged women. *Scandinavian Journal of Medicine and Science of Sports, 12*, 241–247.

Kuyken, W., & Brewin, C. R. (1999). The relation of early abuse to cognition and coping in depression. *Cognitive Therapy and Research, 23*, 665–677.

Lancaster, S. L., Robriguez, B. F., & Weston, R. (2011). Path analytic examination of a cognitive model of PTSD. *Behaviour Research and Therapy, 49*, 194–201.

Lang, A. J., Laffaye, C., Satz, L. E., McQuaid, J. R., Malcarne, V. L., Dreselhaus, T. R., et al. (2006). Relationships among childhood maltreatment, PTSD, and health in female veterans with a history of child maltreatment. *Child Abuse and Neglect, 30*, 1281–1292.

Lang, A. J., Rodgers, C. S., & Lebeck, M. M. (2006). Associations between maternal childhood maltreatment and psychopathology and aggression during pregnancy and postpartum. *Child Abuse and Neglect, 30*, 17–25.

Lange, A., deBeurs, E., Dolan, C., Lachnit, T., Sjollema, S., & Hanewald, G. (1999). Long-term effects of childhood sexual abuse: Objective and subjective characteristics of the abuse and psychopathology in later life. *Journal of Nervous and Mental Disease, 187*, 150–158.

Lange, J. T., Lange, C. L., & Cabaltica, R. B. G. (2000). Primary care treatment of posttraumatic stress disorder. *American Family Physician, 62*, 1035–1040, 1046.

Latthe, P., Mignini, L., Gray, R., Hills, R., & Khan, K. (2006). Factors predisposing women to chronic pelvic pain: Systematic review. *British Medical Journal, 332*, 749–755.

Laws, A., & Golding, J. M. (1996). Sexual assault history and eating disorder symptoms among white, Hispanic, and African American women and men. *American Journal of Public Health, 86*, 579–582.

Lawson, R., Drebing, C., Berg, G., Vincellette, A., & Penk, W. (1998). The long-term impact of child abuse on religious behavior and spirituality in men. *Child Abuse and Neglect, 22*, 369–380.

Lazarus, R. S., & Folkman, S. (1984). *Stress, appraisal, and coping*. New York: Springer.

Lecrubier, Y., Clerc, G., Didi, R., & Kieser, M. (2002). Efficacy of St. John's wort extract WS 5570 in major depression: A double-blind, placebo-controlled trial. *American Journal of Psychiatry, 159*, 1361–1366.

Lemieux, A. M., & Coe, C. L. (1995). Abuse-related posttraumatic stress disorder: Evidence for chronic neuroendocrine activation in women. *Psychosomatic Medicine, 57*, 105–115.

Leserman, J., & Drossman, D. A. (1995). Sexual and physical abuse history and medical practice. *General Hospital Psychiatry, 17*, 71–74.

Leserman, J., & Drossman, D. A. (2007). Relationship of abuse history to functional gastrointestinal disorders and symptoms: Some possible mediating mechanisms. *Trauma, Violence, and Abuse, 8*(3), 331–343.

Leserman, J., Drossman, D. A., Li, Z., Toomey, T. C., Nachman, G., & Glogau, L. (1996). Sexual and physical abuse history in gastroenterology practice: How types of abuse impact health status. *Psychosomatic Medicine, 58*, 4–15.

Leserman, J., Li, Z., Drossman, D. A., & Hu, Y. J. B. (1998). Selected symptoms associated with sexual and physical abuse history among female patients with gastrointestinal disorders: The impact on subsequent health care visits. *Psychological Medicine, 28*, 417–425.

Leserman, J., Li, Z., Drossman, D. A., Toomey, T. C., Nachman, G., & Glogau, L. (1997). Impact of sexual and physical abuse dimensions on health status: Development of an abuse severity measure. *Psychosomatic Medicine, 59*, 152–160.

Leserman, J., Petitto, J. M., Golden, R. N., Gaynes, B. N., Gu, H., Perkins, D. O., et al. (2000). Impact of stressful life events, depression, social support, coping, and cortisol on progression to AIDS. *American Journal of Psychiatry, 157*, 1221–1228.

Leserman, J., Toomey, T. C., & Drossman, D. A. (1995). Medical consequences of sexual and physical abuse in women. *Humane Medicine, 11*, 23–28.

Leshner, A. I. (1997). Addiction is a brain disease. *Science, 278*, 45–47.

Lesperance, F., & Frasure-Smith, N. (2000). Depression in patients with cardiac disease: A practical review. *Journal of Psychosomatic Research, 48*, 379–391.

Lev-Wiesel, R., Daphna-Tekoah, S., & Hallak, M. (2009). Childhood sexual abuse as a predictor of birth-related posttraumatic stress and postpartum posttraumatic stress. *Child Abuse and Neglect, 33*, 877–887.

Levav, I., Kohn, R., & Schwartz, S. (1998). The psychiatric after-effects of the Holocaust on the second generation. *Psychological Medicine, 28*, 755–760.

Leventhal, A. M., Mickens, L., Dunton, G. F., Sussman, S., Riggs, N. R., & Pentz, M. A. (2010). Tobacco use moderates the association between major depression and obesity. *Health Psychology, 29*(5), 521–528.

Levitan, R. D., Parikh, S. V., Lesage, A. D., Hegadoren, K. M., Adams, M., Kennedy, S. H., et al. (1998). Major depression in individuals with a history of childhood physical or sexual abuse: Relationship to neurovegative features, mania, and gender. *American Journal of Psychiatry, 155*, 1746–1752.

Levy, R. L., Cain, K. C., Jarrett, M., & Heitkemper, M. M. (1997). The relationship between daily life stress and gastrointestinal symptoms in women with irritable bowel syndrome. *Journal of Behavioral Medicine, 20*, 177–193.

Lewin, D. S., & Dahl, R. E. (1999). Importance of sleep in the mangement of pediatric pain. *Journal of Behavioral and Developmental Pediatrics, 20*, 244–252.

Lewis, T. T., Aiello, A. E., Leurgans, S., Kelly, J., & Barnes, L. L. (2010). Self-reported experiences of everyday discrimination are associated with elevated C-reactive protein levels in older African-American adults. *Brain, Behavior and Immunity, 24*(3), 438–443.

Lewis, T. T., Everson-Rose, S. A., Karavolos, K., Janssen, I., Wesley, D., & Powell, L. H. (2009). Hostility is associated with visceral, but not subcutaneous, fat in middle-aged African American and white women. *Psychosomatic Medicine, 71*, 733–740.

Lewis, T. T., Everson-Rose, S. A., Powell, L. H., Matthews, K. A., Brown, C., Karavolos, K., et al. (2006). Chronic exposure to everyday discrimination and coronary artery calcification in African American women: The SWAN Heart Study. *Psychosomatic Medicine, 68*, 362–368.

Li, J., Vestergaard, M., Obel, C., Precht, D. H., Christensen, J., Lu, M., et al. (2009). Prenatal stress and cerebral palsy: A nation-wide cohort study in Denmark. *Psychosomatic Medicine, 71*, 615–618.

Libby, A. M., Orton, H. D., Beals, J., Buchwald, D., & Manson, S. M. (2008). Childhood abuse and later parenting outcomes in two American Indian tribes. *Child Abuse and Neglect, 32*, 195–211.

Liem, J. H., & Boudewyn, A. C. (1999). Contextualizing the effects of childhood sexual abuse on adult self- and social functioning: An attachment theory perspective. *Child Abuse and Neglect, 23*, 1141–1157.

Lin, E. H. B., Heckbert, S. R., Rutter, C. M., Katon, W. J., Ciechanowski, P., Ludman, E. J., et al. (2009). Depression and increased mortality in diabetes: Unexpected causes of death. *Annals of Family Medicine, 7*(5), 414–421.

Lindberg, F. H., & Distad, I. J. (1985). Post-traumatic stress disorders in women who experienced childhood incest. *Child Abuse and Neglect, 9*, 329–345.

Lipschitz, D. S., Winegar, R. K., Hartmick, E., Foote, B., & Southwick, S. M. (1999). Posttraumatic stress disorder in hospitalized adolescents: Psychiatric comorbidity and clinical correlates. *Journal of the American Academy of Child and Adolescent Psychiatry, 38*, 385–392.

Little, L., & Hamby, S. (1996). Impact of a clinician's sexual abuse history, gender, and theoretical orientation on treatment issues related to childhood sexual abuse. *Professional Psychology: Research and Practice, 27*, 617–625.

Littleton, H., Breitkopf, C. R., & Berenson, A. (2007). Sexual and physical abuse history and adult sexual risk behaviors: Relationships among women and potential mediators. *Child Abuse and Neglect, 31*, 757–768.

Lizardi, H., & Klein, D. N. (2000). Parental psychopathology and reports of the childhood home environment in adults with early-onset dysthymic disorder. *Journal of Nervous and Mental Disease, 188*, 63–70.

Longstreth, G. F., Thompson, W. G., Chey, W. D., Houghton, L. A., Mearin, F., & Spiller, R. C. (2006). Functional bowel disorders. *Gastroenterology, 130*, 1480–1491.

Lopez, M. A., & Heffer, R. W. (1998). Self-concept and social competence of university student victims of childhood physical abuse. *Child Abuse and Neglect, 22*, 183–195.

Loren, B. (1998). The intimate relationship between chronic pain and depression. In M. Forster, B. Loren, C. Potter, S. Rosloff, S. VonTobel, & B. Voss (Eds.), *Phillips Graduate Institute 1998 progress journal* (pp. 3–10). Available online at: *www.pgi.edu.*

Loucks, E. B., Almeida, N. D., Taylor, S. E., & Matthews, K. A. (2011). Childhood family psychosocial environment and coronary heart disease risk. *Psychosomatic Medicine, 73*, 563–571.

Loucks, E. B., Berkman, L. F., Cruenewald, T. L., & Seeman, T. E. (2005). Social integration is associated with fibrinogen concentration in elderly men. *Psychosomatic Medicine, 67*, 353–358.

Louik, C., Lin, A. E., Werler, M. M., Hernandez-Diaz, S., & Mitchell, A. A. (2007). First-trimester use of selective serotonin-reuptake inhibitors and the risk of birth defects. *New England Journal of Medicine, 356*, 2675–2683.

Lovallo, W. R. (1997). *Stress and health: Biological and psychological interactions*. Newbury Park, CA: Sage.

Low, C. A., Matthews, K. A., Kuller, L. H., & Edmundowicz, D. (2011). Psychosocial predictors of coronary artery calcification progression in postmenopausal women. *Psychosomatic Medicine, 73*, 789–794.

Low, C. A., Thurston, R. C., & Matthews, K. A. (2010). Psychosocial factors in the development of heart disease in women: Current research and future directions. *Psychosomatic Medicine, 72*(9), 842–854.

Luciano, M., Marioni, R. E., Gow, A. J., Starr, J. M., & Deary, I. J. (2009). Reverse causation in the association between C-reactive protein and fibrinogen levels and cognitive abilities in an aging sample. *Psychosomatic Medicine, 71*, 404–409.

Luecken, L. J. (2000). Attachment and loss experiences during childhood are associated with adult hostility, depression, and social support. *Journal of Psychosomatic Research, 49*, 85–91.

Luppino, F. S., deWit, L. M., Bouvy, P. F., Stijnen, T., Cuijpers, P., Penninx, B. W. J. H., et al. (2010). Overweight, obesity, and depression: A systematic review and meta-analysis of longitudinal studies. *Archives of General Psychiatry, 67*(3), 220–229.

Lutenbacher, M. (2002). Relationship between psychosocial factors and abusive parenting attitudes in low-income single mothers. *Nursing Research, 51*(3), 158–167.

Luthra, R., Abramowitz, R., Greenberg, R., Schoor, A., Newcorn, J., Schmeidler, J., et al. (2009). Relationship between type of trauma exposure and posttraumatic stress disorder among urban children and adolescents. *Journal of Interpersonal Violence, 24*(11), 1919–1927.

Lutz, K. F. (2005). Abuse experiences, perceptions, and associated decisions during the childbearing cycle. *Western Journal of Nursing, 27*, 802–824

Lynch, M., & Cicchetti, D. (1991). Patterns of relatedness in maltreated and nonmaltreated children: Connections among multiple representational models. *Development and Psychopathology, 3*, 207–226.

Maccoby, E. (1983). Social-emotional development and response to stressors. In N. Garmezy & M. Rutter (Eds.), *Stress, coping, and development in children* (pp. 217–234). New York: McGraw-Hill.

MacDonald, G., Borsook, T. K., & Spielmann, S. (2011). Defensive avoidance of social pain via perceptions of social threat and reward. In G. MacDonald & L. A. Jensen-Campbell (Eds.), *Social pain:*

Neuropsychological and health implications of loss and exclusion (pp. 141–160). Washington, DC: American Psychological Association.

Macrodimitris, S. D., & Endler, N. S. (2001). Coping, control, and adjustment in Type 2 diabetes. *Health Psychology, 20*(3), 208–216.

Maes, M. (2001). Psychological stress and the inflammatory response system. *Clinical Science, 101*, 193–194.

Maes, M., Bosmans, E., & Ombelet, W. (2004). In the puerperium, primiparae exhibit higher levels of anxiety and serum peptidase activity and greater immune responses than multiparae. *Journal of Clinical Psychiatry*, *65*(1), 71–76.

Maes, M., Christophe, A., Bosmans, E., Lin, A., & Neels, H. (2000). In humans, serum polyunsaturated fatty acid levels predict the response of proinflammatory cytokines to psychologic stress. *Biological Psychiatry, 47*, 910–920.

Maes, M., Lin, A., Ombelet, W., Stevens, K., Kenis, G., DeJongh, R., et al. (2000). Immune activation in the early puerperium is related to postpartum anxiety and depressive symptoms. *Psychoneuroendocrinology, 25*, 121–137.

Maes, M., Yirmyia, R., Noraberg, J., Brene, S., Hibblen, J., Perini, G., et al. (2009a). The inflammatory & neurodegenerative (I&ND) hypothesis of depression: Leads for future research and new drug development. *Metabolic Brain Disease, 24*, 27–53.

Maier, E. H., & Lachman, M. E. (2000). Consequences of early parental loss and separation for health and well-being in midlife. *International Journal of Behavioral Development, 24*(2), 183–189.

Main, C. J., Richards, H. L., & Fortune, D. G. (2000). Why put new wine in old bottles: The need for a biopsychosocial approach to the assessment, treatment, and understanding of unexplained and explained symptoms in medicine. *Journal of Psychosomatic Research, 48*, 511–514.

Mallet, S., & Rosenthal, D. (2009). Physically violent mothers are a reason for young people's leaving home. *Journal of Interpersonal Violence, 24*(7), 1165–1174.

Malt, E. A., Berle, J. E., Olafsson, S., Lund, A., & Ursin, H. (2000). Fibromyalgia is associated with panic disorder and functional dyspepsia with mood disorders: A study of women with random sample population controls. *Journal of Psychosomatic Research, 49*, 285–289.

Maltby, J., Macaskill, A., & Day, L. (2001). Failure to forgive self and others: A replication and extension of the relationship between forgiveness, personality, social desirability, and general health. *Personality and Individual Differences, 30*, 881–885.

Manber, R., Edinger, J. D., Gress, J. L., San Pedro-Salcedo, M. G., Kuo, T. F., & Kalista, T. (2008). Cognitive behavioral therapy for insomnia enhances depression outcome in patients with comorbid major depressive disorder and insomnia. *Sleep, 31*(4), 489–495.

Manuck, S. B., Phillips, J. E., Gianaros, P. J., Flory, J. D., & Muldoon, M. F. (2010). Subjective socioeconomic status and presence of the metabolic syndrome in midlife community volunteers. *Psychosomatic Medicine, 72*, 35–45.

Marcus, D. A. (2000). Treatment of nonmalignant chronic pain. *American Family Physician, 61*, 1331–1338.

Marioni, R. E., Stewart, M. C., Murray, G. D., Deary, I. J., Fowkes, F. G. R., Lowe, G. D. O., et al. (2009). Peripheral levels of fibrinogen, C-reactive protein, and plasmas viscosity predict future cognitive decline in individuals without dementia. *Psychosomatic Medicine, 71*, 901–906.

Marin, T. J., Chen, E., Munch, J. A., & Miller, G. E. (2009). Double-exposure to acute stress and chronic family stress is associated with immune changes in children with asthma. *Psychosomatic Medicine, 71*, 378–384.

Marks, R. (2001). Efficacy theory and its utility in arthritis rehabilitation: Review and recommendations. *Disability and Rehabilitation: An International Multidisciplinary Journal, 23*, 271–280.

Martin, S. L., Mackie, L., Kupper, L. L., Buescher, P. A., & Moracco, K. E. (2001). Physical abuse of women before, during, and after pregnancy. *Journal of the American Medical Association, 285*(12), 1581–1584.

Marx, B. P., Calhoun, K. S., Wilson, A. E., & Meyerson, L. A. (2000). Sexual revictimization prevention: An outcome evaluation. *Journal of Consulting and Clinical Psychology, 69*(1), 25–32.

Marx, B. P., Nichols-Anderson, C., Messman-Moore, T. L., Miranda, R., & Porter, C. (2000). Alcohol consumption, outcome expectancies, and victimization status among female college students. *Journal of Applied Social Psychology, 30*(5), 1056–1070.

Mastorakos, G., & Ilias, I. (2003). Maternal and fetal hypothalamic-pituitary-adrenal axes during pregnancy and postpartum. *Annals of the New York Academy of Sciences, 997*, 136–149.

Matsunaga, H., Kaye, W. H., McConaha, C., Plotnicov, K., Pollice, C., Rao, R., et al. (1999). Psychopathological characteristics of recovered bulimics who have a history of physical or sexual abuse. *Journal of Nervous and Mental Disease, 187*, 472–477.

Maunder, R. G., Peladeau, N., Savage, D., & Lancee, W. J. (2010). The prevalence of childhood adversity among healthcare workers and its relationship to adult life events, distress and impairment. *Child Abuse and Neglect, 34*, 114–123.

McAuley, E., Morris, K. S., Motl, R. W., Hu, L., Konopack, J. F., & Elavsky, S. (2007). Long-term follow-up of physical activity behavior in older adults. *Health Psychology, 26*(3), 375–380.

McBeth, J., MacFarlane, G. J., Benjamin, S., Morris, S., & Silman, A. J. (1999). The association between tender points, psychological distress, and adverse childhood experiences: A community-based sample. *Arthritis and Rheumatism, 42*, 1397–1404.

McCarty, D., Argeriou, M., Huebner, R. B., & Lubran, B. (1991). Alcoholism, drug abuse, and the homeless. *American Psychologist, 46*, 1161–1169.

McCauley, J., Tarpley, M. J., Haaz, S., & Bartlett, S. J. (2008). Daily spiritual experiences of older adults with and without arthritis and the relationship to health outcomes. *Arthritis Care and Research, 59*(1), 122–128.

McCloskey, M. S., Kleabir, K., Berman, M. E., Chen, E. Y., & Coccaro, E. F. (2010). Unhealthy aggression: Intermittent explosive disorder and adverse physical health outcomes. *Health Psychology, 29*(3), 324–332.

McCloskey, L. A., & Walker, M. (2000). Posttraumatic stress in children exposed to family violence. *Journal of the American Academy of Child and Adolescent Psychiatry, 39*, 108–115.

McCullough, M. E., Hoyt, W. T., Larson, D. B., Koenig, H. G., & Thoresen, C. E. (2000). Religious involvement and mortality: A meta-analytic review. *Psychological Bulletin, 19*, 211–222.

McDade, T. W., Hawkley, L. C., & Cacioppo, J. T. (2006). Psychosocial and behavioral predictors of inflammation in middle-aged and older adults: The Chicago Health, Aging, and Social Relations Study. *Psychosomatic Medicine, 68*, 376–381.

McEwen, B. (1999). Development of the cerebral cortex: XIII Stress and brain development: II. *Journal of the American*

Academy of Child and Adolescent Psychiatry, 38, 101–103.

McEwen, B. S. (2003). Mood disorders and allostatic load. *Biological Psychiatry, 54*, 200–207.

McGregor, K., Julich, S., Glover, M., & Gautam, J. (2010). Health professionals' responses to disclosure of child sexual abuse history: Female child sexual abuse survivors' experiences. *Journal of Child Sexual Abuse, 19*, 239–254.

McLewin, L. A., & Muller, R. T. (2006). Attachment and social support in the prediction of psychopathology among young adults with and without a history of physical maltreatment. *Child Abuse and Neglect, 30*, 171–191.

McWilliams, L. A., & Bailey, S. J. (2010). Associations between adult attachment ratings and health conditions: Evidence from the National Comorbidity Survey Replication. *Health Psychology, 29*(4), 446–453.

Meisinger, C., Kandler, U., & Ladwig, K.-H. (2009). Living alone is associated with an increased risk of Type 2 diabetes mellitus in men but not women from the general population: The MONICA/KORA Augsburg Cohort Study. *Psychosomatic Medicine, 71*, 784–788.

Mellman, T. A. (2002). Rationale and role for medication in the comprehensive treatment of PTSD. In R. Yehuda (Ed.), *Treating trauma survivors with PTSD* (pp. 63-74). Washington, DC: American Psychiatric Association Press.

Mellman, T. A., Brown, D. D., Jenifer, E. S., Hipolito, M. M. S., & Randall, O. S. (2009). Posttraumatic stress disorder and nocturnal blood pressure dipping in young adult African Americans. *Psychosomatic Medicine, 71*, 627–630.

Mendelson, T., Thurston, R. C., & Kubzansky, L. D. (2008). Affective and cardiovascular effects of experimentally induced social status. *Health Psychology, 27*(4), 482–489.

Mennen, F. E. (1995). The relationship of race/ethnicity to symptoms of childhood sexual abuse. *Child Abuse and Neglect, 19*, 115–124.

Messman-Moore, T. L., & Brown, A. L. (2004). Child maltreatment and perceived family environment as risk factors for adult rape: Is child sexual abuse the most salient experience? *Child Abuse and Neglect, 28*, 1019–1034.

Messman-Moore, T. L., Brown, A. L., & Koelsch, L. E. (2005). Posttraumatic symptoms and self-dysfunction as consequences and predictors of sexual revicitmization. *Journal of Traumatic Stress, 18*(3), 1–9.

Messman-Moore, T. L., Coates, A. A., Gaffey, K. J., & Johnson, C. F. (2008). Sexuality, substance use, and susceptibility to victimization: Risk for rape and sexual coercion in a prospective study of college women. *Journal of Interpersonal Violence, 23*(12), 1730–1746.

Messman-Moore, T. L., & Long, P. J. (2003). The role of childhood sexual abuse sequelae in the sexual revictimization of women: An empirical review and theoretical reformulation. *Clinical Psychology Review, 23*, 537–571.

Messman-Moore, T. L., Ward, R. M., & Brown, A. L. (2009). Substance use and PTSD symptoms impact the likelihood of rape and revictimization in college women. *Journal of Interpersonal Violence, 24*(3), 499–521.

Meyer, B., & Carver, C. S. (2000). Negative childhood accounts, sensitivity and pessimism: A study of avoidant personality disorder features in college students. *Journal of Personality Disorders, 14*, 233–248.

Mezick, E. J., Matthews, K. A., Hall, M., Kamarck, T. W., Strollo, P. J., Buysse, D. J., et al. (2010). Low life purpose and high hostility are related to an attenuated decline in nocturnal blood pressure. *Health Psychology, 29*(2), 196–204.

Mezick, E. J., Matthews, K. A., Hall, M., Strollo, P. J., Buysse, D. J., Kamarck, T. W., et al. (2008). Influence of race and socioeconomic status on sleep: Pittsburgh SleepSCORE Project. *Psychosomatic Medicine, 70*, 410–416.

Milburn, N., & D'Ercole, A. (1991). Homeless women: Moving toward a comprehensive model. *American Psychologist, 46*, 1161–1169.

Miller, A. H. (1998). Neuroendocrine and immune system interactions in stress and depression. *Psychiatric Clinics of North America, 21*, 443–463.

Miller, D. A., McClusky-Fawcett, K., & Irving, L. M. (1993). The relationship between childhood sexual abuse and subsequent onset of bulimia nervosa. *Child Abuse and Neglect, 17*, 305–314.

Miller, G. E., Cohen, S., & Ritchey, A. K. (2002). Chronic psychological stress and the regulation of pro-inflammatory cytokines: A gulcocorticoid-resistance model. *Health Psychology, 21*, 531–541.

Miller, L. (1999). Child abuse brain injury: Clinical, neuropsychological, and forensic considerations. *Journal of Cognitive Rehabilitation, 17*(2), 10–19.

Miller, L. (2000). Neurosensitization: A model for persistent disability in chronic pain, depression, and posttraumatic stress disorder following injury. *NeuroRehabilitation, 14*, 25–32.

Miller, T. Q., Smith, T. W., Turner, C. W., Guijarro, M. L., & Hallet, A. J. (1996). A meta-analytic review of research on hostility and physical health. *Psychological Bulletin, 119*, 322–348.

Moeller, T. P., Bachman, G. A., & Moeller, J. R. (1993). The combined effects of physical, sexual and emotional abuse during childhood: Long-term health consequences for women. *Child Abuse and Neglect, 17*, 623–641.

Molnar, B. E., Berkman, L. F., & Buka, S. L. (2001). Psychopathology, childhood sexual abuse and other childhood adversities: Relative links to subsequent suicidal behaviour in the U.S. *Psychological Medicine, 31*, 965–977.

Moore, S. A., Varra, A. A., Michael, S. T., & Simpson, T. L. (2010). Stress-related growth, positive reframing, and emotional processing in the prediction of post-trauma functioning among veterans in mental health treatment. *Psychological Trauma, 2*(2), 93–96.

Moorman, A. J., Mozaffarian, D., Wilkinson, C. W., Lawler, R. L., McDonald, G. B., Crane, B. A., et al. (2007). In patients with heart failure elevated soluble TNF-receptor 1 is associated with higher risk of depression. *Journal of Cardiac Failure, 13*(9), 738–743.

Moos, R. H., & Cronkite, R. C. (1999). Symptom-based predictors of a 10-year chronic course of treated depression. *Journal of Nervous and Mental Disease, 187*, 360–368.

Morin, C. M. (2004). Cognitve-behavioral approaches to the treatment of insomnia. *Journal of Clinical Psychiatry, 65*[Suppl. 16], 33–40.

Morin, C. M., & Ware, J. C. (1996). Sleep and psychopathology. *Applied and Preventive Psychology, 5*, 211–224.

Morozink, J. A., Friedman, E. M., Coe, C. L., & Ryff, C. D. (2010). Socioeconomic and psychosocial predictors of interleukin-6 in the MIDUS National Sample. *Health Psychology, 29*(6), 626–635.

Mosack, K. E., Randolph, M. E., Dickson-Gomez, J., Abbott, M., Smith, E., & Weeks, M. R. (2010). Sexual risk-taking among high-risk urban women with and without histories of childhood sexual abuse: Mediating effects of contextual factors. *Journal of Child Sexual Abuse, 19*, 43–61.

Mossey, J. M., & Shapiro, E. (1982). Self-rated health: A predictor of mortality among the elderly. *American Journal of Public Health, 72*, 406–414.

Motivala, S. J., Sarfatti, A., Olmos, L., & Irwin, M. R. (2005). Inflammatory markers and sleep disturbance in major depression. *Psychosomatic Medicine, 67*(2), 187–194.

Mountz, J. M., Bradley, L. A., Modell, J. G., Alexander, R. W., Triana-Alexander, M., Aaron, L. A., et al. (1995). Fibromyalgia in women: Abnormalities of regional cerebral blood flow in the thalamus and the caudate nucleus are associated with low pain threshold levels. *Arthritis and Rheumatism, 7*, 926–938.

Mulder, R. T., Beautrais, A. L., Joyce, P. R., & Fergusson, D. M. (1998). Relationship between dissociation, childhood sexual abuse, childhood physical abuse, and mental illness in a general population sample. *American Journal of Psychiatry, 155*, 806–811.

Mullen, P. E., Martin, J. L., Anderson, J. C., Romans, S. E., & Herbison, G. P. (1994). The effect of child sexual abuse on social, interpersonal, and sexual function in adult life. *British Journal of Psychiatry, 165*, 35–47.

Muller, R. T., Goebel-Fabbri, A. E., Diamond, T., & Dinklage, D. (2000). Social support and the relationship between family and community violence exposure and psychopathology among high-risk adolescents. *Child Abuse and Neglect, 4*, 449–464.

Munroe, C. D., Kibler, J. L., Ma, M., Dollar, K. M., & Coleman, M. (2010). The relationship between posttraumatic stress symptoms and sexual risk: Examining potential mechanisms. *Psychological Trauma, 2*(1), 49–53.

Murberg, T. A., Bru, E., Svebak, S., Tveteras, R., & Aarsland, T. (1999). Depressed mood and subjective health symptoms as predictors of mortality in patients with congestive heart failure: A two-year follow-up study. *International Journal of Psychiatry in Medicine, 29*, 311–326.

Murphy, D. A., Stein, J. A., Schlenger, W., Maibach, E., & National Institute of Mental Health Multisite HIV Prevention Trial Group. (2001). Conceptualizing the multidimensional nature of self-efficacy: Assessment of situational context and level of behavioral challenge to maintain safer sex. *Health Psychology, 20*(4), 281–290.

Murphy, P. E., Ciarrocchi, J. W., Piedmont, R. L., Cheston, S., Peyrot, M., & Fitchett, G. (2000). The relation of religious belief and practices, depression, and hopelessness in persons with clinical depression. *Journal of Consulting and Clinical Psychology, 68*, 1102–1106.

Murray, C. J. L., & Lopez, A. D. (1997). Global mortality, disability, and the contribution of risk factors: Global Burden of Disease Study. *Lancet, 349*, 1436–1442.

Myers, D. G. (2000). The funds, friends, and faith of happy people. *American Psychologist, 55*, 56–67.

Mykletun, A., Bjerkeset, O., Overland, S., Prince, M., Dewey, M., & Stewart, R. (2009). Levels of anxiety and depression as predictors of mortality: The HUNT study. *British Journal of Psychiatry, 195*, 118–125.

National Institute of Mental Health. (2000). *Brief notes on the mental health of children.* Washington, DC: Author.

Nelson, E. C., Heath, A. C., Madden, P. A. F., Cooper, M. L., Dinwiddie, S., Bucholz, K. K., et al. (2002). Association between self-reported childhood sexual abuse and adverse psychosocial outcomes. *Archives of General Psychiatry, 59*(2), 139–145.

Nesse, R. M., & Berridge, K. C. (1997). Psychoactive drug use in evolutionary perspective. *Science, 278*, 63–66.

Nestler, E. J., & Aghajanian, G. K. (1997). Molecular and cellular basis of addiction. *Science, 278*, 58–62.

Newton, T. L., & Sanford, J. M. (2003). Conflict structure moderates associations between cardiovascular reactivity and negative marital interaction. *Health Psychology, 22*(3), 270–278.

Niaura, R., Banks, S. M., Ward, K. D., Stoney, C. M., Spiro, A., 3rd, Aldwin, C. M., et al. (2000). Hostility and the metabolic syndrome in older males: the normative aging study. *Psychosomatic Medicine, 62*(1), 7–16.

Nicholson, A., Rose, R., & Bobak, M. (2010). Associations between different dimensions of religious involvement and self-rated health in diverse European populations. *Health Psychology, 29*(2), 227–235.

Nicholson, N. A., Davis, M. C., Kruszewski, D., & Zautra, A. J. (2010). Childhood maltreatment and diurnal cortisol patterns in women with chronic pain. *Psychosomatic Medicine, 72*, 471–480.

Noell, J., Rohde, P., Seeley, J., & Ochs, L. (2001). Childhood sexual abuse, adolescent sexual coercion, and sexually transmitted infection acquisition among homeless femal adolescents. *Child Abuse and Neglect, 25*, 137–148.

Norman, P., Bennett, P., Smith, C., & Murphy, S. (1998). Health locus of control and health behaviour. *Journal of Health Psychology, 3*(2), 171–180.

Nouwen, A., Ford, T., Balan, A. T., Twisk, J., Ruggiero, L., & White, D. (2011). Longitudinal motivational predictors of dietary self-care and diabetes control in adults with newly diagnosed type 2 diabetes mellitus. *Health Psychology, 30*(6), 771–779.

Nuttal, R., & Jackson, H. (1994). Personal history of childhood abuse among clinicians. *Child Abuse and Neglect, 18*, 455–472.

Nyamathi, A. M., Stein, J. A., & Swanson, J. M. (2000). Personal, cognitive, behavioral, and demographic predictors of HIV testing and STDs in homeless women. *Journal of Behavioral Medicine, 23*, 123–147.

Nyiendo, J., Maas, M., Goldberg, B., & Sexton, G. (2001). Pain, disability, and satisfaction outcomes and predictors of outcomes: A practice-based study of chronic low back pain patients attending primary care and chiropractic physicians. *Journal of Manipulation and Physiological Therapy, 24*, 433–439.

Obasaju, M. A., Palin, F. L., Jacobs, C., Anderson, P., & Kaslow, N. J. (2009). Won't you be my neighbor? Using an ecological approach to examine the impact of community on revictimization. *Journal of Interpersonal Violence, 24*(1), 38–53.

Oberlander, T. F., Misri, S., Fitzgerald, C. E., Kostaras, X., Rurak, D., & Riggs, W. (2004). Pharmacologic factors associated with transient neonatal symptoms following prenatal psychotropic medication exposure. *Journal of Clinical Psychiatry, 65*(2), 230–237.

Oddy, W. H., Kendall, G. E., Li, J., Jacoby, P., Robinson, M., de Klerk, N. H., et al. (2009). The long-term effects of breastfeeding on child and adolescent mental health: A pregnancy cohort study followed for 14 years. *Journal of Pediatrics, 156*(4), 568–574.

Okun, M. L., Schetter, C. D., & Glynn, L. M. (2011). Poor sleep quality is associated with preterm birth. *Sleep, 34*(11), 1493–1498.

O'Leary, P., Coohey, C., & Easton, S. D. (2010). The effect of severe child sexual abuse and disclosure on mental health during adulthood. *Journal of Child Sexual Abuse, 19*, 275–289.

Oliver, J. M., & Paull, J. C. (1995). Self-esteem and self-efficacy: Perceived parenting and family climate, and depression in university students. *Journal of Clinical Psychology, 51*, 467–481.

Oman, D., Thoresen, C. E., & McMahon, K.

(1999). Volunteerism and mortality among community-dwelling elderly. *Journal of Health Psychology, 4*, 310–316.

Ong, A. D., & Walsh, D. A. (2001). Nicotine dependence, depression, and the moderating role of goal cognitions. *Psychology of Addictive Behaviors, 25*, 252–254.

Orbell, S., Johnston, M., Rowley, D., Davey, P., & Espey, A. (2001). Self-efficacy and goal importance in the prediction of physical disability in people following hospitalization: A prospective study. *British Journal of Health Psychology, 6*, 25–41.

Orr, S. T., Reiter, J. P., Blazer, D. G., & James, S. A. (2007). Maternal prenatal pregnancy-related anxiety and spontaneous preterm birth in Baltimore, Maryland. *Psychosomatic Medicine, 69*, 566–570.

Orth-Gomer, K., Wamala, S.P., Horsten, M., Schenk-Gustafsson, K., Schneiderman, N., & Mittleman, M. A. (2000). Marital stress worsens prognosis in women with coronary heart disease: The Stockholm Female Coronary Risk Study. *Journal of the American Medical Association, 284*, 3008–3014.

Ostrove, J. M., & Adler, N. E. (1998). The relationship of socioeconomic status, labor force participation, and health among men and women. *Journal of Health Psychology, 3*, 451–463.

Ostrove, J. M., Adler, N. E., Kuppermann, M., & Washington, A. E. (2000). Objective and subjective assessments of socioeconomic status and their relationship to self-rated health in an ethnically diverse sample of pregnant women. *Health Psychology, 19*, 613–618.

Oxman, T. E., Freeman, D. H., & Manheimer, E. D. (1996). Lack of social participation or religious strength and comfort as risk factors for death after cardiac surgery in the elderly. *Psychosomatic Medicine, 57*, 5–15.

Ozbaran, B., Erermis, S., Bukusoglu, N., Bildik, T., Tamar, M., Ercan, E. S., et al. (2009). Social and emotional outcomes of child sexual abuse: A clinical sample in Turkey. *Journal of Interpersonal Violence, 24*(9), 1478–1493.

Palmer, J. A., Palmer, L. K., Williamson, D., & Michiels, K. (1995). Childhood abuse as a factor in attrition from drug rehabilitation. *Psychological Reports, 76*, 879–882.

Panksepp, J. (2011). The neurobiology of social loss in animals: Some keys to the puzzle of psychic pain in humans. In G. MacDonald & L. A. Jensen-Campbell (Eds.), *Social pain: Neuropsychological and health implications of loss and exclusion* (pp. 11–51). Washington, DC: American Psychological Association.

Pao, M., Lyon, M., D'Angelo, L. J., Schuman, W. B., Tipnis, T., & Mrazek, D. A. (2000). Psychiatric diagnoses in adolescents seropositive for human immunodeficiency virus. *Archives of Pediatric and Adolescent Medicine, 154*, 240–244.

Paras, M. L., Murad, M. H., Chen, L. P., Goranson, E. N., Sattler, A. L., Colbenson, K. M., et al. (2009). Sexual abuse and lifetime diagnosis of somatic disorders: A systematic review and meta-analysis. *Journal of the American Medical Association, 302*(5), 550–561.

Parillo, K. M., Freeman, R. C., Collier, K., & Young, P. (2001). Association between early sexual abuse and adult HIV-risk sexual behaviors among community-recruited women. *Child Abuse and Neglect, 25*, 335–346.

Parrott, A. C. (1999). Does cigarette smoking cause stress? *American Psychologist, 54*, 817–820.

Parrott, A. C. (2000). Cigarette smoking does cause stress. *American Psychologist, 55*, 1159–1160.

Paul, J. P., Catania, J., Pollack, L., & Stall. (2001). Understanding childhood sexual abuse as a predictor of sexual risk-taking among men who have sex with men: The Urban Men's Health Study. *Child Abuse and Neglect, 25*, 557–584.

Perkonigg, A., & Wittchen, H.-U. (1999). Prevalence and co-morbidity of traumatic events and posttraumatic stress disorder in adolescents and young adults. In A. Maercker, M. Schutzwohl & Z. Solomon (Eds.), *Posttraumatic stress disorder: A lifespan developmental perspective* (pp. 113–136). Seattle, WA: Hogrefe & Huber.

Perlis, M. L., Giles, D. E., Buysse, D. J., Thase, M. E., Tu, X., & Kupfer, D. J. (1997). Which depressive symptoms are related to which sleep electroencephalographic variables? *Biological Psychiatry, 42*, 904–913.

Perrott, K., Morriss, E., Martin, J., & Romans, S. (1998). Cognitive coping styles of women sexually abused in childhood: A qualitative study. *Child Abuse and Neglect, 22*, 1135–1149.

Perry, B. D. (2001). The neuroarcheology of childhood maltreatment: The neurodevelopmental costs of adverse chlidhood events. In K. Franey, R. Geffner & R. Falconer (Eds.), *The cost of child maltreatment: Who pays? We all do* (pp. 15–37). San Diego: Family Violence & Sexual Assault Institute.

Perry, B. D., & Pollard, R. (1998). Homeostasis, stress, trauma, and adaptation: A neurodevelopmental view of childhood trauma. *Child and Adolescent Psychiatric Clinics of North America, 7*, 33–51.

Perry, B. D., Pollard, R., Blakley, T. L., Baker, W. L., & Vigilante, D. (1995). Childhood trauma, the neurobiology of adaptation, and "use-dependent" development of the brain: How "states" become "traits." *Infant Mental Health Journal, 16*, 271–291.

Persons, E., Kershaw, T., Sikkema, K. J., & Hansen, N. B. (2010). The impact of shame on health-related quality of life among HIV-positive adults with a history of childhood sexual abuse. *AIDS Patient Care and STDs, 24*(9), 571–580.

Peters, D. K., & Range, L. M. (1995). Childhood sexual abuse and current suicidality in college women and men. *Child Abuse and Neglect, 19*, 335–341.

Phanichrat, T., & Townshend, J. M. (2010). Coping strategies used by survivors of childhood sexual abuse on the journey to recovery. *Journal of Child Sexual Abuse, 19*, 62–78.

Phillips, K. A., Nierenberg, A. A., Brendel, G., & Fava, M. (1996). Prevalence and clinical features of body dysmorphic disorder in atypical major depression. *Journal of Nervous and Mental Disease, 184*, 125–129.

Phuong, D., Dowd, J. B., Ranjit, N., House, J. S., & Kaplan, G. A. (2010). Hopelessness, depression, and early markers of endothelial dysfunction in U.S. adults. *Psychosomatic Medicine, 72*, 613–619.

Pigeon, W. R., Cerulli, C., Richards, H., He, H., Perlis, M., & Caine, E. (2011). Sleep disturbances and their association with mental health among women exposed to intimate partner violence. *Journal of Women's Health, 20*(12), 1923–1929. [E-publication]

Pietrzak, R. H., Goldstein, R. B., Southwick, S. M., & Grant, B. F. (2011). Medical comorbidity of full and partial posttraumatic stress disorder in U.S. adults: Results from wave 2 of the National Epidemiologic Survey on Alcohol and Related Conditions. *Psychosomatic Medicine, 73*, 697–707.

Pilcher, J. J., & Huffcutt, A. I. (1996). Effects of sleep deprivation on performance: A meta-analysis. *Sleep, 19*, 318–326.

Plotsky, P. M., Owens, M. J., & Nemeroff, C. B. (1998). Psychoneuroendocrinology of depression: Hypothalamic-pituitary-adrenal axis. *Psychiatric Clinics of North America, 21*, 293–307.

Poleshuck, E. L., Bair, M. J., Kroenke, K.,

Watts, A., Tu, X., & Giles, D. E. (2009). Pain and depression in gynecology patients. *Psychosomatics, 50*, 270–276.

Pratt, L. A., Ford, D. E., Crum, R. M., Armenian, H. K., Gallo, J. J., & Eaton, W. W. (1996). Depression, psychotropic medication, and risk of myocardial infarction: Prospective data from the Baltimore ECA follow-up. *Circulation, 94*, 3123–3129.

Prentice, J. C., Lu, M. C., Lange, L., & Halfon, N. (2002). The association between reported childhood sexual abuse and breastfeeding initiation. *Journal of Human Lactation, 18*, 291–226.

Preston, J., & Johnson, J. (2009). *Clinical psychopharmacology made ridiculously simple* (6th ed.). Miami, FL: MedMaster.

Preston, J., & Johnson, J. (2009). *Clinical psychopharmacology made ridiculously simple* (6th ed.). Miami, FL: MedMaster.

Pribor, E. F., Yutzy, S. H., Dean, J. T., & Wetzel, R. D. (1993). Briquet's syndrome, dissociation, and abuse. *American Journal of Psychiatry, 150*, 1507–1511.

Price, D. D. (2000). Psychological and neural mechanisms of the affective mechanisms of the affective dimension of pain. *Science, 288*, 1769–1772.

Pritt, A. F. (1998). Spiritual correlates of reported sexual abuse among Mormon women. *Journal for the Scientific Study of Religion, 37*, 273–285.

Purdie, V., & Downey, G. (2000). Rejection sensitivity and adolescent girls' vulnerability to relationship-centered difficulties. *Journal of Personality Disorders, 6*, 109–116.

Raczek, S. W. (1992). Childhood abuse and personality disorders. *Journal of Personality Disorders*, 6, 109–116.

Radke-Yarrow, M. (1998). *Children of depressed mothers: From early childhood to maturity*. New York: Cambridge University Press.

Raikkonen, K., Matthews, K. A., & Salomon, K. (2003). Hostility predicts metabolic syndrome risk factors in children and adolescents. *Health Psychology, 22*, 279–286.

Raj, A., Silverman, J. G., & Amaro, H. (2000). The relationship between sexual abuse and sexual risk among high school students: Findings form the 1997 Massachusetts Youth Risk Behavior Survey. *Maternal and Child Health Journal, 4*, 125–134.

Rao, U., Daley, S. E., & Hammen, C. (2000). Relationship between depression and substance use disorder in adolescent women during the transition to adulthood. *Journal of the American Academy of Child and Adolescent Psychiatry, 39*, 215–222.

Ranjit, N., Diez-Roux, A. V., Shea, S., Cushman, M., Seeman, T., Jackson, S. A., et al. (2007). Psychosocial factors and inflammation in the Multi-Ethnic Study of Atherosclerosis. *Archives of Internal Medicine, 167*, 174–181.

Raphael, K. G., Widom, C. S., & Lange, G. (2001). Childhood victimization and pain in adulthood: A prospective investigation. *Pain, 92*, 283–293.

Read, J. (2001). Child abuse and severity of disturbance among adult psychiatric inpatients. In K. Franey, R. Geffner, & R. Falconer (Eds.), *The cost of child maltreatment: Who pays? We all do* (pp. 103–112). San Diego: Family Violence & Sexual Assault Institute.

Redmond, S. P., & Brackman, J. (1990). Homeless children and their caretakers. In J. Momeni (Ed.), *Homelessness in the United States* (Vol. 2, pp. 123–132). Westport, CT: Greenwood.

Regehr, C., & Marziali, E. (1999). Response to sexual assault: A relational perspective. *Journal of Nervous and Mental Disease, 187*, 618–623.

Reinherz, H. Z., Giaconia, R. M., Hauf, A.

M. C., Wasserman, M. S., & Paradis, A. D. (2000). General and specific childhood risk factors for depression and drug disorders by early adulthood. *Journal of the American Academy of Child and Adolescent Psychiatry, 39*, 223–231.

Resnick, H. S., Yehuda, R., Pitman, R. K., & Foy, D. W. (1995). Effect of previous trauma on acute plasma cortisol level following rape. *American Journal of Psychiatry, 152*, 1675–1677.

Rey, E., & Talley, N. J. (2009). Irritable bowel syndrome: Novel views on the epidemiology and potential risk factors. *Digestive and Liver Disease, 41*, 772–780.

Reyes-Rodriguez, M. L., Von Holle, A., Ulman, T. F., Thornton, L. M., Klump, K. L., Brandt, H., et al. (2011). Posttraumatic stress disorder in anorexia nervosa. *Psychosomatic Medicine, 73*, 491–497.

Rich-Edwards, J. W., James-Todd, T., Mohllajee, A., Kleinman, K., Burke, A., Gillman, M. W., et al. (2011). Lifetime maternal experiences of abuse and risk of pre-natal depression in two demographically distinct populations in Boston. *International Journal of Epidemiology, 40*(2), 375–384.

Rich-Edwards, J. W., Spiegelman, D., Lividoti Hibert, E. N., Jun, H.-J., Todd, T. J., Kawachi, I., et al. (2010). Abuse in childhood and adolescence as a predictor of type 2 diabetes in adult women. *American Journal of Preventive Medicine, 39*(6), 529–536.

Rigby, K. (1998). The relationship between reported health and involvement in bully/victim problems among male and female secondary school children. *Journal of Health Psychology, 3*, 465–476.

Riggs, S., Alario, A. J., & McHorney, C. (1990). Health risk behaviors and attempted suicide in adolescents who report prior maltreatment. *Journal of Pediatrics, 116*, 815–821.

Riley, D., & Eckenrode, J. (1986). Social ties: Subgroup differences in costs and benefits. *Journal of Personality and Social Psychology, 51*, 770–778.

Rios, R., & Zautra, A. J. (2011). Socioeconomic disparities in pain: The role of economic hardship and daily financial worry. *Health Psychology, 30*(1), 58–66.

Roberts, R., O'Connor, T., Dunn, J., Golding, J., & the ALSPAC Study Team. (2004). The effects of child sexual abuse in later family life: Mental health, parenting and adjustment of offspring. *Child Abuse and Neglect, 28*, 525–545.

Roberts, R. E., Shema, S. J., Kaplan, G. A., & Strawbridge, W. J. (2000). Sleep complaints and depression in an aging cohort: A prospective perspective. *American Journal of Psychiatry, 157*, 81–88.

Robin, R. W., Chester, B., Rasmussen, J. K., Jaranson, J. M., & Goldman, D. (1997). Prevalence, characteristics, and impact of childhood sexual abuse in a Southwestern American Indian tribe. *Child Abuse and Neglect, 21*, 769–787.

Robinaugh, D. J., & McNally, R. J. (2010). Autobiographical memory for shame or guilt providing events: Association with psychological symptoms. *Behaviour Research and Therapy, 48*, 646–652.

Robinaugh, D. J., & McNally, R. J. (2011). Trauma centrality and PTSD symptom severity in adult survivors of childhood sexual abuse. *Journal of Traumatic Stress, 24*(4), 483–486.

Robles, T. F., Glaser, R., & Kiecolt-Glaser, J. K. (2005). Out of balance: A new look at chronic stress, depression, and immunity. *Current Directions in Psychological Science, 14*, 111–115.

Roche, D. N., Runtz, M. G., & Hunter, M. A. (1999). Adult attachment: A mediator between child sexual abuse and later psychological adjustment. *Journal of Interpersonal Violence, 14*, 184–207.

Roemmele, M., & Messman-Moore, T. L.

(2011). Child abuse, early maladaptive schemas, and risky sexual behavior in college women. *Journal of Child Sexual Abuse, 20*, 264–283.

Rohde, P., Ichikawa, L., Simon, G. E., Ludman, E. J., Linde, J. A., Jeffery, R. W., et al. (2008). Associations of child sexual and physical abuse with obesity and depression in middle-aged women. *Child Abuse and Neglect, 32*(9), 878–887.

Roizenblatt, S., Moldofsky, H., Benedito-Silva, A. A., & Tufik, S. (2001). Alpha sleep characteristics in fibromyalgia. *Arthritis and Rheumatism, 44*, 222–230.

Romano, E., Zoccolillo, M., & Paquette, D. (2006). Histories of child maltreatment and psychiatric disorder in pregnant adolescents. *Journal of the American Academy of Child and Adolescent Psychiatry, 45*(3), 329–336.

Rorty, M., Yager, J., & Rossotto, E. (1994). Childhood sexual, physical, and psychological abuse in bulimia nervosa. *American Journal of Psychiatry, 151*, 1122–1126.

Rotheram-Borus, M. J., Mahler, K. A., Koopman, C., & Langabeer, K. (1996). Sexual abuse history and associated multiple risk behavior in adolescent runaways. *American Journal of Orthopsychiatry, 66*, 390–400.

Roy, A. (1996). Psychosocial factors and chronic depression. *Journal of Nervous and Mental Disease, 184*, 507–509.

Roy, A. (2001). Childhood trauma and hostility as an adult: Relevance to suicidal behavior. *Psychiatry Research, 102*, 97–101.

Roy, A., Janal, M. N., & Roy, M. (2010). Childhood trauma and prevalence of cardiovascular disease in patients with Type 1 diabetes. *Psychosomatic Medicine, 72*, 833–838.

Rupke, S. J., Blecke, D., & Renfrow, M. (2006). Cognitive therapy for depression. *American Family Physician, 73*, 83–86.

Russek, L. G., & Schwartz, G. E. (1997). Feelings of parental caring predict health status in midlife: A 35-year follow up of the Harvard Mastery of Stress Study. *Journal of Behavioral Medicine, 20*, 1–13.

Russell, D. E. H. (1984). The prevalence and eriousness of incestuous abuse: Stepfathers vs. biological fathers. *Child Abuse and Neglect, 8*, 15–22.

Russell, I. J., Orr, M. D., Littman, B., Vipraio, G. A., Alboukrek, D., Michalek, J. E., et al. (1994). Elevated cerebrospinal fluid levels of substance P in patients with the fibromyalgia syndrome. *Arthritis and Rheumatism, 37*, 1593–1601.

Rutledge, T., Reis, S. E., Olson, M., Owens, J., Kelsey, S. F., Pepine, C. J., et al.. (2006). Depression is associated with cardiac symptoms, mortality risk, and hospitalization among women with suspected coronary disease: the NHLBI-sponsored WISE study. *Psychosomatic Medicine, 68*(2), 217–223.

Rutter, M., & Rutter, M. (1993). *Developing minds: Challenge and continuity across the life span*. New York: Basic Books.

Ryan, K. D., Kilmer, R. P., Cauce, A. M., Watanabe, H., & Hoyt, D. R. (2000). Psychological consequences of child maltreatment in homeless adolescents: Untangling the unique effects of maltreatment and family environment. *Child Abuse and Neglect, 24*, 333–352.

Ryan, N. E., Solberg, V. S., & Brown, S. D. (1996). Family dysfunction, parental attachment, and career search self-efficacy among community college students. *Journal of Counseling Psychology, 43*, 84–89.

Sachs-Ericsson, N., Cromer, K., Hernandez, A., & Kendall-Tackett, K. A. (2009). Childhood abuse, health and pain-related problems: The role of psychiatric disorders and current life stress. *Journal of Trauma and Dissociation, 10*, 170–188.

Sachs-Ericsson, N., Kendall-Tackett, K. A., & Hernandez, A. (2007). Childhood abuse, chronic pain, and depression in the National

Comorbidity Survey. *Child Abuse and Neglect, 31*, 531–547.

Sagi, A., van Ijzendoorn, M., Joels, T., & Scharf, M. (2002). Disorganized reasoning in Holocaust survivors. *American Journal of Orthopsychiatry, 72*(2), 194–203.

Salovey, P., Rothman, A. J., Detweiler, J. B., & Steward, W. T. (2000). Emotional states and physical health. *American Psychologist, 55*, 110–121.

Sandberg, D. A., Suess, E. A., & Heaton, J. L. (2010). Attachment anxiety as a mediator of the relationship between interpersonal trauma and posttraumatic symptomatology among college women. *Journal of Interpersonal Violence, 25*(1), 33–49.

Sanders, B., & Moore, D. L. (1999). Childhood maltreatment and date rape. *Journal of Interpersonal Violence, 14*, 115–124.

Sanz, A., & Villamarin, F. (2001). The role of perceived control in physiological reactivity: Self-efficacy and incentive value as regulators of cardiovascular adjustment. *Biological Psychiatry, 56*, 219–246.

Sapolsky, R. M. (2000). Glucocorticoids and hippocampal atrophy in neuropsychiatric disorders. *Archives of General Psychiatry, 57*, 925–935.

Sareen, J., Cox, B. J., Stein, M. B., Afifi, T. O., Fleet, C., & Asmundson, G. J. (2007). Physical and mental comorbidity, disability, and suicidal behavior associated with posttraumatic stress disorder in a large community sample. *Psychosomatic Medicine, 69*(3), 242–248.

Sarkar, U., Ali, S., & Whooley, M. A. (2007). Self-efficacy and health status in patients with coronary heart disease: Findings from the Heart and Soul Study. *Psychosomatic Medicine, 69*, 306–312.

Sbarra, D. A. (2009). Marriage protects men from clinically meaningful elevations in C-reactive protein: Results from the National Social Life, Health, and Aging Project (NSHAP). *Psychosomatic Medicine, 71*, 828–835.

Scarinci, I. C., McDonald-Haile, J., Bradley, L. A., & Richter, J. E. (1994). Altered pain perception and psychosocial features among women with gastrointestinal disorders and history of abuse: A preliminary model. *American Journal of Medicine, 97*, 108–118.

Schaaf, K. K., & McCanne, T. R. (1998). Relationship of childhood sexual, physical, and combined sexual and physical abuse to adult victimization and posttraumatic stress disorder. *Child Abuse and Neglect, 22*, 1119–1133.

Schachter, C., Stalker, C., & Teram, E. (2001). *Handbook on sensitive practice for health professionals: Lessons from women survivors of childhood sexual abuse.* Ottawa, Ontario: Health Canada, Family Violence Prevention Unit.

Scheier, M. F., Matthews, K. A., Owens, J., Magovern, G. J., Lefebrvre, R. C., Abbott, R. A., et al. (1990). Dispositional optimism and recovery from coronary artery bypass surgery: The beneficial effects of physical and psychological well-being. *Journal of Personality and Social Psychology, 57*, 1024–1040.

Schneider, M. S. (2001). *Pain: Perception and management*. Mountain View, CA: Cortext.

Schnurr, P. P., & Spiro, A. (1999). Combat disorder, posttraumatic stress disorder symptoms and health behaviors as predictors of self-reported physical health in older veterans. *Journal of Nervous and Mental Disease, 187*, 353–359.

Schoedl, A. F., Costa, M. C. P., Mari, J. J., Mello, M. F., Tyrka, A. R., Carpenter, L. L., et al. (2010). The clinical correlates of reported childhood sexual abuse: An association between age at trauma onset and severity of depression and PTSD in adults. *Journal of Child Sexual Abuse, 19*, 156–170.

Schofferman, J., Anderson, D., Hinds, R., Smith, G., & White, A. (1992). Childhood psychological trauma correlates with unsuccessful lumbar spine surgery. *Spine, 17*, S1381–S1384.

Schollgen, I., Huxhold, O., Schuz, B., & Tesch-Romer, C. (2011). Resources for health: Differential effects of optimistic self-beliefs and social support according to socioeconomic status. *Health Psychology, 30*(3), 326–335.

Schuck, A. M., & Widom, C. S. (2001). Childhood victimization and alcohol symptoms in females: Causal inferences and hypothesized mediators. *Child Abuse and Neglect, 25*, 1069–1092.

Schuetze, P., & Das Eiden, R. (2005). The relationship between sexual abuse during childhood and parenting outcomes: Modeling direct and indirect pathways. *Child Abuse and Neglect, 29*, 645–659.

Schulman, E. (2010, June). Abuse screening should be part of the neurology exam. *World Neurology*, p. 4.

Schwarzer, R. (1999). Self-regulatory processes in the adoption and maintenance of health behaviors. *Journal of Health Psychology, 4*(2), 115–127.

Schwartz, D., Dodge, K. A., Pettit, G. S., & Bates, J. E. (2000). Friendship as a moderating factor in the pathway between early harsh home environment and later victimization in the peer group. *Developmental Psychology, 36*, 646–662.

Schwartz, E. B., Ray, R. M., Stuebe, A. M., Allison, M. A., Ness, R. B., Freiberg, M. S., et al. (2009). Duration of lactation and risk factors for maternal cardiovascular disease. *Obstetrics & Gynecology, 113*(5), 974–982.

Scott, J. A., Binns, C. W., Graham, K. I., & Oddy, W. H. (2006). Temporal changes in the determinants of breastfeeding initiation. *Birth, 33*, 37–45.

Scott, K. M., VonKorff, M., Alonso, J., Angermeyer, M. C., Benjet, C., Bruffaerts, R., et al. (2008). Childhood adversity, early-onset depressive/anxiety disorders, and adult-onset asthma. *Psychosomatic Medicine, 70*, 1035–1043.

Seeman, T. E. (1996). Social ties and health. *Annals of Epidemiology, 6*, 442–451.

Seeman, T. E., Lusignolo, T. M., Albert, M., & Berkman, L. (2001). Social relationships, social support, and patterns of cognitive aging in healthy, high-functioning older adults: MacArthur Studies of Successful Aging. *Health Psychology, 20*(4), 243–255.

Segerstrom, S. C., Taylor, S. E., Kemeny, M. E., & Fahey, J. L. (1998). Optimism is associated with mood, coping, and immune change in response to stress. *Journal of Personality and Social Psychology, 74*, 1646–1655.

Segerstrom, S., Taylor, S. E., Kemeny, M. E., Reed, G. M., & Visscher, B. R. (1996). Causal attributions predict rate of immune decline in HIV-seropositive gay men. *Health Psychology, 15*, 485–493.

Seng, J. S., Clark, M. K., McCarthy, A. M., & Ronis, D. L. (2006). PTSD and physical comorbidity among women receiving Medicaid: Results from service-use data. *Journal of Traumatic Stress, 19*(1), 45–56.

Seng, J. S., & Hassinger, J. A. (1998). Relationship strategies and interdisciplinary collaboration: Improving maternity care with survivors of childhood sexual abuse. *Journal of Nurse-Midwifery, 43*(4), 287–295.

Seng, J. S., Oakley, D. J., Sampselle, C. M., Killion, C., Graham-Bermann, S., & Liberzon, I. (2001). Posttraumatic stress disorder and pregnancy complications. *Obstetrics and Gynecology, 97*, 17–22.

Setse, R., Grogan, R., Pham, L., Cooper, L. A., Strobino, D., Powe, N. R., et al. (2009). Longitudinal study of depressive symptoms and health-related quality of life during pregnancy and after delivery: The Health Status in Pregnancy (HIP) Study. *Maternal Child Health Journal, 13*, 577–587.

Shaffer, D. R., Gould, M. S., Fisher, P., & Trautman, P. (1996). Psychiatric diagnosis in child and adolescent suicide. *Archives of General Psychiatry, 53*, 339–348.

Shah, R., & Waller, G. (2000). Parental style and vulnerability to depression: The role of core beliefs. *Journal of Nervous and Mental Disease, 188*, 19–25.

Shakespeare-Finch, J., & De Dassel, T. (2009). Exploring posttraumatic outcomes as a function of childhood sexual abuse. *Journal of Child Sexual Abuse, 18*, 623–640.

Shalev, A. Y., Bleich, A., & Ursano, R. J. (1990). Posttraumatic stress disorder: Somatic comorbidity and effort tolerance. *Psychosomatics, 31*, 197–203.

Shankar, A., McMunn, A., Banks, J., & Steptoe, A. (2011). Loneliness, social isolation, and behavioral and biological health indicators in older adults. *Health Psychology, 30*(4), 377–385.

Shelby, R. A., Somers, T. J., Keefe, F. J., Silva, S. G., McKee, D. C., She, L., et al. (2009). Pain catastrophizing in patients with noncardiac chest pain: Relationships with pain, anxiety, and disability. *Psychosomatic Medicine, 71*(8), 861–868.

Sherin, J. E., & Nemeroff, C. B. (2011). Post-traumatic stress disorder: The neurobiological implications of psychological trauma. *Dialogues in Clinical Neuroscience, 13*(3), 263–278.

Shields, A., & Cicchetti, D. (2001). Parental maltreatment and emotion dysregulation as risk factors in the pathway between early harsh home environment and later victimization. *Journal of Clinical Child Psychology, 30*, 349–363.

Shinn, M., Knickman, J. R., & Weitzman, B. C. (1991). Social relationships and vulnerability to become homeless among poor families. *American Psychologist, 46*, 1180–1187.

Shonkoff, J. P., Boyce, W. T., & McEwen, B. S. (2009). Neuroscience, molecular biology, and the childhood roots of health disparities: Building a new framework for health promotion and disease prevention. *Journal of the American Medical Association, 301*(21), 2252–2259.

Silva, R. R., Alpert, M., Munoz, D. M., Singh, S., Matzner, F., & Dummit, S. (2000). Stress and vulnerability to posttraumatic stress disorder in children and adolescents. *American Journal of Psychiatry, 157*, 1229–1235.

Silverman, D. H. S., Munakata, J. A., Ennes, H., Mandelkern, M. A., Hoh, C. K., & Mayer, E. A. (1997). Regional cerebral activity in normal and pathological perception of visceral pain. *Gastroenterology, 112*, 64–72.

Simon, G., Ormel, J., VonKorff, M., & Barlow, W. (1995). Health care costs associated with depressive and anxiety disorders in primary care. *American Journal of Psychiatry, 152*, 352–357.

Simon, J. G., van de Mheen, H., Van der Meer, J. B., & Mackenbach, J. P. (2000). Socioeconomic differences in self-assessed health in a chronically ill population: The role of different health aspects. *Journal of Behavioral Medicine, 23*, 399–420.

Simoni, J. M., & Ng, M. T. (2002). Abuse, health locus of control, and perceived health among HIV-positive women. *Health Psychology, 21*, 89–93.

Slopen, N., Lewis, T. T., Gruenewald, T. L., Mujahid, M. S., Ryff, C. D., Albert, M. A., & Williams, D. R. (2010). Early life adversity and inflammation in African Americans and whites in midlife in the United States Survey. *Psychosomatic Medicine, 72*, 694–701.

Smith, C. A., Dobbins, C. J., & Wallston, K. A. (1991). The mediational role of perceived competence in psychological adjustment to rheumatoid arthritis. *Journal of Applied Social Psychology, 21*, 1218–1247.

Smith, M. T., Perlis, M. L., Smith, M. S., Giles, D. E., & Carmody, T. P. (2000). Sleep quality and presleep arousal in chronic pain. *Journal of Behavioral Medicine, 23*, 1–13.

Smith, T. W. (1992). Hostility and health:

Current status of a psychosomatic hypothesis. *Health Psychology, 11*, 139–150.

Smith, T. W., Gallo, L. C., Goble, L., Ngu, L. Q., & Stark, K. A. (1998). Agency, communion, and cardiovascular reactivity. *Health Psychology, 17*, 537–545.

Smith, T. W., & Ruiz, J. M. (2002). Psychosocial influences on the development and course of coronary heart disease: Current status and implications for research and practice. *Journal of Consulting and Clinical Psychology, 70*, 548–568.

Smith, T. W., Uchino, B. N., Berg, C. A., Florsheim, P., Pearce, G., Hawkins, M., et al. (2007). Hostile personality traits and coronary artery calcification in middle-aged and older married couples: Different effects for self-reports versus spouse ratings. *Psychosomatic Medicine, 69*, 441–448.

Snyder, C. R., Irving, L. M., & Anderson, J. R. (1991). Hope and health. In C. R. Snyder & D. R. Forsyth (Eds.), *Handbook of social and clinical psychology: The health perspective* (pp. 285–305). Elmsford, NY: Pergamon.

Solomon, Z., & Ginzburg, K. (1999). Aging in the shadow of war. In A. Maercker, M. Schutzwohl, & Z. Solomon (Eds.), *Posttraumatic stress disorder: A lifespan developmental perspective* (pp. 137–154). Seattle: Hogrefe & Huber.

Sorlie, P. D., Backlund, E., & Keller, J. B. (1995). U.S. mortality by economic, demographic, and social characteristics: The National Longitudinal Mortality Study. *American Journal of Public Health, 85*, 949–956.

Southwick, S. M., Bremner, J. D., Krystal, J. H., & Charney, D. S. (1994). Psychobiologic research in posttraumatic stress disorder. *Psychiatric Clinics of North America, 17*, 251–264.

Spak, L., Spak, F., & Allebeck, P. (1997). Factors in childhood and youth predicting alcohol dependence and abuse in Swedish women: Findings from a general population study. *Alcohol and Alcoholism, 32*, 267–274.

Spiegel, D. (1999). Healing words: Emotional expression and disease outcome. *Journal of the American Medical Association, 281*, 1328–1329.

Spitzer, C., Barnow, S., Volzke, H., John, U., Freyberger, H. J., & Grabe, H. J. (2009). Trauma, posttraumatic stress disorder, and physical illness: Findings from the general population. *Psychosomatic Medicine, 71*(9), 1012–1017.

Spitzer, C., Barnow, S., Volzke, H., Wallaschotski, H., John, U., Freyberger, H. J., et al. (2010). Association of posttraumatic stress disorder with low-grade elevation of C-reactive protein: Evidence from the general population. *Journal of Psychiatric Research, 44*(1), 15–21.

Springs, F. E., & Friedrich, W. N. (1992). Health risk behaviors and medical sequelae of childhood sexual abuse. *Mayo Clinic Proceedings, 67*, 527–532.

Stein, M. B., Koverola, C., Hanna, C., Torchina, M. G., & McClarty, B. (1997). Hippocampal volume in women victimized by childhood sexual abuse. *Psychological Medicine, 27*, 951–959.

Stein, M. B., Walker, J. R., Hazen, A. L., & Forde, D. R. (1997). Full and partial posttraumatic stress disorder: Findings from a community survey. *American Journal of Psychiatry, 154*, 1114–1119.

Steel, J. L., & Herlitz, C. A. (2005). The association between childhood and adolescent sexual abuse and proxies for sexual risk behavior: A random sample of the general population of Sweden. *Child Abuse and Neglect, 29*, 1141–1153.

Stepakoff, S. (1998). Effects of sexual victimization on suicidal ideation and behavior in U.S. college women. *Suicide and Life-Threatening Behavior, 28*, 107–126.

Stepanski, E. J., & Perlis, M. (2000). Behavioral sleep medicine: An emerging subspecialty in health psychology and sleep medicine. *Journal of Psychosomatic Research, 49*, 343–347.

Stepanski, E. J., Rybarczyk, B., Lopez, M., & Stevens, S. (2003). Assessment and treatment of sleep disorders in older adults: A review for rehabilitation psychologists. *Rehabilitation Psychology, 48*, 23–36.

Stewart, J. C., Janicki-Deverts, D., Muldoon, M. F., & Kamarck, T. W. (2008). Depressive symptoms moderate the influence of hostility on serum Interleukin-6 and C-reactive protein. *Psychosomatic Medicine, 70*, 197–204.

Stice, E. (2002). The neglect of obesity. *Monitor on Psychology, 33*, 33.

Stock, J. L., Bell, M. A., Boyer, D. K., & Connell, F. A. (1997). Adolescent pregnancy and sexual risk-taking among sexually abused girls. *Family Planning Perspective, 29*, 200–203, 227.

Strathearn, L., Mamun, A. A., Najman, J. M., & O'Callaghan, M. J. (2009). Does breastfeeding protect against substantiated child abuse and neglect? A 15-year cohort study. *Pediatrics, 123*(2), 483–493.

Strawbridge, W. J., Shema, S. J., Cohen, R. D., & Kaplan, G. A. (2001). Religious attendance increases survival by improving and maintaining good health behavior, mental health, and social relationships. *Annals of Behavioral Medicine, 23*, 68–74.

Street, A. E., & Arias, I. (2001). Psychological abuse and posttraumatic stress disorder in battered women: Examining the roles of shame and guilt. *Violence and Victims, 16*, 65–78.

Stuebe, A. M., & Rich-Edwards, J. W. (2009). The reset hypothesis: Lactation and maternal metabolism. *American Journal of Perinatology, 26*(1), 81–88.

Styron, T., & Janoff-Bulman, R. (1997). Childhood attachment and abuse: Long-term effects on adult attachment, depression, and conflict resolution. *Child Abuse and Neglect, 21*, 1015–1023.

Suarez, E. C. (2003). Joint effect of hostility and severity of depressive symptoms on plasma Interleukin-6 concentration. *Psychosomatic Medicine, 65*, 523–527.

Suarez, E. C. (2006). Sex differences in the relation of depressive symptoms, hostility, and anger expression to indices of glucose metabolism in nondiabetic adults. *Health Psychology, 25*, 484–492.

Suarez, E. C., & Goforth, H. (2010). Sleep and inflammation: A potential link to chronic diseases. In K. A. Kendall-Tackett (Ed.), *The psychoneuroimmunology of chronic disease* (pp. 53–75). Washington, DC: American Psychological Association.

Suarez, E. C., Lewis, J. G., Krishnan, R. R., & Young, K. H. (2004). Enhanced expression of cytokines and chemokines by blood monocytes to in vitro lipopolysaccharide stimulation are associated with hostility and severity of depressive symptoms in healthy women. *Psychoneuroendocrinology, 29*, 1119–1128.

Subramani, K., & Janowitz, H. D. (1991). The irritable bowel syndrome: A continuing dilemma. *Gastroenterology Clinics of North America, 20*, 363–367.

Suglia, S. F., Ryan, L., Laden, F., Dockery, D. W., & Wright, R. J. (2008). Violence exposure, a chronic psychosocial stressor, and childhood lung function. *Psychosomatic Medicine, 70*, 160–169.

Suglia, S. F., Staudenmayer, J., Cohen, S., Enlow, M. B., Rich-Edwards, J. W., & Wright, R. (2010). Cumulative stress and cortisol disruption among black and Hispanic pregnant women in an urban cohort. *Psychological Trauma, 2*(4), 326–334.

Sutherland, S. M., & Davidson, J. R. T. (1994). Pharmacotherapy for posttraumatic stress disorder. *Psychiatric Clinics of North America, 17*, 409–423.

Tafarodi, R. W., & Swann, W. B. (1995). Self-liking and self-competence as dimensions of global self-esteem: Initial validation of a measure. *Journal of Personality Assessment, 65*, 322–342.

Talbot, N. L., Chapman, B., Conwell, Y., McCollumn, K., Franus, N., Cotescu, S., et al. (2009). Childhood sexual abuse is associated with physical illness burden and functioning in psychiatric patients 50 years of age or older. *Psychosomatic Medicine, 71*, 417–422.

Talley, N. J., Fett, S. L., & Zinsmeister, A. R. (1995). Self-reported abuse and gastrointestinal disease in outpatients: Association with irritable bowel-type symptoms. *American Journal of Gastroenterology, 90*, 366–371.

Talley, N. J., Fett, S. L., Zinsmeister, A. R., & Melton, L. J. (1994). Gastrointestinal tract symptoms and self-reported abuse: A population-based study. *Gastroenterology, 107*, 1040–1049.

Targino, R. A., Imamura, M., Kaziyama, M. M., Souza, L. P., Hsing, W. T., & Imamura, S. T. (2002). Pain treatment with acupuncture for patients with fibromyalgia. *Current Pain and Headache Report, 6*, 379–383.

Taylor, C. B., Conrad, A., Wilhelm, F. H., Neri, E., DeLorenzo, A., Kramer, M. A., et al. (2006). Psychophysiological and cortisol responses to psychological stress in depressed and nondepressed older men and women with elevated cardiovascular disease risk. *Psychosomatic Medicine, 68*(4), 538–546.

Taylor, M. L., Trotter, D. R., & Csuka, M. E. (1995). The prevalence of sexual abuse in women with fibromyalgia. *Arthritis and Rheumatism, 38*, 229–234.

Taylor, S. E., Kemeny, M. E., Reed, G. M., Bower, J. E., & Gruenewald, T. L. (2000). Psychological resources, positive illusions, and health. *American Psychologist, 55*, 99–109.

Teegan, F. (1999). Childhood sexual abuse and long-term sequelae. In A. Maercker, M. Schutzwohl, & Z. Solomon (Eds.), *Posttraumatic stress disorder: A lifespan developmental perspective* (pp. 97–112). Seattle, WA: Hogrefe & Huber.

Teicher, M. H. (2002). Scars that won't heal: The neurobiology of child abuse. *Scientific American, 286*(3), 68–75.

Tegethoff, M., Greene, N., Olsen, J., Meyer, A. H., & Meinlschmidt, G. (2010). Maternal psychosocial adversity during pregnancy is associated with length of gestation and offspring size at birth: Evidence from a population-based cohort study. *Psychosomatic Medicine, 72*, 419–426.

Thakkar, R. R., & McCanne, T. R. (2000). The effects of daily stressors on physical health in women with and without a childhood history of sexual abuse. *Child Abuse and Neglect, 24*, 209–221.

Thase, M. E., Dube, S., Bowler, K., Howland, R. H., Myers, J. E., Friedman, E., et al. (1996). Hypothalamic-pituitary-adrenocortical activity and response to cognitive behavior therapy in unmedicated, hospitalized depressed patients. *American Journal of Psychiatry, 153*, 886–891.

Thompson, K. M., Wonderlich, S. A., Crosby, R. D., & Mitchell, J. E. (2001). Sexual victimization and adolescent weight regulation practices: A test across three community-based samples. *Child Abuse and Neglect, 25*, 291–305.

Thompson, N. J., Potter, J. S., Sanderson, C. A., & Maibach, E. W. (1997). The relationship of sexual buse and HIV risk behaviors among heterosexual adult female STD patients. *Child Abuse and Neglect, 21*, 149–156.

Thurston, R. C., & Kubzansky, L. D. (2009). Women, loneliness, and incident coronary heart disease. *Psychosomatic Medicine, 71*(8), 836–842.

Ting, H., Hsiao-Sui, L., Chang, S.-Y., Chung, A.-H., Kuan, P.-C., & Yuan, S.-C.

(2009). Post- to pre-overnight sleep systolic blood pressures are associated with sleep respiratory disturbance, pro-inflammatory state and metabolic situation in patients with sleep-disordered breathing. *Sleep Medicine, 10*(7), 720–725.

Tjaden, P., & Thoennes, N. (2000). *Extent, nature, and consequences of intimate partner violence: Findings from the National Violence against Women Survey.* U.S. Department of Justice, Office of Justice Programs, National Institute of Justice.

Toner, B. B., Segal, Z. V., Emmott, S. D., & Myran, D. (2000). *Cognitive-behavioral treatment of irritable bowel syndrome: The brain-gut connection.* New York: Guilford Press.

Toro, P. A., Bellavia, C. W., Daeschler, C. V., Owens, B. J., Wall, D. D., Passero, J. M., et al. (1995). Distinguishing homelessness from poverty: A comparative study. *Journal of Consulting and Clinical Psychology, 63,* 280–289.

Torres, J. B., & Solberg, V. S. (2001). Role of self-efficacy, stress, social integration, and family support in Latino college student persistence and health. *Journal of Vocational Behavior, 59,* 53–63.

Toth, S. L., & Cicchetti, D. (1996). Patterns of relatedness, depressive symptomatology, and perceived competence in maltreated children. *Journal of Consulting and Clinical Psychology, 64,* 32–41.

Trezza, G. R., & Popp, S. M. (2000). The substance user at risk of harm to self or others: Assessment and treatment issues. *Journal of Clinical Psychology, 56,* 1193–1205.

Trickett, P. K., Reiffman, A., Horowitz, L. A., & Putnam, F. W. (1997). Characteristics of sexual abuse trauma and the prediction of developmental outcomes. In D. Cicchetti & S. L. Toth (Eds.), *Rochester symposium on developmental psychopathology: Developmental perspectives on trauma* (Vol. 8, pp. 289–314). Rochester, NY: University of Rochester Press.

Troxel, W. M., Buysse, D. J., Hall, M., & Matthews, K. A. (2009). Marital happiness and sleep disturbances in a multi-ethnic sample of middle-aged women. *Behavioral Sleep Medicine, 7*(1), 2–19.

Troxel, W. M., Cyranowski, J. M., Hall, M., Frank, E., & Buysee, D. J. (2007). Attachment anxiety, relationship context, and sleep in women with recurrent major depression. *Psychosomatic Medicine, 69,* 692–699.

Tucci, A. M., Kerr-Correa, F., & Souza-Formigoni, M. L. O. (2010). Childhood trauma in substance use disorder and depression: An analysis by gender among a Brazilian clinical sample. *Child Abuse and Neglect, 34,* 95–104.

Uchino, B. N., & Garvey, T. S. (1997). The availability of social support reduces cardiovascular reactivity to acute psychological stress. *Journal of Behavioral Medicine, 20,* 15–27.

Uchino, B. N., Holt-Lunstad, J., Uno, D., Betancourt, R., & Garvey, T. S. (1999). Social support and age-related differences in cardiovascular function: An examination of potential mediators. *Annals of Behavioral Medicine, 21*(2), 135–142.

Ulibarri, M. D., Ulloa, E. C., & Camacho, L. (2009). Prevalence of sexually abusive experiences in childhood and adolescence among a community sample of Latinas: A descriptive study. *Journal of Child Sexual Abuse, 18,* 405–421.

Ullman, S. E., Najdowski, C. J., & Filipas, H. H. (2009). Child sexual abuse, posttraumatic stress disorder, and substance use: Predictors of revictimization in adult sexual assault survivors. *Journal of Child Sexual Abuse, 18,* 367–385.

Ulmer, C. S., Edinger, J. D., & Calhoun, P. S.

(2011). A multi-component cognitive-behavioral intervention for sleep disturbance in veterans with PTSD: A pilot study. *Journal of Clinical Sleep Medicine, 7*(1), 57–68.

U.S. Department of Health and Human Services. (2011). The Surgeon General's call to action to support breastfeeding. Washington, DC: Author.

Urquiza, A. J., & Goodlin-Jones, B. L. (1994). Child sexual abuse and adult revictimization with women of color. *Violence and Victims, 9*, 223–265.

Uysal, A., & Lu, Q. (2011). Is self-concealment associated with acute and chronic pain? *Health Psychology, 30*(5), 606–614.

Vaccarino, V., McClure, C., Johnson, D., Sheps, D. S., Bittner, V., Rutledge, T., et al. (2008). Depression, the metabolic syndrome and cardiovascular risk. *Psychosomatic Medicine, 70*, 40–48.

Vaccarino, A. L., Sills, T. L., Evans, K. R., & Kalali, A. H. (2009). Multiple pain complaints in patients with major depressive disorder. *Psychosomatic Medicine, 71*, 159–162.

Vahtera, J., Kivimaki, M., Uutela, A., & Pentti, J. (2000). Hostility and ill health: Role of psychosocial resources in two contexts of working life. *Journal of Psychosomatic Research, 48*, 89–98.

Valham, F., Stegmayr, B., Eriksson, M., Hagg, E., Lindberg, E., & Franklin, K. A. (2009). Snoring and witnessed sleep apnea is related to diabetes mellitus in women. *Sleep Medicine, 10*, 112–117.

van der Kolk, B. A. (1994). The body keeps score: Memory and the evolving psychobiology of posttraumatic stress. *Harvard Review of Psychiatry, 1*, 223–232.

van der Kolk, B. A. (2002). Assessment and treatment of complex PTSD. In R. Yehuda (Ed.), *Treating trauma survivors with PTSD* (pp. 127–156). Washington, DC: American Psychiatric Association Press.

van der Kolk, B. A., & Fisler, R. (1994). Childhood abuse and neglect and loss of self-regulation. *Bulletin of the Menninger Clinic, 58*, 145–168.

van Dulmen, A. M., Fennis, J. F. M., & Bleijenberg, G. (1996). Cognitive-behavioral group therapy for irritable bowel syndrome: Effects and long-term follow-up. *Psychosomatic Medicine, 58*, 508–514.

Van Gerko, K., Hughes, M. L., Hamill, M., & Waller, G. (2005). Reported childhood sexual abuse and eating-disordered cognitions and behaviors. *Child Abuse and Neglect, 29*, 375–382.

Van Gurp, G., Meterissian, G. B., Haiek, L. N., McCusker, J., & Bellavance, F. (2002). St. John's wort or sertraline?: Randomized controlled trial in primary care. *Canadian Family Physician, 48*, 905–912.

van Houdenhove, B., Luyten, P., & van den Eede, F. (2008). Early life stress in chronic pain and fatigue syndromes: Prevalence, consequences, and etio-pathogenic pathways. *Family and Intimate Partner Quarterly, 1*(2), 101–114.

Van Oudenhove, L., Vandernberghe, J., Vos, R., Fischler, B., Demyttenaere, K., & Tack, J. (2011). Abuse history, depression, and somatization are associated with gastric sensitivity and gastric emptying in functional dyspepsia. *Psychosomatic Medicine, 73*, 648–655.

van Tilburg, M. A. L., Runyan, D., Zolotor, A. J., Graham, J. C., Dubowitz, H., Litrownik, A. J., et al. (2010). Unexplained gastrointestinal symptoms after abuse in a prospective study of children at risk for abuse and neglect. *Annals of Family Medicine, 8*(2), 134–140.

Vatnar, S. K. B., & Bjorkly, S. (2010). Does it make any difference if she is a mother? An interactional perspective on intimate partner violence with a focus on motherhood and pregnancy. *Journal of Interpersonal Violence, 25*(1), 94–110.

Veale, D., Kavanagh, G., Fielding, J. F., & Fitzgerald, O. (1991). Primary fibromyalgia and the irritable bowel syndrome: Different expressions of a common pathogenetic process. *British Journal of Rheumatology, 30*, 220–222.

Verdecias, R. N., Jean-Louis, G., Zizi, F., Casimir, G. J., & Browne, R. C. (2009). Attachment styles and sleep measures in a community-based sample of older adults. *Sleep Medicine, 10*, 664–667.

Vincent, N. K., & Walker, J. R. (2000). Perfectionism and chronic insomnia. *Journal of Psychosomatic Medicine, 49*, 349–354.

Virani, A. S., Bezchlibnyk-Butler, K. Z., & Jeffries, J. J. (2009). *Clinical handbook of psychotropic drugs*. Seattle, WA: Hogrefe.

Vitaliano, P. P., Scanlan, J. M., Zhang, J., Savage, M. V., Brummett, B., Barefoot, J., et al. (2001). Are the salutogenic effects of social supports modified by income? A test of an "added value hypothesis." *Health Psychology, 20*(3), 155–165.

Voisin, D. R. (2002). Family ecology and HIV sexual risk behaviors among African American and Puerto Rican adolescent males. *American Journal of Orthopsychiatry, 72*(2), 294–302.

Voisin, D. R. (2003). Victims of community violence and HIV sexual risk behaviors among African American adolescent males. *Journal of HIV/AIDS Prevention and Education for Adolescents and Children, 5*(3/4), 87–110.

Voisin, D. R. (2005). The relationship between violence exposure and HIV sexual risk behavior: Does gender matter? *American Journal of Orthopsychiatry, 75*(4), 497–506.

Voisin, D. R., Salazar, L. F., Crosby, R. D., DiClemente, R. J., Yarber, W. L., & Staples-Horne, M. (2004). The association between gang involvement and sexual behaviours among detained adolescent males. *Sexually Transmitted Infections, 80*(6), 440–442.

von Kanel, R., Hepp, U., Buddeberg, C., Keel, M., Mica, L., Aschbacher, K., et al. (2006). Altered blood coagulation in patients with posttraumatic stress disorder. *Psychosomatic Medicine, 68*(4), 598–604.

Vranceanu, A.-M., Hobfoll, S. E., & Johnson, R. J. (2007). Child multi-type maltreatment and associated depression and PTSD symptoms: The role of social support and stress. *Child Abuse and Neglect, 31*, 71–84.

Wade, T. D., & Kendler, K. S. (2000). The relationship between social support and major depression: Cross-sectional, longitudinal, and genetic perspectives. *Journal of Nervous and Mental Disease, 188*, 251–258.

Wagner, J. K., & Perrine, R. M. (1994). Women at risk for homelessness: Comparison between housed and homeless women. *Psychological Reports, 75*, 1671–1678.

Waldrop, D., Lightsey, O. R., Ethington, C. A., Woemel, C. A., & Coke, A. L. (2001). Self-efficacy, optimism, health competence, and recovery from orthopedic surgery. *Journal of Counseling Psychology, 48*, 233–238.

Walker, E., Katon, W., Roy-Byrne, P., Jemelka, R., & Russo, J. (1993). Histories of sexual victimization in patients with irritable bowel syndrome or inflammatory bowel disease. *American Journal of Psychiatry, 150*, 1502–1506.

Walker, E. A., Unutzer, J., Rutter, C. M., Gelfand, A., Saunders, K., VonKorff, M., et al. (1999). Costs of health care use by women HMO members with a history of childhood abuse and neglect. *Archives of General Psychiatry, 56*, 609–613.

Walling, M. K., Reiter, R. C., O'Hara, M. W., Milburn, A. K., Lilly, G., & Vincent, S. D. (1994). Abuse history and chronic pain in women: I. Prevalences of sexual abuse and physical abuse. *Obstetrics and Gynecology, 84*, 193–199.

Walling, S. M., Eriksson, C. B., Putman, K. M., & Foy, D. W. (2011). Community violence exposure, adverse childhood experiences, and posttraumatic distress among urban development workers. *Psychological Trauma, 3*(1), 42–49.

Wallston, K. A. (2001). Conceptualization and operationalization of perceived control. In A. Baum, T. A. Revenson, & J. E. Singer (Eds.), *Handbook of health psychology* (pp. 49–59). Mahwah, NJ: Erlbaum.

Walsh, J. F., & Foshee, V. (1998). Self-efficacy, self-determination and victim blaming as predictors of adolescent sexual victimization. *Health Education Research, 13*, 139–144.

Ware, J. C., & Morin, C. M. (1997). Sleep in depression and anxiety. In M. R. Pressman & W. C. Orr (Eds.), *Understanding sleep: The evaluation and treatment of sleep disorders* (pp. 483–503). Washington, DC: American Psychological Association.

Warshaw, M. G., Fierman, E., Pratt, L., Hunt, M., Yonker, K. A., Massion, A. O., et al. (1993). Quality of life and dissociation in anxiety disorder patients with histories of trauma or PTSD. *American Journal of Psychiatry, 150*, 1512–1516.

Washington, O. G. M. (2001). Using brief therapeutic interventions to create change in self-efficacy and personal control of chemically dependent women. *Archives of Psychiatric Nursing, 15*, 32–40.

Watari, K. F., & Brodbeck, C. (2000). Culture, health, and financial appraisals: Comparison of worry in older Japanese Americans and European Americans. *Journal of Clinical Geropsychology, 6*, 25–39.

Watson, C. G., Davenport, E., Anderson, P. E. D., Mendez, C. M., & Gearhart, L. P. (1998). The relationship between premilitary school record data and risk for posttraumatic stress disorder among Vietnam War veterans. *Journal of Nervous and Mental Disease, 186*, 338–344.

Weathers, F. W., Keane, T. M., & Foa, E. B. (2009). Diagnosis and treatment of adults. In E. B. Foa, T. M. Keane, M. J. Friedman, & J. A. Cohen (Eds.), *Effective treatments for PTSD: Practice guidelines from the International Society for Traumatic Stress Studies* (2nd ed.) (pp. 23–61). New York: Guilford Press.

Webb, M., Heisler, D., Call, S., Chickering, S. A., & Colburn, T. A. (2007). Shame, guilt, symptoms of depression, and reported history of psychological maltreatment. *Child Abuse and Neglect, 31*, 1143–1153.

Wegman, H. L., & Stetler, C. (2009). A meta-analytic review of the effects of childhood abuse on medical outcomes in adulthood. *Psychosomatic Medicine, 71*, 805–812.

Weinfield, N. S., Sroufe, L. A., Egeland, B., & Carlson, E. A. (1999). The nature of individual differences in infant-caregiver attachment. In J. Cassidy & P. R. Shaver (Eds.), *The handbook of attachment: Theory, research, and clinical applications* (pp. 68–88). New York: Guilford Press.

Weinstock, M. A., Rossi, J. S., Redding, C. A., Maddock, J. E., & Cottrill, S. D. (2000). Sun protection behaviors and stages of change for the primary prevention of skin cancers among beachgoers in southeastern New England. *Annals of Behavioral Medicine, 22*, 286–293.

Weisberg, M. B., & Clavel, A. L. (1999). Why is chronic pain so difficult to treat? Psychological considerations from simple to complex care. *Postgraduate Medicine, 106*, 141–164.

Weiss, E. L., Longhurst, J. G., & Mazure, C. M. (1999). Childhoood sexual abuse as a risk factor for depression in women: Psychosocial and neurobiological correlates. *American Journal of Psychiatry, 156*, 816–828.

Weissman, A. M., Levy, B. T., Hartz, A. J., Bentler, S., Donohue, M., Ellingrod, V. L., et al. (2004). Pooled analysis of antidepressant levels in lactating mothers, breast milk, and nursing infants. *American Journal of Psychiatry, 161*(6), 1066–1078.

Weitlauf, J. C., Finney, J. W., Ruzek, J. I., Lee, T. T., Thailkill, A., Jones, S., et al. (2008). Distress and pain during pelvic examinations: Effect of sexual violence. *Obstetrics and Gynecology, 112*(6), 1343–1350.

Weitzman, M., Rosenthal, D. G., & Liu, Y.-H. (2011). Paternal depressive symptoms and child behavioral or emotional problems in the United States. *Pediatrics, 128*(6), 1126–1134.

Whiffen, V. E., & MacIntosh, H. B. (2005). Mediators of the link between childhood sexual abuse and emotional distress: A critical review. *Trauma, Violence, and Abuse, 6*(1), 24–39.

Whisman, M. A. (2010). Loneliness and the metabolic syndrome in a population-based sample of middle-aged and older adults. *Health Psychology, 29*(5), 550–554.

Whitaker, R. C., Phillips, S. M., Orzol, S. M., & Burdette, H. L. (2007). The association between maltreatment and obesity among preschool children. *Child Abuse and Neglect, 31*, 1187–1199.

Whitbeck, L. B., Hoyt, D. R., & Ackley, K. A. (1997). Families of homeless and runaway adolescents: A comparison of parent/caretaker and adolescent perspectives on parenting, family violence, and adolescent conduct. *Child Abuse and Neglect, 21*, 517–528.

White, C., & Schweitzer, R. (2000). The role of personality in the development and perpetuation of chronic fatigue syndrome. *Journal of Psychosomatic Research*, *48*, 515–524.

Whitehead, W. E., & Crowell, M. D. (1991). Psychologic considerations in the irritable bowel syndrome. *Gastroenterology Clinics of North America, 20*, 249–267.

Whitmire, L., Harlow, L., Quina, K., & Morokoff, P. (1998). *Childhood trauma and HIV: Women at risk*. Philadelphia: Taylor & Francis.

Wickelgren, I. (1997). Getting the brain's attention. *Science, 278*, 35–37.

Widom, C. S., Weiler, B. L., & Cottler, L. B. (1999). Childhood victimization and drug abuse: A comparison of prospective and retrospective findings. *Journal of Consulting and Clinical Psychology, 67*, 867–880.

Widom, C. S., & White, H. R. (1997). Problem behaviors in abused and neglected children grown up: Prevalence and co-occurrence of substance abuse, crime and violence. *Criminal Behavior and Mental Health, 7*, 287–310.

Wiest, M., Schuz, B., Webster, N., & Wurm, S. (2011). Subjective well-being and mortality revisited: Differential effects of cognitive and emotional facets of well-being on mortality. *Health Psychology, 30*(6), 728-735.

Williams, L. M. (1994). Recall of childhood trauma: A prospective study of women's memories of child sexual abuse. *Journal of Consulting and Clinical Psychology, 62*, 1167–1176.

Wilsnack, S. C., Vogeltanz, N. D., Klassen, A. D., & Harris, T. R. (1997). Childhood sexual abuse and women's substance abuse: National survey findings. *Journal of Studies of Alcohol, 58*, 264–271.

Wilson, C. J., Finch, C. E., & Cohen, H. J. (2002). Cytokines and cognition—The case for a head-to-toe inflammatory paradigm. *Journal of the American Geriatrics Society, 50*, 2041–2056.

Wingate, D. L. (1991). The irritable bowel syndrome. *Gastroenterology Clinics of North America, 20*, 351–361.

Wingenfeld, K., Heim, C., Schmidt, I.,

Wagner, D., Meinlschmidt, G., & Hellhammer, D. H. (2008). HPA axis reactivity and lymphocyte glucocorticoid sensitivity in fibromyalgia syndrome and chronic pelvic pain. *Psychosomatic Medicine, 70*, 65–72.

Wingood, G. M., & DiClemente, R. J. (1997). Child sexual abuse, HIV sexual risk, and gender relations of African American women. *American Journal of Preventive Medicine, 13*, 380–384.

Wirtz, P. H., Redwine, L. S., Ehlert, U., & von Kanel, R. (2009). Independent association between lower level of social support and higher coagulation activity before and after acute psychosocial stress. *Psychosomatic Medicine, 71*, 30–37.

Witvliet, C. V., Ludwig, T. E., & Vander Laan, K. L. (2001). Granting forgiveness or harboring grudges: Implications for emotion, physiology, and health. *Psychological Science, 121*, 117–123.

Wolfe, F. (1997). The fibromyalgia problem. *Journal of Rheumatology, 24*, 1247–1249.

Wolfe, F., Clauw, D. J., Fitzcharles, M.-A., Goldenberg, D. L., Katz, R. S., Mease, P., et al. (2010). The American College of Rheumatology preliminary diagnostic criteria for fibromyalgia and measurement of symptom severity. *Arthritis Care and Research, 62*(5), 600–610.

Wolfe, F., Russell, I. J., Vipraio, G., Ross, K., & Anderson, J. (1997). Serotonin levels, pain thresholds, and fibromyalgia symptoms in the general population. *Journal of Rheumatology, 24*, 555–559.

Wong, W. C. W., Leung, P. W. S., Tang, C. S. K., Chen, W.-Q., Lee, A., & Ling, D. C. (2009). To unfold a hidden epidemic: Prevalence of child maltreatment and its health implications among high school students in Guangzhou, China. *Child Abuse and Neglect, 33*, 441–450.

Woods, A. B., Page, G. G., O'Campo, P., Pugh, L. C., Ford, D., & Campbell, J. C. (2005). The mediation effect of post-traumatic stress disorder symptoms on the relationship of intimate partner violence and IFN-gamma levels. *American Journal of Community Psychology, 36*(1–2), 159–175.

Woolf, C. J., & Salter, M. W. (2000). Neuronal plasticity: Increasing the gain in pain. *Science, 288*, 1765–1768.

Wright, L. S., Frost, C. J., & Wisecarver, S. (1993). Church attendance, meaningfulness of religion, and depressive symptomatology among adolescents. *Journal of Youth and Adolescence, 22*, 559–568.

Wright, M. O., Master, A. S., & Hubbard, J. J. (1997). Long-term effects of massive trauma: Developmental and psychobiological perspectives. In D. Cicchetti & S. L. Toth (Eds.), *Rocheter symposium on developmental psychopathology: Developmental perspectives on trauma* (Vol. 8, pp. 181–225). Rochester, NY: University of Rochester Press.

Wyatt, G. E. (1985). The sexual abuse of Afro-American and white-American women in childhood. *Child Abuse and Neglect, 9*, 507–519.

Wyatt, G. E., Guthrie, D., & Notgrass, C. M. (1992). Differential effects of women's child sexual abuse and subsequent sexual revictimization. *Journal of Consulting and Clinical Psychology, 60*, 167–173.

Wyatt, G. E., & Riederle, M. (1994). Sexual harassment and prior sexual trauma among African American and white American women. *Violence and Victims, 9*, 233–247.

Xu, J., & Roberts, R. E. (2010). The power of positive emotions: It's a matter of life or death—subjective well-being and longevity over 28 years in a general population. *Health Psychology, 29*(1), 9–19.

Yehuda, R. (1998). Psychoneuroendocrinology of post-traumatic stress disorder. *Psychiatric Clinics of North America, 21*, 359–379.

Yehuda, R. (1999). Biological factors associated with susceptibility to posttraumatic stress disorder. *Canadian Journal of Psychiatry, 44*, 34–39.

Yehuda, R., Levengood, R. A., Schmeidler, J., Wilson, S., Guo, L. S., & Gerber, D. (1996). Increased pituitary activation following metyrapone administration in post-traumatic stress disorder. *Psychoneuroendicrinology, 21*, 1–16.

Yehuda, R., McFarlane, A. C., & Shalev, A. Y. (1998). Predicting the development of posttraumatic stress disorder from the acute response to a traumatic event. *Biological Psychiatry, 44*, 1305–1313.

Yehuda, R., Resnick, H. S., Schmeidler, J., Yang, R.-K., & Pitman, R. K. (1998). Predictors of cortisol and 3-methoxy-4-hydroxyphenylglycol responses in the acute aftermath of rape. *Biological Psychiatry, 43*, 855–859.

Yehuda, R., Schmeidler, J., Giller, E. L., Siever, L. J., & Binder-Brynes, K. (1998). Relationship between posttraumatic stress disorder characteristics of Holocaust survivors and their adult offspring. *American Journal of Psychiatry, 155*, 841–843.

Young, T. L., Riggs, M., & Robinson, J. L. (2011). Childhood sexual abuse severity reconsidered: A factor structure of CSA characteristics. *Journal of Child Sexual Abuse, 20*, 373–395.

Zanarini, M. C., Frankenburg, F. R., Reich, D., Marino, M. F., Haynes, M. C., & Gunderson, J. G. (1999). Violence in the lives of adult borderline patients. *Journal of Nervous and Mental Disease, 187*, 65–71.

Zanarini, M. C., Williams, A. A., Lewis, R. E., Reich, R. B., Vera, S. C., Marino, M. F., et al. (1997). Reported pathological childhood experiences associated with the development of borderline personality disorder. *American Journal of Psychiatry, 154*, 1101–1106.

Zatura, A. (1998). Individual differences in response to pharmacological treatments: The role of psychosocial factors. *The Health Psychologist, 20*, 10–11.

Zinzow, H., Seth, P., Jackson, J., Niehaus, A., & Fitzgerald, M. (2010). Abuse and parental characteristics, attributions of blame, and psychological adjustment in adult survivors of child sexual abuse. *Journal of Child Sexual Abuse, 19*, 79–98.

Zlotnick, C., Mattia, J., & Zimmerman, M. (2001). Clinical features of survivors of sexual abuse with major depression. *Child Abuse and Neglect, 25*, 357–367.

Zoccola, P. M., Dickerson, S. S., & Lam, S. (2009). Rumination predicts longer sleep onset latency after an acute psychosocial stressor. *Psychosomatic Medicine, 71*, 771–775.

Zuravin, S. J., & Fontanella, C. (1999). The relationship between child sexual abuse and major depression among low-income women: A function of growing up experiences? *Child Maltreatment, 4*, 3–12.

Index

[References are to pages.]

[References are to pages.]

[References are to pages.]

[References are to pages.]

[References are to pages.]

[References are to pages.]

[References are to pages.]

[References are to pages.]

[References are to pages.]

[References are to pages.]